WOMEN'S LIVES

THEMES AND VARIATIONS
IN GENDER LEARNING

Second Edition

SECOND EDITION

WOMEN'S LIVES

THEMES AND VARIATIONS IN GENDER LEARNING

Bernice Lott

University of Rhode Island

Brooks/Cole Publishing Company
Pacific Grove, California

The trademark ITP is used under license.

A CLAIREMONT BOOK

Brooks/Cole Publishing Company
A Division of Wadsworth, Inc.

Printed in the United States of America
10 9 8 7 6 5 4 3 2

Library of Congress Cataloging-in-Publication Data
Lott, Bernice E
      Women's lives : themes and variations in gender learning / Bernice Lott.—2nd ed.
            p.   cm.
      Includes bibliographical references and index.
      ISBN 0–534–15954–0
      1. Sex role—United States.   2. Women—United States—Psychology.   3. Life cycle, Human.   I. Title.
HQ1075.5.U6L68   1993
305.42—dc20   93–5182
                                                                          CIP

Sponsoring Editor: Claire Verduin
Marketing Representative: Ira Zukerman
Editorial Associate: Gay C. Bond
Production Editor: Penelope Sky
Manuscript Editor: Catherine A. Cambron
Permissions Editor: Carline Haga
Interior Design: Wendy Calmenson
Cover Design: Lisa Thompson, E. Kelly Shoemaker
Cover Illustration: Laura Militzer Bryant
Back Cover Photograph: Douglas C. Gamage
Art Coordinator: Lisa Torri
Interior Illustration: Gloria Langer
Photo Editor: Diana Mara Henry
Indexer: Do Mi Stauber
Typesetting: Graphic World, Inc.
Printing and Binding: Malloy Lithographing, Inc.

93, Excerpt from "Some Questions about the Past and the Future," by V. Bullough, pp. 335-354. In V. Bullough, *The Subordinate Sex: A History of Attitudes Toward Women.* Copyright © 1974 by Penguin Books. Reprinted by permission of the author. **137,** Excerpt from *The Moon Is Always Female,* by Marge Piercy. Copyright © 1978 by Marge Piercy. Reprinted by permission of Alfred A. Knopf, Inc. **155,** Line from "Song" reprinted from *The Fact of a Doorframe, Poems Selected and New, 1950–1984,* by Adrienne Rich, by permission of the author and W. W. Norton & Company, Inc. Copyright © 1984 by Adrienne Rich. Copyright © 1975, 1978 by W. W. Norton & Company, Inc. Copyright © 1981 by Adrienne Rich. **157,** Excerpts from *Small Changes,* by Marge Piercy. Copyright © 1975 Fawcett Books. Reprinted by Fawcett Books. Reprinted by permission of Doubleday & Co; excerpts from *Circles on the Water* by Marge Piercy. Copyright © 1992 by Marge Piercy. Reprinted by permission of Alfred A. Knopf, Inc. **254,** Excerpts from "Is This Where I Was Going?" by Natasha Josefowitz. Copyright © 1983 by Warner Books. Reprinted by permission.

This book is dedicated to my granddaughter
Samone,
whose life, along with her generation of women,
I hope will be rich and full.

It is also dedicated to
Sara, Judith, Joshua, Susan, and *Al,*
who keep me dancing.

CONTENTS

P R E F A C E

THIS IS A BOOK ABOUT CONTEMPORARY GIRLS AND WOMEN IN the United States. The complex relationship between being born female and becoming a culturally defined woman is influenced by parents, schools, the mass media, employers, the law, and by religious, political, and other social institutions. The text focuses on how the social construction of gender from prenatal development through old age influences behavior, beliefs, attitudes, and all human relationships.

I bring a social psychological perspective to my analysis of gender, emphasizing that what a person does in a particular situation reflects characteristics, habits, and expectations derived from previous experiences as well as the special demands of the situation itself. It is essential to recognize that gender-identified behavior varies with time, place, and individual and group circumstances, and that it is affected by ethnicity, class, sexual orientation, and other social categories.

Gender is like a prism, and there are women throughout the spectrum of possibilities. We must understand why women in our society are more like each other than like men, attending also to the fact that significant differences in personal development result in diversity among women, and that the same woman will behave differently in different situations.

The Second Edition

Since *Women's Lives* was published in 1987, my files have grown considerably with the provocative new feminist analyses and exciting scholarly articles that have appeared

at a steady rate. My commitment to feminist psychology and to those interested in it made me rethink the text. I was encouraged by the positive response to the first edition by students, colleagues, and the relatives and friends with whom they shared it.

I have integrated new scholarship with important older work. Students invariably ask, "But aren't women's lives different *now* from what they were *then?*" I have drawn from numerous sources to illuminate the past and the present, so that careful readers will be able to answer this question for themselves.

Chapters necessarily vary considerably in length. For example, in the chapter on childhood I examine both how girls acquire gender and the major sources of this learning, subjects that are closely intertwined. Similarly, in the chapter on adult women's behavior I consider the related issues of personality and of mental and physical health.

I want to share all that I can in support of the fundamental principle that women and men are members of the same species. This fact is often lost sight of in scholarship, social policies, and institutional practices, in personal life as well as in politics. Yet the nature of our humanness makes gender learning possible. The potential for women is greater than what we have achieved; as our opportunities increase so does our range of competence and ability.

Acknowledgments

Many individuals have contributed to *Women's Lives,* some indirectly with their provocative ideas, questions, and active pursuit of gender equality, and others more directly with their strong support, constructive criticism, and love. This book reflects the wisdom of students, coworkers, family, friends, and colleagues in psychology and women's studies. There are many who merit mention, but to my colleague Mary Ellen Reilly go very special thanks for many years of encouragement and extraordinary friendship. I also acknowledge the women with whom I have met weekly since 1972 to discuss personal issues and the relationship between our experiences and the larger political, economic, and social context. To all my sisters in this wonderful group of caring, challenging women I offer this public expression of appreciation. Essential too has been the loving sustenance I have always been able to count on from my husband Al Lott and from my children Sara, Judith, and Joshua.

I also thank Claire Verduin of Brooks/Cole for her enthusiasm and the reviewers who commented on the manuscript: Laura Carstensen, Stanford University; Elizabeth McDonel, South Carolina Department of Public Health; Patricia Rozee, California State University at Long Beach; and Bonnie Tyler, University of Maryland. I appreciate the careful and respectful assistance of everyone who helped me at various times during the two-year revision process, permissions and production staffs as well as editors. Special thanks go to Penelope Sky and Catherine Cambron, who painstakingly reviewed every word and offered constructive suggestions.

The final work on this edition was done while I was a visiting scholar at the Institute for Research on Women and Gender at Stanford University during the winter and spring quarters of 1993. I am grateful to the staff and the other scholars in residence for providing an environment that encouraged and supported the exchange of interdisciplinary ideas and methods. In particular I thank Iris Litt and Sherri Matteo for their creative leadership; Gini Gould, Pam Mosher, Sally Schroeder, and Lorraine Macchello for keeping the institute functioning effectively and hospitably; and my respected colleagues and new friends, the visiting and affiliated scholars.

Whoever you are, and whatever your purpose in reading this book, I hope that you find it clear and exciting, that it raises many questions and answers some, that it will deepen your understanding of gender and society, and that it will inspire personal insight and challenges. I have certainly been enriched by teaching feminist psychology and by my own and others' research and writing. I hope that my enthusiasm will be shared.

Bernice Lott

WOMEN'S LIVES

THEMES AND VARIATIONS IN GENDER LEARNING

Second Edition

INTRODUCTION: "AIN'T I A WOMAN?"

The man over there says women need to be helped into carriages and lifted over ditches, and to have the best place everywhere. Nobody ever helps me into carriages or over puddles, or gives me the best place—and ain't I a woman? . . . I have ploughed and planted and gathered into barns, and no man could head me—and ain't I a woman? I could work as much and eat as much as a man—when I could get it—and bear the lash as well! And ain't I a woman?

SOJOURNER TRUTH, 1851 (Flexner, 1975, p. 91)

It's time that people realize that women in this country can do any job that they want to do.

SALLY RIDE, ASTRONAUT (New Woman, 1987, p. 18)

It is not only a question of bringing women into the old roles of men but also of bringing men into the old roles of women.

GRO BRUNDTLAND, PRIME MINISTER OF NORWAY
(New Woman, 1987, p. 18)

AT A MEETING FOR WOMEN'S RIGHTS ALMOST A century and a half ago in Akron, Ohio, a freed slave known as Sojourner Truth responded, in the words that lead off this chapter, to a White clergyman who had argued that because women were weak and helpless they could not, and should not, vote. But the Black slave woman had never been defined in the same way as the White woman on the Southern plantation, just as the definition of the Victorian lady had never fit the working-class woman who had labored in the factories of industrialized cities. Differing conditions of life taught each different ways of being a woman. While the pre–Civil War southern European-American woman of wealth and aristocracy may have been led to believe, like Scarlett O'Hara in *Gone With the Wind,* that she was weak, fragile, modest, and delicate, African-American women labored in the fields, were sexually assaulted by European-American men, and could be stripped naked and whipped. In the preindustrial United States (prior to about 1820), the division of labor among the European-American middle class, with men in the fields and women in the home, did not hold for Native American, African-American, or poor European-American women (Bose, 1987). In today's world, women of all social classes are likely to aspire to any job—including that of astronaut, carpenter, or head of state—and to hope that men will want to do the jobs traditionally ascribed to women.

WHAT WOMEN DO

Women, like men, learn continuously from birth the behavior appropriate to our status. As we grow older or experience changed circumstances in our lives, the earlier lessons may be negated and contradicted, or reinforced and affirmed. At different times and in different cultures, women's behavior has spanned the spectrum of human potential. For example, Margaret Mead (1949/1968) documented dramatic variations in women's approved behaviors among different cultures in New Guinea. At one extreme were the Mundugamor women, who did all the major work of providing food, were assertive and vigorous, detested the bearing and rearing of children, and were, according to Mead, awful mothers. Kola women were described differently, as "sharp tongued and nagging" philanderers who practiced sorcery on their husbands, while Arapesh women were seen as nurturant, maternal, cooperative, and unaggressive, like Arapesh men.

That the meanings of *woman* and *man* vary in different cultures is abundantly illustrated in the data of cultural anthropology. As Sherry Ortner and Harriet Whitehead (1981) have noted, "What gender is, what men and women are, what sorts of relations do or should obtain between them—all of these notions do not simply reflect or elaborate upon biological 'givens,' but are largely products of social and cultural processes" (p. 1). We know that every social behavior performed by men is also done by some or many women, within the same culture or in another. And with the exception of a universal responsibility for the care of infants—not a responsibility all women carry out well or cheerfully—women's tasks and skills vary widely both across and within cultures.

Women in all cultures engage in productive work requiring special training and abilities, and they contribute substantially to their economies, as found in a study of 862 societies (Aronoff & Crano, 1975). Sharon Tiffany (1982) has pointed out that:

> Women may herd reindeer, harpoon seals, carry fifty-pound or heavier loads for miles, labor in fields, dig ditches, haul heavy bags of groceries . . . or spend most of their productive years secluded in courtyards engaged in a routine round of domestic tasks. There is extraordinary variety throughout the world in "women's work" (p. 4).

The photos on pages 3, 4, and 5 show contemporary women engaged in productive work outside of their homes. In the first photograph, two women are hauling huge bundles of sugarcane to be used for fuel; in the second, the woman in the foreground is forking skatefish in preparation for their use as bait. The third photograph, on page 5, is of a U.S. servicewoman working on a helicopter; currently, 10 percent of all soldiers in this country are women (Quindlen, 1991a).

What women do depends on the historical, economic, and social conditions of their lives. During the first several generations of European settlement in the United States, "the exigencies of surviving in the wilderness placed a premium on woman's participation in production, accorded her a central position in economic life, and discouraged any refined notions about her distinctive or feminine temperament" (Ryan, 1979, p. xiv). This conclusion is powerfully and sensitively illustrated in the film *Heartland,* about European settlers in Wyoming in the early 1900s, as well as in *The Dollmaker,* a novel by Harriette Arnow (1954) about a proud Kentucky woman in the 1930s. In one incident, to save her son's life, she purposely runs a soldier's car off the road with her mule and then, with a knife blade, cuts a hole in the swollen

Third-world women hauling sugar cane. (Photograph by Mark Edwards/Still Pictures.)

neck of her desperately ill, barely breathing child—hardly the stereotyped picture of an emotional, dependent woman.

Christine Bose (1987) has pointed out that when our economy was based primarily on agriculture, "monetary income typically came from women's labor in cottage-industry textile work or from selling eggs, butter, or other goods from the home garden" (p. 270). Women earned money from truck farming, weaving, and selling herbs, berries, nuts, flour, cornmeal, and poultry; they also ran newspapers, taverns, and shops. At the beginning of industrialization, women were the first to work for wages in the factories and mills. Although factory labor later became predominantly the sphere of men, by the middle of the nineteenth century "most young urban immigrant and working-class women, as well as most black women, would be engaged in paid labor for a number of years" (Bose, 1987, p. 282).

Dramatic evidence of the responsiveness of sex roles to economic pressures and opportunities comes from a study by Jagna Sharff (1983). Among poor Puerto Rican immigrants living in New York City, she found that children were reared so as to maximize the family's

adaptation to their conditions, leading to different models within the same gender. For example, one girl might be encouraged to develop the traditional docile qualities associated with attracting a lover and husband, and thus function as a "child reproducer," whereas another might be reared as the family's "scholar/advocate" and trained early in life for dominance, assertiveness, and upward mobility.

As noted by Harriet Bradley (1989),

which particular tasks and occupations are defined as "men's" and which as "women's" will vary according to time and place. . . . For example, before the industrialization of the cotton industry men habitually were weavers, while women did the spinning. The introduction of power-driven machinery brought a reversal of these roles. There are few tasks . . . which have not in some time and place been performed by women. (p. 1)

Judith Rossner's 1983 novel *August* tells the story of a young woman who was brought up by two women. One had stayed at home but had also been a superb skier and horsewoman, able to "fix, or build . . . almost anything in the house . . . an excellent cook and a nearly miraculous

Rhode Island women forking skatefish bait. (Photograph by Kathleen Royles, Peacedale, R.I./Courtesy of *The Narragansett Times.*)

gardener" (p. 7). The other parent had cuddled the child and was a skilled dressmaker but didn't like to cook and went to work every day as the head of a high school mathematics department dressed in make-up, jewelry, and skirts. These women's individual patterns of skills and interests shatter our stereotypes but do not contradict what we know about women from our own experience.

ORIENTATION AND OBJECTIVES

These examples of diversity and range in women's work and competencies provide a background for the major thesis of this book—that "one is not born, but rather becomes a woman," words borrowed from Simone de Beauvoir (1949/1961). This book is about learning how and what it means to be a woman.

The enforced silence of women in earlier generations and women's general invisibility in public history has re-

sulted in gaps in our knowledge, but new scholarship has begun to widen our sources of information and to enrich our understanding of women's lives. As pointed out by Arthur Schlesinger, Jr. (1981), "women have constituted the most spectacular casualty of traditional history"; while making up "at least half the human race . . . you could never tell that by looking at the books historians write" (p. 11)—or those written in other fields. This neglect of women, however, is being replaced by reanalyses and new research, and by autobiographies, fiction, poetry, diaries, and essays that provide significant clues to common as well as differing experiences.

Gender as an Organizing Principle in Culture

Careful study of contemporary institutions—the schools, family, mass media, economy, and so on—indicate that social practices are almost everywhere differentiated by gender, that expectations are not the same for women and men, and that serious consequences to the individual

A servicewoman working on a helicopter. (Photograph ©
Bettye Lane.)

follow from both conformity and deviation. Gender organizes social life and thus much of individual experience. It follows, therefore, that gender influences motivation, beliefs, expectations, and social behavior. Because our society is so gender-focused, it is necessary, as Beth Hess and Myra Ferree (1987) point out, "to trace the experiences of people within a gendered social structure" (p. 17).

While the meaning of "man" is as much learned, or culturally constructed, as the meaning of "woman," this book is concerned primarily with the particular experiences shared by girls and women in today's United States, comparing these with the experiences of boys and men whenever necessary. My objective is to trace the continuing socialization of women in this country from birth through old age, weaving the pattern of experiences with strands taken from diverse sources—from fiction, reports of everyday life, and the data of social psychology. Critical aspects of women's experience will be examined chronologically, highlighting the pressures and sanctions that

reinforce the acquiring of gender-appropriate behavior and those that encourage within-gender differences.

We will be concerned with discerning the life conditions systematically related—by cultural prescription, regulation, or arrangement—to being born female in our society. We will try to identify the conditions that contribute to learning how to behave like a woman, noting variations in these conditions during different periods of women's lives and across groups differing in ethnicity, social class, background, and other significant characteristics. Following girls through childhood into adolescence and early, middle, and older adulthood, we will attend to sexuality, relationships, single and married lifestyles, parenthood, employment, health, and the role of hostility and violence in women's lives, with emphasis on shared experiences that link all women as well as variations in circumstances, interests, and concerns. Information about women's lives from a variety of sources—from the psychological laboratory and clinic; from experiments, surveys, observation in natural settings, and statistical summaries of quantitative data; from newspaper accounts of current events; and from biography, fiction, and poetry—will be considered in the hope that from their integration might emerge significant and verifiable themes.

This is a personal book that reflects—like all human work in science as in other spheres—the values and assumptions of its author. I have sampled and selected from the literature, and although I often compare the two genders, women's lives are my central concern. My perspectives are that of a behavior-focused social psychologist and a feminist.

Focus on Social Behavior

Socialization (or enculturation) can be defined as the process of learning those behaviors that are appropriate for members of a particular status group. Some psychologists and other social scientists emphasize childhood socialization, restricting the meaning of the term to the process of acquiring culture during a person's early years. This book, however, uses the concept of socialization more broadly, to refer to a process that continues throughout a person's life. It is assumed that individuals never stop learning cultural meanings.

The differential behaviors we learn as appropriate for girls/women and for boys/men in a given society and historical period constitute the roles identified with sex. Because these behaviors are, in very large part, unrelated to the reliable biological distinctions between the sexes, we use the word *gender* to identify the definitions of women and men that are learned. Whereas *female* and *male* refer to sexual distinctions across all animal species, the terms *woman* and *man* are specific to humans and denote gender—that is, learned attributions about characteristics and behavior.

The language in this book is primarily that of *behavior-focused* social psychology. This approach emphasizes what people do in particular situations and assumes that all human behavior, beyond molecular physiological responses and innate reflex mechanisms, is learned and can be explained by a common set of interrelated principles. Behavior is broadly interpreted to include what persons do and what they say about their goals, attitudes, beliefs, feelings, perceptions, and memories; and explanation involves relating social behavior to its antecedents and consequences.

Within this approach, a *learning-oriented* theoretical model guides my analyses of social behavior. This model requires, on the simplest level, that explanations of behavior take into account the setting in which the behavior occurs; the individual's needs, goals, or motives as they are inferred from what the individual does or says; the range of probable responses that the individual can make in the situation (because of prior learning, physical capacity, and situational properties); and the consequences (provided by self, others, or events) that may follow particular acts. Because of the wide-ranging nature of the material and issues considered in this book, learning theory language is used with varying degrees of specificity, rigor, and consistency. Although not used systematically, learning constructs provide a framework for my thinking and have influenced both the questions I raise and the nature of the evidence I bring to bear on them.

My approach reflects a *social psychological* perspective in that I view people and environments as mutually dependent and interactive. The environment includes the immediate physical and social situation, while the person may be said to comprise motives, habits, memories, physiological/neurological conditions, and structural characteristics (a product of genetic and environmental interaction), reflecting both past and future objectives and expectations. Social psychologists, whether behaviorist or cognitive in orientation, are generally optimistic about the possibilities of personal change, since we see situational variables as important determinants of behavior. Our aim is to understand the relationships between individual behavior and conditions of the social milieu, whether these be the measurable characteristics of small groups, the contents of a persuasive message, or the norms of a culture. We assume that what persons do is relatable to their own direct experiences, to the consequences that follow their behavior, and to observations made of others' behavior.

A Feminist Perspective

In this book, the approach of the social psychologist is complemented by feminist analysis, a perspective that combines clearly articulated values with a set of research priorities. Fundamental to feminism is the value that all persons should be permitted equality of opportunity for full development to the extent that this development does not impede that of others. Since ample historical and contemporary evidence shows that women as a group have experienced significantly fewer opportunities and greater restrictions than men, feminists—who may be either women or men—pay particular attention to women's experiences and circumstances.

A major objective of feminist scholarship is to examine carefully the antecedents and conditions of gender inequality and to specify its consequences for women, men, and children; for social life and institutions; and for social products such as language, art, and science. In addition, a feminist analysis proposes remedies, and feminists actively work to effect solutions and change. These objectives unify feminist scholarship in diverse fields. In literature, economics, art, history, sociology, psychology, and the natural sciences, feminist analyses have produced radical reexaminations of assumptions and reconstructions of previously accepted interpretations. A feminist perspective, as Evelyn Keller (1983) has noted, "leads us to inquire into the simultaneous construction of both gender and science. It also provides us with a particular method for doing so" (p. 15). That method rests upon the recognition that the personal and the political are always related.

The *Association for Women in Psychology* (AWP), an organization of feminist psychologists founded in 1969, cites among its objectives: (a) to end the role psychology has played in perpetuating unquestioned assumptions about the "natures" of women and men; (b) to encourage research on gender; (c) to educate the profession and the public about issues and problems of concern to women; and (d) to work "to eliminate any practices and prejudices that divide women from one another, such as racism, heterosexism, ageism, classism or conflicts arising from differing religious orientations" (AWP Brochure, no date). In 1973, the *American Psychological Association* "accepted a petition signed by 800 members and recognized the psychology of women as a separate division of the association, ending a quarter century of struggle" (Walsh,

1985, p. 199). The major objectives of this group (Division 35), of which I was president in 1990–91, are to promote the study of women, encourage "diversity of approaches and interests," and provide "a forum for the development of a comprehensive feminist and multicultural approach to understanding the psychological and social realities of women" (Division 35 Brochure, no date).

The Impact of Feminism

Feminist scholarship has invigorated, expanded, and transformed traditional disciplines. In psychology as in other fields, the potential for enrichment has come from "critical analyses of the discipline to uncover its androcentric bias in both content and method" and from "the asking of new questions, and the presentation of new hypotheses and theoretical formulations that follow from a focus on the experiences and conditions of women's lives" (Lott, 1985, p. 156). Feminist research in psychology is distinguishable from other research not in the rigor of its methodology or its adherence to the rules of science, but instead in its choice of problems and ultimate objectives. Feminist research satisfies the primary requirements of scientific objectivity, that the relationships described among events be repeatable or verifiable and that the data brought to bear on research questions be accurate and reliable. Like other theoretical positions, a feminist approach must be judged on logical and empirical grounds. Thus, although this book reflects a particular point of view, it does so with due respect for the rules of science and in anticipation of reasoned challenges and continued inquiry into both old and newly arising questions.

The feminist perspective in psychology includes a number of interrelated assumptions and values, many of which are shared with feminists in other disciplines. These include:

> recognition of the patriarchal, sexist nature of most aspects of contemporary life and social institutions; recognition of the negative consequences of gender inequities in power; focus on the entire range of women's experiences; and efforts for change in alliance with others to eliminate barriers to resources based on gender, ethnicity, class, and other social categories. In applying the feminist agenda to our work, our objectives are to promote the interests of women, human welfare in general, and the health and integrity of psychology as a scientific enterprise. (Lott, 1991, p. 508)

While some issues continue to provoke controversy and lively debate, there is a consensus among feminist psychologists on a scholarly agenda. Most of us would agree that science, like other human enterprises, is not value-free; that gender is a cultural construction and an ongoing process; that the social, political, and historical context must always be considered to understand the origin of research questions and to interpret data; that there is always a relationship between researcher and the persons studied; and that multiple methods yield the widest range of information. Similar agendas have been articulated by feminists in other disciplines, particularly in the social sciences (Hess & Ferree, 1987).

Feminist psychologists have been active in research, in theory building, in clinical practice, and in teaching. By the 1984–85 academic year, 209 psychology departments in this country (23 percent of those surveyed) taught at least one course on the psychology of women, a number that grew from 32 in 1972 (Walsh, 1985). Two psychology journals are specifically concerned with women and gender issues (*Sex Roles* and *Psychology of Women Quarterly*), and articles by feminist psychologists appear in dozens of other professional periodicals. The raised consciousness that we have effected among our colleagues, and their recognition of our work, is illustrated in the following assessment by Philip Shaver and Clyde Hendrick (1987):

> When the current wave of feminism began to break twenty-five years ago, few people anticipated one of its notable effects: the revitalization of academic disciplines as diverse as literature, history, biology, and psychology. Anticipated or not, that is surely what happened. (p. 7)

Feminist research has made significant contributions to psychology, including asking new questions, making explicit the role of personal experience and values in science, treating gender as a stimulus to which persons respond, questioning earlier research that ignored or accepted unproven assumptions about women, and studying issues of particular relevance to women. A concern with women's issues is becoming more and more evident in psychology as women's numbers among students, academics, and practitioners increase. As reported by Ann Howard (1987), twice as many women as men now earn undergraduate degrees in psychology, and in 1984, beginning a trend that is continuing, the number of doctorates awarded to women equaled the number awarded to men.

It has been reported that the term *feminist* has negative connotations for many (Bolotin, 1982; Friedan, 1985), conjuring up images of tough, unattractive, bitter women. Most surveys, however, find that a third or more of young women in the United States identify themselves as feminists (cf. DiFilippo & Wexler, 1991; Geyer, 1989). That a negative view may not be as common as the media would have us believe is also illustrated by a study of a large college-student sample (Berryman-Fink & Verderber, 1985). This investigation found, among persons of both genders, that feminists tended to be seen as logical, knowledgeable, intelligent, caring, and flexible women who were likely to be employed, ambitious, independent, active, assertive, and energetic, and who supported equal wages, equal rights, and the Equal Rights Amendment.

Despite such findings—or perhaps because of them—"feminist bashing" seems to be popular in the current press. For example, Georgie Ann Geyer (1989) in a syndicated newspaper column headlined "Is Feminism Dead?" concluded that it was because, even though feminists had "won some of the most extraordinary fights for human equality and justice the world has ever known," women had given up the "truly feminine" in themselves and "climbed into the male value system" (p. A-24). In an equally critical article in *Newsweek,* Kay Ebeling (1990) asserted that feminism had "backfired against women," and that its reality was "a lot of frenzied and overworked women dropping kids off at day-care centers" (p. 9). And an editorial in a new ultra-conservative publication, *Campus,* lashed out at feminism, calling it an "ideology that seeks fundamentally to restructure society" and accusing it of being "about politics and power rather than the traditional objects of academic inquiry" (Lutz, 1991, p. 1).

The reality is that feminists are concerned with politics, power, and with the reliable and valid expansion of human knowledge in all areas. What women want from feminism, as noted by Katha Pollitt (1990), is "respect for women as full and equal members of the human race" (p. 12). The *Doonesbury* cartoon above states this in a way that helps us laugh at feminism's bad press. The majority of college women, a recent poll found, support gender equality on all levels—economic, political, and social (cf. DiFilippo & Wexler, 1991)—supporting Vivian Gornick's (1990) conclusion that "contemporary feminism has changed forever the way we think about ourselves" and the course of our lives (p. 52). At an international conference I attended in February 1993 in San Jose, Costa Rica (the Fifth International Interdisciplinary Congress on Women), where about 2000 women from all over the world met together, the word *feminist* was proudly spoken and heard in presentation after presentation.

Among those who have a feminist orientation, it serves a guiding function in responses to the world around us. What another observer might ignore or find trivial, a feminist may interpret, by putting it in the context of

DOONESBURY. Copyright 1971, 1972, 1973, G. B. Trudeau. Reprinted with permission of Universal Press Syndicate. All rights reserved.

similar events, as having important potential consequences for the lives of women. For example, we laugh but also pay attention when reading about the British postage stamp printed in honor of the (now dissolved) marriage of Prince Charles and Lady Diana that shows him towering over her, even though they are actually almost the same height ("Royal Photo," 1981); the explanation is that Charles, a future king, was photographed standing on a box! Other stories may make us laugh and cry at the same time. In commenting on the often ridiculous situations that former vice president Quayle was found in, two reporters (Jehl & Gerstenzang, 1988) quoted "a well-placed Republican" about the day newly elected George Bush went to call on President Reagan at the White House. "The most telling picture" of Quayle's role, said the informant, was seeing him "three steps behind [Bush], with the women. That summed it all up" (p. A-1)! Not quite so amusing is a story ("Cleveland Clinic," 1987) about a fertility clinic that collects, from donor women, ova that are later fertilized in a laboratory by sperm from

©The Guerrilla Girls. Used with permission.

husbands of women who will have the newly formed embryos implanted in their uteruses; the clinic's guidelines require that a married woman donor must have her husband's consent.

Feminist responses to such reports of gender inequality take many forms—personal, professional, and political. One group of artists, calling themselves "The Guerrilla Girls," has since 1985 "regularly papered sections of lower Manhattan with smartly designed black-and-white posters . . . [that] level charges of sexism and racism at various quarters of the art world" (Smith, 1990). Their posters have been included in art exhibitions and acquired by museums and libraries; an example of their work is shown above. If you don't want to get quite as active as these feminists, try something simpler and more subtle. Ask a friend or relative to solve the following riddle:

> A father and his son are in a car accident. The father is killed and the son is rushed to the hospital for surgery. The surgeon on duty examines the patient and says, "I can't operate on him. He's my son." How can that be?

See how long it takes for the person hearing the riddle to come up with the right answer: the surgeon is the boy's mother.

Sexism as Status Quo

Women's lesser social status relative to men's and women's exclusion from particular places and situations are general conditions in this society. Feminists are concerned with the systematic exclusion of most women from experiences necessary for our full development as human beings, and with our limited access to resources, positions of power, and opportunities for personal growth. We see photographs like the one shown on p. 10 all the time, usually without thinking twice. But look again—what do you see? A group composed only of men is deliberating on still another important issue that affects all of us—in this case, it was the Iran-Contra hearings in Congress.

The scarcity of women in positions of real power in this country should be a source of national embarrassment. In fact, it proved to be so, as well as a stimulus for change, when television viewers in October 1991 saw law professor Anita Hill questioned by an all-male, all-European-American Senate Judiciary Committee on her charges of sexual harassment against Supreme Court nominee Clarence Thomas. Following the elections of 1992, widely acclaimed as the "year of the woman," the number of women in the Senate tripled, from 2 to 6, and

All-male committee in the United States Congress. (Photograph by UPI/Bettmann.)

24 new women representatives joined 23 incumbents in the House of Representatives, raising the number of women in the House to an all-time high of 47 (or 11 percent of the total). Despite these real and impressive gains, the United States probably remains among those countries in the world "with the smallest proportions of women in national legislative bodies" (*The American Woman,* 1988, p. 94). And yet, women traditionally play an active role in U.S. politics; they accounted for 54 percent of the turnout in the 1992 presidential election ("Women Are Victorious," 1992).

Among the most devastating consequences of gender inequality in our country is the impoverishment of millions of women and their children. The data are unambiguous, and the "feminization of poverty" has become one of the catchiest new phrases in the social science lexicon. At the end of the 1980s, "just over 24 percent of all infants were born to mothers who had no prenatal care, 20 percent of all children lived in poverty" ("Children's Lives," 1991), and 43 percent of all African-American children were born poor (Lewis, 1991), as assessed by the most conservative of measures, the Social Security Poverty Index. The statistics for women of color are especially staggering. In the 1980s, out of every 100

European-American women in this country, 9.8 lived below the poverty line, compared with 6.6 out of every 100 European-American men; meanwhile, out of every 100 African-American women, 29.4 were poor, compared with 19.5 out of every 100 African-American men (McClanahan, 1989). Among all households headed by African-American women in 1986, 44.3 percent were poor; among all households headed by European-American women, 25.7 percent were poor (*New York Times,* 1988). Women's poverty, according to most analysts, stems from two major factors: women bear the primary responsibility for rearing children, and women's opportunities in the job market are largely restricted to low-paying jobs with little or no upward mobility. Few middle-class people realize that most poor people are employed: "in 1989 most poor families with children had at least one worker, and paychecks—not welfare checks—were the family's biggest source of income" ("Number of Poor," 1991, p. A-2). We will return to the subject of women's poverty in a later chapter.

Women's absence from high-level decision making and women's poverty are two symptoms or consequences of sexism in our society. What do we mean by sexism? It can be understood in an interpersonal context, in social psychological terms, as having three related components: (a) negative attitudes toward women—generalized hostility, dislike, misogyny, or *prejudice*; (b) beliefs about women that reinforce, complement, or justify the prejudice, including a basic assumption of inferiority—in other words, *stereotypes*, or well learned, widely shared, and almost irresistible generalizations about the nature of women; and (c) acts that exclude, distance, or keep women separate—that is, *discrimination*. A man is most likely to distance himself from a woman in situations where he does not expect nurturance, sexual pleasure, or status enhancement and where he does not expect his behavior to be disapproved of or censured.

Recognition of the patriarchal (male-dominated) nature of our institutions and the consequences of sexism for the lives of women and men is not new; feminist thinkers, scholars, and activists have not emerged full-blown from nowhere. Yet there have been periods of relative quiescence when the social problems associated with gender inequality have been relatively ignored. One such period was the 1940s and 1950s. This period was followed by a growing discontent among women, and similar messages could be clearly heard from a range of different places. For example, in France, Simone de Beauvoir (1949/1961) argued compellingly in *The Second Sex* that "neither men nor women are satisfied with each other"; an American, Betty Friedan (1963), in *The Feminine Mystique,* talked about women experiencing the "sickness without a name"; and Germaine Greer (1970), an Australian in Great Britain, wrote that "ungenteel middle-class women are calling for revolution." A new generation of women began to reexamine their lives.

Feminist scholars began a careful documentation of sexism in all areas of life, tracing its manifestation in attitudes, beliefs, and behavior. For example, a study of top-selling introductory textbooks in psychology (Peterson & Kroner, 1992) found a significant overrepresentation of men as authors, reviewers, and scholars whose work was cited, and in photographs and illustrations. Where women appeared in pictures with a greater frequency than men, it was to illustrate psychopathologies and clients in therapy! Another study underscores the pervasiveness of sexism in our culture. Samples of college students, in response to verbal tasks (Hamilton, 1991), were found far more likely to refer to a particular man as a person but to specify the gender of a particular woman, to report male imagery when remembering a story that had used gender neutral pronouns and nouns, and to be more likely to mention a man than a woman when naming "the most typical person they could imagine."

WOMAN AS DEFINED BY MAN

"Throughout history," asserted Sigmund Freud (1933/1964), "people have knocked their heads against the riddle of the nature of femininity" (p. 113). Considering the brilliance of Freud's contributions to the understanding of human behavior and the fact that the majority of his case studies were clinical analyses of women, his admitted failure to solve the riddle of femininity testifies to his androcentric bias. In a conversation with Marie Bonaparte, a respected disciple, Freud is reported by his biographer Ernest Jones (1955) to have admitted that "the great question that has never been answered and which I have not yet been able to answer, despite my thirty years of research into the feminine soul, is 'What does a woman want?'" (p. 421).

The answers men have given to this question tend to focus on a small number of similar themes. For example, when the movement for women's suffrage in the United States was close to its peak, Congress voted, on May 7, 1914, to give women a national holiday, Mother's Day—their interpretation of what women wanted or ought to want (Rosen, 1973). When the magazine *Self* asked 25 men what they would do if they were women, one 34-year-old writer and editor said, "I'd get a husband who was a big wage-earner. *I'd* be the one who stayed home"; a 32-year-old real estate broker said, "I'd spend eight hours shopping and feel I'd accomplished something—even if I didn't buy a thing but a Tab with lemon" ("If I Were," 1991, p. 161).

Woman as "Other"

Simone de Beauvoir (1949/1961) has argued that men have found it advantageous to identify woman as different from themselves—hard to understand, complicated, ambiguous, and not the same as man. Henry Higgins in *My Fair Lady* asks, "Why can't a woman be more like a man?" but I suspect that he did not really want a woman to be more like himself, preferring to define her as the "other," as distinct from the male "one." Such a view appears to have served men well, providing them with a useful scapegoat to which they could attribute the various evils and temptations of the world, ranging from lust to the excesses of greed and materialism that men claim to pursue for the sake of women (Dinnerstein, 1977).

Some recent examples illustrate how readily (and how foolishly) women are blamed for society's problems. A trend called "grazing"—sporadic munching on the run instead of sitting down to a full meal—has been blamed (albeit with tongue in cheek) on "female careerism. Now that they're spending all day at the office, they're no longer preparing meals" (Patinkin, 1984, p. A-3). A more serious event, the U.S. bombing of Libya in 1986, was attributed by Harvard sociologist David Riesman to our country's need to feel superior as a result of our "loss of face in Vietnam, loss of economic status to Japan and the loss of identity of many men who feel threatened by the women's movement" (cf. Trausch, 1986, p. 76). Similarly, psychologist Joyce Brothers has suggested that the great popularity of Sylvester Stallone's macho film characters is due to, men's confusion about their roles, which is—you guessed it—"the fault of American women" (cf. Canby, 1986).

Woman in Folklore, Myth, and Religion

A broad assessment of the ways women are typically presented in mythology and folklore suggests two general conclusions: women are seen to occupy a smaller, more *constricted* space in the world than men—"so much space for Man and his ideas, such cramped quarters for Woman," in the words of Michele Murray (1973, p. 28)—and attitudes toward women are typically *ambivalent*. This ambivalence appears to relate to the division of women into two categories distinguished by the level of assertiveness or independence a woman exhibits. If *passive,* then woman is *good,* described as a mother, virgin, or saint, as noble, pure, giving, or fruitful, and as an inspiration to man. If *active,* however, then woman is *evil,* a temptress, witch, whore, seductress, or distracter of man from his worldly or religious pursuits.

One of the most enduring and basic Judeo-Christian myths is that of Eve. This prototype of woman, fashioned from man and for man, is said to have damned the entire human species for eternity because of her sinful independent action and pursuit of knowledge—no wonder, then, that an Orthodox Jewish man thanks God each day in his morning prayers that he was not born a woman. In the Judeo-Christian view, woman is second to man in creation and status, and she is the cause of the world's troubles. The Book of Genesis (*Holy Bible,* Revised Standard Version) relates that God said to Eve, after she had eaten of the forbidden apple, "I will greatly multiply your pain in childbearing; in pain you shall bring forth your children, yet your desire shall be for your husband, and he shall rule over you" (3:16).

Eve is said to have erred more out of gullibility than malice, but before Eve there was Lilith, presented in some legends as Adam's first wife. According to Aviva Cantor (1976), "the most ancient biblical account of the Creation

relates that God created the first man and the first woman at the same time. Jewish legends tell us that this woman was Lilith" (p. 5). Adam and Lilith are said to have quarreled over Lilith's refusal to obey Adam's command that she lie below him. Insisting on her equality with Adam, since they had both come from the earth, Lilith flew off in rage. In subsequent tales, Lilith appears not as a symbol of independence or equality, but as a witch/demon who is fearsome and threatening to society, kills pregnant or birthing women, injures newborn babies, and excites men in their sleep in order to manufacture demon children from their sperm. A "female demon" with "many evil attributes," she appears in Jewish folklore as "a vampire-like child-killer and the symbol of sensual lust" (Harris & Levey, 1975, p. 1582).

The symbolism of Eve and Lilith is not unique to the Judeo-Christian tradition but appears in some similar form in the legends of earlier cultures. For example, a Sanskrit myth tells of the creation of woman by Twashtri, who then "gave her to man. But after one week, man came to him and said: Lord, this creature . . . makes my life miserable . . . and so I have come to give her back." After another week, man relented and asked for the woman's return and Twashtri gave her back, but after three days man again complained to Twashtri, "She is more of a trouble than a pleasure to me." Twashtri, angered, refused to accede to man's request. "Then man said: What is to be done? For I cannot live either with her or without her" (Queen & Adams, 1955, pp. 1f.). Not too dissimilar is the familiar tale of Pandora and the box, which so strikingly resembles that of Eve and the apple. In the eighth century B.C., the poet Hesiod, to whom the story is attributed, wrote that when Pandora lifted the lid of the jar, "she let forth gloomy afflictions to give men pain; . . . [and] both the earth and the sea are filled with evil" (Hays, 1964, p. 84).

Ramona Barth (1976) collected ancient "wisdom" from many sources that illustrate considerable agreement about the nature and role of women. In *The Confucian Marriage Manual* (sixth century B.C.) one finds, for example, this description: "The five worst infirmities that afflict the female are indocility, discontent, slander, jealousy and silliness. . . . Such is the stupidity of woman's character, that it is incumbent upon her, in every particular way, to distrust herself and to obey her husband." *The Hindu Code of Manu V* (circa 100 A.D.) similarly asserts that "in childhood a woman must be subject to her father; in youth to her husband; when her husband is dead, to her sons. A woman must never be free of subjugation." Was it feared that otherwise a woman would, like the disobedient Pandora, unleash all the evils of the world?

In the thirteenth century, Thomas Aquinas, in *Summa Theologica,* confidently repeated what Aristotle had preached sixteen centuries earlier—that "woman is defective and misbegotten . . . by nature of lower capacity and quality than man." Three centuries later, leaders of reform Protestantism like John Knox merely varied the theme to assert that "woman in her greatest perfection was made to serve and obey man." Thus, men appear to have found women praiseworthy primarily in passivity, dependency, or nurturant service, while fearing, decrying, and discouraging women's autonomy, activity, and desire for knowledge.

ORIGINS AND CORRELATES OF GENDER INEQUALITY

A number of speculative proposals have been offered to account for the historical sources of patriarchy and beliefs that support women's lesser status. They span many possibilities, including the following: (a) ancient goddess-worshiping matriarchal societies were disrupted by male revolts, and men sought revenge for their earlier inferior status; (b) men were jealous and fearful of women's mysterious birth-giving ability and women's tie to nature and fertility; (c) larger size and greater physical strength may have led men in some cultures to take over the tasks of hunting big game and fighting wars, with the consequence that male children were socialized for aggression and female children for docility; and (d) women sought to avoid dangerous situations, not for the women's own sake nor because they were less competent than men to deal with such situations, but for the sake of their infants, to whom women were biologically tied for gestation and nursing. Woman's designation as the "other" is not likely to be explained by just one of these hypotheses, but rather by multiple interdependent factors varying in significance across cultures.

Women as Mothers

A culture's emphasis on women's reproductive capacities and role in child care is the main factor that many contemporary anthropologists and historians relate to women's lesser public influence. Mary Ryan (1979), for example, has concluded that "child care is the nexus of womanhood in most gender systems" (p. ix). And Peggy Sanday (1981a) has noted that among the "simpler societies of the world . . . women give birth and grow children; men kill and make weapons. Men display their kills . . . with the same pride that women hold up the

newly born" (p. 5). Three explanations have been proposed for the relationship between women's role in child care and their lesser social power (Werner, 1984): (a) child care prevents women from acquiring the knowledge, skills, or followers necessary to exert influence; (b) child care restricts women in their opportunities to obtain economic resources; and (c) child care affects the psychological makeup of caretakers in the direction of inhibiting aggressiveness, a correlate of leadership. Dennis Werner's research in Central Brazil did not provide clear support for any one of these explanations over the others, but he did that the more time women were observed to spend on child-rearing tasks, the less influence in the community they were rated as having by other women.

Not all scholars agree, however, that woman's role as mother is the source of her secondary status, and some question the universality of women's lesser social position. According to Louise Lamphere (1977), for example, the "issue of whether or not there is and always has been universal sexual asymmetry or the subordination of women is far from resolved" (p. 613). In some cultures, like that of the Mbuti Pygmies, power, authority, and decision making appear to have been equally shared by women and men, while in other cultures, like that of the Iroquois, women have been dominant in political and economic affairs (Sacks, 1970). Mary Ryan (1979) has proposed that "the Iroquois social system came . . . as close as any known civilization to the standard of sexual equality" (p. xiii). Iroquois women chose chiefs and tribal council delegates; they distributed surplus produce, chose their children's marriage partners, and held half the positions of religious authority.

Karen Sacks (1979) has used such illustrations to support her argument that the relations between women and men, as well as feminine and masculine characteristics, have taken diverse forms in response to men's and women's relationships to the means of production. That women's status has changed as a result of changes in the means of production has also been emphasized by Sharon Tiffany (1982). A study of 186 tribal and historical societies (Hendrix & Hossain, 1988), however, did not find clear evidence relating women's status to their relation to production.

Michelle Rosaldo (1980), in attempting to reconcile the seeming contradictions among diverse sources and analyses of anthropological data, proposed that sexual asymmetries are fundamentally social constructions and that, while the biological facts of reproduction and lactation "leave their mark on women's lives," biological facts do not by themselves explain sexual hierarchies and inequality. The limitations and constraints placed on women's access to "prestigious male pursuits" may be *understandable* consequences of women's role as mothers, but such constraints are *not necessary* consequences. They are imposed on women to varying degrees in different societies. Regardless of the antecedents of women's lesser status and the variations in its extent, Rosaldo concluded that gender inequality is widespread across cultures:

> In all known human groups—and no matter the prerogatives that women may in fact enjoy—the vast majority of opportunities for public influence and prestige, the ability to forge relationships, determine enmities, speak up in public, use or forswear the use of force are all recognized as men's privilege and right (p. 394).

Almost everywhere, according to Rosaldo, women have functioned primarily in the private, domestic sphere, freeing men to operate in the public sphere where they have "privileged access to such resources, persons, and symbols as would sustain their claim to precedence, grant them power and disproportionate rewards" (p. 398).

Women's Work

Even where both genders contribute to the production of needed and desired commodities, there are typically inequities in what men and women receive in exchange for their labor (Lamphere, 1977), and the work that women do is viewed as less important than what men do (Bradley, 1989). Nevertheless, cross-cultural analyses indicate that societies vary in the extent to which they ascribe different roles, tasks, or "natures" to women and men. Some researchers have proposed that the degree of gender separation in tasks and privileges is correlated with the culture's use of violence. One study that tested this hypothesis, first suggested by Geoffrey Gorer, studied a sample of 17 nonindustrial societies and found, as predicted, a strong positive correlation between sex-role rigidity (or lack of egalitarianism) and use of intra- or extra-communal violence (McConahay & McConahay, 1977). Further, although most societies, in the socialization of their children, tend to emphasize expressive traits more for girls and instrumental traits more for boys, societies differ in the degree to which they stress these attributes for *both* genders. In other words, "socialization varies more among societies than between the sexes" (Hendrix & Johnson, 1985, p. 593).

The findings from an impressive recent study of 93 small nonindustrial societies (Coltrane, 1992) confirm such variation and also highlight the importance of a previously neglected variable, the extent to which fathers participate in the rearing of their children. The investigator found that, of his several independent variables (including frequency of warfare, reliance on hunting, and patrilineal descent), only father-child relations were consistently correlated with "men's display of manliness" (strength, aggression, and sexual potency) and with women's deference toward men, husbands' domination of wives, and an ideology of women's inferiority. There were fewer such indicators of gender inequality in societies in which men were more involved in child rearing. These findings strongly suggest that "only when mothers share child rearing with fathers are women likely to avoid the harassment and humiliation that comes from being simultaneously feared and denigrated by men" (p. 105). Women's control of property was also found to correlate negatively with indicators of male dominance. Thus, there is good evidence that gender equity is more likely in cultures in which fathers contribute substantially to child care and in which women have access to property resources.

It is important at this point to note that among those scholars who stress the universality of men's privileged position vis-à-vis women—whatever its source(s)—and those who stress the variations, there is clear agreement that (a) women's behaviors across cultures span the range of human possibilities; (b) cultures vary in the degree to which sex roles are rigidly distinguished and in the level of overall gender inequality; and (c) where tasks are sharply distinguished by gender, those performed by men tend to be more highly valued despite the fact that one gender's domain is not intrinsically better than the other's.

CASTING A LONG SHADOW

The past has laid a heavy burden upon the present, and ancient myths are alarmingly congruent with some current practices. But as we investigate the conditions of women's lives that serve to cramp and contain us, we should also come to appreciate that without the constraints imposed by ideas of gender and their translations into norms of behavior, the possibilities for women and the variations in what women want and can become are vast.

Early Women

History documents women's oppression, but also verifies women's varied abilities and social positions. In the earliest human groups, gender differences in work and status appear to have been minimal. One theory (Fisher,

1979) is that early evolving humanity was egalitarian and that all members of a group gathered and hunted for food. Evidence suggests that early human mothers did not stay at home with their infants but invented carriers for their babies and for food in order to free their hands and to provide storage for what was gathered.

According to Nancy Tanner and Adrienne Zihlman (1976), females "became innovators in the technology of gathering. They covered a wide range, knew it well, and could protect themselves and their offspring from predators" (p. 607). This finding supports the hypothesis proposed by some that, in the long transition from primate to human, it was the female who not only was responsible for the survival of infants but also played the leading role in the evolution and development of our species. For example, William Calvin (1991), a neurophysiologist, has attributed the development of right-handedness among humans to mothers who calmed their babies by cradling them, using their left arms, next to the sound of the mothers' heartbeats. This kept the infants quiet and left the mother's right hand free for gathering nuts and berries and for hunting small game by throwing stones at rabbits and birds. Other scholars have suggested that many of the achievements that distinguish the New from the Old Stone Age—such as pottery making, weaving, planting, and harvesting—should be credited to women.

The evidence clearly indicates, as noted by Marian Lowe (1978), that "the actual tasks and behavior allotted [to women and men] vary markedly from society to society, with no differences in sex role or behavior common to all, other than behavior directly connected with reproduction and lactation" (p. 122). The diversity of women's roles across cultures and history is being increasingly documented by reappraisals of earlier ethnographic accounts and new investigations. In earlier studies, assumptions about gender influenced the gathering of information and left us ignorant about many aspects of women's lives and experiences. We now know that there is no social behavior performed by men in one culture that is not found performed by some or many women within that same culture or another one. As pointed out by Lila Leibowitz (1978), "who sews, or cooks, or hews wood, or draws water, or engages in market bargaining, or works in the fields, or produces the greater portion of subsistence foods are matters so varied as to defy simple sexual classifications" (p. 35). Thus, it is not the case that among all hunter-gatherers it was the men who hunted and the women who gathered, as some earlier investigators assumed. Indeed, a number of foraging societies in which women hunt have now been identified, including the

Agta of the Philippines (Goodman, Griffin, Bion, Estioko-Griffin, & Grove, 1985). Agta women hunt big game to about the same extent as the men do: they "hunt successfully and effectively . . . [and] are primary hunters, not assistants in male-organized hunting activities. Agta women were observed to hunt during menstruation without reluctance and to carry and nurse babies while on hunting forays" (p. 1204). No significant differences were found between Agta women who hunt and those who do not in fertility, reproductive history, height, weight, or age of youngest child.

The study of archeological finds and ancient sagas has suggested to some scholars (e.g., Daly, 1978a; Sanday, 1981a) that religions organized around mother-goddesses flourished in early civilizations. Merlin Stone (1979) has argued that the written literature and oral traditions of large numbers of cultures, spanning the continents, reveal that women were once viewed as deities and heroines, "as strong, determined, wise, courageous, powerful, adventurous, and able to surmount difficult obstacles to achieve set goals" (p. 3). Images have been found of women as judges, warriors, and teachers; and artifacts from the Mycenaen culture (1400 B.C.) show women driving chariots and leading hunts. Findings in archeological sites of the Neolithic period convincingly support arguments for the importance and visibility of women (Atkinson, 1982).

What Women Want Today

What contemporary women want is what has always been possible—full human status. Women want, in Michele Murray's (1973) words, "to cast a shadow fully as long and as rich as the shadow cast by Man . . . not to be the Other, arranged in her place by comparison with the One, he who makes the comparison" (p. 14). We also want men to cast richer shadows than they have thought possible, by learning from women how to do the tasks that have been relegated to us. Most important, we want there to be many ways of becoming and being a woman and to sing in celebration with Denise Levertov (1973, p. 101):

> There is no savor
> more sweet, more salt
> than to be glad to be
> what, woman,
> and who, myself,
> I am, a shadow
> that grows longer as the sun
> moves, drawn out
> on a thread of wonder.

◆ Discussion Questions

1. Find, and share, a newspaper or magazine article that illustrates gender inequality and one that illustrates equality.

2. Provide supporting arguments for one of the hypotheses regarding the origins of gender inequality.

3. What is the meaning of objectivity in science, and how is it achieved? Does objectivity mean being value-free?

4. Compare the social psychological perspective and the feminist perspective with other perspectives in psychology.

5. Ask a small sample of women, of varied ages, what they "want."

CHAPTER 2

"IT'S A GIRL!":
THE NATURE OF
THE FEMALE INFANT

Girls are maggots in the rice. . . . When fishing for treasures in the flood, be careful not to pull in girls.

OLD CHINESE SAYINGS (Kingston, 1977, pp. 51, 62)

To understand human development we need to know . . . about how the environment affects physical growth and patterns, and how individual variation . . . plays into each different life history to produce adults with different competencies and potentials.

ANNE FAUSTO-STERLING (1985, pp. 88f.)

KILLING NEWBORN CHILDREN, ESPECIALLY GIRLS, was a widespread practice in early societies; whether overt or surreptitious, it was a means to control population growth (Harris, 1977).

Born into a culture that for centuries killed or sold unwanted female children, Maxine Hong Kingston (1977) was never quite certain of her worth as she considered what was said about daughters in the old Chinese sayings that opened this chapter. "I watched such words come out of my own mother's and father's mouths; I looked at their ink drawings of poor people snagging their neighbors' flotage with long flood hooks and pushing the girl babies on down the river" (p. 62). Press reports from modern China in the 1980s and 1990s suggested a resurgence of the ancient prejudice against girl babies and a rise in female infanticide among some peasants in rural areas, believed to have been sparked by the government's one-child-per-family fertility policy.

Disdain for girl babies is not unique to one culture. Among the Zulus, an ox was slaughtered in celebration and to give thanks when a boy was born, but no celebration took place on the birth of a girl, who was considered "merely a weed" (Hays, 1964). Similarly, among Orthodox Jews in eastern Europe (Baum, Hyman, & Michel, 1975), the birth of a son was a time for rejoicing, while the birth of a daughter brought "stoic acceptance." I. J. Singer has described the snickering that accompanied the public naming of his sister by their father: "Siring a female child was a shameful act for which [Hassidic Jews] occasionally flogged a young father with their belts" (Baum, Hyman, & Michel, 1975, p. 10).

GIRLS ARE GOOD, BUT AREN'T BOYS BETTER?

Although our society does not selectively discard female infants in the interest of population control nor ridicule the fathers of girls, girl babies continue to be seen as second best. It should not surprise us that women's lower social value is reflected in parents' attitudes and preferences. The lesser desirability of a girl, especially for a first or only child—a phenomenon we find difficult to believe—is documented by data from a variety of sources.

Patrice Horn (1974) reported the results of two studies separated in time by 20 years. The first investigation in 1954 found that a boy was preferred by 92 percent of a sample of men and 66 percent of the women, if they could have only one child. Different investigators asked the same question of a group of college students 20 years later with comparable results. For an only child, 84 percent of the men and 64 percent of the women preferred a boy. Similarly, Ralph Norman (1974) found that the majority of a sample of nonparent and parent students preferred boys; if they could have only one child, 86 percent of the men and 59 percent of the women wanted it to be a boy. Responses given by 6,000 women below the age of 45 in a national fertility study (Westoff & Rindfuss, 1974) indicated that, among women still childless, 63 percent wanted their first child to be a boy. Among all women who intended to have children in the future, the sex preference ratio in favor of boys was 124 for every 100 girls. Lois Hoffman (1977), in a study of a representative national sample of married women under 40 and their husbands, found that couples who had only girls were more likely than couples who had only boys to continue to have children. After reviewing the relevant literature, Nancy Williamson (1976) concluded that "there is little sign of change in attitudes" since the early 1930s, with American parents continuing to prefer boys to girls. "Even when parents in the United States want one child of each sex, they would like the boy first. If they want an odd number of children . . . most would rather have more boys than girls" (p. 847). The narrator in a novel by Alice McDermott (1987), for example, in talking about the lengths to which her mother and some of her friends went to conceive a child, relates that they tried everything—"headstands and Epsom salts and vinegar douches that would not only guarantee a baby but a boy baby" (p. 65).

One group of investigators (Calway-Fagen, Wallston, & Gabel, 1979) studied parents' preferences for their children's sex by means of a clever behavioral measure. A sample of pregnant women and their spouses awaiting their first child were given a choice of four items of infant clothing as a gift. The investigators found that more than twice as many choices were made for blue rubber pants or a blue tailored shirt as for pink ruffled pants or a flowered bib; and in response to a direct question about preference, these expectant parents chose boys over girls by an even larger margin (39 to 17). Additional evidence of preference for boys has come from medical experiments on sex selection of offspring. A Chicago hospital that made a sex-determining technique available to couples using artificial insemination reported that of the first eight births using this procedure, six were boys and two were girls ("Choosing Baby's Sex," 1979). A subsequent press report of a larger number of couples who used a sex-determining procedure noted that "parents requesting the technique have shown an overwhelming preference for male babies" (Lyons, 1984). Finally, a study of 236 parents who had experienced the death of a child found, sadly, that boys had been grieved for more than girls (Littlefield & Rushton, 1986).

Pseudo-Scientific Claims of Women's Inferiority

Do we continue to prefer boys to girls because we still believe the old myths about the biological inferiority of the female sex espoused by early theologians, philosophers, and scientists? Charles Darwin wrote that women's abilities represent "a past and lower state of civilization" and that intellectual eminence could be expected only of men (Agonito, 1977). The influential philosopher Herbert Spencer came to similar conclusions, and wrote:

> That men and women are mentally alike, is as untrue as that they are alike bodily. Just as certainly as they have physical differences which are related to the respective parts they play in the maintenance of the race, so certainly have they psychical differences, similarly related to their respective shares in the rearing and protection of offspring. (Newman, 1985, p. 17)

Nineteenth-century scientists paraded a continuing array of arguments and "evidence" that females were more childlike and primitive than males, and that males were the agents of evolution and the more advanced representatives of the human species. Females were said to have smaller brains than males; when this notion was shown to be false when brain size was considered in relation to body size, then the argument shifted to the size of particular brain lobes. Females were said to have smaller frontal lobes or smaller parietal lobes, depending on which lobes were being identified with intelligence (Patrick, 1895/1979; cf. Shields, 1975a).

The anthropologist Paul Broca never gave up his view that females were biologically impaired. Stephen Jay Gould (1978) tells us that when Broca was confronted with the possibility that the smaller brain weight of women was related to their size, he argued that "we must not forget that women are, on average, a little less intelligent than men . . . therefore . . . the relatively small size of the female brain depends in part upon her physical inferiority and in part upon her intellectual inferiority" (p. 365). According to Gould, Broca's disciple Gustave LeBon, an early social psychologist, went further, insisting that women "represent the most inferior forms of human evolution," manifesting "absence of thought and logic, and incapacity to reason." Distinguished women were few, he said, and were "as exceptional as the birth of any monstrosity" (p. 365).

THE BIOLOGY OF SEX

Such claims regarding the innate inferiority of human females did not end in the nineteenth century. Beginning in the 1970s, there has been a renewed interest in establishing that sex differences in behavior and capacities originate in biology (or in "nature"), and reports of such hypotheses and related research are widely publicized. As noted by Marian Lowe (1983), "a great deal of media attention is given to biological theories that offer naturalistic explanations for the distribution of wealth and power in this society" (p. 56). Such theories can provide wry amusement and material for cartoons like the one on p. 20, but serious scientific critiques of these theories urge us to examine the evidence carefully and point out the interrelationships among science, culture, politics, and social policy (e.g., Bleier, 1984; Fausto-Sterling, 1985). It has been argued (Lewontin, Rose, & Kamin, 1984) that "biological determinism . . . has been a powerful mode of explaining the observed inequalities of status, wealth, and power" (p. 7), presenting these inequalities as natural conditions.

What are the "natural" characteristics of human females? The answer to this question requires that we first understand the biology of sex. We must know what structural and functional characteristics reliably distinguish a newborn child who is female from one who is male. What, in other words, is the significance of our sexual inheritance?

Sex Differentiation in the Human Embryo

Sex is defined initially by one pair of *chromosomes,* out of the total human complement of 23 pairs, that distinguishes females (XX) from males (XY). The genetic pattern (DNA) on these chromosomes determines whether the embryonic *sex glands* (gonads) will differentiate into ovaries (for females) or testes (for males). Another dimension of sex is morphological, defined by the *external reproductive organs* (vagina and penis), the development of which are under the control of *hormones.* These four aspects of sex, normally concordant, are not always in

SYLVIA, by Nicole Hollander; taken from *Providence Journal-Bulletin,* July 3, 1991. (Cartoonists & Writers Syndicate.)

harmony. The study of sexual anomalies has contributed considerably to understanding the biology of sex; distinguishing among its chromosomal, gonadal, morphological, and hormonal components; and clarifying the relationship between these aspects and psychosexual identity. We will turn to examples of discordant development later in this chapter.

Let us now examine closely how sex differentiation normally proceeds in the human embryo. At first, the newly conceived human organism is in a stage of indifferent sexuality, with a single pair of embryonic gonads that can develop in either a male or female direction. The duct system structures for both are present, as can be seen in Figure 2.1. If the embryo has an XX chromosome pair, then the gonads develop into ovaries, the Wolffian ducts degenerate, and the Mullerian ducts differentiate into fallopian tubes and a uterus. If, however, the embryo has received an X chromosome from its mother and a Y from its father, then the genetic instructions are different; chemical catalysts direct the formation of testes, the degeneration of the Mullerian ducts, and the consequent development of the Wolffian ducts into the vas deferens and seminal vesicles. It is as though "at about week 6 or 7, a switch is flipped and the primitive gonad develops either testes or ovaries, the first and crucial step in the pathway of sex differentiation . . . , [and] the differentiating gonad [then] secretes hormones that govern the subsequent stages" (Roberts, 1988, p. 21).

Until quite recently, it was believed that H-Y antigen, a protein synthesized by genetic information on the long arm of the Y chromosome, was responsible for the formation of the testes. New research, however, now implicates a gene known as the testis-determining factor (TDF), which is located on the short arm of the Y chromosome as well as on the X chromosome (Roberts, 1988). This new discovery complicates our understanding of sex determination, and thus far the biochemical nature of TDF has eluded researchers. David Page, a major contributor to this research, believes that the TDF proteins on the X and Y chromosomes are identical and that one TDF shuts off the other only when an embryo has two X chromosomes, leaving only XY embryos with two active TDF genes (cf. Roberts, 1988). This hypothesis remains speculative, but there is little question about the existence of the same "sex-switch" genes on both X and Y chromosomes.

Once the embryonic testes have been formed, for male development to proceed, the testes must produce the Mullerian regression (or inhibiting) hormone and testosterone. Testosterone is responsible for formation of the male internal genital structure, while its derivative dihydrotestosterone is necessary for development of the external genitals (Wilson, George, & Griffin, 1981). This group of interrelated hormones is called androgen.

In the first stage of human sexual development, then, the reproductive structures are identical for XX and XY embryos. Sexual differentiation proceeds gradually, with structural distinctions evident by the end of the twelfth week of development (the first trimester). The standard description of this process assumes that sexual development proceeds in the female direction unless the embryonic testes produce androgen to direct formation of the

A. Internal Structures

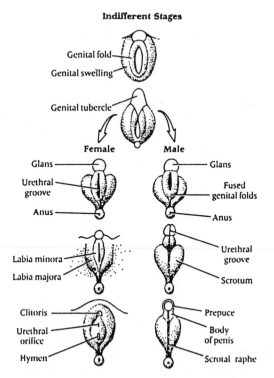

B. External Structures

FIGURE 2.1 *Embryonic development of the female and male genital structures; adapted from J.D. Wilson, F.W. George, and J.E. Griffin. The hormonal control of sexual development. From Science, 1981, 211, 1280.*

male internal and external reproductive structures. This interpretation, however, has been criticized as androcentric (male-centered) by Anne Fausto-Sterling (1985), who questions the assumption that females just naturally "develop from mammalian embryos deficient in male hormone" (p. 81). She has noted the remarkable absence of scientific curiosity about the precise mechanisms underlying female sexual differentiation and cites new work showing that "the XX gonad begins synthesizing large quantities of estrogen at about the same time that the XY gonad begins to make testosterone" (p. 81). Some embryologists have begun to consider that the female hormones (estrogen and progesterone) produced by the placenta and present in high concentration during gestation may be involved in female sexual development. Thus, both female hormones and male hormones are likely to contribute to the sexual differentiation process.

The Influence of Prenatal Hormones on Morphology

Under normal circumstances, from initially undifferentiated gonads and ducts, an XX embryo will develop ovaries and female supportive internal structures, followed by the external genitalia (vagina), while an XY embryo will develop testes and then related internal and external sexual structures. But circumstances are not always normal, and from the consequences of variations our knowledge of the biology of sex has been enhanced.

In some cases, for example, prenatal hormones go wrong and infants are born with sex organ defects. If an enzyme necessary for androgen production is missing or a toxic substance in utero acts as an androgen antagonist, a genetic XY male will be born with the external genitalia of a female (labia, clitoris, and vagina). These "androgen insensitive" (AI) males will typically have a male internal structure (testes) but female external genitals, because their body tissues are insensitive to androgen. Such infants may be labeled as girls and reared as such. When the testes are later discovered, they are surgically removed and estrogen therapy is provided to stimulate breast development and other female secondary sex characteristics. Research on these AI children, summarized by Anke Ehrhardt and Heino Meyer-Bahlburg (1981), indicates that the psychosexual identity of these chromosomal males is typically female, in accordance with their "postnatal rearing history."

A biological error in the opposite direction can occur among chromosomal females exposed to excessive prenatal androgen, producing a condition known as congenital virilizing adrenal hyperplasia (CVAH). In these females, an excessive amount of androgen is released in utero by the cortex of the embryonic adrenal gland (which, like the gonads, also produces sex hormones). Although CVAH can occur in both males and females, the consequences are more serious for the latter, who may be born with sexually ambiguous genitals or a penis but with an internal reproductive system that is female. For such females to be reared as girls, early surgical correction and lifelong hormone treatment are required to ensure fertility and the capacity for normal female sexual functioning. If they go untreated, the girls will "eventually grow thick muscles and a heavy beard" (Hopson, 1987).

Some female embryos are exposed to androgens not as a result of congenital malfunction, as in CVAH, but as a consequence of exogenous hormones being introduced into the blood system of their pregnant mothers and passing through the placental barrier. For example, progesterone given to pregnant women in previous decades to prevent spontaneous abortions (miscarriages) turned out to have an androgenic effect on the embryo, producing a condition called "androgen-induced pseudohermaphroditism," in which the XX infant is born with ovaries but also with a penis or enlarged clitoris. Although it is now well established that treatment with natural or synthetic progesterone (or other hormones) is largely ineffective in preventing problem pregnancies (Ehrhardt & Meyer-Bahlburg, 1981), such treatment was common until the mid-1960s, with unanticipated serious consequences. Pseudohermaphroditism (ambiguous genitalia) was induced in an estimated 18 percent of female offspring of progestin-treated mothers (Reinisch, 1981).

Where prenatal androgen has interfered with the normal progression of female sexual differentiation in the embryo, as in the cases just described, the primitive genital tubercle becomes an enlarged clitoris or a penis, and the labia partially fuse. Chromosomal females born with male genitalia who are labeled male at birth and are reared as boys require surgical removal of ovaries or hormonal treatment to prevent menstruation. Where the condition is recognized at birth, surgical removal of the penis and a program of hormonal treatment make it possible for the child to be reared as a girl.

Intersex Children and Sexual Identity

Evidence from research on such "intersex" children— most of it the work of John Money and his students and colleagues—strongly suggests that the sex assignment at birth and consequent rearing and life histories of individuals is of primary importance in sexual identity. There seems little question that "despite the obvious effects of powerful prenatal hormones on these intersexes, they typically develop sexual identities and orientations in accord with the gender in which their parents reared them" (Hopson, 1987, p. 64). Anke Ehrhardt and Heino Meyer-Bahlburg (1981), major investigators in this field, concluded that "gender identity agrees with the particular sex of assignment, provided that parental doubts are resolved early, and surgical corrections and postnatal hormonal therapy are in agreement with the assigned sex so that the physical appearance of such a child is unambiguously male or female" (p. 1313).

A provocative study (Imperato-McGinley, Guerrero, Gautier, & Peterson, 1974) underscores and illustrates these conclusions. In the Dominican Republic, a group of interrelated families were found who suffer from an inherited deficiency of the enzyme 5-alpha reductase, which is necessary for the conversion of testosterone to dihydrotestosterone. It will be recalled that dihydrotestosterone is essential for the development of a penis; chromosomal males with this enzyme deficiency are therefore born with ambiguous or female-looking genitals. In the investigation by Imperato-McGinley and her colleagues, 18 such children who were raised as girls were studied in adolescence. These intersex children were described as having "a blind vaginal pouch and a clitoral-like phallus" and had undergone no surgical/ medical intervention at birth.

> At puberty, their voice deepens and they develop a typical male phenotype with a substantial increase in muscle mass; there is no breast enlargement. The phallus enlarges to become a functional penis . . . and the change is so striking that these individuals are referred to by the townspeople as "guevedoces"—penis at 12 (years of age). . . . [In puberty] the testes descend . . . and there is an ejaculate. (p. 1213)

Under such conditions—striking physical changes mediated by pubertal secretion of testosterone—it is hardly surprising that the majority of the affected individuals adopted a male sexual identity after puberty.

A lengthy critique of this investigation (Rubin, Reinisch, & Haskett, 1981) suggested that this group of children must have realized that they were different from other girls as pubertal changes gave increasing evidence of their maleness; they are reported to have experienced erections, nocturnal emissions, and to have "initiated masturbation and sexual intercourse." Only 1 of the 18 children continued to dress as a woman after puberty; another lived alone in the hills; and 2 were dead at the time of the investigation. Although it is not clear how much confusion or concern the children's abnormal genitals created, it is very likely that the physical oddness of these children would have been noticed by their parents, siblings, and peers. One hint regarding how the children and their families interpreted their condition is provided by the seemingly good-natured acceptance of these children within the community as ones who "change at twelve," who are first woman, then man, or "machihembra" (Baker, 1980).

Some XY individuals with 5-alpha reductase deficiency have been studied in the United States (Rubin, Reinisch, & Haskett, 1981). These individuals all were reared as girls, in some cases were not treated medically until puberty, and all continued to maintain their female identity. The information available on these cases suggests that as children they were "reared truly unambiguously as females." Susan Baker (1980) has pointed out that, in Dominican culture, gender distinctions are strong and girls marry right after puberty. In such a culture, a person without a functional vagina, who could not have intercourse or bear children, would be unlikely to remain defined as female.

Taken together, the research on intersex children illustrates that sexual identity reflects an interaction of innate and environmental factors and that there is considerable plasticity in the psychological dimension; sexual identification can be continued from infancy or can change in puberty in response to obvious sexual characteristics. As Susan Baker (1980) has suggested, "one's experience of oneself as male or female evolves over time, throughout childhood, and certainly into adolescence with its integration of a new awareness of one's self as a sexual being" (p. 95).

The Influence of Prenatal Hormones on Behavior

As previously discussed, chromosomal female embryos exposed to excessive androgen may develop male external genitalia. Do prenatal hormones also have direct consequences for postnatal behavior? This question is difficult to answer, because androgen-exposed girls differ from other girls not only in prenatal exposure to male hormones but also with respect to such postnatal environmental factors as special treatment by their parents, surgery, medical attention, and hormonal therapy.

John Money and his colleagues have reported a small number of studies on CVAH females who were treated early and reared as girls, the results of which have been summarized as follows:

> The behavior of the prenatally androgenized girls differed significantly from that of the controls in that they typically demonstrated (i) a combination of intense active outdoor play, increased association with male peers, long-term identification as a "tomboy" by self and others . . . , and (ii) decreased parenting rehearsal such as doll play and baby care, and a low interest in the role rehearsal of wife and mother versus having a career. (Ehrhardt & Meyer-Bahlburg, 1981, p. 1314)

These conclusions have been challenged, and it would be premature to conclude that the prenatal presence of androgen has predictable "masculinizing" influences on the later behavior of exposed girls. A number of important questions remain unanswered. For example, were these girls permitted greater behavioral freedom by their parents because of their unusual medical conditions? Also, what was the effect on these girls of their frequent medical examinations and special status? The affected girls clearly differed from comparison girls on variables other than just the prenatal presence or absence of excessive androgen. For example, Estelle Ramey (1976) noted that 7 of the 25 girls in one study were initially identified to their parents as boys and that this sex assignment remained unchanged for as long as 7 months. Others (Quadagno, Briscoe, & Quadagno, 1977) have noted that of the 17 girls in another study, 6 had received surgical correction within the first year of life, 7 between the ages of 1 and 3, and 4 some time later, and that the affected girls had to be maintained on cortisone therapy continually. Moreover, the data obtained in these studies have come from interviews, not from observations of the girls' behavior by unbiased observers. It is likely that ambiguous genitals on a female infant influenced parental perceptions of their daughter's behavior, led to greater tolerance of a wider range of behavior, or both.

Lesley Rogers and Joan Walsh (1982) have noted that CVAH girls in one study were found not to differ from their mothers and siblings in choosing careers over marriage; the CVAH girls, in other words, had aspirations similar to other women in their families. Rogers and Walsh also note the lack of a clear definition of dependent measures in these studies and question how to explain rough outdoor play engaged in by normal girls (i.e., girls who were not exposed prenatally to androgen). One study (Hyde, Rosenberg, & Behrman, 1977) found that a large majority of college women remembered themselves as tomboys in childhood. Since researchers in this area have defined "a preference for male clothing in social and play settings" as a characteristic of tomboys (cf. DeBold & Luria, 1983), large numbers of girls would certainly qualify for the tomboy category today.

No reliable differences have been reported between CVAH girls and others in the incidence of aggressive behaviors, fighting, or other acts of belligerence, nor have differences been found in frequency of reported daydreams about heterosexual romance and dating. Most of the androgen-exposed girls who have been studied have married in adulthood and become mothers. One study (McGuire, Ryan, & Omenn, 1975) found no reliable differences in self-report of tomboyishness, or in any other "femininity/masculinity" comparisons, between a group of 16 CVAH young women and a control group matched in age, height, rural/urban residence, and IQ score.

As noted earlier, female embryos have sometimes been exposed to androgen not because of an adrenal gland defect (CVAH), but because their mothers were treated with natural or synthetic progestins. In the majority of cases in which pregnant women were treated with progestins, their female embryos have not developed male genitalia. Findings from the few studies of behavioral consequences of such exposure are difficult to interpret, because there are two main kinds of progestins—those most closely related chemically to progesterone and those more related to androgenic steroids.* The chemical structure of the synthetic substances varies considerably in the substances' estrogenic or androgenic potential and in their potency; not only do synthetic progestins come in many different combinations but, over the course of a single pregnancy, a woman may have been treated with different progestins or progestin-estrogen combinations (Hines, 1982). In addition, investigations of the behavior of the exposed children have generally utilized inadequate control groups and have not ruled out the influence of pregnancy conditions other than the hormones taken by the mothers (Ehrhardt & Meyer-Bahlburg, 1981).

Estrogen in the form of estradiol or diethylstilbestrol (DES) has also been used, either alone or more often in combination with progesterone, in treating problem pregnancies. Millions of pregnant women in this country took prescribed doses of such hormones in the 1940s, 1950s, and early 1960s without adequate research support for the treatment's effectiveness in preventing

miscarriage. But despite the potentially large research population, few researchers have investigated behavioral consequences of prenatal exposure to estrogen.†

The available data are unclear and difficult to interpret. One study (Reinisch & Karow, 1977) examined the relationship between exposure to synthetic progestin/estrogen combinations and personality factors, as measured by a self-report test, by comparing 71 exposed offspring (of both sexes) between 5 and 17 years of age to their nonexposed siblings. No individuals in the exposed group had genital abnormalities, and some mothers did not recall having taken any medication, although their medical records so indicated. The investigators found no significant personality differences between the exposed children and their siblings. Then the exposed offspring were subdivided into three groups: those exposed mainly to progestins, mainly to estrogens, or to a maximal level of both. When these groups were compared, the children exposed mainly to progestins were found to score higher than those exposed mainly to estrogens on 6 of 16 personality factors—independence, sensitivity, self-assurance, individualism, self-sufficiency, and pathemia (tending to feel rather than think). The investigators concluded from these data that both girls and boys with prenatal exposure to more progestin than estrogen were more inner- or self-directed.

This study presents a number of problems, including whether it was appropriate to use a personality test developed for adults to assess children as young as 5 years old. The group divisions based on the hormone ratios used to treat the mothers may not have been reliable either; the authors themselves noted that many of the mothers received more than one drug during a single pregnancy, and among the mothers treated mainly with progestins 23 different varieties were used. The data do not really support a conclusion that the children who were prenatally exposed mainly to progestin (assumed to be androgenic) manifested more masculine characteristics than the children who were exposed mainly to estrogen, since the obtained differences between these two groups do not reflect or correspond to our culturally stereotyped masculine and feminine patterns. Masculinity, for example, is not typically associated in our culture with sensitivity and feelings.

In a subsequent report of 17 female and 8 male offspring of mothers treated during the first trimester of pregnancy with "synthetic progestins with androgenic

---

* It is instructive to note that the biochemical structures of female and male hormones are fundamentally similar and that each can be converted into the other, as will be discussed later in the chapter.

† The consequences of DES for increased incidence of certain kinds of cancer in prenatally exposed children, especially females, have been studied and widely publicized.

potential," June Reinisch (1981) found that, on a paper-and-pencil measure of "potential for aggressive behavior," these exposed children (ranging in age from 6 to 17 years) scored significantly higher in self-reported physical aggression than their unexposed siblings did. The author does not indicate how these participants were selected; it may be that these are the same children tested in the earlier study and described there as exposed mainly to progestins. If the children in the two reports are indeed the same small group (as suggested by the similarity in numbers and ages), then conclusions about the findings must certainly await replication on independent samples.

Other studies have obtained negative findings. Melissa Hines (1982), for example, found no differences on a paper-and-pencil measure of dominance between 25 women prenatally exposed to DES and their sister controls, and a 1980 study by Kester, Green, Finch, and Williams (reported by Hines) found no differences on a test of personality attributes between a group of men prenatally exposed to DES and a group exposed to progesterone. A longitudinal investigation (Sandberg, Ehrhardt, Mellins, Ince, & Meyer-Bahlburg, 1987) of 34 daughters of women treated with hormones for pregnancy complications compared these girls with unexposed control girls matched for race, birth date, and socioeconomic status. Using a double-blind design and assessment through questionnaires, tests, and interviews with the girls and their mothers at two points in time (when the girls were between 8 and 13 years old and 5 years later when the girls were adolescents), the investigators found no significant differences between the two groups of girls in choice of careers. Careers were categorized as "pioneering"—occupations that are 60 percent male—and "non-pioneering." These studies tend to support Melissa Hines's (1982) conclusions that investigations of girls "who were exposed to unusual hormones prenatally, but who were born without abnormalities, have failed in many cases to find evidence of diminished maternal interest or masculinized play" (p. 72) and that "the history of research on prenatal hormones and human behavior has been typified by reports of suggestive results, followed by realization of potential methodological problems" (p. 73).

Interpretations of research findings in this area have tended to reflect traditional assumptions about women or cultural naiveté, such as interpreting preference for career over marriage as an indication of "masculinity." Despite the ambiguities, contrary findings, and methodological problems, reported effects of prenatal androgen exposure on behavior continue to be exaggerated and overgeneralized from a very small group of female children who were born with genital abnormalities. Hastily drawn conclu-

sions in this area of investigation have typically been followed by negative findings from better controlled studies. One illustration is an early conclusion about intelligence and academic performance: it was first reported that prenatal exposure of females to excessive androgen resulted in higher IQ scores and school achievement, but later research that controlled for socioeconomic factors found that the hormonal exposure had no effect on these measures (Hines, 1982). Thus, the influence of prenatal hormones on human behavior has been confounded by other factors and has not been satisfactorily demonstrated.

Chromosomal Anomalies

We have seen that biological sex is defined by chromosomes, hormones, sex glands, and external genitals and that sometimes these do not match. Other problems of sexual definition arise from abnormal combinations of X and Y chromosomes; these have been revealed as a result of technical advances in the staining of cell nuclei. Chromosomal abnormalities are believed to result from accidents occurring when ova and sperm (gametes) are formed from the division of parent germ cells. (In the case of ova, this process occurs prenatally; in the case of sperm, after puberty.) If the XX or XY chromosomes in the parent cell nucleus do not separate as they are supposed to, or if one member of the pair becomes entwined with other chromosomal material, then an ovum or sperm may be produced that either lacks a sex chromosome or has two instead of one. If such a gamete should participate in fertilization, the zygote resulting from the sperm-ovum union may have one or three sex chromosome(s) instead of the normal two.

Different categories of such sex chromosome abnormalities (SCA) have been identified. According to Daniel Berch and Bruce Bender (1987), "1 in 400 children is born with SCA, although most will never be diagnosed" (p. 54). Males with Klinefelter's syndrome are XXY; have sterile, small testes, delayed puberty, and androgen deficiency; and may have tall, awkward bodies. The occurrence of XXY has not been found to be associated with socioeconomic factors, as is also the case for the occurrence of XYY (Walzer & Gerald, 1975). XYY males—estimated to occur in 1 out of every 1000 to 3000 live births in the United States (Probber & Ehrman, 1978)—are taller than the average XY male, and, perhaps because such males were reported to have been found with unusual frequency within prison populations, they have received a great deal of attention. No causal link, however, has been reliably established between XYY chromosomal abnormality and criminal or violent behavior. Seymour Kessler and Rudolf Moos (1969) concluded, after reviewing the literature, that "no strong correlation exists between the presence of an extra Y chromosome and any specific behavioral, morphological, or physiological parameter," with the possible exception of height. Herman Witkin and his colleagues (1976) found, in a large-scale and well-controlled study, that XYY men were of lower average intelligence than others but no more prone to commit violent or aggressive acts. A review of endocrine studies indicated that plasma testosterone in XYY individuals shows large variability and is "almost always comparable to that in control subjects and rarely above the normal range" (Rubin, Reinisch, & Haskett, 1981).

Female chromosomal anomalies include XO (Turner's syndrome) and XXX. Individuals with the XO anomaly have no ovaries and may be recognized at birth by webbing of the neck and kidney deformities; they tend to be deficient in gonadal hormones, to be short in stature, and to have a number of congenital abnormalities. XXX individuals are morphologically unremarkable but may have speech and learning problems.

From a large screening program of more than 100,000 newborn infants, geneticists in the mid-1960s identified more than 150 children with SCA. These children were subsequently studied by multidisciplinary teams, with the following results:

> First, even though SCA may be associated with some developmental and learning problems, SCA children do not have the serious behavioral abnormalities that had originally been predicted. Second, these children are quite varied; some have severe learning disabilities, but others do well in school and go on to college. Third, the quality of the child's environment is an important factor. . . . SCA children from stable homes tend to have developmental skills similar to their chromosomally normal brothers and sisters. (Berch & Bender, 1987, p. 56)

Recent research has found some individuals with very rare genetic defects that result in sex-reversal. There are males who appear entirely normal but who are chromosomally XX; their unique condition may come to light when they try to have children and are found to be sterile. Similarly, there are XY females who appear normal except that they do not menstruate and are infertile. In the more than 100 such women and men who were studied after being identified by fertility clinics ("Mass. Scientists," 1987), an abnormality was discovered in the position or amount of the TDF gene discussed earlier (Roberts, 1988).

SEX AND THE FUNCTIONING OF THE HUMAN BRAIN

Thus far we have seen that the biology of sex involves genes, chromosomes, hormones, sex glands, and reproductive organs but that sexual identity and individual behavior are more influenced and determined by rearing, experience, and environment. Some scientists have been looking for evidence linking biological sex to human brain functions, a search that has its origins in century-old assumptions. Articles in popular magazines have publicized the idea that there are "male and female brains" (cf. Bleier, 1984) and have suggested that one half of the cortex is more dominant in one sex than in the other, despite the fact that no reliable support exists for any conclusions about sex differences in human brain organization at birth or about the effects of prenatal sex hormones on human brains.

Right and Left Hemispheres

What we do know from research on the human brain is that functions in the cortex, the brain's highest center, are specialized by hemisphere. For right-handed persons, the left hemisphere typically has primary control over verbal, linear-sequential, analytical, and mathematical processes, and the right hemisphere has primary control over spatial, holistic, intuitive, affective, and body awareness processing. For left-handed persons, hemispheric specialization appears to be less developed than for right-handers, and in children with brain injuries (and sometimes in adults), an undamaged hemisphere may take over the activities typically monitored by injured areas.

Whether the right or left brain has been said to be dominant in males (with the opposite hemisphere dominant in females) has varied with ideas about the superiority of different functions. Generalizations about differential hemispheric dominance, as well as generalizations about sex differences in degree of hemispheric specialization (laterality), are not supported by the scientific literature. William Hahn (1987), for example, has concluded from "findings from five lines of research used to examine age and sex differences in normal right-handed children" (p. 388) that consistent sex differences do not exist in the developmental course of specialization of either the left or the right hemisphere and that "neither the male brain nor the female brain is more symmetrically organized" (p. 389).

Marcel Kinsbourne (1982), a major investigator in this field and a critic of "two-package brain" theories, has suggested that scholars and others have rushed to invoke differential hemispheric specialization "to validate their pet formulations" (p. 411) about age, sex, or culture and that "there appear to be as many formulations of the division of function between the hemispheres as there are theorists concerned with this issue" (p. 415). One popular attempt to divide the brain into a "his" and "hers" has given men the left hemisphere, since men are logical, sequential, and analytical (obviously!); this division neatly ignores the fact that verbal skills, which are also a primary function of the left brain, are said to characterize women. Instead, women were given the right brain, since they are intuitive, holistic, and sensitive (of course!); but aren't women supposed to be deficient in spatial skills, which are also a primary function of the right brain?

The newest mythology appears to have reversed the earlier assignment of "his" and "hers"; the left (verbal, sequential) hemisphere has been returned to women, while the right (spatial, simultaneous) hemisphere has been claimed for men. Vivian Gornick (1982) reviewed these claims and noted that "now, suddenly, sequential reasoning is downgraded"; thus old assertions that men are logical while women are "hamstrung by reliance on intuitive perception" (p. 17) have been turned on their heads. As noted by Marian Lowe (1983), "explanations that try to fit brain lateralization to sex stereotypes necessarily end up with some major contortions" (p. 52).

Michael Corballis (1980) has identified ways in which popular translations of the research findings on cortical hemisphericity are similar to ancient myths about differences between the left and right sides of the body and their associations with gender. For example, the Taoist principles of yin and yang associate darkness, passivity, and left-sidedness with femininity and light, activity, and right-sidedness with masculinity. Corballis also noted that hemispheric differences have not been found between persons who presumably depend more upon logical processes, such as lawyers, and those thought to be more visual/spatial, such as sculptors, and that there is evidence that both cortical hemispheres function in both simple and complex tasks, with the left hemisphere monitoring sequences and temporal judgments and the right hemisphere better at perceptual tasks and discriminations.

Roger Sperry (1982), who received a Nobel prize for his empirical and theoretical observations of human lateralization (stimulated by discoveries he had made while working with "split-brain" patients), has concluded that "the two halves of the brain, when connected, work closely together as a functional unit with the leading control being in one or the other" (p. 1224). In other words, under ordinary circumstances, the two hemispheres of the brain work together, their integration mediated by the connecting fibers of the corpus callosum. It is not the case that one hemisphere is "turned on" while the other "idles." When disconnected from the other, each hemisphere has "its own learning processes and its own separate chain of memories," but left and right processes are not antagonistic or incompatible. Instead, they manifest "a mutual and supportive complementarity." In addition, new work has emphasized the unique complexity of individual brain function and intellect, suggesting, according to Sperry, that "the individuality inherent in our brain networks makes that of fingerprints or facial features gross and simple by comparison" (p. 1225). Each human brain, in other words, is wired in a unique fashion with only rough conformity to a general plan. Findings from a study of 520 brain-injured Vietnam veterans have reinforced Sperry's conclusions that the right and left hemispheres work together and that the brain is flexible and adaptive—good news for those concerned with recovery and rehabilitation (Fischman, 1986).

The Effects of Experience

Experts agree that experience affects brain development. As Anne Fausto-Sterling (1985) has noted, "extensive development of nervous connections [in the brain] occurs after birth, influenced profoundly by individual experience" (p. 77). The possibility that differential experiences produce more communication between the two cortical hemispheres in women than in men was suggested by a report (DeLacoste-Utamsing & Holloway, 1982) that a portion of the corpus callosum (nerve fibers that connect the two hemispheres) in women is slightly larger, relative to brain weight. This serendipitous finding was obtained from just one study of nine male and five female brains examined in autopsies; information was not provided about their selection or other characteristics.

In general, conclusions about sex differences in brain organization or function cannot be supported. Many investigators have reported no sex differences, and those that have been found tend to be small. Variation within each sex is always greater than the average difference between them. After reviewing the literature, M. P. Bryden (1979) concluded that "there are no convincing data for sex-related differences in . . . cerebral lateralization" (p. 137). Subsequently, Doreen Kimura (1985) noted that "depending on the particular intellectual function we're studying, women's brains may be more, less or equally diffusely organized compared with men's" (p. 56). Kimura's conclusion is that no single rule holds for all functions and that brain organization patterns vary not only from person to person but also within the same person at different times, with changes occurring in structures and patterns of organization throughout a person's life.

THE BIOLOGICAL IMPERATIVES

As we have seen, chromosomal, gonadal, hormonal, and morphological components of biological sex are not always in harmony; sexual identity is determined more by parental assignment of gender than by any of the above components; later behavior is probably not influenced by prenatal hormones; and brain structure and function have not been shown to differ reliably between the sexes. These findings lead us to an important fundamental question: what, if any, are the inevitable consequences of one's biological sex?

According to John Money (1972), who has posed and answered this question, the biological imperatives associated with sex are only four: for females, menstruation, gestation, and lactation; and for males, impregnation. (These correlates of sex assume normal conditions and a correspondence between chromosomes and morphology.) All other sex-related characteristics either are biological options that display variations or else represent cultural imperatives. Under normal conditions, the four biologically imperative sex differences are the only ones that are invariant for human females and males.

None of the secondary sex differences influenced by hormones released at puberty and in the adult years— such as breast development, distribution of body hair, and voice pitch—is absolute. Although it is difficult for us to accept Money's conclusions because our culture so insistently focuses on female/male differences, the evidence is clear: within-sex variations in the quality, intensity, or frequency of these secondary characteristics "cover so wide a range that, at the extremes, individuals of one sex may be more disparate from one another than from representatives of the other sex" (Money, 1972, p. 14). Individual differences within groups of females and males are as great as the average differences between them.

Even the very limited number of sexual distinctions that constitute the biological imperatives are subject to control. Menstruation, gestation, and lactation may be capacities that are biologically limited to females, but an adult woman may choose never to experience pregnancy,

in which case gestation and lactation will play no obvious part in her life despite the fact that they remain distinguishing features of her femaleness. Menstruation, too, while absolutely predictable for females, is responsive to environmental variation and can be stopped by stress, excessive exercise, or insufficient body fat relative to muscle.

OTHER SEX-LINKED PHYSICAL CHARACTERISTICS

Beyond the biological imperatives and the secondary sex characteristics, the list of reliable sex differences that can be unambiguously attributed to innate factors turns out to be very limited. This conclusion is not surprising when we consider that between genes (the starting materials for inheritance) and completed human structures and functions, a large number of processes intervene in environments that can alter, facilitate, or inhibit any aspect of human development. Victoria Freedman (1983) has summarized this state of affairs as follows:

> There are . . . three fundamental, and new, concepts of the gene which are important in understanding the processes of heredity. First, in some cases, one gene does not determine one protein, but only a part of the protein. For the complete functional protein to be made, several genes must act together [especially in higher organisms]. . . . Secondly, the gene is just the beginning of a complex system of molecular activities which comprise the pathway of gene expression. In many cases, the product of that gene has to undergo many changes before it is in the operational, or active form. . . . Thirdly, the cellular environment plays a tremendous role in the final expression of gene products. (p. 30)

Recessive Genes

Whatever genetic differences exist between the sexes are carried on only one pair of chromosomes, on the X and on the Y. The human X chromosome contains more than 100 genes, accounting for 2.5 percent of the total genetic material, and is much more information-packed and biochemically active than the Y chromosome. Because the Y chromosome is deficient in genetic material, males are more likely than females to inherit recessive characteristics if these are carried on the male's one X chromosome, since everything on the maternal X is likely to be expressed unless modified by genes on the other chromosomes. Males are thus more likely than females to inherit the sex-linked recessive characteristics of baldness, color blindness, hemophilia, Addison's disease, and possibly muscular dystrophy.

Vulnerability in Gestation and Infancy

Newborn males have been found to be more vulnerable than females and to do more poorly on a variety of psychomotor measures (Singer, Westphal, & Niswander, 1972). Natural abortion (miscarriage), stillbirth, and neonatal mortality rates are all higher for males, as are susceptibility to infection and disease in infancy (Eme, 1979). The ratio of male to female conceptions is estimated to be 130 to 100, but at birth the ratio is down to 105 to 100 (P. S. Wood, 1980; "U.S. Study," 1985), indicating a greater risk to males during gestation. Although males continue to be more vulnerable during the early postnatal months of infancy, sex appears to have little relationship to health in childhood. Later on, however, differences in adolescent life-style and activities are reflected in greater male risk in athletic injuries and accidents.

Strength and Athletic Performance

Female bodies differ from male bodies in having a higher fat-to-muscle ratio; female body weight is composed, on the average, of 23 percent fat compared to 15 percent for males (Lowe, 1983). Females also exhale about 40 percent less carbon dioxide than males, differ in nitrogen metabolism, have lower metabolic rates, and a lesser vital capacity (total volume of air expelled after maximal inhalation) (Sherman, 1971). On measures of strength, women, on the average, are two-thirds as strong as men, but the degree of difference varies with muscle group and is smaller when allowance is made for differences in weight and muscle fat (Lowe, 1983).

It is now well known that all the variables relevant to physical strength can be influenced by physical regimen—activity, athletic participation, and exercise. As Marian Lowe (1983) has noted, "there is growing evidence that differences in physical strength could come as much from differences in life experience as from innate factors" (p. 42). Males and females differ most sharply after puberty; at this time hormonal ratios diverge but so also do cultural expectations and restrictions. Thus, for example, the vital capacity of girls is only 7 percent less than that of boys, whereas vital capacity is 35 percent less in adult women than men. Studies have indicated that girls and boys in the United States are equally matched in physical ability until the ages of 10 to 13 (Streshinsky, 1975). During childhood, girls and boys are similar in all

motor skills and physical activity performance, except in throwing a softball for distance.

Evidence from many sources indicates that body structure and function are responsive to variations in physical activity, training, and diet. For example, a newspaper story ("Women Changing," 1978) reported that only 14 out of 1027 female Air Force recruits failed in their performance on a mile-long obstacle course described as "the same difficult test of strength and endurance male recruits have always been subject to." Sports statistics indicate that the gap between the track and swimming records of women and men has been closing fast over the past 20 to 30 years; it has been predicted that women will eventually do better than men in the super marathons (P. S. Wood, 1980).

Such findings and predictions are all the more extraordinary when we remember that up until the 1960s women were excluded from marathon races. In 1967 an entrant in the Boston Marathon named K. Switzer turned out to be a woman, Kathy. She ran the race "bundled in a sweatsuit because women were not allowed to compete" (Gross, 1984, p. E-22). Not until 1984 did the Olympics include a marathon race for women. The woman who won that event, Joan Benoit, had previously set a world record, in the 1983 Boston Marathon, of 2 hours, 22 minutes, and 43 seconds—which was faster than the record set by a man in the 1952 Olympics (Gross, 1984). In 1985, Benoit won the U.S. Amateur Athletic Union's top athlete award, becoming the seventh woman in the Union's 56-year history to do so. This award came one year after Benoit set a world marathon record in Chicago of 2 hours, 21 minutes, and 21 seconds ("Benoit-Samuelson," 1986). In 1979, Lyn Lemaire, a record holder in women's cycling, entered the Ironman triathlon contest in Hawaii (which combines swimming, biking, and running) and finished fifth. Since then, many women have achieved national fame in this competition, including the " 'Ironwoman' champion," Julie Leach, shown on p. 30 (Freeman, 1983).

While adult male athletes still generally outperform females, a review of relevant literature supports the conclusion that the sex gap is narrowing in many sports and that sex comparisons are difficult to make because of differences in coaching, facilities, and training techniques (Wilmore, 1977). Marian Lowe (1983) has cited studies by Jack Wilmore that found that when nonathletic women and men were trained with weights, women's strength increased faster than men's, particularly in the arms and shoulders. This result "was attributed to the fact that in daily life, American women already use their bodies in ways similar to men, but make much less use

Champion triathlete Julie Leach. (Photograph © Budd Symes.)

West Point, where all cadets are trained on the same obstacle course.

> One obstacle is an eight-foot wall positioned between two trees. Cadets are expected to run toward the wall, plant one foot on it, push up and grasp the top, then pull themselves up and over the top. This obstacle requires upper body strength.... [O]ne day, a female cadet approached the wall, grasped the top, and rather than pull up her body weight, she began to use her legs, literally walking up the wall until both her hands and feet were on the top. She then simply pulled up her sagging bottom and disappeared over the wall. (p. 287)

Although it seems likely that males will continue to be bigger and stronger than females on average, we are learning more about physical similarities between the sexes. The abdominal muscles, for example, which assist in a wide variety of sports, are as strong in females as in males.

In addition to the effects of explicit athletic training on muscles, strength, and other physical attributes, dramatic changes have been documented as a function of diet and life-style. Many years ago, anthropologist Franz Boas pointed out the striking difference in height between Asian or eastern and southern European immigrants to the United States and their significantly taller children and grandchildren. Now we have learned that since World War II changes in height and limb length have occurred in Japan for both sexes; the average height of a 20-year-old has increased 3 to 4 inches for males and 2 inches for females, primarily as the result of a change in leg length. The average weight for both sexes has also increased, by more than 15 pounds (Stokes, 1982). These changes are attributable to modifications in life-style, posture, activity, and diet. Other factors known to affect height are incidence of disease, amount of sunshine, and physical and emotional stress (Lowe, 1983). American women are, on the average, 40 pounds lighter than men, and have a body composition of 23 percent fat, compared to 15 percent for men, and 23 percent muscle, compared to 40 percent for men (Kenrick, 1987). Nevertheless, "when trained men and women athletes are compared in the laboratory— muscle pound for muscle pound—there are few actual differences in their performance" (Streshinsky, 1975).

of the upper body" (p. 44). In addition, women in training lose relatively more fat than comparable men do. Today, women's times are about 20 percent slower than men's in the triathlon and about 11 to 15 percent slower in the marathon, but, as pointed out by Patricia Freeman (1983), "scientists speculate that women have a greater physiological capacity for endurance than men do ... [leading] some [to] believe that if the race gets long enough, women may beat men" (p. 101).

Physiological and body build differences between males and females have been said to give each sex an advantage in different sports. Broader shoulders, for example, increase the ability to throw and hit, while greater body fat enhances the buoyancy, endurance, and insulation needed for long-distance swimming (P. S. Wood, 1980). An example of how persons with different physiques can accomplish the same physical task in different ways has come from an observation by Janice Yoder (1983), who studied women in the Army Academy at

Maturation and Size

Females mature physically earlier than males as, for example, in bone development, teeth development, and in age of reaching puberty (although not in age of fertility). Females also stop growing earlier than males. By the time the average girl is 16.5 years old she has typically attained her final height, compared to 17.8 years for boys.

Females mature between 2 and 2½ years faster than males. At birth their skeletal development is 4 weeks in advance of boys and at adolescence, 3 years in advance. Height remains equal for both sexes until age 7, when girls become taller than boys; at age 10, boys become taller than girls. By adulthood there is a 6 percent difference in height and a 20 percent difference in weight in favor of males. At puberty, males begin to show an increase in blood pressure, while a higher pulse rate (2 to 6 beats per minute) develops in females. . . . During puberty, males develop a 20 percent higher metabolic rate. . . . They produce more physical energy, have slower rates of muscle fatigue, and faster recuperative times. (Shepherd-Look, 1982, pp. 407f.)

Females' shorter stature is thought to be related to their greater production of estrogen, which tends to inhibit the growth of long bones. Thus, age of first menses is correlated with adult height, and girls who reach puberty early tend to be shorter than girls who mature late. Some have suggested that if women were treated the same as men from birth, they might be as big and strong, since bone size is a function of calcium development, which is related to degree of muscle use. "Calcium is metabolized best when the muscles that surround the bone are being used, thus stimulating the blood flow to the area. The pull of muscles on bone may also have an effect" (Lowe, 1983, p. 45). Osteoporosis, a bone disease linked to calcium deficiencies in older people (and more common in women), is less apt to develop in individuals who exercise regularly. While large bone lengths generally differ between the sexes, it is in the shape and arrangement of the pelvic bones that female and male skeletons differ most reliably (Leibowitz, 1970). Females typically outlive males, but the gap has been narrowing in recent years in the United States as a result of improved longevity for men. In 1987, life expectancy for women and men, respectively, was 78.3 and 71.5 ("Men Catching Up," 1990).

Hormones

The glands of both sexes release the same chemicals into the bloodstream. During childhood, the adrenal glands and gonads (female ovaries and male testes) produce relatively equal amounts of estrogen and androgen, but the ratios change at puberty. Although differing in relative amount, no known hormone is unique to either sex, including those specific to pregnancy, lactation, and menstruation. The three families of steroid hormones (estrogens, progestins, and androgens) fluctuate daily in their level in any individual and under different physiological and psychological conditions, and the ranges for the two sexes overlap. Each of these hormones has different forms, all closely related in chemical structure. Earlier we discussed the androgenizing effect on some embryos of progestin taken by their mothers. This effect can occur because of the chemical relationship among the sex hormones; all are synthesized from cholesterol, which normally metabolizes first into androstenedione, "the last compound formed before the [prenatal] chain of conversions splits toward either male or female hormones" (Hopson, 1987, p. 63). Progesterone is metabolized to testosterone, a male hormone, which is metabolized to estradiol, a female hormone.

The Limits of Innate Sex-Linked Differences

If the parents of a newborn disregarded culture or the consequences of socialization, the fact of their child's maleness or femaleness would permit them to make predictions about only a very small number of physical traits. The extent of within-sex variability is such that good safe bets could not be made even on some of these traits. Many years ago, geneticist Theodosius Dobzhansky (1967) noted that "the number of human natures is almost as great as the number of humans. Every person is unique, unprecedented, and unrepeatable" (p. 42). New investigations have revealed that even identical twins may not be absolutely identical in cytoplasm or in chromosomes.

BEHAVIORAL PLASTICITY: A KEY FEATURE OF HUMAN BIOLOGY

Each infant with a normal nervous system shares with others the specifically human characteristic of enormous teachability and flexibility. What is universal in the human species is a "capacity to acquire culture" (Dobzhansky, 1972) unmatched by other species and indispensable to human beings. A "fundamental peculiarity of human evolution" is that we have "been selected for trainability, educability, and consequent plasticity of behavior" (p. 528).

Primate Research

Careful studies during the past two decades of our closest animal relatives—group-living mammals and primates—in their natural habitats have found increasing evidence of complex social relationships, individual differences, and nonstereotyped behavior. One review of some of this research (Cheney, Seyfarth, & Smuts, 1986) has highlighted the "sophisticated cognitive mechanisms" underlying primate social relationships. Cynthia Moss (1978) who reviewed the extensive work on elephants, zebras, baboons, lions, and hyenas, concluded that "the roles of the sexes differ markedly from one species to another, and under different environmental pressures may even differ within one species." She noted that although the dominance of an adult male is evident when he can displace a female at a feeding place by virtue of his size and strength, "physical dominance does not imply leadership" (p. 65). An analysis of monkey societies led Sarah Hrdy (1980) to conclude that each has adapted to different circumstances and that male and female roles are not necessarily divergent; she found evidence of highly competitive and sexually aggressive female behavior. Shirley Strum (1987), who studied a troop of baboons for 15 years, found them to be a peaceful group formed around a stable core of females and their infants with no male dominance or aggression. Others have reported that male baboons carry their own offspring when confronting other males (Busse & Hamilton, 1981).

Like others who have examined the results of the new field work among primates, Erik Eckholm (1984) concluded that "an explosion of knowledge about monkeys and apes is overturning long-held stereotypes about sex roles and social patterns among . . . [our] closest kin," with findings of greater female influence on social structure and evidence that "females of many species are fiercely competitive, resourceful and independent, sexually assertive and promiscuous and, in some cases, more prone than males to wanderlust at puberty" (p. C-1). Among the chimpanzees, for example, males have been found to keep closer emotional attachments to their families than females do. A number of reviewers of this literature have pointed out that the new research is largely the work of women scientists like Jane Goodall, Shirley Strum, Jane Lancaster, and Dian Fossey, who spent many years in the field making painstaking observations in close proximity to the animals they were studying. Sarah Hrdy "believes that improved methodology, the broad questioning of sexual stereotypes by the women's liberation movement (influencing scientists of both sexes), and the infusion of female scientists have all contributed to the new understanding of primate societies" (cf. Eckholm, 1984, p. C-3). At this point, it is well to consider again the issues raised in Chapter 1 regarding the relationship between science and society and the role played by values and assumptions.

The Meaning of "Biology"

The term biological, as ordinarily used and applied to descriptions of animal or human capacities, is typically equated with genetic or innate—that is, inherited. But this interpretation is limited and distorted. It is indeed the biological nature of animals, and especially humans, that permits, or fosters, adaptation to environmental conditions through learning. As Helen Lambert (1978) has pointed out, "to equate biological with intrinsic, inflexible, or preprogrammed is an unfortunate misuse of the term biological. Behavior is itself a biological phenomenon, an interaction between organism and environment" (p. 104). Nature and nurture—heredity and environment—always interact, and their independent contributions can rarely be apportioned clearly. The evidence from neurophysiology as well as from anthropology is compelling in support of the conclusion offered by Naomi Weisstein (1982) that "biology is a promise," that "we belong to an order stunningly flexible . . . and capable of great change within species" (p. 85). Similarly, Ruth Bleier (1984) views biology "as potential, as capacity. . . . For each person, brain-body-mind-behaviors-environment form a complex entity the parts of which are . . . ceaselessly interacting and changing" (p. 52). As Stephen Jay Gould simply states it, "biology and culture are inextricable and co-determinant" (cf. Eckholm, 1984, p. C-3).

Female and male infants are similar in that each is unique and born with an extraordinary capacity to learn. Yet, in the eyes of their parents and the culture into which they are born, the fact of the newborn's sex is dominant; sex is so important an identification that, with only rare exceptions, it is the very first thing to be publicly proclaimed at the birth of a child. In the chapters that follow, we will examine the many consequences of that excited announcement, "It's a girl!"

◆ Discussion Questions

1. What defines biological sex in humans?

2. What does discordance among chromosomes, gonads, hormones, and morphology teach us? Distinguish between problems due to hormonal errors and to chromosomal anomalies.

3. How are split-brain hypotheses related to the yin/yang principles and other mythologies?

4. What can we learn about sex roles from primate behavior?

5. What is predictable from being born human and female?

6. Distinguish between the terms innate and biological.

CHAPTER 3

INFANCY AND CHILDHOOD:
LEARNING HOW TO BE A GIRL

We were required to embroider. . . . I mastered the art of crocheting and tatting, and there was a lifetime's supply of dainty doilies that would never be used in sacheted dresser drawers. It went without saying that all girls could iron and wash. . . .

MAYA ANGELOU (1971, p. 87)

I knew I was a girl, but that hardly seemed relevant. Girls did girls' things, but my Mum . . . trudged out and pulled the lever on the gas pumps . . . and so, later, did I, and I could wipe a fine windshield, too, shovel a walk, muck out a pigpen. . . .

MARIAN ENGEL (1979, pp. 29f.)

Grace and Carol look at each other's scrapbook pages and say "Oh, yours is so good. Mine's no good. Mine's awful." They say this every time we play the scrapbook game. . . . I can tell they don't mean it. . . . But it's the thing you have to say, so I begin to say it too.

MARGARET ATWOOD (1988, p. 57)

[S]everal families in our neighborhood gather to play touch football. Lizzy and her pal, Joey, are having fun in the melee, when another family arrives. Their daughter . . . doesn't want to play. Suddenly Lizzy doesn't want to play either, and the adults, within earshot of Lizzy, are clucking about girls wanting to be girls.

ELIZABETH ROMMEL (1984, p. 35)

WHAT DOES IT MEAN TO ANNOUNCE "IT'S A girl"? Such a statement does not simply assert that this child can be expected to mature into a menstruating adult with the capacity for gestation and lactation, who will probably be sturdier in infancy, mature faster, and end up shorter than the average boy. It signifies far more. The gender designation generally carries with it the expectation of numerous personality traits, motives, interests, and capabilities and often the general outline for an entire life script.

COLOR HER PINK: FROM BLANKETS AND BOOTIES TO ASSUMPTIONS AND EXPECTATIONS

For decades, pink has remained the color for newborn girls in hospital nurseries and in wrapping paper and ribbons; it identifies girls in blankets, clothing, and even pacifiers (Pomerleau, Bolduc, Malcutt, & Cossette, 1990). What the color connotes, however, goes far beyond a simple identification of sex. The behavioral predictions that we make from knowledge of sex are ones that we have effected ourselves through differential socialization of our female and male children beginning with their color coding as pink or blue bundles. Culture begins at birth to shape highly flexible and teachable human infants not only into unique individuals but also into two categories of gender.

Expectations

In the musical *Carousel,* the hero, upon learning that his wife is pregnant, sings joyfully about what his son will be like: he'll be a heavyweight champion or president of the United States; "he'll be tall and as tough as a tree." Realization that the baby might be a girl brings an abrupt change in the lyrics, and he begins to picture someone "sweet and petite . . . pink and white as peaches and cream." Such expectations mirror well the still-dominant gender ideology of our culture, although some readers may find this hard to believe. Many contemporary adults anticipate parenthood already prejudiced to some degree against female children. Although girls may be necessary and even very nice, daughters are less expected than sons to fulfill the ambitions of their parents and to maintain continuity of the family name.

When Lois Hoffman (1977) asked women* why they wanted daughters, the most common answer was that a girl would be a companion and fun to dress. She was told that "girls are easier to raise and more obedient, that girls could help with and learn about housework and caring for other children, that girls stay closer to their parents than boys, and . . . are cuter, sweeter, or not as mean" (p. 648). In the same study, adults who had at least one child were asked what kind of person they wanted their sons and daughters to become. For sons, parents focused on career or occupational success and said they wanted their boys to be hard-working, ambitious, intelligent, educated, honest, responsible, independent, strong-willed, successful, and respected in work. Parental hopes for daughters were different, and the themes more often centered on kindness or unselfishness, being loving and attractive, having a good marriage, and being a good parent. In a study done by one of Hoffman's students, a group of university faculty women who were also mothers were interviewed. Most indicated, when asked about goals for sons and daughters, that these goals would be the same regardless of the children's gender. When asked about specific goals for only one of their children, however, it turned out that, "despite their expressed equalitarian ideology, the mothers who discussed sons had higher academic and occupational goals in mind for them and indicated that they would be more disappointed if these goals were not achieved than did the mothers who discussed their daughters" (p. 651). It is not surprising, then, that an ad by IBM in popular magazines in the mid-1980s presented a pair of blue and a pair of pink booties side by side with the statement, "Guess which one will grow up to be the engineer? As things stand now, it doesn't take much of a guess" (IBM, 1985, pp. 14f.).

In an investigation of the expectations of first-time parents (Rubin, Provenzano, & Luria, 1974), one sample was asked to describe their daughters and sons within the first 24 hours after birth. Infant girls were seen as softer, finer featured, smaller, more inattentive, prettier, and cuter than infant boys; although the fathers were more extreme in their judgments, they were largely in agreement with their wives. Objective physical measurements of the babies, however, did not support their parents' perceptions. Medical staff ratings of the infants 5 to 10 minutes after their birth on color, muscle tone, reflexes, heart and respiration rates, weight, and height revealed no significant

---

* The reader is urged to keep in mind that the vast majority of studies cited in this and subsequent chapters have been of European-American, middle-class samples. Exceptions will be noted where known.

If it's a boy—tough and strong; if it's a girl—see her precious dimple. Cathy, by Cathy Guisewhite. Copyright 1986, Universal Press Syndicate. Reprinted with permission. All rights reserved.

sex differences. In another study (Haugh, Hoffman, & Cowan, 1980), a remarkable similarity was found between a sample of 3- and 5-year-old children and adults in their perceptions of girl and boy infants. After watching videotapes of two infants, one labeled a boy and the other a girl, the children described the girl as smaller, more scared, slower, weaker, nicer, quieter, and softer than the boy. In this study, the same infant was sometimes labeled a girl and sometimes a boy.

Research data and our own experience suggest that we often expect and "see" in infant girls and boys different physical and psychological characteristics and potentials. A gender label provides individuals with what they believe is a major clue to the child's behavior, a phenomenon we can sometimes laugh at—as suggested by Cathy Guisewite's cartoon —but that has serious consequences. Some investigators have gone beyond eliciting verbal responses to gender labels and have observed how adults behave in interactive situations with infants presented as girls or boys.

In one of the first of these studies (Seavey, Katz, & Zalk, 1975), graduate students were observed individually as they interacted for 3 minutes with the same 3-month-old European-American infant dressed in a yellow jumpsuit. One third of the participants were told that the infant was a girl; another third that it was a boy; and the others were given no gender information (the "Baby X" condition). Near the infant were a small rubber football, a Raggedy Ann doll, and a plastic ring. What influence, if any, did the infant's gender label have on the toys chosen by the adults

in playing with the child? Both women and men used the doll most frequently in playing with the "girl"; in playing with the child of unknown gender, men used the neutral plastic ring most frequently, while women used either the football or the doll. Although the infant actually was a girl, 57 percent of the men and 70 percent of the women who were not told her gender guessed that she was a boy. Participants appropriately justified their judgments about the infant's gender; those who believed the baby to be a boy "noted the strength of the grasp response or the lack of hair," while those who believed it was a girl spoke of "the baby's roundness, softness, and fragility."

A review of 23 such "Baby X" studies, in which strangers were exposed briefly in laboratory settings to neutrally clothed infants labeled girl or boy (Stern & Karraker, 1989), concluded that young children's reactions are more strongly influenced by the gender label than adults' reactions. Among adults, however, behavioral measures are more affected by gender labels than rating scale measures, with the effects typically "consistent with culturally acknowledged sex stereotypes" (p. 518). Gender labels most consistently influence toy choices, with dolls offered to girls and footballs or hammers offered to boys. One interesting study did not provide observers with gender labels for infants but, instead, simply varied the infant's clothing (Leone & Robertson, 1989). The same 11-month-old girl was dressed as a stereotyped girl in a ruffled dress, or as a stereotyped boy in blue shorts and a striped shirt, or ambiguously in a white shirt and yellow pants. In no condition was the infant identified as a girl or a boy by the investigators. Judgments made by college students who watched videotapes of the infant being held by an adult were found to be significantly influenced by the infant's clothing. Those who saw her in the ruffled dress were significantly more likely than those who saw her in the blue shorts or yellow pants to evaluate her positively (for example, as good and happy), but were less likely to judge her as strong, heavy, hard, and large (concepts connoting potency).

Assumptions about Development

Everyday observations as well as data collected in careful investigations support the conclusion that knowledge of a child's sex continues to influence perceptions beyond infancy of many of the child's characteristics and to affect assumptions about the child's interests, abilities, and development. One study in which a sample of college education majors were asked to pretend they had a 6-year-old daughter or son entering school (Leung, 1990) provides evidence of how prevalent sex-typed beliefs about children continue to be. The participants ranked math, music, physical education, reading and social studies in difficulty, interest, and importance for their make-believe children. These rankings were found to vary with the child's gender: for example, music was said to be more interesting, social studies more important, and physical education more difficult for girls than for boys.

Do such gender-related assumptions reflect real sex differences in physique, temperament, or behavior present at birth? The best answer to this question, in light of the available evidence, is no. During the first 2 to 3 months of postnatal life (the neonatal period), the behavioral repertoire of infants is limited and their responses are extremely variable. Technological advances in observation and recording equipment have increased our knowledge of neonatal capacities and behavior and strengthened the conclusion that few reliable sex differences are present at birth or soon thereafter. Howard Moss (cf. Birns, 1976), after summarizing ten years of his empirical work, noted the instability of early infant behavior and the statistical marginality of sex differences. He had earlier reported (1967) that the most striking characteristic of very young infants is variability, with few behaviors remaining stable from 3 weeks to 3 months after birth. Support for this conclusion with respect to even older infants has come from a study (Feiring & Lewis, 1980) of the same infants at 13, 25, and 44 months, in which no reliable sex differences were found at any of the three ages, and little individual stability was reported over the first 3 years in vigor and activity levels.

An extensive review of the literature revealed that most studies have "failed to show any sex differences in responses to auditory, visual, tactile, olfactory, taste or vestibular stimulation or in . . . spontaneous activities," and thus "labeling a newborn as male or female on the basis of its behavioral characteristics would be extremely difficult if not entirely impossible" (Lyberger-Ficek, cited in Birns, 1976, p. 236). An examination of the later literature on full-term neonates in good health led to a similar conclusion, that "insufficient grounds exist to document the existence of gender differences in neonate behavior" (Brackbill & Schroder, 1980, p. 608). Some small average differences in spontaneous activity were reported (Phillips, King, & DuBois, 1978) in a study of 29 neonates observed for 8 hours at 30-second intervals during non-feeding times. Boys were found to be more often awake and to make more facial grimaces and more low-intensity movements. These observations, while not reported with consistency in the neonatal literature, do support a hypothesis proposed by Howard Moss (1967) that, at birth, males may be operating at a less well-organized level than females and, hence, may be more fussy or irritable and subject to more physical distress.

The most significant characteristic of the newborn of either sex is its capacity for learning. Indeed, evidence from laboratories using refined techniques indicates that the learning potential of human neonates is far greater than we had previously believed. Some studies have shown convincingly that learning begins even before birth, particularly through experience with sounds such as music (cf. Lewis, 1984) and the mother's voice and heartbeat (cf. Kolata, 1984b). Experiments have demonstrated that babies can learn as early as 2 hours after birth (cf. Kolata, 1987). One study found that 36-hour-old neonates could discriminate among happy, sad, and surprised expressions posed by a live model (Field, Woodson, Greenberg, & Cohen, 1982), and another that 6-week-old infants could distinguish the odor of their mothers' breast pads from those of other mothers ("A Baby Learns," 1980). A review of this literature (Friedrich, 1983) led to the conclusion that "babies know a lot more than most people used to think. They see more, hear more, understand more" (pp. 52f.). And Jean Mandler (1990) has suggested that memory, and other forms of symbolic activity mediated by imagery, can occur by the second half of the first year. According to Lewis Lipsitt (1977, pp. 180f.):

The newborn comes into the world with all sensory systems functional . . . [and] may learn to respond differentially based upon sensory preferences and reinforcement contingencies . . . in less than one hour of training. . . . *All of this must have enormous implications for the condition of behavioral reciprocity that characterizes the early interactions of mother* [or other consistent caretaker] *and infant.* [italics added]

Distinguishing Girls from Boys

Research suggests that as child and parent interactions increase and as opportunities for learning expand, girls and boys begin to show those differences in behavior that the culture expects of them. In the ensuing sections of this chapter, we will examine some of this evidence as we focus on the girl's childhood. We will see that the continued purchase by adults of pink or blue blankets, booties, and bibs is not a frivolous issue, but a serious one that signifies a lifelong cultural division based on gender. For example, among a sample of 1- to 3-month-old infants observed in suburban shopping malls (Shakin, Shakin, & Sternglanz, 1985), 75 percent of the girls wore pink (or had pink blankets or toys), but this was not true for a single boy. In contrast, 79 percent of the boys but only 8 percent of the girls were dressed in blue. Girls were also significantly more likely to be wearing red, ruffles or lace, and puffed sleeves. The researchers noted that the parents' answers to interview questions did not reflect the sharp distinction between girls' and boys' clothing that was observed. Regardless of parental awareness, however, as the investigators pointed out, "the sex labeling of infant clothing is simply one more mechanism that maintains the separate worlds of boys and girls" (p. 963).

Decades ago, Sigmund Freud (1933/1964) wrote, "when you meet a human being, the first distinction you make is 'male' or 'female'" (p. 113). This distinction may make us think it will enable us to know what to expect. The behavioral predictions that knowledge of sex permits us to make, however, are the ones we have largely effected ourselves through gender socialization of our children.

Cultural requisites begin at birth to shape highly flexible and teachable human infants not only into unique individuals but also into two categories of gender. Given the human's great capacity for learning, the caretakers of infants and children can provide them environments in which their capabilities will be maximally developed and reinforced and their range of behavioral and cognitive potential expanded. Unfortunately, we know only too well that the ability of parents to provide ideal growth-promoting environments for their children is seriously impaired by poverty, ignorance, illness, discrimination, and lack of access to social resources, and that these

factors are related to social class and minority status. In addition to these social and economic factors, our judgments about the differential "nature" of the two sexes also results in failure to provide our infants with opportunities for full development.

Many beliefs about gender in our society cross the lines of class, color, and ethnicity, and the dominant culture prescribes and enforces a sex-role ideology that is ubiquitous and pervasive, overt and subtle. Although there are important variations in, and deviations from, the dominant norms and ideals, these norms and ideals serve as background in the specification of sex-based expectations. We may nurture our infant girls (and boys) with vision already narrowed by our preconceptions; as they so quickly learn what we teach them, our expectations are reinforced soon enough by their behavior. The female infant begins a lifelong process of becoming a culturally defined woman.

Differences between girls and boys increase as they grow older. Jeanne Block (1976) reviewed a large body of research on children by sorting studies into three groups on the basis of age of the participants (infancy to age 4; ages 5 through 12; and 13 and older), and found more gender differences with increased age. That sex becomes increasingly predictive of behavior as children get older reflects the importance of experience, social pressures, expectations, and contingencies. It is through socialization that sex becomes gender; this process begins at birth and continues over the course of one's life. The socialization emphasis that is focused on gender learning is referred to as *sex-typing*.

HOW GIRLS LEARN ABOUT GENDER

A small number of distinguishable but related processes that operate throughout life help us to understand the acquisition of gender-relevant or sex-typed behaviors. These processes describe ways that behavior is acquired and maintained; while the processes are general, they are of particular relevance in understanding the learning of gender. In the discussion to follow, we will focus particularly and directly on how such learning proceeds in childhood.

Modeling and Imitation

A good deal of evidence supports the proposition that children will imitate, by acting in a similar manner to, those adults and peers who are, first, available (sufficiently present to be perceptually salient), and second, likable. Likability, in turn, derives from the association of persons with positive consequences, rewards, or satisfactions (Lott & Lott, 1968, 1985). Thus, a child will learn to like a person who is nurturant, who directly satisfies the child's needs or helps the child get her or his needs satisfied, or who is consistently associated with positive and pleasant experiences. Persons associated with punishing, frustrating, or unpleasant experiences will tend not to be liked and not to be imitated.

If this analysis is correct, then one parent is as likely to be imitated as the other, and by both girls and boys. But since mothers are usually more available to their children than fathers, and since the mother's role is one of nurturing and ensuring the satisfaction of her children's needs, the mother's behavior rather than the father's is more likely to be imitated by both little boys and little girls. Imitation of mothers' behavior by sons, however, presents a problem to parents in a sex-segregated and patriarchal society. For boys to be too much like their mothers for too long is not acceptable. A girl's imitation of her mother, on the other hand, is expected, approved, and encouraged.

The precise nature of the behaviors a girl acquires by imitating her mother depends on the mother's unique characteristics as well as on those she shares with other mothers. Daughters of mothers who work outside the home have been found more often, for example, to anticipate working when they grow up and to be more independent and assertive as children than the daughters of mothers who stay at home (Hoffman, 1977).

Children tend to imitate the behavior of adults who are available and rewarding, as well as those who have power to dispense or withhold positive outcomes (unless this power is associated primarily with painful consequences to the child, in which case the punishing person becomes one whom the child will tend to avoid rather than imitate). Diana Baumrind (1971) has reported that parents are more likely to take the role of disciplinarian with their like-gender than their other-gender children, and the psychological literature supports the conclusion that the same-sex parent is typically perceived as the more powerful one (Margolin & Patterson, 1975).

In imitating the behavior of an available, likable, and powerful person, a little girl is, for all the reasons given, most likely to model her responses after those of her mother, although not consistently or entirely. In addition, a girl learns at an early age that she is in the same category as her mother when both are referred to as girl, sister, female, lady, or woman. We will return to the significance

of labeling later on, but for now it is important to understand that a mother's similarity—in label, physique, dress, and so on—enhances the probability that she will be imitated by girls (and not imitated by boys).

By preschool age, most children are well aware of their own gender, which parent they are most like, and the gender of family members and peers. One study of a sample of children between 4 and 6 years of age found that with the exception of only one child, boys knew they would be fathers and girls that they would be mothers (Thompson & Bentler, 1973). Spencer Thompson (1975) found that 36-month-old children "consistently applied gender labels . . . to guide behavior" (p. 399). It is not surprising, then, to find, as was reported in a study of preschool children (Bellinger & Gleason, 1982) observed working on tasks with each parent in a laboratory setting, that the girls and boys tended to behave like their same-gender parents. Fathers and sons were found to utter more imperatives (give more orders) and to use more directive speech than mothers and daughters.

Some researchers (e.g., Kuhn, Nash, & Brucken, 1978) have suggested that gender learning is preceded by comprehension of gender constancy—that is, by an understanding that gender is "a permanent, irreversible characteristic" (p. 449)—while others have argued that the attainment of gender constancy is not a necessary antecedent of same-gender modeling. In a study of children from 29 to 68 months of age (Bussey & Bandura, 1984), gender constancy level was found not to affect the imitation of same-gender models. Children with high gender constancy (who were also older) did more imitating than children with lower gender constancy (who were also younger), but they did not differ in their tendency to imitate same-gender adults shown playing a game on television. A study of more than 800 African-American and European-American children between the ages of 4 and 8 (Emmerich & Shepard, 1984) also found that "gender constancy . . . lagged considerably behind the development of sex-stereotyped preferences" (p. 1001). Most evidence supports the conclusion that while children begin to use gender labels reliably between the ages of 21 and 44 months (Hort, Leinbach, & Fagot, 1991), gender learning through imitation begins much earlier.

From an early age, children imitate parents, siblings, and other adults who are available, likable, powerful, and similarly labeled. This process is likely to accelerate with increasing cognitive and discriminating skill and to cover an increasingly wide range of models, including peers and baby sitters, storybook and real-life heroes, and television and cartoon characters. Some research suggests that a child is more likely to imitate a model who is a "good example" of her or his gender. One sample of 9-year-olds (Perry & Bussey, 1979) watched groups of adult men and women make choices among tasks. When the children were subsequently given the chance to make choices, imitation of same-gender adults was more probable if they had behaved in a sharply different manner from other-gender adults. While recall of models' behavior was not influenced by the variable of appropriateness, imitation was, with children of both genders (but with boys more than girls), "matching their behavior to a model known to exemplify sex-typical behavior" (p. 1709). In a subsequent study (Bussey & Perry, 1982), the researchers found that both girls and boys from grades 3 and 4 preferred objects chosen by same-gender children, with boys being more rejecting than girls of choices made by other-gender children and of choices made by both boys and girls.

That selective preference based on same-gender modeling is not a function of selective attention or knowledge is underscored by data reported by Janice Bryan and Zella Luria (1978). Using a physiological measure of attention to stimuli, with samples of children varying in age from 5 to 11, the researchers found no evidence that the children paid more attention to same-gender models, despite their stated preference for the tasks chosen by them. The investigators concluded that "children look at (or have competence about) the behavior of both sexes; but their behavior (or performance) . . . is determined by other factors" (p. 21). Children learn to imitate certain models and certain behaviors, but they also learn not to imitate, by observing the differences between the model and themselves, by noting the divergence in behavior among models, and by observing the consequences experienced by models.

Direct Positive and Negative Reinforcement

Children also learn gender more directly. We know that behavior that is followed by positive consequences tends to be repeated while behavior followed by negative consequences tends to be avoided. Parents, other caregivers, teachers, and peers, by the way in which they react to what children do, provide positive or negative sanctions or reinforcements for behavior. Consider how we let a child know that what she is doing is appropriately "feminine"—we smile, applaud, provide tangible rewards, and repeat "good girl." When she imitates her sister, aunt, mother, or other appropriate female figure, we reinforce the modeling. Negative consequences follow behavior considered inappropriate for girls. These need not involve physical punishment, although they some

times although they sometimes do; more often, we use harshly spoken "no-no's," withholding of desirable rewards, ridicule, or inattention. One form of punishment is to label nonconforming children as deviant and to assume that they need help to become less deviant.

Research findings suggest that pressure for gender-appropriate behavior is applied earlier for boys than for girls. For example, in a study in which two samples of kindergarten children drew Halloween jack-o'-lanterns (Lott, 1979), the boys' drawings were found to match the stereotyped expectations of adults more closely than the girls' drawings. We know that little boys who fail to behave in ways considered "masculine," and who are judged to be "sissies," are more likely to be labeled deviant than little girls who are judged to be "unfeminine" or "tomboys" (Eme, 1979; Feinman, 1981).

Although a preadolescent girl is less likely than a boy to receive serious negative sanctions when she behaves in a gender-inappropriate manner, girls, too, may be considered "problems" and in need of help if they behave too often in ways considered boyish. Girls referred to an outpatient child-guidance clinic by their parents or teachers were found in one study (Feinblatt & Gold, 1976) to be described by these adults as defiant and verbally aggressive, while boys referred to the clinic were more likely to be described as emotional or passive. The researchers also asked parents and psychology students to read hypothetical case studies in which identical behavior was attributed to a girl or to a boy. "The data from the two samples indicated that the child exhibiting the behavior inappropriate to his/her sex was seen as more severely disturbed, as more in need of treatment, and as having a less successful future than the child exhibiting sex-role appropriate behaviors" (p. 109). Similar findings were reported by Paula Caplan (1977), who had college students rate hypothetical children on the basis of the likelihood that they would be assigned to tutors for help. All the hypothetical cases were presented as children "having trouble learning grade-school subjects," but some were presented as girls or boys, and as "acting out" or "withdrawn." Raters of both genders were more likely to send girls for help if they were "acting out" and boys for help if they were "withdrawn" than vice versa.

Social learning theory, a general perspective in psychology, considers the primary mediators of both response performance and maintenance to be positive consequences and opportunities for practice. Consequences are often intertwined with opportunities for practice, which typically precede and provide the setting for behavioral outcomes. And settings, or situations, often present demand characteristics that make some responses more probable (and thus more likely to be reinforced) than others. For example, a doll in a child's hands usually demands hugging, stroking, and tender loving care, responses that adults and peers are likely to reward. A ball, on the other hand, usually demands bouncing, throwing, and kicking. That dolls are more often put into the hands of girls and balls into the hands of boys is, of course, crucial to the explanation of sex-typed behavior in our contemporary culture. As Sandra Bem (1985) has pointed out, "social learning theory . . . locates the source of sex-typing in the sex-differentiated practices of the socializing community" (p. 182), particularly those practices relating to the differential situations to which girls and boys are exposed and to the consequences provided to girls and boys for behaviors considered gender-relevant. Sometimes these consequences are direct and obvious; at other times they are more subtle. An example of the latter comes from a report (cf. Kimball, 1989) of the responses adults gave to a gifted sixth-grade girl who had built a robot. While women asked her "about her design, where she had gotten the parts, and . . . the idea . . . , the first or second question asked by all male visitors (and never by a female visitor) was, Did you build it to do housework?" (p. 209).

Labeling and Cognition

Positive and negative consequences teach children to behave in ways deemed appropriate and to "do the right thing." In addition to such positive outcomes as affection, attention, or approval, and such negative outcomes as punishment, disapproval, or ridicule, words or labels also have powerful reinforcing properties. Once a girl has learned that if she engages in boys' behavior she is not likely to be approved or, worse, may be derided, simply saying to her that "boys do that" serves to increase the likelihood that she will avoid it.

The effectiveness of labels has been demonstrated experimentally. In a number of studies, children were told that particular tasks or toys were preferred by their own gender, the other gender, neither, or both. Such labeling was found to reliably influence the choice of toys in a same-gender direction by 4- to 6-year-old children (Liebert, McCall, & Hanratty, 1971; Cobb, Stevens-Long, & Goldstein, 1982); first graders' success and liking for a task (Montemayor, 1974); children's problem-solving performance (Gold & Berger, 1978); and sixth graders' expectancy for success and achievement on three different paper-and-pencil tests (Stein, Pohly, & Mueller, 1971). In

another kind of investigation, fifth graders were asked to categorize 15 words as masculine or feminine and then to rate their liking for each. The girls (and boys) most preferred those items associated with their own gender (Freeman, Schockett, & Freeman, 1975). Using still a different research strategy, Jerri Kropp and Charles Halverson (1983) found that after being read four different stories, a sample of preschool girls most preferred the one featuring a female character doing a "feminine activity" while boys preferred the story of a male character doing a "masculine activity."

One study (Bradbard & Endsley, 1983) tested preschoolers' retention of "gadget" names after they had been labeled as being for girls, boys, or both. Name recall after a day and after a week was found to be significantly poorer for objects labeled for the other gender. Other-gender labeled objects had also been played with less and had evoked fewer questions about how they worked than had same-gender labeled objects. Thus, gender labels clearly serve as mediators. For the average girl, whatever is associated with a same-gender label makes her anticipate positive consequences, whereas associations with the other-gender label are likely to elicit anticipation of negative consequences. Gender labels probably mediate a very wide array of behavior from the time that children first begin to acquire language. Anyone who has spent time in the average preschool class has undoubtedly heard teachers give instructions by girl/boy divisions, from lining up for milk to picking up supplies for a project. Stories the children are read tend to perpetuate gender division of activities, thus reinforcing gender separateness.

Lawrence Kohlberg (1966) proposed that children form their conceptions of what is appropriate for persons of their own gender by abstracting rules from environmental cues; once having done so, children can direct their own behaviors accordingly. This process can be understood as related to both the mediating effect of gender labels and to learning that it is desirable to act "like a girl" (or "like a boy"). The first step in sex-role learning, according to Anne Constantinople (1979), is "a labeling process." Words like *boy, girl, mommy,* and *daddy* are then joined to clothing, toys, and activities. But while cognitive processes are thought to be vital to comprehending the meaning and content of gender categories, learning principles are called on to explain how children acquire the behaviors that match each category. Constantinople suggests that "linguistic tags" serve an organizing function, while observational learning and positive and negative reinforcement focus the child on relevant stimuli and provide consequences for behavior.

Thus, while gender labels may guide a child's social interactions and activities, other people's responses will affect how well a particular behavior will be learned and the conditions under which it is likely to be repeated.

SOURCES OF GENDER LEARNING

The environments in which children grow and learn are filled with information about gender. Girls (and boys) observe, organize, relate themselves to their appropriate category, try out various behaviors, experience feedback from others, and acquire a gender identity that matches to some degree the ideology of their culture. Gender-identity and the sex-typing of behavior are basic components of socialization, and cultures differ in what is learned and the extent to which the genders are separated. In our own culture, despite its heterogeneity, much of the gender information provided by diverse sources of information (or socialization agents) is remarkably consistent across class, color, ethnic, and geographical divisions. For example, one study (Romer & Cherry, 1980) found that a sample of children aged 10 to 17 from three different ethnic and socioeconomic groups shared the perception that the "typical male" is more competent than expressive. As we shall see, one gender lesson in particular that seems to be present across subcultures in our society is that men and the events, objects, and actions pertaining to them have higher value—are more dominant and powerful—than women and that which relates to them. Thus, in writing about her childhood in New York City as the daughter of Polish Jewish immigrants, Kate Simon (1982) tells us that she learned early that "girls prayers, if they prayed at all, counted for nothing; like animals, they had no souls and no voices to God's ear" (p. 14). In a novel about an African-American family in St. Louis (Shange, 1985), 13-year-old Betsey Brown is taught some lessons about life by her housekeeper.

> These children always playing make-believe in their mother's bedroom with negligees, high heels, feathered hats. There was more to being a woman than that. Carrie knew these things. A Negro man wanted a clean shirt, dinner on the table, and some quiet around the house. (p. 173)

Let us look more closely now at the most significant agents supplying children with information and lessons about gender.

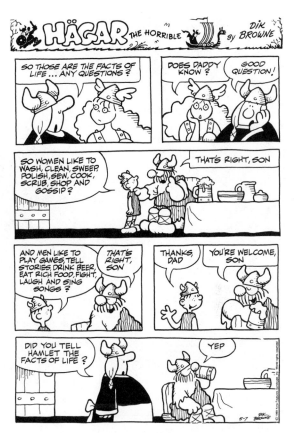

Hagar The Horrible. Reprinted with special permission of King Features Syndicate.

Parents and Siblings

It is unlikely that children learn about gender from their parents in the way that is indicated in the *Hagar the Horrible* cartoon above. One's family, however, is a primary source of sex-typing. Yet, of all the social institutions that provide norms for behavior, the family is probably the most idiosyncratic and the most likely to provide conditions for gender learning that may be inconsistent with the dominant ideology. The family serves so many and such complex social and personal needs that gender requirements may at various times be less important than others, such as economic survival, family tradition, or general nurturance and support. Some theorists, such as Nancy Chodorow (1978), have proposed that the family, particularly the mother, plays a crucial and primary role in teaching girls, from infancy, those attributes that our culture desires in prospective mothers (as illustrated by the photograph on p. 42), so

Like mother, like daughter. (Photograph © Michael Siluk.)

that girls will grow up with the appropriate personality characteristics. Others, however, see the family as only one of many socializing agents. And the family may actually enforce cultural stereotypes least rigidly or consistently, because parents are more likely to respond to the unique characteristics of each particular child. Thus, Anne Constantinople (1979) has suggested that "siblings, peers, and outside figures of all kinds often work harder than parents to enforce sex-role stereotypes" (p. 131). It is not surprising, therefore, that a careful review of the literature (Lytton & Romney, 1991) has found that a child's gender is not a significant influence on many of the parental socialization dimensions that have been studied, with the important exceptions of encouraging sex-typed play and the tendency to show more warmth toward girls.

The part that parents play as agents of gender socialization has been demonstrated in some interesting studies. Beverly Fagot (1974), for example, found that parents of 18- to 24-month-old children may behave in ways that differ significantly from what they say they do. Those who said that most behaviors were appropriate for children of both genders showed as much sex-typing in their actual interactions with their children (when observed in their own homes) as parents who said most behaviors were more appropriate for one gender than another. The studies that demonstrate differential treatment of girls and boys by their parents are more likely to be observational or experimental than to utilize verbal report measures, as noted in the literature review cited above (Lytton & Romney, 1991). For example, one sample of African-American mothers (cf. "The Favored Infants," 1976) were observed to respond differently to newborn girls and boys three days after giving birth. "Once the feeding and caretaking chores were over, the males were rubbed, patted, rocked, touched, kissed and talked to more than the females" (p. 50). Congruent data were reported by Michael Lewis (1975), who found that on the first day of postnatal life mothers tended to feed boy babies more than girls, and by Howard Moss (1967), who observed that mothers of first-born boys held them longer at 3 weeks of age than mothers of first-born girls. After controlling statistically for differences in infant behavior, Moss concluded that two reliable differences distinguished the behavior of girls' mothers from that of boys' mothers. Boys received more physical stimulation while girls received more reinforcement for their verbalizations; girls were more frequently talked to and more frequently imitated. A later study (Wasserman & Lewis, 1985) also reported, from observations of a sample of mothers interacting with their first-born 11- to 14-month-old infants in a laboratory situation, that mothers talked to daughters significantly more than to sons.

Parents' interactions with older preschool children have also been studied. In one investigation (Langlois & Downs, 1980), samples of 3- and 5-year-olds were observed in a laboratory playing alone, with a same-gender peer, or with a parent. When girls played with a toy pre-classified as a "same-sex toy," mothers praised them and gave them affection, but when they played with a "cross-sex toy," their mothers ridiculed them or interfered with their play. Boys received similar consequences, especially from their fathers, who dispensed more vigorous differential treatment of their daughters and sons than the mothers, leading the investigators to propose that "socialization pressure for sex-typed behaviors may come most consistently from fathers" (p. 1245).

Other research also supports the conclusion of greater sex-typing by fathers. Jaipaul Roopnarine (1986), for example, reported, from a study in which 10-, 14-, and 18-month olds were observed playing with each parent separately, that while both parents were less likely to pay attention to the block play of their daughters than their sons, this behavior was even more true of fathers. The fathers were more likely to give dolls to girls than to boys and to attend to the doll play of the former. This study also reinforces the conclusion of Lytton and Romney (1991), noted earlier, from their review of the literature, that sex-typing seems particularly important to parents in regard to their children's play activities. Claire Etaugh and Marsha Liss (1992) found this to be the case with respect to toys. They questioned 245 public school girls and boys from kindergarten through eighth grade and learned that when the children requested toys from their parents they were more likely to receive those that were gender-typed than those that were gender-atypical.

Some investigations point to even more subtle and indirect gender socialization by parents. For example, Robyn Fivush (1989) observed mothers talking with their 30- to 35-month-old children about an event they were likely to remember (for instance, an airplane trip or a movie); whereas mothers used both positive and negative emotion words equally in talking with their sons and attributed both positive and negative emotions to the child, mothers used more positive emotion words with daughters and did not attribute negative emotions to the child. In addition, "mothers talk[ed] about anger with their sons, but never with their daughters" (p. 684). In another study (Birnbaum & Croll, 1984), parents and college students were asked whether they would discourage or encourage emotions depicted in hypothetical situations, and all groups indicated greater acceptance of anger in boys than in girls, with parents more accepting of fear in girls.

Still another demonstration of subtle gender socialization has come from a study in which mothers were observed in a laboratory playroom reading to their 18- to 38-month-old children (DeLoache, Cassidy, & Carpenter, 1987). Where storybook animals were of indeterminate sex, they were referred to as males by the mothers 95 percent of the time. With a different sample of mothers and children, and different books, the investigators found that "child characters [of unknown gender] were nearly always referred to as males when they appeared alone [but] . . . were more likely to be given feminine or neutral labels when . . . in the presence of an adult" (p. 163f). The indirect influence of parents is further suggested by reports (cf. Adler, 1991b) that fathers with challenging jobs tend to spend more time with and to give better explanations to their sons than their daughters; such fathers may also spend more time at work when they have daughters than when they have sons. Finally, some developmental psychologists (Meyer, Murphy, Cascardi, & Birns, 1991) have suggested that parental sex-typing is less a consequence of the behavior parents direct toward their children and more the result of the observations children in two-parent heterosexual families make of "parental interaction that reflects the way most men and women relate to each other," interactions that present distinct messages "about the differential expectations for male and female behavior" (p. 537).

How parents behave with respect to their children, and to each other, contributes to the gender learning of their children and has far-reaching consequences; but parents (and/or other adult caregivers) are not the only family members from whom children learn. Some studies have explored the influence of siblings on gender socialization. The findings from an observational study in the homes of a sample of families with school-aged siblings (Stoneman, Brody, & MacKinnon, 1986) are especially instructive. The investigators reported that "In cross-sex siblings, the sex typing of activities tended to be influenced most by the gender of the older child. . . . For example, little boys with older brothers never played with dolls or played house, while boys with older sisters engaged in these . . . activities as frequently as the pairs containing two girls" (p. 507). Both girls and boys with older other-gender siblings showed less gender stereotyping of objects than those with same-gender siblings.

What Girls Play with and Where They Play

How do the play worlds of our little girls contribute to sex-typing? Consider, for example, the nature of the toys adults see as appropriate for girls: dolls, dress-up clothes, makeup and hairstyling kits, tea sets, kitchen utensils, paint or crayons, cuddly animals. By and large, success in playing with these depends upon someone else's reactions. The little girl asks, Is it pretty, nice, or good? Do you like how it looks, or what I've done with it? Such toys encourage approval seeking and dependence on others. Toys that move or can be manipulated, on the other hand, like trucks, blocks, or tinker toys, provide their own objective test of success by whether or not something the child does works; such toys encourage problem solving through trial and error. Following a review of relevant research on the toys typically played with by children aged 3 to 13, Dyanne Tracy (1987) concluded that the "boys' toys" tend to be "spatial in nature, i.e., vehicles, machine, and construction toys" (p. 124) while "girls' toys are oriented toward domestic pursuits . . . [and] do not encourage manipulation, construction, or movement through space" (p. 127). Toys associated with boys have been found in one study (Rosenfeld, cited in Hoffman, 1977) to have more "potential for inventive use." Both girls and boys gave more varied answers when asked how such toys could be changed to make them more exciting and interesting than they gave in response to questions about "girls' toys." Adult ratings of "girls'" and "boys' toys" yield similar findings (Miller, 1987); the latter are more likely to be described as offering greater opportunities for symbolic play, competition, constructiveness, and handling.

Of the traditional toys given to girls, Barbie dolls are likely to be the most manipulable with their flexible arms and leg joints—a feature that, I suspect, contributes greatly to their popularity. But despite Barbie's physical flexibility, as well as her venture into the career world as astronaut, veterinarian, business executive, and so on, her main function seems to be to represent the essence of feminine glamour and style. The "nation's No. 2 selling toy in 1988" (Garties, 1989), 500 million Barbies and her friends have been sold since her creation in 1959. According to Marjorie Williams (1991), "If you line up 100 little

girls between the ages of 3 and 11, 96 of them will be owners of one or more Barbies" (p. 2). In 1991, the manufacturers of Barbie took the manufacturers of a new doll, Miss America, to court with the charge that the new doll looks too much like Barbie. The lawyers for the Miss America doll agreed that there are similarities in the faces of the two dolls but argued, as suggested by Marjorie Williams, that "if you're going to manufacture stereotypes of feminine beauty, then of course they're all going to look alike" (p. 2)!

Although many people believe that "things are changing," careful observation suggests otherwise. One study (Schwartz & Markham, 1985) found, after examining retail toy catalogs and pictures of children on toy packages, that "sex stereotyping in advertising is strong." In both catalogs and stores, toys for girls and boys tended to be placed in separate sections with "girls' sections . . . characterized by dolls and accessories, doll houses, arts and craft kits . . . , toy beauty kits, and housekeeping and cooking toys [while] building sets . . . , sports-related toys, transportation toys . . . , and workbenches and tools were featured in the boys' sections" (pp. 167f.). The cover of a toy catalog I received in the mail for Christmas 1990 featured a little girl in a floor-length dress and her baby dolls—no different from catalog covers of 40 or 50 years ago. Inside the catalog, girls were shown in fairy godmother dress-up clothes, and next to a stove and sink or doll house, looking much like the photograph shown on p. 45; boys were shown with blocks and planes and in a pirate's costume. A girl and boy were shown together only when playing with a giant floor puzzle. In an advertisement for an air-cleaner to protect children's health, a girl and boy are also shown together but the girl, in stockings and Mary Jane shoes, is hugging her teddy bear while the boy, in jeans and sneakers, is building a tower with blocks. As these examples suggest, the toys we buy for girls are less likely than the ones we buy for boys to evoke energetic movement, to involve objective criteria for mastery, and to encourage both cooperation and competition, as well as risk taking. Consistent with other aspects of gender socialization, the play equipment we frequently purchase for little boys provides training for competence, whereas the toys we buy for girls are more likely to encourage approval-seeking behavior.

An often-heard argument is that girls like and request the toys adults buy for them; so what are adults to do? Let us consider some research that relates to this question. In one study (Serbin, Connor, Burchardt, & Citron, 1979), 4-year-old children were observed alone or in the presence of a same- or other-gender peer in a room equipped with

A little girl "at play." (Photograph © Michael Siluk.)

often as with the housekeeping materials, and girls used the blocks in as relevant a manner as the boys. Another group of researchers (Serbin, Connor, & Iler, 1979) influenced the play behaviors of preschoolers by presenting a group of new dolls and trucks in gender-neutral, nonstereotypic ways. Children who were not given gender labels for the new toys chose them for play with no relationship to gender.

While these studies tell us something about children's toy choices and play under varying conditions, we also have data on the choices adults make for children. Harriet Rheingold and Kaye Cook (1975) inventoried the contents of the rooms of four girls and four boys at each half-year of life from 1 month to almost 5 years old. The boys' rooms and the girls' were found to be sharply and significantly different. Inside the boys' rooms were more vehicles, education/art materials, sports equipment, machines, fauna, and military toys ("activities directed away from the home"), whereas the girls had more play materials in only three categories: dolls, dollhouses, and domestic toys ("activities directed toward the home—keeping house and caring for children"). Girls generally had fewer toys than boys and in fewer categories. We cannot assume that these parents, who were of high educational level and socioeconomic status, simply followed the wishes of their children, in light of differences that appeared even in the rooms of girls and boys as young as 1 month. A replication of this study 15 years later in Montreal (Pomerleau, Bolduc, Malcutt, & Cossette, 1990) obtained similar results. The rooms of boys aged 5, 13, and 25 months were found to differ from the rooms of same-age girls in having more sports equipment, tools, vehicles, and blue bedding and clothing, while the girls' rooms contained more dolls, fictional characters, child's furniture, jewelry, and pink or multicolored clothing.

Parents and other adults continue to be encouraged to make sex-typed purchases for children by other parts of the culture. Thus, for example, a sample of college students, who were shown slides of toys taken from department store catalogs and asked to decide what they would buy for girls and boys, said they would buy guns, soldiers, jeeps, carpenter tools, and red bicycles for boys, but baby dolls, dishes, sewing kits, jewelry boxes, and pink bicycles for girls (Fisher-Thompson, 1990). Men tended to sex-type more than women, and toys chosen for boys were rated as requiring more activity than those for girls. In a different kind of study (Robinson & Morris, 1986), the actual Christmas toy choices of the parents of preschoolers were surveyed. While parents tended to give their children more gender-neutral toys than the children requested,

three toys considered stereotypically appropriate for girls and three toys considered appropriate for boys. The investigators reported significant "effects of peer pressure"; both girls and boys spent less time playing with other-gender typed toys in the presence of an other-gender peer than when alone or with a same-gender peer. In another study (Downs, 1983), letters to Santa Claus written by 7-year-olds were analyzed. Under this private condition, boys were found to be just as likely to request neutral (non-sex-typed) toys as "masculine" ones, but girls requested neutral toys most frequently and more so than "feminine" ones.

Thus, children's toy choices and play behavior vary with the circumstances. For example, when nursery school teachers in one study (Kinsman & Berk, 1979) joined the traditionally separated block and housekeeping areas into one large area, they found "no indication of a sex-typed attraction to either play area." Children of both genders preferred the blocks, playing with them more than twice as none of the parents reported giving boys a toy associated with girls, and only 8 percent of the parents of girls gave her a toy associated with boys.

Nancy Kutner and Richard Levinson (1978) had college students request help from toy salespersons in selecting birthday presents for a 5-year-old niece and nephew (twins). Almost 53 percent of the suggestions the students received were for sex-stereotyped toys, and such suggestions were more likely to be made by salesmen. Even more dramatic results were reported from a later study (Ungar, 1982) which found that 67 percent of 134 toy salespersons approached for suggestions for a Christmas gift for a 5-year-old offered sex-stereotyped advice. Men buyers received more stereotyped advice than women, and salesmen gave such advice significantly more than saleswomen.

In addition to being expected to play with different kinds of toys, girls and boys are expected to play in different places. This form of sex-typing is of great importance because the situations in which children play will tend to evoke responses most appropriate to them. Children who spend more of their time running or playing ball will be practicing and perfecting responses and manifesting activity levels quite different from those of children who spend their time sitting at a table and drawing, lounging on swings, or observing others. In a study I did in New Zealand (Lott, 1978), 4-year-old girls and boys were found to differ significantly in their use of 8 of 21 possible play areas. Girls played less often than boys in the sandpit, with wagons, across situations in make-believe activities, and on an outdoor platform used for dramatic play. On the other hand, girls more often played on the swings; did painting, pasting, or drawing; worked on jigsaw puzzles; or simply observed others. In addition, girls played more often indoors than outdoors and differed reliably in this respect from boys. These findings are congruent with those reported by other investigators. For example, in every season over the course of two years, preschool girls were observed (Harper & Sanders, 1975) to spend less time outdoors than boys. Relevant to these gender differences in play area is the finding in my New Zealand study that children whose observed social behavior did not conform well with adult expectations about gender tended not to play as often in the situations preferred by their own gender. Thus, the girls whose observed behavior did not match adult expectations for girls were found more often than other girls to be playing outdoors.

These data provide suggestive evidence that the situations in which children play are related to the behavior they manifest. One study (Carpenter & Huston-Stein, 1980) addressed this question directly. Preschoolers between the ages of 2½ and 5 were observed in five different classes. Children were found to make more novel and creative use of materials when they were engaged in activities that were not highly structured by teacher feedback and to be more compliant during more structured activities. This finding was true for both girls and boys. Classrooms that differed in degree of structure were also found to have the same behavioral consequences for children of both genders. This investigation was followed up with an experiment (Carpenter, Huston, & Holt, 1986) in which preschoolers were assigned to high or low structured activities for 15 minutes at the beginning of daily hour-long free periods. Each child was given both treatments for 2 to 3 weeks, and the investigators found that when boys or girls were in high structured activities they were more likely to interact with adults. In contrast, when in low structured activities they were more likely to interact with peers and to behave physically and aggressively.

What Girls Read

What children read or is read to them has been the focus of a great deal of attention in the past few years. Narrow, stereotyped images of women and girls, and less narrow but equally stereotyped images of men and boys, have been found everywhere—in nursery rhymes, coloring books, picture books, and Sunday comics, in grade school readers and high school science texts. For example, although in Mother Goose land the "ten-o'clock scholar" who is always late is a boy, the images of girls seem, in general, to be considerably worse, as Letty Pogrebin (1972) has reminded us by pointing to Lazy Mary, frightened Miss Muffet, empty-headed Bo Peep, and Mary Quite Contrary.

Comic strips repeat the lessons of Mother Goose. An analysis by Sarah Brabant (1976) of four popular Sunday family comics indicated that whether the major woman character was domineering or submissive in relation to her husband, she stayed at home, cooked, washed the dishes, and cleaned the house. It was the men who either worked or engaged in leisure activities such as golf, playing musical instruments, or reading. Ten years later, three of these comics were reexamined (Brabant & Mooney, 1986), and, while the investigators reported a narrowing of differences between the major women and men characters, the women "continued to be shown in home and child care more and in leisure activities less than [the men and] . . . were also much more likely to be portrayed as passive onlookers" (p. 147). A content analysis of 100 randomly selected newspaper comics (Chavez, 1985) obtained comparable results. Men not only were presented far more often as main characters, but also were shown to be in the work force more frequently than women. Stereotypic roles predominated, and men were presented more positively than women. In still another analysis of Sunday comics (Mooney & Brabant, 1987), more employed women were found than previously but portrayed in negative ways. According to the investigators, the working woman was shown as a

> superwoman . . . [who] cleans the house, takes care of the children, fixes the car, paints the house, and maintains a career. She is competent, aggressive, and accomplished at a variety of tasks— . . . [but] is also rather 'hard,' 'unfeminine,' and 'mannish,' in her appearance. She can be castrating to males, inappropriately dominating the conversation, and is highly critical of her husband, never seeming to be satisfied with anything he does. . . . She worries a great deal and has stressful sleepless nights. She controls her husband who is ineffectual, weak, and lazy . . . and is even physically stronger than he is. (p. 419)

One of the last of the comic holdouts for the traditional family, the Bumsteads, have finally undergone change, with great fanfare and publicity. The word went out to journalists that Blondie Bumstead, after 58 years as a full-time homemaker, was going to "take a job outside the home. In the World of Comics, this is big news" (Galloway, 1991). So as not to make too many waves, however, Blondie has gone into the catering business. Even such a job, so close to women's traditional sphere, is threatening to Dagwood, as we learn from installments such as the one shown below.

The world of children's books is similar to that of the comics. In one study (Rachlin & Vogt, 1974), 30 coloring books by five different publishers were examined; boys were found to outnumber girls in pictures of outdoor activities, while girls starred in domestic roles. When pictured outdoors, girls were in the sand, on the swings, or jumping rope while boys fished, built things, climbed trees, and rode scooters. An analysis of prize-winning picture books for preschoolers (Weitzman, Eifler, Hokada, & Ross, 1972) found women and girls to be underrepresented in titles, central roles, and illustrations and depicted as passive, as followers, and as serving others. Girls received praise and attention for being attractive, but boys were admired for achievements and for being clever; while women were shown primarily as wives and mothers, men were shown in a wide variety of occupations.

Similar images of women and men emerged from a large-scale study of 134 grade-school readers published by 14 major publishers (Women on Words and Images, 1972). Boys outnumbered girls as major characters in the stories by a ratio of 5 : 2, and biographies of men outnumbered those of women by a 6 : 1 ratio. Boys' themes concerned ingenuity, problem solving, heroism, apprenticeships, and adventurous/imaginative play, in sharp contrast to stories about girls, which emphasized passivity, domesticity, and incompetence, and showed girls being humiliated by boys. In addition, mothers in these books were portrayed not as the nurturant, smiling bakers of yummy cookies, as we at least might have hoped, but as "limited, colorless, and mindless," with fathers shown as more creative and compassionate. According to the authors of the report, "not only does [the mother] . . . wash, cook, clean, and find mittens; these chores constitute her only happiness. . . . She is perpetually on call, . . . available. . . .

BLONDIE. Reprinted with special permission of King Features Syndicate.

Father is the 'good guy' in the family. He's where the fun is" (p. 40). The 15 books that make up the very popular Sesame Street Library have also been found to contain "blatant and pervasive" sexism (Charnes, Hoffman, Hoffman, & Meyers, 1980). Male characters are overrepresented by a 6:1 ratio, and the female characters are "traditional princesses and Little Miss Muffet types" who will "live happily ever after as soon as they find their prince." The girls were frequently "in trouble and in need of rescuing (by a man, of course)" (p. 10).

Data such as these proved sufficiently convincing so that a number of book publishers agreed in the 1970s to make changes in language, stories, and pictures to provide equal treatment for girls and boys, women and men. By 1978 almost all of the major textbook publishers had issued guidelines designed to discourage sexist portrayals of women (Collins, 1978). Some of these new books for children have been studied. Shirley St. Peter (1979) compared 43 picture books for preschoolers identified by publishers as nonstereotyped with 92 conventional picture books. The nonstereotyped books were far more often found to have women or girls as central characters engaged in instrumental activities, but female characters were infrequently shown as behaving expressively. St. Peter concluded that nonsexist books are "overcompensating" for the traditional presentation of women as expressive, dependent, and passive. Another study of newer picture books (Davis, 1984) found that women and girls were presented as more independent than men and boys but that female characters in nonsexist books were shown as more emotional and less physically active than male characters in both nonsexist and conventional books, thus perpetuating traditional stereotypes.

A replication of the 1972 study by Women on Words and Images 17 years later (Purcell & Stewart, 1989) found that gender differences in children's readers were less pronounced than they had been and that there were more stories about girls doing more things. The ratio of boy-centered to girl-centered stories was 1:1, although males still sharply predominated in both animal stories and folk tales. Men were still presented as having a greater variety of careers, and a common theme in the stories about girls still "was that of rescue."

One important study (Tetenbaum & Pearson, 1989) examined 50 works of fiction considered favorites for school-aged children to see how the girls and boys in the stories were shown making moral decisions. The investigators concluded that girls were more likely to be presented as concerned with relationships and the welfare of others (demonstrating a morality of "care"), while boys were more often shown to be concerned with obligations, standards, rules, and principles (demonstrating a morality of "justice"). The authors of this study suggest that "the messages provided by . . . [the] characters in children's literature constitute a powerful source for the modeling of sex role stereotypic behavior in moral decisioning" (p. 392). Such a conclusion is supported by research demonstrating that what children read has measurable effects on their behavior in a variety of areas. In one study (Flerx, Fidler, & Rogers, 1976), preschool children exposed to egalitarian stories for 30 minutes per day for 5 days gave significantly fewer stereotyped responses to questions about children's and parents' activities than children who heard traditional stories about men and women. In another investigation, Eleanor Ashton (1983) found, among a group of 5-year-olds, that those who were exposed to a picture-book story in which a same-gender child played with a particular toy later spent more time with the same toy than children who had not been exposed to the book. The effects of exposure to the picture book were greater on the girls than on the boys.

What Girls See on Television

Studies of television, like those of children's books, have revealed stereotyped images of women and men. Programs produced for children have fewer women than men characters, with women more often in traditional roles and shown as deferent to men. The most extensive monitoring of the television shows and commercials typically seen by children during prime-time was carried out by Women on Words and Images (1975). The authors summarized their findings as follows:

> [Children] see, overall, more men than women on their television screens; on the exciting adventure shows, they see nearly six times as many men. The men they see work in diverse occupations, nearly twice the number of those held by women. . . . Children see that more male than female behaviors show competence, and that more female behaviors display incompetence. On the commercials, children see women taking care of their houses, their families, their shopping and their appearance, while men work and play harder and provide the voice of authority for the purchasing decisions women make.

Some changes have taken place in the relationships between women and men portrayed on television and in their occupations and social status, but children in the 1990s are still, for the most part, seeing women in dramatic shows, comedies, and commercials who do the laundry or who are secretaries or assistants to men. This stereotyping is particularly apparent in shows and advertisements likely to be seen by children in the evening hours before their bedtime and in situation comedies. One study (Atkin, Moorman, & Lin, 1991) found that in the 1980s there was a clear increase in the number of working women leading characters on prime-time network series, such as *Murphy Brown* and *Designing Women.* According to the authors, this positive change was accompanied by "strides women have made 'behind the camera' in . . . the television management 'pipeline'" (p. 684). Nevertheless, an 81-page report of a year-long study (cf. "Report Details," 1990) that examined 80 prime-time programs on ABC, CBS, NBC, and Fox networks concluded that "women continue to fare poorly on television" and to be outnumbered by men. The authors of the report, titled "What's Wrong with This Picture?" note that, "despite working women's breakthroughs on TV, too many female characters remain the extension of male fantasies. . . . Men on TV wear more clothes than women, and they keep them on" (p. G-2). Donald Davis (1990) studied 894 characters in 50 hours of prime-time programming. He found that women characters were significantly underrepresented, appearing only 35 percent of the time, and that they tended to be younger than men, to have red or blonde hair, to have their marital or parental status identified, and to be provocatively dressed. "The portrait . . . is of the young, attractive, and sexy female who is more ornamental . . . than functional" (p. 331).

A study of commercials (Bretl & Cantor, 1988) found some changes from earlier years as well as some continuation of stereotypes and inequities. While women and men were appearing equally as primary characters in evening ads, the women were significantly less likely to have an occupation and were more often shown as a spouse or parent. "The most striking and persistent inequity," according to the investigators, was with regard to the gender of the narrators, who are men 90 percent of the time.

Television cartoons and videotapes popular with children have also been criticized for their unrealistic, stereotyped, and unequal depiction of girls. Katha Pollitt (1991) concluded from watching cartoons with her 3-year-old daughter that she was seeing little that was different from her own 1950s childhood. "Contemporary shows," she wrote, "are either essentially all-male . . . or a group of male buddies will be accented by a lone female . . . [who] is usually a little-sister type. . . . Boys define the group, its story and its code of values. Girls exist only in relation to boys" (p. 22). The major Muppets, the

lovable stars of *Sesame Street,* are all male, with the exception of Miss Piggy. When questioned about this imbalance by Pollitt, the executive producer of the show said, "We're working on it"—this after 25 years of telecasting! As the grandmother of a preschool girl, I share the frustration of adults attempting to find television or video images of active, assertive, intelligent girls. Videos starring boys are in the majority, and it is rare to find a Pippi Longstocking–type heroine or even a central female animal like the spider in *Charlotte's Web.* In the very popular video *The Little Mermaid,* "the bitter message for children," according to Robin Abcarian (1990), "is that girls—even sassy ones . . . —are nothing without their guys. . . . Ariel gives up her whole world for the man she loves" (p. E-3). At least, however, as Pollitt points out, Ariel is "active, brave and determined, . . . and even rescues the prince" (p. 24).

Television has been called a "window on the world" and a "member of the family" (Singer & Singer, 1980), and it has been estimated that grade-school children typically spend 20 to 30 hours each week watching it. It is not surprising, therefore, that children who are frequent viewers have been found to hold more stereotyped beliefs about gender than less frequent viewers (e.g., McGhee & Frueh, 1980). Rena Repetti (1984) reported that, among a group of children aged 5½ to 7½, genderstereotyped responses to questions about toys and occupations were negatively correlated with the amount of educational television the children regularly watched. In other words, the greater their exposure to noncommercial television, the fewer gender stereotypes they held. Michael Morgan (1982) found a significant positive correlation between frequency of commercial television viewing and sex-role stereotyping among a large sample of sixth- to tenth-grade girls, and particularly among high IQ girls, but not among boys, suggesting that television's impact on beliefs may be strongest on those least likely to hold traditional views. The students were tested over a 2-year period, and for girls, especially those of high IQ, amount of television viewing predicted scores on a gender stereotyping measure 1 year later. Among a large, ethnically diverse sample of fourth and fifth graders (Signorelli & Lears, 1992), it was found that those "who watched more television were more likely to say that only girls should do those chores traditionally associated with women and that only boys should do those chores traditionally associated with men" (p. 168). These relationships held regardless of grade, ethnicity, or gender and regardless of the type of chores the children reported actually doing at home. The match between attitudes and reported behavior was stronger among the children who watched more television.

While most studies indicate a relationship between television viewing and children's beliefs about gender, some research has demonstrated that television viewing may have a direct effect on behavior. A 1-year longitudinal study of a sample of preschoolers (Singer & Singer, 1980) found a significant correlation for both girls and boys between observed aggression during free play periods and frequency of overall weekly TV viewing, particularly the viewing of action shows; the correlations were greater and more dramatic for the girls than for the boys. Girls are able to see on television how violence is used as a successful and acceptable means of goal attainment or conflict resolution, a message they are not ordinarily given. Evidence from experimental research also demonstrates that children's behavior can be influenced by what they see on television. In one study (Ruble, Balaban, & Cooper, 1981), 100 preschool children were shown a 1-minute toy commercial inserted in the middle of a Bugs Bunny cartoon. Among the children who understood gender constancy, those who had seen the toy played with by an other-gender child spent less time playing with it when given the opportunity later on to do so than those who had seen it played with by a same-gender child. Considering that the average American child will have spent approximately 15,000 hours watching television by the time she or he is 16 years old, which is 4,000 hours longer than the time spent in classrooms (Women on Words and Images, 1975), the potential of the small screen for teaching about gender relationships, behavior, interests, and expectations is awesome.

Teachers and School

What parents teach their children and what the children play with, read, see, and learn from one another and the media is typically congruent with what teachers model in the schools and reinforce in the behavior of the children in their classes. If we look at the jobs done by women and men in the school system, we see that, as in books and on television, men typically have more power and authority and higher status. The number of women in administrative positions in the schools has increased in the past decade, but while about 75 percent of all teachers are women, they are only 34.5 percent of all principals, and 8.2 percent of district superintendents.* Boys and girls, unaware of these

* Figures obtained by phone from Council of Chief State School Officers and Educational Research Services, January 1993.

figures, still know that ultimate power is found "in the principal's office," most likely occupied by a man. The cafeteria workers and teacher-aides, on the other hand, are most likely women, while the school custodian who helps to retrieve lost balls from the roof and competently opens jammed lockers is typically a man. It is of considerable interest that, in a study of first graders (Paradise & Wall, 1986), those who came from schools with women principals differed significantly from those attending schools with men principals in being more likely to say that either women or men could hold such a job.

Researchers have used several strategies to study teacher contributions to the gender learning of children: (a) relating teachers' judgments about the stereotypical masculine and feminine traits of children to the degree to which the teachers like the children or rate them positively on other dimensions; (b) observing teacher-child interactions, particularly the ways in which teachers reward or punish various behaviors; and (c) measuring teachers' beliefs about gender attributes. In the first category is a study (Levitin & Chananie, 1972) in which first- and second-grade teachers were asked to rate hypothetical children described as behaving independently, aggressively, or in an achievement-oriented manner, by indicating approval and typicalness of the behavior and how likable they found the child. It was found that the teachers liked an achieving girl significantly more than an achieving boy and saw dependent girls and aggressive boys as significantly more typical than the reverse. Also, while the teachers judged dependent and aggressive boys as likable to more or less the same extent, they liked dependent girls far more than aggressive ones. We can guess pretty well how such attitudes toward children are translated into interactive behavior in the classroom.

From studies in which teacher-child interactions have been carefully observed has come information about the different experiences girls and boys seem to have in the classroom. Although not all findings agree, most of the reports on student-teacher interaction support the conclusion that boys tend to receive more attention than girls. Louise Cherry (1975) listened to tape recordings of verbal interaction and concluded that teachers' speech to boys was more directing in nature. A more comprehensive study (Serbin, O'Leary, Kent, & Tonick, 1973) involved direct observation of ongoing activities in 15 preschool classrooms. Teachers were found to respond three times more often to aggressive behavior by boys than by girls and to give boys loud reprimands three times as often as they did girls. Teachers also gave more extended directions to, and had longer conversations with, boys than girls. Girls appeared to receive teacher attention primarily when they were near the teacher, whereas proximity did not influence the amount of attention boys got. Among children who showed neither destructive nor dependent behavior, the rate of teacher response was higher for boys in all classrooms and, furthermore, teachers more often praised and hugged the boys. Boys were twice as likely as girls to receive individual instructions on how to do things on their own, whereas girls were assisted but not sent off to work by themselves. The researchers concluded that boys are encouraged to become involved in the classroom by being given more direction, instructions, and attention, while girls are not encouraged to become involved in problem-solving activities. If girls tend to be ignored except when within arm's reach, directly beside the teacher, it is no wonder that they are more often found there.

That boys tend to get more teacher attention than girls and that certain behaviors by each gender are more likely to be reinforced than others are conclusions supported by data from other studies. For example, among fifth graders observed in English, social studies, math, and science classes (Etaugh & Harlow, 1975), boys were scolded more than girls by both male and female teachers and praised more than girls by female teachers. Beverly Fagot (1981a) observed a sample of 40 teachers in preschool play groups and found that teachers tended to interact verbally more with the girls but to join in more with the play of boys. Another group of researchers (Dweck, Davidson, Nelson, & Enna, 1978) reported that among a sample of fourth and fifth graders, boys received more positive teacher feedback than girls for "the intellectual quality" of their schoolwork. When making negative evaluations, teachers more often attributed girls' failures to their intellectual inadequacies but boys' failures to their lack of motivation. A later study (Sadker & Sadker, 1985) of more than 100 fourth-, sixth-, and eighth-grade classrooms found that, in general, "boys got more than their fair share of teacher attention" (p. 56). This attention included more discipline but also more instruction in how to do things. Teachers were more accepting of boys who called out answers and did not raise their hands—that is, of boys' assertive behavior. A review of the literature led Carol Tittle (1986) to suggest that, compared to elementary school girls, "boys may be getting more instruction in mathematics . . . [and more training in] self-reliance and independent achievement" (p. 1162).

Teachers' differential responses to girls and boys, documented by observational studies, would seem to reflect deeply rooted ideas about how the genders differ.

Indirect evidence of such beliefs among teachers is given in data reported by Mary Gregory (1977). A large sample of elementary school teachers were asked to rate the likelihood that they would refer children with varying problems for special assistance. Boys were found to be significantly more likely to be referred for help than girls (for all problems except reading disabilities), suggesting to Gregory that teachers are "more concerned about male children." In a study aimed more directly at identifying teacher beliefs about gender, George Wise (1978) found that a large sample of public school teachers (representing kindergarten through the 12th grade) perceived girls and boys differently in a consistently stereotypic manner. According to the teachers (both women and men),

> female students tend to be very emotional, do not hide their emotions, easily express tender feelings, are very easily hurt, cry easily, are very affectionate, very gentle, very quiet, and not at all aggressive . . . very aware of the feelings of others, very understanding of others, very helpful . . . enjoy art and literature very much, dislike math and science, are not adventurous, are not at all reckless, are very careful, are very neat . . . [and] are very interested in their appearance. (p. 609)

If adults who teach girls do so with such beliefs, and if girls play and interact with other children whose parents and teachers share these beliefs, then of course these beliefs will be perpetuated and validated through social agreement, and behavior to match them will be learned and strengthened. Such a conviction has led some (e.g., Lee & Gropper, 1974) to suggest that sexist beliefs and practices constitute a "hidden curriculum" in our schools and spurred Congress to pass legislation in 1972 (Title IX of the Education Amendments) that prohibits sex discrimination by an educational program receiving federal financial assistance. Following this law's passage, many state education departments held conferences and workshops and issued guidelines designed to help their districts evaluate their programs, curricula, and textbooks and to devise antisexist strategies.

The federal Title IX regulations have been noticeably effective in expanding opportunities for girls in sports and shop programs and encouraging experimental programs designed to change sexist attitudes and beliefs. Sally Koblinsky and Alan Sugawara (1984), for example, developed such a program for 3- to 5-year-olds in which some were exposed for 6 months to materials and activities designed as a "nonsexist curriculum" while others took part in the regular school program. Girls and boys were found to be equally affected by the special curriculum and manifested significantly less stereotypic views about gender after it than they did before.

The importance of teacher behavior in influencing what children do was demonstrated in an experimental study of preschool classes (Serbin, Connor, & Citron, 1981) in which teachers sat in predesignated areas (ones most popular with only one gender) during free play and interacted with children. Teacher presence was very effective in helping girls overcome "sex role inhibitions against play with 'inappropriate' toys" (such as trucks and blocks). In other words, presence of a woman teacher significantly increased girls' subsequent play in a variety of play areas. Using a different strategy for change, Marlaine Lockheed (1986) tested the effects of a program in which some fourth and fifth grade teachers had children work in small, mixed-gender instructional groups consistently over a 2-year period. Students exposed to this program were found to significantly increase their cross-gender interactions.

Despite Title IX, a 116-page report on schools in the U.S. (The AAUW Report, 1992) concluded that girls and boys still are not treated equally in the public schools. The report, dramatically but carefully entitled "How Schools Shortchange Girls," and presenting a "synthesis of all the available research on the subject of girls in school," offers "compelling evidence that girls are not receiving the same quality, or even quantity, of education as their brothers" (p. v). The authors of the report insist that the current system of education in the U.S. must change if we are to achieve schools that are egalitarian with respect to gender, since "girls do not receive equitable amounts of teacher attention, . . . are less apt than boys to see themselves reflected in the materials they study, and . . . often are not expected or encouraged to pursue higher level mathematics and science courses" (p. 84). We can suppose that a little girl starts school with the very same sense of excitement as a little boy, the same sense of wonder and fear, and the expectation that something important comes from education. It is unfair to shatter these expectations by teaching girls passivity and dependency and rewarding them for "standing by." Experience and research show that stereotypes are modifiable, especially early on, but also throughout childhood.

CHILDREN'S KNOWLEDGE OF GENDER STEREOTYPES

In gender-sensitive societies, children learn early to associate particular behaviors, traits, activities, and occu-pations with women and others with men. Research provides clear evidence that children in the United States learn these associations as early as age 2 and that agreement with adult stereotypes regarding gender-associated personality traits and behaviors increases as children get older.

Behavioral Stereotypes

In a study of 2- and 3-year-olds (Kuhn, Nash, & Brucken, 1978), the children were instructed to select one of two paper dolls as the one who did certain things, such as play ball. Girls and boys at both ages correctly identified the girl doll as Lisa and the boy doll as Michael, and the children indicated by their choices that they believed girls more than boys "like to play with dolls, like to help mother; . . . talk a lot, never hit, [and] say 'I need some help'" (p. 447). The children also believed that when boys grow up they will "be boss," while girls will "clean the house." In another investigation (Cowan & Hoffman, 1986), 2- to 3-year-olds were found to be just as adept as 3 ½- to 4-year-olds in describing both infants and animals in terms of gender stereotypes. Girl babies and female dogs and horses were described as smaller, slower, weaker, quieter, and softer than boy babies and male animals.

In a study of 4-year-olds (Masters & Wilkinson, 1976), it was found that their ratings of 52 common toys as more likely to be used by girls or boys were highly correlated with the ratings of adults; 7- and 8-year-olds rated the toys almost exactly as the adults did. Except at the youngest age, girls and boys exhibited "practically indistinguishable sex-stereotype norms." Stereotyped gender associations to adjectives describing personality have been reported to increase with age among children from 3 to 5 (Reis & Wright, 1982). The stereotypes held by girls and boys were found to be similar, but children with more intellectual ability also had more knowledge of gender stereotypes. According to the children, women (girls) cry a lot, are quiet and afraid, are thankful, weak, gentle, loving, and have good manners, while men (boys) are cruel, strong, get into fights, are self-reliant, and talk loudly. One study (Bardwell, Cochran, & Walker, 1986) has reported more gender stereotyping by 5-year-olds whose parents were more highly educated and by European-American than African-American children, but no difference between girls and boys.

Using a different methodology, Wendy Matthews (1981) videotaped pairs of unacquainted same-gender 4-year-olds for 3 consecutive days as they engaged in an hour of free play in the absence of an adult. From an analysis of the children's imaginative role playing of mothers and fathers, she concluded that they saw wives as relatively helpless in comparison to husbands. Although women were seen as highly competent mothers, their competence decreased dramatically in the role of wife.

Among a sample of older children, in grades 4, 6, and 8 (Connor, Serbin, & Ender, 1978), girls were found to make increasingly positive judgments of passive behavior as they got older while boys increasingly devalued such behavior. The children responded to questions about three stories in which other children were described as behaving aggressively, assertively, or passively in dealing with a problem. Children of both genders viewed passive behavior as more desirable for girls than for boys, and girls more than boys considered the passive approach a good and effective way to solve the problem, were willing to handle the problem in the same way as the passive character, and liked the passive character better. The same study revealed that although verbal hostility was considered a generally undesirable response, children of both genders considered it least desirable for girls. In a different kind of study (Sandidge & Friedland, 1975), 9- and 10-year-old girls and boys were asked to respond to aggressive statements attributed to cartoon figures. Some children were asked to respond as a girl would and others as a boy would. The results indicated that children of both genders share "common expectations in regard to sex-appropriate behavior" and when playing the boy role, both girls and boys displayed, with equal ease, antisocial, aggressive behavior.

Children show early awareness of which gender is expected to be interpersonally sensitive and helpful, and this knowledge increases with age. Beverly Fagot (1984a) observed children aged 19 to 64 months as they interacted with an adult stranger for 5 minutes in a playroom. Among the younger children (under 31 months), neither the child's nor the adult's gender had any significant effect. Among the older toddlers, however, both girls and boys initiated more ball play with men but asked for help more with women, indicating that children learn very early "the different roles that males and females play." In a study of children in grades 4 to 8 (Dino, Barnett, & Howard, 1984), each was asked to indicate how their parents would respond to four interpersonal problem situations. Children of both genders expected fathers to respond to sons by suggesting choices and strategies, but they expected mothers to respond to daughters in terms of feelings. An extensive study (Goldman & Goldman, 1983) of more than 800 children aged 5 to 15 from five industrialized Western countries (including the United States) found that when children were asked in what ways mothers differed from fathers, the vast majority associated their

mothers with "home duties." Also strongly associated with mothers were child care, housework, and such traditional jobs as typing and hairdressing. Mothers were seen as more loving and accommodating and fathers as more disciplining, with these differences mentioned more frequently as the age of the children increased. The authors' conclusion is a simple one: "overall, children view adults in terms of traditional sex roles" (p. 811).

An interesting strategy employed by some investigators is to analyze the content of stories written by children. In one such study (Libby & Aries, 1989), 3- to 5-year-olds were given six story beginnings to complete. Girls were found to be more likely to write about friendly figures who offer assistance, whereas the characters in the boys' stories coped with aggression and made attempts to command or control. While an equal number of the girls told stories involving female and male central characters, "no boy ever told a story specifying a character to be female." Another study (Trepanier & Romatowski, 1985) found that both girls and boys in grades 1 through 6 wrote more stories about male than female characters, with females presented in very few occupational roles, and males "assigned a wide variety of roles, many of which represented power and prestige" (p. 272). Similar findings were reported by Kate Peirce and Emily Edwards (1988) from an analysis of the fantasy stories of a sample of 11- to 13-year-olds; female characters were rarely portrayed as active or working, while male characters were more violent and more varied in occupation.

Occupational Stereotypes

A great deal of research has focused on occupational sex-typing as evidenced by judgments about which gender does what jobs and which gender does what jobs best (as well as by children's expectations about their own future occupations, a question we will leave for a later section of this chapter). The employment status of one's mother seems to make a difference in children's occupational stereotyping, as indicated by the results of one study (Jones & McBride, 1980) that found first- and second-grade children of working mothers to make fewer sex-typed activity attributions than children of full-time homemakers. Not all studies, however, report differences between children of working and nonworking mothers (e.g., Seegmiller, 1980b).

Occupational stereotyping appears to increase with age, like other gender stereotypes, and then to decline. In one study (Gettys & Cann, 1981), the occupational stereotypes of children as young as 2 years old were compared with those of children aged 4 to 5 and 6 to 7.

Each child was asked to assign each of 10 occupations to a male or female doll; stereotyping was found in each group but increased with age. Stereotyping appears to increase from preschool to about third or fourth grade (Tremaine, Schau, & Busch, 1982), suggesting that older children have had greater exposure to cultural expectations and norms. But somewhere in mid-childhood, at about the fifth grade, children's views of occupation and gender appear to become more flexible or "liberal," with a decrease in stereotyping through adolescence (e.g., Franken, 1983; Archer, 1984). A study of children in grades 3, 6, 9, and 12 from a wide range of ethnic and socioeconomic groups (Cummings & Taebel, 1980) reported that by 12th grade, regardless of whether their mothers worked outside the home, students were significantly less sexist in their occupational orientations than younger children.

We can anticipate that girls' beliefs about adult work roles will change as they read and hear more about women astronauts like Sally Ride and Judith Resnick, see more women practicing medicine or law or doing police work, and see more mothers in their neighborhoods carrying briefcases or wearing hard hats. On the other hand, stereotypes are resistant to change. One group of researchers (Drabman, Robertson, Patterson, Jarvie, Hammer, & Cordua, 1981) had a sample of first, fourth, and seventh graders watch a videotape of a child visiting a doctor's office and being attended by a female physician and a male nurse. When tested immediately after the film or one week later, the first and fourth graders assigned female names to the nurse and male names to the doctor! Although the seventh graders gave name assignments in accord with the videotape when tested immediately after the film, one week later their answers were no longer correct and had reverted to the powerful occupational stereotypes.

BEHAVIORAL DIMENSIONS

The preceding discussions and presentation of empirical findings enable us to specify the broad general features of the typical socialization pattern for girls. Different cultural emphases for each gender are established by differences in (a) the situations to which girls and boys are maximally exposed; (b) the meaning and value given to these situations by adults and others; (c) the most probable responses required or demanded by these situations; (d) the opportunities girls and boys are given to practice various behaviors; and (e) the consequences (rewards and punishments) girls and boys experience or receive. Rather than just cataloging observed gender differences in children's behavior, we need to identify how the experiences of girls and boys differ along these dimensions. As an example of this approach, let us consider how the situations in which children play or behave tend to evoke those responses most appropriate to them. Children who spend their time running or playing baseball are practicing and perfecting responses and manifesting activity levels quite different from those of children who spend their time sitting at a table and drawing, lounging on the swings, or observing others.

We know, of course, that within-gender variations exist in childhood experiences and that socialization is influenced by factors other than sex, such as ethnicity, socioeconomic status, and individual variables. Examination of these variations in experience should increase our understanding of the relationship between antecedent conditions and consequent behaviors and enhance our appreciation of the behavioral potential of children of both genders. Unfortunately, most relevant research has not taken this approach but has focused instead on gender comparisons in the form of a simple examination of average differences between girls and boys. As we examine the behaviors typically studied in childhood, we need to consider how the behaviors said to be characteristic of girls may be learned and how the life conditions of some girls may be arranged so that they are particularly suited for the acquisition of certain motives and responses rather than others. The reader is urged to think back to our analysis, earlier in this chapter, of the major sources of gender learning in childhood—parents, toys, teachers, books, television—and to the variety of ways in which female children learn to behave appropriately as girls. As we examine dominant patterns, however, we must not lose sight of variations associated with different experiences.

Dependence/Independence

Passivity, denoting inaction and submissiveness, and dependency, denoting subordination, control by, and reliance on others, are generally measured together in studies of children and are defined by such behaviors as following rather than leading, maintaining physical proximity to an adult, or low level of exploration. Despite the evidence suggesting that female neonates may be somewhat more mature and more biologically sturdy at birth than males (and certainly no less mature or sturdy)—which should lead to the prediction that girls are more able (and certainly not any less able) than boys to acquire independence at an early age—the cultural expectation is just the reverse. Girls are treated as though they are more fragile, and they are expected to be more dependent.

From an extensive survey of the relevant literature, Eleanor Maccoby and Carol Jacklin (1974) concluded that dependency and attachment behavior characterize all human children during infancy and the preschool years, regardless of gender. They further concluded that consistent differences on this dimension between girls and boys have not been found in observational studies of nursery school children, but that rating scales, in which adults make judgments of behavior, more often report greater dependency on the part of girls. In situations that confront children with something strange and unfamiliar, girls and boys generally have not been found to differ reliably on measures such as staying close to the parent (typically the mother), looking or smiling at the parent, exploring the new environment, or becoming upset to a greater or lesser degree at separation from the parent. More gender differences in passive/dependent behavior are observed as children get older.

Peggy Ban and Michael Lewis (1974), for example, reported finding no gender differences with respect to touching, proximity seeking, looking, or vocalizing, in a study of 1-year-old infants in which the children were separately observed in interaction with mother and father. But another study (Brehm & Weinraub, 1977) found in a sample of 2-year-olds that girls differed from boys in their reactions to a situational restriction. When one of two toys was placed behind a barrier, the girls more often than the boys first approached the one that was available and not barricaded. A now classic study by Jerome Kagan and Howard Moss (1962), in which the same group of persons was studied from infancy to adulthood, found that before age 8 girls are not significantly nor consistently more dependent than boys, but in later childhood and adolescence such a difference is more stable. Passive/dependent behavior is also more continuous among girls than among boys, as indicated by a stronger correlation for girls between measures of such behavior in childhood and adulthood. Similar evidence of increasing gender differences in passivity/dependency as children age comes from an investigation by Bonni Seegmiller (1980a) in which children aged 3 to 5 were observed under natural nursery school conditions at 3-week intervals. On dependency behaviors, "three-year-old boys and girls were equal, but the four- and five-year-old boys and girls were increasingly sex-typed" (p. 32), with girls more dependent.

In the New Zealand study mentioned earlier (Lott, 1978) in which I observed 4-year-old children individually during kindergarten free play, I found girls to differ reliably from boys in the following ways: more of their behaviors were adult-oriented; they more often chatted with, smiled at, and followed after adults; they more often played alone, and played quietly; they less often chatted with, cooperated with, followed the lead of, showed off with, followed after, and touched their peers; and they were less noisy and less rough in playing. Although there were actually more similarities than differences between girls and boys, the gender differences that I observed could be characterized by greater sociability and peer interaction on the part of the boys and by adult-centeredness and loneness on the part of the girls. Research with American children generally supports these conclusions (Maccoby & Jacklin, 1974). For example, Gail Nelson (1977) observed 4-year-olds engaged in indoor play in a nursery school over a 6-month period and found that girls played alone or with the leader more than boys, while boys played for longer periods with peers. From an analysis of the functional use of language by preschoolers, in a different kind of study (Cook, Fritz, McCornack, & Visperas, 1985), boys were found to differ from girls in talking more, asserting their desires, and assuming leadership; their words reflected "independence and assertiveness" more than the language used by the girls did.

How does it happen that gender differences in dependence/independence increase as children get older? To answer this question, consider what conditions might be necessary if you were to set out to deliberately produce a dependent child—that is, to encourage a child to be clinging, submissive, and non-risk-taking and to rely on adults. How would you arrange the child's environment, and what experiences and outcomes would you provide? I suggest the following: (a) restrict the child's space and the number of stimuli within it in order to deter exploration of unfamiliar territory or objects—only a limited number of responses should be required so that new behavior need not be tried out or learned; (b) provide as few opportunities as possible for the child to do anything that is self-initiated (independent), by anticipating the child's needs; (c) provide few possibilities for the child's autonomous behaviors to be effective, by withholding positive rewards and ensuring that task success will be unlikely; (d) systematically frustrate independent responses and efforts to solve problems alone by discouraging them or making certain that the efforts will fail to bring the desired results; and (e) positively reinforce dependent, help-seeking, and passive behaviors sufficiently often to encourage their frequent occurrence. The material presented throughout this chapter suggests that this description well matches the environments and experiences typically arranged for many little girls.

Lois Hoffman (1977) has cited a number of investigations that illustrate how, in important and varied ways, a daughter is "deprived of the training in independence that her brother receives" (p. 649). Research by Rosalind Barnett (1981) suggests that the independence training given to daughters is related to the beliefs and attitudes parents have about sex roles. "For parents of girls [but not of boys], non-traditional sex-role ideology was significantly related to lower mean age of independence granting" (p. 841). Thus, while boys seem to be generally encouraged toward independence regardless of their parents' traditional or nontraditional views about gender, such differences among parents makes a substantial difference in the rearing of girls. In a novel about an earlier era, *To Kill a Mockingbird* (Lee, 1960), Jean Louise (Scout), the 8-year-old narrator, tells us what happened when her aunt Alexandra joined the household. As Scout's freedom to explore and romp was suddenly curtailed by her aunt's insistence that Scout wear dresses and play with small stoves and tea sets, she wrote, "I felt the starched walls of a pink cotton penitentiary closing in on me" (p. 147).

Personal experiences, fictional accounts, and evidence from social science research combine to support the proposition that adults systematically encourage girls and boys to have different experiences relevant to independence and dependence. It is not surprising, therefore, that the behavior of girls and boys becomes increasingly differentiable on this dimension as they get older. Independence and dependence are learned behaviors that may be situation-specific or generalizable depending on the conditions of learning and performance. Such behavior can be modified by the way significant persons react to it. This result has been demonstrated experimentally with preschoolers (Serbin, Connor, & Citron, 1978). For a 20-minute period during each of 5 consecutive weeks, nursery school teachers praised one group of children for two kinds of independent behavior—playing with new toys (i.e., exploration) and persisting on a task alone. At the same time, dependent behaviors—proximity seeking and soliciting teacher attention—were ignored. When compared with children who were randomly praised (regardless of behavior), the training was found to be effective in increasing independence and decreasing dependence in both girls and boys. The investigators concluded that "the independent behaviors that were being reinforced were clearly in the repertoire of the children, but were receiving little reinforcement" (p. 874) in the regular classroom.

Activity Level

A child who plays alone, or stays close to adults and depends on their feedback, will also most likely engage in less active play than a child who is exploring the environment, manipulating toys that move, and interacting with peers. As children grow older, therefore, we expect to find that measures of activity level as well as measures of independence distinguish girls from boys.

Activity level is not a stable characteristic of children younger than 3, and no single set of agreed-upon measures exists. Eleanor Maccoby and Carol Jacklin (1974), in summarizing the literature, have noted that "during the first year of life the evidence indicates no sex differences. From this age onward, studies vary greatly as to whether a sex difference is found, but when it is, boys are more active" (p. 177). But not all the evidence supports such a conclusion. For example, one study of 3- to 9-year old children, who were observed playing alone in an open-field situation (that is, a room with several areas, tables, and toys), found no significant gender differences in measures of activity level (Routh, Schroeder, & O'Tuama, 1974). When different measures are used, varied findings are sometimes reported from the same study. Thus, a well-known study (Pedersen & Bell, 1970) did not find preschool girls and boys to differ in the vigor with which they tore down a barrier to get an object, nor in running or tricycle riding, but girls did less walking than boys, and recordings of their large muscle movements yielded lower scores. These findings make sense when one learns that girls spent more time than boys with clay or play dough or on the swings, while boys spent more time with such objects as trucks and blocks. Other studies of children (e.g., Fagot, 1984b) have found that high-activity-level play by preschool girls receives few positive reactions from either peers or teachers, in sharp contrast to the feedback received by boys.

Despite the cultural messages that a high activity level is less appropriate for girls than boys, there is considerable variation in girls' play. The photograph on p. 57 shows my granddaughter, when not yet 2 ½, mixing it up with some other children in a playground. A study by Marriane Bloch (1987) led her to conclude that "girls engaged in as much gross motor play as boys" (p. 298). Using the interesting technique of having a parent report on what her or his preschool child was doing at the time that a telephone interviewer called, the investigator found far more

My granddaughter Samone, at two-and-a-half, roughhousing in a neighborhood playground in San Francisco. (Photograph by Elizabeth Minters.)

similarity than differences in the activities and play settings of girls and boys.

Personal observations and research data suggest that active play by girls is not always discouraged when they are young and may be tolerated in some situations but not in others. For example, in describing her elementary school experience in San Francisco, Maxine Hong Kingston (1977) speaks of how silent and timid the Chinese-American girls were. When her second-grade class did a play in the auditorium, everyone participated except the Chinese girls who were left behind in the classroom: "Our voices were too soft or nonexistent" (p. 194). In the afternoons when she attended Chinese school, however, things were quite different. "The girls were not mute. They screamed and yelled during recess, when there were no rules; they had fistfights" (p. 194f.).

Signe Hammer (1976) talked with a sample of mothers and daughters and found that many preadolescent girls enjoy considerable freedom from gender proscriptions and restrictions and that they "ride bikes, climb trees, play baseball." From three independent samples—undergraduate women who wrote autobiographies, junior high school girls at a summer camp, and adult women in a shopping center who were asked to recall their childhoods—"tomboy" activity was found to be more typical of girls than not (Hyde, Rosenberg, & Behrman, 1977). The researchers concluded that "tomboys do not appear to be abnormal, either by definition as statistically rare or by comparison with nontomboys, from whom they do not differ on many psychological variables" (p. 75).

Some evidence shows that girls who somehow manage to circumvent the sex-typing pressures and expectations toward passivity, dependence, and less vigorous activity are "better off." For example, in a study of children in grades 3 to 6 (Hemmer & Kleiber, 1981), girls identified as "tomboys" by their peers were seen as somewhat "socially difficult" by their teachers in the earlier grades but were later judged to be "popular, cooperative, helpful, supportive of others, . . . and were regarded as leaders." In another study (Plumb & Cowan, 1984), self-identified tomboys in grades 4, 6, 8, and 10 were found to include more than half the girls studied and to differ from both boys and nontomboy girls in enjoying a large and varied repertoire of activities. In my New Zealand study, mentioned earlier (Lott, 1978), no "tomboy" identifications were made, but 4-year-old girls whose behavior did not conform to adult expectations for girls were found to be more creative than more conforming girls on a test of uses for everyday objects.

Where gender differences in motor behavior or physical activity are observed, they are likely to have resulted from differences in opportunities to practice as well as from differences in cultural expectations and encouragement. This conclusion is supported by an investigation by Evelyn Hall and Amelia Lee (1984), who studied the performance of children in grades 3, 4, and 5 during three consecutive years on five standard fitness tests, including running and jumping. Among these participants in daily coed physical education classes, both genders showed continual improvement, and in the last year of the study, girls were better than boys of the same age on most of the tests. The authors concluded that "females at prepubescent ages may be expected to perform at similar levels to boys at that age . . . [if offered] equal opportunities in a coeducational situation" (p. 229).

Attention, Interpersonal Sensitivity, and Prosocial Behavior

Attention to external stimuli can be measured even in neonates, because it relates inversely to such relatively objective measures as heartbeat, muscular activity, and eye fixation. Such methods have not shown consistently reliable gender differences in infants in either hearing or vision. And Eleanor Maccoby and Carol Jacklin (1974) concluded from their large-scale review of the literature that girls and boys are very much alike in the amount and kind of information they are capable of extracting from their environments. Nevertheless, our culture expects girls to be generally more attentive than boys and more sensitive to the feelings of people, and it is likely that socialization in this direction begins very early in the girl's life. A study (Anyan & Quillan, 1971) of the ability of a large sample of children to identify correctly the three primary colors (red, blue, and yellow) at different ages found that, at age 4, the color-naming abilities of boys and girls were comparable, but by age 5, they began to diverge, with girls showing superiority in the sixth year. That differential learning is the major factor involved (and not differential "natures" or capabilities) is strongly suggested by the fact that among the 5- and 6-year-old children of both genders, those attending kindergarten outperformed those who were not in school.

Another interesting investigation of children's attention—this time the attention they pay to one another—was reported by Jerome Feldstein (1976). Girls and boys from the same day-care school were asked to identify by name photographs of their schoolmates. Despite the fact that, on average, the girls had been in the program a shorter time than the boys, the girls made significantly fewer errors in naming their peers, even though standardized measures of intelligence and memory revealed no gender differences. Had the girls already learned the importance of interpersonal sensitivity and practiced paying attention to names and faces? If, like other girls, they had spent more time indoors with a limited range of toys and more time observing "the scene," then the response of attending to persons is more likely to have been learned and less likely to have been interfered with than would have been true if they had spent a great deal of time moving about outdoors or playing in a variety of situations.

In a replication of Feldstein's study (Etaugh & Whittler, 1982), preschool girls were found not to differ from boys in social memory—that is, in the accuracy of their recognition of classmates. Why the two studies obtained different findings is not clear but, as with other behaviors, gender differences in attention or sensitivity to persons are not consistently found. Kay Jennings (1977), for example, tested the widely held assumption that boys are more interested in objects whereas girls are more interested in people by reviewing relevant studies of preschool children. She concluded that the evidence does not support a conclusion of gender differences. She also tested the hypothesis by observing a sample of nursery school children, finding that "both boys and girls divided their attention evenly between people and objects" (p. 71) and that no gender differences appeared in either focus of attention or context of play, so that "boys and girls were indistinguishable" in this behavior.

Our culture expects girls to be more attentive to other persons and to be more empathic than boys, but this expectation is only sometimes supported by the evidence. In a study in which children between 46 and 103 months from 20 families were observed interacting at home with their mothers and a new baby, Judith Blakemore (1990) found that girls had more prosocial contacts with the baby and talked more about it than boys. On the other hand, findings from laboratory studies suggest that "boys are not less 'naturally' nurturant than girls. Until they are 4 or 5, both sexes are equally interested in babies and their care, and even after that, boys are as nurturant as girls in other ways" (Melson & Fogel, 1988, p. 45), such as in the care of pets. Eleanor Maccoby and Carol Jacklin (1974) reviewed 30 relevant studies and found no clear support for the hypothesis that girls are more empathic or sensitive to social cues than boys.

Girls are also expected to be more helpful, cooperative, and considerate than boys and thus to exhibit more prosocial behavior. This set of expectations does not always turn out to be accurate either, especially among younger children. For example, in my New Zealand study (Lott, 1978), teachers and parents of 4-year-olds rated "most kindergarten girls" as being significantly more likely than "most kindergarten boys" to show affection to their peers, cooperate with them, give help to them, smile at them, and give them sympathy. But when I observed the children in free play, I saw no reliable gender differences in any of these behaviors, except that the boys were observed to be more cooperative than the girls. On the other hand, Mark Barnett (1978) found that 10- to 12-year-old girls tended to be less self-serving than boys in dividing up rewards in competitive situations, with boys giving themselves greater rewards than girls did. Perhaps girls have learned to be more concerned with other people's feelings and are thus more likely to be accommodating and generous, or perhaps girls learn that they are most likely to gain approval through such "nice" behavior. Among a sample of preschoolers (aged 42 to 81 months), responses to a story-completion task indicated that boys verbally used more intrusion and domination behaviors than affiliation and inclusion behaviors, whereas girls used the latter more than the former and used affiliation more than the boys did (Cramer & Skidd, 1992). Another interesting finding from this study was that a measure of self-worth was more strongly related to use of the verbally reported gender-stereotyped behaviors among the boys than among the girls. According to the authors, this "is consistent with the fact that there is more pressure [at this age] on boys to conform to sex-stereotyped behaviors and to avoid behaviors that contradict sex role stereotypes" (p. 388).

Janet Lever (1978) has suggested that girls are less competitive than boys as a result of differences in the kind of games they play. She observed and interviewed a large group of fifth-grade children and studied diaries and questionnaires completed by them. Girls' games and play were found to differ from boys' in being freer of rules, providing fewer rewards based on skill, and involving less face-to-face confrontation and more turn-taking activities without explicit goals. Lever concluded that girls generally have less experience with interpersonal competition and with direct face-to-face competition. This conclusion is challenged by the results of a 2-year study during which fourth and fifth graders were observed playing the game Foursquare during recess (Hughes, 1988). The investigator found little evidence to support the general assumption that girls "lack skills in organizing and sustaining large-group activities with highly complex and elaborate rule structures, that they are incapable of competition, or that they fall apart in the face of conflict" (p. 682). On the contrary, the girls were observed to fight vigorously and to manage conflict and competition effectively, as well as to cooperate and to show a concern for close relationships. Cross-cultural data also do not support the hypothesis that girls are universally less competitive than boys. Michael Strube (1981) reviewed 95 independent tests of this hypothesis in studies of children and found that only among Anglo-American and Indian cultures is this expectation supported; it is not supported among samples of Mexican-American, African-American, Israeli, or Canadian children, or those from nine other cultures.

From a review of the literature on altruistic behavior—defined as behavior that benefits another but for which no external reward is expected—J. Philippe Rushton (1976) concluded that measures of altruism in children across situations do not show any discernible patterns of gender difference. As with other behavioral dimensions we have examined, the major research objective should be not simply to assess gender differences or make gender comparisons, but to determine those conditions under which a child of either gender acquires the tendency to behave altruistically or sympathetically. The literature provides some hints. Rushton, for example, noted that children who see the consequences received by altruistic models act more altruistically themselves. Are girls more apt than boys to observe altruistic models, such as their mothers? This possibility seems likely, since girls are encouraged more than boys to stay close to their mothers and to participate in mothers' activities.

A study of empathy (Barnett, Howard, King, & Dino, 1980) tells us something about the relationship between gender differences in behavior and antecedent conditions or past experience. College students were tested for empathy; those who scored high on empathy also reported that their parents had spent more time with them, been more affectionate to them, and discussed feelings more with them than had the parents of students who scored low. This finding held for both genders, but the women students differed significantly from the men in having higher empathy scores and also in reporting having discussed feelings more with mothers and having received more affection from both parents. Thus, two of the factors found to enhance empathy were found more often in the childhood experiences of the girls than of the boys.

In still another research area, that of moral reasoning, some investigators have urged that the focus be less on gender comparisons and more on the conditions under which children learn to be concerned with both care and justice in making moral decisions. The distinction between care and justice considerations was first made prominent by the work of Carol Gilligan (1977, 1982) who has proposed that these considerations are related to gender. But the assumption that girls and boys tend to solve moral dilemmas differently, with the former emphasizing care and interpersonal relationships and the latter emphasizing rules and justice, did not withstand empirical test in a study of fifth and sixth graders (Donenberg & Hoffman, 1988) in which several different tests of moral reasoning were utilized. The investigators found that both genders "use both moral voices in reasoning moral conflicts" (p. 715).

In general, however, the conditions associated with learning helpful or supportive behavior (from which we infer interpersonal sensitivity or caring about others) are suggested by what we know of girls' lives. In her autobiography, *Bronx Primitive,* Kate Simon (1982), the daughter of Polish Jewish immigrants, tells us how different her childhood responsibilities were from those of her brother, especially with respect to the care of their baby sister.

> His role with our baby was to kootchy-koo her as he dashed in from school and down the street while I thumped the carriage down the five flights, up and down again with the pillows and blankets, up and down again with the baby. While he, the grasshopper, sang and danced, I, the ant, sat demurely rocking the carriage. (p. 137)

In a study of eleven cultures varying in complexity and social structure (Whiting & Edwards, 1988), the investigators found that in cultures where girls take care of younger children, the girls are described as helpful, supportive or nurturant, and compliant or accommodating, while the boys are more assertive, attention-getting, and engage in more rough-and-tumble play. However, in cultures where it is appropriate for boys also to care for younger siblings and to do domestic chores, fewer gender differences appear; boys, too, show nurturant and helpful behavior, and girls, too, are assertive and engage in rough play. In commenting on this research, Carol Jacklin (1989) concluded that "if [an] individual spends enough time with infants, he or she will become a nurturer" (p. 131). Clearly, in this realm of behavior as in others, variations are best explained not by differences in biological sex but by variations in conditions and experiences.

Aggression

Eleanor Maccoby and Carol Jacklin (1974) proposed that the evidence for greater aggressiveness—acts that are intentionally hurtful or damaging—by boys than by girls is so consistent and pervasive that it reflects a genuine sex difference, not explainable entirely by differential socialization. But this conclusion is not consistent with the available data and has been criticized and challenged on theoretical as well as empirical grounds. For example, in the previously mentioned cross-cultural study by Beatrice Whiting and Carolyn Edwards (1988), gender differences were found only in provoked aggression in older children and not in all cultures. Todd Tieger (1980) reanalyzed the studies cited by Maccoby and Jacklin and found that, in samples of children aged 6 or younger, boys were not significantly more aggressive than girls. Similarly, Janet Hyde (1984) found, from a statistical analysis, that gender contributed very little to the variance in measures of aggression. According to Hyde, "within-gender variation is far larger than between-gender variation" (p. 732).

Paula Caplan (1979) concluded from an extensive review of relevant literature that in experimental studies, when girls' concerns about adult approval were reduced, the frequency of their aggressive behavior increased. This conclusion supports the view that the aggressive behavior of children, like the other behaviors we have discussed, is sensitive or responsive to changes in the situation or context and that gender differences are more likely to be found in some circumstances than in others. David Barrett (1979), for example, observed 5- to 8-year-old children over a 6-week period in a summer day camp. Although boys were significantly more aggressive than girls overall, the target of aggression made a difference. Boys were more

aggressive than girls only to girls; to boy targets, girls and boys were equally aggressive. Barrett interpreted his data as indicating that "contextual factors . . . may affect the magnitude and even the direction of observed sex differences in children's aggression" (p. 202). Leonard Eron's (1980) research has suggested that other important variables predict aggression. In one study, aggressive behavior displayed in school by 8-year-olds of both genders was found to be related to parental nurturance and punishment: children who were aggressive were more likely to have been punished than nurtured by their parents. In another study, boys and girls who were aggressive were found to share similar "interests, values, and attitudes," as illustrated by preference for violent television programs.

In their reply to Tieger's (1980) criticism of their conclusions about the innate basis of gender differences in aggression, Maccoby and Jacklin (1980) agreed with him that "human behavior is almost infinitely malleable, and the two sexes are alike in their capacity to be influenced by cultural pressures" (p. 977). They noted that there is great overlap between girls and boys in their rates of aggressiveness and that most boys are similar to most girls in this respect, but that boys are more heavily represented in the small group of extremely aggressive children. To understand why this is so, we do not need to assume innate differences, but rather to compare the typical socialization experiences of girls and boys. We know that girls are (a) less likely than boys to have opportunities to practice hurting or inflicting damage; (b) less likely than boys to be assured directly, through adult and/or peer approval and encouragement, or indirectly, through observation of same-gender models, that such behavior is appropriate and expected (even if subject to temporary criticism); and (c) less likely than boys to experience success in this behavior by seeing the results of the damage or hearing the cries of the assaulted. Since we expect that "boys will be boys," their aggressive acts typically bring a mixed message from adults; although the acts may be considered bad, adults recognize them as "inevitable" masculine reactions and believe that it is better to be a "real man" and occasionally be aggressive than to be good but unmanly. (I remember my son's second-grade teacher telling me with great excitement and genuine pleasure that he was beginning to act more like a "real boy"—he was getting into mischief more and working calmly and quietly less!) Girls do not face this dilemma. It is easier for them than for boys to be good—not to hurt others or inflict damage—because these acts are negatively sanctioned and are considered "unnatural" for girls. An aggressive girl thus gets a clear and unambiguous message: aggression is both wrong and decidedly unfeminine.

As the average boy begins to get taller, heavier, and stronger than the average girl, as his metabolic rate, vital capacity, and muscle-to-fat ratio increases, his ability to do damage will probably surpass hers. As Todd Tieger (1980) has noted, "boys [may] have more weight to 'throw around' in . . . play interactions" (p. 957). But physical capacity for inflicting hurt on others is not equivalent to the motivation for doing so, nor does it necessarily imply that aggressive behavior will be practiced. If we assume, however, that in the face of frustration resulting from failure to attain a desired end, a person tends to persist in trying to gain gratification, then a strong response made by a strong person will likely result in damage to someone or something—behavior we label as aggressive. Assuming equal conditions for frustration, we can expect that what big and strong children do in natural response to it will more likely be called aggressive than what small and weak children do. If we put this possibility together with the differential consequences boys and girls are likely to experience following aggressive behavior and the differences in opportunity to practice such behavior, then evidence of a gender difference on this dimension is not at all surprising. The opportunities for aggressive behavior are much greater outdoors, away from the watchful eyes of adults, and in the presence of admiring peers than indoors, near adults, and with no one to approve; and girls are more likely to be found in the latter than in the former scene. In addition, as Dora Ullian (1984) has suggested, if a young girl believes that she is "physically vulnerable- . . . fragile and defenseless" (p. 254), this will contribute to her fear of aggression and concern with potential harm. We know, of course, that young girls are not fragile and that they can be physically effective, but fewer girls than boys are expected or encouraged to practice self-defense or attack.

Conditions for learning an association between expectations for aggressive behavior and gender are present early in the lives of children. Although little evidence has been found generally for significant differences in parental socialization of girls and boys (Lytton & Romney, 1991), parents exhibit "more prohibition of aggression for girls" with considerable consistency (p. 287). The consequences of such early learning are illustrated by the results of a study of preschoolers (Fagot, Leinbach, & Hagan, 1986) that found aggression to vary dramatically with gender-labeling accuracy; "girls who succeeded at the [labeling] task showed almost no aggression in the classroom" (p. 442).

The direct contributions made by teachers and peers to the sex-typing of aggressive behavior has been demonstrated in a number of investigations. For example, in one study (Fagot 1984a), observers of preschool play groups reported that peers or teachers paid attention to boys' aggression 81 percent of the time and to girls' aggression only 24 percent of the time. Dependency behaviors by girls, on the other hand, drew more frequent reaction than did similar behaviors by boys. Not surprisingly, then, aggressive conduct problems were found to be relatively stable for boys but not girls, while dependency problems were more stable for girls. The investigator concluded that "the pattern of reactions that children receive from peers and caregivers is very consistent with the stability of the problem behavior. Behaviors given attention are maintained, while those that result in being ignored tend to drop out" (p. 394). Similar findings were reported from a study (Fagot & Hagan, 1985) that analyzed data on aggression collected over a 4-year period from observations of children's play during their first term of preschool attendance. Whereas fewer than half the aggressive acts by girls received some response, the initial aggression of boys received a response about 70 percent of the time, most often from another boy.

Despite the relative lack of reinforcement that girls receive for aggressive behavior, everyday observations provide countless examples that girls can, in fact, be rough and tough, as illustrated in the photograph on p. 62. A group of elementary school girls in Rhode Island are jeering at their teachers to show their displeasure at a ruling that separated them from the boys in their schoolyard because of the girls' alleged aggression. The principal took this action, he explained to reporters (cf. Johnson, 1985), because the fifth- and sixth-grade girls had been harassing the boys, kicking them, pulling their hair, and grabbing them by the neck. "The girls," he said, "are terrible."

Adult assumptions about girls (and boys) tend to persist despite their frequent inaccuracy. For example, in one study (Lyons & Serbin, 1986), adults were shown slides of playroom scenes containing aggressive girls and boys. Both women and men reported more occurrence of aggression among the boys than among the girls, although this disparity did not actually appear in the slides. Similarly, in my investigation of New Zealand 4-year-olds (Lott, 1978), I found that their teachers and a group of parents believed that girls are significantly less likely than boys to disobey adults, argue with their peers, hit and fight, shout, play roughly, quarrel, and tease. But when I watched the children during free play, I saw no reliable

A group of fifth- and sixth-grade Rhode Island girls judged by their school principal to be terrible to the boys.
(Photograph by Bob Breidenbach/Journal-Bulletin.)

gender differences with respect to disobeying adults, arguing, fighting, or quarreling. The boys did do more shouting, rough playing, and teasing; played outdoors more often; and related to adults less. Since the parents and teachers expected boys to be more disobedient and quarrelsome than girls were (even though boys were not observed to be so), and since boys' opportunities for aggression were greater because they played outdoors more than girls, it is likely that if I had watched older children I would have found a better match between gender ideology and the children's behavior.

The conditions for practicing aggression are generally much poorer for girls than for boys. Thus, Jerome Kagan and Howard Moss (1962) found that the correlation between aggressive behavior in preschool and later childhood was lower for girls than for boys. Early aggression on the part of girls tended not to be maintained, most probably because it was not reinforced. In an investigation of third- to fifth-graders of varied racial and ethnic backgrounds, Robert Deluty (1985) found that girls demonstrated less consistency in aggressive behavior than boys across situations and types of response, supporting earlier findings "that stereotypically male-appropriate behaviors tend to show greater stability for boys" (p. 1062). We know that behavior that is not reinforced

by attention or other positive consequences tends not to be repeated, or to extinguish.

It is not surprising, then, that a review of a number of studies of the effects of exposure to television violence (Turner, Hesse, & Preston-Lewis, 1986) led to the conclusion that "television produces a long-term increase in the aggressive behavior of boys but not of girls" (p. 51). In speculating about why television violence affects girls differently than it affects boys, Leonard Eron (1980), who conducted a 10-year study of a large group of children, noted that, in contrast to boys, "very early in life, girls learn that physical aggression is an undesirable behavior" (p. 247); in addition, there are few aggressive women models on television for girls to imitate. Instead, "the more violent the programs that girls watched, the more they were exposed to female models as victims or as passive observers, and the more they may have associated aversive consequences with aggressive acts" (p. 247), decreasing the likelihood that they would behave in this way.

Although most environments discourage aggression by girls, some girls learn that being bad can bring more immediate rewards than being good. Agnes Smedley (1929/1973) has described such conditions in writing of her childhood in poverty:

> I took my place as one of the leaders of the "toughest kids beyond the tracks." In school I let nothing hurt me—no reprimand of my teacher, no look or word. Swearing had always come easily and naturally with me, for my father had been a very good teacher. . . . I fought boys and girls alike in the alleys beyond the tracks, and my brothers hovered proudly under my protecting wing. (pp. 90f.)

Girls (like boys) can learn to be tough when that behavior is acceptable, brings desired ends, and is not punished.

Cognitive Performance

Most of the earlier research on verbal, visual-spatial, and mathematical abilities shows that in childhood the performance of girls and boys in these cognitive areas overlaps considerably, but that reliable gender differences appear as adolescence approaches. This was the conclusion reached by Eleanor Maccoby and Carol Jacklin (1974) after a review of the literature. But even when girls perform cognitive tasks as well as boys do, girls expect to do more poorly. For example, although no gender differences were found on three measures of cognitive ability among high schoolers (Gitelson, Petersen, & Tobin-Richards, 1982), the girls anticipated doing worse than the boys would, with the girls saying that they had less ability.

Despite our expectations to the contrary, gender differences account for only 1 percent of the variation in scores on measures of verbal ability (Hyde, 1981). The findings in this area are perplexing. Girls' grades in high school English classes are typically higher than those of boys, yet the average boy's score on the Scholastic Aptitude Test has exceeded the average girl's score every year since 1972 when such reports were first issued. We will return to this paradox in the chapter on adolescence. The most recent conclusion from statistical examination of many studies is that "gender differences in verbal ability no longer exist" at any age (Hyde & Linn, 1988, p. 53).

As is true for verbal ability, girls and boys in grade school are similar in their acquisition of mathematical concepts and arithmetical operations (cf. Hogrebe, 1987). But, at about the age of 12 or 13, boys begin to show more improvement in this area than girls. In a review of the literature (Meece, Parsons, Kaczala, Goff, & Futterman, 1982), the authors noted that "sex differences on tests of quantitative skills do not appear with any consistency prior to the 10th grade. . . . Younger boys and girls perform equally well on tests of algebra and basic mathematical knowledge" (p. 325). Even at the high school level, it was pointed out, girls sometimes are found to "outperform boys on tests of computational skills"; differences in mathematics achievement favoring boys are not universally found among seniors and, where found, are small.

Evidence for the smallness of the average difference between boys and girls in mathematical ability has come from a statistical analysis of relevant studies by Janet Hyde (1981), who found that gender explained only 1 percent of the variation in scores. Joseph Rossi (1983), who analyzed the test scores of the mathematically precocious seventh and eighth graders studied by Camilla Benbow and Julian Stanley (1980), found that gender accounted for 4.4 percent of the variation in scores. Among adolescents, the relationship between gender and mathematical test scores, while negligible, is greater than the same relationship among younger children.

As with the verbal scores on the Scholastic Aptitude Test, the average mathematics score for boys has exceeded that for girls since 1972. Why do adolescent boys do better on this test than girls when no differences appear in childhood performance? Why, for example, did my middle daughter, an excellent and enthusiastic math student during her first two years in high school (when her math teachers were women), later lose interest in the subject and confidence in her ability? We will discuss this question more fully in the next chapter on adolescence, where we will find that the answer relates to cultural assumptions

and expectations. For example, Deborah Stipek (1984) found, among a group of fifth and sixth graders who were heterogeneous with respect to ethnicity and social class, that the girls were significantly less likely than the boys to attribute their good performance in math to high ability and were more likely than the boys to attribute their poor performance to low ability. Parents make similar attributions for the success and failure of their children in math. One study (Yee & Eccles, 1988) obtained data from the mothers and fathers of seventh graders and found that "although boys and girls were doing equally well according to achievement test scores and math grades, . . . both mothers and fathers credited [successful] boys with talent and [successful] girls with effort" (p. 330). Talent, unlike effort, is a characteristic that is assumed to be internal and stable. So while girls are said to do well when they try hard, boys are believed to be just naturally smarter and more adept at math.

The importance of attributions and expectations in influencing behavior is demonstrated by an intervention study concerned with techniques for "cultivating competence" (Bandura & Schunk, 1981). Equal gains by 7- to 10-year-old girls and boys in mastery of math were found after they were encouraged to set attainable subgoals for themselves. Not only did these children, who had been identified by their teachers as poor in math, make substantial progress in achievement, but their interest in mathematics activities also increased.

As is the case with verbal and mathematical ability, gender differences in visual-spatial ability are typically not found in childhood and only begin to appear in adolescence (e.g., McGee, 1979; Witkin, 1979). One group of reviewers (Meece, Parsons, Kaczala, Goff, & Futterman, 1982) have concluded that scores on spatial skills tests do not favor boys until about the 10th grade—and, even then, not in all studies, as illustrated by a national survey of more than 3000 junior high and high school students in which girls and boys scored equally well. Thus, the data do not consistently provide evidence for gender differences in spatial skills, even at older ages. A major problem in this area is one of definition and measurement. At least three independent components of spatial ability have been identified by researchers: spatial perception, mental rotation, and spatial visualization. Reviewers of the relevant literature (Linn & Petersen, cited by Tracy, 1987) have concluded that boys appear to do better than girls in spatial perception by age 8, and better than girls in mental rotation, but that "sex differences in spatial visualization do not exist at any point in the life span" (p. 130). Across a range of ages, the percentage of variation accounted for by gender in visual-spatial and field-articulation scores is 4.9 percent and 2.5 percent, respectively, as reported by Janet Hyde (1981).

A number of investigations have demonstrated a relationship between particular experiences and visual-spatial competence. For example, a sample of preschool children of both genders who preferred climbing and playing with transportation toys, blocks, and ring toss were found to score higher on a test of spatial ability than children who preferred to draw or to play with dolls and kitchen toys, while the latter did better on a vocabulary test (Serbin & Connor, 1979). Playing with large toys, moving over large spaces, and manipulating objects are more likely to foster the development of spatial skills than sedentary play in a relatively confined area. The findings of Sharon Nash (1975) also relate to this proposition. She asked a sample of 11- and 14-year-old children to indicate whether they preferred being boys or girls and found that within both gender groups preference for being a boy was related to better spatial performance. Whether the children in this study who said they preferred being boys did what boys typically do—that is, to engage in activities that provide practice in visual-spatial skills—is not known, but when asked to explain their preferences, children of both genders who preferred being boys cited the greater desirability of "male activities" such as sports.

Some have argued that spatial ability is carried by a recessive gene on the X chromosome and is therefore a more probable characteristic of males (who have only one X and are thus more likely to manifest such recessive traits as baldness and color blindness). A direct test of this hypothesis (Sherman & Fennema, 1978) found that the spatial test scores of a large sample of ninth-grade girls and boys did not confirm what a genetic X-linked hypothesis would predict. Similarly, a study that examined spatial ability score correlations between all possible parent-offspring combinations in 200 families (Bouchard & McGee, 1977) found that the correlations did not conform to the expected pattern of zero father-son correlation and greater correlations between mothers and sons. Instead, brother-brother correlations were found to be significantly greater than those between sisters. According to the researchers, the sibling correlations obtained "are compatible with a theory which argues that boys in a family tend to be pushed into activities that foster spatial ability (sports and mechanical activities), while girls are not as consistently channeled into such activities" (p. 335). Thus, the available evidence suggests that the decreasing ability of the average girl to perform well on visual-spatial problems is a function not of some inherent weakness but

of her systematic exposure to play materials and other experiences that offer little opportunity for practice in solving such problems, as well as her increasing familiarity with the cultural expectation that spatial ability is an area in which men, and not women, excel. We will explore such expectations further in the chapters that follow and will find, as new studies suggest (e.g., Adler, 1989; Feingold, 1988), that gender-related differences on all cognitive measures are declining.

School Achievement

It has been suggested (Parsons, Ruble, Hodges, & Small, 1976) that as girls increase in age and experience they begin to (a) underestimate their own abilities and skill relative both to boys and to objective measures, and (b) to attribute their successes to luck or chance and their failures to stupidity or ineptitude. A dramatic illustration of girls' underestimation of themselves is provided by a classic study of a sample of first graders (Pollis & Doyle, 1972). Each student in the class was asked to rank order five peers on leadership. One week later, each child was asked to throw three tennis balls, one at a time, into a box concealed by a curtain so that there were no cues as to whether the throw was accurate or not, and then each child was asked to score his or her own performance (as well as that of every other child). The boys were found to outrank the girls in "class leader" nominations, and these nominations correlated significantly with attributed scores on the ball-throwing task. The boys were given higher performance scores than the girls by their classmates, despite the fact that the actual scores did not differ by gender. Only three children, all girls, achieved perfect scores on the ball-throwing task. How had they scored themselves? They had given themselves scores of 0, 0, and 1 accurate out of three possible throws; this negative view had been shared by their classmates as well.

In a study of more than 800 children in grades 3 to 5 (Cooper, Burger, & Good, 1981), girls were found to attribute their success in school, more often than boys, to an unstable characteristic like effort rather than to ability. Similarly, another investigation of children in grades 4 to 6 (Dweck, Goetz, & Strauss, 1980) found evidence that girls tend to underestimate their school achievement, regardless of the subject matter, despite the fact that their actual performance is consistently better than that of boys. In an experimental situation involving two different tasks, while the fifth-grade girls and boys reacted similarly to repeated failure by lowering their expectations, boys "bounced back" more easily, as when in the presence of a new evaluator or with a new task. Under such conditions, the expectations of the boys rose more than those of the girls.

That adults tend to reward girls and boys differently for achievement is suggested by research findings. For example, a study by Carol Dweck (cited by Parsons et al., 1976) found that teachers explicitly attributed the intellectual failure of boys to "lack of motivation" six times as often as they did for girls. In a different kind of study (Olejnik, 1980), college students played the role of "teacher" and rewarded or punished 6- and 11-year-old hypothetical children for performance in math and spelling. It was found that boys received more reinforcement than girls for their achievement in both areas, were more likely than girls to be rewarded for high effort and positive outcome, and were more likely to be punished for low effort and negative outcome.

School achievement is certainly expected of girls, but the general cultural message, sometimes direct but often more subtle, is that achievement really matters more for boys; girls must attend to schoolwork but also to the things needed to be popular, especially with boys. Girls are expected to get good grades, but they are not typically encouraged to believe that such achievement is predictive of their adult potential for success. Girls come to believe that when they succeed in school it is because they have put forth effort and because they want to please their parents and teachers. When boys succeed in school, our ideology tells us, it is because they are truly bright. We do not necessarily expect boys to expend their best efforts in grade school, which we regard as a "feminine" place staffed primarily by women teachers who do not really count. When boys do poorly, we tell ourselves, it is because they are not really trying. We will return to these issues again in the chapter on adolescence.

As with the other gender differences thus far discussed, the small differences found in achievement attributions and expectancies disappear under some circumstances. Thus, for example, one study of a sample of seventh-grade girls (Van Hecke, Tracy, Cotler, & Ribordy, 1984) used a computerized task that provided its own feedback. Initial estimates of success (provided anonymously by each child) did not differ by gender, and the girls "behaved in ways that maximized achievement more often than boys did," despite the fact that to do so they had to ignore adult feedback in the form of approval for incorrect choices. Once again, these results show the influence of context or situation, as does the work of Marilyn Kourilsky and Michael Campbell (1984) who evaluated the effects of participation in a 10-week simulated economy program by

more than 900 8- to 12-year-old children. At the outset of the program, both the girls and boys viewed the entrepreneurial role as more associated with men than women. But after all the children had received practice in buying and selling goods and services, teacher ratings revealed no significant gender differences in "economic success, risk taking, and entrepreneurial persistence."

The importance of nontraditional gender socialization in raising achievement motivation in girls has been reported in a study of a sample of African-American preschoolers and their mothers (Carr & Mednick, 1988). Mothers' encouragement of their daughters' nontraditional attitudes concerning household duties and occupations were significantly related to the daughters' need-for-achievement scores on three different measures. A different kind of study provides similar evidence for the effectiveness of particular interventions in children's experi-ence. Among a sample of fifth and sixth graders who were given puzzles to do and then praised for their ability and effort (Koestner, Zuckerman, & Koestner, 1989), it was found that "regardless of the recipient's gender, ability praise led children to feel more competent and perform better [on subsequent puzzles] than did effort praise" (p. 68).

Vocational Aspirations

It should not be surprising that in gender-conscious societies children learn early to associate particular activities and occupations with women and others with men and to anticipate that when they are grown up they will do "women's work" or "men's work," respectively. One of the first investigations of children's vocational stereotypes was reported by William Looft (1971), who asked a group of second graders what they would like to be when they grew up and what they thought they really would do. He found that boys nominated a reliably greater variety of vocations, that boys changed more than girls in their responses from the first to the second question, and that the vocational choices were along traditional stereotyped lines. Looft's procedures were repeated in a later study (Papalia & Tennent, 1975), which also found that preschool children's vocational predictions for themselves were highly conventional. The girls saw themselves as potential mothers, nurses, and teachers, whereas the boys' occupational choices tended toward such adventurous and active ones as policeman and fireman.

A later investigation of 540 kindergarten children (Riley, 1981) in which they were asked to draw pictures of what they would like to be when they grew up, and what they would like to be if they were of the other gender, found that girls chose occupations typically engaged in by women and that they selected a significantly smaller variety of occupations than boys. In the gender-reversal condition, the children's occupational aspirations again reflected traditional gender divisions. The author reported that many of the boys found the gender reversal problematic, and "moaned and groaned . . . [and] a great deal of distaste seemed to be associated with the thought of being a girl" (p. 248).

Occupational divisions by gender have been reported in children's own aspirations at a very early age, even before they recognize gender as a constant personal attribute (O'Keefe & Hyde, 1983). In one study (Zuckerman & Sayre, 1982), 4- to 8-year-old children of more highly educated parents were found to express less stereotyped attitudes toward occupations, but parents' educational levels did not affect the children's occupational expectations, which were overwhelmingly traditional. The employment status of one's mother, however, seems to make a difference. Paula Selkow (1984) reported that among children aged 5 to 7 whose mothers were working outside the home, both girls and boys chose more occupations for themselves when they "grow up" than children of non-employed mothers, and girls chose less traditional vocations if their mothers worked at less traditional jobs.

REDUCING THE CULTURAL EMPHASIS ON GENDER

We can discern three general themes in the research on gender comparisons among infants and children. First, gender differences are found less often in the earliest years and more often as children get older and as the experiences of girls vary more and more from those of boys. As socialization pressures and expectations increase, and girls and boys lead more and more different kinds of lives and engage in different activities in different situations, they manifest more differences in behavior.

Second, regardless of gender, children's behavior is positively related to the situations in which the children are observed and in which they have had opportunities to practice appropriate and positively reinforced responses. Many of the studies discussed in this chapter illustrate this point. It may have been with this realization in mind that Marge Piercy (1976a), in her novel *Woman on the Edge of Time,* presented a society in which the sexual identity of children is irrelevant to what they do, where they go, and

with what and with whom they play. She describes a utopia in which children live together with caregivers of both genders and are encouraged to develop individual interests and skills. A visitor to the village society is told:

> Most of what children must learn they learn by doing. . . . They need toys to learn coordination, dexterity; they practice tenderness on dolls. . . . We educate the senses, the imagination, the social being, the muscles, the nervous system, the intuition, the sense of beauty—as well as the intellect. (pp. 136, 140)

Finally, the data suggest that because of individual and group differences in children's experiences and backgrounds, our stereotyped expectations for how girls (and boys) act do not always prove to be reliable predictors of actual behavior. Direct experience, practice, and particular situations have been shown to effectively counteract the dominant socialization of our children. While children learn from their parents, teachers, and each other what is expected from persons of their gender, these lessons are not always compatible with their own experiences, observations, abilities, and interests. Rita Mae Brown (1973) has described such a contradiction in *Rubyfruit Jungle* in a scene in which Molly is playing with her cousin Leroy and with her friend Cheryl.

> Leroy was the patient and we painted him with iodine so he'd look wounded. I wasn't gonna be no nurse. If I was gonna be something I was gonna be the doctor and give orders. I . . . told Cheryl I was the new doctor in town. Her face corroded. "You can't be a doctor. Only boys can be doctors. Leroy's got to be the doctor."
> "You're full of shit. . . . Leroy's dumber than I am . . . and being a girl don't matter."
> "You'll see [retorts Cheryl]. You think you can do what boys do but you're going to be a nurse. . . . It doesn't matter about brains, brains don't count. What counts is whether you're a boy or a girl."
> I hauled off and belted her one. . . . Course I didn't want to be a doctor. I was going to be president only I kept it a secret. (p. 31)

To investigate the reliability of our stereotypes, I asked adults to decide whether each of a series of jack-o'-lantern drawings had been drawn by a 5-year-old girl or boy and to give their reasons (Lott, 1979). The adults said that the girls' drawings were neater, more colorful, better drawn, and had more smiling faces than the boys' drawings and that the latter were sloppier, less careful, less symmetrical, more unconventional, and scarier. Yet, the girls' drawings were accurately identified only 30 percent of the time, and the boys' drawings 60 percent of the time. Thus, the gender beliefs of adults proved to be unreliable guides to the behavior of these kindergarten children.

Even when given more cues than those provided in the study of drawings, what adults associate with gender is not necessarily veridical with what a stranger to the children may observe them actually doing. In my New Zealand study (Lott, 1978), the social behavior of 4-year-old children was assessed in three different ways: direct observation in free-play situations; ratings by teachers of individual children; and ratings of "most girls" and "most boys" by teachers and parents. Direct observation yielded far fewer significant gender differences than teacher/parent ratings of "most girls/boys." More important, however, was the finding that the gender differences obtained by these different assessments were not congruent. What was present in the ideology as measured by the ratings, but missing from the observations, is the picture of 4-year-old girls as dependent, helpful, and pleasant and boys as disobedient and quarrelsome. Conversely, absent from the ideology but apparent in the observations is the picture of the girl at play alone or as onlooker and the boy touching, chatting, and cooperating with peers.

Thus, our gender prophecies frequently fail. But, since we continue, for the most part, to provide girls and boys with differing experiences and opportunities to practice different skills and behaviors, it is not surprising that the average girl, as she grows older, does become distinguishable from the average boy in some of her interests, goals, and responses. If we focus our attention on observing and cataloging gender differences, we shall certainly find them, although not under all circumstances and in all situations; we will tend to forget how these differences have been created by social learning and how they continue to be maintained throughout the life span. We would do better to follow the advice of Michael Lewis (1975), who concluded from his extensive study of infant behavior that "there is no reason to study sex differences" at all. What we should be doing instead, he suggested, is studying individual differences in order to determine how behavior is modified by experience.

Sandra Bem (1981, 1983) has asked why the category of sex has such primacy and importance in organizing ideas and behavior. Her answer is that this primacy is neither inevitable nor necessary but is simply a reflection of the culture's concern. Sex is put forth by the culture as a focus around which we group other material, so most children learn to "encode and to organize information" in terms of gender; they "learn which attributes are to be linked with their own sex and, hence, with themselves" and to evaluate their "adequacy as a person according to the gender schema" (1983, p. 604). Such organization around gender divisions, however, is arbitrary and not inevitable.

As pointed out by John Condry (1984), "gender does not have to be a central fulcrum of our identity, and it does not have to carry the baggage it does today" (p. 506). Parents who wish to raise gender-aschematic children must inoculate them against seeing the world in gender terms by teaching alternative organizing principles, such as individual differences (Bem, 1983). Parents must also come to understand the role played by gender-relevant variables that influence what their children learn to do and to want, and what they expect to be.

◆ Discussion Questions

1. How would you raise a girl child? Describe her room, clothes, and so on, and your aspirations for her.

2. What is meant by sex-typing? Why is this process so important in our society? What are its consequences? What effect does sex-typing have on individual differences?

3. Catalog the contents of the room of a preschool girl and boy that you know.

4. Observe parents at a local playground for direct or subtle examples of sex-typing and non-sex-typing.

5. Ask some parents you know about their specific goals for one of their children. Compare the answers for parents of daughters and parents of sons.

6. What is meant by the term gender-aschematic? Can you imagine a society in which gender is not the most central component of one's identity?

CHAPTER 4

ADOLESCENCE: MIXED MESSAGES AND REAL OPTIONS

I remember how my teacher used to terrify me, my freshman year, by telling me I had talent . . . .

ROSELLEN BROWN (1976, p. 195)

If we were nice-looking and chaste and pleasing in manner and dress, . . . Mr. Right would come and marry us and satisfy all our desires. He would take over our father's functions in caring for us . . . .

GAIL GODWIN (1983, p. 273)

Noonie was boy crazy. . . . But how could she have been anything else when they seemed to hold the key? They had the power to interpret the mystery, how to do it.

ANNETTE W. JAFFEE (1988, p. 72)

THIS CHAPTER EXAMINES THE EXPERIENCES OF girls during the period in their lives when their bodies are rapidly changing in the direction of maturity, and when they are concerned with and preparing for how they will function as adults. We will concentrate on the messages our culture delivers to teenage girls and their personal and social consequences, putting off until Chapter 5 consideration of the physical changes associated with puberty—menstruation and hormonal fluctuations. We will focus on the psychological and cultural significance of adolescence for girls, on the socialization pressures and conditions of childhood that continue, and on the experiences that are new. What expectations are different? What are the available options and likely choices? We will pay particular attention to those aspects of the adolescent world that are most important for girls—the mass media, peers, and school.

Many of us have learned that the main developmental objective of the adolescent period is to establish personal identity—to identify one's adult interests and direction, to determine where one is going and why. While our culture clearly expects this of a young man, a young woman typically receives a double message. On the one hand she is encouraged to follow her interests and skills, to do well in school, and to prepare for an occupation. But at the same time, a multitude of cultural cues proclaim, with varying degrees of subtlety, that a young woman must remain flexible and adaptable because what she becomes and where she goes will depend ultimately upon the man with whose life she will become identified (heterosexuality being assumed). The girl whose active interest in sports may have been encouraged, whose high achievement in school was applauded, and whose aspirations for adventure, exploration, and a career were praised may find adolescence a period of conflict and confusion because of the mixed messages our culture sends to teenage girls.

DOMINANT CULTURAL THEMES

As we shall see, in many ways "the problems of adolescent women," as Patricia Spacks (1975) wrote, "are those of all women writ large" (p. 147). In adolescence, many girls are faced with a narrower definition of women than they had encountered in childhood; this information comes, as before, from representatives of the significant cultural institutions—parents, friends, high school teachers, counselors, and the media. To books and television must be added pop music and films—particularly important sources of information about interpersonal relationships, heterosexual love, and sex, and women's value and social status. Thus, one study found that, among college students who watched an average of 12.1 hours of TV per week, those who watched more sex-role stereotyped programs rated themselves in a more gender-stereotyped way (Ross, Anderson, & Wisocki, 1982). An analogous and supportive finding has come from an experimental study (St. Lawrence & Joyner, 1991); following a single brief exposure to heavy metal rock music, a sample of college men scored significantly higher on a measure of sex-role stereotyping than a comparable group who had been exposed to classical music.

Our society's separation of girls and boys in childhood by activities, interests, and appropriate behavior intensifies in adolescence. Two cultures appear, each with its own characteristics, distinctive language style, dress, informal gathering places, subjects of interest, and worldview. Representatives of the two cultures meet in high school classes, at sports events, and on dates, but sexual excitement is mainly what brings the two worlds together. Some observers have concluded that the "distinctive interaction styles" practiced by girls "put them at a disadvantage" (Maccoby, 1990, p. 513) in mixed-gender adolescent groups and encounters.

Searching for Mr. Right

Our society explicitly encourages the adolescent boy to learn to know himself and to acquire skills sufficient to pursue his ambitions, ideals, and life goals. After he has resolved his problems of identity, he is expected to search for a wife and establish a family. His heterosexuality is taken for granted. An adolescent girl's heterosexuality is also assumed by our culture, and the major developmental task prescribed for her is to enhance her attractiveness and find a boyfriend, lover, or husband. Despite significant changes during the past two decades in women's roles in the family and the economy, the search for Mr. Right is as primary and important for contemporary teenagers in our country as it was for their mothers and grandmothers, and it seems to cross the lines of social class, ethnic group, and geographic area.

Erik Erikson (1968), a developmental psychologist whose ideas are still influential, described adolescent objectives through a cultural lens that views boys as "the figure" and girls as "the background." Thus, for example, he wrote that "much of a young woman's identity is already defined in her kind of attractiveness and in the selective nature of her search for the man (or men) by whom she wishes to be sought'' (p. 283). This message was communicated to young women in the 1950s and 1960s whether or not they were pursuing higher education or career training. Jessie Bernard (1978), in commenting on her daughter's college experience in the early 1960s, noted that "if young women were going to be intellectual, they were made to understand, they better be intellectual in a charming, unchallenging, disarming, appealing—strictly feminine—way" (p. 64). Two curricula seemed to be offered at the women's college her daughter attended: the official one catering to intellectual interests, and the hidden one teaching "feminine style" that would be unthreatening and attractive to men.

Can we dismiss these observations as relics of the past? Current data and the reported experiences of young women suggest not, as does the cartoon by Libby Reid. And what meaning can we ascribe to the different gifts suggested for high school girls and boys in a 1988 catalogue featuring items that deal "with the critical decisions and hard realities . . . [teens] will face upon entering adulthood" (Wieser Educational, 1988)? Offered for boys is a book titled *Challenges;* offered for girls is a book called *Choices.* Whereas the cover of the boys' book shows outstretched arms moving and at work, the cover of the girls' book features lovely pink and white flowers.

Much has changed in the last few decades relevant to woman's place and social recognition of women's abilities and aspirations. The culture, nevertheless, still encourages young women, sometimes subtly and sometimes explicitly, to believe that their fundamental task is to find a man. Not all that long ago, one of the major television networks sponsored a special program entitled "99 Ways to Attract the Right Man," a combination of comic and serious advice on "how to *recognize* him, *meet* him and *keep* him" ("99 Ways to Attract," 1985). So important is this objective for women that it often is presented as taking precedence over same-gender friendships. Screenwriter Susan Isaacs (1990), in elaborating on her thesis that good movies about women's friendship are hard to find, notes that films show women to be less adept at friendship than men because women "simply don't have the time to work at it. . . . Women get sidetracked . . . [when] they get goofy over the opposite sex" (p. H-37).

Messages from almost everywhere encourage a young woman to believe that the activities she engages in before successfully accomplishing her fundamental task should not be taken so seriously that they interfere with finding a man, and to see other activities as instrumental to that search. Certainly, many adolescent women resist and do

Cartoon by Libby Reid, from *Do You Hate Your Hips More than Nuclear War?* Copyright ©1988 by Penguin Books. Reprinted by permission of Libby Reid.

not accept our culture's definition of their fundamental task. These young women seriously prepare for jobs, careers, and personal pursuits vital to their identity, integrity, and self-definition. The dominant culture, however, remains largely uneasy about life-styles for women that do not include happiness with Mr. Right, and it continues to presume that this achievement is the adolescent girl's top priority.

It's Still a Man's World

In our society, men as a class are more important, more highly valued, and more rewarded than women, a fact that continues to be documented by informal and formal observations, personal experience, and research findings (e.g., cf. Carli, 1991). What men do receives higher priority, more social support, and higher status and takes precedence over what women do. Margaret Mead (1949/ 1968) noted long ago that whatever the activity—healing, weaving, doll making, fishing, or what have you—that activity is more valued and honored when performed by men than when it is merely "women's work."

Most girls learn about male supremacy early, but this social fact becomes more and more prominent in adolescence as less time is spent at home and more time is spent in school, the neighborhood, and the outside world. In a story about an adolescent girl (McDermott, 1987) we learn that since her father died she lived with her mother and grandmother; as the neighbors put it, they were living *alone,* "meaning without a man in the house" (p. 9). Adolescent girls find out, by being good observers, that no matter what adults say about boys, boys really count because someday they become men. Marilyn French, in *The Women's Room* (1977), described what Mira, at 15, had figured out but did not quite understand:

> Everybody despised boys, everyone looked down on them, the teachers, her mother, even her father. "Boys!" they would exclaim in disgust. But everyone admired men. . . . Boys were ridiculous, troublesome, always fighting and showing off and making noise, but men strode purposefully to the center of every stage and took up the whole surface of every scene. Why was that? (p. 27)

In this connection, it is interesting to note a conclusion reached by Lawrence Cohn (1991) from an analysis of 65 studies comparing female and male personality development. During adolescence, the research shows, girls are more mature than boys in the sense, for example, of being more self-aware, conscientious, and autonomous. Yet, Cohn notes, "ironically, it is adolescent boys who are granted earlier dating privileges, independence, and freedom from adult supervision . . . , although it is adolescent girls who display greater maturity of thought" (p. 261).

Many girls do not question the greater privileges and status accorded boys, but simply learn well the lessons taught by parents, teachers, and books, including the textbooks they use at school. An analysis of high school history texts (Kirby & Julian, 1981) led to the conclusion that women's concerns were not placed in "the mainstream of American history" and that information about women was frequently misleading or demeaning, with women's suffrage, for example, presented "as a minor advance in the American political system" (p. 206). A very different kind of study also confirms the conclusion of men's greater value in our society. An investigation of the work children do in and around their homes found that parents were more likely to pay boys for the work they did and less likely to pay girls; this pattern also held outside the house, so that girls earned less in general. In commenting on these findings, Jacqueline Goodnow (1988) noted, "mothers do not get paid in money, and their daughters seem to be socialized into a similar pattern of work that is 'for love' " (p. 15); more valued boys's work is done "for pay."

The value of men is a lesson taught not only by parents, teachers, and neighbors, but also by other agents of socialization. The African-American heroine of Alice Walker's *Meridian* (1976) learned from movies not only about how European-Americans lived and loved, but also about "the dream of happy endings: of women who had everything, of men who ran the world" (p. 75). Contem-

porary movies, by and large, present similar images and messages. According to reviewer Janet Maslin (1990), "male stars are dominant. . . . Women are left to play bimbos, and the bimbos take a back seat. . . . The present trend is toward smaller, more submissive roles for women" as is the case in the "fabulously sexist world of rap music and rock video" (pp. 13f.).

Adolescent women are significant consumers of movies, popular music, radio, and television, and from each of these media the message of men's greater value and power is clear and ubiquitous. One study of two top-40 radio stations in Washington, DC (Lont, 1990), for example, analyzed all nonmusic content during peak listening times over a 2-month period and found that men dominated as DJs, newscasters, advertisement voice-overs, sportscasters, and weathercasters. "DJs, the 'stars' of radio, the controllers of the action, are male voices 96% of the time" (p. 667).

An interesting study of the relative size of men's and women's heads in contemporary magazine photographs, in paintings from the 17th to the 20th centuries, and in drawings made by college students found that men's heads are presented as significantly more prominent— that is, larger relative to the total picture—than women's heads (Archer, Iritani, Kimes, & Barrios, 1983). Furthermore, when asked to rate photographs differing in facial prominence, a sample of students judged the more prominent faces to be more intelligent and ambitious. The investigators concluded that the greater facial prominence given to men than to women in photographs and paintings gives men a clear advantage. Another study (Nigro, Hill, Gelbein, & Clark, 1988) examined photographs in *Time, Newsweek, Good Housekeeping,* and *Ms.* from one time in the 1970s and one time in the 1980s and found that, although in all the publications except *Time* women's facial prominence had increased in the 1980s, in 7 out of 8 comparisons, men's facial prominence was significantly greater than women's. Barbara Luebke (1989) studied photographs of adults in four Connecticut newspapers and found that pictures of men outnumbered those of women everywhere except on "life-style" pages. The inequity was especially marked on page 1, the most important page; here the ratio of men's to women's photos was almost 3 to 1. The author concluded that "men are most likely to make page one because they are doing serious, important things; women make page one because they are 'interesting' " (p. 130).

What is true of pop music, radio, films, magazines, books, and newspapers is also true of television, to which we paid considerable attention in the last chapter. A study of prime-time programs during a 4-week period led the investigators (Downs & Gowan, 1980) to conclude that "men are depicted as possessors of both power and status through greater control of both rewards and punishments" (p. 691). Even on TV shows that feature single, independent, working women, the power is shown residing with men, whether or not they deserve to have it. Critic Phyllis Theroux (1987) has argued that the typical scenario is one in which "the men still have the best offices" and the women "accept the man's world as a given that can be mocked and wept over but not changed, at least by them" (p. H-35). Despite some exceptional shows, like "Murphy Brown" and "The Trials of Rosie O'Neil," television in the 1990s presents largely the same picture of women and men as it did in earlier decades. "The Trials of Rosie O'Neil," featuring a divorced attorney working as a public defender, was canceled after one season.

Most young women across regions, ethnic groups, and social classes get the message about male dominance. An important theme in Anne Campbell's (1984) book about adolescent girls in street gangs is their largely unsuccessful challenge of machismo and their emotional dependence on men. Men's superiority is proclaimed in crime, in the intellectual sphere, in work, sports, and entertainment, and in political and economic influence. In one survey (Balswick & Ingoldsby, 1982), more than 1,000 high school students were asked to name their heroes and heroines. Men were nominated overwhelmingly by a 3 to 1 ratio, by both girls and boys, African-American and European-American. Personal friends or relatives chosen as heroes or heroines were just as often women as men, but if public figures were selected, men were chosen by a ratio of 7 to 1. The adolescents in this study came from Georgia; does geography make a difference? Apparently not, since a survey among 1,167 school children in Rhode Island (reported by Major, 1983) found that their 10 top-ranked favorite actors or actresses were all men! It is not surprising, then, to find that a study of college students (Fabes & Laner, 1986) found that both genders perceived men to have more advantages and fewer disadvantages than women, with the judgments based more on social than on physical attributes.

Since men are so highly valued, it is no wonder that adolescent women accept the necessity of finding one. Having a boyfriend greatly enhances a high school girl's prestige or image. A girl may be bright, friendly, competent, and attractive, but without a boyfriend she lacks social validation of these positive attributes. It is as though being selected by a boy tells others that a girl is worth-

while. Thus, a teenage girl in a story by Margaret Atwood (1984) tells us

> Once I started going out with Buddy, I found I could pass for normal. I was now included in the kinds of conversations girls held in the washroom while they were putting on their lipstick. (p. 27)

When Buddy gave her his identification bracelet, he "was putting his name on me, like a *Reserved* sign or an ownership label" (p. 39).

Many college or young working women also feel the need for public display of a boyfriend, despite the fact that they may be experiencing success through academic or other achievements. A cocktail napkin I picked up at a restaurant featured the following "daffynition": "COED—A girl who didn't get her man in high school" (very funny!?). A frequently repeated theme during a meeting of a group of women in science on my college campus was that it was much easier for them to pursue their scholarly ambitions if they already had the security of a personal relationship with a man. To be chosen by a man appears to confer value by showing others that a woman has been found "worthy," and having a relationship with a man may free her to focus on other interests and activities. But young women who make finding a man a top priority accept society's prescription for their adolescent years: they must strive to be popular and feminine, flexible and nurturing.

Be Popular and Feminine

Many contemporary high school girls get up at 6 a.m. to put on their makeup before going to school. Perhaps this is so for the young teenager shown on p. 73 "putting on her face." Girls have learned that to be popular is a coveted achievement and that the route to this goal includes dressing in the latest fashion, covering up blemishes, being friendly and available, and smiling. In a study of boys and girls from grades 1 through 4 and grades 9 through 12 (Berman & Smith, 1984) in which same-gender pairs were photographed, the investigators found that, regardless of instructions or age, girls smiled significantly more often than boys.

A story by Alice Munro (1977) describes how two 13-year-old girls from a previous generation used to spend their time: "We did questionnaires in magazines, to find out whether we had personality and whether we would be popular. We read articles on how to make up our faces to accentuate our good points and how to carry on a conversation" (p. 201). Contemporary magazines for

A young teenager "putting on her face." (Photograph © Michael Siluk.)

TABLE 4.1 *Percentages of editorial pages given to selected topics in* Seventeen *magazine.* (From Kate Peirce, "A feminist theoretical perspective on the socialization of teenage girls through *Seventeen* magazine," *Sex Roles,* 1990, 23, 491–500, Table 1, p. 498.)

	1961	1972	1985
Appearance	48.0	52.0	46.0
Home	9.0	10.0	11.0
Male-female relations	7.0	2.7	6.5
Self-development	7.5	16.6	6.8

young women, like *Seventeen,* have similar questionnaires and features that teach that the more "feminine" a girl looks, the more attractive she will be to boys, and that girls who act and dress appropriately will be admired, approved, and dated. A field experiment (Renne & Allen, 1976) found that college men held doors open for women four times as often as they held doors open for men, but six times as often for women who were wearing "feminine" clothes. An adolescent girl learns what kind of clothes these are from magazines, films, television, and peers. She learns to use cosmetics to highlight her "best" features and hide her "worst" and to behave in ways that will attract and keep the attention of men.

When women behave in ways that men are thought to like—in "feminine" ways—they speak in soft voices, not loudly or shrilly; lower their eyes and look coy; do not talk too much when men are around; and do not sprawl or sit with feet apart (Henley & Freeman, 1976). We might like to think that this definition of what is feminine is outmoded and old-fashioned, but when I asked a high school class in 1985 to list the characteristics they associated with the term *feminine,* they offered the following: intuitive, understanding, caring, graceful, soft-spoken, dainty, and curvy. The characteristics they associated with *masculine,* on the other hand, were muscular, aggressive, brave, ambitious, rough, logical, handsome, daring, competitive, and strong.

Even when advertisements for products for young women portray them as active and adventurous, the associated message is that such young women must retain their femininity. An ad in *Teen* magazine (Maybelline, 1984), for example, presented a girl in pink shorts and sneakers who says, "I always want to look my best, even when I'm riding my bike." This message was echoed in the media treatment of Florence Griffith Joyner, winner of gold and silver Olympic medals and holder of a world record for the 200-meter dash. One newspaper story (Kohl, 1988), in making the point that "feminine beauty can include strength—and sweat," described the athlete's "exotic eye makeup" and fingernails that "were long and painted red, white and blue" (p. B-1).

A study of television (cf. "Shows Blasted," 1988) that focused on images of teenage girls concluded that the major theme was that looks count more than brains and that adolescent girls are "obsessed with shopping, grooming and dating and openly disdainful of studying and planning for a career" (pp. F-1f.). Similar findings have come from a study of *Seventeen,* in existence since 1945 and still widely read and extremely popular with teenage girls. In all the years studied (1961, 1972, and 1985), the investigator (Peirce, 1990) found the topic of appearance to comprise about 50 percent of the nonadvertising content, as can be seen in Table 4.1.

The consequences are serious for adolescent girls who try to match themselves to the media images of women who succeed in getting men's attention. One outcome is that adolescent girls are often regarded as silly and concerned with trivia. For example, the results of a survey of 12- to 19-year-old girls by a marketing company led one columnist (Patinkin, 1987) to write: "What do American girls like to do more than anything else: . . . Shopping. Almost 93 percent said that is their favorite thing" (p. C-1). At the very bottom of the list was school and volunteer work. Another consequence of the pursuit of men's attention is that a teenage girl may not see value in her own qualities until they receive approval from a boy. For example, in the novel *August* (Rossner, 1983), a young woman, Sascha, says:

> The only time I ever think I'm beautiful . . . is when some man is staring into my face in broad daylight and telling me I'm beautiful. And then as soon as he turns away for a minute I think he changed his mind. (p. 376).

Sascha's feelings illustrate an adolescent girl's need to validate her attractiveness and enhance her self-esteem by the responses she elicits from men.

Some young women who pursue men's approval with more than ordinary determination may get caught by our society's limits on how far young women can "properly" go to attract men. The case of Vanessa Williams, chosen Miss America for 1984, is a good example. When a photographer for whom she had posed nude sold her photographs to a magazine for men, she was publicly disgraced and forced to give up her title, as well as the lucrative rewards attached to it. But how did she earn the title in the first place? By having more of "what it takes" than the other young women who paraded, smiling, before judges in body-accentuating gowns or in high heels and bathing suits. Vanessa Williams, however, went "too far." To exhibit one's body scantily clothed and to be seductive conforms to our society's standards for respectable womanhood, but overtly titillating men with nude photos does not. About 80,000 young women enter state beauty contests annually (Nicola-McLaughlin, 1985), participating in the exploitation of women's sexuality, youth, and talent, but little sympathy was expressed for Vanessa Williams in the press, and few saw her as a victim of our culture's mixed messages.

Still another consequence of young women's pursuit of "femininity" is the psychological suffering this pursuit produces for many minority women. In our society's definition of femininity, light skin is often a requisite for attractiveness. Mary Washington (1975) examined the writing of African-American women and found a preoccupation with issues of skin color and hair texture and beauty, as well as other evidence that the image of the European-American "dream girl" has deeply affected African-American adolescents. She noted that "the raving beauties every high school boy coveted were invariably light-skinned with 'good' hair" (p. xvi) and that "the idea of beauty as defined by white America has been an assault on the personhood of the black woman" (p. xvii). One story included in Washington's collection, by Gwendolyn Brooks, is entitled "If You're Light and Have Long Hair." In another story, by Paule Marshall, the heroine Reena tells us that "like nearly every little black girl, I had my share of dreams of waking up to find myself with long blond curls, blue eyes, and skin like milk" (p. 122). Just such a dream is encountered in the opening pages of Maya Angelou's (1971) book about her childhood and adolescence. In the dream, she is wearing a lavender dress that makes her look like a "sweet little white girl"; her hair is long and blond, and her eyes are blue. Chinese-American Maxine Hong Kingston (1977) has also written of how important it was for her to try to become "American-feminine, or no dates" (p. 56).

That not all non-European-American adolescent girls experience their divergence from the majority definition of attractiveness in the same way is well illustrated in the novel *Betsey Brown* (Shange, 1985) about a 13-year-old African-American girl in St. Louis. Betsey's father had "filled her head with tales of Bessie Smith and Josephine Baker . . . [and taken] her to see Jackie Wilson, Etta James, Tina Turner and the Ikettes" (p. 147). Because her heroines were beautiful and talented African-American women like Dorothy Dandridge and Eartha Kitt, Betsey was determined to become like them and to be "Queen of the Negro Veiled Prophet." In the enlightened 1990s, adolescent girls can find African-American models in glamour magazines and TV commercials, but the long-legged, thin, European-American blond continues to dominate and to appear in the dreams of short-limbed, solidly built, brown-haired teenage girls of all skin colors and ethnic groups.

Be Flexible and Caregiving

A persistent message to the adolescent girl is that she should be flexible and not define herself too sharply, because her ultimate identity will be defined by the man with whom she becomes associated. Erik Erikson (1968) viewed adolescence for women not as a time for active searching and exploring, but as a time of fluidity, "a psychosocial moratorium, a sanctioned period of delay of adult functioning" (p. 282). According to Erikson, the young woman's identity will come primarily from the man she marries and for whom she makes a home. While he granted that a young woman also trains herself "as a worker and a citizen," the full context of his discussion makes clear that he believed her final self-definition to be powerfully shaped by the needs, ambitions, goals, and interests of her mate.

Erikson's views reflect a persistent theme in our society. Women are expected to manifest adaptability and flexibility in shaping their lives around the plans and interests of their husbands, and girls are reinforced to consider the wishes of others and to be accommodating. A study of more than 2,500 students in grades 3 and 12 (Rosenberg & Simmons, 1975) found girls to be reliably more self-conscious than boys, with the gender difference increasing over time, so that by age 15, twice as many girls as boys were highly self-conscious or "other-directed." The data suggest that "girls become very worried about what other people think of them, whether they are pleasing and helpful" (p. 158). When asked to choose between success (being "best in things you do") and being well-liked, significantly more girls than boys chose the latter. This concern and its consequences for women is a common theme in contemporary fiction by women. For example, Rosellen Brown (1984) describes one of her protagonists: "The ambitious girl, shaking her glossy curls, making herself soft, Silly Putty in whatever masculine hands. And Alexis, apolitical, had met Roger at Ole Miss and had been formed. Deformed" (p. 54).

Psychoanalytic theory regards women as more pragmatic and less principled—that is, less concerned with abstractions like justice and more with social acceptance—than men. Sigmund Freud (1933/1964) believed that a girl's superego development was inadequate because, unlike a boy, she did not experience an Oedipal conflict or castration anxiety—that is, fear of her father's reprisal for love of the mother. Without an Oedipal conflict to resolve, Freud argued, women's superego development would necessarily suffer, since it is through resolution of this conflict that social rules are internalized. Instead, wrote Freud, when the girl realizes her lack of a penis, she blames her mother, from whom she turns away with hostility, and moves toward her father with a positive attachment. The latter promises love in exchange for her renunciation of aggressive impulses. The result, according to Freud, is a wishy-washy personality without strong personal standards who is intent upon pleasing others. Was Freud describing inevitable feminine development or

cultural prescription? Adolescent women, in their efforts to be pleasing, may continue behaving in many of the same ways that brought them approval when they were little girls. Generalizing from her analyses of English and American novels, Patricia Spacks (1975) concluded that young women are, in many ways, "not encouraged to grow up." Perhaps this is the reason that the word *baby* remains so frequent in the popular music men sing to—and about—women.

That a young woman is encouraged to continue being dependent while learning that she is expected to nurture and take care of others is paradoxical. Among a sample of 7th to 10th graders (Blyth & Foster-Clark, 1987), for example, girls and boys were found to report similar levels of intimacy with family members, but as family ties became more distant, girls were encouraged more consistently than boys to develop intimate relationships. The data suggested that for girls it is expected and required that, with age, "they shift from being nurtured to being nurturant" (p. 713). Our culture expects that a woman will support her family emotionally and be responsible for shaping their home into as ideal an environment as their economic circumstances permit. Beginning in childhood, girls are urged and cajoled to practice domesticity and to view themselves as sympathetic and caring persons. Both middle-class and working-class girls receive the same message, although the timing may differ. Middle-class girls, who are usually encouraged to go to college, can, for a while, be autonomous and make independent choices. But they, too, have practiced and learned much the same domestic and nurturant behavior as working-class girls have. Taking care of people is still a cultural imperative for young women. At 19, having never lived apart from my parents long enough to practice taking care of myself, I remember believing that I would be able to look after the older, more experienced, and troubled man I married. I know other young women who, decades later, did much the same thing.

Be Quiet and Hesitant or Be Bad

An autobiography by New Zealand writer Janet Frame (1982) takes us from her birth through her childhood and ends as she is preparing to go off to college, when she tells us candidly and simply, "I retreated. I was afraid to voice my ideas" (p. 241). Reports of being silenced is a common theme in the stories of girls growing up in the United States as well. According to Maxine Hong Kingston (1977), for example, the voices of Chinese women are typically "strong and bossy . . . [but] American-Chinese girls had to whisper to make ourselves American-feminine" (p. 200). Similarly, Lindsy Van Gelder (1990) recalls experiencing her voice being choked off at adolescence and suggests that "girls at puberty get the message that the culture doesn't value their experience; it literally doesn't want to listen to what they have to say" (p. 77). Such conclusions are shared by others who have carefully examined the content of popular culture. For example, in commenting on the "good girl" image presented on television in earlier decades, one writer (Barreca, 1991) noted that such girls "did not brazenly draw attention to themselves or their ideas. They looked around to see what the other people . . . were doing" (p. H-21) and showed control over their emotions and behavior.

Carol Gilligan and her colleagues (Gilligan, Lyons, & Hammer, 1990) have proposed that this cultural message is still alive and well, a conclusion supported by the results of a 5-year study in which younger girls were compared with older teenagers. Whereas preadolescent girls were found to be generally outspoken or bossy, to express their opinions freely and with confidence, and to discuss their relationships and feelings honestly, many of the older girls appeared to have given up their articulate voices; they were more hesitant, quieter, and more unsure of their positions and ideas. In an interview, Carol Gilligan noted that "by 15 or 16 . . . they start saying 'I don't know. I don't know. I don't know.' They start not knowing what they had known" (Prose, 1990, p. 23). While Gilligan sees this as the dominant pattern, she has also pointed out that some girls resist giving up their earlier certainty and knowledge, taking that attitude "underground." She is quoted in a report on a conference presentation as follows: "The coming of age of girls in this society is accompanied by a falling away of self, a narrowing of psychic parameters" (Moses, 1990, p. 26).

One route out of silence or triviality for contemporary adolescent girls is through participation in sports. This path has been described by the mother of a girl who went from being the girl who was awarded the " 'Best Hair,' female category, in the eighth-grade yearbook" to being a high school varsity basketball player (Whitney, 1988).

> For years, she'd been told at home, at school, by countless advertisements, "Be quiet, Be good, Be still." . . . [She'd been taught that] ideals of femininity are still, quiet, cool females in ads whose vacantness passes for sophistication. (p. 8)

The messages to her daughter as an athlete are different—to be aggressive and intense, to play to win, and to be unafraid to do her best. Other girls learn not to be silent through other interests or pursuits or through the active encouragement of parents or teachers. For example, Ntozake Shange's heroine Betsey Brown (1985), whose ideals of womanhood were not shaped by European-American standards, is drawn to a poem, which she recites in school, that urges people to speak up and express themselves.

Some television and other media portraits in the 1990s are of women who do not lower their voices, who are bold and brash, risk-taking and smart-alecky. In commenting on the "fast-talking, wise-cracking, brilliantly satiric, funny women" on the TV screen in the 1990s (such as Candice Bergen's character Murphy Brown, Roseanne Arnold, or Joan Rivers), Gina Barreca (1991) has pointed out that "we are watching a woman who breaks the rules." We all know what these rules are, and some media women are shown breaking them without negative consequences. Madonna, for example, not only can get away with being brazen and outrageous, but has parlayed her rule-breaking to fame and fortune at the very top of the entertainment world. At the same time, however, even though "she's reveled in changing masks, in contradiction, in putting ironic quotation marks around her various identities" (Ansen, 1991, p. 67), and in not presenting herself as victim or vulnerable, her image remains ultra-American-feminine and sexually provocative. In addition, Madonna is an entertainer who captures our attention, but not usually about serious matters. The same cannot be said of the fictional heroines in the film *Thelma and Louise,* which aroused strong emotional reactions from critics and viewers and provoked a great deal of discussion. Reviewers in *Newsweek* (Shapiro, Murr, & Springen, 1991) noted that the film had "met surprisingly virulent criticism. Commentators in the press and on TV have complained that the two women commit too much social and moral damage to qualify as proper heroines" (p. 63). In the film, Thelma and Louise violently and effectively resist rape and sexual harassment, and change in character and attitudes as they begin to take charge of their lives and accept responsibility for their actions. "Though it tells a tale of violence," according to critic Janet Maslin (1991), "its spirit could not be more benign" since the two women "have no real taste for crime" (pp. H-15f.). The *Newsweek* reviewers suggested that behind the furor raised by the film is the fact that Thelma and Louise are portrayed as having

something on their minds besides men . . . [and that] neither woman needs a man to complete her . . . . [They] have cut their ties to the past; they're free, briefly and wildly free. To some people, that's a scary sight. . . . They're modeling power, not lingerie . . . [And] what triumphs in the end isn't guns or whiskey, it's their hard-won belief in themselves . . . . (Shapiro, Murr, & Springen, 1991, p. 63)

ACHIEVEMENT IN MATHEMATICS AND OTHER ACADEMIC AREAS

Girls as a group in our society typically do as well as boys or outperform them in elementary school, high school, and college classes, attaining better grades in all subjects (Cordes, 1986b; Kimball, 1989). Yet girls have tended to score significantly below boys on important standardized national tests of achievement in cognitive areas. Most of the media and research attention given to the gender disparity in test scores has centered on the mathematics and spatial domains.

It is not uncommon that girls outperform boys in the same math classes. Thus, for example, one study of more than 2,000 high school juniors (de Wolf, 1981) found that although the boys took more math classes than the girls, the latter significantly surpassed boys in their overall math grade point average. Yet, on the Scholastic Aptitude Test (SAT)—a test that is often crucial for college admission and scholarship awards—boys have outscored girls on the math portion of the test by at least 40 points since 1967 (Landers, 1989). Since 1972, boys have also scored better than girls by at least 10 points on the verbal portion of the test. A good deal of effort has gone into attempts to explain this phenomenon.

The results of a study of junior high schoolers of high mathematics ability (Benbow & Stanley, 1980) have been widely interpreted by many, including the investigators themselves, as supporting the hypothesis of innate male superiority. A story in *Science* (Kolata, 1980a) about the research was headlined as follows: "Math and Sex: Are Girls Born with Less Ability? A Johns Hopkins group says 'probably.' Others are not so sure" (p. 1234). Every year from 1972 to 1979 the researchers gave the SAT-M test to groups of mathematically gifted seventh and eighth graders identified through national talent searches, and every year boys scored significantly higher than girls, with the top scorer always a boy. When one carefully examines the actual data presented by the researchers, however, their own figures challenge the conclusion that the gender differences reflect innate male superiority. In 1972, when the number of gifted boys and girls tested was 90 and 77,

respectively, the highest score for a boy was 740 and the highest score for a girl was 590 (a difference of 150 points). In 1979, the last reported sample (Benbow & Stanley, 1980) that included the largest number of children (2,046 boys and 1,628 girls), the highest score for a boy was 790 and the highest score for a girl was 760, a difference of only 30 points. Within just 7 years the gap clearly narrowed between the highest-scoring girls and boys. Surely the most parsimonious explanation is not a transformation of female genes but a documentable change in the culturally acknowledged value of mathematics for girls and a change in experiences, attitudes, and interests.

Environmental Variables

Considerable criticism has been directed at the inferences drawn from the Benbow and Stanley data regarding innate sex differences. Illustrative of the rejoinders is an editorial in *Science* by two women professors of mathematics (Schafer & Gray, 1981) who noted that "anyone who thinks that seventh graders are free from environmental influences can hardly be living in the real world" (p. 231). The results of one study are particularly instructive since they present data from 20 different countries. The International Association for the Evaluation of Educational Achievement (cf. Ruskai, 1991) found that differences among countries are much larger than gender differences. For example, in geometry the average scores of boys and girls from the United States were 39.7 and 37.9, respectively, compared with scores in the 55 to 60 range for Hungarian and Japanese students of both genders. It has also been pointed out (cf. Ruskai, 1991) that the Johns Hopkins group sends a brochure to gifted junior high school students before they are tested in which they are informed that boys outperform girls on the math portion of the SAT; these gifted girls later receive higher grades than the comparable boys in high school math courses.

A considerable amount of research has been directed toward trying to identify correlates or antecedents of mathematical skills in both genders. One intriguing finding is that for girls early grades and test scores do not predict later performance, whereas they are predictive for boys (Wentzel, 1988). What, then, are the predictors for girls? One study (Starr, 1979) found that among a sample of high school seniors, girls with higher scores on a measure of general self-esteem and a greater reported sense of personal control over their environments scored higher on the SAT-M than other girls. For the boys, personality variables were not significantly related to the math scores, suggesting that so many environmental factors may foster the development of mathematics skills for boys that "special personality factors may not be necessary." A review of the research on women's math achievement (Kimball, 1989) led the author to conclude that women who get high grades in math may not continue taking math courses because of two factors:

> The first is the tendency of girls more than of boys to attribute success in math to effort rather than to ability . . . [and] the second factor is sex-role conflict . . . [resulting] both from discrimination against girls' and women's participation in math and from perceived or experienced conflict between parental and career goals . . . . That their male peers stereotype math [as a male interest] more than they do may create in women an uncertainty about their place . . . as mathematics achievers. (p. 209)

Research supports the hypothesis that achievement in mathematics is related to more variables for girls than for boys. Julia Sherman (1980) reported that, among a sample of high school students, significant gender differences in math performance were obtained in 11th grade but not in 8th grade. Accompanying the decline in the girls' performance were significant changes in their attitudes toward math as assessed by a variety of measures. Most important was the perception of math as a male domain. Girls who saw math as something boys do were more likely to do poorly in it. In another study (Sherman, 1983), the best predictor of continued enrollment in math courses for girls was found to be 8th-grade vocabulary score followed by confidence in learning math; for the boys confidence was the most important factor, followed by vocabulary score. Other investigators (Kanarian & Quina, 1984) have reported that 12th-grade boys differ from girls in experience with math, perceived encouragement to study it, and positive attitudes toward it. The importance of the cultural association between math and men is highlighted by a statistical analysis of more than 70 studies (Hyde, Fennema, Ryan, Frost, & Hopp, 1990). Although most gender differences in attitudes and beliefs about mathematics were found to be small, "the one exception is the stereotyping of math as a male domain" (p. 310), a belief subscribed to by significantly more boys and men than girls and women.

Analysis of the content of national standardized tests has led some researchers, like Paula Selkow (cf. Goleman, 1987), to conclude that items tend to be male-centered. From a review of the items in 74 psychological and educational tests, she concluded that there were twice as many references to men as to women and an 8 to 1 ratio favoring men in descriptions of famous people. Others have argued that the gender difference in SAT scores is an artifact that can be explained by the fact that 50,000 to 70,000 more young women than men take the test each year, with greater heterogeneity among the former in social class, ethnicity, and family background. According to Nancy Burton of the Educational Testing Service (cf. Landers, 1989), the women test-takers include more who are from low-income homes with non-college-educated parents and who have taken fewer college-preparatory courses. In a study that "controlled for the variables of family income, ethnic group, high school courses and choice of college major, the differences between men and women taking the SATs vanished" (p. 14). The importance of these findings cannot be overemphasized, since they point clearly to the conclusion that it is not gender but such social variables as income, education, and aspirations that are correlated with high scores on tests of academic aptitude. The seriousness with which data such as that just cited are being taken is indicated by a federal judge's ruling that New York State will have to discontinue its practice of awarding college scholarships solely on the basis of SAT scores (Mitgang, 1989). The judge held that this practice discriminated against women applicants and thereby violated Title IX of the federal Education Amendments of 1972, which forbids sex discrimination in federally funded programs. Using this ruling to underpin their position, others have argued that the National Merit Scholarship Corporation is also unfair to girls in relying solely on the results of the PSAT in determining semifinalists. Such a practice has resulted in a consistent 2 to 1 ratio of boys to girls among National Merit semifinalists.

A recent assessment that appears more and more frequently in the social science literature is that SAT scores are not congruent with information obtained from other national tests; the latter tend to show that gender differences on cognitive measures are declining or disappearing. A study by Marcia Linn and Janet Hyde (cf. Adler, 1989) concluded that "as social roles, job requirements and educational opportunities change, differences in abilities between the sexes in math, spatial and science skills have become almost nonexistent" (p. 6). Similarly, Alan Feingold (1988) concluded, from an analysis of the aptitude test scores of national samples of 8th to 12th graders over several decades, that on all but the upper level of high school mathematics, "gender differences declined precipitously over the years surveyed, and the increases in these differences over the high school years have diminished"

(p. 95). The conclusion that boys have no overall superiority in math was also confirmed by a statistical analysis of more than 259 gender comparisons reported in the social science literature (Hyde, Fennema, & Lamon, 1990).

Computer and Spatial Skills

A number of studies of computer skills and literacy have added to the pool of information accumulating about the achievement and expectations of teenage girls and boys and the opportunities offered to them. It has been pointed out (Merritt, 1986) that women played a central role in the development of computer science and technology, particularly with pioneering work in computer language systems, and that about half of all computer programmers and 20 to 30 percent of programmers and systems analysts are women. In addition, about one third of undergraduate degrees in computer science are earned by women (Lockheed, 1985), and girls and boys in pre-college computer courses perform equally well and include similar numbers of exceptionally talented students (Linn, 1985). Despite these facts, we tend to stereotype computing, like mathematics, as a male domain. One study (Ware & Stuck, 1985), for example, examined pictures in ads and articles in three popular computer magazines and found one woman appearing for every two men. When women were shown, they were likely to be in clerical roles or being used to illustrate computer phobia; women were shown in passive roles while men were pictured "in active, 'hands-on' roles" (p. 212). It is not surprising, then, to learn that boys receive more encouragement than girls to develop computer proficiency. A national survey of computer camps and workshops (Hess & Miura, 1985) found a 3 to 1 ratio favoring boys; this disparity increased with age and was greater in more advanced and more expensive programs. Similarly, a statewide assessment of 6th to 12th graders in California found that more boys than girls reported learning about microcomputers at home, with friends, at school, and from video games (Fetler, 1985). These findings are congruent with those from a survey of home computer use (cf. Holden, 1984), which found that 93 percent of home users are male and that "computer games, educational and otherwise, tend to be oriented to male tastes for violence and destruction" (p. 225). As computers become more linked with what boys do and girls don't, some computer scientists fear that "women are losing many of the gains they made in the first half of the decade" ("Computer Revolution," 1989).

As noted in the last chapter, problems of definition and measurement complicate gender comparison studies with

respect to spatial skills (Caplan, MacPherson, & Tobin, 1985; Halpern, 1986). Although most summaries of the research literature conclude that boys tend to do better on tests of spatial skills beginning at about the 10th grade, contradictory findings have been reported. For example, a large national study of junior and senior high school students found that 13-year-old girls did better than boys on a spatial skills test and that 12th-grade girls and boys did equally well (cf. Meece, Parsons, Kaczala, Goff, & Futterman, 1982). It is also instructive that in Eskimo culture, where both genders participate in hunting, travel over great distances, and must be skilled in spatial visualization and orientation in order to survive, women and men are equal in spatial skills (cf. Hier, 1979; cf. McGee, 1979).

The Eskimo data support the assertion of some that spatial abilities are developed by participation in certain kinds of activities. This hypothesis was tested in one study (Newcombe, Bandura, & Taylor, 1983) in which college students rated a large number of activities as requiring or not requiring spatial abilities and also as "masculine" or "feminine." The activities rated as spatial were also the ones that were rated as masculine, and these were the activities in which men said they participated more than women did. With another group of college students, the investigators found a significant correlation between scores on a test of spatial ability and reported participation in spatial activities, with this correlation higher for women than men. Using a different research strategy, the consequences of specific training have been examined and found to improve visual-spatial performance in children and adults of both genders. For example, the performance of first-graders on an embedded figures task improved after practice (Connor, Schackman, & Serbin, 1978), although there was no generalization to another spatial task (folding blocks). Other studies have documented improvement in the spatial skills of students of both genders in a drafting class (Johnson, Flinn, & Tyer, 1979), among four-person groups given special training (Stericker & LeVesconte, 1982), and among students given practice in a mirror-drawing task (Koslow, 1987). All of these studies have found that whatever initial superiority men may show on spatial tasks disappears when women are provided with opportunities to practice.

Prospects after High School

The evidence with respect to achievement in cognitive areas seems clear. Factors such as practice, family and cultural expectations, interests, opportunities, and self-confidence all seem to be related to whatever gender differences are found. Such differences are not typically found until the high school years, and the differences appear to be shrinking in a changing social climate that includes wider horizons for women.

At the same time, there is evidence that dropping out of school or of being part of a disadvantaged minority may have more serious negative consequences for the achievement of young women than for young men. Nationally, 75 percent of high school students complete school, while the rate in urban areas is only 50 percent; the drop-out rate is similar for girls and boys, as are the reasons for leaving school. The largest number of girls (60 percent) drop out of school for reasons unrelated to pregnancy or marriage, but because of low academic achievement and low self-esteem. After leaving school, they earn 29 percent of what male graduates do and suffer more grim consequences than boys who leave school, according to a study by the National Association of State Boards of Education (cf. "Dropping Out," 1987). Another study (cf. "Girls Lose," 1981) found that among poor African-American children who were part of a special preschool program in Harlem when they were 4 years old, no more of the young women were going to college or working at age 18 to 22 than among a comparable group who were not in the special program. This was not the case for the young men, however; those from the preschool program differed significantly from the others in greater college attendance and greater participation in the work force. Even among the very gifted, the prospects for young women are just not the same as those for young men. Terry Denny and Karen Arnold (cf. Moses, 1991) followed a group of high school valedictorians and other top honor students from Illinois for 10 years and found that

> women students' intellectual self-esteem began to drop shortly after they entered college—despite the fact that they were earning slightly higher grades than the men. After five years, many were achieving and aspiring to lower levels of educational and career attainment than their male counterparts. . . . Women who had lowered their career aspirations did so because they were expecting to marry and have children soon. . . . (p. 47).

The African-American and Hispanic-American students of both genders ran into the most difficulties and experienced the greatest personal and financial obstacles in getting a college degree, despite their high school record of success and accomplishment.

ASPIRATIONS AND ATTITUDES TOWARD WORK AND MARRIAGE

Whether or not a high school girl is planning to go on to higher education or a career, finding a boyfriend and, later, a prospective husband is of highest priority to her if she is heterosexual. One teenage girl in a novel by Annette Jaffee (1988) put it this way: "I never had any serious expectations. If someone had asked me what I wanted to be, I suppose I would have said 'bride' " (p. 113). Despite the fact that the majority of wives and mothers work outside the home, the employment aspirations of adolescent girls lag behind those of boys in terms of prestige and income. Studies indicate that the majority of both genders anticipate a relatively traditional adult life of marriage in which the husband has most responsibility for providing financial resources and the wife has most responsibility for the home.

Traditionalism Is Still the Norm

For most working-class girls, marriage is the way to adulthood. For those who are very poor, or whose ethnicity or race is not respected, school may be a hostile place. For such girls, especially, the high school years may represent a necessary waiting period until a girl is old enough to attract a boy, marry him, and have children. In high school, a working-class girl is likely to be directed either into a commercial or vocational course to learn typing, shorthand, and bookkeeping or into a general course to learn homemaking, child care, and how to be a good consumer. Working-class girls who do go on to college may find that among the barriers to be overcome are the low expectations of parents, teachers, and counselors who assume that marriage represents the poor girl's ultimate ambition, to be realized sooner rather than later. Lillian Rubin (1976) interviewed blue-collar couples in the San Francisco area and found that, even though most married women are in the labor force, working-class girls tend to see work outside the home as temporary. Many of the jobs they see done by older working-class women, in shops, offices, factories, laundries, restaurants, and other people's homes, are low in status and poorly paid, supporting the illusion that one does these things "only for a while" or "part-time" to "help out" and increase the family income. The major breadwinner is still expected to be the husband, and it is the status of his job that matters most.

Regardless of social class, contemporary young women have lower aspirations and expectations than young men of comparable background and ability. For example, in one study (Hurwitz & White, 1977) a group of high school juniors was asked to select from a list of 40 occupations the ones that would be most appropriate for each of five students described in mock profiles; each profile was presented as that of a boy for some of the respondents and of a girl for others. The occupations selected for boys were consistently of higher status (in terms of educational level required and income to be earned) than those selected for girls. Among those students who were given prior information on new occupational opportunities for women, less of a difference showed up between the occupational status scores given to girls and boys.

Not only are the occupational and educational goals of adolescent girls typically lower than those of comparable boys, but the way these are related to such factors as ability or social class seems to differ with gender. Thus, in a review of the literature, Margaret Marini (1978) noted that although the aspirations of teenagers are generally influenced by parental socioeconomic status, parental encouragement, and the teenagers' academic ability, these variables seem to matter less for girls than for boys. Although girls are positively influenced by their mother's employment, "girls from high socioeconomic backgrounds and with high levels of academic achievement are less likely to strive for high occupational goals than boys with similarly high levels of these resources" (p. 747). Supporting this conclusion are data from a study in a midwestern high school ("Teenaged Boys," 1977), in which girls were found to "underplan their future occupational and educational goals" in relation to their academic ability. For example, the girls who anticipated working in the lowest-status occupations had higher grade point averages than the boys who anticipated working in medium-status occupations, so academic achievement did not reliably predict girls' occupational plans. Complementing these findings are those from a study of another sample of midwestern high school students (Danziger, 1983), in which boys' educational aspirations were found to be correlated with their grades, but not girls'. Neither grades nor achievement test scores were significantly related to girls' aspirations, which seemed to be more related to girls' perceptions of actual opportunities.

Studies designed to uncover predictors of occupational plans for girls have been uniformly unsuccessful, leading one investigator (Ihinger-Tallman, 1982), to conclude that "the variables affecting the . . . occupational-educational goals of young women continue to elude us" (p. 544). She observed parents in a laboratory situation as they played a career choice game with a son or daughter aged 12 to 15.

Although the boys and girls achieved similar "attainment value" scores in this game, encouragement from parents was relatively nonpredictive of girls' but considerably predictive of boys' job and income attainment.

Why are the variables that predict girls' occupational goals elusive and not the same as for boys? Is it because occupational goals for most girls are still secondary to finding a husband and supporting him in his movement up the "ladder of success"? In a study of more than 1,000 academically exceptional high school girls who were not planning to major in a science-related field in college (McClure & Piel, 1978), the researchers found that a main reason for not choosing science was "doubts about combining family life with a science career."

Traditional gender relationships, particularly in marriage and parenthood, continue to be anticipated by most teenagers. While many adolescents say they favor egalitarian marriages, their actual descriptions of expected responsibilities, especially for child care and home care, suggest that only a minority hold nontraditional views. A 5-year study of a national sample of teenagers (Canter & Ageton, 1984) found that boys are more traditional than girls, but that there is gender agreement "on the traditional division of labor," with the majority of both genders favoring "males as breadwinner and females as caretaker of home and family" (p. 673). National surveys of high school seniors (Bachman, 1987) have found a greater flexibility among seniors in 1986 than in 1976 with respect to family roles and nontraditional sex roles. Nevertheless, in contemplating "their own marriages, most young men and women don't think a mother should work outside the home full-time while her children are young" (p. 6). When a random sample of undergraduates in a midsize college was interviewed by telephone (Spade & Reese, 1991), both genders reported equally strong commitments to family and work, and both expected to postpone having a family until their late 20s. Nevertheless, congruent with the data obtained in earlier studies, the men were found to hold traditional values about women's home and work responsibilities, were more likely than the women to want their spouses to remain at home, saw their role in the workplace as most central to their future plans, and believed that their wives would have the stronger role in the family. The latter view was shared by the women. The authors concluded that "the value orientation of the men and women . . . interviewed do not support plans for symmetrical relationships in which both men and women share household and work responsibilities" (p. 319).

In general, then, it appears that (a) the occupational aspirations of the average adolescent girl are lower than those of the average adolescent boy; (b) girls' aspirations are typically not predictable from their abilities, high school grades, socioeconomic status, or other factors that relate reliably to boys' aspirations; and (c) these facts make sense in light of the gender ideology prevalent among teenagers, which continues to value traditional roles for women and men in marriage and family life.

The College Experience

Some research suggests that even those young women who begin college with educational and occupational goals similar to men's in prestige show a decline in aspirations as they proceed through college. Whether or not the women themselves value traditional roles, their experiences in college appear to diminish their occupational expectations. For example, Elsie Smith (1982) concluded from a review of relevant research that although African-American adolescent girls demonstrate "higher academic achievement and intellective development" than their male peers, and tend to have higher educational and career aspirations than comparable African-American male and European-American female high school students, these aspirations "begin to erode in college. The environmental press of the college or reassessment of the career opportunity structure appear to lead to traditional career goals for black college females" (p. 278).

Alexander Astin (1977) studied the effects of college on beliefs, attitudes, and knowledge in a 10-year investigation of approximately 200,000 students from 300 institutions and concluded that the undergraduate experience appears "to preserve, rather than to reduce, stereotypic differences between men and women in behavior, personality, aspirations, and achievement" (p. 216). He found that women persisted less in college and showed a decline in aspirations for advanced degrees, whereas men's aspirations for graduate training increased. Attending a women's college, however, may make a difference. Astin reported that students in women's colleges were more likely than those in coed schools to maintain, and even increase, their high aspirations and to persist to graduation. But Janet Giele (1984), in a study of more than 2,000 women who had graduated between 1934 and 1979 from either an elite women's college or a select coeducational college, found that the former, while more affluent, were less likely to have a career or an advanced degree and were more likely to have married and to have children. We will return to the effects of attending a women's college in a later chapter.

What about coed schools that are highly selective and that admit extremely competent and able women? A study of more than 3,000 undergraduates attending six prestigious schools in the northeast (Brown Project, 1980) reported that, compared with men, the women students lost ambition for graduate school or a professional career despite having entered college with aspirations as high as men's and despite having earned grades comparable to men's. Not only did women's aspirations decline relative to men's, but so did women's self-esteem. Although larger proportions of seniors than freshmen gave themselves high ratings on intellectual and social self-confidence and on academic ability, "women were markedly less likely than were men to give themselves high ratings on these three traits, and the proportion [of women] seeing themselves as highly motivated to achieve actually declined" (p. 87). With respect just to Brown University, for example, the researchers concluded that "in general, women enter Brown with a higher achievement level than men and exit with a lower achievement level. At the same time, they do not register gains in intellectual self-confidence to the same degree as do men" (p. 268).

How can we explain women's and men's differential experiences and outcomes in college? In a review of research, Roberta Hall and Bernice Sandler (1982, 1984) identified factors both within and outside the classroom that do not encourage women to the same extent as men and that tend to reduce women's aspirations and confidence.

> Despite women's gains in access to higher education . . . they frequently do not enjoy full equality of educational opportunity on campus. Students attest, and research confirms, that women students are often treated differently than men at all educational levels . . . even when they attend the same institutions, share the same classrooms, work with the same advisers, live in the same residence halls and use the same student services. (1984, p. 2)

Inequities in support services, employment, course-related experiences, and the residential, social, and cultural climate for women and men have been documented. Even college financial aid awards illustrate gender inequality. For example, for the year 1981–82, women were awarded 72 cents in grant money for every dollar awarded men ("Study Shows," 1984).

Sexual harassment has also been implicated as a factor that contributes to a problematic environment for college women. Arlene McCormack (1985), for example, asked a large sample of college students who were majoring in physical or social sciences in 16 different universities about their experiences of unwelcome sexual behavior by their teachers in high school and college; she obtained reports of such behavior from 17 percent of the women and 2 percent of the men. Victimization experiences increased for women as they continued their education, leading the investigator to conclude that "sexual harassment is widespread, not discussed, and appears as an accepted part of the academic environment" (p. 29). Similar data have come from a study at the University of Rhode Island (Reilly, Lott, & Gallogly, 1986). Almost one quarter of the junior, senior, and graduate women surveyed reported having personally received sexually suggestive looks or gestures from male instructors outside the classroom; almost one fifth reported unwanted sexual teasing, jokes, comments, or questions from male teachers; and more than 8 percent reported unwanted deliberate sexual touching. Men students surveyed reported very little personal experience of sexual harassment. The women said they responded to sexual harassment by attempting to handle it on their own or to avoid situations in which it occurred. In essence, then, the women students were being doubly victimized. As noted in an article in *Ms.* (Houppert, 1991), most students respond to sexual harassment silently, by transferring to another school, switching majors, or dropping a class. One student commented that "most women will continue to rebuke professors privately" (p. 57). An introduction to an annotated bibliography on sexual harassment in education (Crocker, 1982) pointed out that "sexual harassment in education is a frighteningly pervasive problem. For a woman, the injury . . . occurs when she is confronted by an educator whose concern is not with her intellectual growth but with the satisfaction of his own sexual needs and a desire for power" (p. 91).

It has been estimated (Dzeich & Weiner, 1984) that, overall, between 20 and 25 percent of the women attending college in the United States have been sexually harassed in some way (that is, offered unwelcome sexual attention) by their male professors. The director of women's studies at the University of Virginia, quoted in a *New York Times* story ("U. of Virginia Considers Wide Ban," 1993), called the "hitting on students" by faculty and staff "academia's dirty little secret" (p. Y-13). The incidence of such experiences seems to be similar for undergraduate and graduate students. In a survey of professional women clinical psychologists

(Glaser & Thorpe, 1986), it was found that 22 percent of recent doctoral recipients had had sexual relationships with an educator, and more than half of those who reported such a relationship currently saw it as coercive. In addition, sexual advances from teachers or supervisors were reported by 31 percent, most of whom judged these advances as harmful or negative in their effects. These data are similar to those reported in an earlier study (Pope, Levenson, & Schoer, 1979). Sexual harassment is experienced by women of all ages, not only in school, but also in social and recreational situations and on the job. Because of the problem's pervasiveness, this issue will be discussed more fully in later chapters.

Against this background of differential gender treatment and outcomes in education, it is important to note that women now generally outnumber men on college campuses in the United States at both the undergraduate and graduate levels. And, despite the accumulated data indicating that a college education is less instrumental for women than men in heightening ambitions and increasing self-confidence, it clearly does significantly benefit women with respect to occupation, income, and life-style. It is also true that reasons for attending college and hoped-for life plans or goals are increasingly similar for both genders. Thus, one study that compared data from 1967 and 1976 (Goldberg & Shiflett, 1981) concluded that both women and men in college are career-oriented. An analysis of data obtained from large national samples of students entering college between 1969 and 1984 found "a dramatic increase in the value that women place on status-attainment goals . . . [and] increasing congruence in the educational and occupational expectations of the sexes" (Fiorentine, 1988, p. 154). The author points out that nearly half of those who indicate that they aspire to advanced degrees are women.

Unfortunately, as we will see in later chapters and as some of the findings cited in this chapter indicate, a large gap exists for women between their aspirations as students entering college and their later achievement. We can begin to understand why this outcome is likely when we discover that most of today's college women want to combine work with marriage and motherhood. Thus, Judith Bridges (1987) found, among a large group of college women, that a role combining marriage, motherhood, and career was evaluated as more attractive than other role possibilities. Women's strong desire for motherhood will be explored in Chapter 10.

Variations among Adolescent Women

So far we have focused on gender comparisons in adolescents' aspirations and attitudes, but it is equally important to examine within-gender variations. Those who are nontraditional in their career choices, in their self-perceptions, and in their general views of what is gender-appropriate also tend to evaluate their abilities more highly, to have higher expectations for success, and to have higher aspirations than more traditional women. Nontraditional adolescent girls appear to have been encouraged and positively reinforced for their attitudes and choices and to have been successful in assertive and achievement-oriented behaviors. They may have had parents who provided direct reinforcement and mothers, or other salient women, who served as models.

One study (Baruch, 1976) found that 10th-grade girls who perceived themselves as very competent also had mothers whose self-perceptions of competence were high and who valued ambition, independence, and being a good student. Such girls also had higher career aspirations and wanted to have fewer children than did girls with lesser feelings of competence. Similar findings were reported in another study (Altman & Grossman, 1977); a group of female college seniors whose mothers worked at careers differed from a group whose mothers were homemakers in their career orientation and their broader conceptions of gender roles. "Daughters of [the] working mothers were unequivocal in asserting that work had provided a major source of satisfaction for their mothers" (p. 374). Some studies, however (e.g., Colangelo, Rosenthal, & Dettman, 1984), have found no significant relationships between the employment status of mothers and the aspirations of their daughters.

There is some evidence that certain beliefs or attitudes distinguish traditional from nontraditional adolescent girls more than background or parental characteristics do. For example, Mirra Komarovsky (1982) found, among a sample of students at an elite private women's college, that what distinguished career-oriented women from others was their greater endorsement of gender equality, lesser belief in gender stereotypes, greater support of the women's movement, greater autonomy and self-confidence, and lesser self-satisfaction. The two groups in this sample were found not to differ reliably on such variables as sexual orientation, high school dating, and mother's or father's education or employment. Data on 1,252 Latina high school seniors, from a national survey, who were followed after graduation (Cardoza, 1991) indicated that, for these women, educational aspiration was the most significant predictor of college attendance and persistence. Other important predictors included having a college-educated mother and willingness to delay marriage and child-bearing.

The influence of models on women's expectations is illustrated by the results of an experiment (Geis, Brown, Jennings [Walstedt], & Porter, 1984) in which some college students were exposed to a set of four TV commercials showing women and men in traditional roles while others viewed commercials in which traditional gender roles were reversed. Following this experience, in a seemingly unrelated task, the students wrote essays "imagining their lives and concerns 'ten years from now.'" When they found that the women who had seen the reversed-role commercials showed a more even balance between achievement and homemaking interests; their achievement scores were similar to those of men and significantly higher than those of the women who had watched the traditional commercials. A group of women who had not seen any of the commercials (the control group) wrote essays that emphasized homemaking, as did the women who had been exposed to the traditional commercials. So the researchers concluded that "the traditional stimulus commercials were not creating the effect, but simply reflecting a cultural image of women's place in society as secondary in relation to men" (p. 522).

We know from the data of social science and our own observations that large numbers of young women do not accept this message and that some manage to rise dramatically above their circumstances. Two novels, Alice Walker's (1982) *The Color Purple* and *Marya* by Joyce Carol Oates (1986), dealing with very different cultural circumstances, explore a young woman's process of development and show her succeeding in her quest for independence, confidence, and competence. The heroines of both stories are born poor, and one is African-American, but the process through which they acquire personal strength and transcend their place and situation is applicable to girls of other backgrounds who are attempting to forge their own rites of passage and find identities that best fit their abilities and interests.

MENTAL HEALTH AND DYSFUNCTIONAL BEHAVIOR

The heterosexual adolescent woman in contemporary U.S. society receives mixed messages about what is expected of her: to develop into a mature woman and, at the same time, to be her lover's "baby"; to be respectable and good and, at the same time, sexy and attractive to men; to be a responsible student or worker and, at the same time, to use campus and work connections to find a husband; to impress others with her self-confident personality and, at the same time, to take a back seat to men on serious matters having to do with public life. It is no wonder, then, that research has been documenting the disheartening phenomenon that adolescence for women often heralds the "twilight" of their self-esteem—their general feeling of well-being or self-worth (cf. Bower, 1991).

Beliefs about Self-Worth

Elizabeth Douvan and Anne Locksley ("Teenaged Boys," 1977), who studied problem behavior among high school youth, found that achievement was a major source of conflict for girls, and that girls reported a reliably higher frequency of feelings of tension and psychosomatic symptoms than boys. Although the girls generally achieved higher grades than the boys, more girls perceived their personal abilities as falling short of expectations, and they tended "to underplan their future occupational and educational goals" relative to their academic ability. In another investigation, eighth graders were required to write down how they were feeling each time a beeper they carried went off. The researchers (Savin-Williams & Demo, 1983) found that girls reported significantly less positive affect than boys. While the boys described themselves as powerful and in control, the girls saw themselves as tense and unsure. These findings are congruent with others. For example, in a longitudinal study (LaTorre, Yu, Fortin, & Marrache, 1983) of first-year junior high school students, girls were found at the end of the year to have increased in measures of neuroticism and alienation while boys' scores decreased.

One study (Webb & Van Devere, 1985) that obtained self-reports from a large sample of 11- to 18-year-old public school students found that girls report more unhappiness than boys, with this tendency increasing with school grade. The authors suggest that this phenomenon is related to "the growing awareness [among girls] of an incongruency between competing and conflicting social expectations" (p. 94). A national survey conducted by the American Association of University Women of 4th to 10th graders, which included almost 25 percent African-American and Hispanic-American students, measured self-esteem in a number of important areas, such as appearance, confidence, family relationships, school, talents, and personal importance. The results indicated that,

whereas "67 percent of elementary school boys reported 'always' feeling 'happy the way I am,' and 46 percent still felt that way by tenth grade," the figures for girls were dramatically different, dropping from 60 percent to 29 percent from elementary school to 10th grade (Bower, 1991, p. 184). Among the girls, European-Americans and Latinas showed the largest drops in all the self-esteem measures. The African-American girls self-reported high self-confidence and personal importance in both the early grades and high school but reported a substantial drop in confidence in their academic abilities as they got older. The conclusions drawn from this study have been debated, and all researchers do not agree that low general self-esteem characterizes more adolescent girls than boys. There is some evidence that girls and boys may behave similarly, but that girls are more likely to deny that they exert influence on others or have control or impact (Smye & Wine, 1980).

Some research has been concerned less with the question of gender comparisons and more with attempts to identify the factors related to adolescents' beliefs about self-worth, symptoms of unhappiness or depression, or both. From these studies has emerged a fairly clear understanding of the variables that promote a sense of well-being and those that promote confusion and self-doubt. A growing literature identifies instrumentality as a necessary ingredient, correlate, or antecedent of self-esteem. This personal attribute, defined by competence, effectiveness, and initiative, is often stereotyped as masculine, a subject to which we will return in a later chapter. Here must be mentioned two studies that relate specifically to adolescents. A longitudinal 6-month investigation (Towbes, Cohen, & Glyshaw, 1989) of 7th, 8th, 10th, and 11th graders, which included non-European-American students, found that for both genders and in all grades, low self-report scores on instrumentality were significant predictors of distress, anxiety, and depression, whereas high scores were positively related to self-esteem. Similarly, Carol Markstrom-Adams (1989) reported that for adolescents of both genders, psychosocial well-being was related to self-reported "mastery of the external world, vocational identity, ideological identity, physical competence, achievement motivation, computer arcade playing, and sports participation" (p. 338).

Other researchers have found that adolescent girls and boys self-report different emotional experiences (e.g., Stapley & Haviland, 1989) and different depressive symptoms (e.g., Baron & Joly, 1988). Janice Stapley and Jeannette Haviland's study of 5th, 7th, 9th, and 11th graders, including minority students, found that girls were more likely to self-report "inner-directed negative emotions" such as shyness, shame, guilt, sadness, and self-hostility, whereas boys were more likely to self-report "outer-directed negative emotions" like contempt. These data are congruent with those from Pierre Baron and Elisabeth Joly's study, a survey of a sample of 7th to 12th graders in Quebec. Boys' self-reported symptoms included irritability, work inhibition, and social withdrawal, compared with girls' reports of body image distortion, loss of appetite, and weight loss.

The salience of body image for teenage girls is well known, of course, to any observer of contemporary society—to any visitor to our high schools, magazine reader, or TV viewer. We will return to a discussion of eating-related problems among women in a later chapter but at this point we must take note of a report issued by the federal Centers for Disease Control of findings from a nationwide survey of almost 12,000 students in grades 9 to 12 (cf. "A Third of High School Girls" 1991). This study found that 34 percent of high school girls, compared with only 15 percent of boys, consider themselves to be overweight. Thus, girls seriously overestimate the extent to which their weight is too high. This is further indicated by the finding that 44 percent of high school girls reported trying to lose weight, "including 27 percent of those who think they're the right weight already." Among all the girls, "80 percent said they had, in the past, gone on exercise regimens in a deliberate attempt to lose weight; 21 percent said they'd taken diet pills and 14 percent said they'd vomited to lose pounds" (p. A-5). A longitudinal study of almost 200 European-American girls in grades 7 to 10 (Attie & Brooks-Gunn, 1989) concluded that eating problems emerged in response to natural (or normal) pubertal body changes. "[T]he rapid accumulation of fat that is part of the female experience of puberty may function as a triggering event, insofar as it elicits the first of perhaps many attempted weight-loss diets" (p. 76). This response is hardly surprising in view of the visual images and stories in magazines and other media that capture the attention of teenage girls and focus on appearance.

Another significant area of problem behavior for adolescent women that has become more recognized in recent years is that of alcohol abuse. According to Iris Litt (1992), an "alarming increase in drinking by adolescent females" has taken place while physicians in general continue to lack training in the detection and management of alcohol use by teenagers. Surveys of high school seniors in 1975 and 1989 indicate a narrowing in the earlier gender difference in the prevalence of alcohol use. For example, by age 19, 90 percent of men and 80 percent of women admit that they are drinking alcohol. While the percentage of heavy drinking by adolescent males decreased in the period between the two surveys, the percentage of heavy drinking by teenage women increased.

Teenage Pregnancies

In addition to an exaggerated concern with eating, dieting, body image, and appearance and shaky self-confidence across many areas, a major personal and social problem for some adolescent women is that of pregnancy. That an adolescent girl's sexuality is no less insistent a concern and no less a source of pleasure than it is for an adolescent boy is increasingly accepted today; but at the same time sex is still often seen as something girls "give" to boys. We will explore more fully issues related to sexuality in Chapter 6; we focus here on the pressures encountered by teenage girls that appear to have consequences for pregnancy and teenage motherhood.

The theme of sexual intercourse as a gift that teenage girls can bestow on their boyfriends appears frequently in the magazine stories and books that teenagers read. Gayle Nelson (1975) analyzed the five novels that were most commonly read by the girls in her 11th- and 12th-grade classes and found that the young women in these books were primarily concerned with clothes, dates, diets, "and whatever makes them more attractive and pleasing to the boys." In each book the heroine was depicted as coming from a nice, middle-class, conventional family and as submitting "begrudgingly to a boy's demand for sexual relations" (p. 54). Each girl was presented as having been "acted upon" and as unable to stand up for her own values. All five heroines were eventually punished; one girl died, while the other four became pregnant.

More than a million American girls between 12 and 19 have been getting pregnant each year during the past few years. Of this number, about 50 percent complete their pregnancies and have babies; half of these mothers are not married. The pregnancy rate among girls aged 15 to 19 increased from 99 per thousand in 1974 to 111 per thousand in 1980 ("Nation Ignoring Problem," 1986), and for girls under 15 from 15.9 per thousand in 1980 to 18.6 per thousand in 1987 ("Fewer Teenagers," 1991), with fewer girls in this age group choosing abortion (1,408 for each thousand live births in 1980, and 949 for each thousand births in 1988). Elizabeth Stark (1986b) has summarized these statistics simply as follows: "One out of ten teenage girls in the United States becomes pregnant every year and almost half of these pregnancies result in births—30,000 of them to girls under the age of 15" (p. 28). The latest figures, as of this writing, indicate a decrease in live births to unmarried teenage girls between the ages of 15 and 19 from 1970, when the rate was 68.3 per 1,000 girls, to 1980, when the rate was 53.0, but then a jump in 1990 to a rate of 59.9 per 1,000 girls ("The Children of the Shadows," 1993).

According to a 2-year study by the National Research Council Panel on Adolescent Pregnancy (cf. Landers, 1987), girls under 15 in the United States are five times more likely to give birth than comparable girls in other developed countries, a fact attributed by the authors of the report to the greater availability of low-cost or free contraceptives in other countries, "where teen pregnancy is viewed more as a health issue than a moral issue" (p. 6). In all age groups, the rates of adolescent pregnancy, abortion, and childbearing are considerably higher in the United States than in comparable countries.

Researchers who have attempted to identify some of the factors responsible for the high rate of adolescent pregnancy in the United States have concluded that level of sexual activity is not implicated, nor is the level of support provided to pregnant mothers. In the other industrialized countries, which have lower rates of teenage pregnancy, more maternity and welfare benefits are available than under the U.S. program of Aid to Families with Dependent Children. What seems most important is the far lesser use of birth control by teenagers in the United States. A Harris poll (cf. "Poll Shows," 1986) found that U.S. teenagers believe easy and free access to contraceptives would increase their use and that teenagers need more adequate sex education.

This conclusion agrees with other information from studies of teenage pregnancy in the United States. A reviewer of the research literature (Phipps-Yonas, 1980) concluded that "there is no unique psychological profile common to most, much less all, pregnant adolescents" (p. 407). Studies indicate that most adolescent pregnancies result from "a quick, often unsatisfying try at sex" (DiPerna, 1984) and that teenagers know about contraceptives but are uncomfortable with them because of their potential danger to health (IUDs and birth control pills) or their messiness (diaphragms, foams, and condoms). There appear to be no peculiarities or special attributes of individual teenagers who get pregnant. The teenagers who get pregnant typically have not planned to have sex. For most of one group of teenage mothers interviewed in New York (DiPerna, 1984), "pregnancy just happened, and most of them didn't believe it when it did" (p. 62).

Others who have studied or worked with pregnant teenagers have suggested that, especially for very young adolescents, the cause of the pregnancy is not eager sexuality but sexual abuse (Barnes, 1989). Other teenagers may see having a baby as a route to adulthood. Related to this is the hopelessness widespread in poor ghetto communities in which young people have little expectation of getting a good job and feel isolated from the larger culture. Harriet Presser (1980) interviewed more than 300 unmarried mothers in New York City in a 3-year study and found evidence strongly suggesting that early parenthood was often a means of achieving adult status in the absence of attainable and desirable employment. A baby can make an adolescent girl feel like an adult and a caregiver, someone of significance and importance in the life of another, and a person from whom competence is expected. One study (Falk, Gispert, & Baucom, 1981) compared a group of pregnant 15- and 16-year-old single African-American girls planning to have their babies with a similar group of girls planning to have abortions and a control group of girls who were not pregnant. Those who planned to have their babies were found to differ from the others on measures that suggested that they were "attempting to fill some void and to demonstrate that they are women by assuming the role of a mother . . . [and] striving to gain status" (p. 744). The previously mentioned report by the National Research Council Panel on Adolescent Pregnancy also noted the probable role played by poverty and feelings of hopelessness in leading some "disadvantaged young people to believe there is no reason to postpone sex or parenthood" (Landers, 1987, p. 6). The conclusion that teenage pregnancy is linked to limited opportunities and a bleak future is shared by other researchers. As noted by Elizabeth Stark (1986b), "Almost everyone who has looked at the problem agrees that poverty-stricken teenagers need to know that opportunities await them before they can be motivated to avoid pregnancy" (p. 35).

That the young men who become teenage fathers are not simply the no-good, macho, irresponsible louts our stereotypes suggest, and that their motivation for parenthood may be similar to that of teen mothers, is suggested by the results of a study of such fathers in 15 cities across the United States (cf. "Teenage Fathers," 1985). Among these fathers, 82 percent reported daily contact with their children even though they lived apart, 74 percent reported contributing to their children's financial support, and 90 percent said they had a continuing relationship with their children's mothers. Another researcher, Irma Hilton (cf. Stark, 1986b), found that teen fathers were generally pleased about their girlfriends' pregnancies, viewing them as an affirmation of the fathers' manhood.

Teenage pregnancy is understandable when we realize that it is compatible with the values and beliefs acquired by young women. If an adolescent girl believes that it is a man's world and that status comes from having a boyfriend; if her sense of self or identity is waiting upon a future role as wife and mother; if she wants to please and be popular and to satisfy the needs of others; if her values are tentative and flexible; if she believes that having a baby and caring for it are the primary signs of womanhood; if she has little reason to expect success in the workplace or good employment opportunities; and if, at the same time, she is confused and uncertain about the various contraceptive options, does not have easy and inexpensive access to them, and is ambivalent about her sexuality—then early motherhood becomes a real possibility. Some research findings support this proposed link between teenage pregnancy and traditional views about gender. Carol Ireson (1984) compared pregnant with nonpregnant but sexually active teenagers and found that the former were more traditional and sex-typed in their activities and educational expectations, as well as being lower in socioeconomic status. In another study, my student Donna Caldwell (1988) compared a group of teen mothers with a group of sexually active teenage women who were using contraception successfully; she found that the teenage mothers had significantly more traditional sex-role beliefs and had also been more sexually victimized.

Added to traditional beliefs and attitudes, which have been with us for a long time, is the increasing sexualization of teenage culture, the increasing age at which couples marry, and a greater visibility of unwed mothers. In the 1950s, as described in a novel by Alice McDermott (1987), unmarried pregnant teens "fell somewhere between criminals and patients and, like criminals and patients, they were prescribed an exact and fortifying treatment: They were made to disappear" (p. 90). If they didn't quickly marry, they were sent to stay with relatives in other cities or states, or to church-run "homes" for unwed mothers; after giving birth, their babies were typically put up for adoption. The situation today is very different; "only one-third of pregnant teenage girls marry the fathers of their children and few consider adoption" (Stark, 1986b, p. 34).

Regardless of the possible pregnancy outcome, contemporary girls face strong pressure to have heterosexual experience at an earlier age than was the case for their mothers and grandmothers. This expectation is transmitted by their peers and the media (especially pop music, movies, and television) and reinforced by their belief that "everyone else is doing it." We will consider this matter more fully in Chapter 6.

CONFLICT AND RESOLUTION

A contemporary adolescent woman will inevitably have to deal with a special kind of dilemma toward which all the years of her life in our culture have propelled her. How she solves the conflict alluded to throughout this chapter will be determined by the particular ways she has been socialized, and by the behaviors she has been able to practice and that are reinforced in her current environment.

A conflict exists when a person must choose between two or more possible objectives that are incompatible and that cannot be attained at the same time. Choosing one means giving up, for the time being, at any rate, the other(s). For a young heterosexual woman, such a conflict is posed by the simultaneous attractiveness of the goals of independence and public achievement, on the one hand, and attaining the cultural ideal for women—identification with a man and homemaking—on the other. Either can bring rewards, but moving in the direction of one goal may mean giving up the other. This is a classic approach-approach conflict, which can be solved only when one goal becomes more attractive and stronger, or when circumstances propel the individual toward one goal and the positive consequences that follow are sufficient to tip the balance in its favor, albeit, perhaps, only temporarily.

We can analyze the conflict a bit differently by examining the variety of consequences likely to follow from attainment of each of the opposing goals. A girl attracted by independence and personal achievement may anticipate positive consequences from their attainment such as recognition, financial rewards, fulfillment, and enhanced self-esteem, but she may also have learned to expect negative social judgment from some who will regard her as less feminine and, therefore, as a less attractive, or more threatening, marriage partner. This consequence is a powerfully punishing one for most young women. In one of the quotations that opened this chapter, Rosellen Brown (1976) shared the thoughts of a fictional young woman, Renata, who recalls feeling terrified when her botany teacher told her she had talent. Renata associated talent with unattractiveness, remembering her botany teacher as "scrawny" with "chapped cheeks and . . . short fingernails," and also with the loneliness of her mother, who was a successful but divorced lawyer.

Negative portraits of career women appear everywhere, including the Sunday comics. One study (Mooney & Brabant, 1987) found the career woman presented in six family-oriented comic strips to be "rather 'hard,' 'unfeminine,' and 'mannish' in her appearance . . . castrating to males . . . , and . . . critical of her husband." The unmistakable message was that "if you are a woman and you want a happy home, do not have a career" (p. 419). On the other hand, in the 1980s TV shows began to show an increasing number of women with jobs outside the home and an increasing number of family-focused nurturing men ("New TV," 1984), a trend that shows signs of reversal in the 1990s.

An individual who expects the same objective to bring both positive and negative consequences of relatively equal strength confronts an approach-avoidance conflict and experiences ambivalence. In such a situation, we tend to move back and forth, first approaching and then retreating from the objective; picture a child on the beach at the water's edge, rushing toward the waves, then immediately running back. Such a conflict can be resolved only when the anticipated (or actual) positive consequences become stronger than the negative ones, or vice versa. Then the ambivalence diminishes, and the person moves forward in pursuit of the positively valued goal or gives it up entirely because its consequences will be too painful.

An approach-avoidance conflict also confronts the contemporary young woman who opts for the traditional role, finding the alternative of independence and achievement relatively unattractive and anticipating personal happiness and fulfillment from the role society considers more appropriate for her. She can anticipate approval and love, a home, a husband-companion, children, financial security, possessions and perhaps luxuries, leisure (for socializing, for helping with community activities, or for doing creative, artistic work), and the vicarious pleasure to be attained through the successes of her husband and children. But today's adolescent girl can also anticipate negative consequences. She knows that as a full-time homemaker her status, power, and influence will be low; her ability to cope with many situations will be impaired; and she may, like other women she sees around her, one day fall victim to the malaise and discontent of middle-class homemakers or be faced with severe economic hardship if she loses her husband through death or divorce.

What has been described is really a double approach-avoidance conflict, as illustrated in Figure 4.1, the most

Public Achievement versus Homemaking

+/– ←————⊚————→ +/–

Anticipated consequences of public achievement	Anticipated consequences of homemaking
Positive	*Positive*
Autonomy	Love/marriage
Excellence	Security
Self-esteem	Vicarious success
Negative	*Negative*
Less chance of marriage	Boredom/discomfort
Less chance of parenthood	Low status/power
Reduced "femininity"	Spouse-derived identity

FIGURE 4.1 *The double approach-avoidance conflict faced by many adolescent women.*

complex and difficult type of conflict to resolve. Resolution is most difficult for those young women who have become competent in nondomestic areas and who have been encouraged to be independent by their parents or other significant persons, but who have also been strongly influenced by the traditional dominant ideology through peer expectations and media models. When a double approach-avoidance conflict cannot be resolved, the person may turn her back on both alternatives and withdraw, unable or unwilling to make a decision. My daughter Sara described such a retreat in adolescence (S. Lott, 1978).

> Mountain peaks—
> strong and serene,
> guide me toward mellow solitude,
> hold me in their power,
> hide me in the land;
> far, far, away . . .
> Moods and energy
> spread themselves out peacefully.
> The mountain calm
> heals,
>   soothes,
>   dissolves all worries into
> tiny particles
> sliding slowly away
> into thin cold air.

Withdrawal, in the form of physical or psychological departure (fantasy), effectively removes the person from the conflict situation until circumstances require that it must again be confronted.

The dilemma faced by today's adolescent girl may not be as exaggerated and extreme as the one illustrated in Figure 4.1, but its ingredients are real. And some adolescent girls do not experience the conflict at all and approach both objectives with equal commitment, anticipating primarily positive outcomes from the attainment of both. Others experience no ambivalence during certain times in their lives, and great ambivalence earlier or later. Some young women are able to take advantage of a comfortable, socially sanctioned delay period prior to making long-range decisions—the period of college study or of job experience before marriage. During these years, successes and failures provide learning experiences that influence later choices by reinforcing particular behaviors or altering the relative strengths of the anticipated positive

and negative consequences. For some young women, public achievement and the pursuit of homemaking may not be incompatible alternatives, and both may be approached without fear of negative consequences.

Some reason exists for optimism about the possibilities for resolving these dilemmas, both for older women who have reevaluated their previous life-styles and acquired new skills and interests and for younger contemporary women now entering or leaving adolescence. For example, contemporary young people of both genders seem to perceive smart, accomplished, and professional women in nontraditional fields as physically attractive. In one study (Lanier & Byrne, 1981), high school students were asked to select, from a group of 20 photographs, those women who were engineers, lawyers, doctors, oceanographers, architects, and executives. Another group of students was asked to select from the same photographs those women who, in high school, had taken mechanical drawing, physics, calculus, chemistry, and political science. They

A reflective teenager, perhaps contemplating her future. (Photograph by Sylvia Plachy.)

asked a third group to divide the photographs into two batches, of more attractive and less attractive women. Judgments of attractiveness, of having taken nontraditional courses, and of working in nontraditional fields were strongly related. These findings suggest that high-achieving women may no longer be viewed as unattractive oddities, and hence the choice of public achievement goals may no longer be strongly associated with the negative consequences of decreased likelihood of marriage and family. On the other hand, a study by Karen Pfost and Maria Fiore (1990) provides little reason to assume widespread change in the perception of women who pursue nontraditional occupations. The responses of a college sample, which included non-European-American students, to descriptions of hypothetical students indicated that women preparing for nontraditional careers were judged by both women and men to be the least desirable heterosexual romantic partners. Nontraditional women were also less likely to be chosen as friends by other women, well illustrating the serious negative social consequences that nontraditional women are likely to suffer.

The less an adolescent girl accepts gender stereotypes, the less willing she will be to choose between the alternatives of doing personally fulfilling work and having a satisfying family life. Most young women today say they want both. The American dream of the young woman shown on p. 90 may be that of combining love with autonomy, connectedness with independence and adventure. Some young women are committed to pursuing both love and relationships and believe, as Patricia Spacks (1981) has argued, that "the ends they seek—independence, control, love—characterize all adolescents—indeed all human beings" (pp. 119f). Many adolescent women believe that, while not easy, it should be possible to attain both satisfying work and family life. And some have also learned that a family is not solely defined by a heterosexual couple with children but also by any number of persons of the same or different generations who care for one another and try to meet one another's personal needs.

◆ Discussion Questions

1. What does femininity mean to adolescent girls? Discuss some variations in these definitions.

2. What gender-related socialization pressures are (a) continued from childhood and (b) new to adolescence?

3. What is learned during adolescence about the differential value of women and men?

4. What special issues and situations face adolescents from different ethnic groups and from different social classes?

5. What are the likely consequences for adolescent women who put relationships ahead of achievement, and vice versa?

6. What is the possible relationship between teen pregnancies and subscribing to gender stereotypes?

CHAPTER 5

MENSTRUATION: POWER, CURSE, OR NATURAL RHYTHM

What would happen . . . if suddenly . . . men could menstruate and women could not?

The answer is clear—menstruation would become an enviable, boast-worthy, masculine event:

Men would brag about how long and how much.

Boys would mark the onset of menses, that longed-for proof of manhood, with religious ritual and stag parties. . . .

Military men, right-wing politicians, and religious fundamentalists would cite menstruation ("men-struation") as proof that only men could serve in the Army ("you have to give blood to take blood"), occupy political office ("can women be aggressive without that steadfast cycle governed by the planet Mars?"), be priests and ministers ("how could a woman give her blood for our sins?"), or rabbis ("without the monthly loss of impurities, women remain unclean").

GLORIA STEINEM (1978b, p. 110)

A flurry of research has found that men, too, suffer waves of hormones—in this case, testosterone. . . . At last men, here's an opening for equal opportunity boorishness.

Why should women be the only sex with license to act like total jerks, then explain: "I couldn't help it, it was just that time."

JUDY ROSE (1990, p. B-3)

OUR GRANDMOTHERS, AND MANY OF OUR MOTH-
ers, did not talk much about menstruating.
Except for occasional reminiscences about the
"first time," how it was handled, what was said,
and the fear or pride it invoked, menstruation was
not typically a subject of much conversation. Yet, for all
the years from puberty to menopause, normally functioning human females of all classes, cultures, and geographic
areas menstruate approximately every 28 to 31 days.
Contemporary women, who are generally healthier than
those of previous generations, reach puberty considerably earlier and normally menstruate for about four
decades (from about age 12 to 52), excluding months of
pregnancy.

Interest in exploring the significance of this uniquely
female experience is growing. Chroniclers of women's
lives in fiction or autobiography have more and more
begun to include in their accounts some attention to
menstrual experiences. Scholarship in this area has also
steadily increased. This new concern can be related to the
influence of the feminist movement, the extraordinary
publicity generated by premenstrual syndrome (or PMS),
and the heightened advertising campaigns of manufacturers with a wide array of menstrual-related products. Five
or six decades ago menstrual supplies consisted of a
"sanitary belt" (a contraption worn around your waist
with two safety pins) to hold a "sanitary napkin"; now
advertisers proclaim the virtues of a variety of different
tampons, maxipads and minipads (in scented and un-
scented varieties), pantyliners, and sea sponges. Relief
from menstrual distress was once rather timidly advertised
by just one pharmaceutical company; now the market has
expanded to include at least a dozen competing brand
names. Supplying women with "personal hygiene" products and drugs to be used prior to or during menstruation,
or both, is big business.

Bonnie Bullough (1974) has described the history of
public attention to menstruation and how it was brought
"out of the closet."

> The belief that menstruating women were unclean,
> cursed, or jinxed is as old as recorded history. Even those
> women in the past who were emancipated enough to
> ignore popular superstitions about menstruation were
> handicapped in their activities by the physical fact. They
> made various kinds of diapers and pads for themselves,
> but one of the reasons they wore so many petticoats
> was to cut down possible odors and hide the bulges;
> inevitably they also cut out many physical activities. . . .
> For this reason the development of the modern dispos-
> able, hygienic, and comparatively inexpensive sanitary

> napkin . . . was an important breakthrough in the eman-
> cipation of women. It first appeared on the market in 1920
> as a direct result of the development of cellucotton prod-
> ucts for surgical dressings during World War I. . . . The
> Kimberly Clark Company hit upon the concept of selling
> them as sanitary pads under the name of Kotex. To be
> effectively merchandised the company had to bring the
> subject out in the open. . . . One of the first effects of the
> introduction of the pad was the shedding of petticoats by
> women, and it was no accident that the new age of the
> emancipated flapper coincided with the introduction of
> Kotex and its competitors. (p. 345)

The availability of tampons (invented in 1933) has
been accompanied by other dramatic changes in women's
clothing such as the widespread wearing of pants, jeans,
and miniskirts, and increased participation of women in
sports and physical activities. Do such changes suggest
that women now take the facts of menstruation more or
less for granted, adapting to its monthly occurence and
giving it little more attention than the periodic rituals of
bathing or teeth brushing? Or is menstruation still overlaid
with superstition and unpleasantness, with anticipations
of tension and irritability? As we shall see, menstruation
denotes a set of relatively clear physiological changes, but
it connotes much more, and it cannot be understood
without considering the acquired beliefs and attitudes
associated with it.

PUBERTY

For most girls, menarche (the first menses) is the most
obvious signal of the beginning of puberty, but it "actually
occurs relatively late in a process that takes about four
years" (Petersen, 1983, p. 65). Body changes associated
with puberty occur between the ages of 9 and 16 and
include an increase in body hair, weight gain, a growth
spurt, increased activity of sweat glands, the growth of
uterus and vagina, and changes in body proportions.
Breast buds begin forming at about age 11, influenced by
secretion of estrogen by the ovaries and prolactin by the
pituitary (Golub, 1983).

Menarche typically occurs after the first stages of pubic
hair and breast development and after the peak spurt in
height. Menarche indicates that the female's reproductive
system is being readied to expel mature egg cells (ova)
from the ovaries on a periodic basis. These ova have been
contained within the ovaries since before birth; the average
girl will have about 75,000 (Weideger, 1976). At puberty,
the ovaries begin their heightened manufacture of estro-

gen, which will change the ratio of female to male hormones from the relative equality of childhood. For the average girl, estrogen production begins to increase at about age 11 and begins to take cyclical form about 18 months prior to menarche. Accompanying these hormonal changes are a growth spurt and the familiar secondary sex characteristics associated with femaleness, beginning with breast development.

Some new research (cf. Kolata, 1984a) has suggested that the onset of puberty in both sexes may be related to a decrease in nocturnal secretions of the hormone melatonin from the pineal gland, a small structure near the center of the brain. The precise role of melatonin is not yet established, however, and the question of what specifically initiates the menarche has no definitive answer. One hypothesis, proposed by Rose Frisch (cf. Weideger, 1976; cf. Golub, 1983), is that the triggering mechanism is a critical weight (somewhere between 94 and 103 pounds) and a critical lean-to-fat body composition ratio (about 22 to 24 percent fat). During puberty, up to the time of menarche, body fat typically increases by 120 percent. By the time regular ovulation has been established—one to two years after menstruation has begun—28 percent of the composition of a girl's body will consist of fat tissue. Somehow the lean-to-fat ratio signals the hypothalamus to begin, and then to maintain, the regular menstrual cycle. That estrogen is synthesized from the cholesterol component of body fat serves to strengthen Frisch's hypothesis about a link between the menarche and body fat.

The average age of first menstruation has been steadily declining in the United States; it is now 12.3 years, with a range from 9 to 17 (Bullough, 1983), and one third of all girls now reach menarche at or before age 11. Good nutrition is reliably associated with physical and sexual maturity, and it appears likely that improved diet, hygiene, and health are responsible for the steady lowering of the age of first menstruation. For example, one study (Goodman, et al., reported in Golub, 1983) found no differences in age at menarche among samples of European, Chinese, and Japanese women living in relatively similar circumstances in Hawaii, supporting the role played by nutritional factors.

CULTURAL SIGNIFICANCE AND BELIEFS ABOUT MENSTRUATION

In most known cultures and historical periods the onset of menstruation has signified to girls, their parents, and the community that the female child is now reproductively mature. Menstruation affirms biological femaleness and the possibility of childbearing, and menstruating persons are distinguished from others in all cultures.

Meanings in Our Culture

Menstruation clearly divides the sexes after childhood and leads to heightened awareness of gender identity. For example, postmenarcheal girls were found in one study (Rierdan, Koff, & Silverstone, 1978) to differ significantly from premenarcheal girls in their drawings of human figures. Comparing different girls, as well as the same girls at different ages, those who had begun to menstruate drew more sexually differentiated figures and more frequently drew a female figure before a male figure. The importance of menstruation to women is highlighted by the finding (Golub & Catalano, reported in Golub, 1983) that a sample of women from 18 to 45 years old clearly remembered their first menstruation and "could describe in detail where they were when it happened, what they were doing, and whom they told" (pp. 17f.)

Since menstruation signifies adult sexuality and reproductive capacity, we might suppose that this indication of female maturity would be culturally interpreted as a symbol of positive power. What we more typically find is the imposition of greater restrictions on girls' freedom of movement, the belief that menstruation is unclean, and increased gender socialization pressures. Parents often begin at this time to curtail and restrain their daughters and to keep a sharper eye on their activities. That menstruation has been associated with restrictions is illustrated by the advice given in films and pamphlets written to instruct menstruating girls on how to care for themselves. A teenage girl in the 1950s might have received, in reply to a postcard to Personal Products Corporation (1957), a free 28-page booklet entitled *Growing Up and Liking It* that urged her to laugh off some "old wives' tales"—for instance, that you shouldn't have a tooth filled while you're menstruating, that loss of menstrual blood weakens you, that you should spend a day or two in bed, and that cold drinks give you cramps. But she would have been alerted to look for a "few little signals" just before menstruation—such as experiencing the "blues," a lack of pep, a backache, or cramps—and been advised to stay out of drafts, not to get a chill, and to dance with moderation.

Comparisons between such earlier messages and more current advice to menstruating girls in pamphlets and educational films indicates that today's messages are more focused on the need to deodorize and sanitize (Delaney,

SYLVIA. From *Mercy, It's the Revolution and I'm in My Bathrobe*, Nicole Hollander, copyright© 1982, St. Martin's Press, Inc., New York, NY. Reprinted by permission of the publisher.

Lupton, & Toth, 1977). This kind of contemporary advice is illustrated by an advertisement in *Seventeen* (FDS, 1984) that informs its teenage readers that a woman's body chemistry doesn't just change during menstruation "but every day," so that she needs a feminine deodorant spray to neutralize and absorb "embarrassing odors." The Nicole Hollander cartoon shown above satirizes this sort of message.

How do today's women feel about menstruation? Pat Barker, in the novel *Union Street* (1983), described the reaction of the character Kelly to the discovery of her sister's used sanitary napkins; Kelly decided that "she certainly didn't want to drip foul-smelling, brown blood out of her fanny every month" (p. 3). Kelly's response, though extreme, does not differ from some among a sample of seventh- and eighth-grade middle-class girls in Boston reported by Elissa Koff and Jill Rierdan (cf. Rubenstein, 1980). Postmenarcheal girls described the first menses of a hypothetical girl as a time when "she wanted to cry, die, or throw up." These girls "seemed especially self-conscious about concealing their condition, and intensely apprehensive about being discovered or being messy or unclean" (p. 38). Similarly, Jeanne Brooks-Gunn and Diane Ruble (cf. Golub, 1983) found mostly negative beliefs about menstruation among seventh and eighth graders of both genders: "Most believed that menstruation is accompanied by physical discomfort, increased emotionality, and a disruption of activities" (p. 27). Lenore Williams (1983) reported that 68 percent of a sample of 9- to 12-year-old girls of varied socioeconomic status believed menstruation to be related to increased emotionality. Other researchers (Woods, Dery, & Most, 1983) asked adult women to recall how they had

felt about their first menstruation. Their recollections revealed ambivalence; most had felt happy (58 percent) and proud (65 percent) but also upset (67 percent) and scared (74 percent). The most frequently reported feeling was that of embarrassment (82 percent). When a sample of adult women were asked to disclose their current feelings about menstruation (Hays, 1987), 54 percent of the responses were categorized as negative, compared with 4.5 percent as positive, and 41.4 percent as neutral.

In a national survey by Tampax of more than 1,000 persons 14 years of age and older (Milow, 1983), it was found that two thirds of the respondents believed menstruation was not a suitable subject for discussion socially or at work; two fifths of the women recalled having had a negative reaction to their first menses; one third believed that menstruation affects a woman's ability to think; and more than one fourth thought that women cannot function normally at work while menstruating. Men's and women's beliefs were found to be generally similar.

In a later section in this chapter we will look at the empirical evidence and find that menstrual "blues" may be more influenced by their anticipation and by other sociopsychological factors than by cyclical physiological changes. But regardless of the evidence, negative attitudes as well as erroneous beliefs persist. Such persistence is understandable in light of our culture's earlier adherence to myths. For example, well into the early part of this century, "some authorities continued to urge . . . that women should not become doctors . . . because menstruation rendered them virtually unclean" (Sayers, 1987, p. 71). Such urging occurred despite the fact that "as early as 1877, women physician-researchers conducted empirical studies concluding that menstruation posed little obstacle to work and social function" (Zimmerman, 1987, p. 451). One of these early studies was conducted by psychologist Leta Hollingworth. Her doctoral research in 1914, which utilized ongoing daily reports by participants who did not know she was studying mental and physical correlates of the menstrual cycle, found no support "for the widespread belief that women suffered periodic incapacity in their physical and intellectual abilities" (Rosenberg, 1984, p. 89).

The continued existence of cover-up expressions, or euphemisms, for menstruation attests to the ambivalence we feel about it. Virginia Ernster (1975) collected euphemisms for menstruation over a period of 10 years from adolescents and adults of both genders and found that negative expressions such as "the curse," "the misery," "unwell," and "under the weather," constituted the largest category of euphemisms contributed by women. Among men, the most common menstrual euphemisms were variations of "on the rag" or "flying the flag." More recently, Terence Hays (1987) reported that the three most commonly used euphemisms by women were "period," "friend," and "that time of the month."

Meanings in Older Cultures

M. Esther Harding (1972) has suggested that in earlier times women were thought to be connected with the moon and its cycles. Woman's power to bear children "was thought to be the gift of the moon" and "her monthly rhythm, corresponding as it does with the moon's cycle, must have seemed the obvious result of some mysterious bond between them" (p. 25). Some cultures have identified the moon as female, and in others the words for menstruation and for moon are the same or are closely related. Perhaps because of this connection, women's blood has been viewed as having powerful effects, as illustrated by negative myths and taboos. Cultural prohibitions include those against cooking food for men, sexual intercourse, religious participation, contact with men preparing for battle or a hunt, or even being in the same room with a man. The Roman writer Pliny warned his readers that menstrual blood would turn new wine sour, dry up seeds in gardens, and kill hives of bees; "to taste it drives dogs mad and infects their bites with an incurable poison" (Delaney, Lupton, & Toth, 1976, p 7).

Even in older cultures that were matrilineal (such as the native American Crow), where women had acknowl-

edged power and rights and occupied positions of high status, the fact of menstruation was used to exclude them from important areas of community life. "Ultimately the line is drawn; menstruation is [considered] a threat to warfare, one of the most valued institutions of the tribe, one that is central to their self-definition" (Ortner, 1974, p. 70).

Many older cultures associate menstruation with contamination, potential evil, and uncleanness. Lois Paul (1974) described a girl's introduction to womanhood at the age of 13 or 14 in a Guatemalan village as follows:

> When a girl suddenly finds herself bleeding and comes crying to her mother, she is given an old rag as protection and told to expect such bleeding each month. . . . No further explanation is given her . . . except for the warning never to divulge the secret of her bleeding to any male and never let any male see her bloody rag, or catch her washing it. Because a girl's blood is "hot" when she is menstruating, she is told not to look directly at infants, turkey chicks, or sprouting beans lest these sicken and die. (p. 291)

That such ideas existed across cultures and persisted across many centuries of social change is illustrated by Simone de Beauvoir's (1961/1949) report of a rule in the refineries of northern France that "forbade women having 'the curse' to enter . . . for that would cause the sugar to blacken." In rural French districts, she noted, "every cook knows that a mayonnaise will not be successful if a menstruating woman is about; some rustics believe cider will not ferment, others that bacon cannot be salted and will spoil" (p. 149). One investigator (Skultans, 1979) was told by a group of 50-year-old women in a small mining village in Australia that each month during menstruation they purged themselves of "bad blood." If they had a "good clearance," this would enable them to better perform their wifely duties, and contribute to their overall good health.

Some anthropologists have suggested that such superstitious beliefs are related to men's envy and fear of women, who bring forth life. Elizabeth Fisher (1979) has suggested that "the wide-spread customs of menstrual restrictions do not necessarily represent disgust or even a low status of women; they may be connected with the mana—the magic and fearful power of the blood" (p. 157). Men's sense of inferiority is believed to be evidenced in the initiation rites of puberty in some cultures, which involve blood-letting and during which young men appear to mimic or pretend to be women.

While men's envy of women may be a factor in the maintenance of menstrual taboos, some scholars have suggested that women have also derived positive benefits from the prohibitions and therefore have taken part in enforcing them. For example,

> in many primitive societies, the menstruating woman was excluded from the most ordinary life of her tribe for four or five days every month. Unable to plant, harvest, cook, associate with her husband, or wander freely around the village, the woman went instead to the menstrual hut, . . . set at some distance from the village. There a menstruating woman might, depending upon her culture, be required to undergo purifying practices or simply enjoy the solitude. (Delaney, Lupton, & Toth, 1976, pp. 7f.)

Thus, as suggested by Elizabeth Fisher (1979), "the menstrual hut or a restriction on housework may well be a welcome monthly vacation to the woman" (pp. 158f.). The taboos may also have served to emphasize women's temporary control over men. For example, "many a New Guinea man will observe his wife's wishes for fear that an angry woman will serve him food while she is menstruating, or step over him, letting blood drip, while he sleeps" (Rosaldo, 1974, p. 38).

Marla Powers (1980) has argued that western anthropologists tend to interpret menstrual customs of other cultures in ways that reflect their own negative attitudes, and she has provided examples of native American peoples where the seclusion of women during menstruation should not be taken as evidence that menstruation is viewed as defilement. She cites the Navajo, among whom the onset of menstruation is regarded "as a time for rejoicing," and the Papago, among whom a menstruating woman is considered a "vessel of supernatural power," conferring the power of childbirth (pp. 56f.). In such cultures, according to Powers, separation of the menstruating women from others in the community is for the purpose of her purification and does not represent fear or hostility. In the puberty rite for Oglala girls at first menses, for example, they are initiated into adulthood as sacred buffalo women in a public ceremony, and a feast is held in honor of their new status. At the end of the ceremony, the girl's "menstrual bundle," which has been lodged in a tree, is passed from the girl's mother to the shaman to her father "indicating that the marginal (dangerous) period has passed . . . and men need not fear contamination" (p. 61). At each menses, women are secluded in special lodges and may not cook for their husbands. Among the Oglala, then, as in other cultures, menstruation may indicate a woman's power and her potential danger to men.

PSYCHOPHYSIOLOGY OF THE MENSTRUAL CYCLE

What has modern science taught us about this phenomenon, so steeped in myths and so poorly understood by earlier cultures? Some of the sequence of physiological changes that occur in a periodic rhythm during a normal female's menstrual cycle are now well established and we can trace the following chain of events. At the beginning of one cycle (and the end of the previous one) the hypothalamus (the major brain center for autonomic functions), in response to a low level of estrogen signaled by neurotransmitters from higher brain centers, produces FSH-releasing hormone, which stimulates the anterior lobe of the pituitary gland to release the follicle stimulating hormone (FSH). This hormone causes several egg-containing follicles in one of the two ovaries to ripen and develop and also stimulates estrogen manufacture by the follicles. The estrogen level in the bloodstream rises, signaling the anterior pituitary to decrease its production of FSH and to release luteinizing hormone (LH). During this part of the menstrual cycle, referred to as the follicular phase, important roles are played by secretions of FSH and LH in preparing an ovum, and by estrogen in thickening the uterine lining (endometrium). During the next, ovulatory, phase, estrogen rises, and FSH first declines and then peaks along with LH. It is LH that suppresses the growth of all but one of the follicles, which then ripens and ruptures, releasing an ovum. This is known as ovulation and occurs on the 14th day of a typical 28-day cycle. Hairlike cells of the fallopian tube sweep the egg into the oviduct, and the empty follicle is converted into the corpus luteum, secreting estrogen and progesterone, which the ripe follicle may have been secreting two to three days before ovulation. During this luteal phase, progesterone helps to prepare the uterine wall for the ovum in case it is fertilized. When the amount of progesterone reaches a critical level, LH production is inhibited. Without implantation of a fertilized egg, the corpus luteum decays, and the manufacture of progesterone (and estrogen) decreases. The withdrawal of these two hormones cuts off the blood supply to the upper layer of endometrial cells; these are then shed, along with blood from the broken blood vessels, as the menstrual flow.

After the first one or two days of menstruation, the hypothalamus again responds to the relative absence of estrogen and the cycle begins again. Had an ovum been fertilized, the corpus luteum would have continued to function, producing progesterone and sustaining fetal

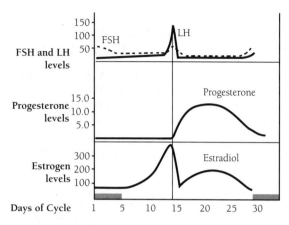

FIGURE 5.1 *Hormone changes in the human menstrual cycle* (taken from *National Women's Health Report*, April 1985, vol. 3, no. 4, p. 3).

development until the placenta, also a progesterone manufacturer, was formed. Figure 5.1 shows changes in the levels of all the relevant hormones during various phases of the menstrual cycle, and Figure 5.2 diagrams the interrelationships among the nervous, hormonal, and reproductive systems.

Accompanying the changes in hormonal levels during the menstrual cycle are other physiological changes, such as changes in the fragility of capillaries. Progesterone, which affects the metabolism of salt and water, causes water retention and consequent temporary weight gain. Estrogen levels affect the quantity of vaginal and skin lubricants and sensitivity to odors and have been shown to affect the sodium/potassium ratio, which is lowest during ovulation and highest during menstruation (DeMarchi, 1976). Sensitivity to pain probably peaks during ovulation (Goolkasian, 1985). Both vision and smell appear to be more acute around ovulation, and hearing seems to peak around ovulation and again at the onset of menstruation (Parlee, 1983). The hypothesis that sensory thresholds are generally low at ovulation is supported by data from a study of lesbian couples (Matteo & Rissman, 1984). Within the sample studied, sexual encounters and orgasms were found to increase during the midcycle portion of the menstrual cycle. The investigators interpreted this finding as evidence "of a general heightening of sensitivities to physical stimuli around the time of presumed ovulation" (p. 253). Data from a lesbian sample are particularly instructive since these women do not generally interact sexually with men and are free of

pregnancy worries and the effects of chemical contraceptives. In contrast to what data from heterosexual women show, this small sample of women, who recorded their daily sexual activity over a 14-week period, did not show a decline in sexual encounters during menstruation, nor did they show a pre- or postmenstrual peak in such behavior.

Hormones other than those just discussed function in reproduction and sexuality: steroids from the adrenal cortex, chorionic gonadotropins from the placenta, and prolactin from the pituitary. These and all the other hormones produced by glands in female bodies are also produced in males and are qualitatively identical in both sexes. Joan Hoffman (1982) has pointed out that "the pituitary hormones involved in reproduction are exactly the same in males and females" (p. 835). That testosterone, produced in females, also fluctuates during the menstrual cycle is now recognized, but little attention has been paid thus far to the role played by this "male" hormone in female physiology. According to Anne Briscoe (1978):

> The hormones produced by the ovary and the testis, as well as by the adrenal cortex, belong to a class of chemical compounds called steroids . . . The capacity of the adrenal cortex to produce hormones which are chemically similar to those of the gonads is explained by [the fact that] . . . the primitive adrenal cortex develops in the embryo adjacent to the site of development of the gonads. (pp. 35f)
>
> Studies of the biosynthesis or manufacture of these sex steroids show that androgens and estrogens are interconvertible in the body and that all are present in both sexes in different amounts. (p. 41)
>
> Males have circulating progesterone in amounts not unlike those of the preovulatory stage of the menstrual cycle in females. . . . Its presence is certain if its role is not. (p. 43)

Recall from Chapter 2 that administration of progestin, a synthetic progesterone compound, to pregnant women to prevent spontaneous abortions has sometimes had androgenizing effects on their female embryos, clearly attesting to the chemical similarity of the sex hormones.

Not only are male and female hormones similar, but recent studies have suggested that sex hormone secretion in men is also rhythmic and cyclical, as evidenced by measurable changes in testosterone concentration in the blood. The data thus far suggest a diurnal rhythm in men rather than a longer cycle, but as Joan Hoffman (1982) has pointed out, without an "external marker" in males, like the menstrual flow, "it is hard to know

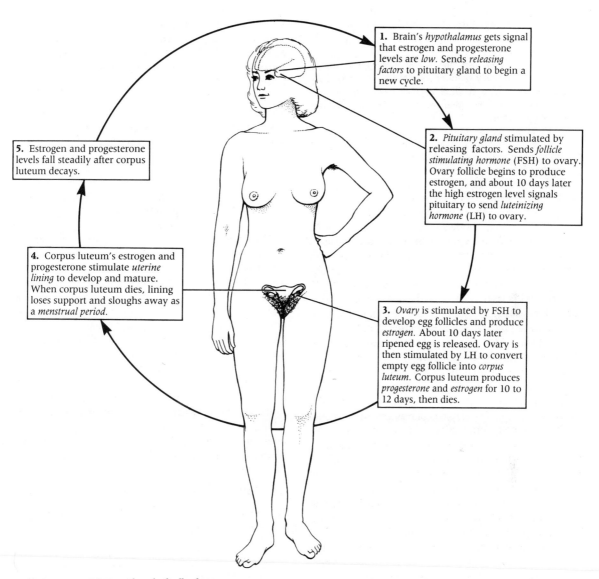

1. Brain's *hypothalamus* gets signal that estrogen and progesterone levels are *low*. Sends *releasing factors* to pituitary gland to begin a new cycle.

2. *Pituitary gland* stimulated by releasing factors. Sends *follicle stimulating hormone* (FSH) to ovary. Ovary follicle begins to produce estrogen, and about 10 days later the high estrogen level signals pituitary to send *luteinizing hormone* (LH) to ovary.

5. Estrogen and progesterone levels fall steadily after corpus luteum decays.

4. Corpus luteum's estrogen and progesterone stimulate *uterine lining* to develop and mature. When corpus luteum dies, lining loses support and sloughs away as a *menstrual period*.

3. *Ovary* is stimulated by FSH to develop egg follicles and produce *estrogen*. About 10 days later ripened egg is released. Ovary is then stimulated by LH to convert empty egg follicle into *corpus luteum*. Corpus luteum produces *progesterone* and *estrogen* for 10 to 12 days, then dies.

FIGURE 5.2 *Menstrual cycle feedback system.*

where to start and to stop looking for cycles" (p. 837). From a physiological perspective, according to Hoffman, the hormonal changes that characterize the menstrual cycle are modest in size, and the fluctuations over 28 days are "really not much more extreme than the diurnal [daily] changes in prolactin levels in both males and females" (p. 839).

Studies of testosterone have disclosed their association

with competitive and aggressive behavior, often interpreted in the popular press as an indicator of testosterone's link to masculinity and as the antecedent or cause of dominant behavior. The very important lesson from the research, however, is quite different. Causality cannot be assumed to be one way, from hormone to behavior. It is as likely to be the reverse—that is, testosterone levels may fluctuate as a consequence of exposure to competitive or aggressive situations. Thus, for example, it has been found that

> testosterone levels can zip up and down by 20 to 30 percent during daily victories and defeats. Men who have just received their medical degrees have more of the hormone than usual. Men being harassed at a military academy have less.
>
> Entering competition, men on a high swing of testosterone feel 'psyched' and optimistic. . . . [W]inning can increase testosterone and losing can decrease it . . . . (Rose, 1990, p. B-3)

In one study, men playing competitive tennis for prize money were found to show a rise in testosterone a few hours after winning; another study found that increased testosterone levels in a group of men were accompanied by high levels of prolactin, a hormone associated with anxiety or stress (cf. Wood, 1986). Because of testosterone's responsiveness to situations, an investigation of 200 teenagers in grades 8 to 10 resulted in the conclusion that "testosterone should not increase sex differences in personality at puberty" (Udry & Talbert, 1988, p. 294). Some studies have not found correlations between testosterone levels in the blood and negative emotions or aggressive behavior, as in the case of a study of more than 100 teenagers of both sexes (cf. Hopson, 1987); but androstenedione, produced by ovaries, testes, and the adrenal cortex, is believed to function as a stress hormone.

That hormone production can be influenced by environmental events is an extremely important phenomenon, which illustrates the psychosomatic nature of human functioning. It is well-known that physiological events, such as blood pressure, heart rate, and hormonal secretion, can be influenced by external environmental stimuli and by psychological events such as cognitions and feelings. Psychological and somatic (bodily) processes are in continuous interaction. Some prefer the term *biosocial* to describe this interaction; others, the term *psychosomatic*. Menstruation, like all other human physiological processes, occurs in a social, psychological, and physical context; variations in this context can produce a variety of modifications in the physiological events.

Menstruation is affected by environmental factors as illustrated by the role of nutrition in decreasing the age of menarche, as mentioned earlier. Nutrition has also been implicated in delaying and in stopping menstruation (amenorrhea). Women who are undernourished as a result of famine, war, poverty, or excessive dieting often do not have menstrual periods. Menstruation is also influenced by exercise. "Women who experience high outputs, such

as ballet dancers and athletes who train intensively, have a later age at menarche and a high incidence of amenorrhea" (Golub, 1983, p. 24). According to Linda Gannon (1988), the most important risk factors for amenorrhea, a condition that is typically temporary and reversible, are being under 30, never having borne a child, and engaging in a highly strenuous exercise program. She has suggested that the stress of competition may be as relevant a factor as strenuous exercise.

MOOD AND BEHAVIOR CORRELATES OF CYCLIC HORMONAL CHANGES

That the levels of various hormones regularly ebb and flow during the menstrual cycle is well established, but the extent to which hormonal changes are related to, and responsible for, predictable changes in mood, feelings, and behavior remains a matter of controversy. Considerable disagreement exists over whether premenstrual tension—sensitivity, anxiety, irritability, depression, and low self-esteem—is a direct consequence of physiological processes, or whether it is a learned interpretation of an altered body state and related to other conditions, beliefs, or circumstances. In this section we will examine the evidence having to do with how the menstrual cycle relates to moods and behavior. After that we will consider the validity of grouping a whole range of diverse symptoms under the recently popularized label *premenstrual syndrome* (PMS); we will also briefly discuss dysmenorrhea.

Do Hormone Changes Cause Shifts in Mood?

Peter Farb (1978) has written, with apparent confidence, that for women throughout history and across cultures,

> fluctuations in hormone levels during each cycle must inevitably produce emotional changes. And indeed, predictable monthly swings take place in the personality of the female that correlate closely with her menstrual cycle. The intensity of these swings . . . may be affected by cultural attitudes toward menstruation and also by the individual's own temperament and predispositions. [But, nonetheless,] . . . emotional changes during the female's monthly cycle are an objective fact related to changing hormone levels. (p. 205)

But Farb himself contradicts this generalization by pointing out elsewhere that in some cultures the emotional changes "are not very marked," and that the "North American and European females, who experience premenstrual tension, apparently [do so] because it is expected of them" (p. 207), whereas Arapesh women of New Guinea, for example, treat menstruation as "a negligible inconvenience." If mood changes are not universally experienced, then they cannot also be said to be inevitable biological facts, unless one assumes that biological femaleness in North America and Europe differs from biological femaleness in Africa, Asia, and South America.

Those who propose a hormone-mood relationship suggest that women experience tension during the premenstruum—variously defined as 2 to 7 days before menstruation—because the levels of estrogen and progesterone are rapidly declining. This period has been related not only to feeling "blue" (anxious and depressed) but also to rates of suicide, crime, psychiatric admissions to hospitals, accidents, and death. Conversely, the high estrogen period that occurs at ovulation has been associated with elevated levels of self-esteem and feelings of well-being and competence. Psychoanalytic theory has encouraged women to believe that sadness accompanies menstruation because it signifies that the woman cannot anticipate imminent childbearing (through which she is said to achieve ultimate fulfillment) and will remain "empty," at least for the time being. Some of my students have reported being told as teenagers that menstruation is a "weeping of the womb" over the lost possibility of a child.

What does the research literature tell us about the proposition that women experience mood fluctuations correlated with phases of the menstrual cycle? The first important critical and careful evaluation of the evidence was undertaken by Mary Parlee (1973), who concluded that the available data were not rigorous or general enough to support a connection between any particular phase of the menstrual cycle and any specific way of feeling. Among the problems Parlee identified was that much of the research had used a single measure of mood, known as the Menstrual Distress Questionnaire (note its suggestive title), which asked women to recollect how they had felt just before, during, and after their most recent menstruation. Information like this tells us only what women say in retrospect in response to questions about menstruation; their retrospective answers may well be influenced by shared beliefs and attitudes. Parlee also concluded that although statements implying "a direct causal relationship between physiological processes and complex psychological experiences and behaviors are abundant in the literature" (p. 461), no research has specified the mechanisms that link these processes to psychological events. Others who have reviewed the literature have

reinforced Parlee's conclusions. Randi Koeske (1983), for example, questioned the concepts and methods that are taken for granted in menstrual cycle research and called for an approach that recognizes the complexity of interacting factors in menstruation and health. Similarly, Anne Fausto-Sterling (1985) characterized this research as filled with inadequate sample sizes and measures, poor statistics, and badly designed studies.

Findings from research that has tried to overcome some of the earlier methodological problems have typically not supported a direct relationship between mood and hormonal change. The new evidence suggests, instead, that anticipating menstruation causes women to respond, both psychologically and physiologically, in ways that are learned. For example, Janet Swandby (1979) found differences between women's self-reports of moods provided in daily assessments (concurrent reports) during a general body awareness study and their recollections of how they had felt during different phases of the menstrual cycle. For 35 consecutive days, a sample of women who used oral contraceptives and women who did not, as well as a sample of men, filled out a mood adjective checklist. These daily assessments showed no reliable relationship between mood and objectively determined phases of the menstrual cycle. There were large individual differences among the participants in mood patterns, and in general the moods of the women who were not using birth control pills did not differ from those of the women who were or from those of the men. When these same persons, however, were asked to report on how they typically felt on menstrual, premenstrual, and intermenstrual days (or, if men, how their female sexual partners felt), responses conformed to stereotyped expectations, with negative feelings and physical complaints reported for the premenstrual and menstrual phases of the cycle. The men, moreover, more frequently reported negative moods for their sexual partners at the premenstrual and menstrual phases than did the women who gave self-reports.

Other investigators have reported a similar lack of agreement between concurrent and retrospective measures of affect. In one study (Golub & Harrington, 1981), anxiety and depression scores were not significantly higher among 10th and 11th grade girls tested during premenstrual or menstrual days than among those tested during intermenstrual days (from the end of the menstrual flow to about four days prior to the next one). Nevertheless, when answering retrospective questions the same adolescent girls reported more negative feelings during premenstrual and menstrual days than intermenstrual days. Using a similar method, Mary Parlee (1982) had a small group of adult women, who were not taking oral contraceptives, report on their mood and activity levels daily for 90 days. No mention was made of menstruation except that menstrual dates were routinely reported on a biweekly health inventory. No woman was found to exhibit significant fluctuations but, as a group, the women were found to show significantly greater activity levels and significantly lower tension and anxiety on weekends than on weekdays—unrelated to the menstrual cycle—and, contrary to expectation, negative feelings were found to be less, and general activity level greater, on premenstrual and menstrual than on intermenstrual days. A close replication of this study (McFarlane, Martin, & Williams, 1988) with women who were asked to report on their feelings daily for 70 days found no negative mood relationships between menstrual cycle phase and concurrent reports of feelings, whereas recollected feelings "were consistent with stereotypes about women's mood fluctuations . . . [and] beliefs about premenstrual syndrome" (p. 212). Both women and men showed more variation in mood over days of the week than over phases of the menstrual cycle, with arousal and pleasantness at their highest levels on Friday and Saturday and at their lowest level on Monday. In addition, the women in the sample were no moodier than the men, and the women's moods were no less stable.

Another study (McFarland, Ross, & DeCourville, 1989) in which women made both concurrent and retrospective reports of menstrual symptoms and feelings found that "the more a woman believed menstruation to have a negative influence . . . , the more negatively she recalled her menstrual symptoms . . . independent of her actual initial ratings" (p. 529). The investigators concluded that their findings provided "little support for the popular belief that women's moods are at the mercy of raging hormones" (p. 530). The conclusion now generally shared by researchers in this field, as noted by John Richardson (1990), is that "the incidence or rated severity of paramenstrual symptoms [shortly before and during menstruation] tends to be higher in retrospective accounts than in concurrent reports" (p. 23). The research of Klebanov and Jemmott (1992) from two samples of women not taking birth control pills provided some support for the importance of both bodily sensations and expectations in influencing the report of premenstrual symptoms. The higher a woman's score on a previously administered retrospective measure of menstrual distress, the more symptoms she reported at a laboratory session held during her premenstrual phase. At the same time, women who were falsely led to believe that they were premenstrual during the lab session reported more

From *Ms.*, January 1983, p. 21.

symptoms than women who were led to believe they were intermenstrual. Two problems with this research that need to be mentioned are, first, that the respondents knew from the beginning of the study that they were being asked questions about menstruation along with other hormonally related issues and, second, that there is no indication whether the number of symptoms reported concurrently by premenstrual women was significantly different from that reported by other women. Despite the largely negative findings from the research literature, myths about women's mood changes in response to the menstrual cycle persist. The cartoon by Mimi Pond can help us laugh at the myths, but dispelling them is more difficult.

One set of studies has focused on the differences between women who often report premenstrual symptoms of negative mood and physical discomfort, such as headaches or backaches, and those who seldom do. Since the pattern of hormonal changes associated with the menstrual cycle is the same in all normal women who menstruate, what explains the variation in psychological and physical correlates? Do those who report going from elevated highs to bluesy lows differ on certain social or personality dimensions from women who do not report such mood swings? This question was raised by Karen Paige (1973) who, in several studies, found evidence that a woman's attitudes toward menstruation relate to other attitudes and behaviors. For example, "women who have physical discomfort and psychological stress during menstruation tend to report such symptoms in other situations as well"; they report higher psychological stress generally, greater use of medication, and more aches, pains, and illnesses. Other investigators have found significant positive relationships between retrospective reports of menstrual distress and general health complaints (Carrie, 1981), general anxiety (Good & Smith, 1980), and self-consciousness and social anxiety (Matthews & Carra, 1982).

In a different kind of study, Edna Menke (1983) found strong evidence of similarity between mothers and daughters in reported attitudes toward menstruation and levels of menstrual distress, suggesting that learning plays an important part in reactions to menstruation. This proposition is supported by data from a study (Ruble, 1977) in which a sample of college women were led to believe that they were closer to the beginning of menses than was actually the case. Those who had been told they were premenstrual reported significantly more pain, water retention, and change in eating habits than another group who were told they were intermenstrual, despite no differences between them in objectively measured cycle phase.

Performance Correlates

While most interest and stereotypes center on moods, some attention has also focused on menstrual correlates of performance on various tasks. The literature does not support a conclusion that fluctuations in objective performance measures are reliably related to the menstrual cycle. Employment records show that it is men who exceed women in monthly absences from work due to illness, and "world and Olympic records have been set by women in all stages of their menstrual cycles" (Wood, 1980, p. 38). A study of more than 1,000 women Air Force pilots during World War II found no relationship between menstrual phase and flying accidents or flying grades; the study also found that women took fewer days off each month from flight training than did their male counterparts (cf. Keil, 1982). Barbara Sommer (1983), in summarizing the research on cognitively demanding tasks, concluded that "among the general population of women, menstrual cycle variables do not interfere with cognitive abilities—abilities of thinking, problem-solving, learning and memory, making judgments, and other related mental activities" (p. 86).

That the mass media grasp at any straws to claim otherwise is well illustrated by a series of events chronicled by Beryl Benderly (1989) and Doreen Kimura (1989). In November 1988, newspapers across the country ran front-page stories with dramatic headlines about the "scientific evidence" that female sex hormones were tied to women's abilities to think and reason and to perform tasks requiring muscular coordination. An analysis of this "evidence," however, does not support the newspaper headlines. Critics have pointed out that the studies by Kimura and her colleagues were of very small samples of women; some of the findings were from a small group of postmenopausal women all over 50; the younger women knew they were being tested at different times during their menstrual cycles (that is, they were not naive about the research); no previous baseline measures had been obtained; and identical tests were not given to younger and older women. The manual dexterity test at which women did better when their estrogen levels were high was one that required them to press the top button of a cabinet with their index finger, pull a vertical handle with four middle fingers, and press down on a bottom bar with their thumb—clearly a task with rather limited generalizability! Kimura's own conclusion from her work is that everyday life is typically not affected by normal hormone fluctuations and that "for most women, they aren't an important factor" (1989, p. 66). They continue to be an important factor, however, for the news media.

The known environmental influences on physiological functioning discussed earlier in this chapter give rise to serious questions about typical interpretations of the higher incidence during the premenstruum of such behaviors as crimes, accidents, suicide attempts, and psychiatric crises. Such correlations have "been viewed as an indication that the hormonal changes associated with menstruation somehow produce increased anti-social or criminal tendencies" without considering the possibility that the "behaviors and concomitant events produce [the] hormonal changes" (Horney, 1979, p. 31). Trauma has been found to shorten cycles and to induce premature menstrual bleeding. Thus, it is as likely that a suicide attempt or psychiatric crisis can stimulate menstruation as that the hormonal changes associated with menstruation can trigger such behavior. Women who have been in automobile accidents as passengers, for example, and who are thus not responsible for the accident, tend to menstruate shortly thereafter (Horney, 1979).

Interpretations and Attributions

Physiological changes associated with increases and decreases in wide-acting hormones (or chemicals) can be understood as producing a state of arousal that requires cognitive interpretation. We learn to ascribe meaning to altered body states and the name we give to what we are feeling is strongly influenced by the situation we are in at the time. A sizable body of literature indicates that what we think or believe about how our bodies are functioning, as well as the social context in which we find ourselves, influences how we feel and behave. A review of this literature led to the conclusion (Harris & Katkin, 1975) that cognitive evaluation of states of arousal is of great importance in the emotions or feelings we experience.

With respect to menstruation, the literature suggests that women learn not only to interpret hormonal fluctuations in certain ways but also to use the fact of their occurrence to explain feelings of irritability or anxiety that may actually stem from frustrations, disappointments, unsolved problems, or unresolved conflicts. Simply put, while earlier research tested the hypothesis that a woman may feel badly when she expects her period, newer research has tested the proposition that when a woman feels badly, she attributes it to her period. It may be more acceptable, to oneself or to others, to attribute negative feelings to menstrual fluctuations than to admit serious problems with personal relationships or with one's work. If "the blues" are due to "that time of the month" then they will go away, at least until next month. This mode of explanation, of course, may leave long-term social or psychological problems unattended. Judith Rodin (1976) had a sample of midcycle and a sample of premenstrual women work on a laboratory task. For some participants the task aroused little anxiety, whereas for others strong anxiety was aroused with threats of shock and testing. Rodin found that menstruating women who attributed their anxiety to their menstruation, and not to the task, performed the task more effectively than equally anxious nonmenstruating women and about as well as women in low-anxiety conditions. In other words, if women associate negative feelings with menstruation, they may not accurately identify other sources of these feelings.

Some studies have found that other persons often attribute a woman's negative or irritable mood to her being premenstrual. One sample of college students (Koeske & Koeske, 1975) read excerpts from an interview with a woman. When she was presented as in a bad mood and also premenstrual, the students attributed her mood more often to her menstrual phase than to other possible sources, such as unpleasant or disappointing news. These respondents discounted situational factors in favor of a biological explanation, reflecting their assumptions about the link between negative moods and premenstruation. In a similar study (Ruble, Boggiano, & Brooks-Gunn, 1982), college students indicated their degree of annoyance with

the various excuses a woman might use to explain her irritability. Men were found to be less annoyed when a woman gave a menstrual excuse than when she gave an ordinary pain excuse or a frustration excuse. The investigators also found a significant relationship between reactions to menstrual excuses for irritability and general attitudes toward menstruation. Those who believed that menstruation is psychologically and physically debilitating were significantly less annoyed at an irritable premenstrual or menstruating woman and were significantly less likely to blame her for being irritable. Men were more likely than women to perceive menstruation as debilitating and to feel that "women are more tired, emotional, do not perform as well intellectually, and should have lower expectations for themselves during menstruation" (p. 633). The investigators noted that their data suggest that women may respond to such beliefs on the part of men by using menstrual-related excuses to justify undesirable behavior or to get away with not doing certain things. A newspaper columnist (Patinkin, 1983) turned this around in a clever piece in which he explained why men drop laundry on the floor, refuse to ask for directions when lost, are insensitive, and don't listen during conversations. It's all due to male hormones, he argues.

> Women's hormones make them hysterical. Ours make us stoic sorts who suppress anger, fear commitment and drink whiskey, instead of having a good cry. . . . Next time I'm told that I'm insensitive, don't listen well, drop socks on the floor and am a lazy bum for refusing to do the dishes, I now have an answer. Don't blame me, I can't help it. It's my hormones. (p. A-3)

PREMENSTRUAL SYNDROME (PMS): WHAT IS IT?

Much media attention has been given in recent years to the claim that a new medical disorder has been discovered that afflicts millions of women and that can be diagnosed and treated. This so-called disorder has brought enormous profits to the pharmaceutical industry, and new comic material to comedians and greeting card distributors, as illustrated on p. 105. One book of cartoons (cf. Chrisler, 1990) describes 38 different types of premenstrual syndrome (PMS) attacks. Melinda, the major character, is shown variously wrecking her house with a hatchet "to rearrange the furniture;" smashing dishes against the wall; sobbing in a movie theater; and devouring the town of Hershey, Pennsylvania. Another book of humor contains

P.M.S. victim

© Jill E. Wright.

quizzes, hints, and lists for women who are called "hormone hostages;" one list presents reasons why women shouldn't want to be president of the United States.

The term *PMS* refers to a constellation of symptoms first discussed in the medical literature in the 1930s but not popularized until the mid-1970s, when the work of Katharina Dalton, a British physician, was reported widely in the press and a number of clinics were established in the United States. A major problem with the writings on PMS is that a large number of varied and sometimes contradictory symptoms are said to indicate it, only some of which need be experienced by the suffering patient. This variation in symptoms makes diagnosis difficult if not impossible. Dalton defined PMS as "any symptoms or complaints which regularly come just before or during menstruation but are absent at other times of the cycle" (cf. Sherman, 1982, p. 10). The symptoms may vary from woman to woman, making PMS quite different from other medical problems. Descriptions of PMS list from 20 to about 150 symptoms, none of which is unique to PMS; these symptoms include tension, depression, fatigue, irritability, backache, asthma, sinusitis, epilepsy, feelings of

bloatedness, breast discomfort, headaches, acne, clumsiness, suicidal urges, herpes, hypoglycemia, sties, hoarseness, weight gain, rage, anxiety, panic attacks, food cravings, mental confusion, and seizures. "There are no medical tests for the syndrome and no psychological evaluation which can predict its occurrence" (Turkington, 1984, p. 28).

Despite the lack of precise definition of PMS, some defendants on trial in Great Britain and the United States have successfully used it as a mitigating factor in responding to assault charges. In one case ("Woman Uses PMS," 1991), a judge dismissed charges against a woman accused of kicking a state trooper who stopped her on suspicion of drunk driving after the woman "contended that PMS, not alcohol, caused her to react violently" to the state trooper. She was found not guilty despite the results of a breath test that showed her alcohol level to have been above the legal limit after a gynecologist testified for the defense that the woman's "behavior was similar to that exhibited by a woman suffering from PMS" (p. A-14).

We find variations not only in the suggested symptoms of PMS, but also in the estimates of its prevalence: from 10 percent to 95 percent of all women have been estimated to suffer from PMS. Assertions that between 5 and 6 million women "cannot hold jobs, . . . cannot maintain relationships . . . [and] fear they are insane" (cf. Turkington, 1984, p. 28) must be carefully scrutinized and questioned; they are not based on reliable and valid data, since PMS has no clear definition and no accepted set of symptoms.

Without precise definition and with wide variation in estimated prevalence, it is not surprising that PMS has no established cause and no agreed-upon treatment. A survey of the literature indicates that "there are at least half a dozen theories as to its cause—ranging from an alteration in the way that the body uses glucose, to excessive estrogen levels—none of which have been convincingly demonstrated (Eagan, 1983, p. 28). The most publicized hypothesis, proposed by Katharina Dalton, is that PMS results from a progesterone deficiency; her treatment therefore includes administering progesterone for about 10 days before menstruation by injection or by vaginal or rectal suppositories. This treatment has been used by doctors in Britain for more than 30 years, but it has not been approved by the Food and Drug Administration in the United States. Reviewers of the literature (e.g., Abplanalp, 1983; Eagan, 1983; Fausto-Sterling, 1985; Laws, 1983) have concluded independently that medical research has thus far failed to support the hypothesis that progesterone deficiency, or any other factor, causes PMS or to support the claim that progesterone replacement therapy, or any other treatment, is helpful.

Studies have found, according to Anne Fausto-Sterling (1985), that "women under treatment for PMS respond just as well to sugar pills [placebos] as to medication containing hormones or other drugs" (p. 100). There is no conclusive evidence that PMS sufferers have lower progesterone levels, or a greater estrogen-progesterone imbalance, than other women (Rubin, Reinisch, & Haskett, 1981). Other suggested underlying factors, such as low blood sugar or insufficient magnesium or vitamin B_6 (cf. Brody, 1986), have also failed to be reliably substantiated. Reviewers of the state of knowledge on PMS have concluded that "nearly every treatment ever tried seems to help PMS, as does a placebo" (Payer, 1989, p. 30), that "its definition, causes and cure are still eluding researchers" (Adler, 1990a, p. 10), and that "there are more than 70 different treatments . . . [many of which] are contradictory, untested, expensive or have unknown long-term effects" (Couzens, 1989, p. B-3).

Despite these conceptual and methodological problems and the paucity of research support, popular articles continue to exaggerate what is known about PMS and to popularize a dizzying array of treatments. These treatments have included, in addition to progesterone therapy, restricting the intake of diuretics; eating frequent small, high-protein meals to prevent a drop in blood sugar; reducing consumption of caffeine; increasing intake of vitamin B_6 (to prevent headache and irritability); taking oral contraceptives; exercising; taking iron and calcium supplements; reducing consumption of red meat; taking tranquilizers; and taking lithium. In a press report ("Premenstrual Syndrome," 1986, p. B-5), the director of a PMS program in New York City was quoted as saying, "There are now 327 different treatments for PMS."

Sophie Laws (1983) has argued that PMS is "a political construct." This argument should not be interpreted as denying the real suffering of women who experience premenstrual discomfort. What Laws questions, instead, is the apparent acceptability in our patriarchal society of attributing women's "bad" behavior to "a pitiable hormonal imbalance." Laws suggests that the PMS concept "isolates the badness in women to a part of themselves which is only sometimes present and results from circumstances (hormones) beyond their control" (p. 21). To illustrate, she described an advertisement in British medical journals for a natural progesterone product (Cyclogest) that shows the same woman before and after treatment. In the "before" photograph, the woman is wearing a black T-shirt and has untidy hair and a sad expression; in the "after" photograph, she has "a shining smile, shining hair," and is wearing a white blouse. A century ago, Laws reminds us, the treatment for "female troubles" was surgical removal of the uterus, ovaries, or both, and the symptoms of "female troubles" were the same as for PMS today: 'nervous prostration,' irritability, mood changes, a tendency to go mad and attack people" (p. 24).

In 1987, the American Psychiatric Association proposed adding the category of premenstrual dysphoric disorder to its official list of psychiatric diagnoses. This suggestion met with considerable opposition from mental health professionals, some of whom did not agree that such a disorder could be reliably identified, and others of whom considered it discriminatory to label experiences reported by women just prior to menstruation as abnormal or symptoms of a mental illness. As a result of the criticism, a set of symptoms now appears in the Appendix of the revised third edition of the *Diagnostic and Statistical Manual of Mental Disorders (DSM)* (American Psychiatric Association, 1987), with the label "late luteal phase dysphoric disorder" (LLPDD). As of this writing, the American Psychological Association plans to include the new diagnostic category "Premenstrual Dysphoric Disorder" (PMDD) in the main text of the fourth edition of the DSM, due to be published in 1994, but the criteria for PMDD will be described in the Appendix, since they are still considered in need of further study. Critics contend that the research on PMS is seriously flawed, preventing conclusions about its definition, treatment, and the reality of its existence as a syndrome. Among the critics is the Board of Directors of the American Psychological Association, which called the new diagnosis "potentially dangerous to women" (cf. Adler, 1990b, p. 12). Others have stressed the economic dangers of such a diagnosis in discouraging employers from hiring or retaining women so labeled, especially in light of the relative ease with which the diagnosis can be made. Paula Caplan (1993) has pointed out that although PMDD will be listed under "Depressive Disorders,"

one does not even have to be depressed at all in order to receive that diagnosis. As long as you are *either* depressed *or* anxious *or* irritable *or* emotionally labile *and* have four physical symptoms such as breast tenderness and bloating, *you will fit the description of this "mental illness"* (p. 3)

The complaints and experiences of women with premenstrual problems must be heeded and taken seriously, but to do so requires better and more sophisticated research, not unskeptical acceptance of a vaguely defined disorder with no verified cause or proven treatment. The issue is complex. Some of the important questions have been raised by Anne Fausto-Sterling (1985):

> Are there women in need of proper medical treatment who do not receive it? Do some receive dangerous medication to treat nonexistent physiological problems? How often are women refused work, given lower salaries, taken less seriously because of beliefs about hormonally induced erratic behavior? In the game of PMS the stakes are high. . . . Some women probably do require medical attention for incapacitating physical changes that occur in synchrony with their menstrual cycle. Yet in the absence of any reliable medical research into the problem it is impossible to diagnose true disease or to develop rational treatment. (pp. 94f)

DYSMENORRHEA

Menstrual cramps are sometimes grouped together with premenstrual distress, but dysmenorrhea is an independent, distinguishable phenomenon. Its symptoms are relatively clear and discrete: lower abdominal cramps (spasmodic pain) that coincide with menstruation, especially during the first day or two, and perhaps also pain in the back and upper legs, nausea, diarrhea, headache, and fatigue. Psychological factors have been implicated in this disorder; for example, a large study of adolescent and college-age women found significant correlations between reported severity of menstrual pain and not having received a clear explanation of menstruation, having been surprised by menarche, and feeling negative about menstruation (Brooks-Gunn & Ruble, 1983). Nevertheless, a widely accepted explanation for primary dysmenorrhea, where there is no known structural abnormality, is that it results from an overproduction of prostaglandins by the endometrium (lining) of the uterus. This overproduction, in turn, has been attributed "to elevated levels of the hormone progesterone during the latter half of the menstrual cycle" (Richardson, 1990, p. 16). A higher prostaglandin concentration has been found in the menstrual fluid of women who suffer from menstrual cramps, and prostaglandins are known to trigger uterine contractions and have been used to induce labor in pregnant women (Marx, 1979a). Prostaglandins have been related to the body's calcium-magnesium balance; they increase the level of the former and deplete the latter. Some have suggested that it is actually magnesium deficiency that causes dysmenorrhea (Friederich, 1983).

Whether directly or indirectly, prostaglandins are said to produce menstrual pain through three mechanisms: "increased [muscle] contraction . . . decreased uterine blood flow . . . [and] increased sensitization of pain fibers to mechanical and chemical stimuli" (Friederich, 1983, p. 97).

Several drugs that function as prostaglandin synthesis inhibitors have been developed to treat dysmenorrhea and include ibuprofen (Motrin), mefenamic acid (Ponstel), and zomepirac sodium (Zomax), in addition to ordinary aspirin. Well-controlled double-blind studies have provided evidence that these new nonnarcotic drugs are effective in reducing dysmenorrhiac symptoms and decreasing prostaglandins. Birth control pills also have been found to alleviate menstrual cramps, probably by preventing the growth and thickening of the endometrium, from which prostaglandins are released (Marx, 1979a). Penny Budoff (1982) compared Zomax with a placebo in a six-month study and found evidence of the drug's effectiveness. While a placebo was also somewhat effective, Zomax was most effective in reducing or eliminating symptoms.

Since prostaglandin synthesis inhibitors "lack selectivity" and "are potentially toxic," some researchers have urged that they be used cautiously (e.g., Chan, 1983). More research must be done to establish the long-term effects of these drugs; to contrast their efficiency with that of aspirin, which is much cheaper; to understand why placebos are sometimes able to reduce the symptoms of menstrual distress; and to identify the conditions under which excessive prostaglandins are produced. Although the symptoms of physical distress that accompany menstruation seem to be directly traceable to prostaglandins, we do not know what triggers their production. Why does the uterine lining of some women but not others release large amounts of prostaglandin and, among the former, in some months but not all? Factors other than the normal menstrual process seem to be at work, and may include exercise, stress, and diet (particularly magnesium deficiency), as well as beliefs, attitudes, and attributions. Menstrual pain can also result from such specific causes as endometriosis (abnormal growth of uterine lining cells), pelvic infection, uterine fibroids, or intrauterine birth control devices (Brody, 1981). Some have argued (e.g., Gannon, 1988) that "stress or anxiety or fear could increase a woman's vulnerability to dysmenorrhea, and the stress-reducing properties of exercise may serve to alleviate symptoms" (p. 109). Exercise may also be effective in alleviating pain by increasing the release of endorphins (natural opiates) which have analgesic properties.

LIFTING THE CURSE

Menstruation is clearly something special for women to deal with. For sexually active women who do not want to become pregnant, signs of the imminent arrival of the menstrual flow will tend to be closely attended to. Anxiety about pregnancy is an important phenomenon that is seldom discussed in the literature on menstrual distress. The personal hygiene aspects of menstruation are real; women need advance supplies of sanitary napkins or tampons, and it is the rare woman who has not found herself, many times, unprepared. For many women, in addition, water retention (edema) elevates weight and bloats abdomens and breasts for some days before menstruation. When some of these relatively minor inconveniences of menstruation are combined with possible dysmenorrhea and the cultural tradition of ambivalence, expectations of distress, and avoidance, this aspect of the female experience may become problematic. Nevertheless, most women handle their monthly menstrual cycles matter-of-factly, routinely, and calmly. Even more of us would be likely to do so if general attitudes and expectations were unambiguously positive.

Women must understand the facts of the menstrual process and the interrelationships among its physiological, psychological, and social aspects. We must come to realize that we should not expect menstruation to be accompanied by distress or pain, and that when it is we must search for the source of the problem. If we accept uncritically the proposition that menstruation is normally associated with distress, then we may fail to identify and treat genuine problems. We must respect our bodies and maintain good health through exercise and a balanced, nutritious diet. And we must also firmly challenge the belief that women suffer from some terrible biological infirmity, some curse that can only be endured by passive resignation or taking to our beds. The fact that women must sometimes think about tampons does not mean that we cannot make decisions, do our work effectively, or lead full, productive, and healthy lives. Any suggestion to the contrary is simply not supported by historical or contemporary evidence.

◆ Discussion Questions

1. Consider how a biological advantage like menstruation can be turned by culture into a "curse."

2. What superstitions do you or your friends follow when menstruating? What others have you heard about?

3. Do you curtail your activities in any way when menstruating? Explain; ask your friends.

4. Review the physiology of the menstrual cycle.

5. Review the literature on moods and the menstrual cycle; what kind of definitive study might you design?

6. Interview some women who believe they suffer from PMS. What questions will you include? Ask their views on the mental disorder diagnosis.

CHAPTER 6

SEXUALITY

Sex is a good gift, a delight; . . . it participates in the fullness of fruit, wine, music, amity, the vitality of the senses.

KATE MILLETT (1978, p. 80)

Lydia had thought of the sex act . . . as something the man "took" and the woman "gave." "He took her quickly," the books would say; or, "She gave herself to him." If anything in these verbal images aroused Lydia, it was the idea of making a present of her virginity to the man to whom she could then "belong."

GAIL GODWIN (1983, p. 141)

SEXUAL EXPERIENCES MIGHT BE ONES THAT "delight" and contribute to the "vitality of the senses," but for many heterosexual women, especially when young, sex is instead something one "gives" to a man. Sexual interaction with a man often proves to be a disappointment to a woman, because the romantic picture she has been led to anticipate is contradicted by the physical, ordinary details of the situation, or because her expectations differ greatly from those of her partner. For example, one teenage girl who participated in an interview study (cf. Fanzo, 1987–88), described her first heterosexual experience as follows: "I expected it to be exactly like the movies . . . Or the soap operas! . . . It really wasn't what I expected. . . . It was like, 'that's what I've been waiting for?!' " (p. 14). Adolescent sexual encounters in an earlier generation have been described by Kate Simon (1986) as

> truncated, gasping ventures made jumpy by the sound of a neighbor's step, an imagined turn of a key in a lock, or the cry of a child with whom one was baby-sitting. The semen spilled on stocking and underpants and inside trousers or, more awkward still, on trouser legs; kitchen rags and towels, hastily grabbed, carried off more semen than the girls did. (p. 176)

Similarly, a poem by Alta (1973) that talks about "a thing/that poked out; you could just shove/it in any body, whang whang come" (p. 295) reflects what social scientists have been validating through more systematic and objective means—the existence of two human cultures divided by gender. Girls and boys learn not just different role expectations and different motives and behaviors but also divergent meanings of sexuality.

SEXUALITY DEFINED BY GENDER

Adolescent boys still appear to be committed to sexuality and encouraged to seek gratification while receiving little training in "the language and actions of romantic love," whereas girls still seem to be "committed to romantic love and relatively untrained in sexuality" (Simon & Gagnon, 1977). In the process of dating, each gender must train "the other in what each wants and expects," but this exchange often does not proceed smoothly.

Investigators continue to document gender differences in the meaning and expectations ascribed to sexuality. For example, Patricia Miller and Martha Fowlkes (1980) have noted that "whereas males are encouraged to give full expression to their sexuality as an indication and demon-

stration of their masculinity, female sexual response has traditionally been thought to be appropriately derived from relationships with men and their needs" (p. 786). This traditional ideology remains dominant and generally descriptive of contemporary adult behavior. Thus, a study of sexual attitudes (Hendrick, Hendrick, Slapion-Foote, & Foote, 1985) reported that a sample of college women expressed substantially less support than college men did for sexual permissiveness and more support than men did for sexual responsibility. Another study (Blumstein & Schwartz, 1983), of 12,000 American couples from varied geographical backgrounds—including heterosexual and homosexual and married and cohabiting pairs—concluded that gender plays a primary organizing role in sexuality. The investigators found that, regardless of sexual orientation, "men and women represent two very distinct modes of [sexual] behavior" (p. 302). With respect to sexual motivation and attitudes, for example, "lesbians are more like heterosexual women than either is like gay or heterosexual men" (p. 303). A more recent survey of adults from age 22 to 57 (cf. American Health and Psychology Today Service, 1990) found that for younger women (22 to 35), 61 percent reported love to be their primary motivation for sex. Among 36- to 57-year-old women, however, this percent dropped to 38. Sex for physical pleasure was reported by 22 percent of the younger women but 43 percent of those in the older group. Among men, too, motivational shifts were reported, but in the opposite direction. Sex for physical pleasure dropped from 44 percent as the prime motive for the young men to 36 percent among the older men.

In earlier periods, women's experiences of sexual arousal and gratification were not much discussed or researched, nor described in literature by women themselves. It was primarily men who attempted descriptions of women's sexual feelings in fiction and in psychiatric and medical texts, basing their descriptions on their own assumptions. Since "our model of sexuality relies on male experience" (Schneider & Gould, 1987, p. 140), it is not surprising that traditional sexual scripts are "heterosexual ones, resting squarely on dichotomously gendered notions" (p. 141). The current climate for sexual discussion by women, however, is more open than in prior decades. Women are talking about their own sexual experiences in autobiography, fiction, and poetry and in response to researchers' questions.

The famous "Kinsey Report," *Sexual Behavior in the Human Female* (Kinsey, Pomeroy, Martin, & Gebhard, 1953), was a landmark work, since the data presented came from women themselves. Almost 8,000 women responded to a variety of interview questions that women typically had not been asked before. Later, valuable information about women's sexual behavior and erotic fantasies came from the work of William Masters and Virginia Johnson (1966) and from the inquiries of journalists like Nancy Friday (1973, 1991) and Shere Hite (1976). Women novelists have also been writing about sexuality. Erica Jong's *Fear of Flying* (1973) and *Parachutes and Kisses* (1984), Judith Rossner's *Looking for Mr. Goodbar* (1976), Marge Piercy's *Braided Lives* (1983), and Lisa Alther's *Kinflicks* (1976) and *Bedrock* (1990)—to name just a few—have jolted readers into recognizing two seemingly contradictory phenomena: first, that women can be just as sexual as men and that typical differences between women and men in sexual attitudes and responses are not inevitable or innate but are consequences of cultural or social learning; and second, that women tend to consider a far broader range of physical experience to be sexual than appears to be true of men.

Sex as Motive and Behavior

Human females do not restrict their sexual behavior to times when they are "in heat" and the probability of conception is maximal. Among our closest mammalian relatives, primates like apes and monkeys, females also engage in sexual play when not in estrus. In general, however, the sexual behavior of lower animals is tied to physiological signs of readiness for mating, when a series of stereotyped, relatively inflexible, and unlearned (instinctive) responses are triggered by appropriate stimuli. As noted many years ago by Frank Beach (1969), however, "as one moves up the evolutionary scale, there is a gradual loosening of the tie between mating [sexual behavior] and reproduction." It has long been recognized that whereas the sexual behavior of lower mammals is controlled by hormones, "in higher mammals, the balance of power shifts toward the central nervous system—and especially . . . toward the neocortex" (p. 33). The erotic responsiveness of human beings, then, depends upon the highest brain center, the cortex, which makes up 90 percent of all brain tissue and is the center for flexible behavior, for learning and memory.

Like other mammals, humans have biological needs that must be satisfied if the individual is to survive. These unlearned (primary or biogenic) needs are related to human physiology and to the maintenance of a stable internal environment (homeostasis). These needs include those for oxygen, for food and water, for waste elimination, and for pain avoidance. Deprivation of nutritional satisfaction or continued exposure to an excessively aversive state (pain, for example) produces a general state of arousal characterized by intense and persistent stimulation, referred to as *drive,* that typically activates an organism and evokes behavior. Some of this behavior is innate—for example, reflex movements—but in humans most behavior exhibited in response to a state of arousal has been learned. This behavior consists of responses that successfully reduce the drive (the persistent and intense stimulation) because they are instrumental in obtaining what is needed, such as food to relieve hunger.

In addition to needs originating from the nature of human physiology, a second category of needs is acquired during the course of a person's life. These needs result from experiences common to all human beings, from experiences common to a group of individuals (cultures), or from experiences specific to a particular person. These needs are variously described as sociogenic, psychological, secondary, or acquired; they may include desires for approval, for love, for affiliation or friendship, for power, for money, and so on. When aroused, these needs, too, result in a state of tension or drive and elicit behavior. Again, the behavior most successful or instrumental in reducing the person's intense state of arousal (drive) will be learned and strengthened and will tend to be elicited again. Figure 6.1 shows how these various concepts are related.

Where do sexual desires stand in this dichotomy between innate/biogenic and acquired/sociogenic needs? Some human needs appear to be closely tied to physiological functions but do not require satisfaction for biological survival. Their satisfaction may simply enhance physical well-being or health or promote more efficient or optimum functioning. One such need is for sensory and physical stimulation. We know that infants who lack such stimulation are not as healthy as those who receive it,

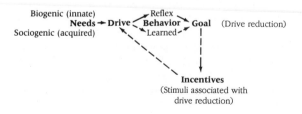

Biogenic (innate)
Needs → Drive ⟨ Behavior ⟩ Goal   (Drive reduction)
Sociogenic (acquired)   Reflex / Learned
Incentives
(Stimuli associated with drive reduction)

———— Unbroken lines indicate innate connections.
– – – – Broken lines indicate learned connections.

FIGURE 6.1 *Basic concepts in a learning model of human motivation.*

perhaps because, as Margaret Ribble (1944) long ago suggested, blood circulation is improved with physical stimulation, exercise, and movement. Adults find sensory deprivation aversive and disorienting—the reason solitary confinement is such a severe and effective punishment. The need for sexual stimulation may be a variant of this more general need category and, when satisfied, may also have the effect of promoting optimum functioning without being biologically essential. As Carol Tavris told an interviewer (Hahn, 1977) after examining the responses of 100,000 women to a magazine questionnaire, female sexuality is "just plain fun . . . . It's jolly. . . . A good, happy sex life is like having good health" (p. D-4).

Hormonal changes at puberty appear to be associated in all cultures with increased attention to and desire for sexual experience, supporting the proposition that sexual motivation has a physiological component. On the other hand, sexual satisfaction is not necessary for the maintenance of either homeostatic equilibrium or life, and the need for sexual stimulation may continue as a strong motivator in individuals with low levels of sex hormones—for example, in postmenopausal women and persons whose sex glands have been surgically removed. In normal persons, no reliable correlation exists between the level of circulating sex hormones and either the experience of sexual arousal or the frequency of sexual behavior. In this connection, it is interesting to learn that, for both adolescent girls and boys, the strongest predictor of sexually active behavior among a large, ethnically heterogeneous sample of 7th to 12th graders was peer association (DiBlasio & Benda, 1992). No major gender differences were found in factors accounting for sexual activity; among both genders what was most important was the degree of sexual activity of best friends.

Sexual arousal is primarily a psychological phenomenon. It can occur under a vast variety of conditions. It is affected by general physical contact or by stimulation of specific body parts, such as the clitoris, or of certain especially sensitive erogenous areas of the skin; it can also occur in response to any stimulus physically present, or to a fantasized or remembered image. Learning-oriented psychologists assume that such motivational stimuli, called incentives (see Figure 6.1), acquire their motivational properties through previous association with gratification or pleasure. For instance, many people attach erotic meaning to, and are sexually aroused by, some special song, situation, look, or memory. This approach to explaining sexual arousal, sometimes referred to as the appetitional theory of sexual motivation, contrasts sharply with Sigmund Freud's libido theory, which postulates a fixed sexual drive. Ethel Person (1980) has distinguished between these two positions simply and succinctly as follows: "In libido theory sexuality is both a motor force in culture and an innate force [in individuals] with which culture must contend. In appetitional theory the content of sexuality is formed by culture" (p. 607). In other words, as expressed by Ruth Bleier (1984), "our consciousness, our world, shapes our libido" (p. 166).

Given a state of sexual arousal, individuals behave in a variety of ways depending on their particular past learning experiences. Among humans, all aspects of sexual behavior (that is, what we do to achieve satisfaction or pleasure) are acquired or learned. Just as the arousing stimuli vary, so too do the specific acts we engage in, the time and the place for the behavior, and the person(s) with whom we interact, if any. All these factors are subject to variation, depending upon one's cultural group and one's particular individual experiences as influenced by family, friends, special circumstances, and unique person-environment interactions. These variations have been well documented by social scientists and complement our personal experiences and observations.

In this view of sexuality, the terms *homosexual, heterosexual,* and *bisexual* are adjectives that denote erotic attraction to same- or other-gender persons or both, and they require no major separation in a general discussion of sexual motivation or experience. Although in our society heterosexuality is the assumed orientation, and only homosexuality is questioned and examined for cause and explanation, all expressions of sexuality have been learned. One conclusion from the study of a sample of women and men who viewed themselves as bisexual (Blumstein & Schwartz, 1977) was that adult sexual preferences are not immutable and that either gender can be eroticized under particular circumstances. The researchers found, especially among the women, that sexual involvement followed "intense emotional attachment," which served as the "prerequisite for sexual attraction, sexual behavior, or a change in sexual identity" (p. 44). Alice Walker's *The Color Purple* (1982), Lisa Alther's *Kinflicks* (1976), and Meg Wolitzer's *Hidden Pictures* (1986) are compelling fictional accounts of such experiences. The conclusion that sexual preferences can change in no way denies the validity of the experience of those persons who, from childhood or adolescence, have felt drawn to a particular sexual orientation. As noted by Carole Vance and Ann Snitow (1984):

There are examples of both persistence and fluidity in sexual desire: for example, individuals who "knew" they were gay at an early age and remained so despite aversion therapy and incarceration, and others who "became" lesbian or gay at different stages of the life cycle in a manner suggesting internal change rather than belated expression of "repressed" desire. (p. 128)

Efforts to find the cause of homosexual and heterosexual orientations in neurophysiological differences have thus far not been successful, as is illustrated by the "failure to find major differences in circulating testosterone levels" between heterosexuals and either lesbians or gay men (Ellis & Ames, 1987). At the same time, we continue to learn from the stories told by lesbian women (e.g., Barrett, 1990) about the complexity of their lives, as is the case for heterosexual women, and about the different times in their lives that loving women became salient.

Psychophysiology of Sexual Arousal and Response

Sexuality can be considered a dimension of personality—a more or less consistent way of responding to a particular class of stimuli—and sexual response can be defined in both physiological and psychological terms. Data obtained from observations and interviews with women (Masters & Johnson, 1966) clearly indicated that sexual arousal can occur in response to anything present or imagined that has sexual meaning, from general body stimulation, or from direct or indirect clitoral stimulation. Orgasm (sexual gratification) was described by women as a complete body phenomenon involving more than just the vagina or the clitoris, and orgasmic experiences were found to vary in duration and in intensity, in extent of body involvement, and in degree of pleasure. Although simple neural reflexes for orgasmic release are involved, orgasm is not an all-or-nothing phenomenon for women, a conclusion reinforced by other investigators (e.g., Hite, 1976; Newcomb & Bentler, 1983).

The clitoris is a woman's primary erogenous or sexually arousing portion of the body. This fact was ignored or denied for a long time by a patriarchal bias in medicine. For example, Sigmund Freud (1905/1938) considered the clitoris to be an analogue of the male penis and believed that clitoral pleasure represented a childish masculinity. Freud insisted that with mature femininity, the vagina becomes the prime focus of women's sexual experience and the locus of adult orgasm. These assumptions, however, are contradicted by data from physiology and by reports of women's experiences. The title of a now classic paper by Anne Koedt (1973), "The Myth of the Vaginal Orgasm," became a challenging call to debate on this issue and a feminist slogan. It is no longer questioned that the clitoris is the major organ involved in the sexual arousal and response of women and that it is a unique human organ in that its sole function is sexual. In this way the clitoris is unlike the penis, although these organs originate from the same embryonic tissue and are similar in structure and function. The clitoris can become erect and enlarged (tumescent), its size changing both in diameter and in length, and its tip (glans), packed with nerve endings, is extremely sensitive to stimulation.

Physiologically, though, more is involved in sexual response than just clitoral tumescence. The muscles in the lower half of the vagina also participate by rhythmically contracting, and a thick layer of veins (venous plexus) in the vagina becomes engorged, thereby narrowing the vaginal passageway and increasing the potential for stimulation of the walls of the vagina, which contain nerve endings. The clitoris and lower third of the vagina function, to a very large extent, as an integrated unit. In addition, vaginal lubricants, resulting from dilation of the venous plexus, are released during sexual arousal.

Vaginal lubricants and clitoral erection indicate sexual arousal in women, while penile erection signifies arousal in men. How similar are the two genders in their subjective experiences and in sexual gratification or orgasm? When William Wiest (1977) asked a group of college students to choose adjectives for their experiences of orgasm, he found no significant differences between the responses of the women and those of the men. Wiest cited an earlier study by other researchers in which judges were unable to distinguish reliably between reports written by women and those written by men of "what an orgasm feels like." Shere Hite (1976) reported that most of her female informants described sexual arousal as involving sensations all over their bodies. They used such words as "tingly," "alive," "warm," "happy," and "feelings of wanting to touch and be touched" to describe sexual arousal, whereas descriptions of orgasm were more confined to the genitals.

Women can experience sequential orgasm more easily than men and retain this ability over most of their lives. This multiorgasmic potential in women has a physiological basis. The engorgement or accumulation of blood (vasocongestion) in the vaginal wall and in the clitoris is reduced with orgasm, but is promptly followed, reflexively, by reengorgement or refilling of the blood vessels. Each orgasm, therefore, produces increased vasocongestion and arousal. Sexual experience thus increases the physiological capacity of women for greater sexual pleasure. The frequency of multiple orgasms, as well as sexual gratification, has been found to increase with age and pregnancies and is potentially greatest when vaginal vasocongestion is maximal, during the postovulatory and premenstrual days of the menstrual cycle.

Differing Views of Women's Sexuality

It has been proposed that women "could go on having orgasms indefinitely if physical exhaustion did not intervene" and that a woman must will herself to be satisfied (Sherfey, 1970). In this view, men in preliterate societies are said to have taken steps to suppress women because, unless women were confined and restricted, there could be no family life, agriculture, or civilization. Regardless of the historical merits or validity of this hypothesis, its basis in female physiology serves to counter the still prevalent view of the insistent nature of men's sexual needs and the lesser importance of active sexuality to women.

The belief that women are less sexual than men has not always been prevalent. For example, the ancient Hebrews assumed that a woman's sexual desires were at least equal to those of a man's, and the marriage contract therefore provided not only for the wife's financial security but also for her sexual satisfaction. In the *Book of Women* compiled in the twelfth century by the physician and rabbi Maimonides (cf. "Holy or Wholly," 1972), the rules governing a woman's "conjugal rights" were presented in detail.

> For men who are healthy and live in comfortable and pleasurable circumstances without having to perform work that would weaken their strength, and do naught but eat and drink and sit idly in their houses, the conjugal schedule is every night. For laborers, such as tailors, weavers, masons, and the like, the conjugal schedule is twice a week if their work is in another city. For ass drivers, the schedule is once a week; for camel drivers once in thirty days; for sailors, once in six months; for disciples of the wise, once a week, because the study of *Torah* weakens their strength. (p. 53)

Clearly, it was women's sexual needs that men were believed to have to satisfy, and not vice versa.

Susan Griffin (1981) has suggested that a dominant idea in Judeo-Christian culture is that "the sight of a woman's body calls a man back to his own animal nature, and that this animal nature soon destroys him" (p. 31). It was Eve, we are told, who tempted Adam, and the belief in witchcraft was closely associated with the belief that carnal lust was insatiable in women. There is some evidence that women in pre-Christian England had considerable sexual freedom, that virginity was considered shameful, that marriage was temporary, and that women took lovers freely (Staples, 1977). The Roman poet Ovid believed that women's lust was uncontrollable; according to Carolyn Heilbrun (1973), he recounted a story about Teiresias, who had been both a woman and a man and was asked to mediate a dispute between the gods Jove and Juno about which sex enjoyed lovemaking more. When "he agreed with Jove that women had greater pleasure, . . . Juno, in a fit of temper at the decision, struck Teiresias blind" (p. 11).

Contrary to such beliefs, contemporary European-American culture maintains that it is male sexuality that is overwhelming, powerful, and more insistent than female sexuality. Women are urged to sympathize with men's sexual needs. Freud presented the libido as masculine, an assumption he accepted from his own time and place and then proclaimed as biological truth. Our society views sexuality as more crucial to men's gender identity and self-worth than to women's, perhaps because, for men, "sexuality represents domination" (Person, 1980). Philip Blumstein and Pepper Schwartz (1983) concluded, from their large-scale study of American couples, that it is the man to whom is attributed "greater appetite" and "greater license." "Women often feel restrained and not in control of their own experience, and men feel pressed to perform" (p. 305). This same imagery, Blumstein and Schwartz assert, is shared by homosexual and heterosexual couples.

Of course, some women's personal histories have reinforced sexual behavior that does not conform to the dominant gender ideology. In addition, the contemporary ideology itself does not present a simple and consistent set of prescriptions. Contradictory expectations coexist, and we receive mixed messages. For example, it has been pointed out that, in movies of the 1960s, unmarried women ("spinsters") were typically depicted as suffering from "sexual malnutrition," looking "pinched and bloodless as a prune, the objective correlative of her unlubricated vagina" (Haskell, 1974, p. 339). The message seemed to be that women really need sex whether they know it or not. In films of the 1980s, sexual overtures were still primarily made by men, but women were shown as acquiescing with far less hesitation than in earlier decades. In contemporary films, women's sexual pleasure is detailed and highlighted by cameras at close range.

Despite the presumed openness of sexual discussion in the present period, women's sexuality continues to be largely described from the perspective of men, a phenomenon that should not surprise us in a sexist culture. Beth Schneider and Meredith Gould (1987) have suggested that descriptions of women's actual experiences of sexuality are suppressed because men are largely ignorant of them and because these experiences do not match "the dominant, expected sexual script" (p. 139). Thus,

> to name adequately and speak of all the experiences women can have that might be considered sexual requires a departure from a male-centered approach to bodily sensation and a positive reappropriation of those features of female experience that men do not have. (p. 140) . . . Constructing the meaning of female sexuality differently may mean taking seriously all those subjective accounts, collected by every sex researcher to date, in which women say that kissing, holding, and touching often mean more and feel better than intercourse . . . For women this *is* sex, not foreplay. (p. 139)

With great frequency, the women who responded to Shere Hite's (1976) survey told her how important body contact and physical closeness were to them. Touching and proximity were valued for their own sakes and not just as behavior leading to intercourse or orgasm. The theme of women's unexpressed sexual attitudes and experiences is also appearing in fiction. For example, the protagonist in Lisa Alther's *Bedrock* (1990) asserts that the AIDS

> epidemic was giving women a chance to express what they'd thought of semen all along. That women weren't as enchanted with the stuff as men assumed, that they in fact felt about as much enthusiasm for it as men did for menstrual blood. (p. 51)

Departure from the sexual scripts prescribed for women raises questions about the "compulsory heterosexuality" (Rich, 1980) so central to mainstream culture and evokes anxiety in a largely heterosexist society. We tend not to openly acknowledge what researchers have known for more than 40 years, since the Kinsey studies—that it is not uncommon for individuals to have some mix of homosexual and heterosexual experiences. Nancy Friday's (1991) exploration of women's sexual fantasies reveals that a common fantasy involves sex with other women. When women's sexuality is freely discussed outside the confines of male-centered expectation, we grow uneasy. An example can be drawn from the heated reactions to a scene in the first episode of the TV drama series *Sisters*. In this opening scene, four sisters were in a sauna talking about multiple orgasms. After a preliminary screening, responses from corporate sponsors who "had threatened to cancel $500,000 worth of ads" (Warters, 1991) forced the elimination of the orgasm-centered conversation.

The contradictions in historical and contemporary views of female and male sexuality, in beliefs about the nature of sexuality, and in beliefs about which gender has the greatest "need," illustrate the significance of learning and culture in defining sexual behavior and in affecting sexual experience. The human brain is the guardian and regulator of the body's hormones. Cognitive processes—thought, fantasies, expectations, and beliefs—function in sexual arousal and nonarousal, in sexual satiation and nonsatiation; and the behaviors used to achieve gratification are learned. All aspects of human sexuality involve the interplay of psychological and physiological factors, and learning and experience are dominant. The biologist Ruth Bleier (1984) has compared sexuality with intelligence, noting that each

> is a learned relationship to the world, with an important and necessary, but not in itself determinate, biological component. For intelligence, it is not enough to have a brain and billions of neurons and synapses. Intelligence develops out of experience and learning. . . . So in sexuality, there is a real biological substrate for a range of sexual responses that involve the brain, hormones, muscles, and blood vessels. . . . But whatever or whoever arouses us . . . are . . . part of one's history of experiences and interactions with the external world . . . . [T]here is nothing about desire, arousal, orgasm, or feelings of transcendant oneness that "comes naturally." (p. 167)

Responses to Sexual Imagery

The belief that women are less apt than men to be sexually stimulated by visual or ideational cues has long been part of our general ideology. Evidence from surveys and laboratory studies, however, seriously challenge this conclusion. For example, Julia Heiman (1975) found that "women like erotica as much as men do, that they are as turned on by sexual descriptions, that their fantasies are as vivid and self-arousing" (p. 91). This conclusion followed the careful measurement of physiological reactions to sexual materials by assessing blood volume and pressure pulse in the penis and vagina of college student volunteers while they listened to tapes of heterosexual interaction that varied in sexual context.

Two separate questions appear to be at issue. First, to what extent do women seek erotic stimulation in pictures, books, and so on? Second, to what degree can women be aroused by such material? With respect to the second issue, experimental findings support the conclusions that any stimulus with sexual significance for an individual can be arousing and that this is no less true for women than for men. Women, however, have learned to experience more "sex guilt" when faced with openly admitting pursuit of sexual interests (Griffitt & Kaiser, 1978; Morokoff, 1985). Fewer women than men actively pursue sexual titillation from visual or auditory imagery.

Some have suggested that women do not actively seek sexually explicit material because such material omits romance. Our culture assumes that women are more romantic than men, more concerned with relationships, and less interested in sexual satisfaction that does not include love. Some evidence supports this view. For example, one study (Kenrick, Stringfield, Wagenhals, Dahl, & Ransdell, 1980) found that a sample of college women chose to view a "loving" erotic film as opposed to a hard-core "lustful" film significantly more often than did a sample of college men. On the other hand, another study (Fisher & Byrne, 1978) found that college women and men responded very similarly to both love and lust themes in erotic films, leading the investigators to conclude that an affectional or romantic emphasis was not a precondition for women's arousal by erotic stimuli. But such an emphasis may be a factor in what women seek out or prefer to view.

An alternative explanation of gender differences in the choice of sexual imagery focuses on the nature or quality of that material. Although many writers and social science researchers fail to distinguish between erotica and pornography and use the terms interchangeably, feminists have been asserting that these terms refer to very different kinds of visual and written materials. In erotica, sexual behavior is instrumental to mutual pleasure. Gloria Steinem (1978c) has pointed out that erotica comes from the root word *eros* and that it pertains "to passionate love or sexual desire" and is defined by the depiction of sexual love. It implies positive choice, acceptance, shared pleasure, communication, and, as Maureen Howard (1983) has suggested, it may "reveal to us the wonders of our sexuality" and encourage "personal revelation." Pornography, on the other hand, stems from the Greek *porne*, which means prostitute, and is not about sexual love or passion but about "dominance and violence against women." Pornography depicts women being sexually dominated—coerced or conquered, degraded, humiliated, or beaten.

> It may be very blatant, with weapons of torture or bondage, wounds and bruises, some clear humiliation, or an adult's sexual power being used over a child. It may be much more subtle: a physical attitude of conqueror and victim, the use of race or class differences to imply the same thing, perhaps a very unequal nudity, with one person exposed and vulnerable while the other is clothed.

In either case, there is no sense of equal choice or equal power. (Steinem, 1978c, p. 54)

In pornography, men are at war against women; sexual acts are used, like weapons, to inflict pain and to defeat the enemy. In pornography, writes Maureen Howard, a woman "becomes no more than a word for a part of her body, a mechanical device acted upon by a male thrust; if not willing to submit, brought to submission" (p. 326). Susan Griffin (1981) has argued that pornography is the antithesis of eroticism and, ultimately, antisexual and antinature. "The pornographer reduces a woman to a mere thing," and the woman, as object, "shows her goods" (p. 36). Although some pornography debases and humiliates men, Griffin has noted that these men are always smaller, weaker, and more "feminine" than their sexual dominators.

Heterosexual pornography is not about the sexual pleasure of women. I periodically receive unsolicited packages of illustrated materials advertising "premiere discount erotica," but these materials are misnamed. They feature incest, animals, and young girls and carry titles such as "Mammaries," "Shaved Naked Twats," "Anal Lust," and "Dominate Women." Such material is pornographic not because it is sexually explicit but because its primary message is the physical and psychological humiliation of women, which, tragically, stimulates sexual arousal in many men. It is understandable, then, why many women avoid pornography. Research that distinguishes between erotica and pornography and that examines women's reactions to each should provide important information. The major research questions being asked currently center on the effect of pornography on men's attitudes and interactions with women. We will discuss these and related issues in a subsequent chapter concerned explicitly with violence against women.

SEXUAL BEHAVIOR IN THE SERVICE OF OTHER GOALS

Sexual behavior serves a number of functions beyond that of being instrumental to sexual gratification. Some of these secondary functions are discussed below.

Sex as Symbol of Personal Identity or Power

Some writers (e.g., Person, 1980) have argued that women are less likely than men to use sexuality to achieve self-identity. Ann Snitow (1980), in reviewing how women novelists have treated sex in their works, concluded that although sex is sometimes presented as a reward for being daring and liberated, it is not presented (as in men's fiction) as a testing ground for the ego, as a way to assert oneself, or as a "symbol of . . . triumph or defeat." Yet, such themes have appeared in contemporary fiction by women, such as *Braided Lives* by Marge Piercy (1983), *August* by Judith Rossner (1983), and Gail Godwin's *A Mother and Two Daughters* (1983). The heroine in *Fly Away Home*, for example, recalls a relationship as follows: "She had slept with Ross, not out of passionate desire, not because she felt swept away, but because she was annoyed with herself for being twenty-one, graduated from college and still a virgin. . . . She was celebrating her independence of body, life, of judgment" (Piercy, 1984a, p. 170). Kate Simon (1982) ends her autobiographical description of emergence from childhood into adolescence by exulting in the discovery of how she can use her sexuality to control men, to mesmerize them, and thereby to become "invincible and immortal" like her favorite female movie stars. At thirteen, she felt "ready for all of them [the men] . . . ; to play, to tease, to amorously accept, to confidently reject" (p. 178).

A young woman began an article about college women with a disclosure about herself: "About all I can remember from spring in sophomore year is that I got myself a double bed. . . . For me, that bed was the ultimate symbol of adulthood—an advertisement that I was not only 'sexually active,' but that my body was my own, to do with as I pleased" (Crichton, 1983, p. 68). Similarly, Toni Bambara (1974) noted, in writing about the attitudes of African-American women, that "you were a 'real woman' when you had knowledge of and control of your sensual gifts" (p. 41).

For some women, then, sex presents a way of defining oneself and gaining power, and for others such an objective has serious negative consequences. During the course of her study of depression, Maggie Scarf (1980) met women who told her that they initiated sexual relationships "to ward off feelings of isolation" and to heighten activity or excitement. But their sexual interactions proved to be poor substitutes for intimacy and were not effective in increasing feelings of autonomy or control.

Sex as Status Symbol

Men boast of their sexual conquests, and women boast of the number of men who find them sexually attractive. Making such reports to friends is an attempt to gain social recognition and to enhance one's social status.

For Sylvia Plath (1972), speaking through a fictional heroine, the world in the 1950s was "divided into people

who had slept with somebody and people who hadn't, and this seemed the only really significant difference between one person and another" (p. 66). Decades later, the same issue is still salient. Since middle-class, college-educated women tend to marry later than working-class women, sexual experience outside of marriage may be a more compelling, status-relevant issue for the former. Writing from the perspective of a college woman, Sarah Crichton (1983) has described the "pressure" felt by sexually inexperienced women to whom virginity "simply means nobody wants you and you feel like shit." She quotes a junior at a midwestern university in the 1980s who echoes Plath's heroine of the 1950s: " 'I've got to get rid of it,' that's all you can think about" (p. 69).

Sex as Commodity

Women have been purchased, won, conquered, taken, and traded, and they have been part of the victor's booty in war. Women are also used to attract attention and to sell products. For example, an ad for a centrifuge in a prestigious science journal reads, "The first beautiful centrifuge," and shows a beautiful blonde woman in a lab coat standing next to the item; a major airline attempts to lure customers by presenting a swimsuit-clad woman under a giant caption that reads, "What's your pleasure?" Women are used as "incentives" for men of varied backgrounds, education, and interests. A newspaper story describing how private companies "use sex to win government contracts" ("How Firms Use Sex," 1980) was relegated to the middle of the paper, presumably because this is not an unusual occurrence. The story informed its readers that sex is "routine" in the world of business and government contracting.

That sex can be exchanged for goods and services is a lesson learned across ethnic groups and is part of the experience of both African-American and European-American women. Thus, Gloria Joseph (1981b), writing about the childhood and adolescence of African-American women, has noted that in our society "sex is the dominant commodity for monetary profit, personal gains and gratifications, and human exploitation" (p. 205). Many adolescent girls are taught to "cash in" on their sex appeal, to use it to manipulate boys for material advantage. Ossie Guffy, an African-American woman, remembered her big sister's advice to her about sex (Guffy & Ledner, 1971):

> Boys lust even more than girls . . . . When a boy lusts after you, that's when you get him to do what you want. You've got to make them feel you're going to let them, and then when they're so horny they can't see straight, you kind of

pull back and whisper you're afraid. Then . . . you start talking about how you'd love to have a charm bracelet, or a new scarf, or see a certain movie, and they'll fall all over themselves getting you what you want, 'cause they figure once you've got what you want, you'll give them what they want. (p. 63)

This advice is straight talk, direct and clear. Other girls receive similar but more subtle, ambiguous, and disguised messages from peers, parents, or the media. For example, in the real-life story of Teresa Cardenas told by Robert Coles and Jane Coles (1978), we learn that her father, a strict, traditional patriarch, responded to knowledge of his 15-year-old daughter's highly paid job in a dance hall by reminding her that "money is not an evil thing." When Teresa considered consulting the priest, her father said, "No—there are some things it's best not to tell priests" (p. 157).

The message that sex is exchangeable for unrelated desired outcomes is well accepted in our culture. Girls and women learn that sex can be exchanged not only for commodities but also for intimacy or commitment. Studies of teenage girls, in particular, suggest that "as girls give more of themselves physically to the male, they want the comforts of intimacy in return" (Fanzo, 1987–88, p. 5). The pleasure of sex is not the major goal; they are trading sex for commitment, as illustrated by answers to questions about their decision to have sex. The reasons given "usually had little or nothing to do with desire" (p. 14).

It has long been understood that women trade sex for the comfort and benefits of a relationship with a man, and this phenomenon seems not to have altered much over the past few decades. Women continue to exchange sex for love, commitment, or security, fearing the consequences of hardship, devaluation, and loneliness if they do not (Ehrenreich, Hess, & Jacobs, 1986). We treat with good humor even the portrayal of very young girls in this role of sex trader. One full-page ad in the *New York Times Magazine,* for example, showed a seductive little girl with a sexy look dressed as half-adult, half-child in an enormous fur coat under the caption, "Get what you've always wanted." Such advertisements rarely produce public complaint or concern because our culture accepts and encourages women to use sexuality as a means of exchange. As noted by Andree Nicola-McLaughlin (1985):

Exploitation of the sexuality of women is a basic element of American enterprise—the blood of Big Business—by which billions of dollars in profit are amassed annually, capitalizing on women's sexuality in . . . corporate-

sponsored media advertising, literature, music, movies, television, medicine, beauty pageants and pornography. (p. 33)

Sex as Sport

Sexual acts are often viewed as requiring skill, expertise, and training; persons boast of themselves or others as expert lovers or, like players of a game, they "score" or win. This attitude is reflected in the extraordinary popularity of how-to sex manuals and in the concern that some mental health practitioners have expressed about the "demands" individuals feel for sexual "performance."

The idea that sex is something a person can do well or badly seems to be an old one and has provided both genders with a source of humor about the other's vulnerabilities. Rayna Green (1977), in an article about the "bawdy lore of Southern women," shared some of the tales told by Southern women about men's sexual errors. "Usually the subject for laughter is men's boasts, failures or inadequacies ('comeuppance for lack of uppcomance,' as one of my aunts would say)" (p. 31). Bawdy lore, according to Green, provided a safe way to laugh at men's pretensions; helped relieve women's sexual disappointments, frustrations, humiliations, and anxieties; and also provided sex education for young girls. What girls did not understand in the jokes, they later inquired about from friends or relatives. Toni Bambara (1974) has presented a similar picture of the sex education of young African-American girls by older women. There is bound to be an aunt, she wrote, who will "encourage you to hang out in the beauty parlor or her living room with her and her friends and eavesdrop," where some woman will look you straight in the eye and warn, "if he don't know what he's doing, pitch him out the bed on his head" (p. 40).

When sex with others falls short of our expectations, and their or our own expertise is found wanting, we invent pleasure machines. William Masters and Virginia Johnson popularized the vibrator, and more recently, women have been offered Tupperware-style parties where they can purchase exotic sex equipment instead of plastic containers. The popularity of sadomasochistic sex can also be viewed as an extension of sex as sport. The influence of "S&M" can be seen in women's fashions, as illustrated by an entire section in *Vogue* magazine on steel accessories worn by wide-eyed, frightened-looking models—arm shackles as bracelets, steel belts, and neck leashes were featured. The appropriate matching clothing, described in fashion jargon as "hard-edged" and "rough," was shown with jagged edges and cut-out pieces, as though ripped (Howard, 1983). The sexual innuendoes were clear from the models' body postures, sultry lips, and tousled hair.

Heterosexual Sex in the Maintenance of Gender Inequality

A well-known ad for men's shoes, which was withdrawn after protests by women's groups, showed a nude woman lying contentedly next to her man's shoe under the message, "Keep her where she belongs." Although we might be inclined to laugh at this rather old cliché, it appears to be remarkably sturdy. In the late 1970s and early 1980s, for example, a top-selling manufacturer of women's underwear (Maidenform) ran a series of full-page, glossy ads in the *New York Times Magazine* that showed women wearing only bikini underpants and bras in outrageous places and in various roles: in telephone booths, in the subway, in an airplane cockpit, conducting an orchestra, playing basketball, as a physician talking with a patient, as a lawyer pleading a case, as a chef, as a businesswoman, as a tourist, as a musician, and so on. In every case, the only other persons in the ad were fully clothed, appropriately dressed men who functioned as obvious counterpoints to the ridiculous, but sexy, women. Although these ads no longer appear in the 1990s—as a result of feminist criticism—those for Guess jeans and Victoria's Secret have replaced them by presenting women in postures, positions, situations, and abbreviated clothing, heavy with sexual meaning, in which the women appear to be waiting "to be taken."

The elevation of men's image through the sexual put-down of women is evident in writing that emerged from the politically passionate period of the 1960s and 1970s, when sizable numbers of African-American and European-American women and men worked together to achieve common social objectives. Even within these groups, sex with men functioned to maintain women's lesser status. Stokeley Carmichael's comment about women in the civil rights movement—that their "only position" within it was "prone"—has been widely quoted. We have paid less attention, however, to how women saw themselves in this arena of radical political activity. Marge Piercy's (1979) character Vida tells us that it was necessary to put "out a certain sexual buzz" as "a way of apologizing for being herself" (p. 124). Similarly, in Rosellen Brown's *Civil Wars* (1984), Jessie remembers herself as a Northern college girl working in the civil rights movement in Mississippi:

She was Teddy's girl . . . . They made room for her, but not for herself; they respected her because they must; she walked in his aura. She was exhilarated and depressed in the same instant; then Teddy would come up behind her, turn her to him, no matter where they were, and suck a kiss so sweetly from her lips (right in the middle of conversation, as her lips formed an important word) that speech and opinion, hers at least, were put in their place. (p. 237)

Other novels about the 1960s, such as Alice Walker's *Meridian* (1976) and Sara Davidson's *Loose Change* (1978), relate how sexual relationships with men served to neutralize and diminish women's bids for leadership in radical political groups and to prevent their equal participation in decision making. Sexual involvement with a politically active man was viewed as a contribution by the woman to the "movement," just as in other times and places sexual relationships with men have been seen as contributing to men's successes and progress by promoting their health and welfare.

A somewhat different motive for sexual behavior, but one that also serves to maintain gender inequality, is to obtain male protection against the demands made by other men. For example, in *Meridian* (Walker, 1976), sex for a high school girl is described as "not pleasure, but a sanctuary in which her mind was freed of any consideration for all the other males in the universe who might want anything of her. It was resting from pursuit" (p. 62).

WOMEN'S AMBIVALENCE ABOUT SEX

Women certainly derive pleasure from sexual arousal and orgasm. The conclusion that the experience of sexual gratification is comparable in women and men, both psychologically and physiologically, is supported by ample data, some of which have already been cited and discussed. However, the social context in which sexual behavior is learned differs for women and men in conditions and circumstances, and these influence women's and men's resultant attitudes toward sexuality. As we have seen, in our culture women's sexuality is exploited to a far greater extent than men's. Consequently, men almost always see sex as a positive goal, but women view it as having both positive and negative aspects; women's ambivalence about sexuality often keeps them from enjoying it fully. Let us look more closely at this issue.

Woman's Role as "Gatekeeper"

Adolescent boys typically learn that sexual activity is desirable and pleasurable, and even necessary for good health. Heterosexual experience confers high status and signifies maturity and manhood. Teenage girls, however, are taught opposite or unclear values in relation to sexuality. Many girls still learn that sexual activity is primarily a means to attract and keep a boyfriend and that a girl should engage in sexual behavior only to the extent necessary to satisfy her boyfriend's needs, not her own. Women are still given the responsibility of restraining and tempering the sexual demands of men, whose needs, they are taught, are greater and more insistent than their own. Naomi McCormick (1979), for example, found that among a group of college students having sex was regarded "as a male goal and avoiding sex as a female goal." A subsequent study (McCormick, Brannigan, & LaPlante, 1984) supported the earlier findings and found evidence that women and men behave in accordance with these stereotypes. Thus, a sample of men college students "reported using strategies more to have sex," while "women reported using strategies more to avoid sex." Researchers continue to find that women report themselves to be less comfortable than men in initiating sex and more comfortable refusing it, thus acting as "gatekeepers." In one study (Grauerholz & Serpe, 1985), the women who did report initiating sexual intimacies were likely to have had more sexual partners and to be more aware of sexual inequalities than the other women. In general, however, these data indicated that "rising sexual intercourse rates . . . do not suggest a fundamental change in sex roles" (p. 1058).

Having sexual relations with boys, though instrumental in keeping their attention, reduces an adolescent girl's status even in the 1990s; it besmirches her reputation, marks her as a "bad girl," and reduces her likability. One study (Garcia, 1982), for example, found that young women described as being well experienced sexually were evaluated less positively than less sexually experienced women by a sample of unmarried college students. Another study of college women (Preston & Stanley, 1987) found "striking evidence" that women and men shared conventional attitudes and adhered to "sexual double standards under which promiscuity is shameful only for women" (p. 218).

Whereas adolescent boys may gain respect from sexual exploits, being sexually free is still considered a sign of deviance among girls, and sexual offenses are used to define female delinquency. This difference is maintained in the legal approach to prostitution. In most states, it is the seller, typically a woman, and not the buyer, typically a man, who is considered more reprehensible, threatening to society, and criminal. These differing standards for women and men were sharply pointed out by tennis star Martina Navratilova in commenting on the public's entirely positive and sympathetic response to the disclosure by basketball hero Magic Johnson that he is HIV positive and to the description of his sexual activity.

> Appearing on Donahue, Navratilova talked about the double standard that society uses in judging the behavior of heterosexual men versus that of women, lesbians and gay men. "I'm staggered that Magic said he had been [sexually involved] with about 1,000 women," Navratilova stated. "If a heterosexual woman had made those revelations . . . [or] that she had been with 100 or 200 men . . . she would be called a slut. And if a male or female athlete [had said they] got it through homosexual contact, they would not be a [national] hero." ("Martina Questions," 1991)

The research literature indicates that although women's sexuality is now more freely and frequently expressed in behavior than during our parents' and grandparents' young adulthoods, attitudes have changed more slowly. J. Roy Hopkins (1977) examined surveys conducted prior to 1965 and compared their results with those obtained from surveys in the 1970s. He concluded that among young adolescents, aged 13 to 15, there "is some evidence for earlier experimentation with intercourse," but that actual incidences have been exaggerated and that more is talked about than is actually done. But, national data on unmarried 15-year-old girls who said they had had sex reveal a change from 15 percent in 1971 to 27 percent in 1988 ("The Children of the Shadows," 1993). A 1990 survey of health habits conducted by the Centers for Disease Control among a large national sample of high school students found that 48 percent had had sexual intercourse by 10th grade, 57 percent by 11th grade, and 72 percent by 12th grade ("Survey," 1992).

Among college-age women and men the data point to a dramatic increase in sexual activity and to "intergender *convergence* in sexual behavior" (Hopkins, 1977). Compared with earlier college surveys, in which 55 percent of the men and 25 percent of the women had reported premarital coitus, surveys conducted after 1965 found at least 60 percent of the men and at least 40 percent of the women reporting such behavior. Other data continue to indicate that young men have greater sexual experience at an earlier age than young women do. Thus, for example, a study of a sample of never-married college students found that almost 30 percent of the women, compared with 15 percent of the men, had never had heterosexual intercourse (Whitley, 1988). Another study found a decrease in sexual activity among unmarried college women from the late 1970s to the early 1980s (Gerrard, 1987).

Regardless of the shifts in frequency of sexual behavior, researchers agree that conventional attitudes and gender relationships persist (e.g., Blumstein & Schwartz, 1983; Peplau, Rubin, & Hill, 1977). Contemporary women are expressing sexuality more openly than in prior generations, but ambivalence seems to be more the rule than the exception. As "gatekeeper," women are expected to know and follow the rules and to confine their sexual experiences to intimate love relationships. In *Cat's Eye* (1988), novelist Margaret Atwood describes sexual experiences of teenage girls that will be immediately recognized by many adult women. "We go to the movies, where we sit in the smoking section and neck, or we go to drive-ins and eat pop-corn and neck there as well. There are rules for necking, which we observe: approach, push away, approach, push away" (p. 252). Married women, too, appear to express their ambivalence in sexual relationships with their husbands. According to Helen Kaplan Singer, director of the Human Sexuality Program at a New York City hospital, wives are more likely to refuse sex than their husbands are, but wives are also more likely to be the ones who complain about the infrequency of sex (Liebmann-Smith, 1987).

Nameless or Shameful Genitals

In addition to women's designated cultural role as gatekeeper, other factors contribute to women's ambivalence about sex. Men experience pleasure in the use of their penises for urination, masturbation, and copulation. Even little boys who may be told horrible tales by their parents about the evils that will befall them if they "play with themselves" have ample opportunities to find out differently from peers, older boys, and personal trial and error. By and large, boys acquire positive associations for the part of their body that is the focus of their sexuality. Girls, on the other hand, learn to expect many negative consequences from their sexuality, to anticipate pain or problems during menstruation, pregnancy, childbirth, and their first act of sexual intercourse.

One study (Gartrell & Mosbacher, 1984) has documented differences in what little girls and boys learn to call their genitals. From the retrospective responses of adults to questions about first words learned for genitalia, the researchers found that girls were far less likely than boys

to have learned the correct anatomical names for their own genitals as children, that both boys and girls learned the word *penis* significantly earlier than they learned any correct name for female genitals, and that the incorrect words taught for the latter were more euphemistic and pejorative than the nonanatomical words learned for male genitals. Thus, while *peenee* or *peter,* for example, were learned by some little boys instead of *penis,* the former terms may be considered derivatives of the latter, whereas *privates, shame, nasty,* or *down there,* words learned by the girls, have no linguistic relationship to *vagina* or *clitoris.* These data indicate that our culture regards the sexuality of boys and men not only as more important, but as nicer, cleaner, and less embarrassing than the sexuality of girls and women.

Woman as Sex Object

Sexuality to many women means being a "sex object." While this concept has been translated into humorous images for cartoons, films, and fiction, it is of utmost seriousness to women, who learn from all areas of the culture that we have "utility." One cartoon given to me by a student shows a sexily dressed woman clerk behind a drugstore counter. A sign on the counter reads, "If You Don't See It, Ask for It." The customer, a genial, well-dressed gentleman in suit, tie, and hat, smiles and asks, "Can I see your tits?" We learn that women can be bought—by favors, by being "wined and dined," or by cash—or exchanged, treasured, or manhandled. I suspect that many women have questioned at some point in a relationship whether they were being sexually used.

The interchangeability of women, as bodies, is the subject of a cartoon (another student donation) in which a movie love scene is about to be filmed. The leading man lies waiting on the bed. The male director has his arm around the voluptuous, naked woman who will also play in the scene; she is faceless, and the director shouts, "Makeup!" The strength of our culture's acceptance of, and blindness to, women's treatment as relatively interchangeable objects on display for the titillation and amusement of men can be illustrated by *Playboy* magazine. Christine Heffner, president of Playboy Enterprises, explained in an interview that "we have come through the sexual revolution and the women's movement and men and women feel more comfortable with each other now" (Geist, 1985). Although she insisted that *Playboy* intended to emphasize relationships and to present "women as more than sex objects," the November 1985 issue featured a group of the smartest women in the United

States, members of the high-IQ association MENSA, posing nude.

Women are confused and pulled in conflicting directions by their objectification as sex goddesses. On the one hand, they are pulled toward making themselves match as closely as possible the sexual image considered attractive to men. On the other hand, they experience the disappointment and pain that stems from the realization that they are perceived only as collections of body parts that titillate men and are useful for men's pleasure. This confusion is illustrated by a tight miniskirt on a woman at work in a public or professional setting, who can't expect her words to be taken seriously when her body is dressed to demand attention. Similarly, the suggestion by some that Madonna is a symbol of women's power and sexual freedom because she is in control of the images she projects is belied by the fact that these images are ones that our sexist culture relishes and pays well to maintain.

The lengths to which many women go to conform to our culture's demeaning standards of sexual attractiveness can be illustrated by two phenomena: the enormous amounts of money spent on cosmetics and beauty aids, and the growth of the practice of cosmetic surgery. As noted by Gloria Joseph (1981c):

> The female image . . . requires women to be simultaneously sensuous, slim, sexy, soft, smooth, shiny, subtle, and seductive! A plethora of aids are needed for women to achieve this image. . . . [Women] use billions of dollars of beauty products annually, plus countless hours, in an effort to 'attain' this image. More than 48 million dollars is spent annually on eye makeup alone . . . . The selling of . . . woman as sex object is big business. (p. 157)

Anyone who has stepped onto the main floor of a large department store can verify that the most space is devoted to selling cosmetics, perfumes, and other personal beauty products for women.

The beauty industry is not confined to over-the-counter products. Cosmetic surgery is also big business for chemical companies and physicians. The grave consequences of one form of this surgery, breast implants, have now been revealed. Well-documented side effects from the use of silicone gel implants include scleroderma, an "autoimmune disease that causes a gradual hardening of the skin and internal organs and can be fatal, . . . systemic lupus erythematosus, and rheumatoid and other kinds of arthritis" ("Breast Implants," 1990, p. 25). So convincing is the evidence of serious side effects that in January 1992 the Food and Drug Administration (FDA) halted the sale and use of silicone implants pending further study. At the time of the FDA action, such implants were already in the breasts of about 2 million women ("FDA Calls," 1992), 150,000 women each year having had the surgery since the implants first became available from the Dow Chemical Company. Among these women, 80 percent requested the implants for cosmetic reasons, not for breast reconstruction following surgical treatment of breast cancer by mastectomy.

Our culture's preoccupation with women as objects has led to serious health problems for women who have turned to surgery to make them sexier and also for women who diet to dangerous extremes—a subject to which we will return in a later chapter. This preoccupation also, however, keeps the cosmetics and fashion industries prosperous and insures that advertisers can profit by creating sexy images of women to sell more and more products. Nowhere do we see the extremes to which advertising has gone in its degradation of women than on MTV, the music video channel. According to media researcher Sut Jhally:

> Women on MTV are most often used as props, put there to entice male viewers. One frequently used technique is to simply flash images of women's bodies at random while a rock star sings his latest hit . . . . Women are objects with no identity apart from that bestowed on them by men. . . . The camera consumes women's bodies, [as it] moves up and down . . . . (Pelka, 1991, pp. 23f.)

Professor Jhally has produced a videotape entitled *Dreamworlds* that seriously and carefully documents his critical analysis of MTV.

That women exist for men's pleasure is a dominant and continuously repeated message in the entertainment media, including television, popular music, movies, and magazines. A study of the 1985 issues of *Playboy* (Matacin & Burger, 1987) revealed that in the cartoons with sexual themes, women were more often shown as the victims of sexual coercion, as sexually naive and childlike, and with more attractive bodies than men. Janet Maslin (1990) called attention to the large number of films in 1990 in which "women are left to play bimbos, and the bimbos take a back seat" (p. H-13); and Leslie Guttman (1991) has commented on the nature of the covers of 1990 mainstream women's magazines. "They stare out from the magazine rack; slim, shapely models in low-cut blouses, cleavage in which you could lose small change forever" (p. E-8). Although intended for women, these magazines are controlled largely by men, and the current "undress for success" fashion clearly illustrates that the objectification of women continues to be trendy.

The objectification of women as bodies is also sometimes a feature of lesbian sexuality, as noted in a

WHAT SHE SAID:

You're a nice guy, but-I'm NOT Sexually interested in you! Besides, I've got a Boyfriend. I Don't like this Rambo approach - there's No WAY I'll go out with you, not a chance, GO AWAY!

WHAT HE HEARD:

You're a sexy, interesting guy! Beside my Boyfriend, you look like an approachable Rambo. There's No WAY I'm going to miss the chance to GO AWAY with you some weekend!

Cartoon by Libby Reid from *Do You Hate Your Hips More than Nuclear War?* Copyright ©1988 by Penguin Books. Reprinted by permission of Libby Reid.

report (Blumenfeld, 1991) on a lesbian nightclub featuring erotic dancers in Washington, DC, modeled after similar popular clubs in New York City. The performers dance in "G-strings, push-up bras, garter belts, and thigh-high stockings" (p. 2); the show has fueled emotional debate within the lesbian community and among feminists. In a similar vein, some heterosexual women attend male strip shows, hire male strippers to perform at pre-wedding parties for brides and their friends, and gain amusement and titillation from the Chippendales, a group of male performers in abbreviated costumes who bump and grind and flex their muscles while welcoming monetary tips from appreciative customers who place bills in the men's bikini shorts.

Sexual Harassment

While some advertisers and entertainment entrepreneurs have introduced the new theme that men, too, can be sexual objects, the predominant image is one that objectifies women. With such media images almost constantly before us, it is not surprising that some men seriously expect women to be immediately and gratefully responsive to the men's sexual interest, as satirized in the cartoon shown above. Some men respond with anger when a woman is not sexually responsive to their attentions and accuse her of not being a real woman. For example, Kate Simon (1990) described what happened when she rejected the sexual advances of a friend's husband. "I laughed as I eluded him from table to bedroom, to hallway, to kitchen. Exhausted, infuriated, he gave up, flinging at me as he reached for his coat a common accusation: 'I always suspected you were a lesbian; now I'm sure'" (p. 108).

This incident illustrates the relationship between the view of women as sex objects and women's experience of sexual harassment and assault, which also contributes to women's ambivalence toward sexuality. Girls learn at an early age that they are vulnerable and largely unprotected from male predators. We try to separate the bad men, who openly leer, catcall, or follow us on the street, from the good ones—our fathers, brothers, and boyfriends—but such a classification becomes increasingly difficult as we encounter more and more men who are fathers or brothers to some other women but pinchers, leerers, or assaulters to us. Male college professors and business executives may be more subtle than the often stereotyped, and probably maligned, blue-collar construction worker, but their sexual allusions and unwanted advances are no less insistent and demeaning. As noted in a report by the Project on the Status and Education of Women (1978):

> Fear of ridicule, and a sense of helplessness about the problem and a feeling that it's a personal dilemma have kept the problem concealed. Many men believe a woman's "no" is really "yes," and therefore do not accept her refusal. Additionally, when a man is in a position of power, such as employer or teacher, the woman may be coerced or feel forced to submit. Women who openly charge harassment are often not believed, may be ridiculed, may lose their job, be given a bad grade or be mistreated in some way. (p. 1)

Research has documented the widespread nature of sexual harassment and confirmed its frequency in social and job settings and on high school and college campuses. Sexual harassment has been reported by patients and clients in medical and legal settings, by students, teachers, employees, vacationers, and women almost everywhere, and the literature on this subject continues to grow. In a later chapter we will consider this issue again. Here, we want to think about how the prevalence of harassment is likely to impact on women's attitudes toward sexuality.

It is the rare woman who has not had some personal experience with inappropriate sexual advances, and such experiences are commonly found in fictional and autobiographical accounts of women's lives. For example, Kate Simon's (1982) introduction to sex as a child included the ugly gropings, fondlings, and abuse of her body by the neighborhood barber, a friend of her parents, and her immigrant cousins. Lynne Schwartz's fictional heroine in *Leaving Brooklyn* (1989) is sexually accosted by a stranger on a subway train and later seduced by her physician. In an autobiographical account, Itabari Njeri (1990) describes an interview for a back-up singing job with a popular entertainer. "He called me from the other room. When I walked in, he was sitting naked on the desk. 'I'd like to make a film with you,' he said, standing now, smiling" (p. 173). Lisa Alther's protagonist Clea in *Bedrock* (1990) is seduced by her art professor in college.

> Professor Galmer had developed a special interest in her work. And in her breasts, where his eyes alighted when he thought she wasn't noticing. He summoned her to his office to show her his portfolio of nudes. (p. 54)

Later, as a working woman, Clea finds that a "sexual favor" is necessary to land a freelance photography job. "Throughout the sex act she stared grimly at a steel I-beam overhead, feeling nothing" (p. 67). Such a situation is presented humorously for male readers in a cartoon in *Playboy*. A leering, obviously satisfied man is getting into his clothes while his secretary is zipping up her skimpy outfit. "By the way," says the boss, "for your raise, you have to ask Mr. Peacock."

When women are sexually harassed, we are often not quite certain that we have not somehow been at fault. Have we enticed the man by our manner or our dress, been too friendly or flirtatious? Women may be reluctant to discuss or report sexual harassment if they are not certain that they did not somehow provoke it. Consider how difficult it is to reconcile the humiliation experienced by receiving the unwanted attentions of a man with the feeling of flattery that comes from being found attractive by him. Among the lessons learned by adolescent girls is that to attract a man is highest on the list of achievements; but just how to do this appropriately and safely remains unclear. As noted by Judith Laws and Pepper Schwartz (1977):

> Those parts of the body which are sexualized in our culture—legs, face, breasts, and to a lesser extent buttocks—are subjected to special routines of display and enhancement. . . . A socialization of the young woman for the role of sex object takes place during puberty. A great deal of attention is focused on the way she looks, and she receives a lot of feedback on her "good points" and "figure faults." . . . She learns the techniques of enhancement, display and artifice. . . . The dialectic between display and concealment, or permissible flaunting and taboo, can be seen clearly in the conventions of dress. (pp. 42f.)

A considerable body of evidence suggests that women and men differ in their evaluations of unwanted sexual initiatives, and that men perceive the same cues as more explicitly sexual in meaning than do women. In a series of studies at the University of Rhode Island (Lott, Reilly, &

Howard, 1982; Reilly, Lott, & Gallogly, 1986; Reilly, Lott, Caldwell, & DeLuca, 1992), my colleagues and I have found that in response to 10 different statements dealing with sexually harassing behavior (such as "an attractive woman has to expect sexual advances and should learn how to handle them"), men exhibit greater tolerance for sexual harassment than women do. In other words, men tend to view sexually related behavior on the job and at school as something to be expected and as less problematic and serious than do women. Other investigators who have used our *Tolerance for Sexual Harassment Scale* have replicated the finding of greater acceptance of harassment on the part of men.

Research has found that men tend to ascribe more sexual meaning than women to a variety of situations and cues. For example, among a sample of adolescents in Los Angeles (Zellman, Johnson, Giarusso, & Goodchilds, 1979), the girls were found to be significantly less likely than the boys to interpret behavioral cues and clothing in sexual terms. In an experimental study, Antonia Abbey (1982) had pairs of mixed-gender observers watch pairs of mixed-gender actors (all college students) carry on a 5-minute discussion, after which the observers rated the actors on various dimensions. The men were found to "interpret women's friendliness as an indication of sexual interest" and to see themselves and other men as well as women in a sexual context. Abbey concluded that "men are more likely to perceive the world in sexual terms and to make sexual judgments than women are" (p. 836). In subsequent studies (Abbey & Melby, 1986) in which college students rated photographs of female-male pairs seated at a table, men raters consistently perceived women "as being sexier and more seductive" than did women raters. Other investigators (Saal, Johnson, & Weber, 1989), using three different methods, have confirmed the general phenomenon that men tend to perceive sexual motives or intentions in women's behavior. The investigators concluded that "men's 'thresholds' for perceiving seductive, flirtatious, promiscuous, and generally sexy behavior in women may be reached more easily—that is, by actions that are less overtly sexy—than women's thresholds" (p. 275).

In an important extension of this work (Johnson, Stockdale, & Saal, 1991), college men who were exposed to videotaped scenes of a professor harassing a student were significantly more likely than women students to report that the woman in the scene, whether a student or a professor, was behaving in a promiscuous, seductive, and sexy manner. These findings held across conditions in which the level of harassment was varied and regardless of whether the student in the scene rejected or accepted the harassment, suggesting the difficulty some men have in recognizing or acknowledging sexual harassment. It seems likely, as well, that the greater primacy of sex in men's interpretations of the world contributes to their sexually harassing behavior and adds to their conviction that women who say "no" are merely being coy and hoping to be pursued further. Some women do indeed say "no" when they mean "yes," but such behavior is less common than men believe. One study (Muehlenhard & Hollabaugh, 1988) found, among a large sample of college women, that 85.2 percent reported saying "no" to intercourse and meaning it. The women who said "no" but meant "yes" were more likely to subscribe to traditional sexual beliefs, more likely "to believe that token resistance is a common behavior among women, that male-female relationships are adversarial, that it is acceptable for men to use physical force in male-female relationships, and that women enjoy it when men use force" (p. 877). My colleagues and I (Reilly, Lott, Caldwell, & DeLuca, 1992) obtained complementary findings; college women who self-reported tolerance for sexual harassment were also more likely to believe in adversarial sexual relations and to subscribe to myths about rape.

Although our culture strongly encourages women to be attractive to men, women also expect to make decisions about which men to accept and about the situations in which they will participate sexually. Too many boys and men, however, do not learn the necessary complementary lessons, such as taking a woman's "no" seriously. Part of men's reality is their higher status and power; they can therefore with relative impunity consider women, no matter what else the women may be or what skills they may have, as fundamentally sexual objects that men have the right to use. Although this cultural message is sometimes at variance with men's self-doubts, fears of incompetence, lack of assertiveness, and needs for acceptance, it seems generally to be the case that sex and the aggressive pursuit of sex are difficult to separate for many men in our culture. Many men do not learn to distinguish well among expressing interest in a woman, asking her for a date, visual ogling, whistling, verbal comments about a woman's body, uninvited touching, and coercion. Such a state of affairs contributes substantially to women's ambivalence about sexuality.

Fear of Pregnancy and Disease

Despite the availability of contraceptives, the fear of an unwanted pregnancy also continues to contribute to women's ambivalence about sex. In *Meridian,* Alice Walker (1976) described a southern college for African-American women in which one common experience brought women from different social backgrounds together.

> Any girl who had ever prayed for her period to come was welcome to the commemoration, which was held in the guise of a slow May Day dance. . . . It was the only time in all the many social activities at Saxon that every girl was considered equal. On that day, they held each other's hands tightly. (p. 45)

Kate Simon (1986) vividly described the fear of pregnancy she and her friends experienced as unmarried college women: "our stomachs turned to burning knots as one week and a third passed without a period" (p. 177). The journals I sometimes collect from contemporary college women contain similar descriptions. Thus, it is the unusual woman who has not experienced, at some time in her life, that awful anxiety associated with being "late," and for whom fear of pregnancy has not interfered in some way with the free expression of sexuality.

The danger of contracting AIDS has greatly added to the anxieties surrounding sexual behavior for women in the 1990s. Among the 200,000 AIDS patients in this country as of the beginning of 1992, 90 percent are men—the majority of whom are homosexual, bisexual, or intravenous drug users—but the percentage of heterosexuals who are HIV positive is growing steadily, particularly among women. An estimated 1 million persons in the USA are believed to be HIV infected—that is, not yet ill with AIDS but carrying HIV, the AIDS virus (Cowley & Hager, 1991). It is ironic, as was pointed out by Deborah Rogers (1988), that, despite the statistics indicating a far greater probability of infection for men, in the soap opera world the three characters who have been presented as having AIDS are all women. One of the fictional women contracted the virus directly through prostitution, another from blood donated by a prostitute, and the third from her drug-using ex-husband. A rather clear message is apparently being sent here about the punishment in store for some women.

An additional irony, of more tragic proportions, is evident in the conclusion reached by a group of medical researchers about "'dramatic' disparities" (Emery, 1991) in the treatment given to women and men AIDS patients. Along with nonwhite, drug-using, or uninsured patients, women were found to have significantly less chance of being treated with the anti-AIDS drug AZT; specifically, "men were three times more likely than women to be offered" this treatment. The investigators, who interviewed AIDS patients in nine cities across the United States, believe their findings may help to explain why women with AIDS die sooner than men. AIDS is believed to have already killed 14,000 women in this country, a figure that is probably an underestimate in the view of some experts because of the underrecognition of AIDS in women and inadequate reporting (Freiberg, 1990b). More than 70 percent of women with AIDS are African-American or Latina and among the former in New York and New Jersey, AIDS is now the leading cause of death.

While the major medical and media focus has been on the spread of HIV and AIDS, women are even more susceptible to the other dangerous sexually transmitted diseases (STDs), which are more difficult to diagnose in women than in men (Rhode Island Women's Health Collective, 1991). The number and variety of STDs and their prevalence are alarming. Federal statistics indicate that almost 13 million new cases arise annually—65 percent in persons under 25, with an estimated 3 million teens affected each year (Family Life Information Service, 1988; Cowley & Hager, 1991). The most common of these diseases from bacterial infections are chlamydia (the most prevalent, with 4 million cases each year), syphilis, gonorrhea, and chancroid. STDs that are transmitted by viruses are genital herpes (where the virus remains in the body for life), condyloma (genital warts), and hepatitis B. STDs have been linked to a higher risk of cervical cancer, infertility, pelvic inflammatory disease (PID), ectopic pregnancy, infection of fetuses and newborns, and fetal death, and some (syphilis and genital herpes) are associated with an increased risk of HIV infection (Rhode Island Women's Health Collective, 1991).

RECONSTRUCTING WOMEN'S SEXUAL SCRIPTS

Given the present social conditions under which young women learn sexual behavior, it seems inevitable that conflict will be experienced by both lesbian and heterosexual women. All women in our culture experience or observe similar consequences for pursuing sexual pleasure. There are positive outcomes from body arousal and sensual excitement, and gratification from physical contact and affection with another person. At the same time, though, there is anxiety about possible negative consequences—concern about sexual exploitation, uncertainty about one's adequacy, fear of pregnancy, anxiety

about disease, social rejection for having (or for not having) a sexual relationship, and concern about the meaning of the relationship. Judith Laws and Pepper Schwartz (1977) have suggested that most young women now subscribe to the standard that sex is permissible if love is present. "But when is love present? . . . [The new standard] that both partners should love in order for sex to be acceptable . . . provides no way to tell if your partner feels the same way you do" (pp. 48f.).

Women's ambivalence about sexuality should decrease as they begin to experience mainly positive outcomes and as they communicate this experience to other women. As women grow older, the pleasures derived from sexual experience and close physical contact with another person should become more potent and the negative associations of badness, of pain, and of being used should weaken. Positive outcomes may also increase as women explore more varied sexual scripts and receive "permission, instruction, and support in learning about their own bodies and the patterns of their own sexual response" (Laws & Schwartz, 1977, p. 62). The possibility of erotic pleasure with another woman is increasingly discussed among women and is being explored in the media. For example, a film presented on network television in 1986 ("My Two Loves") sensitively dramatized the development of erotic attraction between two attractive, upper-middle-class European-American women who had become close friends; and the popular dramatic serial "LA Law" featured a woman attorney who was bisexual. Predictably, however, this character is no longer in the series.

In general, contemporary women appear to differ from previous generations in being more sexually assertive and less passive or simply reactive in sexual situations, in talking more about how they achieve sexual pleasure, and in taking more responsibility for contraception and safe sex. Nevertheless, sexual conflict for young women is unlikely to grow less intense until both genders begin to give similar meaning and value to their sexual experiences. This, in turn, is not likely to occur while men and women continue to be unequal in social status. Changes in sexual standards and greater tolerance for sexuality in an otherwise unchanged world, in which women have less value and power than men, will merely compound the pressures on women, increase the chances for exploitation, and enhance the probability of conflict. We must understand, as noted by Jill Lewis (1981a), that "the conditions and experience of sexuality are enmeshed in the traditions, laws, attitudes, and institutions of a society" (p. 270).

Beth Schneider and Meredith Gould (1987) have outlined some of the new questions that must be asked about sexuality. These questions include "how objects and acts become eroticized, the impact of the sexual revolution on women, and the ways in which race and class shape sexual experience" (p. 146). We need to know a great deal more about how sexuality is defined and experienced throughout the life span, including old age. And "we know virtually nothing about girls' sexual experiences that deviate from cultural experiences, such as in homosexual or autoerotic activity" (p. 147). Heterosexual parents rarely respond to emerging homosexuality in their children with understanding, as we learn from informants in an oral history project (Hall Carpenter Archives, 1989). One woman reported that her mother's "view of lesbians was that they were unattractive women who couldn't get a man" (p. 75).

We take heterosexuality for granted, but we do not appreciate its complexity nor its course of development. The major issue that provides the context for all the others, and that will make a reconstruction of women's sexual scripts possible, is understanding the relationship between women's sexuality and culture. We need to answer the question posed by Beth Schneider and Meredith Gould (1987): "how much freedom [do] women have to be sexual and to set the terms of their own sexuality within the constraints of a heterosexist, racist, sexist, and erotophobic system of domination" (p. 146)?

An important first step in reconstructing our sexual scripts is to appreciate that women's and men's sexualities are fundamentally similar in their psychological and physiological processes and in the learning of motives and responses to sexual cues, although women may find a greater range of behaviors sexually satisfying. This knowledge, however, is not sufficient to eliminate sexual exploitation or women's ambivalent sexual attitudes. We must also dispel other old myths about the nature of women—and men—and work toward eliminating the arbitrary differences in status, power, and role expectations that separate the genders.

◆ Discussion Questions

1. What is sexuality? As defined psychophysiologically? As defined culturally?

2. What do we learn from the mass media about women's bodies? About heterosexual relationships?

3. What is your response to the hypothesis that contemporary women develop ambivalent attitudes toward sex? Do you think that contemporary men learn ambivalent attitudes toward women?

4. What has the so-called sexual revolution meant for women?

5. What is erotica? What is pornography?

6. What do heterosexuals know about lesbian sexual relationships? Ask some friends and acquaintances.

7. Observe 2 to 3 hours of MTV carefully and record how women are presented and photographed.

8. Look at, and bring to class, advertisements from popular magazines in which women are featured in sexual contexts.

CHAPTER 7

RELATIONSHIPS:
LOVE, MARRIAGE, AND
OTHER OPTIONS

The miracle [of love] . . . is its energy . . . the way it actually manufactures more love and further energy for the desire to manufacture more.

ROBIN MORGAN (1982a, p. 137)

One of the young women with whom she had become friendly . . . complained wistfully to Marya that, despite her numerous academic honors and prizes, despite the fact that she would be moving on, with her Ph.D., to Stanford—her family . . . seemed only to be waiting for news that she would be married. Nothing else mattered, evidently; nothing else struck them as ultimately significant.

JOYCE CAROL OATES (1986, p. 207)

Noonie had never understood the title housewife; married to a house! But she knows a lot of women like that; her friend Lola always becomes a little flushed and dreamy when discussing wallpapers or new kitchen cabinets or carpeting for the playroom.

ANNETTE W. JAFFEE (1988, p. 138)

IN CHILDHOOD AND ADOLESCENCE, GIRLS ENTER into positive relationships with family members and peers. They develop affection, respect, admiration, and concern for particular persons of both genders and feel pleasure in their presence. Warm, loving relationships—with parents, siblings, friends, colleagues, and children—continue to be part of adult experience. Such relationships will be discussed in chapters on parenting, adult personality, and employment. In this chapter, we focus on romantic love—on heterosexual and lesbian couples, on marriage, and on the unmarried life-styles seen more and more often among contemporary women for longer periods of their lives.

ROMANTIC LOVE

From our earliest years, women are taught to be concerned with romance. In this respect, little seems to have changed across the generations. Women in the 1990s are still expected to dream of romantic love, long for it, weave our lives around it, and devote considerable skill and energy to its pursuit and maintenance. We get this message in myriad ways from our culture's image producers. For example, in the mid-1980s a large number of best-selling advice books (such as *Women Who Love Too Much*) focused on telling women how they could improve their relationships with men. Many of these books accepted the premise that, although women may be doing all right in the world of paid work, they are failing "miserably when it comes to men" (Lawson, 1986). Among these books were some containing more old-fashioned advice, like *How to Make a Man Fall in Love with You,* and urging women to use any means to get a man. "You laugh a tinkling laugh at his jokes; play hard to get; never show it if you're more intelligent than he is; let him be right, even when he's wrong; and, in short, make your man feel like a king" (Mackey, 1989). Such 19th-century sentiments appear to be alive and well in this last decade of the 20th century.

Our patriarchal, heterosexual majority culture continues to tell women that it is through the love of a man that a woman achieves completeness and mature identity. Not surprisingly, then, when writing about the romantic love of men, women typically describe both passion and pain—an ambivalent experience, sought eagerly but with the anticipation of disillusionment and hurt. Our culture promises fulfillment and happiness from love between a woman and a man, but often the promise is too great and is disconfirmed by the realities of experience. Vivian

Gornick's mother taught her that "love was everything. A woman's life was determined by love. All evidence to the contrary—and such evidence was abundant indeed—was consistently discounted and ignored, . . . refused admission by her intellect" (1987, p. 24). The joy to be found in love is often undermined when the partners are unequal in power and resources. Perhaps, despite films, magazines, and advertisements that continue to sell romantic love with men, many contemporary women no longer really believe in it but nevertheless pursue it because it is expected and brings social rewards. Women's frustration and disillusionment with romantic love relationships with men is heard in the responses of 4500 women to a survey by Shere Hite (1987); 98 percent said they wanted to make basic changes in their relationships, and 79 percent said they are questioning the amount of energy they put into them. These sentiments are illustrated by the personal story of writer Joyce Maynard (1993, p. 18) who has described an ostensible career move to New York City as really being one in pursuit of "the man I might bring home to New Hampshire with me." Her odyssey proved successful but sadly ended in a "long and bitter cold war," compelling her to realize that "no man . . . can make me happy and whole. That task is mine."

Definitions

For many years Albert Lott and I worked together in studying the antecedents and consequences of interpersonal attraction (1968, 1972, 1974). Our basic proposition, supported by considerable empirical data, is that persons learn to like one another if, when they are together, they experience positive outcomes or pleasure. In other words, a person who is rewarded in the presence of another acquires a positive attitude toward that other, and this positive attitude defines liking or attraction. Liking depends on the frequency and quality of the reward that we experience in someone else's presence, and on the infrequency of pain or punishment. When the same person evokes both strong positive and strong negative feelings, the result is ambivalence, and a relationship characterized by conflict. To like a particular person is to expect that we will feel good in that person's company because we will have positive or rewarding experiences. For us to like a person, that person need only be present, in the flesh or symbolically, while we are receiving rewards—whether or not the person has been directly responsible for providing the rewards or has been instrumental in obtaining them. If a person is the direct source of gratification, or if the likelihood of pleasurable consequences is increased as a direct result of interaction with her or him, learning to like that person is even more probable.

Within this framework, love is distinguished from liking when the positive feelings for another person are especially strong, when they are derived from multiple sources or interactions with the person, and when the needs being gratified are particularly powerful and significant. When sexual gratification is a major source of the acquired attractiveness of a person, the term *romantic love* applies. In other words, romantic love is distinguished from liking and other forms of love primarily by the element of sexual pleasure.

Some have suggested that absorption in the relationship (Rubin, 1970) and fantasy (Berscheid & Walster, 1978) also play especially important roles in romantic love. Other descriptions of romantic love "include a sense of urgency; a high degree of possessiveness and jealousy; a diminished commitment to all outside interests; and a feverish amount of sexual passion" (Latham, 1985, p. 98). Some have offered complex models that specify various components (e.g., Sternberg & Grajeck, 1984). Elaine Hatfield and Susan Sprecher (1987) have developed a Passionate Love Scale; Clyde Hendrick and Susan Hendrick (1986) categorized love into six distinct styles or patterns of caring and behaving. But the ambivalence persons in a romantic relationship often feel for their love partners is best explained by the reinforcement/learning model of Lott and Lott. Since romantic love is so strongly associated for heterosexual women in our society with both pleasure and pain, ambivalence is the predicted outcome, and we need to understand its antecedents and consequences. In this chapter we will examine why romantic love in the context of unequal power between partners proves difficult to sustain.

What Love Promises Heterosexual Women

When we love another, we anticipate positive experiences in that person's presence. As a consequence, we tend to approach (to seek after) and to pay attention to those we love; to learn new behavior that the loved individual approves or supports; to model our behavior after theirs; to be sympathetic with a loved person's feelings; and to experience arousal (heightened motivation or drive) in that person's presence. Love, which stems fundamentally from satisfying or positive experiences, endows the object of our love with "good" qualities and leads us to anticipate continued pleasure in the loved person's presence.

But instead of continued pleasure women often experience disappointment and negative outcomes. Our culture makes heterosexual romantic love difficult for women by encouraging us to find our worth and security in relationships instead of in the totality of our lives, and by encouraging us to confuse romance with submission, love with sacrifice, and to juxtapose man's presumed strength against woman's presumed weakness. Women's expectations influence the kind of relationships we seek and settle for, which often turn out to be unsatisfactory. Let us now examine how women's experiences enhance and frustrate the development of heterosexual romantic love and what meaning such love has for women in our culture.

Attention, Prestige, and Self-Esteem. At 15, I fabricated an imaginary boyfriend (complete with photograph) to enhance my popularity and status among my friends. "The woman in love," wrote Simone de Beauvoir (1949/1961), "feels endowed with a high and undeniable value; she is at last allowed to idolize herself through the love she inspires. She is overjoyed to find in her lover a witness . . . [that] she is a wondrous offering at the foot of the altar of her god" (pp. 607f.). *Hannah and Her Sisters,* a 1986 film produced by Woody Allen, resolves the problems of three women by the end of the movie by settling each one into a love relationship with a man.

Critics of the popular love advice books referred to earlier (cf. Lawson, 1986) note that women who are not in a romantic relationship are led to believe that something is wrong with them. Maintaining a love relationship is thus crucial for self-esteem and the satisfaction that comes with having done what is expected. It is considered a woman's responsibility to do whatever is necessary to attract a man and to maintain the relationship. In addition to the positive feelings accompanying the successful establishment and continuance of a relationship, women anticipate other benefits. A woman in a love relationship is courted, feted, admired, extolled, and flattered. Someone is paying attention and she can, by what she does and says, significantly affect another person's feelings and behavior.

Data reported from a study of college students (Rubin, Peplau, & Hill, 1981) suggest that in the earliest part of a romantic relationship women may concentrate primarily on enhancing their attractiveness or desirability, while men place greater importance on the "desire to fall in love." The researchers found that men scored higher on a romanticism scale (which tapped such beliefs as in love at first sight), suggesting that "men tend to fall in love more readily than women," and in the earliest stages of a relationship men reported greater attraction and love for their girlfriends than the men received in return. This state of affairs changed as the relationship continued, supporting the proposition that women may first seek to attract a man—deriving attention, prestige, and self-esteem from his expressed love for her—before her love is expressed in return. Other findings support this proposition. Thus, Elaine Hatfield and Susan Sprecher (1987) found, among a sample of college students, that "men may be the first to fall in love" and that women may be more cautious. In the early stages of dating, men scored higher on the Passionate Love Scale, a difference that leveled off as the relationships continued.

Service, Sacrifice, and Suffering. Both women and men have been led to associate a woman's love for a man with her submission to him. The real man is expected to sweep his lady off her feet while she swoons with delight. Clark Gable as Rhett Butler carrying the half-struggling, half-submitting Scarlett O'Hara (Vivien Leigh) up the staircase to bed, in the film version of *Gone with the Wind,* is still thought of by many as the prototypical romantic scene. Variations on this theme continue to be presented in soap operas where, inevitably, prior to making love, the hero lifts his woman into his arms and carries her to bed. Marilyn French (1977) referred to such love scenes in the movies as "conquest and surrender . . . . A man did one and a woman did the other, and everybody knew it" (p. 31). A man "wins" a woman—if not through brutality, then through the power of his persuasiveness, charm, capacity to protect and support, or simply because he is a man and, therefore, desirable.

Women have been taught that they must be the "soft ones," the yielders, the peacemakers, that men must be "given in" to. My mother found this very difficult to do herself but encouraged this traditional role for her daughters. This message is still prevalent. Toni Grant, a radio psychologist and author of a best-selling late-1980s advice book for women, tells us that "submission can be downright relaxing" (Mackey, 1989).

Folklore and media images send messages to women that we should not expect love to be associated with pleasure alone. In fiction and in popular songs women talk about loving men in whose presence, or at whose hands, they experience pain. The women who "sang the blues" in earlier decades belted out tragic stories about their no-good men who treated them badly, but whom the women could not keep from loving. Their men shoved them around, stayed out late, came home drunk, and ran around with other women, but still the refrain was, "Can't help loving that man of mine." There is some indication that the lyrics in songs sung by women are changing. An analysis of country music tunes from two periods, 1970 to 1972 and 1979 to 1981 (cf. Stark, 1986a), found that some women singers were standing up for themselves, renouncing their older roles, asking for equality and independence and questioning the expectation that they always be nurturing and "forgiving of their philandering, . . . tough and insensitive husbands" (p. 68).

Patricia Spacks (1975) found women's suffering and submission in love to be a major theme of 19th-century literature. Perhaps the most extreme literary example of the ultimate in selfless giving to the man one loves is found in a story by Nathaniel Hawthorne ("The Birthmark," 1843/1973). The male protagonist, Aylmer, is a man of science who becomes obsessed by the need to remove a small blemish from the cheek of his beautiful wife, Georgiana. He sees this mark as an intolerable defect in this otherwise perfect woman, a symbol of her liability to sin or decay, and he convinces her to permit him to perform a series of experiments. In her final moments, realizing that her husband's experiments have succeeded not only in reducing the crimson mark on her cheek but also in killing her, Georgiana speaks these words:

> "My poor Aylmer," she repeated, with a more than human tenderness, "you have aimed loftily; you have done nobly. Do not repent that with so high and pure a feeling, you have rejected the best the earth could offer. Aylmer, dearest Aylmer, I am dying!" (p. 366)

Georgiana symbolizes the conviction that to be worthy of a man's love, a woman must serve him. Such a theme can also be found in contemporary fiction. For example, a young college woman in Judith Rossner's *August* (1983) talks to her psychotherapist about her lover: "He was my first real love. Is. Tom owns me. Do you know what that means? If Tom throws me away . . . I'll be like a rag doll someone threw into the garbage" (p. 57). The ever-present theme of women serving the men they love sometimes receives more comic treatment, as we can see in the 1990 Feiffer cartoon on p. 132. Fiction and humor are supported by the data of social science. Four separate experiments provided evidence for one group of investigators (Sadalla, Kenrick, & Vershure, 1987) that dominance behavior by men increased their sexual attractiveness for college women. Thus, what Simone de Beauvoir (1949/1961) wrote many years ago still seems relevant to the lives of contemporary women.

Shut up in the sphere of the relative, destined to the male from childhood, habituated to seeing in him a superb being whom she cannot possibly equal, the woman . . . will dream . . . of amalgamating herself with the sovereign . . . . She chooses to desire her enslavement so ardently that it will seem to her the expression of her liberty . . . . Love becomes for her a religion. (p. 604)

But, according to de Beauvoir, since most women do not succeed in "deifying" any of the men whom they know, love actually comes to have a "smaller place in woman's life than has often been supposed."

As noted earlier, research suggests that women are more cautious and less starry-eyed than men are when entering romantic relationships. Once committed, however, women appear to become more involved and concerned with the health of the relationship (Rubin, Peplau, & Hill, 1981). Women have been found to be more sensitive than men to negative messages from partners but more likely to interpret their partners' neutral communications positively. This finding was reported in a study of heterosexual couples of varied socioeconomic status who had been living together for at least 6 months (Gaelick, Bodenhausen, & Wyer, 1985). In this investi-

gation, each couple first discussed a problem in their relationship, and later talked about the videotape of that discussion and rated their own and their partner's feelings. The gender differences obtained illustrate and confirm the general cultural expectation that it is a woman's task to nurture her male love partner and to be sensitive to his needs. While the women were accurate in perceiving their partner's hostility, the men were less accurate and tended to distort their partners' neutral communications, perceiving hostility where there was simply an absence of positive affect. Women, on the other hand, perceived the absence of hostility from their partners as indicative of positive feelings. As the investigators noted, "men typically expect women to be affiliative and unassertive, and consequently they interpret behavior that deviates from these expectancies as hostile" (p. 1264). Women are not only more accurate in perceiving hostility, but their degree of satisfaction with the relationship is more strongly affected by their partner's hostility than is true for men.

Gloria Steinem (1978a) described her own feelings and those of other women who have ended relationships as follows: "Creeping self-sacrifice (and creeping resentment of same) meant that sooner or later the only way to regain myself and my own work was to leave" (p. 87). She has argued that love is not possible when one person serves the other, but only when "I can care about the welfare of another person—not more than my own, as I had been trained to do, or less than my own, as men have been trained to do, but as much as my own" (p. 88). To give more to a love relationship than one's partner gives has the effect of lessening one's power and increasing one's uncertainty and vulnerability.

Security. In return for service, sacrifice, and nurturance, a woman may expect recognition, protection, and security. To writers of 19th-century novels, as Patricia Spacks (1975) has pointed out, "the female's compulsion to find some strong male on whom she can rely appears almost as a fact of nature" (p. 58). Although contemporary American women would object to such a description of themselves, many are not so different from the heroines of 19th-century fiction, and the desire for economic and emotional security still enters heavily into romantic relationships.

That heterosexual women tend to look for material security when searching for love is a conclusion supported by studies of personal ads placed in newspapers or magazines by single people indicating their availability and interest in a romantic relationship (e.g., Harrison, 1977). Kay Deaux and Randel Hanna (1984) reported an analysis of 800 such ads collected from four publications equally distributed from the East and West coasts and from both heterosexual and homosexual women and men. Heterosexual women were more likely than any other group to seek financial security or status openly and to request information about the respondents' occupations. At the same time, heterosexual women were the most likely to provide information about their own physical attractiveness—as if offering to trade their looks for material goods. Men, regardless of sexual orientation, behaved in a complementary manner; they were significantly more likely than women to be seeking physical attractiveness in a partner and to be offering financial assets. Heterosexual men were the most likely to write ads with such themes. Laboratory studies, too, have found that women self-report more concern than men with earning potential in judging the attractiveness of other-gender persons (Sprecher, 1989).

Romantic love experienced by women who are financially independent should be less entangled with dependency and therefore ultimately more satisfying. A more independent woman should be more likely to experience pleasure in the presence of her lover without the concomitant frustration or humiliation stemming from the conditions of her dependency. As Vivian Gornick's mother told her, "Don't you see? . . . Love was all I had. What did I have? I had nothing. *Nothing.* And what was I *going* to have? What *could* I have? . . . You have had your work, you *have* your work . . . . I had only your father's love" (1987, p. 203). But women's dependence on men is more than economic. After 10 years of research and more than 4,000 interviews with women and men, Gerald Phillips (1983) concluded that women tend to see men as protectors who lessen their feelings of vulnerability. When the men they trust prove to be untrustworthy, women feel devastated.

Romance: Hers and His

Women often discover that their expectations of a love relationship are not the same as men's. This discovery is not surprising in a society that separates the genders in terms of normative behavior and values. The meanings attached to love, as well as what each gender looks for in a lover, are often found to be distinguishably different for women and men. Studies of different love styles (Bailey, Hendrick, & Hendrick, 1987; Hendrick & Hendrick, 1986) have found significant gender differences. Women are more likely than men to say of themselves that they merge friendship with love, focus on desired attributes of their lover, and are uncertain in relationships; on the other hand, more men than women self-report seeing love as a game to be played with diverse partners and being wary of emotional intensity. Support for these findings can be seen in the results of surveys of women's experiences with love and marriage, such as that by Shere Hite (1987), and by the contents of books offering women advice on love. As summarized by journalists Claudia Wallis and Jeanne McDowell (1987), these "how-to" books instruct women on how to deal with men's "inability to convey their emotions, . . . fear of commitment and intimacy, and . . . obsession with dominance" (p. 70).

One often noted gender difference in approaches to love is the greater importance to men of the partner's physical attributes and attractiveness. A review of the literature (Bar-Tal & Saxe, 1976) found agreement among studies that a woman's judged physical attractiveness is positively related to her "dating popularity" and to her desirability as a mate. The same is not true of men's physical attractiveness. Such findings continue to be reported. One study (Stiles, Gibbons, Hardardottir, & Schnellman, 1987), for example, found that boys between the ages of 11 and 15 who were asked to rate their ideal other-gender person focused on her having good looks and being fun and sexy, whereas the attributes girls ranked most highly for boys were kindness, honesty, being fun, popularity, and having lots of money.

Empirical studies in different settings and using different methodologies confirm the importance of women's physical attractiveness to men (e.g., Howard, Blumstein, & Schwartz, 1987). Among mixed-gender pairs of strangers interacting in a laboratory situation (Garcia, Stinson, Ickes, Bissonnette, & Briggs, 1991), women's attractiveness was found to be significantly related to far more of the observed behaviors and self-reported feelings of the men than the men's attractiveness was related to the behaviors and feelings of the women. In another study, Jeffrey Nevid (1984) had more than 500 college students rate characteristics of prospective romantic partners for a sexual relationship and, separately, for a meaningful long-term relationship. For both types of relationship, men placed significantly greater emphasis on physical characteristics than did women, whereas women rated personal qualities, such as warmth, as significantly more important than did men. David Buss and Michael Barnes (1986) found similar gender differences both within married couples and among unmarried college undergraduates. Whereas men more than women preferred mates who were physically attractive, more women than men preferred partners with good earning potential. In attracting other-gender partners, women were more likely to display their physical appearance, or to consider this an effective tactic, while men were more likely than women to put forward or indicate their resources (Buss, 1988).

We see evidence of the differential use of these tactics by women and men in the personal ads referred to earlier. In the previously mentioned study by Kay Deaux and Randel Hanna (1984), men were found to seek physical attractiveness in a partner significantly more often than women, whereas women, regardless of sexual orientation, more often than men sought and offered specific personality attributes, sincerity, and a permanent relationship. An examination of responses to "lonely hearts" advertisements in a midwestern magazine for singles (Lynn & Shurgot, 1984) revealed that men's responses to advertisements placed by women depended more on "assurances of physical attractiveness" than did the responses of women to male advertisers. Similar findings continue to be reported. A study of more than 500 personal ads placed in a singles magazine in 1989 (Smith, Waldorf, & Trembath, 1990) found that "physical attractiveness easily surpassed all other qualities desired by males, and appeared more than twice as often in males' ads as it did in females' " (p. 681)—in 57 percent of men's ads com-

pared to 26 percent of women's. Of particular interest is that specific reference to low body weight appeared in 34 percent of the men's ads but in only 2 percent of those placed by women. The top five characteristics that men desired in women, as indicated in their ads, were (in order of frequency): physical attractiveness, being understanding, seeking commitment, being athletic, and intelligence. In the top five characteristics that women desired in a partner are three that are shared with men—being understanding, being athletic, and wanting a commitment—but the women also wanted humor and emotional health in the man they sought.

Men's concern with the physical attributes of women seems to cut across social class and ethnic background. Edith Folb (1980) analyzed the language used by one sample of African-American teenagers to describe the other gender and found that, to the young men, women appeared to be equivalent to prized possessions, and were sometimes described as different types of automobiles. Desirable parts of a woman's anatomy were called "g" or "goodies"; and sexually attractive women were referred to as "bitch," "stallion," and "fox," or linked to drugs as "stuff, main stuff, golden girl (very fine cocaine), silk and satin (any combination of amphetamines and barbiturates). These drug-related terms suggest that desirable women get you high and make you feel good. And . . . are addictive" (p. 69). Although the language used by the young women suggested that they also sought attractive physical attributes in men, the women emphasized those qualities less and were interested in a "wider range of qualities," including how men talked and acted, sexual fidelity, intimacy, and earning power.

The primacy of a woman's physical attractiveness to men of varied backgrounds—whether urban teenagers or college-educated adults—has important implications. It is probably related to the consistent finding that men are more likely than women to separate sex from love (e.g., Foa, Anderson, Converse, Urbansky, Cawley, Muhlhausen, & Tornblom, 1987). The primacy of physical attractiveness might also explain why men may fall in love more quickly. For men, romantic feelings may be easily induced by the sight of a pretty face and sexy figure, with parts in the appreciated proportions. Heterosexual men's preoccupation with women's physical attributes is certainly well known to women and obviously encourages them to attempt to gain men's attention by highlighting the attractiveness of their bodies, a consequence of considerable benefit to makeup, perfume, clothing, and diet product manufacturers and advertisers. Nevertheless, physical attractiveness turns out to bear little relation to the probability of maintaining a mutually satisfying relationship.

Women and men bring differences in power and status into love relationships. Thus, in trying to explain their finding that men are more romantic than women early in a relationship, the researchers in the previously cited study of heterosexual college couples (Rubin, Peplau, & Hill, 1981) pointed out that since

> the wife's status, income, and life chances are far more dependent on her husband's than vice versa [she will be] . . . more cautious, practical, and realistic . . . . Men . . . being in a position of greater power both in the larger society and in the marriage market . . . can better afford the luxury of being "romantic." (p. 831)

One symbol of differential power may well be height or physical stature. A study of unmarried college students (Shepperd & Stratham, 1989) found support for earlier conclusions that men prefer shorter women. Such women "were preferred as dates, were dated more frequently, and were perceived as more attractive" (p. 626) than taller women.

Observations of women's behavior in the presence of men they love or are romantically involved with reinforce conclusions about inequities in status and dramatically heighten our awareness of the subtlety and pervasiveness of the consequences. Thus, for example, novelist Annette Jaffee (1988) tells us what one daughter sees when observing her mother in the presence of male suitors:

> her voice was lowered in volume but raised in range; whereas she usually gestured with a whole arm, she tended to use just her fingers and wrists. Her whole frame softened, relaxed, folded, as if she were trying to make herself literally smaller. (p. 47)

Remarkably congruent observations have been reported from a laboratory study (Montepare & Vega, 1988) in which women's conversations with intimate and casual male friends were recorded and rated. The investigators found that both vocal qualities and personal qualities were rated differently depending upon whether the women were speaking to casual friends or love partners. In the latter case, voices were rated as more high-pitched and more variable in intonation, and the speaker was rated as more pleasant, approachable, sincere, submissive, and scatterbrained. Listeners were able to tell whether the speaker was conversing with a casual or intimate male friend with an accuracy better than chance.

Possibilities

Sophie Loewenstein (1977) studied passion in more than 700 women by means of questionnaires and interviews and concluded that passionate heterosexual love is a potential hazard to mental health, disrupting a woman's functioning, producing confusion, and interfering with reason. Are these hazards inevitable consequences of love or do they result from inequalities in status and power?

When one person in a relationship perceives herself as weaker, less competent, more giving, more caring, more identified with the other, more in need of interpersonal reassurance, less powerful, less resourceful, more in need of protection, and so on, the possibility of a satisfying love relationship is dramatically lessened. "It is not the process of love itself that is at fault," as Shulamith Firestone (1971) put it, "but its political, i.e., unequal power, context" (p. 132). For a woman to find satisfaction in love with a man is difficult if she has been taught to lose herself in devotion to, in caring for, and in identification with him. (From the man's perspective, the complementary role that requires him to provide a woman with resources and security and to be grateful and attentive can also be burdensome and frustrating.)

We can learn a good deal about women's beliefs and dreams about romantic love by examining the themes in the romance novels avidly read by millions of American women. The popularity of this genre has increased since 1960; at the same time, the heroines and what they seek have also changed considerably. According to Patricia Lamb (1985), "Harlequin [the major distributor] publishes around 100,000,000 copies annually. Romance novels comprise about 40 percent of the paperback market in this country. Their devoted readers each consume anywhere from half a dozen to one hundred a month" (p. 16). In addition to the Harlequin and Silhouette lines, which are the best known, there are Rapture Romances, Loveswept, To Have and to Hold, Candlelight/Ecstasy, and Love & Life. Together, these publishers "issue some 100 new romances a month." These books constitute more than half of all book sales in the United States and are the most popular among books bought by noncollege women; they run a close second in popularity among college-educated women, for whom historical novels are first (Toth, 1984).

What do these books say about heterosexual love, and why are they so popular among women? Janice Radway (1984) interviewed and administered questionnaires to 42 enthusiastic women readers of romance novels, who were all homemakers in a midwestern community. She analyzed the typical plot and abstracted 13 stages in the structure of the "ideal romance." During the first stage, "the heroine's social identity is destroyed," and in the last stage, "the heroine's identity is restored." In between, the heroine meets the hero and finds him initially cold and unresponsive to her—sometimes even cruel—but toward the middle of the book, she transforms him through the power of her caring and goodness into the warm, sensitive man she knew he was all along, and he confesses his love. This "magic transformation" typically occurs after a separation or misunderstanding but is not explained. According to Radway, it is woman's "sensuality and mothering capacities that will magically remake a man incapable of expressing emotions or of admitting dependency" (p. 128). This same theme is found repeatedly in daytime soap operas. From such stories, a woman obtains reassurance of her worth, an emotional boost, an escape from unexciting domestic worlds, and the hope that her man, too, like the hero, can be transformed through her efforts into the tender, gentle, loving man she seeks.

Sandra Gilbert (1984) and Patricia Lamb (1985) are highly critical of the messages conveyed by romance novels and of their pernicious influence in validating patriarchy and idealizing traditional values. Lamb has suggested that the reader of romance novels is an addict who, like other addicts,

> never learns to come to grips with her world, and . . . therefore seeks stability and reassurance through some repeated, ritualized activity . . . . [But] the problems of their daily lives, the lack of emotional sustenance, the absence of supportive, understanding, caring exchange with a partner—all these await them as they put aside the completed novel, with its happy ending of fulfillment and promise. They will be drained yet again in a day or two or three by the demands made on them and by the absence of other sources of replenishment. So they will buy another batch and read their way through those . . . . Romance novels probably perpetuate the differences and difficulties that exist in our culture between men and women, and between men's and women's expectations of love and marriage. They inoculate, rather than vaccinate, women against the masculine ills of our world, and so the women need booster shots—lots and lots of them, and very regularly. (p. 17)

Since romance novels tend to reiterate traditional sex roles and do not present realistic ways of improving women's relationships or status, Lamb has concluded that they are "inimical to women's real security, growth and freedom."

Janice Radway (1984), on the other hand, is more sympathetic both to the readers of romance novels and to the novels themselves, pointing out that the newer heroines are spirited and rebellious and that the heroes of the "ideal" (as distinct from the "failed") romances are macho only on the surface and are thoughtful, giving, and warm beneath the tough exterior. Radway suggests that it is this expanded version of what men can offer to women in the ideal love relationship that readers of romance novels are seeking. Similarly, Emily Toth (1984) has argued that contemporary romance novels offer readers a newer and more positive or more liberated vision of heterosexual love—that "romances have been updated by feminism." To bolster her thesis, she points out that the heroines of the newer romances "have well-paying jobs and independent lives, and the hero is a partner, not a reason for being." In the Harlequins published since 1982, "the major characters are equals who grow to love one another." Toth argues that romance novels also provide descriptions of sex "from the woman's point of view," emphasizing not moving body parts, but emotion and sensuality. "[T]he ideal romantic hero is not the sullen and moody Harlequin man of the past. His appeal to the heroine is not his being handsome, but his being verbal, and considering her pleasure before his own" (p. 12).

Whatever we may conclude about the ultimate value and influence of romance novels, new themes appear to suggest that ideal lovers are women and men who are competent, strong, and purposeful as well as expressive, nurturant, and sensitive. This matches conclusions from the work of social scientists. Along with the previously noted gender differences in what is preferred in spouses or potential mates and in what is emphasized in attracting partners, a high degree of gender similarity has also been reported. Both women and men, for example, have been found to frequently perform—and to consider highly effective in attracting partners—behaviors "displaying sympathy, kindness, good manners, and humor" (Buss, 1988, p. 625). Citing studies that indicate that romantic love is important for both genders, Francesca Cancian (1986) has argued that the capacity for love is not divided by gender and that it is "both instrumental and expressive" (p. 692). What is necessary for a good love relationship, she notes, are emotional closeness, self-disclosure, providing support and help, sharing time together, and sexual pleasure, all of which are within the behavioral domains of both women and men.

The separation of personal attributes into the strong, silent man and the weak, emotional woman is being found more and more frequently to be an obstacle to the maintenance of love. Evidence that adherence to gender stereotypes is a source of stress and incompatibility has come from a number of studies. In one investigation (Ickes & Barnes, 1977), pairs of pretested strangers were asked to wait together in a room for 5 minutes. Pairs of men and women who were highly sex-typed interacted less, liked each other less, and smiled and laughed less than any other pairs. These data suggest that, contrary to expectation, sharp gender distinctions do not provide for a smooth complementarity between women and men. In another study (Coleman & Ganong, 1985), college students in heterosexual love relationships who self-reported both instrumental and expressive personal characteristics were found to be more loving partners than traditionally sex-typed persons of either gender. The researchers concluded that "to be a loving person it may be necessary to possess instrumental traits such as assertiveness and willingness to take risks as well as expressive traits such as sensitivity and understanding" (p. 174).

Marge Piercy (1984b) has written about romantic love in ways that emphasize the multifaceted contributions that lovers can make to each other when they get beyond gender stereotypes.

> Because we work together we are obscurely
> joined deep in the soil, deep in the water
> table where the pure vulnerable stream
> flows in the dark sustaining all life. In dreams
> you walk in my head arguing, we gallop
> on thornapple quests, we lie in each other's
> arms. What a richly colored strong warm coat
> is woven when love is the warp and work is the woof.
> (p. 67)

And in another poem (Piercy, 1984c):

> We are partially meshed in each other
> and partially we turn free. We are
> hooked into each other like a machine
> that could actually move forward,
> a vehicle of flesh that could bring us
> and other loving travelers to a new land.
> (p. 31)

It is this "new land" that Simone de Beauvoir (1949/1961) was pointing toward when she wrote, "On the day when it will be possible for woman to love not in her weakness but in her strength, not to escape herself but to find herself, not to abase herself but to assert herself—on that day love will become for her, as for man, a source of life and not a mortal danger" (p. 629). This possibility is being envisioned by more and more contemporary women. In an autobiographical novel, Erica Jong (1990), for example, wrote:

I learned that if you stopped looking at a man as someone to give you an orgasm or a baby or save your life, you could really be friends with him and find him quite as human as yourself. I realized that my whole life I had regarded men as both enemy and prey—entirely without being aware of it—so therefore they must have regarded me the same way. (p. 132)

MARRIAGE

For most women, marriage continues to be, as it was for our mothers and grandmothers, a social statement that affirms the end of girlhood and assures us of a recognized place in the adult world. Lillian Rubin (1976) has pointed out that contemporary middle-class girls can delay marriage and extend the period in which they make preparations, explore talents and aptitudes, and enjoy such privileges of adulthood as "separate domiciles and sexual relations." This luxury, however, is less available to working-class women, for whom adult privileges are expected to be accompanied by adult responsibilities, both of which come with early marriage. But for any woman to remain permanently unmarried is still relatively rare, although, as we shall see, this option is an attractive one for some women.

In general, despite a high divorce rate, the popularity of marriage remains much the same as it was in earlier generations. Mary Ellen Reilly (1976) analyzed the demographic data on marriage in the United States over a 100-year period and noted that 9.6 persons out of every 1,000 got married in 1867; 7.9 in 1932 during the Great Depression, when the marriage rate reached an all-time low; 16.4 in 1946 following the end of World War II, the highest peak; and 9.9 in 1952. The marriage rate rose a bit in the 1960s and declined again very slowly in the 1970s. In the 1980s the marriage rate first climbed, reaching 10.6 in 1982, and then declined slowly to 10.2 in 1985 ("Marriages Down," 1986). About two thirds of U.S. adults in the 1980s were in married couple relationships ("Singles Enjoy," 1985).

Although marriage remains popular for the vast majority of women and men in the United States, Census Bureau data also indicate a trend toward remaining single longer. Table 7.1 presents a historical look at the percentage of women and men in different age categories who were never married. Looking just at the figures for women, we can see that from 1950 to 1986, the percentage of single women increased in every age category except age 40 and over. Census Bureau figures

TABLE 7.1 *Percentage of never-married persons in the United States by gender and age.* (Data taken from U.S. Bureau of the Census, 1985a, Table B, p. 2, and from "The way we live," *New York Times*, December 14, 1986, p. E-9.)

Women					Age	Men				
1950	1960	1970	1980	1986		1950	1960	1970	1980	1986
32.3	28.4	35.8	50.2	57.9	20 to 24	59.0	53.1	54.7	68.8	75.5
13.3	10.5	10.5	20.9	28.1	25 to 29	23.8	20.8	19.1	33.1	41.4
9.3	6.9	6.2	9.5	14.2	30 to 34	13.2	11.9	9.4	15.9	22.2
		5.4	6.2	7.5*	35 to 39			7.2	7.8	11.6*
		6.2	5.1	5.0*	40 & over			7.4	5.7	5.8*

*These figures are for 1984.

show that, in 1990, the percentage of unmarried women in their 30s rose to 16.4 (cf. "It's Taking Longer," 1991). In 1986, as can be seen in Table 7.1, 95 percent of all women were married (or had been married) by age 40 or over, a figure higher than that for 1970. In general, and across the decades, 95 percent of Americans have married by the time they are 50.

Related to these data is the phenomenon of a significant increase in the median age of first marriage. In the first half of this century, the median age of first marriage for women in the United States declined steadily from a high of 22.0 in 1890 to a low of 20.1 in 1956. Since then, however, the median age has been rising: it was 20.3 in 1960, 20.8 in 1970, 22.0 in 1980, and 23.9 in 1990. The trend among men has been similar and complementary; the median age of first marriage was 26.1 in 1890, reached a low of 22.5 in 1956, and has been slowly increasing ever since, reaching its highest level yet in 1990, when it was 26.1 ("It's Taking Longer," 1991). For women, age of first marriage is related to education. Jeanne Morman of the Census Bureau found that high school graduates tend to marry sooner but that the better educated woman is more likely to get married at a later age (cf. "Census Says," 1987). Thus, at age 30, single high school graduates have a 55.9 percent chance of eventually marrying, compared with a 66.3 percent chance for college graduates and a 67.8 percent chance for women with graduate training. Overall, for college-educated women at age 25, the chance of marrying before the age of 65 is 89.1 percent.

Despite the later age of first marriage and the increase in number of single adults in their 20s and 30s, marriage remains the preferred way of life in the United States. Annual studies of national samples of high school seniors ("The Future of the Family," 1981) have found that four

fifths of the teenagers studied said they expected to marry at some point. Daughters whose mothers are employed full-time outside the home have not been found to differ in their desire for marriage from those whose mothers are full-time homemakers. While preferring a less traditional, more egalitarian marriage, daughters from dual-career families choose to marry no less frequently than daughters from single-career families (Rollins & White, 1982).

Most modern women, like their mothers and grandmothers before them, believe that marriage brings social approval and recognition and that not marrying is a sign of failure. Vivian Gornick (1987) learned this lesson as a child and adolescent from many sources:

> Wasn't my mother as good as saying with every breath she drew, "Life without a man is unlivable"? And wasn't Nettie actually saying, "Men are scum but you gotta have one"? The message was not open to interpretation, a three-year-old could have repeated it: "If you don't get a husband you're stupid. If you get one and lose him you're inept." I knew, beyond knowing, this was non-negotiable truth. (p. 113)

Similarly, in a novel by Gloria Naylor (1985), a young African-American woman thinks that

> marriage would set her free . . . . Finally free. Freed from those endless luncheons with other lonely women . . . [for whom] something must be missing if they only had each other across the table week after week. Freed from the burden of that mental question mark on her left ring finger. What's wrong with you if no one's wanted you by now? (p. 117)

In the sophisticated 1990s one still hears undergraduate women talking about their pursuit of the MRS degree in college. And an African-American professor touched off debate and controversy when he told a class at San Francisco State University that African-American women should be concerned with husbands and family first—that they should choose a good man over a career (Lang, 1991). Many young women feel that, regardless of what else they do or accomplish, their parents will be disappointed in them if they never marry, and their self-concepts will suffer. But what does it mean to be a bride or a wife? Let us explore this question now.

Wedding Belles

To be a bride in our society brings joy, excitement, and intensity. On the day of her wedding, and during the months preceding it, the bride is center stage—the object of plans, inquiries, gifts, conversation, admiration, and envy. Her hair, figure, and clothes are noticed and described. She is finally that bride doll that she has fussed over and rehearsed with during the many years of her childhood. The groom seems necessary only to validate the bride's status. Newspaper supplements that appear in local newspapers shortly before the spring wedding season still focus primarily on the bride: how she looks, what she wears, her dreams and needs. The "Wedding Planner" (1990) supplement to my local newspaper has remained much the same through the years, featuring stories and advertisements focused on brides—as, for example, "Cordless iron offers ease and convenience for the busy bride." Bride books remain big-selling items, and marriage announcements in the press are still typically accompanied by photographs only of the bride, as you can see by a glance at your own local paper.

Women who marry in the traditional manner—in a wedding attended by family and friends and preceded by announcements, invitations, and plans for flowers, the ceremony, receptions, food, drink, and decorations—will, for a short time, have all eyes on them. Such traditional preparations are accompanied by a kind of consumer power not typically enjoyed again with such freedom. Although the number and nature of the purchases made varies with social class, a period of euphoric spending is experienced by both working-class and middle-class brides. That traditional marriages are once again in vogue is certainly good news for business. Department stores have reported that the compiling of bridal registries (lists of wedding gifts the young couple would like to have) has increased after a decline in the 1970s. In 1988 the bridal business was estimated to bring in $27.5 billion a year; the average cost of a formal wedding, including the bridal party's clothing, reception, flowers, music, and photographs, was $10,379, and more in big cities (Wells, 1988).

Marge Piercy's book *Small Changes* (1975) opens with a description of a wedding that does not seem too out-of-date. Beth is 18 and marrying her high school boyfriend. She feels proud and grateful, and her parents have spent a great deal of money to celebrate this wedding. "This is the happiest day of your life!" her mother tells her, "The happiest day!" She tells Beth's younger sister, "And I want *you* to remember this, Nancy Rose Phail—that's how it's supposed to be. Just like we're doing for your sister Bethie, if you're a good girl and do right by your parents, your parents will do right by you" (p. 8). Because a daughter's marriage is of major significance to working-class parents and a sign that the parental responsibility of caring for her can be relinquished and transferred to her husband, they may spend large sums of money, painstakingly put aside for this purpose, to mark the occasion. The wedding proclaims to the neighbors and to relatives that daughter and parents have "done right" by one another. The daughter has been found desirable, and all the years of parental preparation have been rewarded.

The wedding is a symbol that a young woman and a young man have done the right thing, the culturally approved thing. Society's representatives—the clergy, parents, merchants, relatives, neighbors—all smile with approval at a marriage since it is through families that new members of a culture are provided for the production, distribution, and consumption of goods. Marriage, in other words, has significance for the culture for a number of reasons, including social, religious, and economic ones. Marriage remains a serious goal, extolled by all our major social institutions. That wedding bells have retained their traditional meaning and desirability for most women, then, is not surprising.

Being a Wife

For the typical married woman who does not divorce or separate from her husband, the role of wife lasts longer than that of mother to children at home. Gerda Lerner (1977) pointed out that this phenomenon is relatively recent historically, citing demographic data showing that marriages in the United States prior to 1810 were apt to end with one spouse's death while there were still small children in the family. After 1910 a couple could anticipate less than a year of marriage without children at home. It was not until the middle of the 20th century that wives and husbands could expect to spend a significant period of time together without children to rear, due to a steady decrease in the number of years devoted to childbearing and an increase in longevity.

Social Class. A working-class woman whose formal education ends with graduation from high school will typically marry soon thereafter or after 1 or 2 years of employment. The young couple will try to settle in a neighborhood close to relatives or friends, so that the wife will have the support of continued relationships with other women as her world and that of her working husband gradually begin to separate. She and her husband will be linked together primarily by shared meals, children, a common bed, and common financial concerns. Even before children are born, while the wife may also be employed outside the home, her husband's life will tend to diverge from hers. The working-class wife will spend more time with her home than with her husband. Being a wife for her literally means being a housewife. This was true of my mother and the mothers of most of my friends; it remains true today of working-class women whose self-images are enhanced by compliments about their homes and by pride in their children's accomplishments or good behavior.

Working-class wives are especially dependent on their husbands if they have little work experience, little personal knowledge of the world outside their neighborhoods, and only limited education. A working-class wife may have few options and little sense of personal control over events outside the limits of her home. Lillian Rubin (1976) reported that the most often-heard phrase among the working-class women with whom she spoke was "he won't let me," spoken "unselfconsciously with a sense of resignation."

> On the surface, working-class women generally seem to accept and grant legitimacy to their husband's authority, largely because they understand his need for it. If not at home, where is a man who works on an assembly line, in a warehouse, or a refinery to experience himself as a person whose words have weight? . . . But just below the surface, there lies a well of ambivalence. (p. 113)

A homemaker with few financial resources spends a great deal of time doing endless, monotonous, exhausting chores. Lillian Rubin described a composite scene of what she saw as she visited working-class neighborhoods. At ten in the morning

> mothers are catching their first free breath of the day, perhaps perched on a stool in the kitchen, coffee cup in one hand, telephone in the other. Since five-thirty or six

they have been up and about—preparing breakfast, packing lunches, feeding and changing a crying baby, scolding this child, prodding that one. (p. 15)

Being a working-class wife means experiencing financial instability that strains relationships and increases frustrations. Yet, despite hardships, disappointments, quarrels, and unrealized dreams, divorce is not more common among working-class couples than among their more affluent middle-class cohorts. In fact, the probability of divorce increases with income. Working-class women, who have little opportunity for economic independence, traditionally work very hard at making their marriages work. Marriage and motherhood are what working-class girls have aspired to, expected, and been taught to value most highly.

Lillian Rubin (1976) argues that working-class and middle-class wives have different expectations. She found that middle-class wives "tended to focus on such issues as intimacy, sharing, and communication and . . . on the comforts, status, and prestige that their husband's occupation affords" (pp. 93f.) Although the working-class wives also said they valued sharing and intimacy and quarreled with their husbands about lack of communication, the wives felt guilty about doing so, as though they were asking for more than they had a right to and should be content if their husbands worked hard, brought home steady money, and were not abusive. Many of the women felt that they were much better off than their mothers had been and thus had no right to be dissatisfied, despite gnawing feelings of doubt.

A decade later, journalist Anne Fleming (1986) found many of the same themes identified by Rubin in the stories told her by the working-class and more affluent wives she interviewed. For the former, problems were "exaggerated . . . by the lack of money." But wives in both groups worried about whether they should stay home with their children and why their husbands weren't more helpful and more tender. Today's wives across social classes appear to expect more than simply the "marriage to a man who will provide" (French, 1987) hoped for by poor women in earlier generations. But it is more often middle-class women who have voiced the disappointments, disillusionment, boredom, frustrations, isolation, and lack of personal fulfillment experienced in the role of wife. For example, in *A Perfect Woman* by Carolyn Slaughter (1985), Beth, a middle-class wife, reflects upon her marriage: "That trading-in of a solitary life for one which was subject to the demands and needs of one man? Of a child? Of a lifelong ritual of always being second?" (p. 14). The growing aspirations of women for egalitarian marriages and expressive, sensitive, caring husbands, illustrated so dramatically in the popular film *Thelma and Louise,* are in sharp contrast to the traditional marriage roles. These contradictions decrease the probability of satisfaction in marriage.

Traditional Values and Egalitarian Hopes. An analysis of the opinions of high school seniors, surveyed nationally each year since 1976, indicated that

> both the young men and the young women want a family arrangement in which the husband consistently works full-time outside the home . . . . When small children are part of the family, the young people say they want a wife who is not spending large portions of her time working in outside employment. ("The Future of the Family," 1981, p. 8)

Data from other studies reinforce the conclusion that, in general, traditional family arrangements are still strongly endorsed even as the traditional full-time wage-earning husband and full-time homemaking wife becomes a smaller and smaller minority of American families. In one study (Hollender & Shafer, 1981), a sample of college men viewed videotapes of five women who expressed different aspirations about having a career versus homemaking, after which the men rated the likelihood that they could be interested in marrying someone like each of the five women. Most preferred was the woman who articulated the "Immediate Nurturer" role—that is, who desired marriage and a family first, then pursuit of a job or career after her children were in school. The second-highest preference was for the "Delayed Nurturer," who would work right after marriage and then take time out for a family. Next preferred was the "Homemaker," for whom home and family are primary and continuing priorities, and then the "Integrator," who wanted both a career and a family at the same time. Least desirable was the woman for whom "Career" was the primary focus.

Among both genders we find contradictions between egalitarian goals and the well learned traditional values. In a novel by Gail Godwin (1983), for example, a daughter recalls how her mother's behavior in the presence of her husband had confused her and her sister; they had noticed as little girls that "their mother suddenly became smaller and smoother when Daddy came home" (p. 223). A survey of 452 husbands conducted by a New York advertising firm (cf. Rice, 1980) found that 65 percent believed that wives and husbands should share family responsibilities, including providing income for it, while at the same time 70 percent agreed that "a family is better off if the woman of the house does not work" and 60 percent felt that "a woman's place is in the home." Only 13 percent of the men surveyed could be classified as consistently nontraditional (egalitarian or progressive) on the basis of their responses. The investigators concluded that most of the men were ambivalent, or characterized by more talk than action.

One pair of investigators (Gillis & Avis, 1980) checked bank records for the heights of couples who maintained joint checking accounts and found that, whereas the overall possibility of a woman being taller than a man is 2 out of 100, the actual incidence of taller wives among the married couples was 1 out of 720, far less than might be expected by chance. In other words, there is a systematic bias in marriage that the husband should be taller than his wife. A similar systematic bias occurs with respect to age, in that husbands are typically older than their wives. Gloria Cowan (1984) had a large sample of college and high school students respond to scripts about heterosexual couples in which the ages of the pairs were varied and found evidence for a "double standard." Respondents expressed "less optimistic views towards relationships in which the female is older than the male" (p. 22).

There is evidence that contemporary women and men have different preferences with regard to decision making and performance of household chores. Marcia Kassner (1981) questioned a sample of college seniors graduating from a midwestern university and found "incongruency in attitudes between the two sexes," with men preferring traditional marriages and women preferring egalitarian ones. A survey of 60,000 women conducted for *Woman's Day* magazine found that "women want more equality in marriage, with men helping out more at home and women being able to hold jobs" (cf. "Women Want," 1986). While 70 percent of the respondents described the ideal marriage as one of shared responsibilities for earning money and caring for the home and children, only 53 percent felt that this ideal characterized their own marriages.

Similar findings have come from other sources, suggesting that more men than women continue to want and expect traditional roles in marriage. For example, a survey of a national sample of more than 7,000 couples who were seeking marital counseling (Fowers, 1991) found that the wives endorsed more egalitarian roles and reported less marital satisfaction than the husbands did. One sample of European-American, upper-middle-class suburban men aged 35 to 55 told researchers that "work and making money is the man's job. Child care and homemaking is for women'' (cf. "Study: Men's Attitudes," 1990). Whatever income is earned by women was seen as "helping out." Janice Steil and Karen Weltman (1991) interviewed a sample of highly educated European-American couples in which both partners were employed full-time. In half the couples the wife earned more, and in half the husband earned more. Although the higher earner of either gender had "more say" in family decisions, men "were reluctant to rate their wives' careers as more important regardless of their relative earnings" (p. 174), and the higher-earning wives shared this reluctance. Partners who earned less, but wives in general, were viewed as having more responsibility for children and the household. The investigators concluded that the persistence of "the traditional differences in career valuation and the allocation of domestic influence . . . [highlight] the tenacity of cultural expectations associated with the roles of husband and wife" (p. 177). We see this tenacity expressed with some humor in a column by journalist Mark Patinkin (1986). He describes the division of household tasks that he and his wife have settled into, explaining that "most men are genetically incapable of reading a recipe. Just as we're genetically incapable of closing drawers or cabinets. It's not in the DNA."

Housework: The Bottom Line. The reality of married women's day-to-day lives suggests that both working-class and middle-class wives are primarily associated with *things,* with duties and responsibilities, rather than with relationships. In *The Fiddler on the Roof,* Golde answers her husband Tevye's insistent question, "Do you love me?" by reminding him that she has washed his clothes, cooked his meals, cleaned his house, given him children, and milked the cow. "If that's not love," she asks, "what is?" From Golde's old-world perspective, proof of her love is found in the meals she has cooked and the clothes she has washed. Modern Americans, especially those who are educated, professional, and middle-class, are not likely to describe marital love in Golde's terms, but the traditional view she expressed is still prevalent. For example, a marriage counselor quoted by Janet Harris (1976) reported that a couple told him about what each saw as lovable in themselves.

> The wife began by telling me that she thought she was deserving of love because she was a good housekeeper, a good cook, a good mother, that she did a lot of things for her family, that she put them first. The husband, on the other hand, thought he was lovable because he saw

himself as a kindly person, with a good sense of humor, a lively imagination . . . . She perceived herself only as an object of service. (p. 109)

In April 1990, I received in my mailbox, along with a discount coupon, an ad for a household product for the cleaning of toilets and sinks being cheerfully used by a smiling and happy wife.

A woman typically expects to perform services when she marries, and her husband expects to receive them. Girls have practiced being housekeepers and cooks from earliest childhood play and have been encouraged to put others first and to be good managers and tidy cleaners. If a woman can also sew or knit and manage the budget and chores economically and efficiently, so much the better. Women have been assured that if we do these things we will be appreciated and taken care of. In *A Mother and Two Daughters* (Godwin, 1983), for example, Lydia, now divorced, reflects that

> during her marriage, her compartment system had served her well. Her compartments organized her. If she had labeled them in her neat handwriting, they would have read something like: MOTHER. COOK. HOSTESS. INTERESTED WIFE . . . WELL-DRESSED LADY SHOPPER. AMIABLE BED PARTNER. (p. 268)

In *The Women's Room* (1977), Marilyn French described the "grimy details" of a housewife's life as not "background," but "the entire surface . . . . When your body has to deal all day with shit and string beans, your mind does, too" (p. 46). Research supports this grim picture for working-class wives. For example, interviews with more than 3,000 adults in Los Angeles, including 668 Mexican-Americans, reported that women did significantly more household labor than men did and that, among the women, "household strain was a direct consequence of housework, and depressive symptoms were an indirect consequence" (Golding, 1990, p. 113). But even among the more affluent, wives as well as husbands believe that the wife is responsible for most of what one associates with the home. In a wonderfully funny essay called "Click! The Housewife's Moment of Truth," Jane O'Reilly (1982) wrote, "I have never met a woman who did not feel guilty . . . when a man we are attached to goes out with a button off his coat; we—not he—feel feckless" (p. 29).

For most women, excluding those whose housework is done by paid domestic workers (who are primarily women), being a wife means doing housework. The family is the unit in which the housework is done and, in Marxist economic terms, "consists largely in purchasing commodities and transforming them into usable forms" (Hart-mann, 1981, p. 373). Since this labor is traditionally and typically done by women, the result is exclusion from equal competition with men in the wage labor market, where husbands are supposed to provide for their families by earning a "family wage." Unlike the breadwinner, the full-time homemaker does not create surplus value (that is, the difference between the price at which a product is sold and the cost of wages). Instead she exchanges her labor for the financial responsibility her husband assumes for her and her children, and she is part of an unpaid labor force. Her contributions to the nation's economy are not included in our nation's gross national product (GNP), making such labor economically "meaningless" or "nonexistent" (Porter, 1985). The increasingly large share of home nursing and medical monitoring tasks performed at home for family members has added to the number of services done for free by women. Nona Glazer (1990) has called attention to this new burden placed on women in the home, brought on by insurance reimbursement policies and the high costs of health care. More and more women are doing medical home care, which can include giving injections and monitoring technical equipment as well as attending to bodily needs and offering loving support.

The modern family and the housewife role are relatively recent phenomena. As Angela Davis (1983) has pointed out,

> housework during the colonial era was entirely different from the daily work routine of the housewife in the United States today . . . . In the agrarian economy of pre-industrial North America, a woman performing her household chores was . . . a spinner, weaver and seamstress as well as baker, butter-churner, candle-maker and soap-maker . . . . Colonial women were not "housecleaners" or "housekeepers" but rather full-fledged and accomplished workers within the home-based economy. Not only did they manufacture most of the products required by their families, they were also the guardians of their families' and their communities' health. (pp. 225f.)

Women also ran taverns and sawmills, caned chairs, built furniture, ground eyeglasses, made rope, and were housepainters and undertakers. Jessie Bernard (1981) has also traced changes in the family and noted that "the good provider as a specialized male role seems to have arisen in the transition from subsistence to market—especially money—economies that accelerated with the industrial revolution" (p. 2). This change, according to Bernard, kept women from direct access to money earned through their own skills and made it necessary for them to win "a good provider who would 'take care of' them."

Time Spent on Housework and Childcare for Married Couples with Children

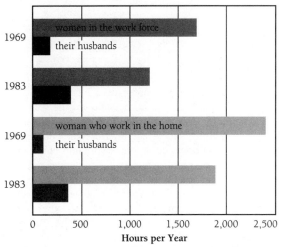

FIGURE 7.1 *Status report: who does the work?* *(Taken from chart by Andy Christie. (Ms., February 1988, p. 19.)*

Although it is the unusual wife today who doesn't share the "provider" role with her husband, he far less frequently shares the household chores with her. Little change seems to have occurred in women's responsibilities for household tasks among dual-earner couples, and being a wife means doing housework even when you are also employed outside the home in full-time work. As can be seen from Figure 7.1, married women in the work force, according to a large-scale study reported in 1983, spent three times as much time as their husbands on housework and child care. These findings are consistently replicated in other studies. According to Heidi Hartmann (1981), regardless of whether she works outside the home, "the vast majority of time spent on housework is spent by the wife, about 70 percent on the average, with both the husband and the children providing about 15 percent on average" (p. 385). A study of a sample of predominantly European-American middle-class couples (Nyquist, Slivken, Spence, & Helmreich, 1985) found that few women received "any appreciable amount of help from their husbands on a regular basis, even when they had full-time outside employment . . . [and that] in less than 2% of the couples did the husband and wife share equally or the husband contribute more" (p. 31). While husbands did more of the house and yard maintenance work than their wives did, such work is done less regularly and frequently than household chores; moreover, wives contributed more to maintenance jobs than husbands contributed to household jobs.

Data on 1,565 married couples (cf. Grant, 1988) indicated that, whether or not the wife worked full-time outside the home, husbands do about 4 to 6 hours of housework each week, a 14 percent share. Women who are full-time homemakers do 83 percent of the housework, while employed women do 70 percent. Also of considerable interest is that the status of the wife's job makes no difference: women with high-powered careers, just like nonprofessional employed wives, put in three times as many hours doing housework and childcare as their husbands. This phenomenon of unequal responsibility for household labor when both spouses are employed is found to characterize rural as well as urban couples, with the same 3 to 1 difference as other studies report. One investigation (Lawrence, Draughn, Tasker, & Wozniak, 1987) reported that wives spent an average of 3.9 hours per day in household work, compared with 1.7 hours a day for husbands. Although rural wives spent more time in housework than urban wives did, the husbands did not differ in the share they performed. It will come as no surprise, in view of these data, that the Virginia Slims poll in 1990 found that the two issues causing women the most distress were not having enough money and men's inadequate sharing of domestic and child-care responsibilities (cf. Faludi, 1991). Ethnicity and social class seem to make little difference. As Angela Davis (1983) has pointed out, housework has never been the central focus of African-American women's lives because throughout their history in the United States they have had to work outside their homes, but "while they have seldom been 'just housewives,' they have . . . carried the double burden of wage labor and housework" (p. 231).

A longitudinal study of 160 couples who got married in the first half of 1981 and who were interviewed periodically during the early months of their marriages provides interesting data. The researchers (Atkinson & Huston, 1984) found that, regardless of their employment situation, from more than half to more than three fourths of the household chores were done by the wives. Although differential skills predicted division of household labor better than such factors as attitudes or personal attributes, how skillful a wife was at doing the traditional "feminine" tasks (cooking, shopping, laundry, and so on) did not predict how much she participated in them. In other words, wives did these chores, regardless of their level of skill, because they were wives. As one group of researchers concluded from a survey of husbands (cf. "A Man-

Sized Resistance," 1981), "it's easier for men to accept the possibility of women as brain surgeons than to release their own wives from the drudgery of laundry and cleaning the bathroom." Similar conclusions have come from research done in other countries (Bernard, 1981).

That the common availability of so many mechanical and electrical household appliances has had so little effect on the time women spend on housework is an interesting phenomenon. To help explain why studies have found "no relationship between the presence of household appliances and women's hours of housework" (p. 25), Bonnie Fox (1990) analyzed 70 years of ads in the *Ladies Home Journal,* from 1910 to 1980. She found that although the messages presented in these ads varied somewhat with the time period, after 1930 they tended to define housework in ways that increased women's responsibility. The ads presented "ideals of better housekeeping" and invoked images of housework as a "labor of love." Only 6 percent of the ads in 1979–1980 presented new products as ways to reduce household work, suggesting that advertisers were not interested in raising "the possibility that women's interests might lie outside the confines of domesticity" (p. 33).

Women who live with men do most of the housework even if not legally married. Observations in communities that provide alternatives to conventional marriage have indicated that such arrangements did not free women from traditional gender-related responsibilities (Estellachild, 1971). Under the leadership of men, many American communal groups continued to support the older gender distinctions of our patriarchal society. Kate Wenner (1977) described what she saw on a visit to an alternative community in Tennessee: the men were doing the outside work while the women were taking care of the house and the children. "Sex roles are clearly defined: Household, health, food and child care are the exclusive domain of women; manual work, leadership and administration are jobs for the men" (p. 81). These observations are confirmed by a study that compared a sample of married couples with a sample of cohabiting couples (all European-American, college-educated, and middle-class). The researchers (Denmark, Shaw, & Ciali, 1985) found that although the difference between women and men in the "numbers of weekly hours spent on housework was greater for married couples, unmarried females still reported spending nearly twice as many hours on housework as unmarried males" (p. 623). Unmarried couples did differ from married couples in exhibiting less consistency and greater variability in jobs done around the house, but the women did more of them, more often.

Reduced Social Status. By taking on primary responsibility for care of the home (and children), women enable their husbands to put time and energy into the pursuit of occupational success. It is the husband's work outside the home that typically has top priority in family decisions and that provides the family with its social standing in the community. Since it is the husband's occupation that matters in the community's evaluation of the family, it is not surprising to find that women make personal and career sacrifices for the men to whom they are engaged or married.

Mark Kotkin (1983) documented this process in a study of graduate student couples at the University of Pennsylvania who were interviewed and then followed up a year later. He compared married with cohabiting engaged and nonengaged couples and found that 70 percent of the married women had made sacrifices for their husbands' career advancement, whereas only 10 percent of the husbands had made sacrifices for their wives' careers. These sacrifices included providing economic support, relocating, postponing their own careers, and typing papers or doing labor for the spouse. Cohabiting women had made fewer sacrifices than married women. Most married couples (55 percent) said they were living in Philadelphia because of the man's career or education; only 5 percent specified the woman's. Attitudes and plans or strategies favoring the man's career were most common among the married couples (80 percent), followed by the engaged couples (64 percent), and least common among the nonengaged couples (44 percent), reflecting a spectrum from least to most egalitarianism. Kotkin concluded that

> most women in the sample had already subordinated their own careers to their husbands' . . . , and most engaged women apparently were prepared to do likewise upon entrance to matrimony. Having all but guaranteed the greater earning capacity of the husbands, neither partner will be likely to risk this investment in the future. Male career precedence is thereby perpetuated. (p. 984)

It is because of a husband's position in society, and not because of his particular personal characteristics or motives, that he has significantly more power in marriage than does his wife. A contemporary employed wife may be shocked to realize that her social status is derived from her husband's and is determined by his socioeconomic position, just as was true for her mother and grandmother. She is still formally identified in many places as Mrs. John Doe. I was disturbed to find that a center for battered women in my community maintained this practice in the early 1990s in their public listings of charitable donors.

In the eyes of the community, a married woman takes on the status of her husband and the generally lower status of wife. This is well illustrated by a study (Richardson & Mahoney, 1981) that had groups of college students each read a different vignette of a family with two children in which the wife and husband were both employed full-time. What varied among the stories were the occupations of the adults. Receptionist, office manager, and English professor were used to identify women's low-, middle-, and high-status occupations, respectively, whereas bus driver, insurance salesman, and dentist were used for the men's jobs. When respondents were asked to rate separately the wife's and the husband's general social standing in the community on a 21-point scale, the results were clear and dramatic. The status given to the wives was not at all influenced by their own occupations, but was instead significantly influenced by that of their husbands. The social standing of the husband, on the other hand, was influenced only by his own occupation and not at all by his wife's, with only one exception: low occupational status husbands whose wives had higher-status jobs were judged to be lower in status than other husbands, presumably because their situation violated the "traditional male prerogative to confer status" rather than to derive it. Although the wives derived their social status from their husbands' occupations (and not their own), the wives of high- and middle-status husbands were judged to be significantly lower in status than their husbands and not equal to them. The researchers concluded from these data that "being a woman has a powerful ceiling effect on attributed social status . . . [while] the general social status scores assigned to men reflect sex-role status plus or minus occupational status" (p. 1196).

With such differences in social status between wives and husbands, we should not be surprised to find related differences in role—that is, in expected ways of behaving. Thus, for example, in one study (Barnes & Buss, 1985) husbands were reported by themselves and by their wives to behave in ways judged by the investigators as reflecting initiative. Within marriage as outside of it, men have greater power—that is, greater access to resources. This greater power is reflected in men's greater influence on the quality of the marital relationship. A study of 106 couples interviewed over the course of two years, beginning soon after their marriage (Huston & Vangelisti, 1991), found that it was the negativity of husbands early in the marriage that predicted their wives' later levels of satisfaction with the marriage and their wives' later negativity. The early socioemotional behavior of the wives did not predict—that is, did not seem to influence—the later behavior of husbands.

Men's greater power in marriage is often portrayed in fiction. In a novel by Jimmy Breslin (1986), for example, we read the following exchange between husband and wife.

> "Come here."
> "Why?"
> "I want to talk to you."
> His voice, equal parts plea and command, created one of those humiliating instances that she had been raised by gender and landscape to accept. She now thought of how many times she had answered that call, walking to bed like a servant girl in bare feet. (p. 233)

In this novel the characters are European-Americans living in New York City. The marital relationship, however, is not too dissimilar from that described in a novel by Gloria Naylor (1988), who writes about African-Americans. In the following passage, a young woman is thinking about marriage.

> You fear sometimes for women, that they would just fold up and melt away. She'd seen it happen so much . . . .But who needed to wake up each morning cussing the day just to be sure you still had your voice? A woman shouldn't have to fight her man to be what she was . . . . (p. 203)

Men's power relative to their wives seems to be a widespread phenomenon in our society, one that is related to the fact that they are men. Conversely, women's lesser power is related to our lesser access to resources by virtue of social position, and not because of individual personal qualities.

Disappointment and Divorce

In fiction, poetry, essays, and diaries women have described disappointments in marriage that seem to reflect the differential roles our society allocates to husbands and wives. Husbands may also find their marriages disappointing and experience dissonance between their expectations and the realities, but there is evidence from a variety of sources that married women are less satisfied with their lives and marriages than married men are. The previously mentioned survey of 60,000 women conducted in 1986 by *Woman's Day* found that 38 percent of the respondents said they would not choose the same husband if they could do it all over again; and an analysis of 15 years of national survey data compiled by the Opinion Research Center of the University of Chicago found that wives

reported getting less out of marriage than their husbands did (cf. Wallis & McDowell, 1987). Among the divorced women surveyed by Shere Hite (1987), 91 percent said that they had initiated the divorce. Other studies, too, have reported that women are more likely to begin the process of putting an end to a painful marriage (cf. Gray & Silver, 1990).

Contemporary marriages may fail for the same reason that love relationships do. Husbands and wives are not equal in status or power and have different expectations of marital roles. A comparison of a sample of European-American, middle-class couples involved in marriage counseling with similar couples who were not in counseling (Nettles & Loevinger, 1983) found a greater average discrepancy between wives and husbands on sex-role attitudes and beliefs in the troubled marriages. The investigators concluded that "what differentiates problem marriages is not [personality] differences within the couples . . . but different expectations and attitudes about behavior and division of labor" (p. 685). Wives appear still to be burdened by the responsibility for nurturance in the marriage. This conclusion comes from an analysis of advice books for couples (Ross, 1980) as well as from studies of couples. For example, one investigation (Levenson & Gottman, 1985) found that a husband is likely to withdraw emotionally in a problematic marriage much earlier than his wife and that his wife's initial reaction may be to increase her level of positive affect and support "to coax him back into the emotional life of the marriage" (p. 90). Eventually, the husband's continued withdrawal is accompanied by an increase in the wife's negative emotional responses.

What presents problems for marriages are our cultural prescriptions for gender, which are tied to differential access to resources—that is, to power. In today's world these gender prescriptions and discrepancies are sources of discomfort, disillusionment, distress, and real disadvantage to large numbers of women. Even when the inequality is tolerated by the wife, her husband, possessing the social advantages of worldliness and economic independence, may grow dissatisfied with his wife's contributions to his ego, physical comfort, or sexual pleasure and seek to replace her with a wife who is younger, sexier, better-looking, or more adoring. This pattern is not unusual and is a frequent source of satirical humor, as illustrated by the Doonesbury cartoon on p. 147.

In some marriages, when the wife is in the work force a husband may feel that his power and authority is threatened by the priority she gives to her work. As a wife devotes more attention to pursuits outside the home, she

has less time and energy to focus on her husband. While wives expect their spouses to be work-oriented, many husbands resent the fact that their wives' employment leaves less time for attention to them and to household chores. A national survey of 6,000 married or cohabiting couples (Blumstein & Schwartz, 1983) found that conflict over the woman's job was most often responsible for the breakup of heterosexual couples and that women were less likely to stay in an unhappy relationship if they were economically independent. But other researchers have found a gradual convergence in divorce rates among different socioeconomic groups (cf. Arendell, 1988) and no significant relationships generally between economic factors and divorce. One study of nearly 1,800 families that had been periodically surveyed for 12 years (Johnson & Skinner, 1986) reported little relationship between divorce and a wife's employment or the educational level of either spouse. Women preparing to end their marriages, however, tended to increase their work hours or to try to find more highly paid jobs.

Some data suggest a woman's dissatisfaction with her marriage leads her to search for emotional satisfaction and support in friendships with other women or in extramarital relationships. For example, Shere Hite (1987) reported that 87 percent of the married women who responded to her survey said their deepest emotional relationship was with a woman friend and 70 percent of the women married for five or more years said they were having affairs. Similarly, among a sample of African-American women (Brown & Gary, 1985), almost three fourths of the married women did not cite their husbands as being among their three closest relationships. For a majority of these women, while a marital partner provided psychological benefits associated with the spouse's wages or salary, he did not provide a "socially supportive relationship." The social support networks of married African-American women appeared to be very similar to those of unmarried women, centering on children, siblings, and other relatives. The nature of extramarital relationships has been found to differ significantly for women and men among a sample of middle-class, highly educated European-Americans, (Glass & Wright, 1985) in ways that reflect the data on social supports. The married women reported that their extramarital involvements were more emotional than sexual, whereas men reported the reverse.

The severity of the problems encountered in marriage in the U.S. is indicated by the divorce rate. A Harris poll in 1987 found that one in eight marriages (12.5 percent) end in divorce (cf. "Divorce Rate," 1987). Compare this figure with those from previous years: among the population of persons who had ever been married, 9 percent were divorced in 1984, 4 percent in 1970, and 3 percent in 1960 (U.S. Bureau of the Census, 1985b). There is disagreement about long-range forecasts. Whereas some have projected, for example, that nearly half the marriages begun in the mid-1970s will end in divorce (cf. Barber & Eccles, 1992), others emphasize that "in any single year . . . only about 2 percent of existing marriages will break up" and that "nearly nine out of 10 marriages are surviving" ("Divorce Rate," 1987). As the reader can see, statistics on the incidence of divorce in the U.S. are presented in various ways, making clear conclusions difficult. Some believe that because of the later age of marriages the divorce rate leveled off or slowed in the 1980s (cf. Lopata, 1987), yet one still reads that "about 50 percent of marriages end in divorce" (Pearce, 1993). Looking just at women in the United States between the ages of 25 and 44, 11.4 percent were divorced in 1990, a figure that is the highest among all the "developed" countries of the world (*The World's Women*, 1991). We also know that more divorced men remarry after divorce and that they do so sooner than women ("More Women," 1986); and that marriage dissolution rates are higher among African-American couples than among European-American couples (Lopata, 1987).

Among the distresses and dislocations that accompany divorce is the tendency for a woman to blame herself for the failure of her marriage. Anecdotal reports of such feelings of guilt are common in women's conversation and women's literature. Joyce Carol Oates has captured the essence of these feelings in Monica's words in *Solstice* (1985):

> She was prevented [by losing herself in work] from lapsing into self-pity and self-recrimination and self-loathing of the kind she so abhorred in women acquaintances of hers whose marriages had "also" ended disastrously. How did I fail, these stunned women asked themselves, what did I do wrong, how could I have avoided . . . ? I, I, I . . . (p. 12)

Such feelings among divorced women are not surprising, given our culture's view that it is the wife's job to keep the family together, that it is her responsibility to do the emotional work in the family and to supply the glue for connectedness among members (Gelman, 1990a).

A divorced woman often finds that her social activities and friendships are seriously dislocated after her marriage ends. Accustomed to being part of a couple, a divorced woman becomes an "extra" guest or a third wheel, a source of discomfort to her acquaintances. Her phone doesn't ring as often with invitations from married friends. In *Fly Away Home* (1984a), Marge Piercy has written about a recently separated middle-class woman whose friend Annette cancels an invitation to dinner when she hears of the separation, suggesting that it would be "awkward."

> She wanted to call Annette back and berate her. What would it cost them to have one unattached woman to supper? A beggar at the banquet? Did they think she would crawl into the laps of her neighbors' husbands? They were always afraid of the damaged marriages. Avoiding the plague. (p. 192)

Beyond such problems, the most clearly established aftermath of divorce is economic hardship for women and their children. In the chapter on parenthood, we will pay particular attention to the economic circumstances of single mothers and the conditions of poverty in which vast numbers of women and children in the United States live, but here we must attend to the fact that divorce is a major contributor to this poverty. After a 10-year study of divorce in California, Lenore Weitzman (1985) concluded that divorced women with children suffer an average immediate 73 percent drop in standard of living, whereas that of their husbands increases in the first year after divorce by an average of 42 percent. Weitzman attributed this disparity to the way property settlements are mandated under new no-fault divorce laws (although she did not compare divorce settlements under old and new laws). She argued that dividing family assets equally between husband and wife typically means that the husband gets half while the other half goes to the wife and children (in nine out of ten divorces involving children, when custody is not disputed, the mother gets legal responsibility for the children). If a family home is sold to obtain liquid assets, the wife and children must relocate to housing of lesser value, since their income has been drastically reduced. Weitzman argued that current judicial practice does not divide a couple's assets acquired during marriage equally because omitted from the legal definition of assets are those associated with the job of the husband, who is typically the major, if not the only, breadwinner. Husbands are allowed to retain their occupational assets—professional licenses, pensions, health insurance, and future earning capacities—despite the fact that their wives have invested heavily in time and human capital in their husbands' educations and occupational advancement.

Weitzman urged that divorce laws take into account the difference between husbands and wives in current and potential economic position, that a woman's contributions to home life as well as her impaired earning capacity during marriage be acknowledged and credited, and that women who have primary responsibility for their children after divorce be provided with special economic supports. An older woman whose marriage is dissolved after decades of full-time management of a home and tending to the needs of children and husband may be left with no job, few prospects of reasonable employment, no pension, and no health insurance. Such women, Weitzman noted, have earned alimony. For them, it is a pension to which they are entitled for their contributions to the marriage partnership.

While Weitzman's suggestions for greater equity in divorce settlements have been largely applauded by feminists and others, criticism has been directed at the statistical conclusions drawn from her data. Saul Hoffman and Greg Duncan (cf. Faludi, 1991) tracked the effect of divorce on income for two decades and found a 30 percent drop in women's living standards in the first year after divorce (not 73 percent as Weitzman claimed), and a 10 to 15 percent improvement for men. They also found that, 5 years after divorce, the average divorced woman's living standard was higher than when she was married. The Duncan and Hoffman findings have been supported by a subsequent study conducted by the Census Bureau. Among the problems with Weitzman's study, as pointed out by Susan Faludi (1991), are that Weitzman used a very small sample of divorced people in only one state, relied on self-reported financial information, and carried out no comparison with couples who divorced prior to no-fault settlements.

Although there is disagreement about the precise economic effect of divorce on women and children, all experts and studies agree that the effect is substantial. As noted by Terry Arendell (1988), "men leave marriage with their earning abilities and social statuses intact" (p. 123). Divorced women spend significantly less than divorced men on food, recreation, and clothing and are less likely than any other group to be covered by any kind of health insurance. Arendell has summarized the situation as follows:

> The differential economic impact of divorce on men and women is largely the result of four factors: the continuation, for most women who are mothers, of the primary family caretaking role and the time that such nurturing requires; women's sudden financial responsibility for themselves and their children in a society where women's earning potential is limited by wage discrimination; divorce laws that reinforce and increase the financial inequities between men and women in general; and public assistance programs that fail to facilitate divorced women's transition from dependence to autonomy. (p. 128)

These conclusions are supported by a study of 600 divorces in Rhode Island in the 1980s. The custodial parent, typically the mother, ended up after the divorce with 47 percent of the family's previous income; the parent living alone without the children, typically the father, ended up with 53 percent of the family's previous income—a 36 percent increase in buying power (cf. Macris, 1992). To remedy this unequal outcome, three bills were introduced into the Rhode Island legislature: one to allow judges to

award long-term alimony, a second to encourage judges to postpone the sale of the family's house, and a third to require judges to consider pension benefits as part of the couple's combined assets. These recommendations are similar to changes in the divorce laws of other states; New York, for example, now includes career and education investments in its definition of community property.

In the United States today, fewer than 15 percent of divorced women receive alimony, and the average award lasts only for 25 months. Of divorced mothers, 44 percent are awarded child support, and the average amount is $200 a month for two children, a sum that typically covers less than half the support costs and is difficult to collect. The rate of delinquent and defaulted payments is very high among fathers of all income levels. A federal law passed in 1984 now mandates that defaulting fathers be found and child support payments be provided by withholding money from the fathers' paychecks, imposing liens against their property, or withholding income tax refunds. Most states have found implementation of this law difficult, and a federal audit in 1988 discovered that 35 states were not complying with federal child support laws (cf. Faludi, 1991).

Of the children of divorced parents, 90 percent live with their mothers, largely the result of fathers not requesting residential custody. In recent years, more fathers are beginning to make such a request either at the time of the divorce or later. A study by Phyllis Chesler (1985) found that in custody challenges, mothers lost custody to fathers in 70 percent of the cases examined. Among the fathers making the custody challenge, 87 percent were not previously involved in primary child care, 67 percent had paid no child support, and 62 percent had been accused of physically abusing their wives. Chesler found that mothers most at risk for losing custody of their children when challenged by the fathers were those who were sexually active, were lesbians, had careers, or were economically disadvantaged.

Divorced women without young children and without jobs may find themselves suffering the consequences of being "displaced homemakers." This group is defined as those who are over age 35 and who had been out of the labor market for an extended time period (Arendell, 1988). Such women lose their sole source of income, are ineligible for unemployment insurance, do not qualify for Aid to Families with Dependent Children if their children are over 18, and find it extremely difficult to get jobs because of their age and lack of recent paid employment experience. Some women in this situation, who have no sources of support from their families, must turn to public assistance programs in order to survive.

Studies of divorced women have found that the majority are interested in remarriage, but such chances for women are 75 percent compared to 80 percent for men (Phillis & Stein, 1983). This disparity comes about because the pool of eligible men for divorced women is restricted by age and status factors. For example, whereas men with higher educations have the highest rate of remarriage, "women with high incomes and/or high educations have the lowest remarriage rate" (Finlay, Starnes, & Alvarez, 1985, p. 641). Divorced and widowed men tend to marry women who are younger and have lesser socioeconomic status. Another factor that diminishes a divorced woman's chances for remarriage is that her attitudes regarding marriage and gender-appropriate behavior tend to be significantly more liberal and egalitarian than those of divorced men. Interviews with a national cross section of divorced persons found that divorced women have difficulty finding divorced men who share their views, and it is these men who are "their most likely source of partners" (The Virginia Slims Opinion Poll of 1979, in Finlay, Starnes, & Alvarez, 1985).

In our discussion of divorce, the emphasis has been on the problems that unequal settlements present to women and their children. We must not, however, lose sight of the reasons for divorce, and the consequent benefits to women who dissolve painful and miserable marriages. One study (Buehler, 1988) of 177 divorced single parents found that the women and men in the sample reported similar levels of life satisfaction, social support from relatives, and social, emotional, and familial well-being. The women, however, reported more improvements in their health since the divorce and a higher level of family feelings of togetherness, respect, and openness.

Joy and Growth

If inequality in status and power produces unhappiness in marriage, then it should follow that women have a greater chance for marital happiness the more liberated both they and their husbands are from restrictive and debilitating gender roles. Some men, in response to the women's movement and to economic forces that have weakened the family wage system, have begun to question their traditional role as provider and breadwinner and have come also to enjoy what used to be women's prerogatives—self-adornment, home decorating, cooking, and consumerism. Jessie Bernard (1981) described the decline of the "good provider role" for

men but cautioned that while men are finding personal benefits in sharing breadwinning responsibilities with women, they are not as eager to share women's traditional responsibilities for the household. Barbara Ehrenreich's (1983) analysis of what she labeled "the male revolt" is even more disquieting. She concluded that contemporary men seem to have "abandoned the breadwinner role" without changing their sexist attitudes. Some men appear to have discovered, with pleasure, that, as unmarried men, they can do their own cooking and laundry, spend their own money, and enjoy the company of adult women and men. It is not clear whether these discoveries are accompanied by the reduced desire to commit oneself to a long-term relationship with a woman, as Ehrenreich suggested. As noted earlier, it is the age of first marriage for women, not for men, that has increased dramatically over the decades, and marriage is chosen at some point by 95 percent of all adults in our society.

For marriage to be enhancing and growth-producing, we must, as Ehrenreich suggested, "learn to be brothers and sisters" and be guided by the "feminist principle . . . that women are also persons with the same needs for respect, for satisfying work, for love and pleasure as men" (p. 182). Social science data support this view. Studies of couples (married, cohabiting, heterosexual, gay, and lesbian) have found that partners of both genders most prefer expressiveness or kindness and consideration in the other and believe a relationship is enhanced by partner characteristics that promote positive interpersonal relations (Buss & Barnes, 1986; Howard, Blumstein, & Schwartz, 1987; Kurdek & Schmitt, 1986a). What it takes for a marriage to succeed is suggested by the results of a study by John Antill (1983), who found that both wives and husbands were looking for the same characteristics in the other, namely "sensitive, nurturant, and gentle qualities." Another study (Neiswender-Reedy, Birren, & Schaie, 1981), of a sample that included young adult, middle-aged, and older married couples, with and without children, concluded that the most important factors in a successful marriage were "feelings of concern, caring, trust, comfort and being able to depend on one another" (p. 62).

Studies of intact marriages find greater harmony and satisfaction in those characterized by relative equality. A review of the literature (Gray-Little & Burks, 1983) concluded that the majority of post-1960 studies found evidence linking high levels of marital satisfaction to egalitarian patterns of decision making, with egalitarianism sometimes defined as joint decision making and sometimes as separate control over separate areas. Most studies continue to find that marital satisfaction is more likely in couples who perceive equity or fairness in their marriage and when the partners are not sex-typed but instead self-report a wide range of personal qualities (cf. Kohn, 1987b). A study of 185 married couples of diverse ethnicity and socio-economic status (Zammichieli, Gilroy, & Sherman, 1988) found higher marital satisfaction in couples in which husband and wife self-reported a wide range of attributes rather than sex-typed characteristics. Marital satisfaction was related to both partners being adaptable, flexible, and situationally effective, "aggressive and competitive or gentle and nurturing depending on the nature of the situation" (p. 752). Working wives also reported greater marital satisfaction than did wives who did not work outside the home. Similarly, one study (cf. Zinn, 1982) found Mexican-American couples in which both partners are in the labor force to be more egalitarian and more satisfied.

LESBIAN COUPLES

As noted by historian Megan Marshall (1986), "there was a time" in the late 19th century "when women walked arm in arm across Boston Common without attracting attention, when teenaged girls swore eternal devotion, when households run by two cultivated ladies who loved each other 'dearly' could become gathering places for polite society" (p. 71). Such a relationship between two women, considered a "union of hearts," became known as a "Boston marriage." Today we speak of sexual orientation and refer to partnered women as a lesbian couple. In the 1980s a good deal of attention was focused on the nature of lesbian relationships, sometimes in comparison with heterosexual couples and sometimes in comparison with male (or gay) couples.

Letitia Peplau (1981) and her colleagues studied, over the course of four years, a sample of mostly European-American middle-class lesbians and gay men and compared them to each other and to a sample of heterosexual couples. Differences between genders were found to be greater than differences in sexual orientation regarding what the individuals considered important in an intimate relationship, with women giving higher priority than men to emotional expressiveness. The lesbian women were found to care more than any other group about shared political attitudes and about having an egalitarian relationship.

What has emerged, generally, from the research on lesbian couples is that butch-femme roles, which recreate traditional heterosexual scripts, are infrequent. What is more common is "role flexibility and turn-taking" (Peplau, 1982), relationships that resemble friendships with the addition of erotic attraction, and a concern with equal power and equal involvement (Caldwell & Peplau, 1984). Jean Lynch and Mary Ellen Reilly (1985–1986) concluded from a study of 70 middle-class lesbian couples who had lived together for one or more years that "the majority of these women believed in egalitarianism and, in most areas of their lives, achieve" it (p. 66). In general, each partner was found to make relatively equal financial contributions and to participate equally in day-to-day decision making. Others have reported very similar findings (e.g., Blumstein & Schwartz, 1983). Lawrence Kurdek and his colleagues found the highest level of shared decision making in lesbian couples, as compared with gay and married or cohabiting heterosexual couples (Kurdek & Schmitt, 1986b); they also found that lesbian couples report more rewards from their relationships than gay couples do (Kurdek, 1991).

The conclusion from the majority of studies on lesbian couples is clear: these relationships are characterized by a belief in, and the practice of, egalitarianism in the relationship and a high degree of relationship satisfaction. Margaret Schneider (1986), for example, found that while her sample of cohabiting lesbian and heterosexual couples showed "striking similarity" in their day-to-day life patterns, the lesbian couples were distinguished by greater equality. In lesbian couples, household tasks tended to be divided equally and not to follow stereotypical patterns, suggesting flexibility and tasks allocated more by preference than role. One illustration is given of a lesbian couple in which one partner was responsible for home repairs and dusting, while the other's chores included mending, laundry, and car repair. This may remind the reader of the description given in Judith Rossner's (1983) novel *August,* mentioned in Chapter 1, of a family in which one of the adult women did the house repairs, cooking, and gardening while the other woman partner did the dressmaking and child-cuddling and worked as a mathematics teacher.

It would be a mistake to conclude that lesbian relationships are free of stress, conflicts, jealousy, frustrations, and the fear of dissolution. Lesbian couples do have problems, and do split apart, but those that remain together are consistently found to value and achieve egalitarianism in the relationship more than other types of couples do. Thus, a study of 275 lesbian couples from 39 states (Eldridge & Gilbert, 1990) concluded that the partners valued both "dyadic attachment and personal autonomy"—that is, that both intimacy and independence were important. Both partners reported a sense of power in their relationships, "suggesting that an egalitarian relationship is the reality for most of these couples" (p. 58).

BEING SINGLE

Although marriage remains the life-style preferred by a large majority, the percentage of single adults in this country living alone or with unrelated adults of either gender continues to rise. In 1985, persons over 18 years of age living alone or with nonrelatives made up 28 percent of all U.S. households, compared with 19 percent in 1970 and 8 percent in 1940 ("Living Alone," 1984; "More People," 1985). Of all persons 18 years of age or older, 35 percent were single and living alone or with other adults in 1980 (Phillis & Stein, 1983). This number includes a wide range of persons—those never married, widowed, divorced, or separated and single parents—but it does not include college students who reside with their parents when school is not in session. Among the women who lived alone in 1980, 23 percent were never married, 5.6 percent were separated, 56.4 percent were widowed, and 15 percent were divorced. Comparable figures for men, in respective categories, were 45.5 percent, 13 percent, 16.1 percent, and 25.4 percent (Wolfe, 1981–1982).

Among unmarried adults three different trends in living arrangements have been noted. First, there has been a sharp increase in the number of unmarried couple households; these include cohabiting couples as well as any other shared domicile arrangement between any two adults. Such households numbered close to 2 million in 1984 (U.S. Bureau of the Census, 1985a). U.S. households comprising unmarried couples have steadily increased from 0.8 percent in 1960 to 2.5 percent in 1986 ("The Way We Live," 1986). At the same time, more adults between 18 and 34 years of age have been living in the homes of their parents, with this more true of young men than women. Thus, among men between 25 and 34 years of age, 12.4 percent (including college students) were living with their parents in 1984 compared with 8.8 percent in 1970, whereas among women of the same age, 5.4 percent were living with their parents in 1984 compared to 5 percent in 1970. Contributing to this

change were such factors as "postponement of marriage, rise in divorce, emphasis on advanced education, employment problems, and high housing costs" (U.S. Bureau of the Census, 1985a, p. 6). The largest group of unmarried adults, however, consists of one-person households. In 1986, 24 percent of all households were of this kind—meaning that more than 1 adult in 10 lived alone—compared to only 13 percent of all households in 1960 ("The Way We Live," 1986; "More Women Postponing," 1986).

In 1986, news stories were reporting an unpublished study by Neil Bennett, David Bloom, and Patricia Craig, that came to be known as the Harvard-Yale study, that had concluded from a statistical analysis of 1982 census data that

> college-educated white women who have not married by the time they are 25 years old have only a 50 percent chance of marrying . . . . Just 20 percent of the women who reach the age of 30 without marrying can be expected to marry, 5 percent of those who reach the age of 35 . . . and for those beyond 40 . . . 1 percent. (cf. Greer, 1986)

As journalist Susan Faludi (1991) has since noted, these "statistics received front-page treatment in virtually every major newspaper and top billing on network news programs and talk shows . . . wound up in sitcoms . . . ; in movies . . . ; in women's magazines . . . ; in dozens of self-help manuals, dating-service mailings, night-class courses on relationships, and greeting cards" (pp. 9f.). Unmarried women all over the United States were suddenly questioning their life-styles and career decisions and feeling anxious and uncertain. But a close examination of the Harvard-Yale study by Jeanne Moorman and Robert Fay of the Census Bureau revealed a major error; and an independent study by Moorman of a much larger number of households (13.4 million compared to the 60,000 examined by Bennett, et al.) led to very different conclusions.

> At thirty, never-married college-educated women have a 58 to 66 percent chance at marriage—three times the Harvard-Yale study's predictions. At thirty-five, the odds were 32 to 41 percent, seven times higher than the Harvard-Yale figure. At forty, the odds were 17 to 23 percent, *twenty-three* times higher. And . . . a college-educated single woman at thirty would be *more* likely to marry than her counterpart with only a high school diploma. (Faludi, 1991, p. 11)

The press has granted Moorman's findings only scant attention; but when the Harvard-Yale study was finally published, 3½ years after making national headlines, it did not include the much publicized but erroneous marriage statistics (Faludi, 1991).

The press had seized upon the Harvard-Yale statistics, frightening unmarried college-educated women, as reflected in the reports of psychotherapists and in the findings of surveys. One study conducted for women's magazines by Mark Clements Research (cf. Faludi, 1991) found that one year after the press had reported the Harvard-Yale statistics, the proportion of single women who feared they would never marry jumped to 27 percent from 14 percent the year before; this figure was 39 percent for women 25 and older. Yet, as is evident from Table 7.1, there is no shortage of single men; their percentage is greater than that of single women in every age category. As Susan Faludi (1991) has pointed out, the only place a surplus of unattached women could be found in the 1980s was in retirement communities. In 1986 the median age of women living alone was 66, compared with a median age of 42 for single men. That the press continues to misrepresent the situation for single women can be illustrated by the cartoon shown below. The image of a single woman looking wistfully in the mirror and imagining a man at her side appeared in a news story in the *New York Times* (Barringer, 1991) that reported the latest Census Bureau figures showing 16.4 percent of women between the ages of 30 and 34 to be unmarried.

©P. C. Vey. Reprinted from *The New York Times* through The Cartoon Bank, Inc.)

The story conveniently neglected to cite the comparable figure for men.

The message conveyed by the sad cartoon figure is at variance with data from a variety of sources. For example, single men in the 1980s far outnumbered single women in dating services and matchmaking clubs. Susan Faludi (1991) concluded, from interviews, that males outnumbered females in the membership rolls of video dating services by a 3 to 1 ratio. Similarly, a study of personal ads (by Theresa Montini, cf. Faludi, 1991), found that the majority were placed by 35-year-old heterosexual men.

Contemporary women who lead independent lives and do not marry tend to be well educated, well employed, and financially secure and to manifest fewer signs of psychological distress than single men do. A study of a sample of childless, never-married women between 25 and 55 who were employed and not living with a romantic partner found that these women did not differ from women in other marital-status or relationship groups in degree of self-reported psychological distress or well-being (Augustoni, Barnett, & Baruch, 1988). Contributing to their well-being was feeling good about being single, having a good job, perceiving available social supports, having positive relationships with parents, and preferring not to have children. Similarly, a study of a sample of African-American women (Brown & Gary, 1985) found no differences between those who were not married and those who were married in either the range or number of their supportive social relationships.

Research on unmarried adult women without children supports the conclusion that those who live alone or with other adults score high on physical, psychological, economic, and other criteria of well-being or life satisfaction. In some instances single women are found to do better than comparable groups of married women and, as noted above, never-married women are generally better educated and employed and more satisfied with their lives than never-married men. David Bersoff and Faye Crosby (1984) analyzed data obtained, in nine national opinion surveys conducted between 1972 and 1982, from 13,500 European-American adults aged 25 to 40 who were employed at full-time jobs. They found that, of all categories of respondents, single men contained the smallest percentage who indicated that they were very satisfied with their jobs—39.5 percent versus approximately 50 percent for all other groups. Single women and married women did not differ from one another on this dimension. A study of adults who had been identified in 1921 as highly gifted children (Sears & Sears, 1980) found that, in their 60s, the women who were unmarried, childless, and employed reported the highest level of occupational satisfaction of any group of women. Lynn Gigy (1980) studied a sample of childless women over 30 years old who had never married and found that they had significantly more education and were more likely to be employed and to have professional status than a comparison group of married women. There were no systematic differences between the single and married women in morale or personal adjustment, but the single women placed a higher value on personal growth and achievement and manifested a "continuing theme of self-assertiveness, determination, or independence" (p. 335).

Others have reported similar findings. One group of investigators (Loewenstein, Bloch, Campion, Epstein, Gale, & Salvatore, 1981) interviewed 60 women between the ages of 35 and 65 who were single with no young children at home, half of whom lived alone. What contributed to the feelings of satisfaction among these women were their health, living situations, friendships, and work. Only 15 percent rated their lives as unsatisfactory, and only about 30 percent of the childless women regretted not having had children. Data from the 1990 Virginia Slims poll indicated that close to 60 percent of the single women surveyed believed their lives were easier and happier than that of their married friends (cf. Faludi, 1991).

Some never-married women have begun to publicly proclaim their single status and to find it as worthy of celebration as marriage. Beverly Stephen (1984), for example, has described the turning point as no longer waiting for Mr. Right. Some women, with a party or a card, then send a message to their friends that "I am an adult. I want a whole life, not half a life. I am not willing to let life pass me by because I don't have a partner to share a mortgage or a vacation" (p. 55).

Among women's reasons for choosing not to marry, the desire for personal independence has been found to rank high, as well as not having found a suitable partner, incompatibility between marriage and career, and preferring to live with a woman. Lynn Gigy (1980) found among a sample of never-married women over 30 years old that 30 percent cited their sexual orientation as an important factor. Most homosexual women are not likely to marry, but a sizable number have married and an even larger number are parents.

Despite the positive images of single women that emerge from the research literature, old images of the "spinster" or "old maid" linger on in the pictures of never-married women we carry in our heads and see reinforced in films, television, and fiction. To the image of

the sexually repressed "dried-up old prune" has been added that of the liberated "swinger" who searches actively for sexual satisfaction and the company of men. The dark side of such pursuit of sexual experience by dissatisfied, unhappy single women has been fictionalized by Judith Rossner in *Looking for Mr. Goodbar* (1976). The title suggests the theme; in this case the heroine's frantic and bewildered search ends in tragedy and violence. *Fatal Attraction,* a hit film of the late 1980s, presented a similarly insidious and frightening picture. A single career woman, intelligent, beautiful, and competent, becomes obsessed with a married man; her pursuit of him is marked by her pathological behavior and ends with her terrible murder.

The popular TV series "Thirtysomething" also treated unmarried women harshly—as neurotic and always searching for a man or as tough career women who experience breakdowns or finally succumb to romance. Susan Faludi (1991) quotes one of the staff writers for the show, Ann Hamilton, as follows: "When you look at the characters on this show you get the sense that all single women are unhappy. You look at these women and you think, 'God, I wouldn't want to be single now'" (p. 166). Among the primarily negative images of single women on television, Murphy Brown and Jessica Fletcher of "Murder, She Wrote" stand out as exceptions. But Murphy Brown became a mother, and Jessica Fletcher was once married. Fletcher is a childless widow living delightfully alone in a seacoast town in Maine. She is a successful writer of mysteries, competent, confident, assertive, busy, with many friends, places to go, and things to do; she is respected, admired, liked, and sought after. No reasons are presented to the viewer to pity her single status; one sees, instead, a life in which involvement with work and personal relationships are sources of satisfaction.

Some stereotypes of the unmarried woman include unusual dedication to some pursuit or career. She may be romanticized as a ballet dancer, executive, scientist, or reclusive poet, or as someone who devotes her life to a cause or a person. She may then be viewed with some pity, since her life, though worthy, is nevertheless narrow and restricted. In fiction or films we have seen such women as teachers or daughters of demanding old parents, sometimes bitter, or, like Mary Poppins, as ever cheerful, clever, and good.

Along with the continuation of such stereotypes, the late 1980s witnessed two other phenomena: the virtual disappearance of the single woman from major positive roles in television dramas or comedy, and the media's "preoccupation with single women's miseries" (Faludi, 1991). Aside from those who function in all-female worlds (such as those of "The Golden Girls" or "Designing Women"), a single woman is typically shown, according to Susan Faludi (1991), as a "coldly calculating careerist or . . . deeply depressed spinster. Either she had no emotions or she was an emotional wreck . . . . She had traded in her humanity for a paycheck, and spurned not only men but children" (p. 159). Supporting the argument that the media has tended to focus on the problems rather than the strengths of single women, Faludi (1991) cites a study that found that, between 1983 and 1986, national magazines ran 53 feature articles about single women—almost all of them "critical or pitying"—compared to the 5 articles they ran between 1980 and 1982. During the same period, in 1987, the CBS Morning News did a 5-day special on the regrets of single women, and ABC had a 3-day special in 1986 and a 4-day series in 1987. Strangely, similar attention has not been given to the single man!

Mary Washington (1982) has written movingly about how damaging the negative images and assumptions about single women can be, expressing the wish to have singleness "acknowledged as a legitimate way to be in the world." To assume that single people do not have responsibilities, she points out, equates them with children, treats them with contempt, and "keeps the single woman feeling perilous about her sense of personal success" (p. 80). Washington quotes the following lines from a poem by Adrienne Rich ("Song") to illustrate her own feelings.

> You're wondering if I'm lonely;
> OK then, yes, I'm lonely
> as a plane rides lonely and level
> on its radio beam, aiming
> across the Rockies
> for the blue-strung aisles
> of an airfield on the ocean.

One woman, writing to a newspaper's "share your thoughts" column, expressed her annoyance with people who responded to her singleness "with shock, dismay, gloating or pity."

> My sister is a successful career woman [unmarried and childless] . . . . Our childhood was normal and loving, and my parents are still happily married. We both date and enjoy men's company. When I tell people about my sister's life and accomplishments, the question always comes, "Is she married?"
> Am I mistaken in thinking that people ask this question as a further evaluation of worth? Is it my imagination that in this day and age there is the

unfortunate concept that single men are wisely so by choice, and single women just "couldn't catch one"? ("She's Single," 1984)

Among single women, those living with young children do tend to face serious economic hardship in this country and differ substantially on many measures from other single adults. Thus, for example, although data from a national study revealed that adults of both genders who live alone typically do so by choice and are likely to be more socially integrated and to have more social contacts outside their household than adults who live with others, the women who lived alone with young children revealed "significantly negative feelings about their life circumstances" ("Living Alone," 1984). Single parents, the vast majority of whom are women, constituted 19.5 percent of U.S. households in 1980. In the chapter on parenthood, we will discuss the special problems of single mothers related to their grossly inadequate access to economic resources. At this point it is important to recognize that single mothers are not a homogeneous group. In 1980, over 20 percent of the more than 5 million female-headed households in this country were headed by college-educated mothers (Wolfe, 1981–1982).

NEW DEFINITIONS OF FAMILY

Accompanying the steady growth of single women who live alone or with other unrelated adults is a new conceptualization or an expanded understanding of what constitutes a family. Persons on whom one can depend for emotional support, who are available in crises and emergencies, or who provide continuing affection, concern, and companionship can be said to make up a family. Members of such a group may live together in the same household or in separate households, alone or with others. They may be related by birth, marriage, or a chosen commitment to one another that has not been legally formalized. Thus, for example, Donald Bloch, the director of a family therapy center, reported that he views family therapy as appropriate for people who consider their family members to be friends, lovers, companions, work colleagues, or some combination of these (cf. Wolfe, 1981–1982).

We know that what we used to think of as the typical family can no longer be so described. As indicated by data from the Bureau of Labor Statistics, only about 6 percent of all households in the United States now have an unemployed wife at home with two or more children and a breadwinner husband ("Fascinating Facts," 1989). Nontraditional couples, both heterosexual and homosexual, are demanding legal rights and recognition, including the pension benefits of a deceased partner, child custody and visitation privileges following separation from a partner, work leaves to care for ill partners, tax benefits, and public registration as "domestic partnerships" (Beck, 1990). In other words, nontraditional couples are pressing for the same respectful treatment and benefits accorded traditional heterosexual marriages. As Philip Gutis (1989) has pointed out, "redefining the family is not only a gay rights issue" but involves other kinds of adults living together as a functional unit. Such functions, as enumerated by a 1987 California State Task Force on the Changing Family, include "maintaining physical health and safety of members, providing conditions for emotional growth, helping to shape a 'belief system,' and encouraging shared responsibility" (Gutis, 1989, p. E-6).

It seems reasonable to expect families to perform such functions and to call a group of persons who do a family. By so doing we include blended families (of stepparents and stepchildren), single-parent families, gay and lesbian families, and other groups of persons who have chosen to live together and take responsibility for one another's welfare. Carol Stack (1974) long ago described the importance of such families within an African-American community. Recognition of the expanded meanings of family are necessary to deal with the realities of 1990s arrangements and to enhance the satisfactions unmarried adults derive from a single life-style and from relationships with persons of varied marital categories and both genders.

In addition, as Lillian Rubin (1986) has argued, clinging to a traditional—now faded and unreal—image of families is hypocritical in light of our society's failure to support them. "We are, after all," she noted, "the only advanced industrial nation that has no public policy of support for the family, whether with family allowances or decent publicly-sponsored childcare facilities" (p. 89). As of this writing, we finally have a federally mandated family leave program (passed by Congress in 1993) that allows *leave without pay* for childbirth, adoption, and family illness; and an improved health insurance system is under study. We will return to these issues in later chapters.

◆ Discussion Questions

1. What variables in today's society contribute to equality in heterosexual relationships, and what variables interfere with achieving equality?

2. Analyze the lyrics in a sample of pop music for what they say about romantic relationships.

3. Discuss the pros and cons of marriage, first for women, then for men.

4. Who has "more say" in heterosexual and lesbian relationships you have directly observed?

5. Ask a sample of your friends or acquaintances about their images of single women in their 30s or 40s.

6. What kind of a family do you anticipate being part of? What kind of a family are you a part of now?

CHAPTER 8

VIOLENCE AGAINST
WOMEN AND GIRLS

*There is no difference between being raped
and being pushed down a flight of cement steps
except that the wounds also bleed inside.*

*There is no difference between being raped
and being run over by a truck
except that afterward men ask if you enjoyed it.*

*There is no difference between being raped
and being bitten on the ankle by a rattlesnake
except that people ask if your skirt was short
and why were you out alone anyhow.*

*There is no difference between being raped
and going head first through a windshield
except that afterward you are afraid
not of cars
but of half the human race.*

MARGE PIERCY (1976b, p. 88)

*Late at night
I chase you home.
I say I wanna stay,
You say you wanna be alone.
You say you don't need me,
But you can't hide your desire,
'Cause when we kiss, oohh—
Fire . . .*

*Well, now your words, they spit,
But your words, they lie,
'Cause when we kiss, oohh—
Fire.*

THE POINTER SISTERS (''Fire,'' 1981)

VIOLENCE AGAINST GIRLS AND WOMEN OCCURS with alarming frequency in our culture. The roots of this violence are in gender stereotypes and unequal power. When one gender dominates, the stage is set for the hostility and violence we will now explore in detail.

The Marge Piercy poem that opens this chapter describes the reality of sexual abuse for women; the fictional character in the Pointer Sisters pop song (recorded by Bruce Springsteen) expresses why this abuse is so frequent. As Katherine Imbrie (1986) noted, even though the woman says "no," the man is convinced she really wants to have sex as much as he does. This point of view illustrates "the centuries-old, culturally ingrained expectation that women want to be persuaded to have sex, and that to be successful, men must be aggressive persuaders" (p. E-4). Such an expectation is part of the complex web of beliefs; attitudes; responses; laws; and economic, social, and political realities that define and illustrate sexism and provide the ever-present context for women's experiences in our society. The most tragic outcome of sexism is the violence inflicted on girls and women by men. A recent example of such an outcome is seen in the actions of a group of male high school athletes from a suburb in California. This group, known as the Spur Posse, has been accused by a large number of girls and their parents of sexual coercion and assault. The boys—who have braggingly admitted their sexual prowess in "scoring," a requirement for Posse membership—claim consent in all cases, and have been treated to guest appearances on national TV talk shows. According to Anna Quindlen (1993), while some of the parents have been upset and dismayed by the behavior of their sons, one father said with apparent pride, "Nothing my boy did was anything that any red-blooded American boy wouldn't do at his age" (p. E-13). Another recent example is the Tailhook scandal during which, according to a Defense Department report, 83 women and 7 men were sexually assaulted and abused by naval officers at a convention of Navy and Marine fliers in Las Vegas in 1991. As of this writing, it is expected that "as many as 175 officers, including admirals and generals, may face disciplinary action" (Gordon, 1993, p. E-2).

It has been proposed that violent responses to women lie at the extreme end of a continuum of hostile or misogynistic behaviors (Hughes & Sandler, 1988; Reilly, Lott, Caldwell, & DeLuca, 1992; Quina & Carlson, 1989). This continuum would begin with humorous put-downs, jokes, and leering and end with sexual assault, battering, and

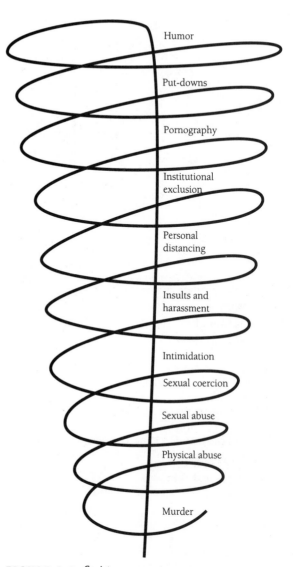

FIGURE 8.1 *Sexist responses to women.*

murder. In its center, we find pornography, harassment, and the exclusion of women in public and institutional domains such as employment, as well as face-to-face discrimination in interpersonal situations. Figure 8.1 presents a possible model of the relationship among such sexist responses to women.

Positive relationships (correlations) among negative behaviors, cognitions (beliefs), and feelings (attitudes) toward women have been identified and supported by empirical research (e.g., Briere & Malamuth, 1983; Check & Malamuth, 1985; Malamuth, 1981, 1986). In one study (Pryor, 1987), men who self-reported a high likelihood of engaging in sexually harassing behaviors were found to differ from men who reported less of a likelihood in that the former group also subscribed to more adversarial sexual beliefs, reported more likelihood to rape, and behaved in a more sexually exploitive way when their motives could be disguised. Another study (Reilly, Lott, Caldwell, & DeLuca, 1992) found positive correlations in the self-reports of college men among measures of tolerance for (acceptance of) sexual harassment, likelihood to rape, experience as a sexual victimizer, acceptance of rape myths, and the belief that heterosexual relationships are adversarial. Self-reported use of coercive techniques and force to obtain sexual intercourse has also been found to be positively related to men's greater adherence to beliefs about their sexual dominance and adherence to traditional sex roles (Muehlenhard & Falcon, 1990). Hostility toward women is thus found to be manifested in a great many interrelated ways.

PORNOGRAPHY

Some men experience pleasure when they see, hear, or read about the sexual humiliation and abuse of women. In our society such images are easily obtainable for sale or rent. The formal, intentional pornography business is more profitable than the popular recording industry, earning billions each year. According to David Friendly (1985), "every week Americans buy an estimated 2 million tickets to X-rated films resulting in an annual box-office take of about $500 million even before they reach the burgeoning home-video market" (p. 62). Videocassettes have now become the major product in the pornography business, with 42 percent of video shops selling or renting "adult" videos (cf. Cowan, Lee, Levy, & Snyder, 1988). A Gallup poll in 1985 found that 20 percent of 13- to 18-year-olds had seen an X-rated movie (cf. Linz, Donnerstein, & Penrod, 1988).

In a study of the contents of readily available pornographic material (Cowan, Lee, Levy, & Snyder, 1988), trained raters watched 45 rented X-rated videos and coded scenes in them for a variety of themes. They found that an average of 47 minutes of each approximately 78-minute film was devoted to explicit graphic sex (primarily heterosexual) and that, within such scenes,

dominance and exploitation were major themes 54 percent of the time. Using the films rather than scenes as the unit of analysis, 82 percent were found to feature dominance and 78 percent to feature exploitation, primarily of women by men. A rape occurred in 51 percent of the videos, and 90 percent of these presented the rape of women by men. In 97 percent of all the heterosexual sex scenes, a man was shown ejaculating on a woman.

In addition to material that is clearly identified as pornography, incidental and free pornography is present in advertising on billboards, in fashion magazines, on record covers, and on television, especially the MTV cable channel. Images of women as dehumanized objects, with focus on body parts, or as chained, bound, treated with contempt, or abused, are familiar to all of us and are found in magazines, films, and on the television screen. I have a file of such magazine advertisements, which presumably are designed to sell clothing, perfume, and so on; this file continues to grow even in the 1990s. Should such material be considered pornographic? Definitions vary but, following the lead of Gloria Steinem (1978c) and others cited in the chapter on sexuality, I suggest that pornography is any symbolic material that shows women being sexually exploited, demeaned, humiliated, dehumanized, threatened, or abused, when this presentation is not for educational purposes but for the economic gain of those who produce and distribute it with the intent of providing viewers with sexual titillation, arousal, or pleasure. Acceptance of such a definition leads to the conclusion that pornography is systemic in our society and that it serves to reinforce and maintain gender inequality. As argued by law professor Catharine MacKinnon (1989), in pornography "women exist for the end of male pleasure" and such material "dispossesses women of the same power of which it possesses men" (p. 209).

Some African-American feminists (e.g., Collins, 1991) have argued convincingly that pornography illustrates "the interlocking nature of race, gender, and class oppression" (p. 170). Thus, whereas European-American women are shown as objects, African-American women are more often depicted as animals, typically in situations of submission or bondage to European-American men, and Asian-American women are shown being tortured. Alice Walker views pornography as a system of images that "entraps everyone" and urges minority men to understand how they are affected by it and how pornography defines them "as being capable of fucking anything . . . even a piece of shit" (cf. Collins, 1991, p. 173).

A February 1992 Jordache ad. What is it selling? (Photograph courtesy of Jordache Enterprises Inc.)

A critique and analysis of the music videos we see on MTV (Jhally, 1991) convincingly demonstrates that women of all ethnicities are presented in this medium primarily as props or objects to decorate and arouse, to stroke men's egos and satisfy men's fantasies and needs for power, sex, and violence. In his videotape, *Dreamworlds,* Sut Jhally documents, through the use of MTV footage, the sexual objectification and degradation of women in a medium that reaches millions of children, teenagers, and adults in living rooms all over this country. These music videos have never been declared obscene or pornographic by any formal judicial body, yet their negative, hostile messages about women are clear. It is of interest to note in this connection that a group of college men in one study (St. Lawrence & Joyner, 1991) that was randomly exposed for a brief period to heavy metal rock music subsequently self-reported significantly more adherence to gender stereotypes and negative attitudes toward women than did a group exposed to classical music. Such a finding is not surprising when we pay attention to the lyrics of

heavy metal performers. Axl Rose, for example, sings about rape as a cure for boredom and Ice-T raps about raping a woman with a flashlight. Bryan Turner of Priority Records, a $53-million-dollar business, was reported (McCarroll, 1993) to have "refused to publish a rap group whose songs advocate gang violence" (p. 63) while finding lyrics by the rap group N.W.A. in their hit song *One Less Bitch* acceptable. Among the images projected in this song is the following: "And she lets you videotape her/ And if you got a gang of niggers the bitch'll let you rape her." This kind of pornography is found in films as well as in pop music and advertisements and on MTV. In horror movies, for example, the majority of victims are young women (Maio, 1990). The audience first watches the victim undress or soap up in a shower and then observes her being murdered.

Feminists who are critical of pornography do not object to its explicit sexual content but rather to its degrading, demeaning, and potentially dangerous portrayal of women as objects to be used by men for their satisfaction. As discussed in the chapter on sexuality, the dominant view among feminists is that pornography is distinguishable from erotica. Whereas erotica portrays mutually satisfying and consensual sex or the beauty of human bodies, pornography presents women as men's toys, things, pets, servicers, or meat.

The consequences of exposure to pornography is the subject of considerable debate, and many questions remain unanswered. Most of the current debate centers on pornography's effects on men's attitudes, beliefs, and behavior, largely ignoring how exposure to pornography may affect what women feel, think, and do. Although research has thus far been unable to show a clear and direct link between a man's exposure to pornography and his sexual assault of a woman, there is considerable evidence that exposure has demonstrable effects on men's attitudes and beliefs and on aggressive behavior toward women in laboratory situations.

Edward Donnerstein (1983) concluded from a summary of relevant literature that a positive relationship exists between men's exposure to pornographic materials and their sexual arousal, self-generated rape fantasies, lessened sensitivity to rape, increased acceptance of rape myths and interpersonal violence, and increased self-reported likelihood of sexually assaulting a woman. Illustrative of this research is an experiment in which college students were first exposed to slides (varying in content for different groups of viewers) and then asked to read the testimony of a rape victim and make judgments about the case (Wyer, Bodenhausen, & Gorman, 1985). Exposure to visual materials that portrayed women as sex objects significantly decreased men's belief that the rape victim was telling the truth and increased their belief that she was responsible for the sexual assault. Especially important "in influencing men's perceptions and attitudes about rape," according to Edward Donnerstein and Daniel Linz (1986), are "messages that women find force or aggression pleasurable" (pp. 57f.). Among the most significant and chilling consequences of pornography is its desensitization of viewers to sexual violence. One study (Linz, Donnerstein, & Penrod, 1988) found, among a sample of college men exposed to a number of films over the course of several days, that "sexually violent material that was originally anxiety provoking and depressing became less so with prolonged exposure" and that "films once found degrading to women were judged to be less so after prolonged exposure" (p. 765). Men who had seen sexually violent films became less able to empathize with rape victims. As concluded by active researchers in the field, studies consistently indicate "that exposure to violence against women . . . results in callousness toward female victims of violence, especially rape" (Linz, Wilson, & Donnerstein, 1992, p. 146). The implications for real-life situations outside the laboratory are frightening.

Beliefs about women are clearly influenced by media images. Other data indicate that such images also directly mediate aggressive acts against women. Edward Donnerstein (1980) and his colleagues found (a) that men in a laboratory situation, when given a second chance to apply electric shocks to others, gave shocks of higher intensity to women than to men if they had first been exposed to a sexually explicit film; (b) that men who had first seen an "aggressive-erotic" film gave higher intensity shocks to women than to men even if they were not angry at the women they shocked; and (c) that, when angered, men exposed to either an "aggressive-erotic" or an aggressive film in which a woman was physically abused, behaved more aggressively toward women targets than did men who had not been exposed to such materials. In another study, Neil Malamuth (1983) found that, after men had been angered, those who were more accepting of rape myths and who had previously been sexually aroused by a rape depiction were more likely to deliver aversive noise to a woman as punishment for incorrect responses on a laboratory task.

Repeated laboratory studies have thus demonstrated that men exposed to pornographic materials are likely to experience rape fantasies; to report greater acceptance of rape myths; to question the credibility of rape victims; to be more likely to say they might sexually assault a woman,

if no possibility of punishment exists; and also to be more likely to behave aggressively toward women, whether angry at them or not. Finding relationships between what people see and hear and what they consequently feel, believe, and do is not surprising. To expect that pornography would not affect attitudes, beliefs, and behavior would counter much of what we know about human learning, although we clearly must learn more about the conditions that mediate the connections with action. We must take seriously the myriad messages in our media that present the abuse of women as a source of amusement and pleasure to men in the context of male privilege and dominance. Catharine MacKinnon (1989) argues that "men treat women as who they see women as being. Pornography constructs who that is" (p. 197). Until we make serious changes in these messages, too many women, and men, will continue to experience pornography as reality.

SEXUAL ASSAULT

On the extreme end of the continuum or spiral of sexist responses to women is rape or sexual assault, typically defined as forced sexual intercourse or contact without the partner's consent. Such a definition is found in the legal statutes of all states, all of which treat rape as a violent crime, a felony, punishable under the law. Because forced sexual acts may involve penetration of various body parts or other acts of a broadly sexual nature, and because attempted rape is sometimes successfully thwarted, some state laws now refer to forced sexual acts as sexual assault rather than rape. New laws are also gender-neutral in recognition of the fact that boys or men may also be sexually molested and that women are sometimes, although rarely, the perpetrators. One example of such legislation is the Rhode Island law (State of Rhode Island, 1979) that defines first degree sexual assault as forced or coerced "sexual penetration with another person." Force or the threat of force must be demonstrated unless the victim is under 13 years of age or mentally or physically incapacitated. Second degree sexual assault is defined as forced or coerced "sexual contact with another person" if the intentional touching of intimate body parts "can be reasonably construed as for the purpose of sexual arousal, gratification or assault." The use of force or its threat, and the victim's resistance to it, is central to current legal definitions, as it appears to have been for centuries in western societies. According to

Louise Fitzgerald (1992), 4,000 years ago "the Hebrews declared that if a virgin was raped within the walls of the city, she was to be stoned to death along with her attacker; the patriarchs reasoned that if she had screamed, she would have been rescued" (p. 2).

Cultural Significance

The full meaning of sexual assault is more complex than the legal definitions, as the above example from ancient law indicates. Because rape is an act performed primarily by men against women, it symbolizes women's *vulnerability*. In cultures in which rape occurs frequently, as in our own, girls grow up fearful of the possibility that they will be overpowered and sexually violated. The possibility of rape increases a woman's need to seek out a man who will serve as her protector and thereby increases her dependency. Rape connotes men taking women in the same way they take money and other goods, out of greed or temptation—thus specifying women's status as objects rather than persons. Rape flourishes during wars as an accompaniment to other violence and looting. Men tend to think of rape as an affront to the man with whom his victim is identified—her father or husband. The victim suffers from the brutality inflicted on her and also from shame and guilt, as though she has somehow been an accessory.

The ancient legend of the rape of Lucretia, dating from the sixth century B.C. and later retold by Shakespeare, contains all the major elements mentioned above. Sextus Tarquinius, the son of the Etruscan king, was determined to have Lucretia, wife of a kinsman, because she was chaste, hardworking, and beautiful. He came to Lucretia one night and forced himself upon her. If she resisted, he told her, he would kill her and a male slave and then claim that he caught her in an act of adultery; by Roman law he would have the right to kill an adulterous relative. In the morning, Lucretia told her father and husband what had happened, entreated them to "avenge her dishonor" and stabbed herself to death in disgrace. The account of what took place is said to have so enraged the Romans that they overthrew the king, Tarquinius Superbus, and drove the Tarquins out of their city (V. Bullough, 1974).

The story of Lucretia enlists our sympathies but also teaches a cultural lesson. We are meant to see the rape as an act of dishonor against her father and husband that must be avenged by them; their rights and property have been trespassed against. Because Lucretia was a party to their disgrace, she is implicated and must suffer beyond the rape itself with her death. Despite her reputation for

chastity and the fact that she was forced to submit to Sextus by threat of his sword, she is presented as the source of his temptation and therefore tainted by the deed. Such attitudes persist today, many centuries later, and are part of our patriarchal heritage.

Women are seen as objects of desire to men who sometimes feel so passionate or, in modern language, so "turned on" that they cannot curb their behavior. Consider the following poem by Baudelaire used by a colleague (Duffy, n.d.) in teaching about human sexuality.

Mad woman who maddens me,
I hate thee as much as I love thee!

Thus, I would like, some night,
When the hour of lust strikes
To crawl, I, a craven, in silence,
Towards the treasures that are thine.

In order to chastise thy joyous flesh,
To bruise thy pardoned breast
And to inflict on thy surprised flank
A deep and hollow wound.

And, giddy with the sweetness of it,
Through these new lips of thine
More beautiful and more radiant,
Infuse in thee my venom, O sister of mine!

We have all come across similar sentiments, although perhaps less poetically expressed. As noted by Catharine MacKinnon (1989), "to woman is attributed both the cause of man's initiative [by her desirability] and the denial of his satisfaction. This rationalizes force" (p. 175). MacKinnon argues, as have others—and as is illustrated by Beaudelaire's poem—that our culture legitimates a woman's taking by her male lover. Thus, "forced sex as sexuality is not exceptional in relations between the sexes" (p. 178); under conditions of male dominance, it is sometimes difficult for both women and men to distinguish rape from heterosexual intercourse.

Whatever one may think of MacKinnon's thesis, sexual assault by men against girls and women is clearly related to women's subordinate status, to the differential socialization of girls and boys, and to the sanctioned belief that it is a woman who attracts a man and is either his prize or prey. Sexual assault can be understood as an almost inevitable consequence of our gender stereotypes. Fear of its occurrence is part of learning what womanhood means, along with the lessons that women defer to men and depend upon them for self-definition and identity. A woman learns to expect that "her man" will defend and protect her against other men, and she is continually reminded and warned of the potential dangers awaiting her in unlit hallways, deserted streets, lonely roads, or strangers' cars. What women are less often warned of—but, unfortunately, learn from experience—is that the danger is greater in their own homes, not from strangers but from men they have been urged to trust—friends and relatives. In our society, it is the rare woman who is free of the fear of sexual assault. As men learn that women exist for their pleasure, women learn about their vulnerability.

Studies of other cultures suggest that sexual assault is not attributable to human nature and that cultures vary greatly in the incidence with which rape and related acts occur. Peggy Sanday (1981b) examined 95 older tribal societies (from previously gathered ethnographic reports) and classified 18 percent as "rape prone," compared to 47 percent classified as "rape free" and 35 percent as intermediate. She concluded that sexual assault is not a universal phenomenon and that rape-prone societies share certain attributes that distinguish them from societies in which sexual assault is absent or rare. In the rape-prone societies, intergroup and interpersonal violence was at a high level, with frequent wars; macho ideology predominated; men had more power, authority, and public decision-making responsibility than women; women were poorly regarded; the sexes were largely segregated; and the natural environment tended to be exploited. Sanday interpreted these findings as indicating that rape is "the playing out of a socio-cultural script" by men for whom the expression of their "personhood" involves violence and toughness.

Among contemporary societies, the United States would undoubtedly be classified as rape-prone, since it has the highest rate of sexual assault of any industrialized country in the world. The United States can be said to share some of the characteristics of other rape-prone cultures described above. Sexual assault is part of a cultural configuration that includes a view of men as predators and of women as prey who have something men desire, need, lust after, and have a right to. Supporting the proposition that sexual assault reflects the culture in which it occurs are data from a study (Straus & Baron, cf. "Northeast Has Lowest Levels," 1985) that examined the 50 U.S. states in terms of a violence index indicating the degree to which violence is legitimated or accepted. This index includes tolerance of corporal punishment for children in the schools, National Guard enrollment and financial support, popularity of violent TV shows, and ratio of executions to murders. A strong correlation was found between a state's incidence of reported rape and its ranking in "legitimate violence" level. In other words,

states high in acceptable violence tended also to be high in sexual assaults.

In Susan Brownmiller's (1975) now-classic sociopolitical analysis of rape, the men who rape are said to perform an important function for all other men. "That some men rape provides a sufficient threat to keep all women in a constant state of intimidation" (p. 209), with rapists functioning, in effect, as "front-line masculine shock troops." This conclusion, though extreme, does not seem to be greatly at variance with what we know about sexual assault—its prevalence, the difficulties many people have in distinguishing between rape and seduction, the low conviction rate of accused rapists, and the divergent attitudes toward rape expressed by women and men. Katha Pollitt (1985), for example, has noted that, in cities like New York, "public space is . . . male turf," and women are rarely seen in public parks or rest areas alone or in small groups, unaccompanied by men. Women gather together outdoors primarily with their children—in playgrounds, near sandboxes and swings. While we can probably find exceptions to Pollitt's generalization, the grim picture she paints is nevertheless hauntingly familiar.

> There's the male sense of entitlement—on the street, men march boldly down the middle of the sidewalk, swinging their arms and looking ahead . . . . Women scurry along, clutching their shoulder bags, head down, weaving a zigzag path through the crowd. (p. C-2)

Prevalence

Sexual assault is believed to be the least reported but most frequently committed violent crime in the United States. In the early 1980s the rate for reported rapes was nearly twice as great as for all other violent crimes and four times as great as the overall crime rate (cf. Faludi, 1991). These statistics, however, reveal only a small part of the problem. It is well known that sexual assaults are grossly underreported; the FBI has estimated that only 1 in 10 are reported to the police (cf. "Sexual Assault," 1986). Estimates are even higher if they include assaults on children by their fathers or stepfathers (usually categorized separately as incest), childhood sexual abuse in general, or incidents of statutory rape—that is, sexual relations with a child, generally between 12 and the "age of consent" (variously defined by state laws but typically 16). FBI statistics on rape do not include these categories of sexual assault, nor do they include marital rape.

Because FBI data depend on the number of reported rapes, a better estimate of prevalence comes from the

National Crime Survey, a report issued by the Justice Department from its periodic interviews with a representative national sample of households. These interviews provide more reliable data than FBI statistics because respondents are asked to talk about crimes they have not necessarily reported to the police. In 1987, the National Crime Survey (cf. "Rape Attempts," 1991) estimated that the rate of completed and attempted rapes during the preceding 6-month period was 1.3 for every 1,000 women and girls over the age of 12. The survey also concluded that 53 percent of sexual assaults are reported to the police. In 1990 the estimated rate was 1 per 1,000 (Rowley, 1992). Although these figures get closer to the true picture than FBI statistics do, other investigators have found "a far higher incidence of rape than is revealed by the [justice] bureau's National Crime Survey" (Freiberg, 1990). For example, in one study of a random sample of teenagers (cf. Linz, Wilson, & Donnerstein, 1992), 14 percent of the girls reported having been raped, in most cases by men they knew. In addition, there is evidence that whereas violent crimes against men and boys over 12 have been declining, the same is not true for crimes against women ("In Crime," 1991).

Psychologist Mary Koss testified before a Senate committee about the deficiencies of the Justice Department's National Crime Survey approach. She pointed out that family members may be present during an interview, serving to discourage victims from revealing sexual abuse by those known to them and their families as well as from revealing assault experiences that they never shared with their families. In addition, the screening question about rape is extremely vague; after a respondent is asked about having been knifed, shot at, or attacked with another weapon during the last six months, the interviewer asks, "Did someone try to attack you in some other way?" The words *rape* and *sexual assault* are not used in this question nor in follow-up questions, and respondents are not informed that rape is a form of attack. Because of these deficiencies in gathering information, Koss (1992) has estimated that the frequency of rape may be 6 to 10 times higher than what is reported by the National Crime Survey. One outcome of Koss's criticisms has been a decision by the Bureau of Justice Statistics to improve their questions by asking directly about sexual assault and family violence (Freiberg, 1990a). We should expect to get more realistic and reliable data from future studies.

Among the most carefully prepared estimates of the prevalence of rape in the United States is one that examined age-specific rape rates and accumulated the risks over all ages to estimate the risk over a woman's

entire life (Johnson, 1980). The conclusion from this study was that if reported rapes are in fact the only ones that occur, and if conditions in the United States remain the same, then 12-year-old girls have an 8.5 percent chance of being subjected to a completed or attempted rape sometime during their lives. Since reported assaults represent only a small portion of the number that actually occur, a conservative assumption, in Johnson's view, is that reported sexual assaults reflect two fifths or one third of their actual number. In that case, he has concluded, "20–30 percent of girls now under twelve years old will suffer a violent sexual attack during the remainder of their lives" (p. 145). This estimate, he reminds us, is based on data that exclude children under 12 and wives sexually assaulted by their husbands. According to Johnson,

> the average American woman is just as likely to suffer a sexual attack as she is to be diagnosed as having cancer, or to experience a divorce. . . . The numbers reiterate a reality that American women have lived with for years: Sexual violence against women is part of the everyday fabric of American life. (p. 146)

Studies that have asked respondents about their experience of sexual assault at some time in their lives provide support for Johnson's conclusions. For example, a survey conducted by *Cosmopolitan* magazine in 1980, to which more than 106,000 women responded anonymously, revealed that 24 percent had been raped at least once; more than half the reported assaults had been perpetrated by acquaintances, relatives, or husbands and only 38 percent by strangers (cf. Beneke, 1982). Diana Russell and Nancy Howell (1983) have reported results from a sample of 930 randomly selected adult women in San Francisco who were encouraged in full disclosure by well-trained interviewers matched to respondents in race or ethnicity. Within this group, 44 percent reported having experienced rape or attempted rape at some time during their lives. Based on their data, Russell and Howell calculated the probability of being the victim of attempted or completed rape during a woman's lifetime to be 46 percent; they found the most vulnerable ages to be 16 to 24, similar to other reports. For example, in 1985, according to the Rhode Island Rape Crisis Center, nearly 20 percent of the sexual assault victims were under the age of 13, and nearly 23 percent were between 13 and 15 ("Sexual Assault," 1986). Although the age of victims has ranged from infancy to old age, women aged 12 to 24 are the most frequent targets, according to Justice Department statistics ("In Crime," 1991). A nationwide survey conducted in 1990 concluded that five times as many rapes of women at least 18 years of age had occurred that year than had been estimated by the Justice Department; nearly 60 percent of all rapes are committed against girls younger than 17; 39 percent of victims had been raped by boyfriends or other acquaintances, 36 percent by relatives, and 22 percent by strangers; and "one of every eight adult women in the United States has been a victim at least once" ("1 out of 8," 1992, p. A-1).

In a study conducted at the University of Rhode Island (Lott, Reilly, & Howard, 1982), my colleagues and I found that among a random sample of more than 500 women (students, staff, and faculty), 29.4 percent, or almost one out of every three women, reported a personal experience of sexual assault sometime during her life. Our definition of sexual assault included any sexual intrusion without consent, by force, deception, or threat of violence. Mary Koss (1985) found in a survey of more than 2,000 college women that 12.7 percent reported having been forced to have oral, anal, or genital sex against their will and that another 24 percent had been forced to have other kinds of sexual contact or had experienced attempted rape. Among women whose experiences met the legal definition of rape (37 percent of the sample), only 57 percent acknowledged their experiences as rape. Further, among the acknowledged victims, only 8 percent had reported the rape to police, 13 percent had gone to a rape crisis center or hospital, and 48 percent had told no one. Among the sexually victimized women, 59 percent of those who called their experience rape knew their assailants and 100 percent of those who did not call it rape knew their assailants. Similar findings were obtained from a national survey of more than 6,000 college students (Koss, Gidycz, & Wisniewski, 1987): 27.5 percent of the women reported sexual experiences since the age of 14 that met the legal definition of sexual assault. Most of the women had been victimized by acquaintances, and virtually none had reported the assault to the police.

Sexual assaults can occur anywhere and at any time, but are more likely to take place on the weekend, during evening or early morning hours, during summer months, and in urban areas. In 1985, almost one third of the assaults reported to the Rhode Island Rape Crisis Center occurred in the victims' homes, 15 percent in the assaulters' homes, and 15 percent in homes the victim and assaulter shared (cf. "Sexual Assault," 1986). My colleagues and I (Lott, Reilly, & Howard, 1982) also found that homes are places of risk. Among those in our university sample who had experienced sexual assault, 42 percent were assaulted in someone's residence and 39 percent in their own homes, as compared to 32 percent

outdoors and 24 percent in a parking lot. National data support the conclusion that the single most common place of attack is in a woman's own residence—approximately 30 percent of all reported cases.

The victim and the attacker are of the same ethnicity 93 percent of the time ("The Problem of Rape," 1978) and typically also of the same social class. According to Susan Brownmiller (1975), those who run the greatest risk of being assaulted are African-American, teenage, urban working-class girls. There has been little change in this conclusion. Justice Department statistics continue to show that the women who are most frequently victimized, sexually and otherwise, are poor, African-American, and living in metropolitan areas ("In Crime," 1991). On the other hand, there is evidence that among women of comparable education and socioeconomic background, the incidence of sexual assault is similar for African-American and European-American women. Lengthy face-to-face interviews with 126 African-American and 122 European-American women in a study by Gail Wyatt (1992) revealed no significant ethnic differences in the women's rape experiences, but African-American women were found to have disclosed or talked about their experiences less often.

Reports of sexual assault have been increasing among all segments of the population, including college students, and women have reported sexual abuse by their lawyers, psychotherapists, and other trusted professionals. Among respondents to a survey by *Nolo News,* published in California, 18 percent said that they had had sex with their attorneys; the same percentage of lawyers in a July 1992 poll reported having had sex with a client ("Lawyer-client sex," 1992). Although forced assault is not indicated in the majority of these cases, coercion and taking advantage of a client's vulnerability is. Thus, only 15 percent of the polled lawyers considered sex with clients to be unethical, compared with 71 percent of the respondents to the *Nolo News* survey. A number of studies have provided documentation of the seriousness of the problem of sexual assault by psychotherapists. For example, a national survey showed that 5.5 percent of male clinical psychologists had had sexual relations with their clients (Holroyd & Brodsky, 1977). In a subsequent study cited by Trotter (1982), 700 licensed clinical psychologists in California responded anonymously to a mailed questionnaire and gave details on 559 cases of sexual intimacy between patients and therapists, in the vast majority of which some harm to the patients was reported. Almost all the offending psychotherapists were men, while almost all of the patients involved in the intimacies were women, ranging in age from 13 to 58. Sexual intimacies between psychotherapists and their minor clients (children and adolescents) occur with some frequency (Bajt & Pope, 1989).

The true prevalence of sexual assault can only be estimated since, as already noted, most victims do not report to official agencies and many do not talk about their molestation to anyone. But it is a rare autobiography or novel about women's lives that doesn't contain some description or report of a forced sexual experience. In *Leaving Brooklyn* (Schwartz, 1989), for example, a mother responds as follows to her teen-age daughter's recounting of having been sexually molested by a man in a crowded subway train:

> "Ugh!" She thrust me from her to look at my face. "It's disgusting. It never fails. You can't go through life without something like that. . . . Look, sweetheart, there's not a woman I know who hasn't had that happen at least once. It's part of being a woman. Men can be animals, it's the honest truth. You have to fight back. Let them know you won't stand for it."
>
> "It was too crowded." I wept again. The telling of it, and her response, revived the horror. That it happened to everyone made it worse, not better.

When women report the reactions they encounter when they discuss their experiences of sexual assault, we gain some insights into the reasons this crime continues to remain underreported. In testimony before a U.S. Senate committee, for example, in June 1992, women currently and formerly in the military talked of how they had been discouraged from reporting sexual assault, derided and made to feel at fault, and poorly treated at Veterans' Administration medical facilities (cf. Youngstrom, 1992). For these and other reasons, sexual assault victims in all sectors of U.S. society are often unwilling to report a rape or its attempt.

A woman may not report sexual abuse because she doesn't realize that what happened to her is a legally punishable offense. She may have been assaulted on a date, by a family member, or while intoxicated. She may be embarrassed and ashamed; she may wish to avoid the unsympathetic, and sometimes callous, treatment she anticipates from the police and in the courts; she may want to avoid continued references and attention to a deeply painful experience; or she may simply feel helpless and confused. A child may not report a sexual assault for the same reasons as an adult; in addition, the child may fear reprisals, may not fully comprehend what has occurred until later, or may be convinced that she is now a "bad" girl and that no one can help her.

Child Sexual Abuse

One of the earliest estimates of the sexual abuse of daughters by fathers (Herman & Hirschman, 1977), based on the reports of psychotherapists, was that at least 2 to 3 percent of women have been the victims of father-daughter incest. The age of onset of such a relationship was reported to be from 4 to 14, and the occupation of the father was found to span socioeconomic categories. Similarly, Louise Armstrong (1978), who interviewed 183 women who had been sexually assaulted by their fathers, reported that these women came "from all classes, all races, all parts of the country" (p. 232). David Finkelhor (1979) surveyed almost 800 New England college students and found that 19 percent of the women (and 9 percent of the men) reported having been sexually abused as children, primarily by male friends or acquaintances of the family or by family members. The probability of sexual abuse by an adult was greater in poor and rural families but was also found within suburban and urban families of all social classes. Approximately 1 percent of the women had been sexually victimized by their fathers or stepfathers. The Children's Bureau (Executive Summary, 1982) estimated that 1 person out of every 1,000 is a victim of child sexual exploitation, while emphasizing that this figure is "a bare minimum number." Among anonymous respondents to a *Cosmopolitan* survey, 10 percent indicated that they had been victims of incest (cf. Beneke, 1982), and a survey of 1,000 college women in Rhode Island (Crook, 1986) identified 30 as father-daughter incest survivors, an incidence rate of 3 percent.

A summary of all available national data (*Developing a National Agenda*, 1985) led to the conclusion that "incest is estimated to occur in 14 percent of families and is found in all family types and social classes" (p. 12). In 75 percent of the cases, fathers have abused daughters; when boys are victimized, they are also likely to be sexually assaulted by men in their own families. Some estimates of the prevalence of child sexual abuse are even higher. For example, analyses of the survey literature suggest that "about one in six Americans may have been sexually victimized as children" (Kohn, 1987a, p. 54)—25 to 35 percent of all women and 10 to 16 percent of all men. According to Kohn,

> the abuser is almost always a man and . . . he is typically known to the child—often a relative. In many cases, the abuse is not limited to a single episode, nor does the abuser usually use force. No race, ethnic group or economic class is immune. (p. 56)

Important new information has come from a year-long intensive study of child abuse cases that reached the offices of district attorneys in eight judicial jurisdictions across the United States (Gray, 1993). The alleged victims ranged from 1 month to 17 years, with the average age being 9. The majority were between 9 and 12 years of age, while 18 percent were 5 years old or younger. Among the victimized children, 80.3 percent were girls and 19.7 percent were boys. Among the cases examined in this study, 79 percent involved male perpetrators and female victims, 19 percent involved male perpetrators and male victims, 2 percent involved a woman abusing a girl and 1 percent a woman abusing a boy. The author of the study points out that the number of cases reaching the judicial system is smaller than the true prevalence of sexual abuse of children and that, of the cases presented to prosecutors, more than 90 percent are never brought to trial. This may come as a great surprise, in view of the media publicity that surrounds trials of accused child molesters. But, most cases are diverted to some treatment program or settled through plea-bargaining.

> If you are a very young child, chances are your case will be plea-bargained or dropped. If you are five or six years old, chances are greater that the case will go to trial. If you are a teenager, however, chances are very slim that a trial will be held. (Gray, 1993, p. 3)

Although estimates of the true prevalence of sexual exploitation of children by adults (and particularly by family members) vary, as the reader has surely noted from the figures cited, investigators agree that the number is far greater than was suspected two or three decades ago. Slowly, reports by women of childhood sexual victimization by men in their families have been matched and corroborated by data gathered by social scientists. According to Maria Sauzier, a leading researcher in this field (cf. "Disclosure of Sexual Abuse," 1990), victim disclosure is a lifelong process, with few disclosures occurring immediately after the sexual abuse. One study found that 39 percent of abused children never told anyone, with the percentage varying with the relationship between offender and victim: when the offender was a natural parent, 53 percent never told; when the offender was a parent figure, 22 percent never told; when the offender was another relative or not a family member, 40 percent and 32 percent never told, respectively. That some adult women appear to recover the memory of sexual abuse at the hands of a family member only after entering a program of counseling or psychotherapy has led some to question the reality of the memory and the role played by the therapy process,

and to suggest that the memory might be "therapeutically induced" (e.g., Tavris, 1993a, 1993b). This suggestion has been met with dismay and anger by women who consider themselves to be survivors of abuse and by some mental health practitioners (e.g., "Real Incest," 1993). There will continue to be discussion, debate, and research on this issue for some time to come; at this point we can only identify the problems.

Maya Angelou (1971) has written of her experience as an 8-year-old when she went to live with her mother and her mother's friend, Mr. Freeman, who used to hold and fondle her and press his "thing" against her leg. Eventually he raped her. After telling what happened, and testifying in court at Mr. Freeman's trial, Maya was unable to speak for many years. In a novel by Marian Engel (1979), the heroine recalls her childhood experiences with Uncle Eddie, who would "put his arm around me and tell me what a good girl I was and try to get his finger up my pants. I hated him, but I knew if I told my mother she'd think I invited it or invented it" (p. 23). Gail Godwin (1978) has told a similar story about a young girl who would awaken in the middle of the night to find her stepfather "kneeling and panting in the dark beside her bed" (p. 311); and Kate Simon's (1982) childhood included sexual exploitation by her cousins, a family friend, and the neighborhood barber, incidents she never disclosed to her parents.

The central plot of a powerful novel by Joyce Carol Oates (1987) is the rape of a 14-year-old girl, Enid, by her uncle Felix.

> Two days later back in the city he telephoned . . . . Felix's voice was low and quick, hurried, all he had to say was that he'd been drunk out there and hadn't meant what happened.
>   It wouldn't happen again, he told her. . . . Enid said nothing, listening to her uncle's low, nervous voice; he was assuring her he'd been drunk he hadn't known what he was doing it was just something that happened out on the island and it wouldn't happen ever again. Then after a pause he said, "Don't tell anyone, Enid."
>   "No," said Enid. "I won't tell anyone." (pp. 106f.)

Later, he tells her, " 'You led me on, acting the way you did fooling around the way you did you knew damn well what you were doing didn't you! . . . You led me on . . . ' " (p. 132). Former Senator Paula Hawkins of Florida, who disclosed that she had been sexually molested as a child, reported being subsequently "bombarded by letters" from women who had been similarly victimized ("Molestation Story," 1984). More recently, a former Miss America, Marilyn VanDerbur, revealed sexual abuse by her father, a "millionaire businessman, socialite, philanthropist and pillar of the community" ("I Survived," 1991).

Because the sexual abuse of a child often begins before she understands its significance, the abuse often does not involve the use of force. Accounts by women who have told their own stories, like Katherine Brady (1979), Louise Armstrong (1978), and others, suggest that the process described by Ellen Weber (1977) is typical. When the girl begins to understand what has been happening to her, "she may feel both betrayed by the offender, and guilty and ashamed . . . . [She] will usually resist the relationship, only to be frightened with stronger and stronger threats; but her own sense of complicity may prevent her from asking anyone else for help" (p. 64).

Most studies, like that reported by Ellen Gray (1993), have found that children are sexually abused by persons they know. She concluded from the cases entering the judicial system that

> noncustodial acquaintances made up the largest single group of alleged abusers. Second in preponderance . . . were the victim's stepfather or her mother's boyfriend. In general, most biological and step-relatives abused children under eleven years old . . . . Strangers abused children eleven and older much more often. (p. 104)

While no consistent profile of the sexually abusive father appears in the literature, one general attribute is typically reported; the abuser is described in retrospect by his victimized daughter as having been authoritarian, punitive, dominating, threatening, and intimidating. The victim of incest tends to feel "overwhelmed by her father's superior power and unable to resist him; she may feel disgust, loathing, and shame" (Herman & Hirschman, 1977, p. 748). Louise Armstrong (1978) concluded that the abusive father "must have a sense of paternalistic prerogative in order to even begin to rationalize what he's doing. . . . He must have a perception of his children as possessions, as *objects* . . . as there to meet his needs" (pp. 234f.). Joan Crook (1986) found that the fathers of incest survivors were reported by their daughters to have been more verbally aggressive, violent, punishing, and less supportive than the fathers of a comparison group and that most survivors did not tell anyone about the abuse when it was occuring because they feared the abuser.

The traditional psychiatric literature has tended to blame the mother for her daughter's abuse (especially if the molester is the father or stepfather), either because the mother presumably shut her eyes to what was going on and refused to believe her daughter's claims or hints or because of a presumed overly dependent personality.

Thus, for example, in a report on the wife in cases of father-daughter incest, it was noted, without supporting data, that she usually "has an extremely passive personality" ("Paper Urges," 1982). A widely held view is that the mother is somehow responsible for her husband's behavior, by her passivity, her unavailability for sex, or her failure to protect her child. Critics of this view, however, have pointed out that the negative assumptions made about the mothers of incest victims are "based on scarce documentation and no data from well-designed empirical studies" (Gavey, Florence, Pezaro, & Tan, 1990, p. 4). There is little support for the usual descriptions of an incest victim's mother "as passive, weak, submissive, emotionally dependent, sexually withdrawn from her husband, or as having abdicated her parenting role or, . . . being incapacitated or absent" (p. 3).

A study by Margaret Myer (1985) concluded that mothers of incest victims cannot be grouped into any one category and that they vary in personality attributes and in their initial responses to the revelation of the sexual abuse of their daughters as well as in their ability to protect them. Of the 43 mothers she studied, 56 percent were found to have protected their daughters and rejected their husbands when the incest was discovered or disclosed, and at least 75 percent of the mothers had not known about the sexual abuse. Similar findings were reported by Joan Crook (1986), who compared 30 college women incest survivors with a matched group from a large sample. She found no evidence that the mothers of incest survivors had played any role in maintaining the father's behavior. These mothers did not differ from other mothers on any measure "except that they seemed to be more verbally aggressive, perhaps their way of acting out under the stressful conditions of their lives" (p. 58). The daughters reported that their mothers had been unaware of the abuse, and that most had been "helpful and supportive" when they did learn of it. Perhaps, as Crook suggests, the incest survivors who are supported by their mothers (the majority in her sample, 22 of 30) do not consult psychotherapists, whereas those who have had little or no parental assistance are more likely later to be seen in therapy. She concluded that "incest happens in a large number of families whether or not the mother is a strong and protective parent figure" (p. 56).

While empirical studies have been finding no support for the assumptions traditionally made about the mothers of incest survivors, mother-blaming continues. This phenomenon is not surprising in a culture that views women as "responsible for emotional and physical well-being within the family, and for protecting . . . [its members] from abuse and trauma. . . . It is the mother's job to make things right in the family and if they are not right, it is her fault" (Gavey, Florence, Pezaro, & Tan, 1990, p. 16). Traditional psychiatric analyses of incest sometimes have blamed not only the mothers but the victims themselves for being seductive. That such views are still held is illustrated by the public statements of two judges from different regions of the United States. In sentencing a man convicted of first-degree sexual assault, a judge in Wisconsin said of the 5-year-old victim, "I am satisfied we have an unusually sexually permissive young lady. And [the defendant] did not know enough to refuse. No way do I believe [he] . . . initiated sexual contact" ("Judge's Recall Sought," 1982). Similarly, a judge in Rhode Island suggested that some victims of incest "really enjoy it," don't complain "until they get hurt or something," and thus must share guilt with their abusers ("Judge Defends Comments," 1982).

When Sigmund Freud proposed in 1896 ("The Aetiology of Hysteria") that women's neuroses were caused by childhood experiences of sexual abuse within their own families, the medical community responded with outrage, and Freud was ostracized. He soon abandoned this hypothesis in favor of one that was more acceptable—namely, that the women were obsessed with sex and that their stories about seduction and sexual violence were not memories but rather wish-fulfilling fantasies. This process of change in Freud's position has been carefully studied (Masson, 1983; Westerlund, 1986). When Freud changed his theory of neurosis, he argued that it was inherent in a daughter's nature to fantasize an incestuous relationship with her father, because "of her physical deficiency and intrinsic biological inferiority. Seduction fantasies were inevitable . . . [because] of the innate female need to compensate themselves for their lack of a penis" (Westerlund, 1986, p. 307). Through such reasoning, according to Westerlund, Freud ended up protecting the sexual offender and betraying the victim.

Date or Acquaintance Rape

As we have seen from statistics cited earlier in this chapter, more than half to three fourths of sexual assaults are committed by someone known to the victim. This is especially true when the victim is a child, but is also the case for older victims. Judge Patricia Gifford, who sentenced boxer Mike Tyson to a 6-year prison term for the sexual assault of an 18-year-old woman with whom

he'd had a date, urged that we cease talking about date rape as though it were somehow different from any other kind. "Rape is rape," she said ("Prisoners," 1992). The media and social scientists, however, continue to give special attention to sexual assault by an assaulter who is known, and often trusted by, the victim. Date rape requires special attention because of its frequency and because, for the most part, victims remain invisible and offenders are rarely detected. Indeed, a sizable number of both victims and victimizers fail to identify such an incident as rape despite the fact that it meets the legal definition.

Because assault by someone with whom the victim has voluntarily interacted in social and other situations is far less likely to be reported than assault by a stranger, the perpetrator is far less likely to be prosecuted and convicted. Figures for 1985 reported by the Rhode Island Crisis Center ("Sexual Assault," 1986) indicated that the assaulter was a stranger to the victim in only 18.7 percent of the cases: 31.8 percent of the time, the assaulter was a relative; 26 percent of the time, someone the victim knew well; and 23.5 percent of the time, an acquaintance. These data, from only one state, are similar to those from others, and to information from nationwide studies cited earlier.

Reports of the widespread sexual exploitation of women by men whom women know and trust enough to go out with have come from a number of studies. On one college campus (Koss, Leonard, Beezley, & Oros, 1985), almost 32 percent of approximately 2,000 men surveyed admitted having used some degree of physical or emotional coercion to have sex with an unwilling woman. In all cases the nonconsensual sex reported was with an acquaintance. The men who reported having threatened or browbeaten women into sexual contact with them were undetected offenders, since their assaults were never reported; the women in these cases were hidden rape victims. Elsewhere, Mary Koss (1981) reported that the women in this same study who did not label their experience of forced sexual intercourse as rape tended to be romantically involved with the offenders. For approximately 40 percent of the hidden rape victims, their first sexual experience had been a sexually aggressive one!

Findings reported from a number of studies on college campuses are remarkably, and sadly, similar. The percentage of college women reporting sexual experiences since age 14 that were coercive, abusive, or assaultive was 47.3 percent in a study on my campus (Reilly, Lott, Caldwell, & DeLuca, 1992), and close to 55 percent in studies by Koss and her colleagues (Koss & Oros, 1982; Koss, Gidycz, & Wisniewski, 1987). Using a different measuring instrument, other investigators (Muehlenhard & Linton,

1987) found that 70 percent of their women respondents reported having experienced unwanted sexual activity on a date. Only a minority of women who experience victimization in the form of acts meeting legal definitions of sexual assault, however, label or recognize their experience as rape. Only 43 percent did so in the study by Reilly, Lott, Caldwell, and DeLuca mentioned above; only 34 percent did in the study by Koss and Oros. The percentage who identify their assault as rape is higher among women assaulted by a stranger: 55 percent, as compared to 23.1 percent among women assaulted by an acquaintance, as reported in one study (Koss, Dinero, Seibel, & Cox, 1988).

It is not surprising, in view of these data, that "virtually none of these victims [of date rape] or perpetrators had been involved in the criminal justice system" (Koss, Gidycz, & Wisniewski, 1987, p. 168). In one study of more than 2,000 college women (Koss, 1985), only 8 percent of acknowledged rape victims said they had reported the assault to the police; 13 percent had reported it to a rape crisis center or hospital, and 48 percent had told no one. Among the victims who did not label their assault as rape, 100 percent knew their assaulter. What are some of the factors that contribute to women's failure to identify their assaults as rape, and why, even when they do, do they tend not to report it to the police or, sometimes, to anyone?

Among students at an eastern university, one man told an interviewer (Barrett, 1982) that when he hears "no," he keeps on going anyway, since "nobody complains afterward." Another man told her:

I guess it's hard to believe a girl could really mind that much. Because the guy's never even imagined a negative sexual experience, he can't quite relate to the significance of coercion. After all, sex is fun, right? (p. 50)

Such attitudes and beliefs help us to understand the cultural context in which date rape occurs and why it is so prevalent. A study of sorority women (Copenhaver & Grauerholz, 1991) found that more than half of the reports of "unwanted sex play due to the man's continual arguments and pressures" (p. 36) either occurred during a fraternity party or involved a fraternity member. In another study, a sample of college women who responded to a videotaped seduction scene (Lewin, 1985) provided qualitative information about the complex conflicts women face in such situations. If a woman refuses to have sex, she anticipates negative reactions from the man who is pressuring her. Typically, a woman has learned to put a man's needs ahead of her own but also believes that she

is supposed to set limits. The researcher concluded that the "conflicting norms can be reconciled only by convincing the man that he supports her refusal. That's a lot harder than just saying no" (p. 192). Twenty-two percent of the women reported having experienced unwanted intercourse at least once.

The expectation that coercive sex is normative for women is reinforced in television dramas and in films. Gerard Waggett (1989) has discussed the daytime soap opera phenomenon of turning rapists into heroes, portraying rape as an act of love rather than violence and leading audiences into a forgiving attitude toward sexual assailants. In confusing the issue and lessening the crime, soap operas "idealize rape as a seduction, or as a rite of passage into heroism" (p. 11) and contribute to our acceptance of this criminal, dehumanizing, and damaging behavior. Robin Warshaw (1991) has presented similar arguments regarding the treatment of date rape in movies. "Hollywood," she noted, "rarely depicts forced sexual assault as rape when it occurs between acquaintances" (p. H-17). In addition, acquaintance rapes in films tend to be stereotyped as occurring primarily in working-class, rural, or southern settings among uneducated persons, a portrayal that has no basis in fact. It has been suggested, on the contrary, that rape is more prevalent on college campuses than in other environments (cf. O'Brien, 1989). Others believe that the rate of sexual assault is probably the same on campuses as it is within the general population but that college men are more likely to get away with sexual assault, because victims are reluctant to report fellow students and tend to meet with little sympathy and much blame, and because college officials, fearful of bad publicity, prefer not to deal with date rapes as crimes (Hirsch, 1990).

Attempts to identify attributes common to victims of date rape have been unsuccessful. Using a number of self-report measures, Koss (1985) found no support "for the influence of victim attitudes or personality characteristics on victimization status" (p. 210). College student victims, in other words, did not differ from non-victims, a finding replicated on my own campus (Reilly, Lott, Caldwell, & DeLuca, 1992). Among the more than 500 women in our study, no attitude or belief measure was found to predict whether or not a woman had experienced coercive, abusive, or assaultive sex. Men who are victimizers, however, have been found to be distinguishable from men who do not coerce or assault women, a subject to which we will return later in this chapter. We need to know more about the men who are most likely to behave in sexually aggressive ways as well as about the situational variables or circumstances under which sexual victimization by an acquaintance is most likely to occur. Alcohol or drug use has been identified as a significant factor in some studies, especially of college students (e.g., Copenhaver & Grauerholz, 1991).

Marital Rape

Another group of rape victims who tend to remain hidden are wives forced to submit to their husband's sexual demands. Husbands have typically been excluded from state rape laws, on the assumption that marriage is a contract that gives a man the right to "carnal knowledge" of his wife; wife rape, in other words, has not been considered a criminal offense. It is understandable, then, that it is rarely reported to the police or to other agencies.

In a sample of women respondents in San Francisco, 14 percent reported having been sexually assaulted by their husbands (Russell, 1982). Another study (Frieze, 1983) found that marital rape is embedded in violent marriages. In a sample of almost 300 women in Pittsburgh, 73 percent of those who reported being physically assaulted by their husbands also said they were pressured to have sex, and 34 percent said they had been raped. Among the women in a supposedly nonviolent comparison group, 37 percent reported pressure for sex and 1 percent reported rape. Another study of a random sample of adults in Texas (Jeffords, 1984) found that persons who have tolerant attitudes toward forced marital intercourse are also likely to be highly traditional in their sex-role attitudes. These data complement Frieze's findings that husbands who forced sex on their wives did so, according to their wives, to prove their manhood and to obtain services they believed their wives were obligated to perform.

As is so often the case, women's experiences as reported by social scientists are mirrored in fiction written by women. In *Vida,* for example, by Marge Piercy (1979), two sisters are talking about rape and one is reminded of experiences with her husband.

> She saw herself pinned on the bed under Vasos, unable to cry out because there was nothing but humiliation in screaming when your own lawfully wedded husband exercised his conjugal rights . . . .
> "But it isn't rape if you know the guy."
> "If you murder somebody you know, it's murder. If you rob somebody you know, it's robbery." (pp. 200f.)

As noted by Mildred Pagelow (1992), "in the United States, a man could rape his wife with impunity from the law until 1977, when Oregon became the first state to repeal the marital exemption" (p. 103). In December 1978, an Oregon man went on trial for raping his wife—the first such prosecution in this country—but he was acquitted by a jury of four men and eight women who deliberated for 3 hours. Almost 6 years later in Florida, in August 1984, a man was convicted for marital rape for the first time. Between these two events the laws in several states had changed so that spousal rape became a criminal offense. At the same time, 13 of our states moved backward on this issue, broadening their marital rape exemptions to include unmarried cohabiting couples (*Docket Report,* 1983–1984). By 1989, 36 states had specified that it was a crime for a husband to rape his wife, but marital rape remained legal in 14 other states (cf. Pagelow, 1992). In contrast, the High Court of Australia ruled in 1991 that the country's criminal law does not distinguish between rape committed by a spouse or by anyone else ("Australian Court," 1991).

Who Commits Sexual Assault?

Information about the characteristics of sexual assaulters comes primarily from those who have been identified, arrested, tried, and convicted. What we know about men who sexually assault women is thus very limited, since most perpetrators are never identified and even fewer are punished. For example, the Rhode Island Governor's Justice Commission reported that in 1981 and 1982, although arrests were made in the majority of sexual assault cases reported to the police, the number of arrests was only one third the number of sexual assaults reported to the Rape Crisis Center (cf. Landis, 1983). More reports are made to such agencies than to the police, but still more assaults are suffered painfully alone or shared only with a friend or relative.

An arrest does not always follow the reporting of a sexual assault, and prosecution does not always lead to a conviction. According to Susan Brownmiller (1975), "in reported rape cases where the police do believe the victim, only 51 percent of the offenders are actually apprehended, and of these, 76 percent are prosecuted, and of these 47 percent are acquitted or have their case dismissed" (p. 175). Reports of conviction rates around the country have varied from 10 to 50 percent, but Karen Barrett (1982) reported only a 16 percent national rate. Of the four major violent crimes—rape, murder, aggravated assault, and armed robbery—rape has the highest rates of acquittal and dismissal and the lowest rate of conviction. In addition, "for those who are convicted, probation with mandated treatment . . . is the most common disposition" (Furby, Weinrott, & Blackshaw, 1989, p. 3f.). Thus, even among apprehended and convicted assaulters, only a small minority are ever jailed. The situation is different for those tried for child sexual abuse, among whom prison sentences are "given to the overwhelming majority of tried cases and over 60% of . . . pled cases . . . [with] sentences rang[ing] from 3 to 37 years . . . [and] the most likely sentence being 5 years" (Gray, 1993, p. 106).

No "typical portrait" of a potential rapist has been identified in terms of demographic attributes. He may be single, married, or divorced; of any stature, physique, or degree of intelligence; drunk or sober; in any occupation; and aged 14 to over 50. Nicholas Groth (1979) studied more than 500 convicted rapists and concluded that

> rape is a complex act that serves a number of retaliatory and compensatory aims in the psychological functioning of the offender. It is an effort to discharge his anger, contempt, and hostility toward women—to hurt, degrade, and humiliate . . . to assert his strength and power—to control and exploit . . . . Sexuality is . . . the means through which conflicts surrounding issues of anger and power become discharged. (p. 60)

Others (e.g. Becker & Abel, 1978) who have studied men convicted of sexual assault have concluded that rapists select their victims on the basis of availability and vulnerability and that rape is a "crime of opportunity."

According to Neil Malamuth (1981), reliable differences between rapists and non-rapists in personality characteristics have not been identified, but the former have been found to be more likely "1) to hold callous attitudes about rape and to believe in rape myths, and 2) to show relatively high levels of sexual arousal to depictions of rape" (p. 142). One study (Hall, Howard, & Boezio, 1986) compared, on a number of measures, a group of convicted rapists, a group of men convicted of other violent crimes, and a non-prisoner control group. The two prisoner groups did not differ significantly on any measure, and both were more tolerant of rape than the control group. On the other hand, a very similar study (Scott & Tetreault, 1987) of matched groups of convicted rapists, men convicted of non-sex-related violent crimes, and non-convict controls found differences in attitudes toward women's equality, with the convicted rapists being the most traditional and adhering most to gender stereotypes. The rapists were significantly more opposed than the other two groups to women's equality in the workplace and were more in favor of "subservient, stereotyped, passive roles for women in male-female relationships" (p. 379). There were also similarities between the groups of men. The three groups did not differ, and were similarly conservative, in their attitudes toward women's marital roles; and there was no significant difference between the two groups of offenders in their attitudes toward women's freedom and independence.

In an important study of 79 convicted rapists, Diana Scully (1988) interviewed each man for more than 4 hours. She was able to categorize the men as either an "admitter" or "denier" with respect to the crime for which he was imprisoned and found both differences and similarities between them. For both groups of men, Scully concluded

> victims had no value outside of the roles they were forced to play in the rape . . . . Some of the men viewed women as opponents to be reduced to abject powerlessness. Others, adopting the cultural view of women as sexual commodities, reduced their victims to meaningless objects. (p. 211)

When asked how they would feel if "their significant woman was raped," approximately three fourths expressed anger, and most said they would get personal revenge; if they felt the woman was at fault, she'd be beaten.

Adolescent sex offenders are virtually all male and are estimated to account for about 20 percent of the assaults on adult women and 30 to 50 percent of child sexual abuse (Davis & Leitenberg, 1987). These adolescents are rarely apprehended, convicted, and sentenced. Compared with other male adolescents, apprehended sex offenders more frequently report having been the victims of abuse and report more sexual experience, but they do not differ from other delinquent youth in frequency of behavioral or school problems. The studies to date have not been able to identify the major variables on which adolescent sex offenders differ from either other delinquents or ordinary adolescents.

The data reported on undetected offenders are particularly significant because such men represent the majority of rapists. Among a national heterogeneous sample of more than 6,000 college students from 32 colleges, 25.1 percent of the men anonymously self-reported having engaged in some sexual aggression since the age of 14. The behavior reported by 7.7 percent of the total group of men met the legal definition of rape or attempted rape. On my campus, 39.4 percent of male respondents were classified as sexual aggressors or victimizers (Reilly, Lott, Caldwell, & DeLuca, 1992). One study (Koss, Leonard, Beezley, & Oros, 1985) found that men who have threatened or actually used force to gain nonconsensual sexual intercourse with female acquaintances differed from sexually nonaggressive men in their degree of adherence to several rape-supportive attitudes. The more sexually aggressive a man had been, the more likely he was to attribute adversarial qualities to interpersonal relationships, to accept sex-role stereotypes, to believe myths about rape, to feel that rape prevention is the woman's responsibility, and to view as normal an intermingling of aggression and sexuality. (p. 989)

It is important to note that, while sexually coercive men differed sharply from other men in their attitudes and beliefs about gender attributes and about rape, they were not distinguishable on any measure of psychopathology, a finding that has also been reported by others (e.g., Malamuth, 1986). Several investigators have found some important attitudinal and belief correlates of sexual aggression among self-reported but undetected sexual victimizers. Predictors include reported and observed sexual arousal to rape scenes, a high level of dominance motivation, hostility toward women, and acceptance of interpersonal violence (Malamuth, 1986). Another study found that the best predictors were tolerance for (acceptance of) sexual harassment and self-reported likelihood to rape (Reilly, Lott, Caldwell, & DeLuca, 1992). In addition, sexually aggressive college men have been reported to differ from nonaggressive men in being more likely to see themselves as having been hurt, deceived, or manipulated by women, in feeling a greater need to assert themselves, and in seeing themselves as more likely to lose control under the influence of alcohol (Lisak & Roth, 1988). Another group of investigators (Malamuth, Sockloskie, Koss, & Tanaka, 1991) analyzed the responses of a large national sample of college men to a survey on their sexual behavior. Among this group, 30 percent reported some physical aggression against a heterosexual partner within the previous 12-month period. How did these young men differ from their peers? The investigators concluded that sexual aggression in this sample was related to "relatively high levels of hostile masculinity and sexual promiscuity" (p. 680). Hostile masculinity was assessed by self-reported personal attributes, adherence to adversarial sexual beliefs, and responses to a scale measuring hostility toward women.

Unfortunately, all the belief and attitude factors identified with college perpetrators of sexual assault appear to be reinforced and encouraged in U.S. fraternities. Peggy Sanday (1990) concluded from an interview study that fraternities attract particularly insecure young men, who are drawn by the fraternity's promise of self-assurance in exchange for conforming to its rules. Others have identified fraternities as "rape-prone social contexts" (Martin & Hummer, 1989, p. 458). An in-depth multisource analysis of the fraternity system on one college campus led the investigators to conclude that fraternities value and stress dominance, conflict, drinking, and heterosexual prowess; "fraternities knowingly, and intentionally, *use* women for their benefit . . . as bait for new members, as servers of brothers' needs, and as sexual prey" (Martin & Hummer, 1989, p. 466). Members are encouraged to view the sexual coercion of women "as sport, a contest, or a game," to view "scoring" as part of interfraternity rivalry and as a sign that the fraternity is "successful and prestigious." The sequence of events leading to fraternity gang rapes, an all too frequent accompaniment of fraternity parties, has been described by Kathleen Hirsch (1990).

A series of studies by Neil Malamuth and his colleagues have revealed that sexual assault is not beyond the realm of contemplation for a surprisingly large number of ordinary, middle-class, college men. Instead of asking men to report on their actual behavior, the procedure developed by Malamuth is to ask participants to read a description of a sexual assault and then to indicate, on a 5-point scale, the likelihood that they would behave like the assailant under similar circumstances if they were assured of not being caught and punished. This measure yields a Likelihood to Rape (LR) score. Among various samples of college men, 35 percent have indicated some likelihood that they would engage in sexual acts with a woman forcibly and without her consent. These men, in other words, did not respond to the question by saying there was no likelihood at all that they would behave in this way. When compared with men who self-reported no likelihood of rape, those with higher LR scores were found to have more callous attitudes toward rape, to score higher on a measure of sex-role stereotyping, to believe more in rape myths, to be more sexually aroused by depictions of rape, to be more inclined to perceive rape as a sexual act that women enjoy, to be less likely to view rape as an act of violence with serious consequences to the victim, and to more often report that they have personally used force against women in sexual relationships and might do so again (Malamuth, 1981; Check & Malamuth, 1983). Thus, ordinary college men who admit that they might assault a woman under certain circumstances are similar in attitudes and beliefs both to undetected offenders and to convicted rapists.

Attitudes and Beliefs

Louise Fitzgerald (1992) suggested that the most common beliefs about rape can be divided into six basic categories: women lie about rape; women enjoy sexual force; men are justified in their behavior; rape is a trivial event; and rape, by real rapists, is a deviant act. Such beliefs, the basic ingredients of rape myths, are found in popular culture and in the answers many people give to questions about rape and are likely to influence the low frequency with which rape is reported; the judgments made in rape trials; the reactions of victims, their friends, and their families; and the social and personal consequences of sexual assault.

What people believe about rape is related to other beliefs about what is appropriate behavior for women and men and about gender-differentiated responsibilities and attributes. These beliefs affect judgments about the guilt or innocence of accused offenders and about whether a particular incident constitutes sexual assault. Even when a described incident is one in which sexual relations were forced without consent—thus meeting the legal definition of sexual assault—persons asked to make judgments about the situation appear to be influenced by other factors, particularly their beliefs about rape, whether the victim and offender were acquainted, and characteristics of the persons involved. Research indicates that these factors often support a judgment that the victim was somehow to blame for her assault.

Evidence from varied sources suggests that men in general do not consider sexual assault to be as serious a personal violation as women do and that they are more likely to subscribe to myths about rape. Many men seem really to believe that a woman can "lie back and enjoy it"; that she has somehow "asked for it" by her manner of dress or speech or her walk, or by the fact that she was out alone, hitchhiking, or in a bar; and that women entice and lure men and really want to be "taken" by strong and forceful ones. For example, in one study (Malamuth, Heim, & Feshbach, 1980), when the reactions of college men and women to a depiction of rape were compared, the men were found to be significantly more aroused when the victim was described as experiencing both orgasm and pain. In addition, the men, overall, self-reported significantly less frustration, anger, and negative feeling than the women after reading rape stories.

When victims were described to a sample of women and men in another study (Krulewitz, 1978) as having come to a rape crisis center for help, the women expressed more interest in talking with the victim, saw her as more upset and frightened, expected her to experience psychological problems as a consequence of the rape, were consistently more supportive, and perceived the situation as more serious than the men did. Similarly, Hubert Feild (1978) found in comparing 528 adult women with an equal number of men from the same community that the men believed more than the women that it is women's responsibility to prevent rape, that victims "precipitate rape" by how they look or behave, that rapists are not motivated by a need for power over women, that a raped woman becomes less attractive, that women should not resist during rape, and that punishment for rape should be harsh. Except for the opinion about punishment, each of the beliefs about rape held by the men was also found among a group of convicted rapists. The views of the men were closer to those of the rapists and to a sample of male police officers than they were to those of rape crisis counselors. Like the rapists, the male police officers believed that rape is motivated by a desire for sex and not by a need for power, that rapists are not mentally normal, and that after a rape a woman is a less desirable person. A college study (Deitz, Littman, & Bentley, 1984) found the men to believe, more than the women, that the victim somehow encouraged the rape, that the psychological impact of the rape was not too severe, and that rape is not a very serious crime. The men identified less with the victim and more with the defendant, had less positive feelings toward the victim, and were less certain of the defendant's guilt. That these findings are not "just academic" is illustrated by the comments of boxer Mike Tyson after his highly publicized rape trial and conviction. He told the judge before being sentenced, "I'm sorry Miss Washington [the victim] took it personally" ("Prisoners," 1992).

Ethnicity has been found by some investigators to be related to beliefs about sexual assault. For example, a sample of Latino college men were found to be more accepting of date rape and to ascribe to more rape myths than a sample of nonminority college men (Fischer, 1987). For Latina women, the more they were assimilated into the majority culture, the less they accepted or tolerated date rape. Another study (Giacopassi & Dull, 1986) reported that among a sample of college students, both African-American and European-American women were less likely than men to accept the common rape myths and to believe that "normal males do not commit rape." But African-American men self-reported more acceptance of rape myths and stereotypes than European-American men were.

Jurors' acceptance of rape myths affects trial outcomes, the reluctance of victims to press criminal charges against their assailants, and the hesitancy of prosecutors to go forward with a case. Gary LaFree, author of a book on rape for which he interviewed jurors, concluded that "rape is not defined so much by statute as by social attitudes. . . . Rape is defined first by the victim, and in the end . . . [by] whatever a jury says it is" (cf. Mansnerus, 1989, p. E-20). According to a prosecutor in Atlanta (Carole Wall, cited by Mansnerus), jurors are "the clog in the system"; to be convinced that sexual assault occurred, they want the victim "dragged off the street and raped in front of a TV camera."

Although women are generally more upset and disturbed than men by stories or reports of rape, some women also believe the culturally supported myths about rape and ascribe blame to the victim. The following public letter, for example, was written by a woman in response to the trial of several men accused of having raped a woman in a bar in Massachusetts. The events of this trial and what led to it (the "Big Dan" case) served as the basis for the acclaimed movie *The Accused*.

> There are women who ask to be raped, and they get what they deserve. There are also women who are raped and don't deserve it. The first kind are those who dress themselves indecently and flaunt themselves in front of men or throw themselves at men and go into barrooms by themselves . . . .
>
> I was one who didn't deserve it . . . . I was raped because the boyfriend I was seeing was trying to prove his masculinity to his mother. . . . I'll tell you what I intend to do if a women's libber ever approaches me. I'm going to shove her teeth down her throat . . . [because] it's you I blame for my getting raped. (Barb, 1984, p. A-16)

Many women and men perceive a victim as somehow implicated in, or responsible for, her assault. Martha Burt (1980) found, among a random sample of almost 600 Minnesota adults, that one half agreed with the following statement: "In the majority of rapes, the victim was promiscuous or had a bad reputation." Such myths persist, and the victim is blamed for somehow provoking, if not actually enjoying, her assault. Burt found that acceptance of rape myths was not related to personality variables but, among both genders, was "strongly connected to other deeply held and pervasive attitudes such as sex role stereotyping, distrust of the opposite sex (adversarial sexual beliefs), and acceptance of interpersonal violence" (p. 229). Acceptance of violence in personal relationships correlated most strongly with acceptance of myths about rape.

People seem less ready to call an attack *rape* when the victim was previously acquainted with the offender, even though between 50 to 75 percent of all sexual assaults are committed by persons who are not strangers to the victims. In one study (Klemmack & Klemmack, 1976), more than 200 adult women in Alabama were interviewed and asked to evaluate the degree to which they believed a rape to have occurred in seven different situations that met the legal definition of rape. When the victim in the situation had any prior relationship or acquaintance with her attacker, fewer than 50 percent of the respondents considered the described incident of forced nonconsensual sex to be a rape. The situation labeled as rape by the largest percentage of respondents described a woman assaulted by a stranger in a parking lot after 11 p.m. as she was walking to her car after work. But even this seemingly unambiguous rape story was judged not to be rape by 8 percent of the respondents.

A study of college students who read stories of rape trials (L'Armand & Pepitone, 1982) found that they were significantly more likely to recommend more lenient sentences, to perceive less damage to the victim, and to blame the victim more and the rapist less if the victim and rapist had dated or been previously intimate, than if they were strangers. Similarly, another sample of college students (Johnson & Jackson, 1988) perceived the victim less favorably and the assaulter less harshly if the woman had allowed kissing before refusing intercourse. Both women and men college students were found (Check & Malamuth, 1983) to perceive the victim of an assault as having reacted to it more favorably if assaulted by an acquaintance than if assaulted by a stranger; persons with highly stereotyped gender beliefs were even more likely to perceive favorable reactions on the part of acquaintance-rape victims, despite the complete absence of such cues in the stories read.

Studies of teenagers have found a startling degree of rape tolerance and a great degree of influence of victim-offender acquaintance on judgments about rape. One group of investigators (Giarrusso, Johnson, Goodchilds, & Zellman, 1979) asked a sample of 4,000 teenagers in Los Angeles (evenly divided by gender and including equal numbers of European-Americans, African-Americans, and Hispanic-Americans), "Under what circumstances is it OK for a guy to hold a girl down and force her to have sexual intercourse?" Only 44 percent of the girls and 24 percent of the boys maintained that it was *never* acceptable to use force. Girls and boys ranked nine specific circumstances under which they believed force to be acceptable in very similar ways and believed it was most acceptable "when a girl gets a guy sexually excited." The researchers found that nonconsensual sex was most likely to be labeled as rape by both girls and boys in situations in which the boy used physical force and the couple had just met, and least likely when nonconsensual sex occurred between dating partners and a minimum of force was used. They concluded that "victims of nonstranger rape are likely to receive little sympathy from individuals or institutions" (Zellman, Goodchilds, Johnson, & Giarusso, 1981, p. 8), because they are likely to be seen as having provoked or enjoyed the violent encounter. Similar data and conclusions have come from a survey of 1700 sixth- to ninth-graders in Rhode Island (cf. Banks, 1988). As can be seen from Figure 8.2, an overwhelming number of both girls and boys said that a man has the right to intercourse without a woman's consent if she is his wife

or if they are planning to marry. And 65 percent of boys and 47 percent of girls believed forced intercourse is acceptable if the couple has been dating for 6 to 10 months, while 24 percent of boys and 16 percent of girls found the behavior acceptable if the man had spent money on the woman.

Another circumstance likely to influence judgments about sexual assault is evidence of resistance. To convict an accused rapist, many state laws require proof that the victim actively resisted; the greater the number of cuts, bruises, and broken bones, therefore, the more believable is the accuser's story. Studies of judgments about rape victims and their assailants have found that degree of victim resistance is an important variable. Mary Kanarian (1980) reported that a sample of college men attributed more responsibility for a sexual assault to the victim when

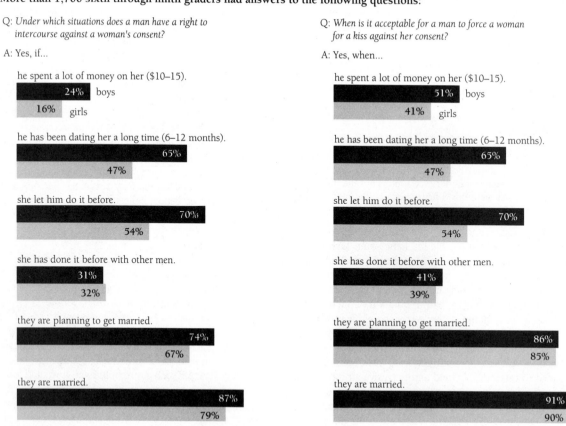

More than 1,700 sixth through ninth graders had answers to the following questions:

Q: *Under which situations does a man have a right to intercourse against a woman's consent?*

A: *Yes, if...*

he spent a lot of money on her ($10–15).
24% boys
16% girls

he has been dating her a long time (6–12 months).
65%
47%

she let him do it before.
70%
54%

she has done it before with other men.
31%
32%

they are planning to get married.
74%
67%

they are married.
87%
79%

Q: *When is it acceptable for a man to force a woman for a kiss against her consent?*

A: *Yes, when...*

he spent a lot of money on her ($10–15).
51% boys
41% girls

he has been dating her a long time (6–12 months).
65%
47%

she let him do it before.
70%
54%

she has done it before with other men.
41%
39%

they are planning to get married.
86%
85%

they are married.
91%
90%

FIGURE 8.2 *When is rape OK? Ask your kids* (taken from Adelle M. Banks, "Is rape sometimes OK?" *Providence Sunday Journal,* May 1, 1989, p. A-29). Data from Rhode Island Rape Crisis Center Survey.

she did not physically resist. Another group of investigators (Wyer, Bodenhausen, & Gorman, 1985) found that a victim who did not resist was judged by student raters to be less credible, less likely to have been harmed, and more responsible for the incident than one who resisted.

Sometimes, however, even corroboration of resistance is not sufficient to convince others that a rape has occurred. For example, a district attorney told a reporter (Mansnerus, 1989) about the following case:

> A 21-year old woman had gone to her former boyfriend's apartment at his request to pick up some belongings. As the jury heard it later, he tied her wrists with telephone cord, raped her and broke her nose. The jury convicted him of assault and acquitted him on the rape charge. (p. E-20)

In a Massachusetts case, five young men were acquitted of raping and beating a woman who was left nude, battered, and abandoned on a winter night, but they were convicted of wrecking her car ("5 Acquitted," 1983). The defendants had previously pleaded guilty to the rape charges in a plea bargaining agreement and had received $500 fines and suspended sentences. A new trial was ordered when additional evidence was brought forward, but despite testimony against the defendants from an admitted participant, the men were judged not guilty. The victim was a former beauty queen whose character was questioned by the defense attorney; the attorney claimed the victim had offered the defendants sex for money but that things had gotten "out of hand."

The respectability of the victim and her sexual history have been found to influence the extent to which she is blamed or held responsible for her sexual assault. In the previously mentioned "Big Dan" rape case, six men were accused of sexually assaulting a woman, in front of onlookers, on a pool table in a tavern. During the trial she was questioned by the defense attorneys about whether she had tried to keep her legs together, how much she had had to drink, whether she had ever had psychiatric treatment, and whether she had violated the welfare code by living with her boyfriend while collecting public assistance. Despite these efforts to discredit the victim and to influence the jurors to perceive what had occurred as something other than rape, some of the defendants were convicted.

Considerable research supports the conclusion that the victim's respectability is a prime determinant of how she is viewed and treated and of what juries decide. Jurors interviewed for a study of the Indianapolis justice system by Gary LaFree (cf. Mansnerus, 1980)

often made comments like "I don't think a woman can be raped." When they were asked what influenced them in cases where consent was at issue, medical evidence and the extent of injury were factors that counted, but the victim's 'moral character' counted more than either. (p. E-20)

In one study (Luginbuhl & Mullin, 1981) in which college students read a description of a rape, men recommended a significantly lighter sentence for the offender when the victim was described as a topless dancer who took drugs than when she was described as a married social worker. Similarly, in another study (Acock & Ireland, 1983), when a rape victim was described as a service station attendant who had given a man a ride, college students of both genders perceived her as more to blame for her assault and the rapist as less to blame than they did when the victim was described as a college student on her way home from the library. Other studies have shown a greater assignment of responsibility (or blame) to a forcibly assaulted victim if she failed to take precautions in avoiding a poorly lighted street (Pallak & Davies, 1982); if she was intoxicated (Richardson & Campbell, 1982); if she was attractive (Jacobson & Popovich, 1983); and if her previous sexual history was part of the material presented to evaluators (L'Armand & Pepitone, 1982). Some states now bar evidence about a rape victim's past sexual conduct from the trial proceedings under a rape shield law, or leave the matter up to the judge's discretion.

Victims of sexual assault have often found their treatment by law enforcement officers to be less than sympathetic and to range from harsh and superficially objective to leering and insulting. Complainants have been made to feel that they committed some crime—the crime of being out alone at night, of having accepted a ride in someone's car, of having been at a bar, of having gone to a man's apartment, of having bathed away the signs of rape, of improperly securing their doors, of simply of being women and available targets! In the face of widespread criticism, police departments have begun to sensitize their officers to try to understand rape from the victim's perspective, to ask questions sympathetically, and not to assume that the complainant is lying or at fault. Many departments are now assigning rape cases to female officers.

In a rape trial, the victim is on trial along with the accused. She is expected to recall in minute detail and with detachment small fragments of information about what took place. A trial in 1991 of three male college students in New York City accused of raping a woman after they had got her drunk resulted in their acquittal, primarily because of the victim's failure to recollect details and her failure to notify the police immediately afterward. We know, however, that, even in the absence of alcohol, incoherent memory often accompanies traumatic experiences. As pointed out by E. R. Shipp (1991),

> a victim is likely to remember only fragments of what happened. She often delays going to the authorities because she is shocked that someone she knew, and perhaps trusted, has treated her in such a beastly way. She may be filled with shame and overcome by feelings of guilt. (pp. E-1f.)

In a commentary on the nationally publicized rape trial of William Kennedy Smith, journalist Anna Quindlen (1991b) noted that there are actually two people on trial in such cases. "[D]efense attorneys have been known to attack dress, drinking, drug use, gynecological, psychological and sexual history to fashion an acquittal independent of the central issue, whether certain acts were performed without consent" (p. A-15). In the trial, which ended with Smith's acquittal, private investigators were hired by his lawyer to "dig up any dirt" on the victim, her friends, and family (Martz & Reiss, 1991).

The reader may wonder whether the different verdicts in the Mike Tyson and William Kennedy Smith trials, both of which captured media attention in 1991 and 1992, were perhaps influenced by the fact that Tyson is African-American, poorly educated, and from a ghetto background, whereas Smith, the nephew of a senator and of a dead president, is from a powerful and wealthy European-American family. We will never know to what extent these differences affected the outcomes of the two trials, but research has disclosed that characteristics of defendants do make a difference in judgments about sexual assault. Judgments ascribing less responsibility to the defendant are influenced by such factors as his physical attractiveness (Jacobson, 1981), his having retained a female defense attorney (Villemur & Hyde, 1983), and a description of him as having been intoxicated at the time of the assault (Richardson & Campbell, 1982). The latter study found that, in contrast, the victim was judged to be less moral, less likable, and more responsible for the assault when she was drunk than when she was sober.

The color or ethnicity of a defendant accused of rape has been found to be an important factor in influencing judgments. Hubert Feild (1979) found in a study of European-American students who served as jurors in a mock rape case that when the victim was also European-American, African-American defendants were punished more severely than were European-American defendants. The use of excessive penalties against African-American men for the sexual assault of European-American women is a matter of historical record (Brownmiller, 1975). Death was the prescribed punishment for rape in 14 states before the Supreme Court in 1972 voided states' capital punishment laws (which have now been reenacted by many states, specifying particular conditions). Of 455 men executed for rape between 1930 (when national figures began to be published) and 1972, 405 were African-American; these were overwhelmingly men who had been convicted for raping European-American women. Whereas 38 percent of convicted African-American rapists in Georgia, for example, were sentenced to death before 1972, only one half of 1 percent of convicted European-American rapists were similarly sentenced (Lear, 1972).

The greater readiness of our racist culture to hold African-American men responsible for sexual assault has prompted some in the African-American community to pressure African-American women to stay silent about their victimization by African-American men. Law professor Anita Hill faced this predicament when she came forward in 1991 to accuse Supreme Court nominee Judge Clarence Thomas of sexual harassment. As noted by Rosemary Bray (1991), when "Anita Hill put her private business in the street, and she downgraded a black man to a room filled with white men who might alter his fate—[this was] surely a large enough betrayal for her to be read out of the race" (p. 94). Such pressure to keep silent, however, has angered some African-American women who have publicly denounced it—for example, by taking out a quarter-page ad in the *New York Times* headlined "African-American Women in Defense of Ourselves" (cf. "Black Women," 1992).

Victim Reactions and Long-Term Consequences

Considering the continued strength of myths about rape, it is not surprising to find that victims of sexual assault suffer not only from shock, physical bruises and lacerations, disruption of their lives, invasion of their safety and integrity, but also from embarrassment and confusion about responsibility for their victimization. Some victims blame themselves, as cultural beliefs have taught them to do, and retreat into an isolation of shame and helplessness. One study (Meyer & Taylor, 1986) of 58 women who had reported a sexual assault to a rape crisis center found that nearly half "mentioned some form of self-blame" and, that self-blame was reliably related to poor adjustment.

Some women do not forcefully fight back against an attacker. The average woman is generally physically weaker than the average man and has had very little practice in physical self-defense. Many rapists have weapons—knives or guns—and women fear for their lives if they resist. In the past, parents and police urged girls and women not to resist so as to avoid serious injury or death at the hands of an enraged attacker. At the same time, evidence of resistance (and injury) is often required in order to convict an accused rapist. Pauline Bart and Patricia O'Brien (1985) described this dilemma as follows:

> Women threatened with rape are in a double bind. On the one hand we are told, "Fighting back will only excite him . . . ." We are warned . . . that resistance will result in serious injury, if not mutilation and death. . . . On the other hand . . . in order to prove legally that what happened was rape, the woman has to prove that it was indeed against her will . . . . The best way to prove that the act is not mutually consensual is by physically resisting. (pp. 83f.)

Recent advice from feminists, rape crisis counselors, and psychologists who have worked with rapists is that women facing assault should scream, make a scene, attempt to break away, and fight back, if at all possible. The efficacy of such responses was recognized more than 20 years ago by James Selkin (1975), who based his advice on what he had learned from clinical experience with rapists, which suggested that a woman's best strategy is to resist immediately, because most rapists first test and then threaten a prospective victim. From their interview study of 94 women who had experienced rape or attempted rape, Pauline Bart and Patricia O'Brien (1985) found that those who had effectively avoided rape differed from those who had not in having used more varied and multiple strategies against the attacker, and in having used some combination of screaming or yelling and physical resistance. Successful avoiders were also likely to be taller and heavier and to have had more childhood experience in contact sports and in fighting. Fighting back was found not to have resulted in more injury than not fighting and thus to have been an effective response. Talking, the most often employed avoidance strategy, was found to be largely ineffective. "Only environmental intervention proved more likely than flight/attempted flight to be associated with rape avoidance" (p. 110). This relatively new message to women—to attempt escape by physically resisting or by creating a scene—may add to the negative consequences experienced by a rape victim; having been unable to fend off an attacker, she may feel the additional pain of having failed to fight back effectively.

Two women made headlines in the 1970s by fighting back and killing their assailants. In March 1974, Inez Garcia of Soledad, California, after having been beaten by two men and raped by one of them, pursued her attackers with a rifle and shot one to death. She was tried and found guilty of second-degree murder but, after a national campaign that brought psychological and financial support, she was acquitted in a second trial in 1977. Joan Little, a 20-year-old African-American woman, fought off with an ice pick her 62-year-old European-American jailer who was sexually molesting her in a cell in Beaufort County, North Carolina; she fled the jail, leaving the man dying of stab wounds. She was acquitted of first-degree murder after a widely observed trial. Both of these cases captured the public's attention at a time when the women's movement was openly discussing sexual assault, violence, and their consequences for women's lives.

Personal testimony and more formal research indicates that the lives of sexual assault survivors are not only temporarily disrupted but often permanently altered. Ann Burgess and Lynda Holmstrom (1976) provided 24-hour-a-day immediate counseling for rape victims who came to the emergency room of a Boston hospital, later following up with telephone counseling or home visits. They found serious disruptions in the performance of important life tasks and diagnosed 79 percent of the victims they saw as having suffered from "rape trauma," or acute disorganization. Among students, 41 percent either stopped attending classes or changed their schools; unemployed married women experienced disruptions in homemaking and parenting; and among the women whose main activity was employment, half changed or quit their jobs within 6 months after having been assaulted. The assaulted women made changes in their residences, phone numbers, and transportation habits. The sexually victimized sorority women studied by Copenhaver and Grauerholz (1991) found themselves forced either to continue interacting with their assailant or else to withdraw from their sorority house and sorority activities or quit school. As noted by Kathleen Hirsch (1990), on college campuses

> victims drop out of the classes they share with their assailants. Their grades go down. They experience chronic depression and have trouble concentrating. Eventually, many . . . leave school for a period of time, or drop out altogether. (p. 55)

Gail Wyatt and her colleagues have compared African-American and European-American women victims of rape or attempted rape and reported similar consequences for both groups, depending on the mediation of particular circumstances. Negative effects on attitudes toward sex and intimacy were found to be more likely if the victim blamed herself, had suffered repeated rapes, had experienced severe coercion, or had been interviewed by the police (Wyatt, Notgass, & Newcomb, 1990). Many women reported having received "little support" even after having been raped "in the most severe circumstances" (p. 168). Other researchers have also noted that victims do not generally find support among peers or family or within their communities, "but instead may experience isolation and shame" (Koss & Burkhart, 1989). Alice Sebold (1989) told her personal story of being raped as a college freshman in a park near her dormitory. The rapist was convicted and sentenced to 25 years in prison, but her own father, she wrote, "who has spent his life working with young people, confessed . . . that he did not understand how [she] . . . could have been raped if [she] . . . didn't 'want to' be" (p. 18). From her own experience, supported by research findings, she concluded that "shame and pressure to forget are the most common reactions, not only for the victim of rape but for the victim's family" (p. 18). A personal report by Susan Brison (1993) sadly adds yet an additional illustration of this conclusion. She was the victim of a brutal sexual assault by a stranger who left her for dead in a country ravine and who was later caught and indicted for rape and attempted murder. Despite the lack of ambiguity about what had happened, and the fact that Brison had to be hospitalized for 11 days and then spend many months physically recovering from the attack, she found herself surrounded by denial, particularly in the form of silence. She has described what happened as follows:

> During the first several months of my recovery, I led a spectral existence, dissociated from those around me, and my sense of unreality was reinforced by the fact that most of my relatives didn't phone, write or even send a get-well card. These are all caring, decent people who would have sent wishes for a speedy recovery if I'd had, say, an appendectomy . . . . I learned later they were afraid of reminding me of what had happened. Didn't they realize that I thought about the attack nearly every minute of every day and that their silence made me feel as though I had, in fact, died and no one had bothered to come to the funeral? (pp. 20, 22)

An often debated issue relevant here is whether the current journalistic practice of not identifying a rape victim by name or photograph serves the purpose of protecting her from further abuse and pain or, instead, contributes to the view that rape, unlike other violent crimes, somehow implicates and shames the victim. This debate was fueled in 1990 when, a month after her attacker was convicted of raping her, Nancy Ziegenmeyer of Iowa shared her story openly and in great detail with the public through a series of front-page stories in the *Des Moines Register* written by its editor, Geneva Overholser. One objective of these stories and of the decision to identify a rape victim publicly was, according to Overholser, to bring us closer to the day when "we will treat rape more like other crimes" (Margolick, 1990). The issue of "naming" has strong adherents on both sides. Some (e.g., Benedict, 1991; Estrich, 1991) believe that not identifying rape survivors encourages more to report the crime, who would otherwise fear the inevitable digging into their pasts and abuse of their privacy by the press. Others believe just as strongly that not naming the victim encourages the belief that rape is shameful and different from other crimes of violence. A *Newsweek* poll revealed that 77 percent of those surveyed believed the names of rape victims should not be revealed by the media and that 86 percent believe disclosure would discourage reporting of the crime (Kantrowitz et al., 1991). In light of these views, it is interesting to note that the two women who had brought charges in the highly publicized acquaintance rape trials of 1990 and 1991 mentioned earlier—those of Mike Tyson and William Kennedy Smith—each came forward after the verdict and identified herself.

In-depth interviews by Gail Wyatt have revealed that African-American women were less likely than European-American women to report an assault to authorities and were more likely to blame the attacker than to blame themselves (cf. O'Brien, 1989). And a number of studies (e.g., Frazier, 1990; cf. Quina & Carlson, 1989) have found significant relationships between the degree to which a woman blames herself and the extent of post-rape depression. A review and analysis of the literature on long-term effects of sexual victimization (Koss & Burkhart, 1989) concluded that rapid recovery is unlikely and that such victimization is typically followed by continued sexual difficulties, restricted dating, suspiciousness, fear of being alone, and depression. No significant differences in psychological symptoms were found in a large sample of college students between victims of stranger and acquaintance rape (Koss, Dinero, Seibel, & Cox, 1988).

The consequences for children who have been sexually abused, especially for those who have been repeatedly assaulted by family members, may be even more severe than for adult survivors of sexual assault (Herman, 1992).

For example, in psychiatric populations, two thirds of women have been reported to have been victims of childhood abuse ("Disclosure of Sexual Abuse," 1990). Many adolescent runaways, drug abusers, and prostitutes are reported to have been abused (Bianco, 1984; Herman & Hirschman, 1977; Kohn, 1987a; Weber, 1977). A panel of psychologists who participated in a national symposium on the subject of childhood sexual molestation reported that "adults who were sexually abused as children are more likely to be more depressed, to abuse drugs and alcohol, and have difficulty in sexual relationships than those who were not abused" (cf. Fisher, 1985, p. 12). Psychotherapists were urged to be more aware of child sexual abuse as a root of psychological problems in adult women. A review of research on long-term effects led Angela Browne and David Finkelhor (1986) to conclude that "adult women victimized as children are more likely to manifest depression, self-destructive behavior, anxiety, feelings of isolation and stigma, poor self-esteem, a tendency toward revictimization, and substance abuse" (p. 72). The greatest negative impact was found to be suffered by women who were abused by their fathers or stepfathers. This conclusion was reinforced by data from a study of client files from a university clinic (Feinauer, 1988). The most serious psychological effects of childhood sexual abuse—that is, depression, interpersonal difficulties, and thought disorder—occurred "when the victims were abused by a trusted person who was known to them" (p. 105).

Others have noted that disclosure of the sexual abuse of a child, especially if the abuser is a parent, has widespread and continuing effects on the entire family. "Disclosure of incest usually means that a mother and her children face change in almost every aspect of their lives" (Gavey, Florence, Pezaro, & Tan, 1990, p. 23). The child may be removed from the home for some period of time; the family may break up by separation or divorce; the father's income may be lost to the family if he is jailed; and the family must face shock and questioning from neighbors, relatives, and school officials.

Among the most significant and general social consequences of the widespread prevalence of sexual assault by men against women is that girls and women learn to be fearful, perceive themselves as vulnerable, and curtail their activities. Martha Burt and Rhoda Estep (1981) interviewed a sample of college seniors and found that the women differed significantly from the men in experiencing more fear in places usually associated with possible danger (such as vacant lots and bus stations) and in receiving more warnings from others. The findings suggested that

this gender difference emerged in adolescence. The researchers concluded that

> adult women report a sense of sexual vulnerability both in their own concerns and in the concerns for them expressed by their family and friends as warnings designed to increase their vigilance and safety. Adult males do not share this sense of the world as a sexually dangerous place, and . . . report less overall sense of danger. (p. 520)

Similar findings were reported from an interview study of a sample of urban adults (Riger & Gordon, 1981): 44 percent of the women, compared with 18 percent of the men, reported being very or somewhat afraid when out alone at night. Elderly African-American and Latina women, those with the least formal education and lowest incomes, carried "the heaviest burden of fear." The precautions taken by women result in a restriction of freedom: 75 percent of the men but only 30 percent of the women reported that "they never let fear deter them" from doing what they want to do. Thus, as the investigators concluded, "high fear seems to shrink the scope of women's choices about their lives by restricting their movement through time and space" (p. 87).

PHYSICAL ABUSE

Sexual assault and physical abuse, resulting in bodily harm and psychological damage to women, are on the extreme end of the continuum or spiral of sexist responses to women by men. Such consequences appear to be a source of pleasure to many men. Consider, for example, how some men in movie audiences react with hoots of delight to events on the screen that demean women; when a woman gets slapped, roughed up, or insulted in a film, some male voices in the audience invariably cheer.

Until very recently, it was acceptable in our culture for a man to hit a woman in a family argument. In an experiment in which college students observed staged assaults (Shotland & Straw, 1976), some student observers were told that the assaulter and victim were strangers, while others were told that the two persons were a married couple. Despite the fact that the fight was identical under both conditions, students intervened more frequently when they believed the fight involved strangers. Under the married couple condition, the woman was less often perceived as in danger or as wanting help. When observers were given little information about the conflict, they were more likely to see the quarrel as between "dates, lovers, or married couples" and were less likely to intervene even though they were observing a man physically attacking a woman.

The assumption that a woman is hit "for a reason" is still often made and may help account for the slowness with which we have come to recognize and talk about the widespread prevalence of wife battering in this country. It has been estimated that each year 3 to 4 million women in the United States are beaten in their homes by their husbands, ex-husbands, or male lovers ("On the Legislative Front," 1990). A national study reported in the press found that "attacks by husbands on wives result in more injuries requiring medical treatment than rapes, muggings and auto accidents combined" ("Carnage of Violence," 1984, p. A-2). Current estimates are that between 22 and 35 percent of women's emergency room visits are for domestic assault injuries (Gibbs, 1993). Richard Gelles (1974) found that one fourth of the women who were beaten by their husbands were pregnant; and the March of Dimes has indicated that more birth defects result from the battering of pregnant women than from the children's diseases for which they are immunized (cf. Gibbs, 1993). According to Susan Faludi (1991), almost half of all homeless women in the 1980s were running away from abusive husbands. Some investigators, focusing attention on the children of battered women, have estimated that 10 to 30 percent of children in the United States live in violent homes and that most children of abused mothers do not escape being abused themselves (cf. Adler, 1991).

Erin Pizzey's (1974) now classic book, *Scream Quietly or the Neighbours Will Hear,* startled some of us into public recognition of what we had really known for a long time, that large numbers of women were being physically and emotionally brutalized by their husbands or cohabiting boyfriends and that these women had virtually no place to go for advice, support, or assistance. Since then a great deal of attention has been paid to the problem, much research has been done, and many cities and towns have established facilities to assist battered women. We now know that family violence cuts across socioeconomic classes as well as across ethnic categories (Martin, 1976; Straus, Gelles, & Steinmetz, 1981; Walker, 1979). Neither the men who batter nor the women they abuse fit into clear categories or support our stereotypes. Men of all skin colors, ethnic groups, and socioeconomic strata have physically abused their wives or lovers.

Women have been battered by doctors, lawyers, dock workers, judges, school teachers, ministers, cab drivers, and every other variety of worker . . . . [And] a battered woman may be elderly, teen-aged, or middle-

aged. . . . She may work inside or outside the home as a housewife, teacher, prostitute, student, or laborer. (Massachusetts Coalition, 1981, p. 9)

A story carried by the national press dramatically illustrates the fact that wife abuse occurs at all social levels. The head of the Securities and Exchange Commission appointed by President Reagan resigned his position after his wife alleged, in suing for divorce, that he had repeatedly abused her during their 18-year marriage ("SEC Enforcer," 1985). Like other abused wives, this woman had tolerated the abuse because she thought she was alone in being subjected to it and had blamed herself for not pleasing her husband. An autobiographical account (Njeri, 1990) of life with an African-American college professor father and nurse mother includes descriptions of violence and abuse.

For days, maybe weeks, a tense calm would reign in the apartment. Then without warning the hall was filled with harsh voices; he stood in the narrow, shadowy space hitting my mother. (p. 67)

[Years later, my mother] said she didn't know how she could have gotten herself into such a mess. She didn't know how she could have married such a man. And once she had, she was ashamed of her predicament and emotionally paralyzed. (p. 130)

Such personal stories have become all too commonplace. Miss America of 1991, from Hawaii, revealed in an interview that she had been beaten by her boyfriend and had once escaped being pushed by him from a speeding car ("New Miss America," 1991).

For men who engage in the physical abuse of their wives or lovers, violence is an acceptable and effective method of wielding power. This use of violence has been amply reinforced by historical precedent, prior family experiences, cultural sanction, personal identification with stereotyped "masculinity," and toleration by neighbors, police, and judges, and because it has evoked few, if any, aversive consequences from friends, relatives, or society.

Murray Straus (1978) proposed that family violence is related to the level of conflict and stress experienced within the family. This hypothesis was tested in a national interview study of more than 2,000 adults who were living as heterosexual couples: it was found that "the higher the stress score the higher the rate of assault between husband and wife" (p. 10). Family violence was also found to be related to the husband's dominance. "Men who believe that husbands should be the dominant person in a marriage, and especially husbands who have actually achieved such a power position, had assault rates from one and a half to three times higher than the men without such values who were also under stress" (p. 16). Similar findings were reported by Irene Frieze (1979), who interviewed a sample of battered women and compared them to a sample of women who had not been battered. She concluded that violent marriages are characterized by high levels of husband dominance and use of coercive power.

The relationship between traditional sex role attitudes and marital violence was investigated by Jerry Finn (1986). Among a large and ethnically heterogeneous sample of college students, he found that African-American and European-American women and men "who believe a man should 'wear the pants' in the family . . . are also likely to believe he ultimately has the right to maintain his position with physical force." A traditional orientation was "the strongest predictor of attitudes supporting marital violence" (p. 241). Complementary findings were reported from another college student study (Mason & Blankenship, 1987) in which respondents reported their own experience in inflicting physical abuse on intimate heterosexual partners. Men with higher levels of power motivation were found to be the most likely to use physical abuse as a way to settle conflicts.

The sequence of events that involve a husband's abuse of power and use of violence has been described by Lenore Walker (1978), who has proposed a "cycle theory of battering incidents." In phase one, tension builds and "the woman usually attempts to calm the batterer . . . She may become nurturing, compliant and anticipate his every whim, or she may stay out of his way" (pp. 146f.). During phase two, the tension is released destructively, and the batterer's rage is out of control. It may be triggered by a specific incident—almost any excuse will do—or occur without an obvious reason. According to Walker, "it is not uncommon for the batterer to wake the woman out of a deep sleep to begin his assault" (p. 151). In the third phase, the batterer knows he has gone too far; is contrite, kind, and charming; begs forgiveness; and promises that he will never again hurt the woman he loves and that he will change. In this phase, "the woman gets a glimpse of her original dream of how wonderful love is . . . [which provides] reinforcement for staying in the relationship" (p. 152), so she will "try again."

Phase three may not be reached if the battering ends in murder. One fourth of all murders in the United States occur within a family, and half of these are husband-wife killings (Gee, 1983). It has been estimated that from one third to one half of all women murdered are killed by

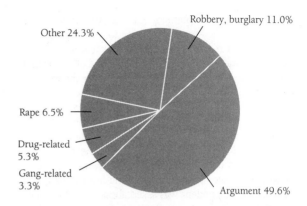

FIGURE 8.3 *Femicide: related circumstances—California, 1988 (out of 689 willful femicides where related circumstances are known).* (Taken from Jane Caputi and Diana E.H. Russell, " 'Femicide': Speaking the unspeakable," *Ms.*, September/October 1990, p. 34.)

spouses or lovers, compared with only 4 percent of male murder victims (cf. Gibbs, 1993), and that almost 1,700 women in this country die each year as a direct result of spouse battering (Strube, 1988). Figure 8.3 indicates the circumstances surrounding the willful murders of 689 women in California during 1988 (Caputi & Russell, 1990). Almost 50 percent of these murders were the result of arguments, primarily with male family members or friends.

The long-range consequences of continued physical abuse by one's husband or lover may be murder, scars, broken bones and other bodily damage, or psychological and emotional injury—feelings of valuelessness, extreme helplessness, and disillusionment. In describing her feelings as a battered wife, Andrea Dworkin (1978) reflected the experiences of others. To be physically abused by one's husband is particularly shattering and life-diminishing because his violence contradicts everything that we have "been taught about life, marriage, love and the sanctity of the family" (p. 34); "the fear does not let go. The fear is the eternal legacy" (p. 35).

A great deal of press attention was given to a report by Suzanne Steinmetz (1977–1978) that more women batter husbands than vice versa, data she obtained from the same national survey of more than 2,000 U.S. families referred to earlier (Straus, 1978; Straus, Gelles, & Steinmetz, 1981). Critics responded that the statistics were taken out of context of the total investigation and were misinterpreted. Richard Gelles (1979), for example, who along with Steinmetz and Straus had been one of the project's major investigators, pointed out that the violent acts reported by the wives tended to be "protective reactions"—acts of self-defense against physical attack or its threat—and that "irrespective of the kind of hitting that goes on, women are much more likely to get the worst of it" (p. 72). The data gathered in this survey do not tell us what proportion of the violent acts committed by wives were in response to violence initiated by their husbands, but that proportion is likely to have been high.

The Conflicts Tactics Scale used by the researchers measures acts of violence, not their outcomes. It is also important to know that the data came from self-reports; that is, each respondent was asked about acts of violence that he or she had committed. Murray Straus (1978) cited evidence from another study that husbands tend to underreport their own acts of violence, and he suggested that they do so "probably because the use of physical force is so much a part of the male way of life that it is not salient for men" (p. 22). Straus also noted that husbands have higher rates than wives in the most injurious forms of violence (beating up and using weapons) and that husbands repeat violent acts more than wives do. The Conflicts Tactics Scale does not separate defensive from offensive acts, and "when victimization occurs in marriage, it is the wife who is injured approximately 95% of the time" (Gerber, 1991, p. 442).

Despite the problems associated with use of the Conflicts Tactics Scale, researchers continue to use it while admitting its limitations. Thus, for example, Edward Thompson (1991) had 336 college students respond to it with respect to their physical violence in dating relationships and found no differences in the reports of women and men either in their own use of physical violence in conflict situations or its use by their partners. But Thompson himself points out that the scale "does not incorporate the context in which the aggressive behavior occurs, the injury that results, or whether the aggressiveness is defensive or offensive" (p. 265). His findings do, however, indicate a high prevalence of violence among heterosexual dating couples, approximately 25 percent, and suggest that physical abuse is not just a problem in marriage.

Within marriage, a review of the literature by Mildred Pagelow (1992) indicates that the preponderance of studies of marital violence have reported a small proportion of abused husbands. Just as the potential victim of rape is any woman, the potential victim of wife-beating is any wife. Those who remain in marriage with a brutal spouse do so for some combination of a number of very powerful reasons: they have children to care for and no resources for outside child care; they have fulfilled the prophecies of a sexist society and have learned behaviors appropriate to low-status persons; they are embarrassed and ashamed; they are discouraged by unsympathetic police officers who typically do not arrest abusive husbands and by a legal and social service system that generally attempts to preserve the family at all costs; they may fear reprisals from their husbands; and most have literally "no place to go"—no psychological or physical refuge.

Both indirect and direct studies suggest that 50 percent of the women who seek refuge in crisis shelters return to their homes and continue to live with their abusive partners. A number of psychological mechanisms have been suggested as relevant to understanding this phenomenon (Strube, 1988). For example, having invested effort and energy in a relationship, we tend to become more and more committed to it and to become "psychologically entrapped." This kind of entrapment is especially likely for women, who are expected by the culture to be responsible for the smooth functioning of a relationship; if it "is failing, she must not be trying hard enough" (p. 241). Entrapment is also more likely if the abuse is intermittent rather than constant, that is, if it is interrupted by calm and pleasant periods; if saving the relationship is viewed as socially desirable; and if a woman has few alternatives. Others have discussed the role played by learned helplessness (Walker, 1979, 1989a)—the result of having no control over negative outcomes and attributing such outcomes to some deficiency in oneself. Lenore Walker (1989a) has emphasized the powerful effect of the batterer's apologies, promises never to inflict hurt again, and entreaties of love and need, which function as intermittent rewards to the woman and reinforce her remaining in the relationship. "A battered woman believes that if she somehow could find the right way to help this man . . . then the mean part of him would disappear" (p. 697). Mary Romero (1985) has argued persuasively that wife battering is "an instance of social control tactics utilized to maintain unequal power relations" (p. 538) and that the strategies used by abusive husbands are very similar to those used on prisoners of war by their captors. She has noted three important commonalities: (a) psychological abuse in an atmosphere of violence and fear; (b) emotional dependency, intermittently reinforced; and (c) isolation from friends and family.

The cognitive and affective outcomes of such experiences have been identified by Lenore Walker as "the battered woman's syndrome," and the extensive documentation of such outcomes have led the American Psychological Association to prepare amicus briefs for use in the defense of some women on trial for the murder of their allegedly abusive husbands (Walker, 1989a). Wives are seven times more likely to murder their husbands in self-defense than vice versa (Jones, 1980). The nationally televised dramatization in October 1984 of Faith McNulty's (1981) book *The Burning Bed* presented the true story of such a murder to millions of viewers. Francine Hughes, a Michigan wife and mother, after years of abuse and unsuccessful efforts to dissolve her marriage, poured gasoline around the bed on which her husband was sleeping and set fire to the house, killing her husband. She was acquitted by a jury that found her not guilty by reason of temporary insanity. Expert testimony about the behavior of women who have been repeatedly abused by their spouses, and the reality of their fear of imminent danger, was not admissible as evidence to help establish her claim of self-defense at the time of Hughes's trial in 1977. Since then, however, nine states have passed legislation to permit such testimony, while in other states it is up to the discretion of the judge (Gibbs, 1993). Although some women have been acquitted on the grounds of self-defense for murdering husbands who physically abused them for many years, many more women have been convicted and jailed. It is important to note that whereas the average sentence for a woman who kills her husband is 15 to 20 years, the average sentence for a man who kills his wife is 2 to 6 years (cf. Gibbs, 1993).

According to Lenore Walker (1989b), women who kill their abusers have lived out

> the full consequences of domestic violence, riding its spiraling cycle to one irrevocable, inevitable end: . . . kill[ing] in self-defense. (p. 4)

> . . . Battered women who kill have almost invariably done so after having experienced . . . an uncontrollably savage acute incident, or after the recurrent onset of tension-building phase behavior, in order to prevent such an acute incident from happening again. Each woman seems to feel that she just cannot cope with the impending brutality . . . any longer . . . ; all say that they simply wanted to stop him from hurting them like that again . . . . They are seeking . . . to put an end to their pain and terror. (p. 106)

A number of state governors, influenced by the psychological arguments supporting a plea of self-defense and the acceptance of expert testimony by the courts on the battered-woman syndrome, have reviewed the sentences of women convicted and jailed for the murder of their husbands or lovers. For example, at Christmas in 1990, the governor of Ohio granted clemency to, and commuted the sentences of, 26 such women. As of this writing, 26 states have now reviewed the cases of women who have killed their abusive husbands or partners (Gibbs,

1993), and it seems likely that more will do so. In the case of California, the governor recently denied clemency for 14 women who claimed to have killed their husbands in response to their abuse, while he reduced the sentence of one woman (Mydans, 1993).

INTERVENTIONS AND SOLUTIONS

Men have said very little about the sexual or physical assault of women until quite recently. It is primarily women who have spoken out; recounted their experiences in interviews, essays, autobiographies, fiction, and poetry; protested; examined the problem; and suggested solutions.

How to deal with the potential danger to women posed by pornography is an issue on which feminists and others are divided (cf. Kahn, 1993). One study that analyzed and categorized the conflicting points of view (Cottle, Searles, Berger, & Pierce, 1989) found three identifiable major positions. These are the religious-conservative view, which emphasizes the dangers pornography poses to moral development and traditional family values; the antipornography feminist position, represented by Catharine MacKinnon and Andrea Dworkin, which emphasizes pornography's role in maintaining women's social status and views pornography as sex discrimination; and the liberal view, which fears the consequences of possible censorship and emphasizes guarantees of free speech. Some feminists, while convinced of the dangers of pornography, are also opposed to legal solutions that involve censorship. A route supported by some is legislation that defines pornography as sex discrimination and gives victims the right to sue for damages under civil law if they can support the claim that they were injured by it. Another proposal (Kahn, 1993) is that part of sex education in the schools "be instruction in how to read both mainstream media and pornography to expose the myths they promulgate about women's sexuality . . . . Pornography unveiled and taken out of the realm of the unmentionable and the illicit is pornography defused" (p. 246).

In contrast to obscenity laws in the United States, which are about lewdness, nakedness, and overt sex, the Canadian criminal code defines obscenity in terms of the "undue exploitation of sex." In a unanimous decision in February 1992, the Supreme Court of Canada upheld the conviction of a hard-core pornography shop owner under this law and, in so doing, redefined "obscenity based on what subordinates or degrades women" (Lewin, 1992a,

p. B-7). The government's legal brief in this case was drafted with the help of Catharine MacKinnon; in its ruling, the Canadian Supreme Court "explicitly accepted the argument that pornography harms women."

In 1986, a federal panel in the United States known as the Meese Commission, convened to study the effects of pornography, concluded that there was a relationship between most pornography and violence against women and made a large number of recommendations (cf. Shenon, 1986). Critics of the Commission's report feared that its intent was to interfere with the distribution of all sexually explicit material—including erotica and images of homosexuality—and to dictate standards of morality and restrict and legislate sexual behavior. Among those who share this fear are persons who also view pornography as a clear and present danger to women. With or without legislation, feminists and others believe that we must launch educational campaigns, organized demonstrations, and personal protests and continue to discuss the issues and search for ways to protect women without interfering with legitimate civil liberties. The Canadian solution recognizes that its antipornography law does infringe on the freedom of expression but does so in the interest of achieving true gender equality. The unanimous opinion of the Canadian Supreme Court reads, "we cannot ignore the threat to equality resulting from exposure to audiences of certain types of violent and degrading material. Materials portraying women as a class as objects for sexual exploitation and abuse have a negative impact on the individual's sense of self-worth and acceptance" (cf. Lewin, 1992a, p. B-7). Excluded from the law are materials presented in artistic or other serious contexts.

An end to violence against women is possible. A number of significant legal reforms with respect to the crime of sexual assault have already taken place. Some states now define rape in terms of the rapist's conduct (that is, the use of force) rather than by the victim's behavior (resistance) or state of mind (lack of consent). Many states define rape as gender-neutral and use the broader term *sexual assault*. Catharine MacKinnon (1991) suggested a more far-reaching and radical change, permitting victims of rape to sue for civil damages on the ground that their civil rights, protected by the 14th amendment's guarantee of equal protection under the law, were violated. She argued that rape, like lynching (which is recognized in federal law as a civil rights violation), is an act of bigotry and violence systematically directed against members of a particular social class. Placing sexual assault in the context of civil law means that a victim does not have to prove rape

beyond a reasonable doubt, as required by criminal law, but only by a preponderance of the evidence.

Some solutions have taken the form of treatment programs for sex offenders. The first of these, for imprisoned offenders, was begun in California in 1948. Since then, many other states have provided intensive therapy opportunities in prisons, with some claiming successful outcomes. For example, it is reported (Freeman-Longo & Wall, 1986) that of the men who completed all three phases of such a program in Oregon, fewer than 10 percent became repeat offenders. The multi-focused Oregon program attempts to change attitudes and beliefs about rape, to enhance social skills, and to improve general psychological and sexual functioning. It is a voluntary program, however, from which more than 50 percent drop out before completion. Like other prison-run interventions, the Oregon program reaches only a small number of convicted sexual assaulters. And, as we know, convicted rapists represent only a very small proportion of offenders. A review of 42 studies in which 7,000 convicted male sex offenders were followed up after their participation in treatment programs (Furby, Weinrott, & Blackshaw, 1989) concluded that "there is as yet no evidence that clinical treatment reduces rates of sex reoffenses in general and no appropriate data for assessing whether it may be differentially effective for different types of offenders" (p. 27).

Concerned women around the country have organized rape crisis centers and telephone hot lines to help victims deal with the psychological and physical trauma of sexual assault, to work cooperatively and innovatively with law enforcement and medical agencies, and to encourage increased rates of reporting, arrest, and conviction. The most typical intervention involves immediate assistance in dealing with the crisis, an opportunity to talk, and assistance in regaining control over daily tasks and more long-term pursuits. Rape victims are reassured that they were not at fault, are assisted in putting the incident into a realistic perspective, and are offered emotional as well as practical support (Quina & Carlson, 1989). A survey of rape crisis centers around the country (King & Webb, 1981) found that 62 percent of clients receive at least one follow-up contact and that a third of the centers provide two to five contacts. The investigators noted that while these centers are recognized and lauded for contributions to their communities, their funding "remains tenuous and professional staffing is minimal" (p. 102). The situation has not improved in the decade since this survey.

Lynda Holmstrom and Ann Burgess (1978), who followed almost 150 rape victims from the time they arrived at a city hospital emergency room to the final outcome of legal proceedings, concluded that what was necessary for change was, first and foremost,

> to *delegitimize* rape . . . [to see it] as an act of aggression and violence, motivated primarily by power and anger, rather than by sexuality. And it means seeing that rape . . . can occur in many circumstances . . . between people who are not strangers, when the victim is not a virgin, when there are no bruises because the victim did not dare to fight . . . (p. 262).

Efforts directed at reducing child sexual abuse have involved community- and school-based prevention programs as well as changes in the law. Unfortunately, evaluations of prevention programs directed at educating children have not been entirely positive, despite the considerable time and financial resources expended on the programs. While children in such programs have been found to show a slightly increased knowledge about sexual abuse (Reppucci & Haugaard, 1989), "there is no evidence . . . that primary prevention has ever been achieved" (p. 1274). Thus, the effectiveness of current programs may with good reason be questioned. On the legal front (Mithers, 1990), some states have passed laws permitting adult victims of childhood abuse to file suit against their molesters years after the abuse—that is, beyond the usual statute of limitations. Although the right to file such a lawsuit will not abolish the sexual abuse of children nor undo its negative consequences, it does "make public the fact that incest happens, that it is wrong and that it should be punished" (p. 63).

Such a message is not always clearly delivered by our law enforcement agencies or judges. For example, Dr. Elizabeth Morgan, a plastic surgeon, spent more than 2 years in a Washington, DC, jail on contempt charges for refusing to disclose the whereabouts of her daughter Hilary, who had reported being sexually abused by her father. Hilary, in hiding with her grandparents, would have been forced by a judge's ruling to have long unsupervised visits with her father despite evidence presented in support of Hilary's allegations and despite the fact that the same charge had been made by another daughter from a previous marriage. As of this writing, the judge's order forcing Hilary to visit her father still stands, and the child and her mother must continue to reside in New Zealand, where they have found safety and legal support.

Sexual assault of children and adults is a cultural problem. Educating women and men about the facts of rape and how it can be prevented must be the focus of programs in local communities, schools, colleges, corporations, and smaller employment settings. Martha Burt

(1980) concluded from her investigation of the acceptance of rape myth beliefs that the most fruitful long-range strategy for change was to counter children's gender stereotypes at very young ages. She argued that, since "rape is the logical and psychological extension of a dominant-submissive, competitive, sex role stereotyped culture . . . the task of preventing rape is tantamount to revamping a significant proportion of our societal values" (p. 229).

Physically abused women who try to avoid beatings by seeking assistance from relatives, friends, the police, social service agencies, and the courts typically meet barriers in their attempts to improve their situations. A study of 45 women who succeeded in getting out of violent relationships, and staying out of them for at least 1 year, provides information on the factors that contributed to their success (Wagner, n.d.). The women reported that they managed to get out primarily on their own or with the help of a friend or relative rather than through the assistance of a traditional community service. Among the institutional services used, the police were mentioned by 55 percent of the women, a private attorney by 53 percent, the clergy by 18 percent, and counseling by 12 percent. The most significant factor that enabled a woman to leave her husband was finding employment.

It was not until 1974 that shelters for battered women were opened in the United States, following their inauguration in England 3 years earlier through the efforts of Erin Pizzey (1974) and her colleagues. Such shelters were a response to the impossible situation that faces most battered wives: police reluctance to intervene in "family squabbles"; the focus of social workers on "reconciliations" to save the family; lack of financial resources or a place to go; and fear of further harassment from their husbands or partners. Most shelters, staffed by volunteers, provide 24-hour telephone hot lines; emergency temporary shelter for women and their children; support groups; information about legal services, welfare, housing, and counseling; and community education. By 1978, a national directory listed 2,000 shelters across the country (cf. Dworkin, 1978). Yet, the number of emergency shelters are too few, and those that exist are underfunded. Of the 1 million women who have been seeking shelter each year, one third can find none (Faludi, 1991, p. xiv).

As a result of public concern and publicity about wife abuse and efforts to reduce its incidence, new police policies have been implemented and new state laws have been passed. For example, an analysis of 300 cases in Minneapolis revealed that arrest of the husband was significantly more effective in preventing future wife battering than either attempting to counsel both parties or sending the assailant away from home for a few hours ("New Police Policy," 1984). Previously, arrests could be made only if an assault was witnessed by a police officer or if the wife made a citizen's arrest. The new policy in Minneapolis permits an arrest for probable cause—that is, if there is reason to believe that an assault took place within 4 hours before the police arrived on the scene. In Oakland, California, the police department changed its arrest policy in response to a class action suit filed by a group of battered women who claimed that their constitutional right to equal protection (guaranteed by the 14th amendment) had been violated by the police department's reluctance to arrest assaulting husbands. The police policy of nonintervention

> was argued to be an invidious discrimination against the plaintiffs on the basis of sex, in that it encourages violence against women and is based on "biased and archaic" sexist assumptions that what a man does in his home is not the state's business and that a man has a legal right to punish and restrain his wife physically. (Gee, 1983, p. 558)

This case was settled out of court in November 1979 with a promise from the police to treat domestic violence as they would any other criminal behavior and a promise from the city to provide support services for the victims of such violence.

Settlements in similar cases have provided models for change elsewhere. In Rhode Island, for example, an abused spouse can now get a temporary restraining order against the alleged abuser without the aid of a lawyer. This protective order removes the abuser from the family for up to 30 days, until a hearing is held before a judge. Unfortunately, as noted by Mildred Pagelow (1992), "even after obtaining these orders, battered women are often subjected to repeated abuse, harassment, threats, and murder by men whom the courts had ordered to stay away" (p. 99), and convicted wife batterers typically get lighter sentences than they would have if they had physically assaulted a stranger.

In Connecticut, a federal jury ruled in 1986 that police in the town of Torrington had not adequately protected an abused wife from her husband, thus denying her equal protection under the law. After an unsuccessful appeal by the Torrington Police Department, the woman, Tracey Thurman, scarred and paralyzed, was awarded $1.9 million. Despite numerous prior complaints, the husband had not been taken into custody until after he had stabbed her 13 times. When the police arrived 25 minutes after Tracey Thurman's call for help, she was lying wounded in her front yard and her husband was standing over her with a knife. As a direct result of this case, the state of Connecticut passed a family violence law in 1986 "that ranks among the strongest in the nation. Under the law, Connecticut becomes the seventh state to require an arrest in cases of probable domestic assault, regardless of whether the victim is willing to sign a complaint" (Johnson, 1986, p. E-9). Connecticut's law requires court hearings the day following an assault, establishes court-appointed advocates for victims, and provides special training on domestic violence for law enforcement personnel. Tracey Thurman's husband was convicted of assault and sentenced to 20 years in prison. Despite such celebrated and well publicized cases, however, sexual assault by a spouse is still legal in 30 states, and arrest for domestic violence is mandated by law in only 10 states (Faludi, 1991).

It is clearly necessary to continue improving the quality and extent of services to victims of aggression, to improve our justice system, and to educate the general public and law enforcement personnel about hate crimes committed against women. Representative Barbara Boxer and Senator Joseph Biden introduced legislation in Congress in 1991 and again in 1992 that would define gender-motivated crimes as civil rights violations. Other provisions of the proposed Violence Against Women Act would fund rape education programs, require restitution in sex crime cases, provide additional funding for shelters for battered women, create special spouse abuse units in courts, mandate treatment for convicted sex offenders in federal prisons, and urge states to consider evidence of spouse abuse in child custody cases ("On the Legislative Front," 1990; Russ & Goldfarb, 1992; Youngstrom, 1992). As of this writing, such legislation has not yet been approved.

While pressing for legal reform and improved community services, we must continue discussing the cultural significance of hate crimes against women. As many have noted, the ultimate solution is to change "the unequal power relationships between men and women" (Romero, 1985, p. 545), and make "the traditional male role . . . the focus of public education efforts" (Finn, 1986, p. 241). Women must both seek physical competence and maintain feminist consciousness. Most important of all, we must continue to question and evaluate what we teach our children about the differential roles of women and men.

◆ Discussion Questions

1. Why does this chapter on violence appear in the middle of the textbook?

2. How has the wide prevalence of violence against women affected you personally? Others you know?

3. Discuss the probable relationship among sexual harassment, sexual and physical abuse of women, childhood sexual abuse, pornography, and sexism in general.

4. When are forced sexual relations acceptable?

5. Why do battered women stay in relationships with lovers or husbands?

6. Plan a workshop for college groups on violence against women. What information would you include and how would you present it?

CHAPTER 9

CHOICES IN BIRTH CONTROL, CHILDBEARING, AND CHILDBIRTH

No woman can call herself free who does not own and control her own body. No woman can call herself free until she can choose conscientiously whether she will or will not be a mother.

MARGARET SANGER (1920, p. 94)

I had insurance that covered my daughter. She saw an obstetrician in town who was reputed to be one of the best. She had the choice of a birthing room. She had the finest care. Despite this, I once again battled with a system in which physicians are taught the art of healing by dissecting cadavers. . . . I was warned that if I took her out of the hospital so her labor could occur naturally my insurance would cover nothing.

JOY HARJO (1991, p. 30)

I have lain down and sweated and shaken
and passed blood and feces and water and
slowly alone in the center of a circle I have
passed the new person out
and they have lifted the new person free of
                                        that
language of blood like praise all over the
                                        body.

SHARON OLDS (1980, p. 44f.)

ALL THREE OF THE BIOLOGICAL IMPERATIVES, discussed in Chapter 2, that distinguish females from males are related to childbearing. Menstruation is a precondition for natural reproduction; gestation is the prenatal sheltering and nourishing of a developing new human organism; and lactation provides for maintaining the life of a newborn child. The female's ability to become pregnant, carry, and bear a child is what identifies her as biologically distinct from the male and provides the primary definition of the female sex.

Although this has always been true, women have never before had so many choices to make about childbearing capabilities and possibilities. A woman today can truly "choose conscientiously whether she will or will not be a mother," as urged by Margaret Sanger almost 75 years ago, with contraception, abortion, and role models for a child-free life available. Among women who choose motherhood, many can choose the timing and the conditions for conception, pregnancy, and childbirth. New reproductive technologies have expanded the possibilities for conception, but the primary relationship between femaleness and childbearing remains the same.

CHILDBEARING AND CHILDLESSNESS

Like marriage, pregnancy is still very much the norm for women, regardless of any other decisions pertaining to education, work, career, or life-style. More than 90 percent of married women and approximately 85 percent of all women in the United States end up having at least one child. Still, the number of childless women is increasing, and a trend toward having fewer children, and starting later in life, is growing.

Frequency and Timing

Women seem to be making different choices about children than their mothers and grandmothers did; indeed, women today are far more able than were their mothers and grandmothers to regulate the number and timing of children that they have and to make the more fundamental decision as to whether or not they want to experience pregnancy at all. In 1988, the proportion of women with no children was 25 percent for women in their early 30s, 18 percent for women 35 to 39, and 15 percent for women in their early 40s (cf. "Census: Women Waiting," 1989). According to Marcelle Clements (1992),

the current estimate is that "16 to 17 percent of women in this country will remain childless their whole life, some with regret, some by choice" (p. 208).

The number of children the average American woman will have in her lifetime has been declining steadily since 1800, when the rate was seven children per woman. During the last hundred years, the fertility rate has been gradually decreasing (except for a high point in 1957), settling at 1.8 in the 1980s (cf. Faludi, 1991), but reaching a low of .96 in 1992 (cf. "Family Size," 1993). This decrease in the birth rate is believed to be associated with the reduction of unplanned pregnancies and unwanted births.

In addition to average family size, another measure of fertility is the number of births per 1,000 women of childbearing age (between 15 and 44 years old). Among women in the United States, this rate was 67 in 1976, 68.4 in 1980, 66 in 1984, and 70 in 1988 ("Nation's Birthrate," 1985; "Census: Women Waiting," 1989). Thus, despite yearly fluctuations, the birth rate seems not to have changed substantially in the past two decades. In 1980, Hispanic-American women had the highest fertility rate (95.4), European-American women the lowest (62.4), with African-American women in between (90.7) (Amaro, 1986). Compared with married women, births to single women have been increasing, particularly among teenaged women and women between 35 and 39 years of age. In 1983, one out of every five births in the United States was to an unmarried mother (cf. "U.S. Study," 1985), an increase in out-of-wedlock births that is attributed to European-American women (cf. Faludi, 1991).

Regardless of marital status, the proportion of women in their 30s having babies was 33 percent in 1988 (compared with 19 percent in 1976), and 33 percent of all births in 1988 were to women in their 30s ("Census: Women Waiting," 1989). The contemporary trend for a woman to have her first child at a later age is not an entirely new phenomenon. Ravenna Helson (1986) found, for example, in studying the alumni of an upper-middle-class college for women, that those who had graduated in the 1920s and 1930s had had their first child at age 30. Age at marriage and age at first childbirth both moved downward in the 40s and 50s and then began an upward reversal with graduating classes in the 1960s.

How can we account for the present trend toward later parenthood? A study of first-time parents from diverse backgrounds found that the older mothers tended to be better educated, more affluent, more likely to hold professional jobs, and more "settled" in their lives (Weingarten & Daniels, 1981). They had put off having children until they had the "right man" in their lives, had achieved a secure relationship, or had experienced some degree of success in their careers.

Another correlate of the increased birth rate among women over 30 may be the insistent message of the mass media that they should "hurry up" and have their babies. Some doctors and the press have been quick to suggest to women over 30 that they consider motherhood before their "biological clocks" click to midnight. For example, newspapers all over the country publicized the findings of a group of French researchers (Federation CECOS, Schwartz, & Mayaux, 1982) that among a sample of more than 2,000 women, the infertility rate rose from 26.5 percent for women under 30 to 39 percent for women between 31 and 35, and to 46 percent for women over 35. What was also true, however—but infrequently included in the news reports—was that the women in the study were married to sterile men and had been artificially inseminated with frozen sperm, known to be less potent than the naturally delivered, fresh variety. The same investigators had found that women were more likely to get pregnant through intercourse on a regular basis than through artificial insemination (cf. Faludi, 1991). In addition, the definition of *infertility* used in the much publicized study was not getting pregnant after 1 year of trying, a more stringent definition than that used in other studies.

A report in 1985 by the U.S. National Center for Health Statistics indicated that American women between 30 and 34 had only a 13.6 percent chance of infertility, which was only 3 percent higher than for women in their early 20s (cf. Faludi, 1991). Similarly, a study by Alan Guttmacher (cf. Brickman & Beckwith, 1982) found that it took couples in the 15-to-24 age group 2 months to succeed in a planned first pregnancy, as compared to 3.8 months for couples in the 35-to-44 age group—a modest difference of 1.8 months. Overall, the percentage of women unable to have babies has "fallen—from 11.2 percent in 1965 to 8.5 percent in 1982" (Faludi, 1991, p. 29), and studies have shown lower rates of infertility among college-educated, higher-income women than among less educated and less affluent women, a phenomenon probably associated with better health and nutrition. We also know, despite fears to the contrary, that women over 35 are no more likely than younger women to have problem pregnancies or problem infants. An analysis and review of more than 100 studies dealing with the pregnancies of older mothers led Phyllis Mansfield (cf. Woodall, 1983) to conclude that maternal age by itself is irrelevant to the prediction of such negative outcomes as miscarriage,

intense labor, problem pregnancies, birth defects, and so on. The only possibly greater risk statistically linked to maternal age is that of having a child with Down's syndrome, a subject to which we will return in the section on pregnancy. Having a baby even after 40 appears to be just as safe for both the mother and the child as having a baby during one's 20s, if the mother receives good prenatal care. This conclusion is based on new research, such as a study in Chicago that found no significant differences on relevant maternal and neonatal measures between a large group of women over 40 and women between 20 and 30 if the older woman's weight was "normal" at the time of delivery (cf. Kasindorf, 1989).

Motives

The old argument that motherhood is the direct result of an instinctive biological mechanism can no longer be taken seriously. There is no evidence that human females are universally driven to perform a series of complex, unlearned, species-specific acts, triggered by discrete stimuli, that result in impregnation. The more sophisticated biological argument—that "anatomy is destiny"—is, nevertheless, still persuasive for many. Freud's view was that childbearing is a woman's ultimate destiny, not only because the female body is supremely equipped and fashioned for it, but also because it is in this way that women can resolve our early envy of the penis.

> The wish for a penis is replaced by one for a baby. . . . Not until the emergence of the wish for a penis does the doll-baby become a baby from the girl's father, and thereafter the aim of the most powerful feminine wish. Her happiness is great if later on this wish for a baby finds fulfillment in reality, and quite especially so if the baby is a little boy who brings the longed-for penis with him. (Freud, 1933/1964, p. 128)

How cleverly Freud turned our anatomy against us by arguing that we must have babies not so much to realize our reproductive capacities—which is at least a positive approach—but in order to compensate for our anatomical deficiency. By having a baby (especially a male baby), according to Freud, a woman can provide herself with a substitute for the unattainable penis. Psychoanalytic theorists after Freud modified his thesis, but in ways that embellished and strengthened it. Helene Deutsch (1944), for example, who could not as a woman take the penis envy proposition too seriously, suggested that women's urge for motherhood stemmed from our tender and erotic motives. Our sexuality, she said, serves reproduction; and the major goal of the truly feminine woman is motherhood, a goal toward which the development of a woman's entire personality has been directed. In this view, a woman who does not accept motherhood is deviant and suffers from a "masculinity complex." Erik Erikson (1968) suggested that the design of women's bodies focuses our adult motives on receiving, enclosing, and protecting. Without a child, Erikson told us, a woman feels unfulfilled and empty. Even Karen Horney (1931/1967), who recognized the patriarchal bias in Freud's assumptions and the role of culture and socialization in the development of personal motives, believed, nevertheless, that a woman's desire for a child is a primary unlearned drive "instinctually anchored deeply in the biological sphere" (p. 106).

Ideas such as these have served to reinforce the belief that pregnancy, even more than marriage, certifies that one is a genuine woman. In *Small Changes,* a novel by Marge Piercy (1975), we listen to a professionally employed couple consider reasons for having a child. The husband, Neil, speaks first, as follows:

> Here we are in our own house. A big house with plenty of room. I'm thirty, you're twenty-six. We're not kids. I was so late finding my own woman, we're behind for our ages. Shouldn't we start a family? It would get Mother off our backs. I know you don't like needling. But they say it's harder to have a baby later on, harder to conceive, harder to carry and deliver. (p. 376)

Miriam, the wife, considers:

> A baby in her arms. That whole adventure. To feel life in her quickening, to grow large with life. She would be a real woman then, she would be what they all tried to prove she was not. . . . She would prove that Neil was right to love her and marry her, to take a chance on her. She would validate her womanhood. . . . She saw herself stepping proudly through her pregnancy, ripe as a pear and glowing, full and beautiful as a sheaf of ripe wheat. Suckling her own baby. . . . She would have Neil's child and he would love her even more, they would really be bound together securely. . . . He wanted that from her. . . . She would satisfy him. She would be a mother, a good mother, warm and nurturing and protective. Why not? (p. 377)

Between them, Neil and Miriam seem to have mentioned all the usual reasons for having a child except the economic ones—another pair of hands for the farm or another potential wage earner. Contemporary women, like their mothers and grandmothers, also want to please their husbands and to prove that they are true women. They also want to experience the special sensations of pregnancy, actualize their biological potential, provide nurturance and guidance for a developing human being, and embark on an adventure unique to their sex. These were my own objectives, and I was eager to partake of woman's grand experience, to know what it felt like to have another's life and body inside of me, to follow its development and marvel at its possibilities.

None of these motives, however, are simply "natural" to women. Women have learned them all and are reinforced for pursuing them. As Marcelle Clements (1992) has argued, because childless women are considered second class and are not honored, "no woman lightly relinquishes motherhood, whether by choice or not" (p. 208). Women without children must cope with stereotypes, patronizing and disrespectful attitudes, and media images like that of TV's Murphy Brown, whose motherhood was presented as having made her a more complete human being. Thus, in a novel by Carolyn Slaughter (1985), a woman leading a nontraditional, liberated life, is described as reacting to her pregnancy as follows:

> Sylvie got out of bed and lifted her arms high. She was naked, her body, so taut and well-tuned, was touching now because of the round, hard belly. She put her hands to her large breasts and felt them, womanly and large, but with reason now for being so. She was complete. (p. 162)

But this reaction is no more natural than that of the Mundugumor of New Guinea, who, as described many years ago by Margaret Mead (1949/1968), did not welcome pregnancy and punished it by social disapproval.

Among contemporary American women the desire to bear a child has remained strong at the same time that family planning and women's right to reproductive freedom are supported. Thus, researchers consistently report that more than 90 percent of European-American women plan on having children (e.g., Gerson, 1980; Knaub, Eversoll, & Voss, 1983; Shields & Cooper, 1983), while many also support delayed parenthood and reject the traditional ideas that children are necessary for a woman's fulfillment.

Women who have borne and reared children learn that the reality is far different from the idealized expectations, and national studies have found that young married women without children tend to be the happiest of all groups (e.g., Campbell, 1984; Morgan, 1980). Angus Campbell (1984) concluded that "children are not necessary either for a successful marriage or for a happy and satisfying life. Married men and women over 30 who do not have children are more positive than the parents of young children . . . and have about the same feelings of well-being as married people who are parents of grown children" (p. 5). Such findings, from studies of representative national samples, contradict our stereotypes but have altered neither the strong pronatalist pressures in our society nor our negative views of women who choose not to bear children.

In one study of a sample of college students (Shields & Cooper, 1983), a happily pregnant 25-year-old married career woman was consistently evaluated positively and described as radiating "happiness and competence." In sharp contrast, an unhappily pregnant woman was described by the women respondents as confused and dissatisfied. The men were even harsher, judging her to be bitter, fearful, moody, resentful, and self-centered. Such adjectives as mature, understanding, or warm were seldom used to describe her. In another sample of college students, it was reported that among those who felt that childbearing was a "way to achieve adult status and social identity," 78.6 percent were women (Gormly, Gormly, & Weiss, 1987). And Mary-Joan Gerson (1986) found, among a large sample of childless adults of heterogeneous ethnicity, that younger persons considered childbearing more compelling than older women and men, wanted children more, and "saw them as more instrumental to expressing life values" (p. 59). Among women, in addition, childbearing motivation was related to lower self-esteem and to memories of a father's love during childhood.

Among feminist women, too, having a baby has remained a strong personal motive, although less so than among nonfeminist women (Lott, 1973). As noted by Ann Snitow (1991), "since 1980, we [feminists] have apologized again and again for ever having uttered a callow, classist, immature, or narcissistic word against mothering" (p. 37). It is probably not coincidental that the 1980s were also a time when the popular media went to great lengths to increase the pressure on women—especially career women—to reproduce. According to Rebecca Jones (1991), "everywhere today's childless women turn they are bombarded by this message: Have a baby . . . they're surrounded by images of . . . powerful and trendy women—who are" (p. D-5). Among the media's pregnant women are the protagonists of popular movies like *Baby Boom* or TV shows like "L.A. Law," "Thirtysomething," "Designing Women," and "Murphy Brown." The anecdotal stories of women who leave careers for motherhood are also featured in popular magazines and presented as trends without supporting data (e.g., Basler, 1986; K. Gerson, 1986). But, as Alfie Kohn (1991) has cautioned, while Hollywood and the other media sources are

telling us that becoming a parent is a sobering experience that can turn the self-absorbed into the other-directed . . . [t]here's no good evidence of a relationship between childlessness and immaturity, and there are good data showing that . . . childless couples have more satisfying marriages. . . . [H]aving a child does not automatically make one a responsible adult. (p. 65)

Our society, like others, provides the appropriate institutional pressures and rewards, and the necessary conditions for learning that a woman should want to have a child. This process has been described by Nancy Chodorow (1978) as the "reproduction of mothering." Girls receive consistent encouragement and practice in caring for children, planning for children, and in expressing delight about motherhood. The 1990s, for example, have spawned pregnant dolls designed, in the words of one manufacturer, to give little girls "a special look at the magic of becoming a mommy" (cf. Corrigan, 1992, p. C-3). A child can hear a heartbeat and feel a baby kick inside one of these dolls and, in another, the belly can snap open to reveal a baby.

The anticipation that a woman will be perceived negatively if she chooses not to bear a child is supported by pressures to have a baby that come from family, friends, community, and the media. Such negative expectations must surely evoke anxiety, and avoidance of anxiety is a powerful motivator of behavior. We can reasonably suppose, therefore, that one reason young women continue to seek motherhood is to gain approval and to avoid being judged as self-centered, immature, and cold. Adrienne Rich (1977) has pointed out how difficult it is in our culture to talk about women who, through choice or necessity, do not have children. We speak of such women as barren or childless, both terms implying some lack, failure, or emptiness; or we use the word child-free, suggesting a refusal to be a mother. Voluntary childlessness was viewed by one sample of college students (Peterson, 1983) as a temporary or misguided intention, while another group of students (Ross & Kahan, 1983) projected selfishness, loneliness, and regret as consequences. Children were seen as more important for a woman's life satisfaction than graduate school or job advancement.

The strength of the motivation for motherhood on the part of contemporary women can be illustrated by the large number of lesbians choosing to bear a child. At the Sperm Bank of Northern California, for example, about 40 percent of the women artificially inseminated were reported to be lesbians ("Increase Seen," 1989). A number of books offering advice and support to lesbian (and gay) parents have been published recently, suggesting, as Louise Rafkin (1993) noted, that "the lesbian baby boom" is being acknowledged by mainstream publishers and society in general. We will return to the subject of lesbian mothers in a later section of this chapter. Many infertile women, or those married to sterile men, also go to great lengths in pursuit of the opportunity to bear a child. They voluntarily endure pain and discomfort and submit their bodies to a variety of exploratory, problematic, and unreliable techniques, some of which will be discussed later on.

Choosing Not to Have Children

Despite the strength of our traditional ideology and the fact that most women bear at least one child, millions of women choose not to have children, and perhaps even larger numbers have them but would have preferred not to. We know something about the characteristics of these women and how they differ from the majority. For example, within a college sample, I found that both women and men who were not too eager to rear children differed reliably from those whose attitudes were highly positive in viewing child rearing as a less creative activity, in believing less strongly that child rearing is of value to society, and in remembering less energy and attention being devoted to their care as children by their mothers and by their fathers. In addition, among women, those who were less eager to have and rear children had stronger pro–women's liberation views than those who were more eager to be mothers (Lott, 1973). Replications of this study have found comparable results (Gerson, 1980; Biaggio, Mohan, & Baldwin, 1985). Among a group of unmarried college women, Mary-Joan Gerson (1984) found that those most supportive of, and identified with, the feminist movement believe that "motherhood offers opportunities for active mastery and assertiveness" but, at the same time, that there are costs associated with motherhood centering on "loss of freedom with regard to self and career" (p. 395).

In one study, Susan Bram (1984) compared three groups of married women; those who were childless and wanted to remain so, those who intended to have children, and mothers. She concluded that the childless women differed from those who were already parents as well as from those who were delaying parenthood in being less traditional in behavior, attitudes, and self-image. For the childless woman

> the themes of achievement and egalitarianism emerge repeatedly. The childless woman is more committed to

her work . . . views her marriage as a source of personal companionship and growth . . . adheres to principles of equal participation of the sexes in public and private life . . . [and] views herself in strongly individualistic terms. (p. 203)

Other studies of voluntarily childless women (reviewed by Veevers, 1982) have found that they are more likely to be employed outside the home, to be committed to a career, to be earning higher incomes at higher-status jobs, and to value independence as a personal characteristic.

CONTRACEPTION

While some women devote considerable energy to efforts to bear a child, many others are deeply concerned with finding safe and reliable ways to prevent pregnancy, if only temporarily. Women in all cultures have attempted to plan the size of their families, and societies have regulated their birth rates in one way or another. Women everywhere have sought to control their own bodies and have practiced some form of birth control with varying levels of knowledge and varying degrees of safety and success. Many different natural, artificial, and social means of birth control have been identified, including abstinence; the rhythm method; taboos on intercourse with lactating women; vaginal douches; the use by men of penis sheaths and by women of cervical plugs or caps (pessaries); sponges, potions, and powders; abortion; and infanticide (Newman, 1972). Prior to the 19th century the only truly effective method of pregnancy prevention was abstinence.

The earliest contraceptive used by women was the pessary—some material placed over the cervix to prevent the sperm from reaching the uterus. Pessaries were made of many substances "including leaves, gum arabic, grasses, camel [crocodile or elephant] dung, cork, honey, cotton and hemp" (Newman, 1972, p. 8). Vaginal washes (douches), of vinegar, lemon juice, gum arabic, boric acid or other substances, have also long been used, their contraceptive effectiveness dependent upon their degree of acidity to counteract the alkaline environment necessary for the survival of sperm. The diaphragm was developed in the 1880s; and, after the vulcanization of rubber was perfected, relatively safe and cheap condoms replaced the types made from such materials as fish skin, bladders, intestines, and the skins of goats and sheep. The modern condom is used to protect against venereal disease and AIDS, as well as to prevent pregnancy.

Methods

Although as yet no one method of birth control available to women (outside of abstinence) is both infallible and completely nonhazardous to health, a number of relatively safe and effective alternatives can be chosen by women in the 1990s.

Sterilization. Surprisingly, voluntary sterilization is now the most popular method of birth control in the United States and is used by 24 percent of adults—9.6 million women having had tubal ligations and 4.1 million men, vasectomies (Cowley, 1990). Sterilization is most popular with women over 35 and with middle-class married couples with at least one child.

Surgical sterilization is almost always irreversible, and although it is most often a matter of informed choice, some poor women, especially minority women on welfare, have been bullied or coerced into accepting such a procedure. Sometimes doctors have agreed to perform an abortion only as a "package deal" that includes sterilization. Some women have reported signing papers they didn't understand and then discovering, after an abortion or their baby's birth, that they had had their tubes tied (Dreifus, 1975). Joy Harjo (1991), a Cherokee Indian, was asked to consider sterilization by her doctor when she became pregnant at the age of 17. She later learned that many Indian women signed the consent form thinking it was related to a birth procedure, while "others were sterilized without even the formality of signing" (p. 29). Such experiences on the part of women of color impelled them to demand of feminist groups "that the fight against sterilization abuse be as integral to the struggle as the right to abortion itself" (Lewis, 1981b, p. 50).

The Pill. The second most widely used contraceptive method is the birth control pill, used by 18.5 percent of women of childbearing age, or 10.7 million women (Cowley, 1990; Rubin, 1991). Most users of birth control pills are European-American, and 82 percent are under 30, with the largest group between 20 and 24 years of age (Kash, 1984a). Birth control pills are 98 percent effective; and recent research has indicated that they are safer than previously thought and may even protect women against cancer of the ovaries and uterus, pelvic inflammatory disease, toxic-shock syndrome, rheumatoid arthritis, and dysmenorrhea ("The Pill," 1982). An 8-year follow-up study of a group of 120,000 nurses found no difference in heart disease risk between those who were taking, or had taken, birth control pills and those who never had

(cf. "Contraceptives," 1989). On the negative side, some studies show that early use of birth control pills by teenagers and women in their early 20s increases the risk of breast cancer ("Study: No Link," 1989).

The changed evaluation of birth control pills' safety is mainly due to changes in their production. Sequential pills (a series of only estrogen, followed by a shorter series of only progestin) have been replaced by combination pills (a mixture of the two hormones); and the dosage has decreased dramatically from the 5 to 10 mg. per day in the 1960s to today's .5 to 1 mg. (Djerassi, 1981). Progestin is the active contraceptive agent that inhibits ovulation, thereby preventing pregnancy, while estrogen is added to overcome the menstrual irregularities that would otherwise occur. Since the cardiovascular risks previously found to be associated with birth control pills are attributable to the intake of large dosages of estrogen, some experts advise taking an oral contraceptive with the lowest possible estrogen content. High-progestin pills, however, have been found to increase the level of LDL, the dangerous form of cholesterol (cf. Emery, 1983). What is important is clearly the proper balance between progestin and estrogen. Women over 35 are still advised against using birth control pills, but recent evidence suggests that only heavy smokers are at greater risk for cardiovascular complications. "The consensus now is that for healthy young women, the pill is the most effective contraceptive method and probably one of the safest" (Djerassi, 1989, p. 357). Some women, however, remain skeptical about the steady ingestion of hormones that alter normal body chemistry and the menstrual cycle.

Diaphragms and IUDs. Another birth control method commonly used by women is the diaphragm, preferred by higher-income women. Often used in conjunction with a spermicidal cream, it has about a 13 percent failure rate and no identified side effects. The IUD (intrauterine device), widely used until the mid-1980s, had a 4 percent failure rate but adverse and serious side effects, particularly pelvic inflammatory disease and perforations of the uterus. The most serious offender, the Dalkon Shield, was removed from the market by its manufacturer in 1975 and was the target of 320,000 lawsuits brought by women who had suffered serious consequences (Hilts, 1990). Women who had used IUDs were found to be at serious risk for infertility as a result of infection. All U.S. manufacturers have now ceased production of IUDs, but they are still used by .7 million women in this country (Cowley, 1990). How an IUD works is not completely understood, but its presence in the uterus is thought to produce a local inflammation that destroys sperm or inhibits the implantation of a fertilized egg.

Natural Birth Control and Other New Methods. A sophisticated form of the rhythm method, "natural birth control," depends for its success on accurately assessing when a woman has ovulated (Skolnik, 1983). Monitoring of body temperature is essential since, just prior to ovulation, temperature drops slightly and then rises about one degree, remaining high until about a day or so before menstruation. One technique requires monitoring the cervical mucus to check for changes in amount, translucency, and elasticity. Some newly developed methods have combined the essentials of the rhythm method with modern computerized technology. For example, a "bioself" invented in Switzerland registers a woman's temperature and calculates the days of the month she is fertile; and a "sexometer" developed in England transmits a woman's body temperature through an electronic sensor in her mouth to a miniature microcomputer that stores the daily information.

Another relatively new birth control device is the contraceptive sponge, a variation of the diaphragm. This two-inch polyurethane cushion contains a spermicide that is activated by being put in water; it is low in cost and available over the counter. A female condom has also been recently introduced (Millenson, 1992). In addition, 1.5 million American women use only a spermicidal foam or suppository; these can be purchased without a prescription and have an estimated failure rate of 15 percent (Kash, 1984a).

Norplant. The newest form of birth control available to women, approved in 1990 by the FDA, is Norplant (Anstett, 1991). Figure 9.1 shows the procedure necessary to use it. Implantation into a woman's arm takes 10 to 15 minutes, is painless, and protects against pregnancy for 5 years with a 99 percent success rate. Although the initial cost may be $500, this is less than the cost of birth control pills over a 5-year period. Norplant works by gradual release of the synthetic hormone progestin, which blocks ovulation and thickens the cervical mucus, obstructing the entry of sperm into the Fallopian tubes. Side effects may include irregular periods and light bleeding that diminishes with time, headaches, nausea, weight fluctuations, dizziness, and breast tenderness; Norplant is not recommended for women with liver or heart disease, breast cancer, or blood clots (Rubin, 1991). Fertility returns when the implant is removed. As with other contraceptives, more research is needed on Norplant, and some

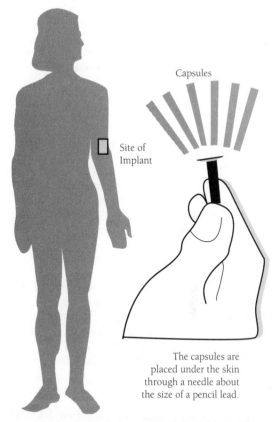

Capsules

Site of Implant

The capsules are placed under the skin through a needle about the size of a pencil lead.

FIGURE 9.1 *Norplant—the long-term contraceptive. The implants are the size of matchsticks.* (Taken from Patricia Anstett, "Armed with birth control," *Providence Journal Bulletin,* July 2, 1991, p. B-1.)

critics are cautioning against its too enthusiastic early reception because we know little about its long-term safety (Norsigian, 1989).

Methods for Men. The contraceptive methods currently available to American men are withdrawal (which is very unreliable), the condom, and vasectomy. An ancient form of birth control, condoms were used as decorative penile sheaths as early as 1350 B.C. by Egyptian men, and linen condoms were recommended in the mid-1500s by Fallopius for disease protection. In the 1930s, "when latex was substituted for rubber and condoms could be made thinner and more flexible," their popularity rose, and "today one can buy condoms that are lubricated, textured, colored, latex or natural lambskin (from the lining of the intestine)" (Hendricks, 1987, p. 98). Condoms are bought by 4.5 million women, generally under age 30, as well as by men (Kash, 1984a). The sales to women are about 30 to 40 percent of the total sales (Hendricks, 1987). The failure rate is estimated to be about 10 percent.

After a long period of contraception research concentrated mainly on methods for women, methods for men are now being investigated. One contraceptive being studied involves a synthetic form of the hormone that turns off testicular function (LHRH); this method could be available by the year 2000 ("Male Birth Control," 1991). Another involves gossypol, a derivative of cottonseed oil, which interferes with sperm production (Brody, 1983b). Gossypol has been tested on a large scale in China and found to be safe, effective, inexpensive, and reversible; it can be taken orally and is relatively economical (Djerassi, 1981), but is not available in the United States.

Contraceptive Development

Among all women of childbearing age in the United States, 60 percent use some form of contraception (Cowley, 1990). The modern woman is thus close to having complete control over her procreative capacities. Women today are far more able than were our mothers and grandmothers to regulate the number of children that we have and to decide whether or not we want to experience pregnancy at all. We have certainly come a long way since the time Margaret Sanger opened the first birth control clinic in 1916 and was arrested and jailed. Unfortunately, U.S. pharmaceutical companies and research biologists are focusing more effort and dollars on the study of infertility than on the study of contraception. According to Carl Djerassi (1989), developer of the birth control pill, contraception has become a less "fashionable," less prestigious area of study. Thus, for example, although birth control pills in the United States have had no new active ingredients since 1960, three new ones were introduced in Europe in the 1980s. Only one U.S. company is now doing significant research on contraceptive development, compared with nine large companies in the 1970s (Hilts, 1990).

A new contraceptive, RU 486, manufactured in France, is called by some an abortion pill but is considered a contragestion pill by its developer (Dowie, 1990; Palca, 1989). If taken shortly after conception (as indicated by a missed period), it has a 96 percent chance of preventing a fertilized egg from attaching to the uterine wall because its active ingredient (the steroid mifepristone) is an anti-progesterone agent that interferes with the utilization of progesterone, necessary for a pregnancy to continue. By

blocking necessary hormonal messages, RU 486 prevents gestation. Forty-eight hours after taking 600 mg. of RU 486, a woman should be given a small dose of prostaglandin to stimulate the uterus to contract and shed its lining as in a menstrual flow.

RU 486 has been widely used in France since 1988 and has been approved for use in England, Holland, and Sweden, but has been opposed by powerful anti-abortion groups in the United States and, as of this writing, is not yet being marketed in this country. The FDA has approved its use for limited research purposes, since there are good indications that it can induce labor for the delivery of a full-term neonate in cases where the cervix isn't opening well, thus serving as a safer alternative to a cesarean section. The use of RU 486 in treating breast cancer and endometriosis is also being explored. Among the first actions taken by President Clinton after his inauguration in January 1993 was to direct "federal regulators to reassess whether RU 486 is safe and effective and should be available in this country" ("Changing the Rules," 1993, p. A-19). A birth control pill, *Ovral,* has been used in the United States in a similar way to RU 486. Two tablets within 72 hours of unprotected sex, and two more pills 12 hours later, are effective in preventing pregnancy, but questions remain about safety (Hoffman, 1993).

ABORTION

We all know that reasoned and thoughtful decision making does not precede every pregnancy, and women throughout history have become pregnant as a result of force, coercion, ignorance, thoughtlessness, or carelessness. A pregnancy begun under such conditions may not be wanted; this may also be the case if the pregnancy threatens a woman's physical or mental health or her obligations to herself or to others, or if it is known in advance that if the pregnancy continues, a child is likely to be born with serious mental or physical handicaps. Once begun, pregnancies can only be terminated by natural or induced abortion.

Worldwide, an estimated 30 to 55 million abortions were performed in 1980, about half of them illegally, according to a United Nations report (cf. "A Look at Abortion Laws," 1981). Thus, for every 10 live births in the world, there were 4.5 interrupted pregnancies. After the Portuguese parliament voted to legalize abortion in 1984, Ireland and Belgium remained the only Western countries in which abortion is forbidden by law under all conditions. In 12 Western countries, abortion on demand is permitted during the first 3 months of pregnancy (Francke, 1982).

In the United States, the number of legal abortions performed varies widely among states. U.S. Bureau of the Census (1985b) data indicate that the national rate is 426 abortions for every 1,000 live births (similar to the worldwide figure). New York has the highest abortion rate (731 per 1,000 live births), while Utah has the lowest rate (100 per 1,000 births). The number of legal abortions in this country has remained the same since 1980, about 1.6 million each year, "representing almost a fourth of all pregnancies" and supporting the estimate "that more than 46% of American women will have had one by the time they are 45" (Johnson, Painton, & Taylor, 1992, p. 28). The number of abortions has remained relatively stable in the U.S. since legalization in 1973, with about 70 percent of the legal abortions now performed having merely replaced the earlier illegal ones. Data from 1987 indicated that 82 percent of women having abortions are single; half are already mothers; almost 60 percent are under 25; nearly 69 percent are European-American; and about one third are from low-income groups (Adler, David, Major, Roth, Russo, & Wyatt, 1990; Russo, 1992). The vast majority of abortions (95 percent) are performed during the first trimester, when they are safest, simplest, and least problematic.

Legal Status

"Hardly any society is known that has not at some time and for some reason practiced abortion," according to anthropologist Lucile Newman (1972, p. 8). But although abortion is a universal occurrence, not every culture has recognized it as legal. In the United States, abortions were relatively common and not punished or censured until about 150 years ago. In the 19th century statutes prohibiting abortion began to be passed, and by 1850 to 1890 every state had enacted legislation specifying that abortions could be performed only if the pregnancy was life-threatening and then only by a doctor. The practice of abortion did not cease, however; it just went underground. Before the modern liberalization of abortion laws by some states in the late 1960s, a vast black market in abortion was thriving in the United States. Each year 1–1.5 million abortions were performed illegally, with women risking their lives and health to terminate unwanted pregnancies, and resulting in the deaths of between 5 and 10 thousand women (Kanowitz, 1969; "The Risks," 1989).

After decades of debate and state reforms of restrictive legislation, the Supreme Court ruled in 1973 (in Roe v. Wade and Doe v. Bolton) that no state can pass laws prohibiting or restricting a woman's right to an abortion during the first trimester of pregnancy. The Court intended that a woman and her doctor should be free of state interference for the first 3 months in determining whether an abortion is in the best interests of the mother, with attention paid to her psychological, emotional, and physical circumstances. During the following 6 months of a pregnancy, according to the ruling, a state can regulate abortion procedures in ways that reasonably relate to maternal health, and only in the last 10 weeks can a state ban abortion entirely, except where it is necessary to preserve the woman's life or health. The plaintiff Jane Roe in the historic Roe v. Wade decision is Norma McCorvey; in 1973 she was a 25-year-old divorced waitress from Texas who 5 years earlier had been gang-raped and severely beaten. Too poor to seek a legal abortion outside of Texas, which did not permit one, she had sued the state. When the Supreme Court finally decided her case, the child that she had given up for adoption was 4 years old (Brasher, 1983).

As of this writing, the Court's decision in Roe v. Wade, guaranteeing a woman the unconditional right to terminate her pregnancy during the first trimester, is still the law of the land, but it has been subjected to repeated attempts by state legislatures to impose restrictions. Some of these restrictions have been declared unconstitutional by federal district judges and by the Supreme Court, but others have been allowed. The continuing legal efforts of anti-choice groups to abolish abortion for everyone have included unsuccessful attempts to pass a constitutional prohibition amendment and legislation that would specify that human life begins at conception. A cartoon by Nicole Hollander, shown on p. 200, highlights the humorous side of the continuing debates and legislative actions.

The Supreme Court permitted the federal government to deny public funds to poor women who wish to exercise their constitutional right to an abortion but cannot afford to pay for it themselves. The Hyde Amendment, passed by Congress in 1977 and still in effect, prohibits the use of federal funds for abortion except in cases of promptly reported rape or incest or when the mother's life is endangered. This legislation enables states and cities to issue similar prohibitions with regard to the use of public funds. In 1980, a federal district judge in New York declared the Hyde Amendment unconstitutional on the grounds that it interfered with a woman's religious beliefs favoring abortion, violated her right to privacy, and

Cartoon by Nicole Hollander (1982), from *Mercy, It's the Revolution and I'm in My Bathrobe* (New York: St. Martin's Press, pp. 10–11).

represented unequal treatment for indigent women. The Supreme Court disagreed, and in a 5 to 4 decision in 1980 (*Harris v. McRae*) upheld the constitutionality of the Hyde Amendment. The majority opinion was that Congress had the right to establish the favoring of childbirth as national policy and to further that objective by denying the use of federal funds for abortions. The Court argued that a woman still had the right to have an abortion; if her poverty prevented it, that was not the fault of the government.

As a consequence of the Hyde Amendment and the *McRae* decision, poor women and those in the military, whose health care is federally funded, are restricted in the exercise of their right to terminate a pregnancy. It is estimated that the number of women so restricted is 44 million (Faludi, 1991). Although the states are free to use their own funds to finance an abortion for a woman who cannot pay for it herself, only 15 states do so, under conditions that vary from state to state (Bakst, 1984). No one knows for certain how many women each year are still forced to face the shame, terror, pain, and potential danger of back-room abortions simply because they are poor. Among the first recommendations of President Clinton after his 1992 election was that Congress lift the ban on federal financing of abortions. To date, there has been no definitive action on this request. "Still ahead," as noted by Robin Toner (1993), "is, perhaps, the most significant struggle: whether to include abortion in the benefits expected to be guaranteed for all Americans under health care reform" (p. 2-E).

Rural women, in addition to women who depend on public funds for health care, are also being denied their legal right to terminate a pregnancy through lack of abortion services. "For most rural women . . . the availability of abortion services is increasingly rare. By 1989, according to the Alan Guttmacher Institute, 83 percent of U.S. counties had no doctors, clinics, or hospitals that would perform abortions" (Blakely, 1991, p. 25). It has been estimated that about 20 percent of women in this country who want abortions cannot get them. The 2,500 places in the country where abortions are available are mostly clustered around cities; and this number is down from the 2,908 sites that were available in 1982 (Johnson, Painton, & Taylor, 1992). In addition, "fewer and fewer doctors are trained to perform abortions, and many say they are unwilling to brave the pickets, protests and bomb threats that come with the practice" (Lewin, 1992, p. 1). For example, the National Abortion Federation reported that in just one year, 1992, 116 clinics were vandalized; there were 21 reports of completed or attempted arson, 5 burglaries, and 1 bombing (Lacayo, 1993). And in March 1993, a doctor who performed abortions in a clinic in Pensacola, Florida, was shot and killed by an anti-choice activist. Reports of doctors resigning from other abortion clinics have followed this murder.

An effort to intrude further on the rights of poor women, referred to in the press as the "gag rule," was first passed by Congress in 1988 and was upheld by a 5 to 4 Supreme Court decision in 1991. It prohibited "health care providers who receive any federal dollars under Title X of the Public Health Services Act from giving out any information—even when asked—about abortion" (Dermody, 1992). This rule affected approximately 4,000 clinics, serving 4.5 million women, mostly low income

(Kaplan, McDaniel, Glick, & Picker, 1991). Most Americans, as indicated by poll responses, disagreed with this decision. For example, a CBS News national poll found that 71 percent of respondents believed federally funded family planning clinics should be allowed to give pregnant women information about abortions ("Policy vs. Polls," 1991). Perhaps in response to such opinions and widespread criticism, President William Clinton issued an executive order shortly after taking office that removes the ban on the providing of abortion information by federally financed family planning clinics.

Although women remain free to choose abortion in principle—if they can pay for it and find a facility—only 7 states imposed no restrictions on this right as of 1992. These restrictions include counseling bans, notification of husband or parents of minors, and a 24-hour waiting period. Figure 9.2 provides a summary of abortion laws in each state and the District of Columbia.

To impose a delay in carrying out the termination of a pregnancy has been opposed on mental health grounds by the American Psychological Association (APA). With respect to spousal notification, an amicus brief filed by APA with the Supreme Court identifies extensive research that has found

> good reasons for women not to report their intentions. . . . These include situations in which women fear notification will harm their marriages; that the news will negatively affect their spouses; and that they will be psychologically or emotionally abused if they tell their husbands. (DeAngelis, 1992a, p. 6)

The brief also notes that spousal notification is "strikingly one-sided," since husbands are not required to inform their wives prior to a vasectomy and unmarried adult women are not required to notify anyone about an abortion decision.

Adolescents obtain a little over 25 percent of all abortions in the United States (Adler & Tschann, 1993). APA committees reviewing the literature on decision-making by adolescents and its relevance to abortion decisions concluded that legally imposed delays would have negative consequences. As summarized by Gary Melton (1987),

> the available psychological research and theory suggest that special provisions for judicial review of adolescents' abortion decisions have served as obstacles to protection of privacy and to diminution of stress. At best, they are benign but costly and purposeless legal procedures. At worst, they increase pregnant minors' delay in seeking

medical attention and induce embarrassment, anxiety, and family conflict. (p. 82)

A report by the National Academy of Sciences similarly concluded that "on the basis of existing research . . . the contention that adolescents are unlikely or unable to make well-reasoned decisions or that they are especially vulnerable to serious psychological harm as a result of an abortion is not supported" (cf. "Parental Notification," 1990).

Many state legislatures have apparently not been influenced either by psychological and medical data or by the fact that teenagers are 24 times more likely to die from childbirth than from a first-trimester abortion (cf. Suisman, 1990). Nor have they been moved by such tragic stories as that of Becky Bell of Indiana. Her parents have recounted to groups across the country the story of their daughter, who at 17, wishing to avoid hurting her parents by telling them she was pregnant and unable to terminate it in her state without telling her parents or a judge, somehow underwent an illegal abortion and subsequently died of an infection.

In a very important case—the most recent abortion ruling as of this writing—the Supreme Court, in a 5 to 4 decision, ruled in June 1992 in *Planned Parenthood of Southeastern Pennsylvania v. Casey* that women still have the constitutional right to an abortion but that states may impose restrictions. These restrictions, however, may not impose "an undue burden" on the woman. Using this as a guideline or new standard, the Court overturned the Pennsylvania requirement that spouses must be notified about the abortion, as urged in the brief presented by the American Psychological Association. The Court, however, did uphold the requirements that abortion providers give women information about possible negative effects of abortion, that women wait 24 hours after receiving this information before terminating a pregnancy, and that minors under 18 obtain one parent's consent or a judge's approval (cf. DeAngelis, 1992a).

Attitudes

A summary of the results of nationwide opinion polls indicates that 80 to 90 percent of Americans support abortion when a woman's health is endangered, when there is a chance of serious fetal abnormality, or when the pregnancy has resulted from rape or incest. Support for abortion for economic, social, or personal reasons is also found among 40 to 50 percent of adults ("Views on Sex," 1985). An ABC TV poll in 1985 found that 52 percent of

	Alabama	Alaska	Arizona	Arkansas	California	Colorado	Connecticut	Delaware	D.C.	Florida	Georgia	Hawaii	Idaho	Illinois	Indiana	Iowa	Kansas	Kentucky	Louisiana	Maine	Maryland	Massachusetts	Michigan
Medicaid funding unavailable unless a woman's life is in danger.	■		■	■		■		■		■	■			■	■		■	■	■	■			■
Abortion prohibited in public facilities; public employees may not participate.			■															■	■				
Counseling required for women; often a 24-hour minimum delay.	■	■						■		■			■		■		■	■	■	■	■		■
Parental consent required for minors.	■			■						■					■			■				■	■
Woman required to notify husband.						■				■					■				■				
Health-care providers prohibited from abortion counseling.																			■				
Virtually all abortions prohibited.	■		■	■		■		■		■							■		■		■	■	■
Governors favor criminalization	■	■								■					■	■			■				■
Both houses favor criminalizing abortion.	■																	■	■				■
Houses split or very close.				■				■					■	■	■	■							
Both houses support legal abortion.		■	■		■	■	■		■	■	■	■					■			■	■	■	

Minnesota
Mississippi
Missouri
Montana
Nebraska
Nevada
New Hampshire
New Jersey
New Mexico
New York
N. Carolina
N. Dakota
Ohio
Oklahoma
Oregon
Pennsylvania
Rhode Island
S. Carolina
S. Dakota
Tennessee
Texas
Utah
Vermont
Virginia
Washington
W. Virginia
Wisconsin
Wyoming

FIGURE 9.2 *Abortion laws state-by-state. This is a selection of the laws that affect the availability of abortion. Some, like the outright bans and husband notification, are not enforced, pending consideration by the Supreme Court.* (Based on "Abortion: The future is already here," by Richard Lacayo, *Time*, May 4, 1992.)

respondents favored abortion on demand, 36 percent approved of it for health reasons, and 11 percent were opposed under all circumstances (cf. Lake, 1986). In 1990, 73 percent in a national poll "were in favor of abortion rights" (Rosenblatt, 1992). Despite the majority support for legal abortion, lobbying for anti-choice legislation has remained strong, and women entering abortion clinics, as well as clinic personnel, have increasingly been harassed by members of organized anti-choice groups. Such clinics as well as family planning centers around the country have been threatened with or victimized by violence, as noted earlier.

It has been argued (English, 1981; Luker, 1984) that women who are most strongly anti-choice differ from those who are pro-choice, not so much in ideology, religion, or the value they place on children and families, but in social circumstances. Those who adamantly oppose anyone's right to terminate a pregnancy by choice tend to be less well educated and to be married to husbands who are skilled workers or small business operators. They have typically married young, had relatively large families, and devoted their adult lives to homemaking and motherhood. They perceive legalized abortion as a profound threat to their way of life. Those who have been in the vanguard of the movement for legalized abortion, on the other hand, are more likely to be women eager to enter or retain their positions in the work force.

Methods

Pregnancies have been terminated throughout history in ways that have varied with the technology available and with the legal status of the procedures. Linda Francke (1982) has described some of the ancient methods as follows:

> Over 5,000 years ago in China, women drank quicksilver fired in oil or swallowed fourteen live tadpoles three days after they had missed a menstrual period in the hope of bringing it on. . . . In more modern times, Russian women attempted to abort themselves by squatting over pots of boiling onions, while members of certain Indian tribes climbed up and down coconut palms, striking their stomachs against the trunks. (p. 24)

Before 1973, when legal abortion was available only for narrowly defined medical reasons, millions of women in this country underwent humiliating and dangerous procedures to end their pregnancies. Many novels about women's lives in the 1950s and 1960s such as Marge Piercy's (1983) *Braided Lives* and Joyce Carol Oates'

(1987) *You Must Remember This,* or autobiographical accounts like Vivian Gornick's (1987) *Fierce Attachments,* present unforgettable accounts of the way it used to be for women whose only means of terminating a pregnancy was an illegal abortion in a back room or on a kitchen table. As Kate Simon (1986) noted in her own story, "illegal abortionists were not difficult to locate; everyone had a friend who had a friend who had an address and telephone number. . . . Those who couldn't raise the large sums could find a faceless room, a table, and a wash bowl . . . no refinements assured or expected" (pp. 178f.). Often, the abortionist was a doctor, as described by a woman recalling her experience in the novel *Father Melancholy's Daughter* (Godwin, 1991), "who'd been disqualified because of drugs or something" (p. 399). A woman in Barbara Raskin's (1990) novel *Current Affairs* recalls her abortion as follows:

> Shay [her sister] had found two med students who agreed to do it and borrowed enough money to pay for it. Eli had driven us to St. Paul to get it done and let me use his apartment while I recuperated from the little illegal operation that left me with a perforated uterine wall [and permanent infertility]. (p. 34)

In *You Must Remember This* (Oates, 1987), Enid, who later undergoes an illegal abortion, recalls a girl in her school:

> they were saying somebody's got her pregnant was it her own daddy? then they were saying somebody got rid of it was it her own mommy?—aborted with a coat hanger, maybe it was an ice pick, she didn't die but they didn't let her back into school and afterward the family moved away. (p. 9)

Part of becoming a woman, for me, was going very early one morning to a fashionable address in New York City with a brown paper bag containing a supply of sanitary napkins and $350 in cash. When I arrived (alone), the physician gave me an injection of penicillin and took me to a small room behind his office. There, with no nurse in attendance and no anesthetic, I was aborted as I screamed and he angrily shouted at me to keep quiet. For an hour afterward I was able to rest on a cot but, before his office filled with his regular patients, I had to leave as surreptitiously as I had come. My experience was not unusual, and in some respects it was much better than that of other women, as we can see from the list prepared by Adrienne Rich (1977) of the methods resorted to by women unable to obtain legal abortions:

> Wire coat-hangers, knitting needles, goose quills dipped in turpentine, celery stalks, drenching the cervix with

detergent, lye, soap, Ultra-Jel (a commercial preparation of castor oil, soap, and iodine), drinking purgatives of mercury, applying hot coals to the body. The underworld . . . abortionists, often alcoholic, disenfranchised members of the medical profession, besides operating in septic surroundings . . . frequently rape or sexually molest their patients. . . . An illegal or self-induced abortion is no casual experience. It is painful, dangerous, and cloaked in the guilt of criminality. (p. 272)

In these days of safe, legal abortions by professional medical personnel, the most common procedure is vacuum aspiration (suction), which can be performed during the first trimester (up to 12 weeks) under local anesthetic and takes about 10 minutes. Dilation and curettage (D&C), also a first-trimester procedure, involves scraping the uterine lining and may require a night in the hospital. Second-trimester abortion procedures (which represent only 5 percent of those performed) include injection of saline solution, intra-amniotic prostaglandin injection, and dilation and evacuation (D&E). The least traumatic and safest of the late-pregnancy techniques, a D&E, involves a combination of suction and curettage, takes less than half an hour, and requires only a local anesthetic (Francke, 1982).

First-trimester abortions need not be performed in a hospital, but states may regulate the location of second-trimester abortions, most of which are done in hospitals. Most facilities in which abortions are performed provide counseling before and after the procedure and are staffed by empathetic personnel. According to Linda Francke (1982), "the legalization of abortion has brought with it the development of an abortion industry that is at the same time profitable to its members and supportive and safe for the women seeking its services" (p. 40). Most abortions are now performed in specialized clinics and only about 10 percent in hospitals because of the relative lack of doctors trained to perform abortions and the reluctance of many to "deal with the hassle" of emotional demonstrations (Kirshenbaum, 1990).

Motivations and Consequences

Terminating a pregnancy is a decision made by a very large number of women, but I have never spoken with, or read or heard about a woman whose abortion decision was made quickly and effortlessly. The very personal decision to end a pregnancy is made in a social context in which abortion is negatively evaluated by many persons, hysterically condemned by a highly vocal minority, considered sinful by a significant and powerful church, and not approved for support by public funds and in which abortion was illegal and criminally punishable until the early 1970s. As noted by Jeanne Lemkau (1988), "the sociocultural environment in which women make abortion decisions reinforces ambivalence at best, and at worst introduces negative thoughts and feelings" (p. 461). It is not surprising, therefore, that for most women in this country abortion is a last resort. Religious, moral, and medical considerations enter in; so do fear for one's health and safety and for one's future ability to have children. Issues must also be resolved relating to a woman's relationship with the man who participated in the conception. New reproductive technology has increased the dilemma of choosing for some women, as pointed out by Barbara Rothman (1986). Diagnoses in utero can now be made of certain kidney diseases, Tay-Sachs disease, anencephalus (absence of brain and spinal cord), and chromosomal abnormalities, in addition to Down's syndrome. Thus, a decision to terminate a pregnancy may be based on probable outcomes for the fetus if it is carried to term, multiplying the factors to be taken into account and adding to the stress of decision making.

Following an abortion, the emotions a woman experiences may range from renewed self-confidence to guilt and depression, or some combination of these. Linda Francke (1982) interviewed women who had had abortions and found examples of all these emotions and reactions. Questions about the psychological consequences of abortion have been raised and answered. The conclusion is clear. Women who choose legal abortions invariably feel good about their decision, experience relief, and very rarely suffer serious emotional harm. Lisa Shusterman (1976) reviewed the literature on psychosocial factors in abortion and concluded that women who obtain legal abortions on request are typically young and unmarried, are not in a good position to bear or care for a child, and are influenced by social and economic factors in their decisions to abort, and that the psychological consequences for them have been "mostly benign." Women who experience negative effects tend to be less certain of their decision and to be involved in less stable heterosexual relationships. Nancy Adler (1979) reached a similar conclusion from a review of research findings. She found that most women who had legal abortions experienced relief and positive emotions afterward, although not unmixed with some negative feelings. She and her colleagues have pointed out (Adler, 1979, 1992; Adler & Tschann, 1993) that much of the stress experienced by women who terminate a pregnancy stems from the discovery of an unwanted pregnancy and the need to decide what to do about it. Although no studies have focused on the direct relationship between the degree of unwantedness of a pregnancy and reactions to abortion, many women, according to Adler, "generally report that the time of greatest distress is between the discovery that they are pregnant and the abortion" (1979, p. 112).

In testimony before a congressional committee, Adler (1989) summarized a review of the relevant literature conducted by a panel of experts for the American Psychological Association. The conclusion reached was that severe negative reactions to legal abortions are rare, that the greatest distress is experienced before the abortion, and that the predominant post-abortion emotions are positive. Reactions to an unwanted pregnancy and to the decision to end it are strongly influenced by a woman's social and economic circumstances, by the meaning the pregnancy has for her, by the resources and support available to her, and by her previously developed skills in coping with stressful situations. Following an examination of all the available research on abortion outcomes, a group of experts (Wilmoth, deAlteriis, & Busell, 1992) concluded that "the available U.S. studies with control groups have consistently shown that the amount of negative psychological responses following abortion is either the same or less than postpartum" (p. 62). For example, one study (cf. Adler & Tschann, 1993) that compared women who had a first-trimester abortion, who had a second-trimester abortion, and who carried a fetus to term—and who were matched in age, number of previous live births, ethnicity, and marital status—found few differences between the groups on personality and adjustment measures 13 to 16 months later. "If anything, the early abortion patients showed the most favorable psychological responses" (p. 200).

A study that offers some insight into the decision-making process of women faced with an unwanted pregnancy was carried out by Carol Gilligan (1977). She interviewed 29 women, varying in age, ethnicity, and social class, who had been referred to her by abortion and pregnancy counseling services. Of this group, 4 decided to complete their pregnancies, 21 decided to end them, 1 woman miscarried, and 3 remained in doubt about what to do. Gilligan found that in confronting their dilemma the women tended to define the moral problem as "one of obligation to exercise care and avoid hurt" (p. 492). Once they extended the concept of care to include themselves, they were able to make judgments and choices. The decision to end a pregnancy is made within the same moral and psychological framework as the

decision to initiate or continue it and involves concern about other persons as well as oneself and one's responsibilities.

In a study of a small sample of women who had had abortions, a colleague and I (Quina & Lott, 1986) found that, for most, it had been a reasoned decision, and 75 percent of the women had consulted their sex partners, all of whom had agreed with the decision to terminate the pregnancy. In retrospect, 65 percent felt that their decision had been very wise, and an additional 25 percent that it had been moderately wise. All the women said that they would support a friend in her decision to end a pregnancy, but 20 percent would probably not have an abortion again. The women in our sample varied in current age from 21 to 52 and varied in the age at which they had had an abortion from 15 to 43. They also varied in the number of years that had passed since they had had this experience, the conditions of the abortion, and its legality. The sample was heterogeneous with respect to ethnicity, religion, sexual preference, and marital status. What unified this group of women were the reasons they gave for having decided on an abortion and the ways in which this decision had affected their lives. The abortions, in most cases, had served an enabling function by permitting the women to move ahead in their lives. The women told us that the abortions had enabled them to provide care and affection for the children they already had; to complete their education; to find better employment; to solve debilitating problems (such as drinking); to mature emotionally or psychologically before having a child; and to avoid financial hardship or going on welfare. Most of the women recognized both positive and negative outcomes, and their immediate and longer-range reactions revealed complex experiences, but 75 percent believed, strongly or moderately, that their abortion had changed their lives for the better.

Congruent findings have been reported by others. A review of studies dealing with the motivations of women seeking abortions (Russo, Horn, & Schwartz, 1992) revealed that women's reasons for seeking abortions are generally "linked to their inability to provide for a child and to their responsibilities and relationships to others" (p. 198). Reasons mentioned by women include socio-economic factors, problematic relationships with partners, health-related concerns, and lack of readiness or ability to be responsible for a child (or another child).

The statistics on abortion indicate that members of all social classes, all regions of the country, and all ethnic and religious groups (with only a few exceptions), have taken the opportunity now provided by law to exercise choice over their pregnancies and to make decisions about their bodies and their lives. As noted by Randall Lake (1986),

> abortion is a morally complex subject with no easy answers. Abortions in the first trimester are different than those in the third; abortions by poor women already overburdened by large families are different from those by the well-to-do; abortions because of rape or incest are different from those performed because the parents would rather have a boy. (pp. 498f.)

Many women have children out of needs to validate their womanliness, to do the correct thing, to please others, or to fulfill the expectations of parents and culture; many women do so also because few attractive alternatives exist. If these are her motives, then the willful termination of a pregnancy may leave a woman confused, uncertain of her worth, questioning her womanly qualities and her goodness as a person. On the other hand, a woman may choose to experience pregnancy, childbirth, and motherhood because she wishes to extend her experiences and personal development through caring interaction with a growing human being; she may want to share her skills and use her adult competencies to assist a helpless infant; she may want to give and receive attention and love. If such objectives are not likely to be realized—if childbirth is likely to result in both the woman and child being diminished, exploited, and hurt—then a decision to end a pregnancy becomes one that is made out of a sense of morality in which responsibility and the avoidance of hurt are key elements.

Based on its study of the empirical data and its commitment to the promotion of human health and welfare, the American Psychological Association reaffirmed its 1969 resolution declaring the termination of pregnancy to be a civil right of pregnant women and passed an additional resolution in 1989 directing the "Chief Executive Officer to undertake an immediate initiative to disseminate scientific information on reproductive freedom to policy makers, [and] to the public" ("Council Resolutions," 1989).

REPRODUCTIVE TECHNOLOGIES

While some women choose to terminate an unwanted pregnancy, others undergo lengthy, expensive, painful and invasive procedures in order to bear a child or to contribute genetically to its conception. These women may have dysfunctional, impaired, or absent ovaries, fallopian tubes, or wombs; be married to, or in relation-

ships with sterile men or men with low sperm counts; or desire to bypass heterosexual intercourse. The incredible variety of options that have been developed to assist such women and their partners are referred to as reproductive technologies or noncoital reproduction (NCR). The most well-known of these will be described and discussed briefly in this section with information compiled from several sources (Buttenwieser, 1991a; Hopkins, 1992; Raymond, 1986, 1991; Rowland, 1987; Robison, 1989; Thom, 1988).

Artificial or Donor Insemination (AI or DI). This technology, first utilized medically in 1790, has been available in this country for nearly 100 years. Sperm from a nonpartner, typically frozen and stored in a sperm bank, is inserted into the vagina of a regularly ovulating woman. A new variant of this procedure is *intrauterine insemination* (IUI) in which semen is placed directly inside a woman's uterus by means of a catheter.

In-Vitro Fertilization ("Test-Tube Babies" or IVF). Eggs (ova) and sperm are joined in a petri dish where fertilization occurs. The resultant embryo can be frozen for later implantation or implanted immediately in a female body. It is important to appreciate that anyone can be the donor of the eggs and the sperm—not necessarily those who will rear the child—and that any healthy, willing female can host the implanted embryo. All possible variations of donor and host have been utilized by the 200 U.S. institutions that perform IVFs. The first "test-tube" baby was born in 1978.

Laparoscopy and Cryopreservation. These are technologies used in conjunction with IVF. The former is a surgical procedure to collect the eggs from a woman's ovaries, and the latter is a way of freezing eggs, sperm, and embryos and storing them for later use.

Superovulation. This process also typically accompanies IVF; it involves the use of powerful fertility drugs and hormones (for example, pergonal) given to donor females to "coax" their ovaries into maturing more than the usual one ovum per month—sometimes as many as eight.

Sex Predetermination. X-bearing sperm can be separated from Y-bearing sperm (gynosperm and androsperm), and parents-to-be can request that only one kind of sperm be used to fertilize eggs with the IVF procedure. As the reader may have guessed, such a request is made more often for androsperm.

Surrogate Embryo Transfer (SET or "Lavage"). A fertilized egg or embryo incubating in the uterus of one woman is surgically transferred to the uterus of another after 5 days of gestation by "flushing" it out and then implanting it.

Gamete Intrafallopian Transfer (GIFT). Eggs and sperm are injected separately into a woman's fallopian tube to permit fertilization there instead of in a laboratory dish.

Zygote Intrafallopian Transfer (ZIFT). In this variant of IVF, fertilized embryos are transferred from a laboratory dish to a woman's fallopian tube instead of to her uterus.

Surrogacy. A woman agrees to be a birth mother only— that is, to carry and gestate a fetus and then turn the child, at birth, over to others who will rear it. The child may be the result of artificial insemination or in-vitro fertilization with sperm and eggs from one or both of the rearing parents or from neither. An unusual example of surrogacy is that of a mother in South Dakota who gave birth to twins "produced from her daughter's eggs, fertilized in a laboratory dish with sperm from her daughter's husband" and implanted in her uterus (Kolata, 1991).

Considerable criticism has been directed against many of these technologies, particularly surrogacy and the various IVF-related procedures. Although these technologies have made some women and men very happy, questions have been raised about the ways they may be damaging to women, generally. Critics of surrogacy contracts, for example, have argued that they "have created a national traffic in women—a system in which women are movable property, objects of exchange" involving "the procurement of women for breeding" (Raymond, 1991, p. 30). It is primarily poor women who agree to act as surrogates, for the usual fee of $10,000; it has been estimated that at least 40 percent of all surrogate mothers are on welfare (cf. Buttenwieser, 1991b). Some critics have urged Congress to ban commercial surrogate contracts, particularly after the much publicized Baby M case in which the birth mother changed her mind and wanted to retain custody of the child she had borne. Her petition was denied by the New Jersey Supreme Court, which awarded custody of the child to the couple who had contracted for her. In contrast to the state of affairs in the United States, "France's Supreme Court has outlawed surrogate mothering, stating that it violates a woman's body and improperly undermines the practice of adoption" (Greenhouse, 1991).

Some critics of contractual surrogacy have distinguished between surrogacy for payment and surrogacy for love or friendship, and been more accepting of the latter arrangement, arguing that it involves sacrifice and altruistic gift-giving. Others, however, have questioned this position. Sharyn Arleu (1992), for example, has pointed out that even surrogacy in the case of close friends or relatives is exploitative in that it is based on patriarchal assumptions and expectations about women's roles. Because a woman lends her body to another for "private" as opposed to "marketplace" reasons, she may be considered to be behaving appropriately. But, argues Arleu,

> conceptions of womanhood and motherhood underpin all discussions of surrogacy, specifically that motherhood is essential to women and that motherhood must be based on biological or genetic links. In these pronatalist pressures, *all* women are exploited. (p. 45)

With respect to the IVF technologies, Janice Raymond (1986) has argued that they tend to further medicalize pregnancy and birth and to separate women from control over their own bodies and reproductive processes. As Robyn Rowland (1991) has pointed out, the use of these technologies encourages us to view a woman's body as a collection of interchangeable parts—"eggs, ovaries, wombs—[and] leads to the retranslation of the woman's body . . . into a kind of laboratory" (p. 39); at the same time, it encourages "the perception of babies as a new 'product' to be marketed to the infertile" (p. 41). In some cases the cost of a baby through the use of these technologies can be as high as $100,000. Thus, it is clear that those who can benefit from these new procedures are primarily affluent European-American women in western countries. Joan Robison (1989) has cautioned that "payment for germinal materials, embryos, or gestational services can be seen as leading to . . . dehumanization through the commercialization of human reproduction" (p. 4).

The IVF and related procedures are invasive, painful, and exhausting, last anywhere from 6 months to 6 years, and have a very limited success rate in guaranteeing a "take-home baby." A congressional committee in 1989 reported this rate to be 9 percent. In addition, the complications these technologies may raise for a child are almost too strange to contemplate; one child may have a genetic mother, a gestating mother, a rearing mother, a genetic father, and a rearing father (Elias & Annas, cf. Robison, 1989). That the technologies can also be a source of humor is illustrated by the cartoon on p. 209.

Cartoon by Signe Wilkinson. Cartoonists & Writers Syndicate.

PREGNANCY

As we have already seen, most women in our society continue to want babies and to have them, although women now want fewer babies than their mothers and grandmothers did and to have them at later ages, spaced at more convenient intervals. The unique female capacity to sustain developing human life remains a source of delight, excitement, and awe; and the remarkable months of pregnancy continue to be experienced at least once by the vast majority of women.

What's Going On and How It Feels

The normal changes that occur inside a pregnant woman's body during the nine months of gestation are extraordinary and intricate, involving practically every organ and all major physiological systems. Some of the profound physical changes a pregnant woman undergoes include rapid increase in production of progesterone, which will be maintained throughout the pregnancy; heightened and continued production of estrogen; high expenditure of energy; tiredness; possible nausea; frequent need to urinate as the growing embryo presses on the bladder; the possibility of dietary deficiencies (perhaps associated with specific food cravings), since the fetus must obtain from its mother all nutrients and vitamins and makes particularly heavy demands on calcium, iron, and protein; rapid weight gain (approximately 24 pounds); and the physical

discomforts and postural adjustments that may accompany changes in body weight and distribution (Newton & Modahl, 1978).

Although all pregnant women undergo the same general physical and physiological changes, their subjective experiences of pregnancy can vary widely. How a woman experiences her pregnancy reflects her past history and present situation; its meaning and consequences vary in accordance with differing circumstances. Yet, as Myra Leifer (1980) has noted, few psychological studies "have dealt with women's subjective reactions to pregnancy" (p. 758). Much of what we know of these has come from feminist literature and the women's health movement. The empirical findings regarding psychological changes typically fluctuate between an emphasis on positive feelings of well-being, hope, eager anticipation, and calm, to descriptions of pregnant women as vulnerable and stressed. A pregnant woman may confront fears of death, unattractiveness, or loss of figure and beauty or fears that the child will be born defective or deformed. A pregnant woman is nurturing a developing human being—literally giving it all she has—and at the same time is typically enjoying some special care and attention from her partner and from friends or relatives. Both positive and negative experiences may fluctuate or occur simultaneously.

How the pregnant woman will react to the changes taking place in her body depends on the interaction between these changes and the environment in which she experiences them, with *environment* broadly defined to include cultural, social, economic, and physical conditions as well as her attitudes toward herself, the pregnancy, her marriage, her job, and so on. Myra Leifer (1980) concluded from a review of the literature on pregnancy that the degree to which it "is experienced as a time of well-being or stress may be critically related to the quality and extent of social and interpersonal support received" (p. 760). Studies have found that pregnant women with poor marital relationships are more likely to feel depressed or anxious than those whose marriages are happy ones and that there is a relationship between a woman's general feeling of well-being or satisfaction and the extent to which she will enjoy or feel positively about her pregnancy (cf. Newton & Modahl, 1978). In one study (Carrie, 1981), responses to a lengthy questionnaire were collected from a large sample of pregnant women, and it was found that the report of negative symptoms was most related to general health and to a tendency to report symptoms in general.

What we have learned to expect, and how we define or label our experiences, greatly influence how we feel and what we do. Nausea, for example, accompanies the first trimester of pregnancy for many, but by no means all, women. It is instructive to note what Margaret Mead (1949/1968) long ago observed among women in different cultures of the South Seas regarding how variations in personal experience are correlated with cultural emphases:

> Morning-sickness in pregnancy may be completely ignored, or it may be expected of every woman, so that the woman who displays no nausea is the exception or it may be stylized as occurring for the first child only. But in those societies which . . . ignore it . . . there are still a few women who have extreme nausea. . . . We may say of morning-sickness that where it is culturally stylized as appropriate . . . , a large majority of women will show this behavior; where it is not, only a very few will. Convulsive vomiting is a capacity of every human organism, which can be elaborated, neglected, or to a large degree disallowed. (p. 221)

After reviewing the relevant literature, Myra Leifer (1980) concluded that little is known about "what proportion of women actually experience [nausea and vomiting] . . . , nor do researchers agree on the biological, psychological, or sociological factors associated with them" (p. 756).

A pregnant woman's feelings and view of herself is influenced not only by general cultural emphases but also by the way her neighbors, family, employer, and others react to her. Pregnant women may make those around them, particularly men, feel uneasy. In one study (Taylor & Langer, 1977), people in an elevator were found to show a strong preference for standing next to a nonpregnant as opposed to a pregnant woman, even when the former took up as much space with a package; the pregnant woman was avoided more by men than by women. In another study, Dianne Horgan (1983) found that department stores differentially frequented by upper- and working-class pregnant women displayed maternity clothes in very different places. High status stores displayed maternity clothes adjacent to lingerie or loungewear, whereas lower status stores placed them near uniforms or clothes for large women. These findings suggested to Horgan that perhaps "in the high status stores, pregnancy is seen as feminine, delicate, luxurious, joyous, personal, and private [while] in the lower status stores, pregnancy is viewed as a job, a period when one is fat" (p. 336). Complementing Horgan's department store data are differences in attitudes assessed from responses to a brief survey filled out by women who were waiting to see their obstetricians. Upper-middle-class women were found to differ from working-class women in reporting that they felt sexier,

were treated differently when pregnant, and were more likely to be returning to work after giving birth.

Laws in the United States treat pregnancy as a disability, and many regulations, policies, and practices still treat women differently from men on the job because women are potential childbearers. We will return to this issue in the chapter on employment.

Fears and Taboos

In addition to physiological and physical changes, feelings about the extent to which the pregnancy was planned or desired, and fears for her own safety and competence in a new role, yet another factor can contribute to the stress of pregnancy for contemporary women. This is our feeling of responsibility for the health of the fetus and our awareness of the large number of potential threats to normal development. In many cultures, special regimens, rituals, or taboos are related to such fears. For example, within the Guatemalan village of San Pedro (Paul, 1974), a pregnant woman is believed to be especially vulnerable to harmful influences. It is considered dangerous for her to be outside at midday when the sun is strongest or during a thunderstorm or for her to look at the full moon or point to a rainbow.

Even if we do not subscribe to superstition and magic, even if we know that it is safe during pregnancy to swim, ski, dance, work, look at the moon, and be out in thunderstorms, modern women have other things to worry about, other proscriptions and another list of "don'ts." Most of us have learned how intimately fetus and mother are connected, how vital it is that our health be good, that we walk enough and rest enough, that our diet be nutritious, and that our spirits be high. Everything we do and ingest will have some consequence for the developing fetus. Despite the fact that doctors were responsible for the tragedy of deformed children born to mothers who took prescribed thalidomide in the 1960s, and for the tragedy of cancer in the reproductive tissues of children born to mothers who took prescribed DES, it was the mother who undoubtedly felt the guilt. Pregnant women feel responsible for the new human being growing in their bodies; they are concerned about avoiding X rays, drugs, alcohol, and cigarettes and are wary of contracting German measles and herpes.

Research indicates that pregnant women should be very cautious about consuming alcoholic beverages. Evidence documents the existence of a fetal alcohol syndrome, characterized by a set of abnormalities evident after birth: growth deficiencies, mental retardation, body organ defects, psychomotor disturbances, or some combination of these. A review of the research (Streissguth, Landesman-Dwyer, Martin, & Smith, 1980) concluded that "the lower limit of alcohol necessary to produce a harmful effect has not been determined" (p. 359), but clear indications exist that alcohol is a teratogen—that is, it freely passes across the placental barrier and affects fetal development. Although the mechanisms through which alcohol affects the fetus are still unclear, and variations among individuals in alcohol metabolism are poorly understood, adverse effects have been found in the offspring of women reporting an average consumption of two alcoholic drinks per day. Binge drinking has been found to be particularly harmful and can produce different congenital abnormalities at different times during fetal growth. More recently, considerable attention has been given to "crack babies," and tentative findings suggest serious potential consequences for infants born to cocaine-using mothers.

Smoking and aspirin have also been found to adversely affect prenatal development. Data from a national study of more than 50,000 pregnancies implicated smoking as a factor in spontaneous abortions, stillbirths, premature births, and crib death. The danger of smoking stems from its reduction of blood flow to the placenta; aspirin is believed to interfere with the circulation of oxygen. New research has indicated that caffeine consumption, too, may be dangerous to the fetus, as well as sexual intercourse during the second and third trimesters of pregnancy (cf. Connelly, 1981). Heavy caffeine use (equivalent to about five cups of coffee a day) is associated with an increased likelihood of breech births, miscarriages, low birth weight, stillbirths, and premature births. The danger of sexual intercourse comes from the possibility that seminal fluid may introduce or activate bacterial infection that can spread to the amniotic fluid surrounding the fetus and cause premature labor. Such infections are the most frequent cause of premature birth in the United States.

Sherryl Connelly (1981) listed the following other things that are "not good for the unborn": gaining too much weight or too little weight (the new medical advice is 25 pounds for a woman with a normal pre-pregnancy weight); eating a diet deficient in vitamins and minerals; using diazepam (marketed as Valium); and being exposed to cats or cat litter. A Boston University study recently reinforced the common wisdom that a mother's mood affects her unborn child. Women who were depressed during pregnancy were twice as likely to give birth to irritable infants as were non-depressed mothers (cf. "Mom, Please," 1990). Similarly, a UCLA study found

that next to diabetes, hypertension, or drug use, high maternal stress is the second most important factor in causing premature birth and low birth weight (cf. "Stress Causes," 1990). The net effect of these considerations is that a pregnant woman can hardly avoid feelings of apprehension and concern about whether or not she is doing all that she can to enhance the health and proper development of the fetus. If her baby is born defective, will it have been her fault?

The many "don'ts" for contemporary pregnant women has led to an overreaction on the part of some, dubbed by the media "the pregnancy police," and to fears about invasions of privacy and interference with civil liberties. "Since 1987, there have been about 60 criminal cases in 19 states against pregnant addicts; the charges have included child abuse, assault and manslaughter" (Kantrowitz, Quade, Fisher, Hill, & Beachy, 1991b). As noted by Isabelle Pinzler (1989) of the American Civil Liberties Union, "some people—the number is undetermined— . . . believe that if a woman chooses to carry a pregnancy to term then she takes on a 'duty of care' to the fetus . . . [that] may override her right to decide what she will eat, drink or smoke, what medical treatment she will or will not undergo, what job she will hold, whether or not she will have sex . . . [and] the state should have the power to force her to do so" (p. 3). Those who oppose intervention point out its dangers, using as an example the strong suggestion given to women to avoid sex near the end of their pregnancies and asking how far the pregnancy police wish to go. An actual incident in Seattle in which a pregnant woman was refused a drink in a bar prompted the "Sylvia" cartoon shown on p. 212.

Although some fears for the newborn can be handled by doing or avoiding certain things, we have no control over some dangers, originating from genetic or chromosomal errors. Some of these errors can be discovered prior to the birth of a child through modern advances in prenatal screening technology; parents are then faced with the choice of terminating the pregnancy. The most common prenatal tests are briefly described below (Gilbert, 1993; "Glossary," 1990; Klass, 1989).

Alpha-Fetoprotein Test (AFP). The protein AFP can be extracted from a small sample of the mother's blood after the fourth week of gestation or later on from amniotic fluid. Abnormally high levels indicate malformation of the spine or brain (for example, spina bifida), abdominal wall malformations, or kidney disease, whereas abnormally low levels can indicate Down's syndrome or other chromosomal anomalies. Additional tests are used for follow-up

Sʏʟᴠɪᴀ by Nicole Hollander. Cartoonists & Writers Syndicate.

diagnoses. Spina bifida is found in 1 in 1,000 fetuses regardless of the mother's age and is the most common birth defect.

Amniocentesis. Cells from the amniotic fluid, extracted from the uterus by means of a long needle inserted through the mother's abdomen, are analyzed to reveal their chromosomes, which will indicate sex of the fetus and certain abnormalities.

> The fluid contains two clues to a fetus's health. One is sloughed-off fetal skin cells, which can be analyzed for hundreds of chromosomal and genetic defects. . . . The other clue is the level of . . . alpha-fetoprotein. (Gilbert, 1993, p. 71)

Down's syndrome, the most common chromosomal disorder, is indicated when the 21st pair has three instead of two chromosomes, which can result from defects in the ovum, the sperm, or from abnormal conditions present during cell division. It used to be the case that amniocentesis was not performed until the 16th or 17th week of pregnancy, but it is now routinely done at 14 weeks, and by some doctors in the 12th or 13th week.

Chorion Villus Sampling (CVS). This procedure has gained in popularity as a substitute for amniocentesis because it can be performed earlier, generally at 9 to 11 weeks of pregnancy. It involves the removal of cells for chromosomal analysis from the placenta. CVS has a number of important shortcomings. It cannot diagnose spina bifida; it is inconclusive about 1 percent of the time; and the risk of miscarriage from the procedure is about 2.4

percent, twice as high as the risk from amniocentesis. There have also been reports of fetal limb and mouth deformities as a consequence of the test.

Ultrasound. High-frequency sound waves produce an echo of the uterus and can show the size and position of the developing fetus as well as very obvious malformations. Ultrasound also permits accurate pregnancy dating and sex determination, and it is often used in conjunction with the other tests.

Down's syndrome has been linked to the age of the parents. Early research focused only on the age of the mother at pregnancy, ignoring the possible role played by the sperm-contributing fathers, but paternal age has now been identified as being as important a predictor of Down's syndrome as maternal age (cf. Schmeck, 1980). The two variables are highly correlated, since older women are usually impregnated by older men. Taking only maternal age into account, the risk of having a child with Down's syndrome is 1 in 1,500 for women under 30, 1 in 952 for a 30-year-old woman, and 1 in 385 for a 35-year-old, and the risk doubles every 2½ years after 35 (Francke, 1982; Gilbert, 1993).

CHILDBIRTH

Nancy Dean and Myra Stark (1977) have suggested that childbirth is a woman's biological test of courage, a natural occasion for bravery that men have tried to match by constructing battlefields. In childbirth women risk their lives, demonstrate strength, and withstand pain. The result of such courage is the bringing forth of life. Individual women probably do not usually see childbirth in this way, and certainly women's strength can be exhibited in every sphere of human activity, but childbirth does contain elements of challenge and risk.

What triggers the end of gestation and the beginning of parturition (birth) is not entirely clear. Believed to be involved are hormones from the pituitary, namely oxytocin and prostaglandins, as well as progesterone. The first sign of impending childbirth is the expulsion of a mucus plug from the cervix, followed closely by the rupture of the amniotic sac housing the fetus and release of its fluid contents (the "bag of waters"). This should normally be followed by the first stage of labor, uterine contractions that take place at regular intervals while the cervix dilates. This first stage may last from 2 to 16 hours or longer. During the second, briefer, stage, the fetus is expelled (normally head first) down the vaginal canal, accompanied by a different kind of uterine contraction. During the last stage the placenta is expelled.

The Cultural Context

How a woman experiences childbirth varies widely from culture to culture, and within our own culture variation exists among groups of women who have received different kinds of prenatal preparation and whose babies are born under different conditions. Niles Newton and Charlotte Modahl (1978) have pointed out that "in societies that look upon birth as a fearful and secret experience, women often have long, difficult labors. In societies that are open about childbirth and expect it to be simple, women usually have short, uncomplicated labors" (p. 47).

In some cultures, childbirth is a relatively public event at which other individuals are expected to be present and to assist; in other cultures, childbirth is private. For example, in the Guatemalan village of San Pedro (Paul, 1974), a childbirth is attended by the husband, his parents, possibly the woman's parents, and the midwife. Women are expected not to cry or scream "lest the neighbors hear them," and the husband assists by supporting his wife from behind "as she squats to deliver her child." In contrast, among the Siriono Indians of Bolivia (Newton, 1970) birth takes place in a communal hut where the mother lies in a hammock and her groans appear to disturb no one; labor tends to be short, and the woman is not usually assisted.

Cultures vary in the number and kind of special taboos observed just before the birth is expected. The woman may be required to leave her village, go alone into the bush, and care for her own needs entirely, or food may be brought and left for her. In still other cultures, the father may be encouraged to behave in a manner paralleling that of his childbearing wife, so that he becomes more closely involved in the birth of his child; this is known as couvade. As Sheila Kitzinger (1979) noted, anthropological data clearly indicate that

> human childbirth is a cultural act in which spontaneous physiological processes operate within a context of customs, the performance of which is considered essential or desirable for a safe outcome. . . . [Birth] is surrounded and shaped by ritual and myth, injunction, prohibitions and taboos. (p. 83)

Our society has tended to encourage fear of childbirth, the expectation of terrible pain and helplessness, and an increasing dependence upon a male-dominated medical system. In earlier times, childbirth took place in a different context: it was the domain of women. Historian Nancy Dye (1980) noted that

> until the late eighteenth century, birth [in the U.S.] was an exclusively female affair, a social rather than a medical event, managed by midwives and attended by friends and relatives. . . . From the late eighteenth century [and] throughout the first decades of the twentieth century, [there] was a long transition between "social childbirth" and medically managed birth. Gradually, male physicians replaced midwives and transformed birth into a medical event. By the 1920's . . . the medical profession [had] consolidated its control of birth management. (p. 98)

Viewing childbirth as a medical event transfers its control from the woman to medical personnel. Childbirth is equated with illness and the baby is "delivered" in a hospital by a doctor. The entire experience encourages dependence, passivity, uninformed reliance on authority, and anxiety. The pregnant woman is virtually powerless; the doctor, still usually male, is powerful and in control. The powerlessness and helplessness of the woman is even further aggravated by what happens to her in the hospital. She is undressed, her genital area is shaved ("prepped"), and she is given an enema and sedated; later she is typically drugged more heavily, wheeled out, and strapped down. She is probably also patronized, poked and prodded by nurses and interns, and told to be a "good girl."

Such experiences elicit anxiety and increase the probability of a painful and prolonged labor. Giving birth is not an easy thing to do. It is stressful; it is a physiological, psychological, and emotional challenge. But we know that a woman's discomfort in labor is greatly increased if she is fearful.

> The excessive amounts of adrenaline that fear can place in a woman's bloodstream may counteract the work of hormones like oxytocin that help labor progress. Anxiety may cause the mother's muscles to become tense, converting simple contractions into painful cramps. (Newton & Modahl, 1978, p. 47)

A study by John Kennel in a Guatemalan hospital (cf. Newton & Modahl, 1978), for example, found that women who were assisted during labor and delivery by a friendly woman companion (an untrained stranger) were in labor fewer than half as many hours, had simpler deliveries, and were more affectionate to their babies during the first 45 minutes after birth than were a comparable group of women who received traditional childbirth care from medical personnel.

Our culture's dominant view of childbirth as a medical event can have negative consequences not only for the mother, but also for the child. Obstetrical procedures such as the use of forceps, overdependence on anesthetics and other medication, the use of epidural (spinal) blocks, artificial induction of labor, delaying birth until the doctor arrives, and separation of mother and infant right after birth have been found to be potentially harmful to the newborn, to prolong labor, and to increase the probability of damage to the child. For example, an epidural block can lower the mother's blood pressure, decrease the oxygen supplied to the fetus, and interfere with effective pushing by the mother in the second stage of labor. Babies who have been heavily drugged during birth (as a consequence of drugs administered to their mothers) have been found to have trouble learning to suck, to have slower heart and circulatory rates, and to have an impaired ability to clear mucus from air passages (Gould, 1979).

The connection between fear and pain was articulated very persuasively by Grantly Dick-Read (1959), the champion of "natural" childbirth. He asserted that the "fear-tension-pain" syndrome worked to counteract the birth process by pitting two sets of muscles against one another. Fear produces tension in the muscles controlling the cervix, acting to close it, while the muscles farther up in the uterus continue to contract, producing even greater pain. To prevent this, argued Dick-Read, a woman should know in detail what takes place inside her body during the birth process and should practice a series of exercises designed to gain control over relevant muscles, learn to breathe deeply and to relax completely, and rid herself of fear. With such preparation, Dick-Read argued, a modern woman can give birth without drugs and excruciating pain if she is supported in her efforts during labor by sympathetic attendants.

Despite the popularity of natural childbirth classes in the 1970s and 1980s, there has been some tendency for women in the 1990s to return to the use of pain-relief medication during childbirth, including epidural blocks, and the use of drugs to induce labor (cf. "Refusing to Bear," 1990). At the same time, pressure for increased control by women has led to some significant changes in the current obstetrical approach to childbirth and to the provision of a considerable number of options, including the use of Lamaze procedures and the widespread availability of childbirth-preparation classes for prospective parents. The Lamaze program, based on Pavlovian conditioning techniques and brought to us by way of France from Russia, involves massage and breathing and muscle control; its success depends on blocking out sensations of pain through distraction and making competing responses to stimuli that ordinarily evoke the perception of pain. This method involves the mother more actively than Dick-Read's relaxation approach and uses the father or another concerned adult as an assistant.

Many women now prepare for a childbirth experience that involves them more actively in the process. One option available in some hospitals is a birthing chair, which permits a woman to give birth while reclining comfortably in a chair with a strategically located hole in the seat. In older societies, women in labor did not lie down but moved about, changed positions, and stood or squatted during the final stage. The modern birthing chair recognizes the wisdom of the older, more natural posture, which enlists gravity as an aid to both mother and neonate. Many hospitals are now also offering LDRs, a combination of labor, delivery, and recovery rooms.

Renewed support for midwifery and home births also aims to increase women's participation in the management of childbirth. Most of the world's babies are still delivered by midwives, and in some modern countries, such as Holland and New Zealand, midwives are highly trained and respected professionals. In the United States, however, midwives were effectively forced out of business by restrictive laws passed in the early part of the 20th century. Interest in midwifery is currently experiencing a resurgence, but states vary widely in laws and practice: some states permit lay midwives to practice; others permit only nurse-midwives to practice as part of an obstetrics team; in some states all midwifery is prohibited; and in others the laws are confusing and difficult to interpret.

More than 95 percent of all births in the United States take place in hospitals, but home births have been increasing. Some teams of doctors and midwives offer women this option, although the dominant response by traditional medicine is largely negative. Opponents of home birth emphasize the risks and point out that many hospitals now provide a more humanistic, family-centered approach to childbirth. Home birth advocates counter that skilled midwife-physician teams will promptly move a woman to a hospital if problems arise that cannot otherwise be handled. The personal experiences of women are often at odds with the new rhetoric about humanized childbirth, even by enlightened medical practitioners.

The Cesarean Epidemic

One way that medicine in this country is reasserting its dominant role in childbirth is illustrated by the increased use of surgical procedures. This increase has occurred just when women have achieved success in demands to participate more actively in the birthing process and to improve the quality of prebirth education and preparation. Women have succeeded in reducing childbirth anxiety and increasing the option of drug-free and instrument-free procedures; but paralleling these gains has been an alarming rise in cesarean deliveries.

In the 1970s, the national rate of cesarean births tripled from 5.5 percent (up from 4 percent in the 1950s) to 18 percent by the end of the decade. This increase prompted an investigation by the National Institutes of Health (cf. Kolata, 1980b), which called the rapid increase in cesarean interventions "a matter of concern." No reduction in infant mortality was found to be associated with cesarean births among normal-sized infants, and a task force concluded that the number of cesareans could be reduced without added risk to babies or their mothers. The rate has continued to rise, however, reaching 24.4 percent in 1987 ("Half of Caeserean-Section Births," 1989). Thus, about one out of every four newborns in the United States is surgically removed from its mother's uterus, a national rate that is considered by some to be twice as high as it should be.

What is responsible for this epidemic, as it has been labeled by Gena Corea (1980) and others? From a medical perspective, cesareans are said to be indicated for the following kinds of problems: breech birth; failure to progress in labor (dystocia); the baby's head being too large for the mother's pelvis; or a decreased oxygen supply to the fetus (Heilman, 1980). It is widely agreed that electronic monitoring, now used routinely to check on the conditions of the fetus, is partly responsible for the increase in cesareans, because the information it provides can be misinterpreted or given greater significance than it deserves. A study of nearly 35,000 pregnant women found that fetal monitors, which are used in about two thirds of all deliveries, were not associated with fewer birth defects or decreased infant mortality but did motivate doctors to perform twice as many cesarean sections on low-risk mothers (cf. Emery, 1986).

Some doctors are so enthusiastic about cesareans that they believe even more women should have babies that way because they are safe and can be scheduled at the doctor's convenience. Cesareans make more money for medical practitioners. "According to government statistics, the average doctor and hospital charge in 1986 was $2,620 for a normal delivery and $4,330 for a C-section" ("Doctors," 1988). In addition, many doctors contend that more cesareans are performed because obstetricians fear malpractice suits. Obstetricians/gynecologists (along with neurosurgeons and orthopedic surgeons) are most likely to be sued. The blame for surgical intervention is thus said by some to lie with parents who sue doctors for unfavorable childbirth outcomes.

Once a woman has had a cesarean, she is very likely to have one again for her next child. The number of women who deliver vaginally after having had a cesarean is very small, and at least a third of abdominal births in this country are a consequence of prior cesareans. Perhaps this practice will change as a result of the public position taken by the American College of Obstetricians and Surgeons that 50 to 80 percent of women who have undergone surgical birth with a low transverse scar can deliver their next child vaginally (cf. Diamond, 1985).

Peak Experience?

If a woman is actively involved in preparing for childbirth, if she is knowledgeable about the physiological changes involved in pregnancy, and if she knows what to expect during childbirth, she is likely to be less anxious throughout the gestation period and to have less need for medication during labor, thus benefiting her child. This wisdom should be reassuring to those preparing for childbirth. Also reassuring should be the knowledge that some women have found childbirth to be a rapturous, exhilarating, exultant "peak experience" (cf. Tanzer, 1973; Odent, 1984). But emphasis on natural, relatively pain-less, and joyful birth sometimes makes women even more anxious about being able to measure up to the new expectations. Will they, like the women they read and hear about, be strong, involved, calm, and capable?

Miriam in *Small Changes* (Piercy, 1975) dutifully practiced her breathing and did her exercises; she and her husband prepared for childbirth. In the hospital awaiting the birth of her child, however,

> the labor went on and on. Sometimes she felt exhausted and just wished the whole damn thing would end and forget the idiot panting and counting and carrying on. Contractions, my ass. It was pain and big pain and it hurt like hell. However, she continued. Partly she was ashamed to act as if she couldn't handle it. . . . And she wanted to be awake, she wanted that desperately. . . . She panted instead of screaming. She counted instead of crying. . . . Neil was with her, she held his hand, she held tight to him, but she could feel always his fear that she would not be good enough, . . . that she would back down from the way they had chosen. (pp. 393f.)

Miriam did not want her husband to be disappointed in her; she did not want to be a "Lamaze failure." She thought that perhaps things might have been different for her if she were giving birth as she had seen her friend Sally do, surrounded by women who rubbed her stomach, kissed her, and spoke softly.

Still, despite the pain and fear they may have felt during the process, women who have observed their own children being born under normal or non-traumatic conditions have described a breathlessness, an incredulity, and excite-ment that cannot be duplicated by any other experience. The mundane and the sublime appear in unique combination. This is Miriam's description:

> The head was blooming . . . Huge coming through her. Ridiculous. A dark wet head emerging from the nest of towels and large sheet . . . In the mirror a pile of laundry was giving birth. A person was emerging. Then she was laughing, because it looked ridiculous in the mirror . . . . "I did it" she cried out. . . . Gradually, gradually, the baby slipped out of her, oh, beautiful creature thrust into the world glowing and bright. (pp. 394f.)

◆ Discussion Questions

1. How has the availability of contraceptive methods made your life different from your parents or grandparents? Ask them to discuss this with you.

2. What difference has the legalization of abortion made to you or your peers?

3. Discuss the benefits and problems associated with the new reproductive technologies.

4. Ask 5 friends of each gender whether or not they want to be parents, and why.

5. Ask 4 women who are mothers—one each in her 30s, 40s, 50s, and 60s—to describe their childbirth experiences.

PARENTING

For me, the experience of motherhood has been passionate, uprooting, harsh, full of sacrifice, a sense of humility and the opportunity to experience the most powerful love I have ever known. Being a mother is one road to a deep regard for all human life.

JANE LAZARRE (1985, p. 30)

Grown don't mean nothing to a mother. A child is a child. They get bigger, older, but grown? What's that supposed to mean? In my heart it don't mean a thing.

TONI MORRISON (1987, p. 45)

WOMEN'S EXPERIENCE AS MOTHERS RECEIVED little serious analysis until the 1960s, when feminist scholars began to explore its content and significance. By and large, motherhood was simply taken for granted by social scientists, while popular images focused on aprons and home-baked cookies or on frazzled nerves and endless chores. What does being a parent mean for contemporary women, and what are the behaviors that define this role? It is no surprise to find that these behaviors are related to motives, attitudes, and responses reinforced during childhood and adolescence and also to the typical conditions of motherhood that socialize women into nurturant, caregiving, family-oriented persons.

In our society, as in most others, we assume that a baby's primary caregiver will be its biological mother, and that if she is not available another woman will be sought as a substitute. Indeed, the meaning of the verb "to mother" is to care for and protect; in contrast, "to father" means to have contributed to the conception of a child, not to its care.

To be a middle-class mother in our society is usually to be the primary caregiver to one's own children in a relatively isolated and relatively small family unit. This is less true for some working-class ethnic minorities. For example, Carol Stack (1974) described a cooperative communal exchange network among women (relatives or friends) within a poor urban African-American community in the Midwest. In many African-American families, roles are interchangeable and "aunts, grandmothers, older sisters, cousins and nieces . . . frequently play major roles in the care and raising of younger children" (Joseph, 1981a, p. 82). Some mothers who are not part of extended families or friendship networks form support groups to decrease their isolation, to share resources and strategies, and to provide services to themselves not otherwise available (McCoy, 1980).

Today's mothers include women of diverse life-styles and circumstances: heterosexuals and lesbians; married and single women; those who are at home with their children full-time for varying numbers of years and those who are employed outside the home in jobs at all occupational levels and on widely varying work schedules. In 1982 almost 49 percent of married mothers and 54 percent of unmarried mothers with preschool children were employed outside the home (Shreve, 1982). In 1988, the percent of mothers in the labor force was 73.3 for those with children between 6 and 17, 56.1 for those with children under 6, and 50.8 for those with children 1 year old or less (cf. Darnton, 1990). Women experience motherhood in varied personal, economic, and family circumstances and also at diverse ages.

Mothers with children at home now vary widely in age. As noted earlier, about one third of women in the United States are now delaying the birth of their first child until they are in their 30s. A growing number of women are not waiting for marriage before having a child and are choosing single parenthood as a preferred life-style or because they have not found a marriage partner. Our discussion of mothers, then, includes married women who begin having a family in their 20s and stay at home for many years to care for their children (a minority of today's mothers); married women who combine paid employment with family responsibilities in varying ways; single mothers—divorced, widowed, or never married; and mothers in complicated family situations who may share care of their children with relatives, share custody with ex-husbands, or who may be noncustodial mothers or stepparents to a new partner's children. Not all mothers are heterosexual, a subject to which we will return later.

RESPONDING TO AN INFANT

We will explore the consequences of the mother's role as primary parent in later sections. First, we will consider the mother's experiences, beginning with the early days and months of her parenthood. If she has given birth to her child, a woman's body must adjust to post-pregnancy changes. With lactation, she can, if she chooses, provide directly for the nutritional needs of her infant. The infant also has other needs, however, and filling these needs does not come naturally for any mother. She must learn to nurture her child and to fill the role that society has prescribed for her as a mother. Some of this learning has already occurred in her childhood and adolescent years but some of it can only be done in interaction with her baby.

Postpartum Blues?

While most women are led from childhood to the role of childbearer, later on we are taught that motherhood is likely to begin with a period of sadness, or a big letdown. Friends, neighbors, magazine articles, and doctors reinforce the expectation that after birth of the baby, the mother can expect to experience a temporary period of depression and confusion. For example, Jane Brody (1983a), in a *New York Times* story, wrote that for up to two-thirds of new mothers, something unexpected and mystifying happens during the first week after childbirth. For no apparent reason, sadness sets in and the initial elation dissolves in teary confusion that may last for days, weeks or months.

The mother may feel irritable, hypersensitive, fatigued, restless, unable to sleep, depressed or ambivalent toward her baby. She finds herself crying at the drop of a hat. . . . This reaction . . . is so common that it is considered a normal part of the postpartum experience. (p. C-6)

Little seems to have changed in the 1990s relevant to this frightening picture. A story in a popular magazine ("Women's World," 1991) is headlined "One in every seven new mothers falls victim to a depression so severe it threatens to ruin her life and endanger her baby's." Accompanying the story is a picture of a distraught mother, holding a crying baby and exclaiming, "I wanted to kill my baby."

As is true for other aspects of women's lives, inaccurate generalizations about the postpartum experience have been widely circulated and promote the expectation of dysfunction and negative mood without a firm empirical basis. Childbirth is followed by a dramatic decrease in pregnancy's very high levels of estrogen and progesterone, but the accompanying body changes during this puerperium period—in tissue fluid retention, in chemical balance, metabolism, and so on—must be interpreted by the person experiencing them, as is true for the hormonal changes that occur during pregnancy and the menstrual cycle. To be told, in advance, that one should expect to feel blue and let down after the birth of a baby provides new mothers with a cognitive framework that explains, labels, and identifies their feelings. But no necessary connection exists between a decrease in progesterone and estrogen and feelings of depression. A review of the relevant literature (Hopkins, Marcus, & Campbell, 1984) concluded that "evidence of a direct link between hormone levels and depressed mood is lacking" (p. 506). For example, one group of researchers (Treadway, Kane, Jarrahi-Zadeh, & Lipton, 1975) found that all the postpartum women in their sample showed reductions in norepinephrine, but only some were depressed whereas others were not. Such data are important because they indicate that factors other than normal biochemical changes following childbirth are responsible for the blues experienced by some women during this period.

Most women will be physically tired from the strain of labor, from inadequate hours of rest or sleep, and from focusing attention on the needs of their newborn babies. Few researchers have attended to the influence of such factors on mood. Many women do not experience a period of sadness or general disequilibrium after childbirth, but all must cope with a variety of increased stresses—new stimuli (both internal and external), hormonal and metabolic changes, fatigue, new responsibilities, and changes in tasks and daily routines. Kate Simon (1990) has described this period after the birth of her child.

Lifted and whipped around by breezes of ecstasy, I did not sleep for two days and nights, calling everyone I knew . . . to tell them about the wonderful thing I had done. A few days later, sitting at home among a luxury of presents . . . I gathered around myself a vulnerability I had never before experienced. . . . A child was my passport to all of humanity. (pp. 68f.)

The responses women make to the changed circumstances of their lives following the birth, or adoption, of a child will vary across groups and individuals, just as will responses to pregnancy and childbirth. Women who are more eager for a child, knowledgeable about their body changes, prepared for the changes that will take place in their lives, who feel generally good about themselves and their situations, and who receive encouragement and support from family members, significant persons, and community resources are less likely to feel depressed after their children are born and more likely to continue feeling positive excitement and pleasure.

We know that the birth of a child generally affects the relationship of heterosexual married couples in a negative way. Two major research projects, in California and Pennsylvania, have found that for half the couples studied, marital satisfaction declined after the birth of a first child, when the wife and husband tend to assume traditional gender roles even if both are employed outside the home (cf. Rubenstein, 1989). In both studies, couples were followed over several years. Among the dissatisfied couples, the major problem was the division of family labor and, for the women, "the gap between their egalitarian expectations for family life and reality. . . . [The] expectation . . . that their husbands will share household and parenting chores—is often unrealized" (p. 40). Other investigators have reported similar findings. In one large-scale study (Ruble, Fleming, Hackel, & Stangor, 1988), first-time mothers reported "less positive feelings about their husbands during the post-partum period than during pregnancy, . . . [and] reported doing much more of the housework and child care than they had expected" (p. 78). More than 40 percent of the women reported a large discrepancy in the child care division of labor and that they had expected their husbands to do more. If we are searching for factors contributing to a woman's letdown after childbirth, it is likely that such violated expectations are more relevant than hormonal changes.

Breast-Feeding

Following childbirth, only one of the behaviors that define the mother role or motherhood is dependent upon biological sex or femaleness. Breast-feeding is made possible by hormonally controlled lactation but is, as we know, optional for today's mother. All other experiences of motherhood are a function of the tasks performed and not of the sex of the caregiver. In Marge Piercy's (1977) utopian novel about a nonsexist future society, *Woman on the Edge of Time,* males, too, can nurse if they choose to undergo special hormonal treatment, making all aspects of child rearing available to both women and men.

The science fiction image of a breast-feeding male may be funny or shocking, but it is not impossible. Similarly, an adoptive mother can nurse with the help of a device strapped between her breasts that contains "a formula-filled plastic bag." When an infant sucks at the breast, it also sucks at a spaghetti straw attached to the bag. By so doing, the infant both gets milk through the straw and stimulates the mother's breast to lactate (cf. VonBergen, 1990).

Lactation normally begins during the second or third day after the birth of a child; the mammary glands swell and manufacture a milky substance filled with nutrients and antibodies. If she chooses not to breast-feed her baby, the mother must bind her breasts tightly, be given hormones to suppress the lactation, and may be uncomfortable for several days. The proportion of mothers who breast-feed their babies in U.S. hospitals was reported to be 52 percent in 1989, 59 percent among European-American mothers and 23 percent among African-American mothers (cf. Spears, 1991). Among those who breast-feed, 85 percent stop nursing by the time the baby is 10 to 12 months old (Myers & Siegel, 1985).

Women may choose to bottle-feed their babies because of the easy availability of store-bought supplies and milk products and because someone else other than the mother can then feed the child, an important consideration for working women or those with obligations to a large family. Some women associate nursing with poverty; others find it embarrassing; others want their breasts to return as soon as possible to their pre-pregnancy size and shape. Low-income women, especially, are encouraged by advertising and government policies to formula-feed their

babies. They are misinformed, being told that formula is just as good as breast milk and that nursing will spoil the child and make it more needy. "[T]he biggest promoter of bottle feeding is the federal government, which provides nearly $500 million in free formula annually to poor women under the Women Infant Children feeding program" (Spears, 1991, p. F-4).

We know that breast milk is nutritionally better, safer, and easier to digest than store-bought formulas. Most nursing women find the experience of breast-feeding pleasurable and believe it provides a unique closeness and relaxed communication with their child; some like the ease—no fuss, no bottles to sterilize; and some feel a sense of pride in the fact that their bodies can provide nourishment and natural immunities for their infant. Breast-feeding also has immediate physical benefits for the mother; it releases hormones that trigger uterine contractions that reduce the size of the uterus and speed the process of its descent from the abdomen back into the pelvic area.

Groups like La Leche League extoll the pleasures and benefits of breast-feeding; some have described nursing as a "sensuous experience." The pleasure that nursing mothers derive from the experience (whether from feelings of intimacy, power, giving, or sensuality) is conditioned to the infant, who is always present, and as a mother continues to breast-feed, the strength of her motivation to do so increases. Mothers who breast-feed and those who do not have not been found to differ in age, education, religion, or other social variables, but have been distinguished on the basis of attitudes and beliefs (Berg-Cross, Berg-Cross, & McGeehan, 1979; Manstead, Proffitt, & Smart, 1983).

No woman who chooses to bottle-feed should feel as though she has failed some test of motherhood. For some women, nursing is not successful: it is painful or frustrating. A working woman who must be away from her infant for a considerable period of time each day may find it impossible to nurse comfortably. It is not always possible or desirable to breast-feed an infant in the special circumstances of a particular woman's life. Like most other behavior, the naturalness of nursing, and its frequency or duration, is influenced by an array of environmental factors. Although nutritionists and pediatricians may recommend breast-feeding for its benefits to the infant during the first months or year of life, choosing to breast-feed may require strong-willed commitment, and a nursing mother may meet with only grudging cooperation from hospital staffs, surprise from neighbors and relatives, and frustration when trying to find a quiet spot outside her home.

Caring and Connection;
Joys and Frustrations

The process of bonding with and nurturing an infant begins in pregnancy but requires behaviors that are learned in interaction with the child. For example, Ann Murray (1979) concluded from a review of the literature that infant cries are not "invariably effective in eliciting care-giving behavior" (p. 211) on the part of women (or men), but that caregiving responses depend upon sensitization and exposure to young children.

Mothers are typically exposed to a helpless infant whose survival and development depend upon attention and care. Mothers are rewarded unambiguously, amply, and immediately by an infant when its cries cease; when it snuggles or sucks; when it smiles, coos, and babbles; when it laughs, talks, or rests peacefully. A mother soon learns that these positive responses from her infant are contingent upon her behavior: on changing a diaper; providing a bottle; giving a hug, a caress, or a cookie; giving a bath; soothing or calming the infant; and so on. Thus, a mother's nurturant behavior is powerfully reinforced, strengthened, and maintained by (a) her child's reactions of pleasure and gratitude; (b) the success of the mother's behavior in effecting a desired change in the child's responses or circumstances; (c) the consequent feeling of competence the mother experiences; and (d) her feelings of pride and self-satisfaction for having done the right thing and having done it well. In this way, mothers learn to nurture. Caring behaviors are ones all human adults have the capacity to manifest, but such behaviors are acquired and maintained only by those who are provided with the appropriate conditions in which such responses will be evoked and rewarded.

Reinforcements are not always forthcoming, however, and a mother's nurturant behavior will not always be successful or instrumental in effecting changes in her child's environment or behavior. A mother may be frustrated; tired; overburdened; lacking in resources, relevant knowledge, or skills; abused by others; or frightened. Child–mother interactions can thus yield both positive and negative outcomes.

The ambivalent feelings of mothers who inevitably experience both pleasure and pain, gratification and suffering, as they interact with their children have been expressed by many women in fiction and autobiography. For example, a mother in a novel by Lynne Schwartz (1985) recalls

> when my infants cried . . . my impulse was not to run and comfort them but to hide my head under a pillow, which

I sometimes did. Of course most of the time I went to comfort them, but I didn't run. (p. 16)

> That mothers gladly endure pain so that their children may thrive is a useful, sustaining myth. Also something of a cultural joke; the mother as sucker. And between saint and sucker, two sides of one thin coin, is little room to maneuver. (p. 220)

Adrienne Rich (1977) has described motherhood in terms of the "alternation between bitter resentment and raw-edged nerves, and blissful gratitude and tenderness" (p. 1); and Theodore Dix (1991), in an article reviewing the literature on emotional responses to parenting, noted that "raising children involves more joy, affection, anger, and worry than do most other endeavors in life" (p. 3).

A mother's continuing, unbreakable connection to her children is underscored by Toni Morrison (1987) in *Beloved*. And, in a novel by Marilyn French (1987), a mother speaks as follows about her children.

> I adore them. I would not be without them. . . . My heart is tied to them with unbreakable cord. The cord is scarred, pulled thin . . . [but] strong enough to rip apart the heart before it breaks. (p. 654)

Mothers experience both connectedness to their children and separation. Jane Attanucci (1982) asked a heterogeneous sample of mothers to describe themselves and found variation in their reported relationships to their children. Mothers' self-definitions were found to reflect more separation as they grew older, were married longer, and had more children.

For women with few personal or community resources or inadequate preparation or skills, motherhood may not provide the optimum conditions for the acquisition of nurturant, caring, empathetic behavior. By and large, however, mothers do "come through" and validate our image of people who care; who provide and protect; who teach, explain, and expect; who wait and forgive. Mothers are givers, healers, and workers of miracles. The benefits and costs of such a role can be illustrated by the results of two studies. In one (Helson, Mitchell, & Moane, 1984), a sample of mothers in their early 40s showed a significant positive change in responsibility, self-control, and tolerance over their earlier scores when tested as college seniors. However, Anne Wells (1988) found, among a sample of European-American employed mothers, that responses to a self-esteem survey yielded lower scores when the women were with their children than when they were with adults.

Like the Great Mother or Great Goddess of antiquity who appears in the mythology of widely separated cultures, mothers are associated with life, peace, tenderness, concern for human welfare, and unconditional love (Harding, 1972; Rich, 1976). There is great similarity in the ancient myths: the mother goddess represented a generative power, whose relation to her children (that is, the community) defined her special quality as a giver of life and transformer of power, able to function as priestess, potter, healer, artist, wise woman, and weaver. Contemporary mothers, too, are seen as doers of magic and lesseners of hurts—the ultimate alchemists who can transform the ordinary into glitter and gold. For example, in Carolyn Slaughter's *A Perfect Woman* (1985), a daughter describes her mother as "pulling it all together somehow, making a net into which she scooped all the misery and laughter, the anguish and tears, shook it about a bit until it settled again" (p. 89).

MUST THE MOTHER BE THE PRIMARY PARENT?

Our discussion of parenting thus far must be understood within the context of the present system, in which women are expected to fulfill the role of primary caretaker for their children, whether or not they are employed outside the home or have other significant interests or skills. Although the children of many mothers are looked after for many hours each week by relatives, neighbors, fathers, and child care workers, our society continues to regard the mother as the primary parent and child care as her responsibility. She must provide it herself or find someone else who will do it for her. Recognition of men's potential for parenting and men's responsibilities for child care is increasing but is not yet a dominant theme in our culture. Motherhood continues to encompass the bulk of parental responsibility, especially for very young children, while fatherhood still represents only general support and assistance. One sees this allocation of responsibility reflected in the lives of most women in our society, of all social classes and all ethnicities, among women who are not employed outside the home and among those who are, among the undereducated and the highly educated, among those with unknown talents and those with known skills. Not all contemporary women who have borne children accept the role of primary child rearer, but those who do not must often apologize for their choice and experience guilt and frustration. Child care is considered a "woman's issue," a woman's problem.

Interviews with a group of Harvard and Radcliffe students (Klein, 1977) revealed that although both women and men talked about having careers and families, "no woman said she would put career before her family. . . . In contrast, a few men admitted that their careers would probably always come first" (p. 12). Similarly, a longitudinal study of women who had graduated from a women's college (Helson, 1986) found that during the time when they were between 27 and 37 years of age, being a mother took precedence over their roles as marriage partners and employed workers. The ensuing decades seem to have brought little change in the expectation that the mother has primary responsibility for child care. This continuing expectation can be illustrated by the personal stories of career women in the 1990s who have spoken of adjustments made in their work to accommodate child rearing. Commenting on such reports is a letter to the *New York Times* (Gazzaniga, 1991), pointing out how these stories illustrate "the burden . . . on women to find ways to juggle family and career. . . . [Yet] there is another possibility: demand that men share the pain of those difficult choices," and identify parenthood as "an equal priority for mothers and fathers" (p. E-12).

I first became a mother a little more than three decades ago. I was as highly educated as my husband, with more job experience and professional background, but it was I who shifted to working part-time while his career was put on a firm, full-time basis. We both believed that we would be much better at rearing our children and would enjoy it more than paid babysitters, but we never seriously questioned that this responsibility would be primarily mine. When my husband stayed home one half-day each week to care for his first child all by himself his colleagues were astounded, and we considered ourselves to be radical; now our naïveté seems unbelievable. The association of mothers with children, ancient and powerful, persists despite our growing knowledge that fathers (and other adults) are physically, intellectually, and emotionally as capable as mothers are of learning to care for children.

One study (Yorburg & Arafat, 1975) surveyed the beliefs of a large sample of adults in offices, campuses, and shopping centers about men's and women's responsibilities for the care of infants and children. The authors reported that only 44 percent of the men and 54.8 percent of the women agreed that a woman should be both employed and a homemaker if she had children under 6 years of age. In another study (Kellerman & Katz, 1978), a group of parents rated child-rearing tasks by specifying the percentage of maternal and paternal responsibility for each task. Judged to be primarily the mother's job was physical caretaking and emotional support, while primary responsibility for activity and recreation was more often given to fathers. (You may recall that in children's books, too, fathers are typically shown to be "where the fun is!") In total, 53 percent of all the child-rearing responsibilities were seen as primarily the mother's, 38 percent were seen as shared with the father, and only 9 percent were seen as primarily the father's. Of special interest is the fact that when tasks were categorized into groups relating to age of the child (infant, preadolescent, and adolescent), it was found that the younger the child, the greater the attribution of primary maternal responsibility.

That a mother's attention is vital to the health and full development of a young child is an assumption reflected in the language used by scientists in discussing parenting and in the nature of their research. Thus, a report in *Science* entitled "Need for mother's touch is brain-based" (1988) reports a study that found that touching premature human infants is good for them and that they "thrive better with extensive skin-to-skin contact" (p. 142). But must this touching be done by the mother, or even by a woman? The obvious answer is "no," although this question is not addressed in the report, and its answer is misleadingly implied in the article's title. Another example is an extensive review of the literature on adaptive and maladaptive parenting (Dix, 1991) that cites study after study dealing only with mothers.

It is not surprising then to find that social scientists have labeled situations in which a maternal figure is missing from a child's environment as "maternal deprivation," but have used the term "father absence" to refer to situations in which a paternal figure is missing. The difference in meaning between these descriptive phrases is not accidental, has important implications for the behavior expected of a child's two parents, and is reflected in the ways in which mothers employed outside the home are perceived and judged. For example, research has found (Etaugh & Nekolny, 1990; Etaugh & Poertner, 1991) that samples of both adults and college students rate working mothers more negatively than mothers who do not work outside the home, describing the employed mothers as less dedicated to their families, less sensitive to the needs of others, and less well adjusted. Joan Riedle (1991) also found that college students described an employed mother of preschool children as less feminine, more masculine, and as having generally less desirable characteristics than a full-time homemaker mother. The ratings of a mother whose employment status was not specified were similar to those of the at-home mother, suggesting that, without information to the contrary, a mother is expected to stay at home. Such findings persist despite the fact that they do not mirror contemporary realities: "the 'average mother' is not at home with children supported by her employed husband" (Attanucci, 1989), and

two-parent households of all kinds made up only 27 percent of all households in 1988.

Although our society clearly views primary parenting as a woman's job, the strength of this conviction appears to weaken considerably when the mother is a lesbian. Estimated to be about 5 million in number in the United States, lesbian mothers are poorly regarded and poorly treated. The National Gay and Lesbian Task Force has estimated that 15 to 20 percent of all lesbians are mothers, among whom about two thirds were married when their children were born (cf. Beck, 1983). As noted by Judith Worell (1988), the lesbian mother "is always under threat of losing custody to her former husband, to grandparents, or even to stranger foster parents" (p. 7). Lesbian mothers are believed to cause their children to become sexual deviants and to damage their peer and community relationships, although no evidence supports these stereotyped beliefs (Evans, 1990; Freiberg, 1990b). No significant differences were found, for example, between a sample of homosexual and heterosexual single mothers in their self-descriptions or in their descriptions of preferred behaviors for children in general and for girls and boys separately (Kweskin & Cook, 1982). Each mother tended to describe her ideal child as having attributes similar to her own, but these attributes were not related to sexual orientation.

Despite such data, it has been extremely difficult for lesbian women to adopt a child or to serve as foster parents, as illustrated by the case of a couple in Massachusetts—Lorraine McMullin and Liz Offen (n.d.)—who were denied the chance to look after a troubled teenage girl even though they met all of the state's placement criteria except for one: they were homosexual women. As a result of efforts on behalf of this couple, the state subsequently changed its discriminatory policy. A more enlightened ruling was later made by a New York State judge who granted a lesbian couple's request to legally adopt a son who had been born to one of them ("Motherhood," 1992). As of this writing, two appellate courts will be ruling for the first time on cases involving lesbians' requests to legally adopt their partners' children ("2 Gay Adoptions," 1993).

While facing social disapproval and legal difficulties, lesbian women in large numbers are responsible, committed, and loving parents. The role of the nonbiological parent is especially difficult and has been described as "born of love rather than biological imperative" and as having "no official recognition, no legal recourse, no hope for visitation rights if the relationship between lovers should end," with "financial requirements" but no legal tax allowance (Tortorillo, cf. Evans, 1990).

Parenting as Learned Behavior

Except for breast-feeding, the care and nurturance of a human being at infancy is not dependent upon the sex of the caregiver nor upon the caregiver's biological relationship to the child. Parenting behavior ("mothering"), bonding, or attachment depends instead on certain features of the environment, expectations, practice, and contingencies, and on previously acquired attitudes and behaviors. Important factors are (a) the physical presence of an infant; (b) the expectation that one will be caring for a child; (c) previously acquired nurturant responses; (d) opportunities for practice and reward; and (e) the quality of one's own remembered childhood—that is, the behavior of one's own parents. We have evidence of this from other cultures and other times as well as from contemporary research.

Children in different cultures and in different historical periods have been cared for in a variety of ways by a variety of different persons: looked after by siblings, grandparents, neighbors, kinfolk, nannies, or nursemaids. Extreme role specialization for mothers, with child care as a mother's major task, was the exception and not the rule in older, traditional societies (Greenfield, 1981). Full-time mothering, by a woman who stays home just for that purpose, is a relatively recent phenomenon, which coincided with the development of a socioeconomic middle class in 19th-century industrialized urban societies. As Diana Baumrind (1980) noted, "there is no evidence of a biological or psychological need for an exclusive primary bond, and certainly not a bond to a particular person" (p. 645). Children can develop important relationships with several people, and neither the gender of the person nor the biological tie with the child is an important variable.

A small number of cultures are known in which both father and mother participate in all aspects of child rearing. Among the Arapesh of New Guinea, for example (cf. Mead, 1935/1950), this shared responsibility began at conception and continued during pregnancy, when the father's presence and adherence to certain rituals was considered vital to the feeding and shaping of the child in its mother's womb. After the child was born, both mother and father fasted together for the first day and performed rites to "ensure the child's welfare and their ability to care for it." Despite the physical ties between the mother and child in pregnancy and breast-feeding, both mother and father were said to have borne the new child and to be equally responsible for it; thus, the care of children was said by the Arapesh to be the work of both parents.

Nancy Chodorow (1978) has argued that little girls are taught early to be affiliative and nurturant and are therefore both motivated for motherhood and prepared to do its work. She suggests that caring, concern, and connectedness are attributes of women prior to their experience as mothers and contribute to their desire to bear and rear children. Society, in other words, reproduces motherhood by "inducing [appropriate] psychological processes" in girls. Thus, we would expect to find, as reported in one study of college students (McBride & Black, 1984), that women and men would respond differently to stories about parent–child interactions, with women showing more empathy and understanding of the children's failures and problems. The investigators concluded that "even before a woman has been through the biosocial experiences of pregnancy, labor, delivery, and lactation . . . socialization into gender roles by late adolescence has already paved the way for different approaches to parenting" (p. 244).

It is the mother–daughter relationship in particular, according to Chodorow (1978) and Carol Gilligan (1982), that encourages attachment and connectedness on the part of girls and prepares them for maternal work. Such preparation for motherhood, however, is more likely to be a function of a continuing socialization that extends across the life span; it is not likely either to be limited to the early years nor to be primarily a function of the mother's behavior. The preparation of girls for motherhood varies with culture, historical period, and situation. Judith Lorber (1981), for example, has noted that social structures are the crucial explanatory variables, not personality or intrapsychic needs. Contemporary women continue to be their children's primary parents because "intensive mothering is the choice most likely to maximize their social rewards" (p. 84).

Because it has been assumed for so long that women and infants will naturally display bonding or attachment toward each other, men have seldom been placed in situations where their interactions with babies could be observed over a sustained period of time. But evidence is accumulating in support of the proposition that attachment to an infant is a function of its presence and interaction with an adult, regardless of gender. Infants and children play an active role in getting their needs satisfied, thus helping adults develop effective responses; a child's choice of an attachment person depends primarily on the social setting in which it is reared; and attachment depends upon the interaction between children and caregivers.

Of particular significance are investigations that have demonstrated the very early and well developed capacities of infants to identify and respond to their caregivers. For example, 3-month-old infants were conditioned to increase their vocalizations in response to a tape-recorded human voice (Banikiotes, Montgomery, & Banikiotes, 1972), and the conditioning was found to be just as rapid and effective to a man's voice as to a woman's. Another study (DeCasper & Fifer, 1980) found that infants who had had no more than 12 hours of postnatal contact with their mothers were able to discriminate between the voices of their mothers and other speakers, as indicated by the infants' displaying more sucking behavior to produce their mother's voices. By demonstrating such remarkable early learning, this study and others dramatically illustrate the importance of environmental stimuli for attachment between infant and adult. We have every reason to believe that a newborn infant would learn to respond to the voice and face of its father (or another adult), as well as its mother, if this other person were present and interacting with the child during the early days of its life.

Whether women do intensive mothering because they have been psychologically prepared since infancy or because this choice is most socially acceptable and reinforcing, maternal behaviors by girls and women become strengthened through practice, whereas boys and men are typically deprived of the opportunity to acquire them. The differential responsibilities of women and men for the care of children results in the heightening of empathy, sensitivity, and interpersonal concerns in women and the strengthening of assertiveness, public achievement, and risk-taking behaviors in men. Thus, asymmetrical parenting perpetuates differential strengths as well as "gender-related insufficiencies" (Baumrind, 1980) in both women and men.

Consequences of Child-Care Asymmetry

Our present child-care system, which gives women primary responsibility for child rearing, has a number of interrelated consequences of enormous significance—for women, for men, and for children. What children learn in such a society can be summarized as follows: they become overattached to their mothers and overinvested in her reactions and attention; they learn the cultural definition of sex roles by observing firsthand what their mothers and fathers do within the family and outside of it; and they learn ambivalence toward women, who become associated at an early age with both intense pleasure and intense anger as the child's needs are satisfied or frustrated by the mother's actions. Dorothy Dinnerstein (1977) has emphasized this last consequence and has argued that the fact

that children's earliest experiences are almost always with a woman has far-reaching and important consequences for the personality development of both genders and for their relationship with one another.

The consequences for men are equally serious and wide in scope. By not doing the work of primary parenting, and not being expected or encouraged to behave appropriately in child-care situations, men lose the opportunity to practice and to learn behavior that is nurturant, sympathetic, patient, and cooperative. Opportunities to do maternal work strengthens those attributes and behaviors associated with it. Being denied the chance to do such work hurts fathers, as Paula Caplan (1986) has noted, because then "we expect too little warmth, humanity and involvement from them, assuming these to be somehow 'unnatural' in men" (p. 70). And, as noted further by Letty Pogrebin (1990), "we raise boys to be men but not fathers, and . . . raise girls to let men get away with it" (p. 19).

As for women, their role as the primary caregiver has the effect of narrowing and restricting the social environments of mothers; encouraging women to be perceived and reacted to as doers of tasks and servicers of children and men; reinforcing women for a preoccupation with, and focus on, personal relationships; reinforcing women for giving primary attention to private, domestic, and interpersonal issues rather than public and institutional ones; and ensuring that women's economic potential and access to resources (power) will always lag behind that of male partners because family will take precedence over job, or will be expected to by employers and community. Two major consequences for women that we will examine in detail separately are the tendency to hold mothers accountable for family failures (that is, to blame mothers for just about everything), and the greater risk of poverty for women than for men.

Many full-time mothers, although eager to do the right thing and to excel in their role, may also feel that their lives are not as exciting, not as interesting, not as challenging or as pleasant as they had anticipated. They may feel dissatisfied when they compare how they spend their days as mothers with how they used to spend them and with how their husbands, and women who are not mothers, spend theirs. If full-time mothers have personal objectives in addition to motherhood, the likelihood of achieving them becomes more remote and the barriers become more formidable as the months at home with small children accumulate.

Women who combine motherhood with a full-time job or career may also become disillusioned with their role as primary parent and distressed by the definition of that role as selfless devotion and service. One study (Feldman & Nash, 1984) investigated the impact of a firstborn child on a sample of educated, middle-class parents and found that the firstborn child brought more changes into the lives of mothers than fathers. It is not the fact of motherhood that is inevitably stressful but its contemporary definition in our society. For example, when a sample of television commercials was analyzed for the way they presented women (Mamay & Simpson, 1981), it was found that motherhood was equated with service. The investigators concluded that

> children appear to exist primarily to be fed and doctored, get their clothes muddy, and dirty up the house. There is little indication of parent-child interaction except in mothers' services to small children. . . . Mothers do not impart moral values to their children; they give them things to consume and expect nothing in return. . . . [Children's] mothers keep them healthy and supply their material wants. It is a one-way obligation. (pp. 1230, 1231)

The "Cathy" cartoon below illustrates this view of a mother's role.

Motherhood, which most often begins with eager anticipation and determination, may become burdensome in a society that simultaneously offers women educational and occupational options and regards women as primarily responsible for the psychological and physical welfare of their children, regardless of whatever else the women may also do. It is no wonder that a number of recent investigations of large national samples have reported greater well-being on the part of women whose children are grown and no longer at home than among mothers of young children (e.g., Gerson, Alpert, & Richardson, 1984). We will return to this issue in the chapter on mental health.

The diverse expectations we have for mothers and fathers in our society provides the basis for much humor. In a newspaper column designed to make us chuckle (Fleming, 1992), we are told "how kids distinguish moms from dads." Among other things, moms remind kids to wear a hat and to make their beds, and dads don't; dads don't hassle kids about brushing their hair, unlike moms, and dads let kids eat lunch on the floor in front of the TV—moms, of course, do not!

It is through maternal work—that is, caring for others—that mothers are said to develop a distinctive perspective. This thesis was elaborated by Sara Ruddick (1989) who has suggested that maternal thinking, an outcome of doing maternal tasks, has a special quality characterized by concern for others, cooperative solutions, and healing rather than harm-doing. As pointed out by Ruddick and other feminist writers, anyone who does maternal work can learn its lessons, and this work can be done by men as well as by women. According to Ruddick, a "mother" (who does not have to be a woman) is "someone who responds to the three main demands of preservation, growth, and social acceptability" (p. 51).

In a society in which women are the primary caregivers of children, it is women who will experience both the positive and negative consequences of doing maternal

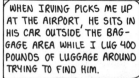

CATHY. Copyright 1986, Universal Press Syndicate. Reprinted with permission. All rights reserved.

work. Such a society must arrange conditions so that girls are socialized to want to do the work associated with motherhood and to do the job well. Girls must learn attitudes and motives congenial to the maternal role and antagonistic to other roles. For women to continue in the role of primary child rearer, women must learn to want to do this, to expect to do this, and that such work defines womanhood more than public achievement does. Thus, the familial division of labor is reproduced because girls acquire appropriate attributes for motherhood and boys do not. The reader may recall a study cited in Chapter 1 (Coltrane, 1992), of 93 small, preindustrial societies, which found that when men did little child rearing, the culture was more likely to include displays of manliness, an ideology of women's inferiority, women's deference to men, and husband's domination of wives, characteristics that were less likely in cultures in which men played a larger role in caring for children.

Women do intensive mothering because they have been psychologically prepared for it since childhood and because this choice is most socially acceptable and reinforcing, with the result that certain behaviors like interpersonal sensitivity become strengthened through practice, whereas boys and men get to practice other behaviors like assertiveness and risk-taking. We know, of course, that not all mothers are nurturant and peace-loving and, as we have already seen in earlier chapters, girls learn to perform a far greater range of behaviors than those related to preparation for motherhood. Adult women, too, continue to learn and display all human qualities in appropriate situations.

Blame and Guilt

While our literature provides us with images of mothers who work miracles, who feed, clothe, protect, and adore their children (the "real" mothers), it also shows us the witches, the mean, cruel, unfeeling, ever-demanding, and cold women (the "stepmothers" into whose evil hands children may fall). A mother's power is double-edged; she can give or withhold. We see mothers in supermarkets scowling at their children, pushing, slapping, and shouting, and we shiver as we recall the evil witches in all the fairy tales of our childhood.

Mary McLaughlin (1974) has described changes in western views of the "good mother." During the middle ages she was pious and responsible for the spiritual as well as the physical well-being of her children. Later, she came to be seen as tender, gentle, and noble as well. Yet mothers have little power in our society. They are important figures primarily in the eyes of their children, over whose resources and desired outcomes they have control. A mother provides positive or negative sanctions for her children's behavior; she can indulge, satisfy, support, frighten, threaten, or tyrannize her child.

Despite our expectations for caring, nurturant mothers, we have grown accustomed to seeing contemporary mothers satirized as controllers and dominators, as destructive wielders of power and destroyers of children's psyches; women respond to this image more typically with guilt than with anger. Even women-friendly cartoonists like Cathy Guisewite can't resist using mothers as easy and laughable scapegoats, as the cartoons below and on p. 228 illustrate. Lynn Caine, in a book entitled *What Did*

I Do Wrong? (1985), has argued that guilt and self-blame are occupational hazards of motherhood, that mothers tend to accept responsibility for anything that happens to their children, and that most mothers have self-denouncing tapes playing continuously in their heads. In a society in which mothers are given the primary responsibility for their children's welfare, such feelings are hard to avoid; so much of what happens in the child's life is seen to be the mother's responsibility and under her control. She is accountable daily for providing good food, clean clothes, concern, love, advice, safety, permission, and answers. She is accountable for how her children turn out in the long run, but she is more likely to be blamed for failure than praised for success.

In a novel by Nancy Hayfield (1980), a young mother is remembering newspaper stories of child accidents:

> they always make it a point to tell you in those stories what the mother was doing wrong—she just ran to the store for a pack of cigarettes—she just dozed off for a minute—she was talking on the phone when the kid, who was jumping on the bed, flew out of the tenth-story window. (p. 29)

A mother, who was also a psychotherapist, in Judith Rossner's *August* (1983) had received a similar message from her husband, who

> made it clear in a variety of ways that he considered Lulu responsible for her daughter's defection. This . . . [was the] justice under which mothers are held responsible for everything from life's random negative quality to the

genesis of every neurosis developed by those passing through it. (pp. 126f.)

The pressure on women who work outside the home to put their children first is especially strong, since when things go wrong it can be said, "Aha! Look what happens when there's no mother at home." A mother who works outside her own home, who pursues career or other interests, may be accused of neglecting her children—an accusation not likely to be leveled against a working father. Women who must work to support a family face less disapproval, but if we work because we want to use our talents or to feel the pleasure of achievement in areas outside the home, then we may be said to be selfish and more concerned with personal development than with the welfare of our children. Such attitudes, verified by social scientists, may be illustrated by a brief newspaper report ("Working Moms," 1992). The popular film hero Arnold Schwarzenegger (himself married to a working wife) is quoted as blaming the physical unfitness of slouching couch potato children on "women's equal rights. Women go out and get jobs and the husband has a job. . . . Where does this leave the children? When they come home they sit down in front of the TV set" (p. B-2).

But mothers who stay home and devote maximum time and energy to motherhood are not immune from criticism, and have been accused of smothering their children with too much attention, of crippling their initiative and prolonging their dependency. We are said to overfeed, overcontrol, overmotivate, and overwhelm. And so we mothers blame ourselves for not having done enough (or

for having done too much), for not having done the right thing (or for having overdone the right thing), for having shouted too much (or too little), for having expected too much (or not enough). Our guilt is amply reinforced by the mass media, fiction, and the mental health profession. Mothers have been blamed for their children's overstriving or underachievement, schizophrenia, school problems, suicide, drug and alcohol problems, and abuse by others.

One study of 125 articles in mental health journals published between 1970 and 1982 found that mothers were held responsible for 72 different kinds of psychological disorders in their children (Caplan, 1986). The conclusion that mother blaming remains a dominant theme in clinical psychological and psychiatric literature and practice is reinforced by others' analyses as well. Jamie Holten (1990), for example, pointed out that "the literature of family therapy is laced with both overt and covert assumptions regarding the role of mothers in the development of family dysfunction" (p. 54). A good illustration is an article in *Newsweek* on psychiatric interventions for infants and preschool children (Gelman, 1990). Only mothers are pictured in the three parent–child photographs used to illustrate the story. Even some feminist writing slips too easily into mother blaming. In reviewing a 1991 book edited by Gilligan, Rogers, and Tolman, "Women, girls, and psychotherapy," Susan Contratto (1992) noted that one dominant theme is that "women are responsible for the development of their daughters and almost always fail (virtually every clinical example is mother blaming)" (p. 544).

Gilliam Michell (1988), in commenting on the anti-mother bias in the mental health literature, noted that discussions of the negative consequences of bad parenting for children have focused almost exclusively

> on the details of the mother's behaviour . . . disregard[ing] . . . other aspects of either the child's or the mother's environment: it is as if mothering took place in a vacuum, unaffected by anyone or anything else. Two important omissions are: (1) the father/husband figure; and (2) the context of the mothering—or parenting—experience. (p. 39)

Thus, we can immediately identify with the humor in a "Doonesbury" cartoon, shown above, in which someone is interrupted while telling his therapy group from his car phone about how his mother hated him.

Middle-class mothers tend to blame themselves for psychological mistakes, for not having been better, calmer, or wiser, more permissive or less permissive. Working-class mothers blame themselves, in addition, because they could not do enough, provide enough in the way of resources, money, and opportunities, or because they were too tired or overburdened to pay attention to all of their children's needs. Mother, as Great Goddess, giver of life, seems thus to blend well with Pandora, on whom can be blamed all the hopes that are unfulfilled, the calamities, misfortunes, and problems of her children. Astoundingly, men, like Adam, have managed to retain their purity. Only rarely is some feeble voice heard asking, "But where was the father? What was he doing? What part did he play?"

Mothers may accept the reality of their imperfections but fear that their children will not. A mother in a novel by Louise Erdrich (1987) says,

I learned the lesson parents do early on. You fail sometimes. No matter how much you love your children, there are times you slip. There are moments you stutter, can't give, lose your temper, or simply lose face with the world, and you can't explain this to a child. (p. 236)

Of course, mothers do not only experience guilt and sorrow over their own and their children's difficulties, but also pride and joy in their affection and accomplishments. A mother is rewarded by the respect of her children, friends, and neighbors. The existence of children validates a working-class woman's importance and respectability; the successful rearing of her children is dramatic testimony to the world that she has done well. She wants above all else, as my mother did, for her children to grow up to be respectable, self-supporting, and happy, and she hopes that her love will be reciprocated and that her children will value her. Middle-class mothers may expect something more, some tangible sign of achievement or success.

Some ethnic groups, such as Italian-Americans and African-Americans, have ritualized and elaborated respect and idolization for mothers. Gloria Joseph (1981a) has described "Mother's Day on the Block" in African-American communities as "bigger than Easter, and more of a religious rite than Christmas" (p. 86), and has told how an escalating series of insults is exchanged by African-American urban youth when someone's mother is spoken of disparagingly. But Joseph has also cautioned that although the African-American mother is exalted publicly, in private she may be "used, bruised, and abused"; the "ritualization of motherhood as precious . . . has its roots in African tradition and is a part of Black culture," but all is not "love, honor, respect, and appreciation" on the part of one's children (p. 92).

Poverty in Families Headed by Women

Along with the probability that mothers will be blamed for their children's missteps in a society that gives them primary responsibility for childrearing, another major consequence of asymmetrical parenting is the great risk of poverty for families headed by women. The number of such families has grown enormously during the past two decades (Pearce, 1993).

In 1986, 60.1 percent of African-American families and 20.8 percent of European-American families with children present were single-parent families compared with 35.7 percent and 10.1 percent, respectively, in 1970 ("More One-Parent," 1986). The vast majority of such families (90 percent) are headed by women. While families headed by

23.2% of all American Families with Children Are Headed by Single Mothers.
Of these:

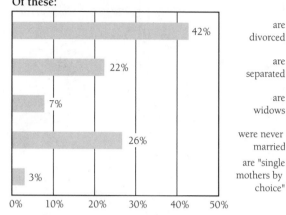

FIGURE 10.1 *Who are the single mothers?* Based on "Mothers Alone: Strategies for a Time of Change," by Sheila B. Kammerman and Alfred J. Kahn, Columbia University School of Social Work

women represent approximately 23 percent of all families in the United States, they constitute 55 percent of all poor families.

> Over one-third of female-headed families live below the poverty level and many more live marginally close to the poverty level. In fact, in 1985 approximately one-half of all families headed by women were poor or near poor. (Arendell, 1988, p. 121)

A congressional report indicated that 25 percent of all children in this country now live in single-parent families ("Report Says," 1990) and, as pointed out by Mary Jo Bane and David Ellwood (1989), the "poverty rates for children in single-parent homes have averaged roughly 50% since 1965 with very limited changes." Figure 10.1 shows how single-mother families get to be that way.

To get some sense of what poverty means in dollar terms, the federal poverty index in 1991 was an annual income of $11,140 for a family of three (cf. CAPLine, 1991), and $13,924 for a family of four ("The Children of the Shadows," 1993). Federal guidelines, which have remained virtually unchanged since the mid-1960s, are based on calculating how much a family needs "to maintain a minimally adequate diet" and then multiplying that figure by three, since low-income families are assumed to spend one third of their income on food (Bane & Ellwood, 1989). To understand the full meaning of a poverty level, one should contrast it with average family income. In 1987, for example, when the poverty index for a family of four was $12,000, the median income for such a family was $36,800!

By the end of the 1980s, according to a report by the Center for the Study of Social Policy, "just over 24 percent of all infants were born to mothers who had no prenatal care, 20 percent of all children lived in poverty and 19.5 percent were not covered by health insurance" (cf. "Children's Lives," 1991). Another study found that 12.8 percent of all children under age 12 in this country are hungry (cf. "Study: 1 in 8," 1991). The worst off economically among low-income groups are Hispanic-Americans; in 1989 33 percent of Latino children were poor ("Hispanic Children," 1991).

An important index of poverty, used by international agencies, is the infant mortality rate—infant deaths within the first year of life, a figure influenced by the mother's prenatal care, the infant's birth weight, available health care, nutrition, and so on. Federal statistics for 1990 indicated that our national infant mortality rate was 9.2 deaths per 1,000 live births. Although this is a better figure than that reported in the mid-1980s, it is not as low as that in other countries. In 1988, for example, when the infant mortality rate in the United States was 10 deaths per 1,000 live births, it was 5 in Japan, 6 in Finland and Sweden, and between 7 and 9 in Austria, Australia, Belgium, Canada, Denmark, France, German Federal Republic, Hong Kong, Ireland, Netherlands, Norway, Singapore, Spain, Switzerland, and the United Kingdom (The World Bank, 1990). In the United States, there is great disparity among the states, the rates ranging from a low of 6.2 in Maine to a high of 20.7 in the District of Columbia ("D.C. Rates Highest," 1993). The meaning of these numbers becomes clearer when we know that international agencies such as UNICEF and WHO use the infant mortality rate as a measure of the existence of hunger, since "three out of four who die of hunger [anywhere in the world] are children" (The Hunger Project, 1985, p. 384).

Single mothers and their children constitute two thirds of all persons defined as poor by the federal government and are the fastest growing segment of poor in this country; the "feminization of poverty" has become one of the catchiest new phrases in the social science lexicon. Research shows that women's poverty stems from two major causes: the fact that women bear the primary responsibility for rearing children (and are typically left rearing them alone after separation or divorce, with little or no financial assistance); and the fact that women's occupations are limited primarily to low-paying jobs with

little or no upward mobility. As argued by a major contributor to this literature, sociologist Diana Pearce (1993),

the two sets of factors that make women's poverty distinctive—the economic burden of children and women's disadvantaged labor-market status—are only analytically separable. When a woman's wages are inadequate, she cannot pay rent on housing that is large enough for her and her child(ren). When child and other income support is lacking, women are forced into jobs, but the cost and availability of child care often limit her occupational choices and work hours. . . . There are almost no programs or policies that provide after-school care. . . . This makes it difficult for women to take full-time, better-paying jobs. Welfare programs, in addition to stigmatizing the recipients, offer little access to training or education beyond basic literacy; furthermore, they hurry women into employment, no matter how low the wages or how poor the future prospects, thus continuing the cycle of poverty. (p. 90)

It can be seen from the chart on p. 230 that most single mothers have been married (71 percent), but are divorced, separated, or widowed. Among single mothers whose families are living in poverty, fewer than a third have never been married. To understand the poverty of African-American women, according to Rose Brewer (1988),

requires a hard look at political and economic changes in urban inner cities, in rural southern towns, and in the marginalization of black men and women from the labor market. . . . [W]omen generally are segregated in low paying, secondary jobs, but black women are highly concentrated in the lowest paying and lowest status women's work, from nurse's aid to private household worker. (p. 335).

Reductions during the 1980s in federal spending for human services have directly affected women and worsened conditions for the poor. These reductions have been in funding for food stamps, legal aid, energy supplements, Medicaid, nutritional supplements for mothers and infants, and Aid to Families with Dependent Children (AFDC). AFDC welfare benefits vary widely from state to state, with Mississippi and Alabama paying the least and Alaska and Hawaii the most. These variations are shown in Table 10.1, from which the reader can also see that AFDC grants have *decreased* nationally by an average of 27 percent between 1972 and 1991. One can also see that not a single state provided welfare benefits that reached the 1991 poverty level of $13,924. It is also of considerable interest that, in contrast to the myths often heard as political propaganda, the average number of

TABLE 10.1 *The welfare pinch*

Changes in state welfare grants over two decades. Figures combine Aid to Families with Dependent Children and food stamps. Amounts are in 1991 dollars.

	1972	1991	Percent change
National average	$10,169	$ 7,471	−27%
The 16 states that pay the most			
Alaska	$16,489	$13,114	−21%
Hawaii	14,539	12,089	−17
California	11,752	9,906	−16
Connecticut	12,419	9,788	−21
Vermont	12,074	9,730	−19
New York	13,882	9,114	−34
Rhode Island	11,637	8,791	−24
Washington	11,959	8,738	−27
Massachusetts	11,959	8,604	−28
Minnesota	12,005	8,545	−29
Wisconsin	12,666	8,419	−34
New Hampshire	11,499	8,411	−27
Oregon	12,568	8,365	−33
Maine	9,498	7,882	−17
Kansas	12,028	7,805	−35
New Jersey	11,545	7,728	−33
The 5 states that pay the least			
Mississippi	$ 5,172	$ 4,764	−8%
Alabama	6,899	4,812	−31
Texas	7,083	5,532	−22
Tennessee	7,060	5,543	−21
Louisiana	7,359	5,604	−24

House Ways and Means Committee.

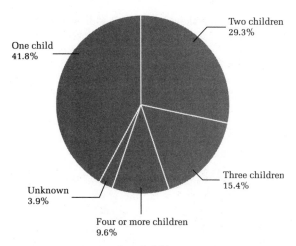

FIGURE 10.2 *Number of children in welfare families. Figures are from fiscal year 1991.* (Department of Health and Human Services. From Jason De Parle; "Why marginal changes don't rescue the welfare system," *New York Times*, March 1, 1992, p. E-30).

children in welfare families is small, as can be seen in Figure 10.2. One or two child families constitute 71.1 percent of all families receiving AFDC assistance.

Poignant and detailed descriptions of the daily lives of poor mothers such as that in Carolyn Chute's (1985) *The Beans of Egypt, Maine* give life to the statistics supplied by economists and help us to understand the experiences of single mothers living in poverty. If you are poor, you experience crowding. Whether in an urban ghetto or a rural shack, you have little chance of having privacy, or maintaining a separate space. You live in substandard, deteriorating housing, surrounded by peeling paint, decay, rodents, insects, crumbling walls, the odor of garbage and urine, leaking pipes, inadequate water, inadequate heat, and poor lighting. Your home is dreary and unlike the sparkling clean "house beautiful" seen on TV. You eat a poor-quality diet of low nutritional value that affects your health and decreases your energy level. You are likely to be overweight and dressed in clothes that do not match the glowing, slender, well-groomed image of women in the media. You are constantly searching for bargains and haunting the flea markets and thrift stores, not out of chic but necessity. You have inadequate access to private and public resources—to police protection, political power, education, and to networks leading to jobs. You provide a body "on which physicians train, research and practice" in hospital clinics for the poor, testing out their newest chemical, procedural, and medical technologies (Hurst & Zambrana, 1980). You shop in smaller stores to which you can walk and that give you credit but sell you older and damaged food at higher prices. You make frequent moves due to fires, raised rent, eviction, or a constant search for something better, cheaper, cleaner, safer. Or your housing is condemned as unsafe and torn down for renewal and profit by those who buy the land and gentrify the community.

Clearly, for women with few personal or community resources, motherhood does not provide the optimum conditions for nurturant, effective behavior. If you are poor, you are more likely to have been sexually assaulted; be without a spouse; marry a low-earning man and marry earlier; be in poor health; have had an abortion; have had a child without being married; be less well educated; have children suffering from all varieties of disease, more often, with greater severity and chance of complications; be widowed at an early age; and to be insulted and humiliated by representatives of society's public institutions (the schools, social service agencies, and the justice system). You are more likely not to be in a stable heterosexual relationship, and to be doing endless chores and leading a burdensome, monotonous, and physically tiring life. If you are poor, you are more likely to give birth to a low-weight infant who is at greater risk for infant mortality; to receive inadequate prenatal care; to experience dysfunctions during pregnancy and in giving birth; and to bear and rear more children. If you are poor, you are constantly saying "no" to your children. You are called in by teachers who tell you that your children are slow, dirty, undisciplined, unruly, absent too often, or sick. And your children are more likely to be assaulted, victimized, murdered, arrested, unemployed, addicted, school drop-outs, or social failures. That more than one out of five children in the United States was growing up in such circumstances in 1991 ("The Children of the Shadows," 1993) is a sobering thought. A nationwide 6-year investigation of 7,200 families by Greg Duncan and his colleagues recently reported that family income is more strongly related to a child's tested intelligence at age 5 than all other variables studied (cf. "Poverty Scars Kids," 1993).

Toward Shared Parenting

Some feminists believe that asymmetrical parenting is the single most important obstacle to gender equality and is closely tied to inequalities in all other spheres of social and personal life. More equal involvement by fathers or other caring adults, more high-quality community resources, and a national and social commitment to shared parenting are necessary to reduce the negative consequences of asymmetrical child-care and achieve the benefits of greater parenting involvement beyond the mother.

An increasing number of contemporary fathers are eager to experience child rearing on an equal basis with the mothers of their children and are learning, like the Arapesh described earlier, to find the care of little children "congenial." Letty Pogrebin (1982a) has commented on the discovery by men of the "joys of fatherhood," and suggested that "fathering is becoming a new kind of verb—an active verb—that describes a new kind of role and a new set of behaviors" (p. 43). Play groups for dads have been established (Korpivaara, 1982); workshops are being held for fathers to improve their skills as co-parents or single parents; more divorced fathers are winning custody of their children either alone or jointly with their ex-wives; and some corporations permit paternity leaves for men. In most states, mothers no longer have an automatically greater claim than fathers to the legal custody of their children, and in cases of contested custody fathers are now almost as likely to win as mothers. In some circumstances fathers are even more likely to win, if not necessarily for positive reasons (Chesler, 1985). Citing Bureau of Census figures, Dennis Meredith (1985) pointed out that by the mid-1980s, there were

> some 893,000 fathers heading single-parent families . . . , rearing more than one million children. These fathers are discovering what single mothers have long known: that rearing children alone while trying to make a living is inevitably hard work. . . . But most importantly, they are discovering that they can manage a household successfully, nurture their children and derive immense satisfaction from watching them develop into successful adults. (p. 60)

Fathering is now a subject of concern to young adults planning marriage and families, and an issue considered and examined in research and in the mass media. Much of this research has been encouraged and motivated by feminist concerns and analyses. When Winifred Shepard (1980) asked a group of college students to report on their remembered interactions with their parents, she found more similarities than differences reported for mothers and fathers. Although mothers were seen to have had prime responsibility in areas that may be particularly important for a child's emotional life, differences between mother and father in behavior and influence were small. Shepard concluded that "in general the fathers in this sample were not distant authoritarians but concerned participants in activities involving their children" (p. 425); and both parents behaved similarly toward sons and daughters, suggesting "that, in principle, parents can be interchangeable" (p. 432).

Men who have assumed a sizable share of responsibility for the day-to-day rearing of their children have reported an increased respect for, and appreciation of, "maternal work," and that their experiences have expanded their sensitivities and human capacities. Kenneth Pritchford

(1978), for example, wrote about his equal involvement in the raising of his son and the mixed, largely uncomprehending reactions he received from other men. He admitted that it's been "rewarding *and* tiring . . . to be so deeply involved in the care and feeding of another miraculous human being" (p. 98). One of the most important consequences of his participation in child rearing is the effect he believes it has had on his son.

> One of the most touching things about him is that he "instinctively" loves to take care of younger children. . . . It's because his earliest memories include not solely his mother but, as far back and just as often, this grumpy lovable old shoe of a person who snored sometimes when cuddling his baby asleep. It's what a Real Man does. Like his father . . . I know . . . a child's crying will pierce his sleep as much as mine. Inherent? Instinctual? On the contrary, it's something that men can do in learning the work of love. (p. 99)

And Robert Miner (1980) has written very similarly about his experience as a single parent to two preschool children.

> [L]ike most mothers I . . . think it was . . . far and away the most important experience I'd had in my life. I learned how to love, and I learned how to be emotionally available to others. I also learned that most of us men have little to congratulate ourselves for on Father's Day. (p. 6)

Grace Baruch and Rosalind Barnett (1986) found from an interview study of a sample of European-American middle-class parents that fathers who participated more in parenting felt more involved and competent than men who participated less, and recognized both "the problems as well as the pleasures" of daily involvement with children. Congruent findings have come from an important study by Barbara Risman (1987) that compared 55 single fathers with 73 single mothers and 155 dual parent pairs, all matched on age of youngest child, on a variety of self-report measures. She found similarities between women and men who had primary responsibility for their children. The most important predictor of responsibility for housework and reported affection between parent and child was not gender but parental role, and "parental role was the only variable directly related to reports of parent-child intimacy" (p. 25).

One interesting consequence of our contemporary "discovery" and growing acceptance of fathers as active co-parents or primary caregivers is their treatment by the mass media as somehow heroic or extraordinary in this role—a treatment, of course, not given to mothers. The "Doonesbury" cartoon below helps us laugh at this discrepancy. Popular films like *Kramer vs. Kramer* and *Author, Author* have poignantly portrayed men as better parents, once they put their minds to it, than their wives. Having discovered that a man can be a caring, sensitive parent, the media occasionally now present his role as superordinate. For example, a story headlined "'F' Is for Infants Favor Fathers' Favors" (1982) reported a pediatrician's findings that not only is "the father's role in infancy . . . more important than previously thought," but, in addition, "a father's physical play elicits more response from infants than a mother's soothing manner does"! Similarly, another news story reporting on a study that found babies to prefer playing with their fathers

because mothers are overburdened with chores was headlined "Fathers Are More Fun" (1986).

Community resources like day-care centers or nurseries can encourage shared parenting but are still viewed primarily as aids for mothers. Although public day-care facilities for children are important, they are not the only solution. If adults worked shorter or more flexible hours, and if child-care leaves were considered as necessary as sick leave and vacation time, then fathers and mothers might both be able to contribute equally to the rearing of their children, with minimum dependence upon other facilities during the first 1 or 2 years of their children's lives. Until 1993, the United States was the only industrial nation without a federal policy on parental leave to enable working parents to take time off from their jobs for child care without fear of being fired. We will discuss this issue more fully in the chapter on women's achievement and employment.

Current efforts at shared parenting in our society are typically undertaken with few institutional supports, resulting often in resentful fathers and still overburdened mothers. Thus, for example, among a sample of European-American middle-class parents, higher levels of participation by fathers in family tasks had negative effects on the marital relationship (Baruch & Barnett, 1986). Similarly, Ann Crouter (1987), who compared fathers in dual-earner families with sole-earner fathers, found that the former spent more time caring for their children but reported greater unhappiness with their marriages. Another study of dual-earner families (Gilbert, 1985), undertaken over a 10-year period, found that 40 percent of the fathers contributed virtually nothing to the family's care and maintenance beyond financial resources, while the mother did it all and functioned as a "Superwoman." Another 30 percent of the men were "participant fathers" who helped with the parenting and were involved with their children, but wouldn't do any of the housework. A final 30 percent, labeled "Supermen" by Gilbert, were intimately involved in parenting and shared family responsibilities in and outside of their homes equally with their wives. Such fathers, Gilbert noted, like Superwomen mothers, were often torn between their responsibilities at home and at work. It is important to remember that the parent categories of "Supermom" and "Superpop" are far from equivalent, however. While the former "does it all," the latter simply shares parental and home chores with his wife!

Adrienne Rich (1976) has made an important theoretical distinction between motherhood as a *relationship* between a woman and a child, and motherhood as an *institution* that has been used to imprison women—to "ghettoize," degrade, and restrict. This analysis can be extended by noting that while motherhood as an institution has imprisoned women, it has also denied entry to men. While it has tended to incapacitate women in the pursuit of public achievement, it has incapacitated men in the expression of positive affect and sensitivity. If a society wishes to avoid such consequences, the care and responsibility of its children must not be restricted to adults of one gender.

Modern technology has made parenting and work force participation compatible and feasible. Flexible time schedules, for example, are used widely in several European countries. A suburban community in Maryland has moved six of its schools close to parents' work locations, near major employment centers and traffic routes. These "work place schools" are open from 7 A.M. to 6 P.M. and offer extra instruction in regular and special subjects, for a small weekly fee for each child (Wallace, 1985). Cooperative child care can be encouraged by designing housing that builds in such arrangements. As noted by Dolores Hayden (1984), "to recognize the desire of women and men to be both paid workers and parents is to search for a way to overcome the physical separation of paid jobs and parenting inherent in many urban settings" (p. 69). In the 1960s, a pioneering housing project that brought homes and jobs together for single parents was built in London. Interior corridors "doubled as playrooms, with carpeted floors and windows from each apartment looking in, so that a parent cooking could watch a child at play. Intercoms linked apartments, enabling parents to baby-sit for each other by turning on the intercom and listening for children crying" (Hayden, 1984, p. 70). Other variations are possible.

Although the data from social scientists in this country do not provide an optimistic picture of the results of shared parenting from the perspective of fathers who are also employed outside the home, and though the obstacles are great, shared parenting remains a necessary objective in order to avoid the negative consequences of asymmetrical parenting. The psychological separation of men from women—a major symptom of what Dorothy Dinnerstein (1977) has called the "human malaise"—can be prevented, she argues, only if parenthood is a shared enterprise from the very beginning.

When men start participating as deeply as women in the initiation of infants into the human estate, when both male and female parents come to carry for all of us the special meanings of early childhood, the trouble we have reconciling these meanings with personness will finally be faced. (p. 94)

Susan Suleiman (1988) has urged that one means to this end be "a system of excellent universally available day care that would . . . encourage all of us to think of motherhood and self-creation as complementary rather than as mutually exclusive categories in women's lives" (p. 41). Without such a system, she argues, mothers do not feel secure in straying from the path of primary responsibility for their children and in relinquishing "the stubborn belief that mother is the one who really counts" (p. 39). What is needed, she urges is a society committed to assisting women in the pursuit of full integrated lives containing work and family. Many other voices in social science have now been raised in support of a national program of high quality day care. For example, "shared child care across the boundaries of public and private, male and female, elder and young," Jane Attanucci (1989) has argued, "is not a threat to our future, but a failure to recognize our shared responsibility . . . undoubtedly is" (p. 601). Similarly, Sandra Scarr and her colleagues (Scarr, Phillips, & McCartney, 1990) have concluded that "child care is now as essential to family life as the automobile and the refrigerator" (p. 26), and Ed Zigler, an architect of the Head Start program, has called for a day-care program for 3- and 4-year olds to be run by the public schools (Trotter, 1987).

What must change if we are to have a high-quality system of day care in this country is the wages paid to day-care workers. The average annual income earned by the highest paid child-care center teacher is $15,488, a figure $4,000 lower than the annual income earned by women with high school diplomas and $2,500 lower than the annual earnings of people who look after zoo animals (Noble, 1993). This tells us something about the value our society places on children and on those who care for them. Information from a sample of day-care centers from five representative cities across the United States indicates that 98 percent of the workers are women, and about 33 percent are women of color.

Reviews of research on the effects of nonmaternal child care (Etaugh, 1980; Scarr, Phillips, & McCartney, 1990; Silverstein, 1991) have concluded that such care, if of good quality, does not adversely affect maternal attachment, intellectual development, or social-emotional behavior. What is important is the kind of care provided, not the caregiver's gender or biological relationship to the child. Not all child care provided outside the home is good, but the same is true of child care within homes, and by mothers. But good quality care in community centers has been found not to harm children and, in some cases, to be associated with accelerated cognitive and social development (cf. Moss, 1987; Scarr, Phillips, & McCartney, 1990).

If parenthood is shared by the adults responsible for a child's well-being, and if mothers, like fathers, are encouraged to pursue personal goals, work at meaningful paid jobs, and live full busy lives, children will not represent the only means of experiencing satisfaction with one's life. Fulfilled and liberated parents will continue, of course, to suffer anxieties, worries, disappointments, and frustrations, and experience elation, pride, satisfaction, and pleasure as their children grow, change, and lead autonomous lives. Typically, only women are expected to acquire the many responses that make up caring, but this is alterable and in the process of change. Committed parenting is maintained and strengthened by the rewards of society and by reinforcement from children and one's own assessment of how well one has done as a parent. The joys and agonies that inevitably accompany parenting can be shared by the adults who care.

◆ Discussion Questions

1. Discuss the consequences for women, men, and children of having women be the primary caregivers for children.

2. Find examples of common cultural images of mothers from popular magazines, TV shows, and movies.

3. List three dominant characteristics of *your own mother* and, separately, of *your own father* that immediately come to mind. Ask 10 friends to do the same.

4. Discuss the special issues faced by single mothers; by lesbian mothers; by low-income mothers.

5. What social and personal changes are necessary to achieve shared parenting? Is this a worthwhile goal?

CHAPTER 11

WORK OUTSIDE THE HOME:
INEQUITIES AND CHALLENGES

The major campaign [during World War II] conducted by OWI [Office of War Information] was the one to recruit women into the labor force. Thus . . . magazines published romances in which women who entered defense industries found fulfillment in performing important work for the nation. . . . Women [were shown obtaining] great satisfaction from employment . . . heightened . . . self-esteem . . . [and] developing into mature strong adults through meeting the challenge of long hours and hard physical labor.

MAUREEN HONEY (1983, pp. 677f.)

[W]omen have always worked. What has dramatically altered over the centuries has been the relationship between paid and unpaid labors. . . . Women's current values and visions regarding work reflect not only the changing large-scale economic realities, but also the limits of the outdated mythology that holds that women's only proper workplace is in the home or in caregiving. How individual women struggle to reconcile this prevailing, out-moded myth with present economic and cultural conditions in the U.S. informs the meaning of work today for women's lives.

PAULA RAYMAN (1990, p. 11)

A SOCIETY'S VIEWS OF GENDER CAN UNDERGO dramatic changes to accommodate varied circumstances and demands. An example is given in the quote that opens this chapter.

Maureen Honey (1983) found sharp differences in the ways employed married women were presented in government propaganda and in mass media fiction in the 1930s and 1940s. During World War II, when recruiting women workers into defense and other industries became essential, popular magazines carried stories about heroines "who successfully coped with both family and work responsibilities"; in the earlier fiction from the 1930s, on the other hand, employed married women had been depicted as "selfish and destructive to their families" (p. 678).

Between 1941 and 1945, approximately 6 million new women workers entered the work force. Rosie the Riveter became a national symbol of the wartime American woman—strong, capable, confident, and responsible. After the war, when men returned to the factories, farms, and offices, the media presented Rosie as graciously relinquishing her job, taking off her work clothes, and happily returning to the bedroom, to the kitchen, and to the older image of traditional femininity. Although 75 percent of the women interviewed in a 1944 Women's Bureau study said they wanted to keep their jobs after the war, 1 million were laid off when it ended, and another 2.25 million quit (Gregory, 1974).

WHO ARE TODAY'S WORKING WOMEN?

In this chapter we will describe the daughters and granddaughters of Rosie the Riveter—the women who work for wages or salaries. We will explore their motives and sources of satisfaction and frustration and discuss the many interrelated issues relevant to women's participation in the work force. Use of the term *working women* to designate those who are employed outside the home should in no way be interpreted as denigrating the work of full-time homemakers; as we know, however, work within one's own home is unpaid and is typically also done by women who are in the paid work force. A fuller discussion of homemaking was presented in the chapter on relationships.

Women's participation in the world of paid employment has steadily increased during the past three decades. In the United States, the percentage of all women in the labor force (holding jobs or actively seeking them) rose from 37 percent in 1960 to 60 percent in the late 1980s (cf. "Labor Department," 1990). By the end of the 1980s, the United States was second only to Scandinavia in its proportion of working women. Women are now 46 percent of the total work force, a figure expected to rise to 50 percent by the year 2000 (Noble, 1993a). Among the women in the labor force in 1988, 25 percent were single (never married), 12 percent were divorced, 4 percent were widowed, 4 percent were separated, and 14 percent were married to men earning less than $15,000 a year. Rates of participation in the labor force among African-American, Hispanic-American, and European-American women are almost equal (Rayman, 1990); and in two-parent families, 71 percent of mothers are employed outside the home (Hoffman, 1989). This figure was projected to reach 75 percent in the 1990s; "fewer than 7% of families now reflect the two-parent model of husband as breadwinner and wife as homemaker" (Silverstein, 1991, p. 1025).

Today, women workers can be found in virtually all areas of the economy, performing jobs at every level of skill, from blue-collar work to public service to business and industrial management, in technical, scientific, and professional fields. Although most women continue to be employed in a narrow range of jobs—an issue we will discuss later in this chapter—breakthroughs have occurred in just about every occupation typically associated with, and reserved for, men.

The range of paid jobs done by women is illustrated in Figure 11.1, which also shows the areas that have experienced the most dramatic changes since 1970. Women can now be found among the ranks of rock musicians leading their own groups, not just decorating all-male bands, and seemingly "unafraid to vent fury and flay guitars" and explore a wide range of emotions (Reynolds, 1992). Women are in every branch of the armed forces, comprise 10 percent of all persons on active duty (Hoff-Wilson, 1988), and, as of April 1993, have been given a role equal to men in flying combat missions. Among all servicewomen, African-American women constitute 30 percent and other women of color are 8 percent (Fuentes, 1991). Reflecting the role of women in today's work force are new media images. In both established women's magazines like *Redbook* and newer magazines like *New Woman*, the majority of articles about particular women's lives were found in one study to be about women employed full-time (Ruggiero & Weston, 1985).

Women are now a majority among "insurance adjustors, bill collectors, psychologists and assemblers" (Serrin, 1984), as well as bank tellers and real estate agents (Noble, 1985). By February 1986, more women than men were

Percentage of Jobs Filled by Women in Each Year	1970	1986
Managerial and professional specialty (such as administrators, financial managers,buyers)	33.9%	43.4%
Professional specialty (such as lawyers, teachers, writers)	44.3%	49.4%
Sales occupations	41.3%	48.2%
Administrative support, including clerical	73.2%	80.4%
Service occupations	60.4%	62.6%
Precision, production, craft and repair (such as mechanics)	7.3%	8.6%
Operators, fabricators, and laborers	25.9%	25.4%
Transportation and material moving occupations	4.1%	8.9%
Handlers, equipment cleaners, helpers, and laborers	17.4%	16.3%
Farming, forestry, and fishing	9.1%	15.9%

FIGURE 11.1 *The gains of working women: percentage of jobs filled by women in each year.* (U.S. Bureau of Labor Statistics.)

Bobbie Hammond riding the Kansas range she manages.
(Photograph by David Hutson/NYT Pictures.)

employed in the 50 occupations categorized by the U.S. Labor Department as professional, with the exception of executive, managerial, or administrative jobs ("Women Now Hold," 1986). Women can be found among working poets (Ostriker, 1986), orchestra conductors (Kozinn, 1985), narcotics agents (Gross, 1986), artists (Russell, 1983), scientists (Bruer, 1983), and jockeys (Duckworth, 1985); women are engaged in commercial fishing ("Life of Fishing," 1980) and in farming. Women make up 15 percent of all persons who receive compensation for work on farms, either through wages or profits from self-employment, and 1.4 percent of all employed women are farm workers; they are "in the fields, operating farm machinery and making farm decisions" (Pearson, 1980, p. 564). A woman who manages a 40-square mile range

in Kansas is shown on her horse in the photograph above. The largest proportion of farm women, however, can be found on small farms, doing all the chores necessary to keep them going. As noted by Mona Vold (1987), "sacrifice is part of the tradition of farming, especially for women" (p. 80).

More and more women are preparing for careers by attending college and earning advanced degrees. Women now account for more than 52 percent of all college students, a phenomenon partly due to the large increase in college attendance by women aged 25 to 44 returning to school to complete their educations. Women have made great progress in traditionally male-dominated areas, as illustrated by their increased share of science and engineering degrees, up from 7 percent in 1965 to 26 percent in 1983 ("Chartbook Shows," 1985), and their increased share of science and engineering doctorates, up from 13 percent in 1973 to 25 percent in 1983 (Walsh,

1984). In 1980, women earned 23 percent of the medical degrees, compared to 8.5 percent in 1970, and 12 percent of the dentistry degrees, compared to 1 percent in 1970 (Vetter, 1981). About one third of the students now entering medical school in the United States are women, and in 1990 almost 17 percent of all physicians were women (Joyce, 1993). As noted by Perri Klass, a physician and writer, patients are "no longer surprised or make a big deal" out of being treated by a woman (cf. Chavez, 1987). By 1983, women were 15.3 percent of all lawyers, 13.5 percent of law professors, 6 percent of judges, and 37.7 percent of law students (Briscoe, 1989); 9 percent of women lawyers were African-American (Simpson, 1984). Within science and engineering, the highest proportion of professional women are in the biological sciences, followed by the computer field, in which 25 percent of the software specialists are now women (Schmidt, 1985). Among African-Americans, more women than men earn doctoral degrees (Wyche & Graves, 1992).

The 1980s witnessed many occupational "firsts" for U.S. women. In June 1983, Sally Ride became the first woman astronaut. After her first mission, she talked about how the questions asked her by journalists had changed from the previous year ("Ride Claims," 1983).

> They started off primarily addressing questions to me about whether I would wear makeup, how my husband felt, privacy, whether I cried in the simulator. And now they seem very happy to ask me how the arm [of the space shuttle] worked. That's very gratifying.

In 1988, Julie Krone, a jockey, was the first woman to "ride fast horses for big money. . . . Although women have been jockeys for almost 20 years, and now make up an estimated 25 percent of all licensed riders, most race at smaller tracks on pokier poniers" (Vader, 1988, p. 28).

Evelyn Handler became the first woman president of a publicly supported land grant university, the University of New Hampshire, in 1980; in 1981, Sandra Day O'Connor became the first woman to be named to the Supreme Court, and Elizabeth Jones the first woman to be appointed as chief sculptor-engraver at the U.S. Mint. The first woman to head an elite U.S. law school is Barbara Black, appointed dean of Columbia Law School in 1986 ("Woman to Head," 1986); Eleanor Baum, dean of the Pratt Institute School of Engineering in Brooklyn, was the first woman in the United States to head a college of engineering (Teltsch, 1985). In December 1985, Wilma Mankiller was installed as the first woman chief of a major native American tribe, the Cherokee Nation of Oklahoma (Reinhold, 1985). In the 1980s, Dorothy Cousins in Philadelphia and Penny Harrington in Portland, Oregon,

became two of only a handful of women in this country to be named police chief of a large metropolitan area. Although the Episcopal Church and Reform and Reconstructionist Judaism began ordaining ministers and rabbis in the 1970s, it was in 1983 that women were first admitted to the rabbinical studies program in Conservative Judaism.

Jeannette Rankin from Montana was the first woman elected to the U.S. Congress, in 1916, and it was she who introduced legislation for women's suffrage 3 years later (she was also the only person to vote against U.S. entry into both world wars). In 1932, Hattie Caraway, from Arkansas, became the first woman to be elected to a full term in the Senate, but it was not until 1984 that a major political party nominated a woman, Geraldine Ferraro, for the high office of vice president. Of course, Congresswoman Ferraro did not win the 1984 election, but in that same year Arlene Violet of Rhode Island became the first woman ever to be elected a state attorney general. In 1992, 108 women ran for seats in the House of Representatives and 48 women won; 11 women competed for Senate seats that year and 4 won, bringing the total of women in the Senate to 6 ("Women Crack," 1992). These figures can be compared with those for 1970, when 12 women won House seats, out of 25 who ran, and no woman was elected to the Senate (only 1 woman ran). In 1992, the percentage of women in Congress doubled, from 5 percent to 10 percent, and the number of women of color increased from 6 to 14. Carol Moseley Braun of Illinois became the first African-American woman elected to the Senate. In the Clinton administration, there are women in the cabinet and in other significant high-level positions. Women were 17.1 percent of all mayors of cities with populations greater than 30,000, and 18.2 percent of all state legislators were women in 1991. The largest percentage of women state legislators (34.4 percent) was in Arizona, and the smallest (2.1 percent) was in Louisiana. In 1992, women held 20 percent of the elected executive offices in the states and constituted 20 percent of all state legislators ("Women Crack," 1992). We will return to a discussion of women in high places later in this chapter.

The early 1990s saw more women "firsts." For example, the Library of Congress named the nation's first woman poet laureate, Mona Van Duyn; 73-year-old Gertrude Belle Elion, a Nobel Prize winner in medicine, became the first woman to be voted into the Inventor's Hall of Fame ("Getting Ideas," 1991); and psychologist Judith Rodin was appointed provost at Yale University.

Women today occupy managerial and administrative posts in such varied fields as health administration,

A woman mining coal in Ohio. (Photograph by UPI/Bettmann.)

building supervision, general office management, finance, the food service industry, the movie industry, charter jet business, banking, marketing, philanthropic foundations, and consumer products. Women are still largely absent, however, from the heavy industry and manufacturing sectors and from the boardrooms of the largest and most prestigious companies, a subject to which we will return. It has been as difficult for women to enter the skilled trades as the executive suite, but women can now be found working as bricklayers, auto mechanics, construction workers, utility servicepersons, maintenance workers, and electricians. By the end of 1981, 8 years after women were first permitted to work in underground mines, there were almost 4,000 women coal miners across the country, out of a total of approximately 200,000 miners ("Superstition Crumbles," 1981). The photograph above shows a woman miner at work in Ohio, shoveling coal onto a

moving belt. Certain hard-hat opportunities have become more available to women than have others, as the following figures indicate: by the early 1980s women were 5.7 percent of construction and maintenance painters; 1.6 percent of electricians; .4 percent of plumbers and pipefitters (Kerr, 1982); 1.1 percent of construction workers; and 8 percent of precision production, craft, and repair workers (Kleiman, 1989a). In Rhode Island, 95 percent of all the flaggers assigned to construction sites in 1987 were women (Rakowsky, 1987). And some large industrial companies appear to be especially committed to hiring women as skilled workers. For example, the Ford Motor Company ad shown on p. 242 features a woman engine tester under the headline "Quality is Job 1."

Although some women can now be found in practically every occupation in the United States, women's numbers are still small in jobs traditionally done by men. In

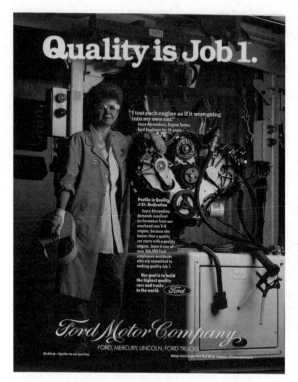

A Ford Motor Company ad features a woman engineer.
(Photograph courtesy of Ford Motor Company.)

addition, as we will see in later sections of this chapter, the average woman earns considerably less than the average man, receives fewer benefits, and works under poorer conditions. Women have been permitted entry into the world of paid employment, but the nature of that entry reveals an ambivalence. Women come into the work force largely through the rear door and from the end of the line—especially women who are poorly educated or who are non-European-American.

WHY DO WOMEN WORK?

Although women in the United States still typically learn that their primary roles have to do with the care of home and family, most spend many years contributing human capital to the nation's economy in the form of paid employment. Women work at jobs outside the home for the very same reasons that men do. Studies of varied samples of women (e.g., Andrisani, 1978; Astin, 1978; Beckman, 1978; Moore, 1985) have shown that full-time workers report wanting to obtain needed financial resources (money and goods); become independent; have greater control of their environment and future; contribute meaningfully to the needs of society; interact with other adults engaged in productive work; develop and use skills and talents; achieve recognition; experience growth, change, challenge, creativity, mental stimulation, and personal fulfillment; and gain self-definition and esteem.

Some studies have directly compared sources of job satisfaction among women with those reported by men. For example, Patricia Voydanoff (1980) found, among a national sample of persons over age 20 who were working for pay at least 20 hours per week, that for both women and men the variable correlating most highly with job satisfaction was opportunity for self-expression. Also important for both genders were financial rewards or promotion, working conditions, minimal role strain, and quality of supervision. The author concluded that, despite the significant gender difference in earnings, "men and women generally . . . require similar job characteristics to be satisfied with their jobs" (p. 185).

In all the occupations where both genders are found, women are found to be just as involved and committed to their jobs as men are and to report similar levels of job satisfaction under similar conditions of work. For example, among a sample of husband-and-wife motel managers for a national chain (Summers & DeCotiis, 1988), no gender differences appeared in reported satisfaction with work, work relationships, or company policies and procedures. A statistical review of 124 published studies on organizational commitment led to the conclusion that gender is unrelated to strength of identification with and time and energy devoted to one's employer (Mathieu & Zajac, 1990). Similarly, a statistical review of studies of gender differences in work stress (Martocchio & O'Leary, 1989) found no support for the belief that women and men differ in experienced occupational stress.

A common finding among studies of employed women—whether they are hard hats, white-collar workers, or professionals—is that their jobs provide needed financial resources, independence, and personal satisfaction. According to *9to5*, a national organization of working women, almost 60 percent either are the sole family wage earner or have husbands who earn less than $15,000 a year ("The 1989 *9to5*," 1989). Molly Martin, a maintenance electrician since 1983 and author of the book *Hard-Hatted Women*, noted that women go into the trades for the same reasons men do. We like to build things and see completed the product of our labor. We like to fix things, to work outside—and to make money. (Kleiman, 1989a, p. B-5)

Linda Brown (1979) concluded from a review of research on women and men in business management that both groups had the same job expectations and "like[d] solving problems, using their talents, and managing others" (p. 286). Among a sample of women coal miners, for example (Hammond & Mahoney, 1983), the most common response given to the question about what they liked most about their work was "good money" and the satisfaction that came from providing for their children; the miners also said that they enjoyed the interactions with other workers and the feeling of camaraderie on the job. Of the 25 women interviewed, 22 were the primary or sole providers for their families. The responses given to Gwyned Simpson (1984) by a group of African-American women lawyers were not too different from the responses of the women who worked in the coal mines; 47 percent listed independence, mobility, or money as reasons for choosing law as a career. A group of farming women interviewed by Jessica Pearson (1980) cited the following as the satisfactions they derived from their work: being outdoors, growing crops, "battling with the elements, contact with animals, and the independence of farm work . . . identical to the satisfactions of farming articulated by the men who were interviewed" (p. 566). Thus, women look for employment that pays well, is challenging, and provides opportunities for both social and intellectual stimulation in a positive environment. The human motives for activity and exploration are reflected in the desire to work. Women and men work for the same reasons, but their success in reaching their objectives and the rewards they are able to obtain differ considerably and significantly for the two genders.

OBSTACLES TO JOB SATISFACTION AND ACHIEVEMENT

Most employed women in this country are in narrow-option jobs in a small number of low-status fields that, for the most part, neither do justice to their education or skills nor provide the satisfactions and rewards generally sought for in employment.

Gender-Segregated Occupations

In 1988, women made up 80 percent of all administrative support clerical workers and 69 percent of all retail sales and personal service workers (Rayman, 1990). Among employed women, 40 percent are found in just 10 traditional women's occupations (Pearce, 1985). In the 1980s, for example, women constituted 99.1 percent of all secretaries, 95.6 percent of registered nurses, 98.5 percent of preschool and kindergarten teachers, 70.7 percent of all schoolteachers, and 70 percent of sales clerks; but women were only 1.4 percent of miners, 6 percent of engineers, 6.7 percent of police officers and detectives, 9 percent of architects, 14.6 percent of doctors and dentists, and 15.5 percent of lawyers ("Careers and Paychecks," 1984; "Change over a Decade," 1985; "Poll: Women," 1986). Although clear gains have been made in many fields, the largest number of employed women are still in "pink ghetto" occupations, which pay considerably less than the jobs usually done by men. Among all employed women, 75 to 80 percent still work in "support" jobs—that is, clerical, sales, and service, as can be seen in Figure 11.2.

Segregation of jobs by gender has far-reaching consequences. For example, in one study college students rated the general standing or prestige of a selected group of occupations; the study found that the prestige associated with an occupation reflected the gender of the typical incumbent and thus the "sex-segregated nature of the occupational world" (Jacobs & Powell, 1985, p. 1070). A report by the Carnegie Corporation noted that "among the 503 occupations listed in the 1980 United States Census, 275 were greater than 80 percent male or female" (cf. Noble, 1985, p. A-20); but "women's jobs" and "men's jobs" are not equal. "Women's jobs" are lower in status and lower in pay than "men's jobs," and are also found in fewer areas. Nine out of 10 women work in only 10 occupational categories (Rayman, 1990). Alice Ilchman (1986), who chaired a national committee that studied gender segregation in the workplace, concluded that although some previously "men's jobs" have now become "women's jobs" and vice versa, "overall, the amount of sex segregation in the U.S. workplace has been virtually stable since 1900" (p. A-11). Occupational segregation also contributes most directly to the disparity between women's and men's earnings, an issue we will consider more fully later. For example, the vast majority of home-care workers (who tend the homebound sick, disabled, and elderly) are women; in New York City, these workers are also primarily women of color. In 1991, their

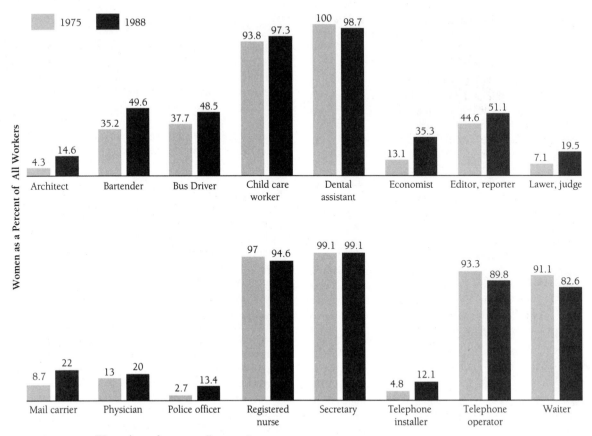

FIGURE 11.2 *Women's employment: collar it pink.* (U.S. Bureau of Labor Statistics.)

average yearly earnings for a 37-hour week were $11,500, well below the poverty line if they were the sole contributors to family income ("Full-Time Work," 1991).

Gender segregation in employment is reflected in the fact that the average woman's job tends to be unrelated to her level of education or background. One study (Scarr & McAvay, cited in Bridgwater, 1983) found that among a sample of unmarried adults in their mid-20s, men with impressive family backgrounds and academic records were the most likely to have high-status jobs, but such a relationship was not found for women: "women who did well in college were just as likely to go into relatively low-status and traditionally 'female' occupations such as public-school teaching or nursing as they were to pursue more socially prestigious professions" (p. 74).

Coinciding with the massive entry of women into the U.S. work force has been the rapid expansion of the service sector of the economy. By 1980 this sector contributed

nearly 55 percent of the gross national product; it is into this sector that women workers have been most welcomed (Smith, 1984). The service sector has the capacity to sustain high labor turnover and derives its profits from "low-wage, intermittent, and part-time work" (p. 292). More than 75 percent of the recent growth in financial, real estate, and insurance businesses and 60 percent of the growth of service-producing and retail food industries is attributed to the contribution of women's labor; but most of these women work primarily in low-salary occupations. According to Jennie Farley (1985), "about a third of all male workers produce goods (as opposed to services), while only 17 percent of female workers are in goods-producing industries" (p. 585). As noted previously, women are poorly represented among blue-collar workers, comprising only 4 percent (cf. Kleiman, 1989a).

According to Natalie Sokoloff (1987), "the twin growth of low-wage occupations and low-wage industries is the major source of employment growth for women, at least since World War II" (p. 16). Not only are most women workers in the service sector but, within this sector, more women than men are part-timers and do not work year round. The consequences of this for women, Sokoloff argues, are serious: they can be paid less (part-timers earn 29 percent less than full-timers); they are kept attached to domestic duties in their homes and dependent upon men; and their attachment to the labor force is tenuous. While gender segregation in occupations affects all women, interactions among gender, social class, and ethnicity result in differential effects, as pointed out by Evelyn Glenn (1987).

> Racial ethnic women perform the more menial, less desirable tasks. They prepare and serve food, clean rooms, and change bedpans, while white women, employed as semiprofessionals and white-collar workers, perform the more skilled and administrative tasks. The stratification is visible in hospitals where . . . the majority of health care aides and housekeeping staff are blacks and Latinas. (p. 72)

Gender segregation exists even within the same general job category. For example, women in the professional-technical category are more likely to be at the bottom of that rung, and women scientists are less likely than men to get jobs in prestigious educational institutions or in private industry, and more likely to advance at slower rates to managerial responsibility or higher academic rank. Thus, according to Peggy Schmidt (1985), "although a growing number of young women are studying the quantitatively based disciplines that prepare them for careers in science, engineering and computer science, their prospects for employment and advancement in industry and academia drag woefully behind those for men" (p. 14).

Regardless of occupation, if both women and men are represented, it is men who tend to have the more powerful, prestigious, and remunerative jobs—in the arts as well as in the professions, and in manufacturing as well as in the service sector. For example, while half the musicians in U.S. regional and metropolitan orchestras are women, the figure for large, major orchestras is only 26 percent, and less than that in 10 of the 12 largest orchestras. The New York Philharmonic did not hire its first regular woman member until 1966, and it did not assign a woman to a first-chair position until the early 1980s. In 1983, the orchestra had 18 women on its roster of regular members out of a total of 105 (Henahan, 1983). In medicine, gender segregation exists in the specialties

and in teaching and administration (Sherman & Rosenblatt, 1984). Few women physicians are found in some areas, such as surgery, and across all specialties women tend to be overrepresented in teaching and research and underrepresented in administration, with the most powerful and financially rewarded positions primarily occupied by men.

Discrimination in Earnings, Benefits, and Job Security

Employed women earn less than employed men, and Latina women earn the least of all. The wage gap has remained an economic reality, although it has begun to narrow as ever increasing numbers of women enter and remain in the labor force. In 1968, the average woman earned 58.5 cents for every dollar earned by the average man; in 1976, 60 cents; in 1986, 65.1 cents ("Wage Gap," 1989). This figure was reported by the U.S. Bureau of Labor Statistics to have been 75 cents in the first three quarters of 1992 (cf. "Decade of the Woman," 1992). The situation remains worse for women of color than for European-American women. "African-American women earn 61 cents and Latinas only 55 cents on a white man's dollar" (Colatosti, 1992, p. 1).

The wage gap reflects, first of all, the facts of job segregation, as discussed above. Women tend to be employed in occupations and industries, and at status levels, that pay less than those in which men are employed. But the gender difference in earnings reflects an additional economic fact: even when women and men are in the same occupational category, the men receive more money for comparable work. Data from all areas of employment continue to show evidence of this startling phenomenon, with only rare exceptions.

For every dollar earned by men, women in the same occupation earned 73 cents as a bookkeeper, 80 cents as a computer programmer, 76 cents as a cook, 75 cents as a lawyer, 61 cents as an office manager, and 80 cents as a social worker. A woman motor vehicle operator averages $307 a week while a man averages $408 (Colatosti, 1992). Similar gender differentials are found among engineers, physicians, and accountants (Schreiner, 1984), and a study of computer software specialists (cf. Schmidt, 1985) found that even though women in this field "earn more than do 98 percent of all working women . . . [they nevertheless] earn $9000 a year less than men do" (p. 15). According to comedian Diane Ford (cf. Leader, 1991), unequal pay for comparable work also exists in the world of comedy clubs. She told a reporter that she had sold out eight shows at an Atlanta club and still . . . was paid $2000 less than a man. . . . If a man and a woman share headline status, the woman frequently will get paid $100 less. . . . And if I complain about it, I don't work. (p. A-10)

The gender gap is also in evidence among the most highly paid people in the United States. For example, while Bryant Gumbel of the *Today* show made $2 million in 1991, his co-anchor, Jane Pauley—"who got up just as early"—earned only $750,000 (cf. Kleiman, 1991). While we might find Pauley's salary eminently desirable, the gender difference is perfectly clear and staggering. Another example comes from a poster that appeared in prominent places along Sunset Boulevard in Hollywood in response to Hollywood's "Year of the Woman" slogan. As reported by columnist Liz Smith (1993), the poster showed Al Pacino and Michelle Pfeiffer in a scene from their film "Frankie and Johnny," with their salaries printed over their heads—$6 million for him, and $3 million for her! MBA graduates are not in the same league, financially, as TV anchors or movie stars but do earn substantial sums. Here again, however, "men . . . outdistance women in salary and promotions" (Doyle, 1993, p. 1), as found in a study of 855 Stanford MBA recipients who earned their degrees between 1973 and 1985. Regardless of work hours, experience, job responsibilities, and other factors, single women's average annual salaries were 14 percent less than men's, while married women were paid 30 percent less than married men ($101,124 for women compared with $144,461 for men). These findings are similar to those reported by others. One study of business college graduates concluded that women were earning

> substantially less than the men even though they were all graduates from the same business schools, were all employed on a full-time basis, and were very much alike in terms of their work experience and socioeconomic origins. Moreover, they reported using similar strategies when attempting to influence their superiors and held positions in organizations of essentially the same size. (Dreher, Dougherty, & Whitely, 1989, p. 545)

In higher education, at all ranks from lecturer to full professor, and in all types of colleges and universities, men earn a greater annual salary than women, a phenomenon that has remained relatively unchanged over many years. The gap is greatest at the higher levels, so that women and men full professors' incomes are further apart than instructors'. Thus, for the 1991–1992 academic year, in all categories of higher education combined, the average salaries for male and female full professors, respectively, were $59,180 and $52,280, and the average salaries

earned by male and female instructors, respectively, were $28,220 and $26,390 ("Average Salary," 1992). At Harvard, during the 1992-1993 academic year, the average male full professor earned $93,600, compared to the average woman of the same rank who earned $79,900 (De Palma, 1993).

Among public school teachers, too, men earn on average $2000 more a year than women, and men superintendents earn almost $3000 more a year than women (Kleiman, 1983). A survey of lawyers in Massachusetts ("Survey: Women," 1990) revealed a $30,000 annual earnings differential between women and men, which was only partially accounted for by a greater number of years of experience on the part of the men.

A college education generally increases a person's earning power, but this is considerably more true for men than for women, as is clear in Figure 11.3. Among full-time working adults between 35 and 44 years old, the average man with only a high school diploma earns more than a woman with 4 years of college; this gap in favor of high school–educated men compared with college-educated women widens with age. Across ages, the average annual wage for a woman with a bachelor's degree or more education was, in 1992, $33,615 compared to a comparable man's earnings of $51,804. A woman with a high school diploma earned $19,309 compared to the $27,865 earned by a man with a high school diploma (Noble, 1993). At every educational level, European-American men earn the most, followed by African-American men, and then European-American women, followed by African-American women, and, in all age groups, as women and men get older, the difference in their earnings increases, as can be seen in Figure 11.3.

One group of researchers (Steel, Abeles, & Card, 1982) who studied a large national sample of women and men from high school through age 29 concluded that differences between the genders in pattern of adult roles explained very little of the significant sex differences in earnings. Similar conclusions have come from other data, from a national sample of more than 5,000 American families studied in depth since 1968 (Corcoran, Duncan, & Hill, 1984). All the variables examined—such as education, work experience, work continuity, self-imposed restrictions on work, and absenteeism—"explained only about one-third of the wage gap between white men and white women and only about one-quarter of the wage gap between white men and black women" (p. 239), strongly suggesting the existence of "institutionalized discrimination against women in the working world." The researchers found that men were favored over women in finding better jobs through old-boy networks. In obtaining

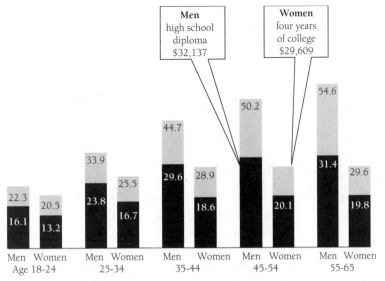

Men
high school
diploma
$32,137

Women
four years
of college
$29,609

Pay for full-time working
men and women, by age and education:

■ Earnings with four years of high school

▦ Earnings with four years of college

FIGURE 11.3 *Unequal pay for equal education* (from *Providence Journal Bulletin,* November 14, 1991, p. A-1. Based on Bureau of Census data).

positions with longer training periods and advancement opportunities, and most important, in obtaining jobs that gave them authority over others. A study with rather extraordinary implications of 140 persons who underwent medical sex changes found that "all of those who became men increased their earnings [while] all but two who changed from male to female experienced a loss in subsequent earnings" ("News from the United Nations," 1991, p. 11).

In addition to earning less for her labor than her male counterparts, an employed woman may find that her employer reacts negatively to her request for maternity leave, that she is without a pension after years in the work force, or that she is among the first to lose her job during slow periods in the economy. A law passed by Congress in 1978, the Pregnancy Discrimination Act, specified that a pregnant woman is entitled to temporary disability benefits for pregnancy, childbirth, and related medical conditions if her employer provides disability benefits to other workers. However, the law did not require an employer to guarantee that the woman's job would still be available to her when she returned if she stayed away for more than her disability leave allowed. The law also did

not apply to companies that provide no disability benefits. Before Congress passed the Family and Medical Leave Act in 1993, more than 60 percent of women did not have maternity leave protections, and the United States was the only industrialized country in the world that had no national policy for paid and protected parental leave. The "Cathy" cartoons on p. 248 tell the story of how it was for working women before 1993.

The new Family and Medical Leave Act mandates that workers of either gender must be granted up to 12 weeks of *unpaid* leave each year, if they request it, as time off for the birth or adoption of a child, for personal sickness, or the serious illness of a family member. Employers must continue the health insurance coverage of the employee on leave, and employees are assured of their old jobs when they return. While this new legislation is a vast improvement over the situation that prevailed prior to 1993, it applies only to businesses with 50 or more workers, or to only 40 percent of the work force. In contrast, Finland provides 35 weeks off with full pay; Germany offers 14 to 19 weeks; and Canada allows new parents to take 15 weeks off with 60 percent pay (Colatosti, 1992). The minimum paid leave in continental Europe is 3 months,

with most countries moving toward six months (Zedeck & Mosier, 1990).

The new law is not likely to affect "the maternal wall" documented in a study by Deborah Swiss and Judith Walker (cf. Painton, 1993). A survey of 902 women graduates of Harvard's schools of business, law and medicine revealed that this group of successful professionals "often faces punishment on the job for daring to get pregnant, taking a few weeks of maternity leave and shortening their work week" (p. 45).

The National Federation of Business and Professional Women's Clubs ("Women's Pay," 1982) found that only 21 percent of working women are covered by pension plans. Companies that employ large numbers of women tend to lack such plans; and interrupted work patterns and job-changing also contributes to women's low rate of coverage. In addition, when a woman takes time off from work to care for children at home, her Social Security contributions during that time are zero. Legislation and a Supreme Court ruling have addressed and corrected some inequities between women and men with respect to pension benefits. In 1984 Congress passed legislation requiring the spouse's written consent before a retiree can waive survivor benefits and allowing former (divorced) spouses of federal workers to receive survivor benefits. A case brought to the Supreme Court by a working grandmother from Arizona changed the insurance industry practice of paying out less each month in pension benefits to women after retirement than to retired men, whether or not the women had made contributions to the plan equal to the men's—a practice insurance companies justified on the ground of women's greater average longevity. In the 1983 *Norris v. Arizona* decision, the Court ruled that this practice violates Title VII of the Civil Rights Act and discriminates against women. In other words, pension or retirement benefits must be gender-neutral, and calculated without regard to the beneficiary's gender.

Inequities are also found in the health insurance coverage of private sector full-time employed women and men. Health insurance is the second most widely received fringe benefit, next to paid vacations. Yet, only 67 percent of women were found in one study (cf. Perman & Stevens, 1989) to have group coverage through an employer plan, compared with 79 percent of men. Women's lower rates of health coverage were primarily the result of their greater employment in the nondurable manufacturing, retail trade, and services industries, which are the most poorly unionized and in which the gender difference in health coverage is greatest. These three industries together employ 60 percent of all women workers in the private sector.

The statistics on unemployment have also reflected discrimination against women, since more women than men are typically out of work and looking for jobs. According to Diana Pearce (1985), "women's unemployment rate has historically been higher than men's, with the ratio between the two ranging from 1.09 to 1.46" (p. 445). This has been true in virtually all fields, including middle managers in business (Kleiman, 1988), and in almost every area of science, as indicated by data from the National Science Foundation ("Data Points," 1992).

The differential impact of industry layoffs on women and men can be illustrated by data from the steel industry. Among employees laid off by U.S. Steel in South Chicago, 63 percent of the women were reported by a union study (cf. Greenhouse, 1984) to be still unemployed 5 years after the layoff, as compared with 44 percent of the men. Women went from being 9 percent of the nation's steelworkers in 1980 to less than 2 percent in 1984 ("Women Face Low Pay," 1984). Similar statistics have been reported from studies of other industries.

> [W]omen who have been laid off from blue-collar jobs in declining industries have the poorest prospects of ever making it back into those same jobs. The seniority rules governing layoffs and recalls are the reason . . . dislocated female workers . . . appear to have a harder time finding work and . . . end up earning less than their male counterparts. ("Recovery of Women Workers," 1984, p. A-15)

In addition to being more likely to lose her job and less likely to find a new one than a comparable man, a woman will typically receive less money in unemployment benefits. An analysis of such benefits led Diana Pearce (1985) to conclude that the unemployment compensation system in this country "is structurally biased against women . . . [who] find themselves disqualified as claimants or allotted reduced benefits more often than men do" (p. 444). The bias stems from the greater probability that an unemployed woman has been employed part-time or earned wages so low that they do not meet the minimum earnings requirement.

Few Women in Powerful Positions

When we do not see others like ourselves occupying certain positions or visibly achieving in particular careers, we are not likely to believe it suitable or advisable to train for and aspire to those positions or careers. Role models for boys and men are found in great areas of human endeavor covering the spectrum—from brawn to brains, active to the sedentary, risky to the safe, and routine to the creative. Gender segregation serves to restrict men's aspirations as well as women's, but men are restricted from far fewer areas. Girls who look outside the home for the presence of women do see a small minority in nontraditional fields and high-status jobs, as noted earlier. But the greatest number of women are still found in a relatively small number of fields that are limited with respect to personal growth or advancement. We hear a great deal about the enormous strides taken by women and about the new career options available. For example, "25 percent of all graduates in law, medicine and business are women, compared with only one in 20 two decades ago" ("Wage Gap," 1989, p. A-5). Yet, within the nontraditional fields, women are largely absent from the positions of highest status and power.

Turn on your television set and note the gender of the persons who are shown conferring with the president, your governor, or the president of some major company; or conducting a congressional hearing; or giving an important speech. A woman's face is still hard to find, except as an accompanying wife or staff member. President Clinton has made an effort to change this state of affairs with respect to his cabinet and other high-level appointments, signaling, perhaps, greater sensitivity to gender equity in other important places.

The U.S. State Department, which implements our nation's foreign policy, has been overwhelmingly male in terms of senior posts with important decision-making responsibilities. In 1989, in response to a court ruling, the State Department publicly acknowledged that it disproportionately assigned women to relatively low-status consular jobs and to jobs below their civil service rank, and that it assigned disproportionately fewer women than men to the deputy chief of mission position and undervalued women on their "potential" in annual ratings (cf. "State Department," 1989).

The situation in the business world is similar. Only rarely have women moved beyond the middle rung of responsibility, prestige, and power. Studies in the 1980s found that women hold only between 2 and 5 percent of executive positions in the top companies in this country (cf. Loden, 1986). According to Marilyn Loden, "most women in middle management today believe that their careers have reached a plateau" (p. F-2) and that they do not have the same chance for promotion as equally qualified men. As a result, the corporate world may be losing some of its best and brightest women. In 799 major companies, according to a study by *Fortune* magazine, the top executive positions were held by 3,993 men and only 19 women (Kleiman, 1991). Within the Fortune 500—

the most powerful businesses in this country—1.7 percent of corporate officerships and 3.6 percent of board directorships were held by women in 1988; 8.6 percent of senior executive personnel in the federal government were women in 1989 (Morrison & Van Glinow, 1990). Among federal employees, the high rank of GS-15, with a starting salary of $61,643, comprises 85 percent men, whereas the majority of those with a rank of GS-14 or below are women (Zeman, 1991).

In colleges and universities, as of 1988, women were only 10 percent of college presidents, or 296 in number, of which 38 were women of color (Wilson, 1989). Most of the college presidencies held by women are on small and not highly prestigious campuses. U.S. colleges and universities have an average of 1.1 senior women administrators (Morrison & Van Glinow, 1990), and 4.3 percent of college administrative posts below that of president are held by women of color (Wilson, 1989). A study of African-American women administrators at a large, predominantly European-American university in the East provides some insight into the obstacles faced by this small minority (Wilson, 1989). Many reported having to fight racism and sexism and having their ability questioned by subordinates and peers. Only a small number said they wished to remain in higher education administration and to move up in the status hierarchy.

In college faculties, according to data presented in *Science* ("Data Points," 1992), "women are overrepresented in non-tenure-track positions such as adjunct faculty and lecturer, but higher up the career ladder there are fewer women" (p. 1376). Thus, for example, while women are 40 percent of all lecturers, they are only 11.6 percent of full professors. According to a *New York Times* report by Anthony DePalma (1993), while women constitute more than half of all college students, they make up only 27.6 percent of faculty members nationwide. The greatest progress by women has been made "at community colleges, where the pay is lowest, [and where they] hold 38 percent of faculty positions" (p. Y11). The situation at Ivy League colleges is the worst for women faculty: they are only 7 to 13 percent of full professors (an average of 10 percent) but 30 percent of associate professors and 30 percent of untenured assistant professors. Minorities are also poorly represented in college faculties generally at 11 percent (approximately 2 percent women), although 19 percent of all higher education students are minority group members.

In law schools, women constitute only 13.5 percent of the faculty (Briscoe, 1989) and 7 percent of the deans, with minority women in the least secure position of all groups. One study found that 44 percent of minority women began their law school teaching job in a non-tenure-track position, compared with 29 percent of minority men (cf. "Minority Women," 1992). There are only four women in tenured positions in the top ten mathematics departments (Selvin, 1991). Bernardine Healy (1992), former director of the National Institutes of Health, noted that a National Science Foundation study had found that 68 percent of men in science departments have tenure compared with only 36 percent of women and that in medical schools full professors are only 9.8 percent women. She concluded that "in view of some negative treatment in the classroom and discouraging employment and funding prospects, the astonishing thing is that young women pursue careers in science and medicine at all" (p. 1333). Susan Blumenthal of the Society for the Advancement of Women's Health Research (cf. Joyce, 1993), noted that 21 percent of medical faculties across the United States are women, but two thirds are instructors or assistant professors, and there is only one medical school dean. In a meeting at Stanford University she cited a study that "looked at the careers of 2,196 men and 699 women who were appointed to junior full-time faculty positions in 1976. By 1991, 22 percent of the men, but only 10 percent of the women had reached the level of full professor" (p. 9). These data clearly point to the difficulties facing women in terms of the evaluation of their competence and other barriers that impede achievement.

One study matched more than 5,000 triads of one woman and two men scientists by year of doctoral award, field, and race; the study found differences in rank (and salary) between the men and women even when they had earned their degrees and were currently employed in similarly prestigious institutions (cf. "Misconceptions," 1982).

> Women were more likely, at each level of academic employment, to be in a non-faculty or junior faculty position than their matched male counterparts. Males were 50 percent more likely than females to have reached the status of full professor among men and women who received their doctorates between 10 and 19 years ago. . . . [And] unmarried women or women without children fared no better with faculty promotions than women with children. (pp. 6f.)

Not until 1971 was a woman, mathematician Mina Rees, elected to the presidency of the American Association for the Advancement of Science, an organization founded in 1848; since that time she has been followed by only five others. The situation in other national scientific societies is similar. In psychology, for example, although women are now in the majority in the 100-year-old American Psychological Association, only eight women have been elected president since Mary Calkins was in 1905.

What do we see in other career areas? An analysis of the situations of high-profile women in TV network news reporting and commentary led the National Commission on Working Women to conclude that such women may be working in a "hostile or nonsupporting environment." This conclusion was echoed by a former network vice president, who noted that "women are still not power players. The power is behind the scenes and all you have to do is look and see who the executives are . . . mostly men" (cf. Rosenthal & Rudolph, 1991, p. 30). And the men, of course, are primarily European-American. Movie directors, the powerful shapers of culture, are also primarily (European-American) men. While women constitute 20 percent of the membership of the Directors Guild of America, they were asked to direct only 5 percent of Hollywood's feature films, according to a study of the deals made in 1990 (Rohter, 1991). In television, during this time period, women directed 12 percent of the half-hour shows, 9 percent of hour shows, less than 3 percent of TV movies, and none of the miniseries. "When women do get work, they earn significantly less than their male counterparts" (p. H-14), an average of $70,000 during the first 10 months of 1990, compared to $135,000 for male directors. A similar situation exists for women in the print media. The National Federation of Press Women reported that women hold only 19.4 percent of the important editing jobs at daily newspapers around the country (cf. "Few Women," 1993). Women publishers, who constitute only 8.7 percent of the total, are found at primarily small papers with low circulations.

This paucity of women in top positions in private industry, government, the media, and educational institutions—a paucity that exists despite the enormous influx of women into all of these areas in the 1970s and 1980s—has been labeled the "glass ceiling" and has been the subject of considerable research and analysis. As the term *ceiling* suggests, women and members of minorities appear to bump into "an invisible, artificial barrier . . . when trying to rise within the workplace" (Hawkins, 1991). The "mommy track" has also been discussed in analyses of the limits placed on women's upward movement in organizations. Those who have proposed such a track, or who have based promotion decisions on it, assume that employed mothers require or should require a career path different from that of employed fathers—a path where mothers forgo upward mobility to have more time for their children.

A "mommy track" seems to be alive and well in the legal profession, for example, and has created "a new category of law firm associates who work with no prospects of advancement" ("Few Woman Lawyers," 1988). In such two-tier law firms, the full-time partners (mostly men) have all the perks and prestige, according to the executive director of the New York Bar Association, while the bottom tier is made up largely of women. Next to private practice, corporations are the largest employers of lawyers in the United States, employing 13 percent. A study of 12 such corporations, involving interviews with 68 full-time attorneys (Roach, 1990), found that although there were few gender differences in "quality of law school . . . , academic performance, prior legal employment, and legal specialty . . . there were salient gender differences in job-finding routes, current position, salary, promotion, and type of firm and size of department" (p. 212). Among the men, 44 percent had learned about their current job through employer-initiated contacts, compared with 68 percent of the women who had used employee-initiated methods. In addition, the women were less likely than the men to be in the more lucrative manufacturing firms or in large, prestigious departments.

The "mommy track" has been called a "devil's bargain" (Deutsch, 1990) and is the subject of considerable criticism. Trudi Ferguson and Joan Dunphy (1991), for example, interviewed some exceptional women in high places who have managed successful careers in conjunction with family life and parenthood and found that their lives challenge the "mommy track" assumption that women must choose between motherhood and high professional achievement.

Research generally continues to show, despite popular myths, that women and men in positions of authority are extremely similar in how they do their jobs and in their work-related attitudes and beliefs. One study of 51 chief executive officers of nonprofit organizations (Heimovics & Herman, 1988) found that gender was not a relevant variable; both women and men viewed their successes as a consequence of hard work and ability and took responsibility for their failures. The investigators concluded that the organizational leadership role takes precedence over gender in influencing the behaviors of women and men at the top. Congruent data were reported from a study of 250 senior public administrators (Russo, Kelly, & Deacon, 1991). Both women and men considered ability and hard work as most important to their own success and that of their colleagues, and professional contacts were considered more important than luck.

The research literature continues to point consistently to the same conclusion: women and men doing similar work in high-status positions are remarkably similar in

interests and attributes. Thus, a study of college student leaders (Offerman & Bell, 1992) found that the achievement profiles of women leaders were closer to that of men leaders than they were to their female non-leader peers. In a different setting, the responses made by a large group of women and men managers to self-report questions indicated that they "were strikingly similar in self-confidence" in both at-work and social family situations, with both genders scoring higher in the former than the latter setting (Chusmir,Koberg, & Stecker, 1992). Still another study, this one of small business owners (Smith, Smits, & Hoy, 1992), found no clear pattern of gender differences in personal characteristics of the 27 women and 29 men who were compared. While the women had had less industry experience, were less likely to be married, and were more likely to hire female employees, there was no gender difference in scores on measures of nurturance and dominance.

The "glass ceiling" is thus not easily explainable by gender differences in perspective, ability, or job performance. Nor can it be explained by some women's parenthood responsibilities. To what, then, can it be attributed? An analysis of gender and power in organizations by Belle Ragins and Eric Sundstrom (1989) provides some clues. They reviewed the relevant literature in an attempt to understand why "women are clustered in positions with relatively little power . . . ; [do] not advance as far or as fast in the organizational hierarchy as their male counterparts . . . [and] seldom reach top-level positions" (p. 51). Women, they concluded, are put into organizational positions where they cannot accumulate resources as easily as men or have access to resources from multiple sources. For women, they found,

> the path to power contains many impediments and barriers and can best be described as an obstacle course. In contrast, the path to power for men contains few obstacles that derive from their gender and may actually contain sources of support unavailable to their female counterparts. (p. 81)

Over time, "power begets power," and "powerlessness perpetuates powerlessness," so that existing differences in power between women and men are escalated.

Some women who have achieved important decision-making positions find that they are frequently bypassed and undervalued. Their suggestions may be ignored or recognized only later, when they are repeated by a male colleague. As a college dean for 6 years, I often found myself in groups in which I was either the lone woman or among a very small minority of women, and my experiences matched those reported by other women in similar situations. For example, Mary Rowe (1973) has described some of "the minutiae of sexism," petty incidents that when taken together serve to impede women's job progress: a woman's name may be oddly missing from a list of announcements or invitations; her opinion may not be solicited or her work not cited; she may be loaded with extra work or given an undesirable office. Rosabeth Kanter (1977) studied a large corporation and reported that when only a few women were at the managerial level, they were highly visible and under particular pressure to succeed, felt isolated, and had few others with whom to share their feelings and perceptions. Their chance for success was diminished by their lesser power and by others' perception that they were less able than men to reward those whom they supervised.

Stereotypes and Devaluation of Women's Competence

The conviction that women just cannot do certain jobs as well as men continues to be strong and persistent despite the dramatic changes in women's participation in the work force. In virtually every field that has been examined, evidence has been uncovered to document the devaluation of women's achievements, while new scholarship has unearthed the important contributions of women to art (e.g., Nochlin, 1979), to music (e.g., Wood, 1980), and to other creative, scholarly, and scientific endeavors.

Maria Goeppert-Mayer, winner of the Nobel Prize in physics in 1963, was not offered a full-time faculty appointment in a U.S. university until her imminent award was widely rumored a year or two earlier (Dash, 1973). The case of biologist Rosalind Franklin is even more tragic. In an extraordinary book, Anne Sayre documented Franklin's contributions to the discovery of the molecular structure of DNA, which were not acknowledged by the three male scientists who received the 1962 Nobel Prize for this work, although they were well aware of her research. There have been other apparent negations of the important work of women scientists. Jocelyn Bell's contributions to the discovery and understanding of pulsars were not recognized when the Nobel Prize for this work was awarded to two men, in the laboratory of one of whom she had worked (Wade, 1975). For her work in genetics, Barbara McClintock had to wait until she was over 80 years old to be awarded the Nobel Prize in 1983; some believe recognition would have come to her sooner had she been a man.

A large research literature suggests that such a supposition has merit. I reviewed this literature (Lott,

1986) and concluded that a competent woman (or her work) is likely to be devalued relative to an identically credentialed competent man (or his work). This phenomenon of devaluing a woman's competence is found across a wide range of settings, but most often in realistic contexts in which the evaluator is a real employer or personnel manager and the evaluation is believed to have some real consequence or significance. A more encouraging conclusion was drawn from research in which evaluations were made of women whose work was already known well. Negative evaluations of competent women were less likely to occur in such studies. However, other evidence indicates that when women are in direct competition with men for rewards, factors that are not directly work-related may be utilized in making job decisions or evaluations. For example, a field study involving interviews and analysis of job performance records of 651 employees of five different companies (Gupta, Jenkins, & Beehr, 1983) found that "while opinions (evaluations) may be positive, actions (promotions) still follow tradition" (p. 183). Women subordinates received the fewest promotions, and men subordinates of men supervisors received the most frequent pay raises, regardless of the evaluations of their work.

Situations in which women are likely to be evaluated negatively are best illustrated by investigations that do not rely on college students responding to hypothetical target persons and questions. An example of such a more realistic study is one in which managers, mostly men, evaluated applications for both a purely technical job in chemical engineering and a technical-managerial job (Gerdes & Garber, 1983). A woman candidate for the technical-managerial job was rated significantly lower than a man candidate, despite identical credentials and competence. The researchers speculated that the greater ambiguity of qualifications required for a managerial position may have increased the role played by prejudice, and they concluded that "credentials that demonstrate competence . . . are not sufficient protection from sex bias when the candidate applies for a demanding job" (p. 317). A different kind of study analyzed the actual records of 341 applicants to a medical school (Clayton, Baird, & Levinson, 1984) and found that women received lower interview ratings than men and that the interview evaluations were significantly more important for women than for men. Despite no reliable gender difference in objective test scores (grade point average and MCATs), because women received lower interview ratings they received lower overall evaluations than men.

A study of the hiring practices of a sample of psychology departments revealed that "given equal qualifications, men tend to be hired at higher position levels and at more prestigious institutions than women" (Bronstein & Pfennig, 1988, p. 669), and a 1983 study in which mathematicians rated identical math papers thought to be written by either John or Joan McKay found that the former were rated more highly (cf. Selvin, 1992). In still another study, when a large sample of business professionals were asked to evaluate the resumes of applicants for three different jobs, men were preferred for a heavy machine company sales manager and women were preferred for a dental receptionist, while gender did not influence evaluations for a bank administrator assistant's job. Yet, for all three jobs, so-called masculine traits (for example, independence, reliance, leadership) were positively related to the likelihood that applicants would be interviewed (Glick, Zion, & Nelson, 1988).

Two recent reviews of the relevant literature (Swim, Borgida, Maruyama, & Myers, 1989; Top, 1991) have concluded that there is, overall, little or no general tendency for men's products or performance to be evaluated more positively than women's. This conclusion is questionable, however, in light of the fact that the first review cited was primarily of studies using college student raters, and the second was a review of studies in which "the evaluations were without any consequences" (p. 103). That studies in which the stimulus materials are resumes or applications show greater male bias, as noted by Swim et al., supports the hypothesis that such bias is likely to be manifested when the ratings matter for real decisions.

A great deal of evidence supports the conclusion that women and men in the workplace are perceived differently and are thought to have different attributes, skills, and interests. For example, one group of investigators (Schein, Mueller, & Jacobson, 1989) found that contemporary male management students as well as male managers continue to believe what they did in the 1970s—that "men are more likely to possess the characteristics necessary for managerial success" (p. 109). Other studies (e.g., Frank, 1988; Hartmann, Griffeth, Crino, & Harris, 1991) have also reported that such stereotypes and preferences for men in management persist.

An insightful and humorous list of the different interpretations given to the same office behavior by women and men, prepared by Natasha Josefowitz (1992), follows. Supporting the proposition that what women and men do is perceived quite differently are the results of a study of "office romance" (Anderson & Fisher, 1991). Employed recent business school graduates were asked to comment on an intimate heterosexual relationship they were aware of in their firm. The respondents said that men were more likely to enter such a relationship for "ego satisfaction, excitement, adventure, and sexual experience," whereas women's motives were (predictably) perceived as "job advancement" and "in order to move up the organizational ladder" (p. 174).

IMPRESSIONS FROM AN OFFICE

The family picture is on HIS desk.
Ah, a solid, responsible family man.
The family picture is on HER desk.
Um, her family will come before her career.

HIS desk is cluttered.
He's obviously a hard worker and a busy man.
HER desk is cluttered.
She's obviously a disorganized scatterbrain.

HE is talking with his coworkers.
He must be discussing the latest deal.
SHE is talking with her coworkers.
She must be gossiping.

HE's not at his desk.
He must be at a meeting.
SHE's not at her desk.
She must be in the ladies' room.

HE's not in the office.
He's meeting customers.
SHE's not in the office.
She must be out shopping.

HE's having lunch with the boss.
He's on his way up.
SHE's having lunch with the boss.
They must be having an affair.

The boss criticized HIM.
He'll improve his performance.
The boss criticized HER.
She'll be very upset.

HE got an unfair deal.
Did he get angry?
SHE got an unfair deal.
Did she cry?

HE's getting married.
He'll get more settled.
SHE's getting married.
She'll get pregnant and leave.

HE's having a baby.
He'll need a raise.
SHE's having a baby.
She'll cost the company money in maternity benefits.

HE's going on a business trip.
It's good for his career.
SHE's going on a business trip.
What does her husband say?

HE's leaving for a better job.
He knows how to recognize a good opportunity.
SHE's leaving for a better job.
Women are not dependable.

NATASHA JOSEFOWITZ

From Is This Where I Was Going? by Natasha Josefowitz, *Copyright*
© *1983 by Warner Books. Reprinted by permission.*

Clearly, women who try to achieve in areas outside the home, particularly in nontraditional fields, begin with a handicap of serious proportions—namely with negatively biased perceptions of their motivations and competence for the job. Nevertheless, the objective data that exist on the comparative quality of men's and women's work in various fields suggest that competence varies only with individual characteristics, not with gender. Women who achieve distinction in fields like engineering, science, art, business, or politics have been found to be similar to men who achieve distinction in these fields and different from persons who do not. This conclusion is supported by the work of Louise Bachtold (1976), who studied 863 high-achieving women in four different career categories, and by the work of Frieda Gehlen (1977), who compared the women and men who served as elected representatives to the 91st and 93rd U.S. Congresses. Gehlen found that women and men were not distinguishable in the ratings given them by political interest groups, nor in how often they voted with or against their own party, their general effectiveness, the percentage of legislation they sponsored, or the percentage of sponsored legislation Congress acted upon. I know of no evidence in any field that indicates a gender difference in competence among similarly trained and functioning persons. Thus, for example, in a Marine Corps program to teach women recruits to shoot a rifle, while only about 40 percent of the women were expected to qualify as marksmen, 98 percent ended up qualifying— the same rate as for men recruits ("Women Marines," 1986).

Accumulated data support the conclusion that where social categories, roles, or demands are more relevant or salient than gender, those roles will be most likely to influence behavior (Lott & Maluso, 1993). As noted by Alice Eagly and S. J. Karau (1991), when "other roles [e.g., occupational roles] are salient, the expectations associated with them would tend to control behavior, and comparisons between men and women who are in the same role . . . should reveal few sex differences" (p. 8). Thus, a

statistical analysis (Eagly & Johnson, 1990) of studies comparing women and men on leadership style found little gender difference within ongoing organizations in real settings where people are functioning in accord with the demands of their jobs. Similarly, when Andrew DuBrin (cf. Kleiman, 1989b) studied how 337 high-level employees (with an average of 14 years of work experience) "get things done," he found that "women and men virtually behave the same" in their use of various influence techniques.

Family Responsibilities

Most women, including those with jobs or careers, are also wives and mothers at some time in their lives. Those who leave the work force in order to assume primary responsibility for child care run the risk of losing out on new skills, opportunities, and promotions.

While professional women must be prepared for adverse career consequences after a temporary withdrawal from active participation in their fields and association with their professional colleagues, the less educated woman will confront an even more difficult situation. A Census Bureau report (cf. "Women Working Less," 1984) indicated that 72 percent of employed women interrupt their jobs or careers for 6 months or longer, compared to only 26 percent of men. While men spend an average of 2 percent of their potential work years out of the work force, the average woman spends 23 percent of these years unemployed. The major reason for this difference is that women interrupt their employment to have children and to care for them at home. Among a group of women faculty members, one study (Yogev & Vierra, 1983) found that 66 of the 68 who had children reported one or more interruptions in their careers, and 83 percent of these interruptions were to have or care for children.

Deeann Wenk and Patricia Garrett (1992) studied almost 2,000 working women who had given birth to a child between 1979 and 1986 in order to identify variables associated with remaining at work during the childbirth period and being employed one year later. The factors that made the most difference and had the consistently most positive effect on continued maternal employment were presence of a husband or an additional adult in the household. Other contributing factors were more education, being older, and having a higher-status job. In summing up their findings, the authors noted that most likely to remain employed is "a married white woman whose first child was born after age 24 and who completed some years of college. Least likely to be employed is the young minority mother with a high-school education or less" (p. 62).

As we have seen, women who work outside the home tend also to work inside of it almost as much, in terms of chores done, as women who are full-time homemakers. An employed woman who is also a wife and mother remains primarily responsible for the good health, comfort, cleanliness, and happiness of her husband and children. Regardless of her type of employment—blue-collar, white-collar, managerial, or professional—the average woman with children tries to find ways to accommodate her schedule to the needs of her family. Employed mothers typically devote substantially more time than employed fathers to caring for their children and their homes, to meeting the needs of family members, and tending to household responsibilities. This disparity between mothers and fathers has been the subject of a great deal of study in samples of working women from different parts of the country, in different social classes and varying occupations. Thus, for example, women who work in coal mines (Hammond & Mahoney, 1983) reported that they arrange their work shifts to be home at the same time as their school-age children. Similarly, among a sample of employees in a large corporation (Englander-Golden & Barton, 1983), although women and men without children had similar work attendance records, mothers were found to use significantly more of their sick-leave hours than fathers to attend to a child's illness or other child-related matters of importance. An interview study of working couples in the San Francisco area (Hochschild & Machung, 1989) confirmed the heavy burden on working mothers found in more quantitative research.

Professionally employed mothers seem not too different from other employed mothers in their concern for their children's well-being and in the lack of equal time and effort forthcoming from their husbands. Among a group of married full-time practicing physicians whose professional productivity was unrelated to their gender, the women had primary responsibility for significantly more domestic tasks than the men and spent more than twice as much time on them (Pyke & Kahill, 1983). A similar picture of inequality in household chores was also found to exist among a sample of employed psychologist couples (Bryson, Bryson, Licht, & Licht, 1976). The researchers concluded that "sharing a profession evidently does not involve sharing the housework" (p. 15). In another study (St. John-Parsons, 1978) of 10 dual-career couples, spanning 14 different professions, in which the wife had only minimally interrupted her career for childbearing, it was found that

not one husband took sole care of the children in emergencies or illness, although four couples shared this responsibility. Where the families had hired helpers, they were invariably brought in. In the two families where the husbands were physicians, though specialists in psychiatry, the wives took sole care of sick children. (p. 35)

That the responsibilities for home and children fall primarily to the professionally employed wife rather than to her husband continues to be documented by recent research. Monica Biernat and Camille Wortman (1991) interviewed 139 women who were mothers of preschool children and also university professors or in business, and also interviewed their husbands who had comparable job status and incomes. Although the husbands were found to contribute significantly to some home chores and to be involved in interactive play with their children, the husbands were not the primary care providers on any of 10 tasks that were studied. Although the men were clearly not doing an equal share of home tasks and child care, their wives expressed general satisfaction with their husband's contributions and were more self-critical than the men. These findings suggest that even professionally employed adults are using traditional standards to judge themselves and their spouses, so that men who take on some home responsibilities (but not an equal share) are seen by themselves and their wives in a positive light, while women who run a home as well as work full-time tend to be critical of themselves in comparison to traditional expectations of wives and mothers.

In a seriocomic vein, Kathleen Parker (1991) wrote about one of the consequences for employed women of being the primary parent. Because mothers understand that "children sometimes come first" but that "to openly care about one's children is not considered professional," the solution to occasional conflicts between the two demands is to lie—to cover for one another on the phone when a mother/worker is not around. Sometimes, then, being "at a meeting" really means "she's taking her child to the dentist . . . [or] out to lunch . . . [or] home for cookies and milk" (p. C-3).

Whether we look directly at women's personal experiences or through the filtered lens of social science research, we find much the same indication of the conflicting pressures married women (especially mothers) encounter in trying to fulfill the cultural expectations for being good homemakers while at the same time fulfilling work obligations or pursuing careers. A husband may expect his employed wife to behave in the traditional manner and may be uninterested in her achievements outside the home, or he may resent them and attempt to stand in her way. In Marge Piercy's *Fly Away Home* (1984a), when the daughter of a successful cookbook writer remarked to her mother that some of her friends had seen her on television, the mother replied, "Well, does that bother you?" and quickly changed the subject. "Talking too much about her work or the modest measure of celebrity it had brought felt dangerous around the house, even if Ross [her husband] wasn't in earshot" (p. 22). Many successful women I have known have expressed the same feeling of diffidence or discomfort about discussing their public achievements in the presence of their children or husbands, as though the public aspect of their lives were either not relevant or disturbing to those to whom the women were mothers or wives.

Role overload—the necessity to fulfill many responsibilities associated with both home life and employment—is clearly greater for married women than for married men. For example, Dalia Ducker (1980), who interviewed a sample of women physicians in four different specialties, found that those with strong family commitments were likely to experience feelings of strain and conflict between personal and professional demands. Similarly, among a group of 232 married women doctors, lawyers, and professors, Janet Gray (1983) found that 77 percent said they often experienced strains between home and career. A study conducted among 651 employees of a Boston company (cf. Dietz, 1985) found that women spend twice as many hours on homemaking and child-care tasks as men, even if their income equaled or exceeded their husbands'. Figure 11.4 shows the total number of hours spent on job and family responsibilities by all categories of workers in the company; from it we can see clearly the greater load carried by working mothers than working fathers. Nevertheless, this study found that the balancing of work and family did not contribute more to depression among women than among men.

Despite the reported experience of problems associated with trying to balance home and job responsibilities, and the unequal share of home responsibilities that falls to women, research on the effects of role overload do not support a conclusion of negative consequences for the married employed women—for her job productivity, job satisfaction, or her family. Sara Yogev (1982) reviewed relevant research on dual-career couples and concluded that for women, "the act of coping and the challenge of this lifestyle seem to outweigh the disadvantages, and there is no harm to the family unit" (p. 603). Others who have studied varied groups of employed women have reached similar conclusions with respect to family and personal functioning. After reviewing the sizable literature

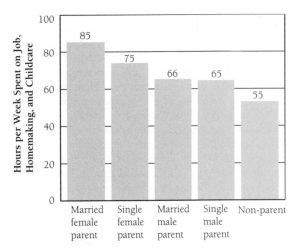

FIGURE 11.4 *Job–family responsibilities.* (Taken from Jean Dietz, "Family Job Stress Found in Hub Study," *Boston Globe,* November 14, 1985. Information from Boston University/C.O.P.E. 1985.)

on working women and stress, James Terborg (1985) concluded that "working women as a group differ little from working men in rates of turnover, absenteeism, and illness, and both groups report similar levels of job satisfaction" (p. 254). Some research has found that not only is employment not detrimental to a woman, but it in fact enhances her mental health. Lois Hoffman's (1989) review of relevant literature led her to conclude that "maternal employment is often a boost to the morale of mothers and a buffer against other anxieties" (p. 290). And Louise Silverstein's (1991) review of findings in this area led to a similar conclusion: "women who work outside the home report better physical and emotional health than do women who are full-time homemakers" (p. 1028). Findings from a long-term study of a sample of European-American women in California go beyond verbal reports. The working women were found to have a significantly lower risk of heart disease and lower levels of total cholesterol and blood sugar, than the women who stayed at home (cf. Abrahamson, 1992). We will explore issues relevant to women's health more fully in a later chapter.

Harassment on the Job

Even the most highly motivated woman, who knows she has the aptitude for a particular job, is confident that she will succeed, and manages to receive the appropriate training, may find that she is treated differently from her male coworkers. She may be the target of hostility or suspicion. She may not be taken seriously, or she may be expected to outperform the men with whom she works. She may be the butt of tasteless jokes, pursued as easy sexual prey, or humiliated. Such reports have come from almost every occupational area—from the armed forces, coal mines, corporate offices, universities, and factories.

Marian Swerdlow (1989), for example, who worked as a conductor for a major rapid transit system for 4 years while taking notes and making observations, concluded that her male coworkers (who were 96 percent of the conductors and train operators) showed no evidence of trying to force the women out of their jobs. Instead the men harassed them in more subtle and aggravating ways.

> Willingness to 'teach the ropes,' encouragement, and support were by far the most common attitudes of subway workers toward 'new women.' However . . . the men adopted practices and interpretations . . . that reconciled the fact that women were successfully performing their jobs with a continuing belief in their own superiority. These . . . took the form of the sexualization of work relationships, the exaggeration of women's errors, depicting women's routine competence as exceptional, and perpetuating a myth of 'preference.' (p. 386)

Similar findings were reported from a study comparing the job climate for samples of tradeswomen, women transit workers, and school secretaries (Mansfield, Koch, Henderson, Vicary, Cohn, & Young, 1991). The women in the traditionally male fields differed from the secretaries in reporting that their supervisors were more unfair, critical, and prejudiced; and the women in the trades (skilled crafts, repair, and construction) rated their supervisors as most sexist and their coworkers as most disrespectful. "More than half of the tradeswomen, and over a third of the transit workers reported incidents of sex discrimination or harassment; incidents for blacks exceeded those for whites" (p. 75).

Large numbers of women experience sexual harassment—unwanted, unsolicited, and nonreciprocated sexual behavior or attention. Surprisingly, however, this subject was rarely discussed openly until the late 1970s, so well had women learned to expect such behavior by men in the workplace as in all other settings. The reader is referred to the chapter on violence in women's lives for a general discussion of sexual harassment. Here we will deal only with workplace examples and issues.

In 1980, the federal Equal Employment Opportunity Commission (EEOC) interpreted the prohibition of sexual harassment under Title VII of the Civil Rights Act of 1964 as a form of sex discrimination and defined harassment as "unwelcome sexual advances, requests for sexual favors, and other verbal or physical conduct of a sexual nature." It is illegal for sexual submission to be made a condition of employment or assignment, and for sexual conduct to interfere with an employee's work performance or to create a hostile work environment. The commission's guidelines hold employers liable for the behavior of their supervisors and for sexual harassment between coworkers if the employer should have known about it.

The EEOC guidelines were in response to assertions such as that by the Working Women's Institute (1980) that "sexual harassment is the single most widespread occupational hazard women face in the workforce" (p. 1). This conclusion was supported by the data from many studies, including the most extensive and carefully executed research on this issue, involving the largest number of randomly sampled respondents (federal employees). The investigators (Tangri, Burt, & Johnson, 1982) had found that 42 percent of the women and 15 percent of the men reported having been sexually harassed at work within the past 2 years. Of those with this experience, 78 percent had been harassed by men. Most incidents were found to involve coworkers, but women's harassers were also likely to be older married men, and more women than men were harassed by a superior. The victims of harassment seldom reported it to anyone, a common finding in other studies as well, including that by Barbara Gutek (1985) who conducted the most extensive study of the workplace in the private sector using telephone interviews of a random sample of women. She found that 53 percent of the women said they had experienced at least one sexually harassing incident at work during the course of their years of employment. These included insulting comments, looks, or gestures; sexual touching; expected socializing; and expected sexual activity.

While younger, unmarried women are the more likely targets of older supervising men, women are not immune from sexual harassment at any age or in any job category. According to 9to5, sexual harassment is "near the top of the list of complaints" received on its job problem hotline ("Hot News," 1991). Figure 11.5 shows the number of complaints filed with the EEOC in 1981 and 1990, and the frequency of different harassing behaviors. In 1991 the number of complaints filed was 6,883, whereas in 1992, largely in response to Professor Anita Hill's testimony against Judge Clarence Thomas, the number soared to 10,522 (Salholz, Beachy, Miller, Annin, Barrett, & Foote, 1992). In October 1992, a Newsweek poll found that 21 percent of women respondents said they had been

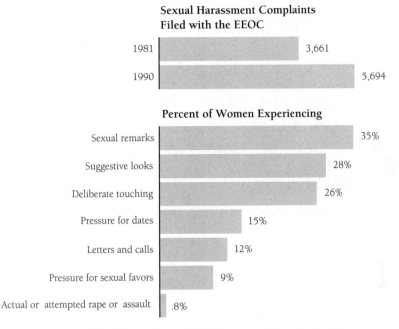

Sexual Harassment Complaints Filed with the EEOC

1981	3,661
1990	5,694

Percent of Women Experiencing

Sexual remarks	35%
Suggestive looks	28%
Deliberate touching	26%
Pressure for dates	15%
Letters and calls	12%
Pressure for sexual favors	9%
Actual or attempted rape or assault	.8%

FIGURE 11.5 *A disturbing pattern*   (EEOC Merit Systems Protection Board.)

harassed at work, and 42 percent said they knew someone who had been harassed.

Some workplaces may be more dangerous for women than others. Thus, 64 percent of the military women questioned told Defense Department investigators in 1990 that they had been sexually harassed (cf. Kantrowitz, Barrett, Springen, Hager, Wright, Carroll, & Rosenberg, 1991c). And, sexual harassment continues to be a serious issue in the entertainment industry. Most people in the industry, according to Mary Murphy (1986), agree that harassment

> is the centerpiece of a pervasive problem in Hollywood: exploitation of women. So pervasive is it, in fact, that the Screen Actors Guild has set up a 24-hour hotline to deal with sexual-harassment and other complaints. (p. 3)

> The cliches . . . are all true—the casting couch, the porno-movie producers on the prowl, the agents who trade time for sexual favors. (p. 11)

In 1991, a pioneering woman neurosurgeon, Frances Conley, resigned from her position at the Stanford Medical School

> after what she said was a quarter-century of subtle sexism . . . from insensitive language to physical harassment. . . .

Academic medicine is a particular hothouse for sexist attitudes, medical professionals of both sexes say, because of the rigid educational hierarchy, the traditional inequality between doctors and nurses, which sets the tone for other working relationships, and the many opportunities to make rude anatomical remarks. (Gross, 1991)

The high frequency of sexual harassment in the medical profession and also among lawyers and business executives has been documented by research. A study of female doctors and medical students in 1989 by the American Medical Women's Association found that 27 percent of female doctors and medical students reported having experienced sexual harassment; 60 percent of 3,000 high-ranking women lawyers responded to a *National Law Journal* survey in 1989 that they had been sexually harassed sometime during their careers; and a 1990 survey of 1,300 female executives found that 53 percent reported harassment by male supervisors (cf. Kleiman, 1992).

In 1992, Senator Brock Adams of Washington, with a long record of public service, ended his reelection campaign after he was accused of sexual harassment by a number of women who had worked with him in various capacities. These accusations followed in the wake of the dramatic and nationally riveting testimony in October

Cartoon by Stayskal. Reprinted by permission: Tribune Media Services

1991 by Anita Hill, a law professor, against her former boss at the EEOC, Judge Clarence Thomas. Professor Hill's charges of sexual harassment, though shocking and sobering to some, were minimized, trivialized, and disregarded by others and had no effect on the confirmation of Judge Thomas as a Supreme Court justice.

Our society's resistance to serious discussions of sexual harassment is illustrated by the cartoon shown above, which appeared in my local paper but was probably not unlike others that appeared in newspapers across the country following the Senate hearings on Judge Thomas' confirmation. Many have noted the difficulty women have in reporting workplace harassment when it occurs, an issue made salient by Professor Hill's testimony. For example, attorney Laura Mansnerus (1991), in discussing her own experiences, admitted that she had not complained, but went on being "nice," enabling her to continue her employment and move on in her career. Her argument that "nobody likes a tattletale" is presented not with bravado but with sadness; "to squeal on one's mentor," she writes, "is an idiotic thing to do."

Some women have resorted to legal action; an example of a successful outcome from litigation is the "peephole case." Seven women coal miners from West Virginia won a lawsuit against the Pittston Company for its negligence in not having protected them from being watched by their male coworkers through peepholes as the women showered and dressed in the bathhouse. Another successful outcome that took 4 years of hearings, negotiations, and lawsuits involved Mary Lebrato, a psychologist employed by the State of California. After she had reported being sexually harassed by one of her supervisors (an incident

witnessed by many), she was passed over for a promotion promised to her. After a "long, hard road" through the courts, Lebrato's case was settled in her favor out of court. The state awarded her $150,000 and agreed "to finance for two years a project to study problems in sexual harassment in private and public employment and to pay Lebrato's salary as its manager" (Cunningham, 1984).

Some landmark court cases have helped to sharpen the legal meaning of sexual harassment. For example, in *Barnes v. Costle,* an appellate court in 1977 overturned an earlier decision and ruled that "if a female employee was retaliated against because she rejected the sexual advances of her boss, this is sex discrimination in violation of Title VII" ("Development of the Law," 1992). In *Bundy v. Jackson,* an appeals court in 1981 endorsed the EEOC's position that sexual insults and propositions create a hostile work environment even if no tangible job benefits are lost, and constitute sexual harassment and discrimination. In 1988 another appellate court found in *Hall v. Gus Construction Co.* that the hazing of female colleagues by male construction workers constituted gender-based harassment prohibited by law. And in a final example, *Ellison v. Brady* in 1991, a court ruled that behavior that might appear to be inoffensive to a man might offend a woman so that "the appropriate standard to use in sexual harassment cases is that of a 'reasonable woman' rather than a 'reasonable person'" ("Development of the Law," 1992).

Sexual harassment in the workplace may have begun to be taken seriously by the courts, employers, and employee organizations. Following the issuing of the EEOC guidelines in 1980, many large companies (and universities) developed anti-harassment policies, procedures, and programs that defined sexual harassment and explained to managers that the company could be held legally liable for such behavior. An example of the "protective measures" taken by companies are the seminars on sexual harassment that all AT&T employees are required to attend (Lewin, 1986). An article in *Newsweek* (Salholz, Beachy, Miller, Annin, Barrett, & Foote, 1992) reported that many businesses reviewed their sexual harassment policies or developed new ones following the Clarence Thomas hearings, and that a survey in June 1992 found that 81 percent of Fortune 500 companies offered their employees sensitivity-training programs. Another sign of increased attention is a 7-page fact sheet for employees published by the Bureau of National Affairs' *Labor Relations Week* ("Preventing Sexual Harassment," 1992), which defines sexual harassment and presents guidelines for employee responses to it.

Women have waited a long time for the issue of sexual harassment on the job to be taken seriously and have endured in a mainly patient and quiet manner too many indignities. While the subject is no longer a hidden one and some women have publicly protested their victimization, most women still "grin and bear it" or try a variety of individual solutions—including leaving their jobs, suffering psychological pain and financial hardship. In summing up the available data on incidence, Barbara Gutek (1992) concluded that "from one-third to one-half of all women have been sexually harassed at some time in their working lives" (p. 8), with the frequency greatest for women in nontraditional jobs and in nontraditional industries. Despite a paucity of careful studies focusing directly on harassment's effects on women who experience it, a good deal of incidental evidence has accumulated to support a list of probable outcomes. These have been reviewed (Gutek & Koss, 1993) and include a variety of negative work-related outcomes (such as leaving one's job) as well as psychological and physical health outcomes (such as lowered self-confidence, headaches, and so on). Some literature has also addressed the negative effects of sexual harassment on the workplace or organization itself. The reviewers suggest, on the basis of their examination of the existing literature, that "sexual harassment is hardly benign—either for the individual or the organization" (p. 16).

HIGH-ACHIEVING WOMEN

Some research has attempted to determine whether particular personality or background factors distinguish women who persist in the work force and who make exceptional progress in their jobs or careers. Women who achieve in the public sphere have been found to come from families in which independence, personal excellence, and assertiveness were stressed and encouraged. Women in nontraditional occupations, in particular, have been found to come from homes where they were encouraged to explore a wide range of behaviors and to manifest high levels of independence, assertiveness, and adventurousness as well as nurturance and expressiveness (Lemkau, 1979). In her investigation of a sample of employed women with master's degrees, Jeanne Lemkau (1983) found that occupationally atypical women differed from a group of equally well educated traditionally employed women in being more assertive, in having been more frequently first born, and in having had mothers who had

worked before their daughters were born. Women with master's degrees, whether in traditional or nontraditional jobs, differed from women in general in scoring higher on measures related to competence and in manifesting less sex-typing, but the occupationally atypical women were more likely "to have been exposed to parental models and values that do not enforce a division between femininity and competence in any occupational field, to a cultural milieu more supportive of female innovation, and to early experiences contributing to . . . high confidence in being able to succeed in male domains" (p. 164). Similarly, Gwyned Simpson (1984) reported that the African-American women lawyers she studied were taught by their parents that they must be autonomous and capable of taking care of themselves. Both their parents valued self-reliance and economic independence.

Some researchers have reported that high-achieving European-American women have a greater percentage of foreign-born parents and non-college-educated parents than would be expected by chance. Women physicians who persist in their work and do not take significant periods of time out for child rearing were found to be likely to come from "lower social class origins," to have established their career goals early, and to have been socialized in less traditional directions (Mandelbaum, 1978). Similarly, Helen Astin (1978), who followed a large group of women from their entry into college until 8 years after graduation, found that the married women who had worked continuously since graduating differed significantly from those who had not yet worked in being more likely to have foreign-born or non-college-educated parents, as well as in having been more involved in extracurricular college affairs and having majored in nontraditional fields such as natural science or business. Astin suggested that women who work continuously are likely to be motivated by a concern with social mobility—that is, to be striving to improve their social status relative to that of their parents. The college-educated women who did not work after college were more likely to have majored in fields such as the arts and the humanities, to have married men with graduate and professional degrees, to have started families early, and to have come from middle- and upper-middle-class backgrounds. Rita Mae Kelly (1983), who studied the lives of eminent women, also found that 65 percent of those who had attained political prominence had come from working-class or poor families; this was not the case for politically eminent men.

Having women role models has also been identified as an important correlate of work achievement by women.

Thus, Mary Walshok (1981) found that most women in a sample of blue-collar workers (primarily European-American and from rural backgrounds) came from families in which the mother was strong, resourceful, and employed. Similarly, among a group of African-American college women, Ann Burlew (1982) found that those aiming for nontraditional professions were more likely to have had more highly educated mothers who had worked in nontraditional fields than those making career choices traditional for women. A study of a group of women ministers (Steward, Steward, & Dary, 1983) reported the presence of influential mothers who served as role models for their daughters. And within Rita Mae Kelly's (1983) sample, very eminent women in politics or business were almost three times as likely to have had mothers who had worked at professional, business, or skilled jobs than women whose eminence derived from that of their husbands. Mothers who served competently in an independent public role seem to have made a difference for the leadership potential of their daughters, but not of their sons.

These findings support the conclusion that mothers serve as models for their daughters in the world of work; other women have also been found to function as models. M. Elizabeth Tidball (1980) found that "graduates of women's colleges are approximately twice as likely to be listed [on registers of public achievement] as are women graduates of coeducational institutions" (pp. 506f.). One reason proposed for the greater achievement by graduates of women's colleges is that they have been exposed to large numbers of women faculty. Tidball found an almost perfect positive correlation for colleges of varying sizes between the ratio of women achievers (cited in *Who's Who in America*) to women graduates and the ratio of women faculty to women graduates. Conversely, the correlation between the proportion of men enrolled in a college and its proportion of women achievers was found to be a strongly negative one.

Other researchers who have compared graduates of women's colleges with women graduates of coeducational institutions (e.g., Oates & Williamson, 1978) have found no significant differences between them in the percentage who have gone on to careers in nontraditional fields such as science, medicine, or business. Another study (Rice & Hemmings, 1988) examined the information provided on women listed in *Who's Who of American Women* and replicated Tidball's findings of an advantage for women's college graduates for women who had graduated in earlier decades. No difference, however, was found in achievement between graduates of women's colleges and gradu-ates of coeducational colleges for women who had graduated in the 1960s and 1970s.

In a different kind of study (Gilbert, Gallessich, & Evans, 1983), women doctoral students who self-identified with a woman faculty member were found to score significantly higher in self-report measures of self-esteem, instrumentality, work commitment, and career aspirations than women students who identified with a male professor. Of course, women students already high in self-esteem may tend to select women mentors, but the relationship found in this study is nevertheless of considerable interest. Others have also reported the advantage of a woman mentor or of attending women's schools. For example, a national survey found a substantially greater proportion of women in women's colleges than in other colleges majoring in the natural sciences and mathematics (cf. Lorimer, 1990). Another national study found that 12th graders in all-girls high schools were twice as likely to plan on majoring in math or science in college as 12th-grade girls in coeducational schools (cf. Rogers, 1992). My own experience in an all-girls high school supports such data: while I cannot be sure, I think at a coeducational school I would have been less likely to pursue 4 years of science and math and win the science medal at graduation.

With respect to personal demographics, it is not surprising to find that more women than men in comparable high-achieving careers remain unmarried and that career women are more likely than other women to not have children. Among 500 employees of a midwestern university, twice as many women as men were found to be unmarried (Herman & Gyllstrom, 1977). Others have found that women with Ph.D.s are less likely to marry than men with Ph.D.s. For example, one study (Glenwick, Johansson, & Bondy, 1978) found that proportionately more women assistant professors in two universities were either never married or divorced than a comparable group of men; and in another investigation (Yogev & Vierra, 1983), a higher rate of childlessness was found among a sample of university faculty women than in the general population for every age group sampled. A study of 300 top women executives (cf. Fowler, 1982) found that only 40.7 percent were married, compared with 94 percent of a group of men executives surveyed in an earlier study. The percentage of women who had never been married was 27.6 compared to 1 percent of the men.

A sample of corporate women was found to be more nonconforming, independent, and willing to take risks than a comparable sample of corporate men (Hatcher, 1991). Rosabeth Kanter (1977) has argued that an important correlate of a woman's achievement, beyond personal characteristics, background factors, or role models, is her location or position in the work structure. According to Kanter, it is more likely that "the job shapes the person" than vice versa; one's position in an organization has more relationship to one's productivity, self-esteem, and competence than socialization or background factors do. She studied a large corporation and found that a woman's success within it depended upon whether or not she was a lone woman among men and thus highly visible and vulnerable; able to reward and punish subordinates; and perceived as having power.

ENDING SEXISM IN THE WORKPLACE

Efforts to decrease or eliminate sexism in the workplace have taken many forms.

Legislation and Litigation

Congress has enacted a number of laws that, if strictly enforced and interpreted, would help reduce the current differential in the status of women and men in the work force. The first of these was the Equal Pay Act, passed in 1963, prohibiting wage discrimination and requiring that women and men "performing work in the same establishment under similar conditions must receive the same pay if their jobs require equal skill, effort, and responsibility" (U.S. Department of Labor, 1980, p. 1). This act applies to most workers in both the public and private sectors except those in small retail and service establishments. Since 1979 this act has been administered by the EEOC. Title VII of the Civil Rights Act of 1964, as amended by the Equal Employment Opportunity Act of 1972, prohibits discrimination based on sex, race, color, religion, and national origin in hiring, firing, wages, fringe benefits, classification, training, apprenticeships, or any conditions of employment. It covers establishments employing 15 or more workers and labor unions. According to Joan Hoff-Wilson (1988), "it took over a decade to put teeth into" the legislation, primarily through presidential executive orders, guidelines, and other laws. Some of these require contractors doing business with the federal government not to discriminate against any employee or applicant because of sex, color, religion, or national origin; that qualified women have access to job training programs; and that no educational institution

receiving federal assistance discriminate on the basis of gender in any of its programs or activities.

The U.S. Department of Labor urges women to assert their job rights by discussing them with personnel officers or supervisors, instituting grievance procedures through appropriate programs, and filing complaints with a state or federal agency. From the brief summary of legislation given above, one can see that the machinery exists to counter gender discrimination in employment. Unfortunately, this machinery has proven cumbersome; time-consuming; painfully slow; and a drain on the energy, financial resources, and self-confidence of those who bring forth individual complaints. A satisfactory solution is rarely achieved without years of struggle and frustration. One reason is that a huge number of claims are filed with federal agencies not able to handle them quickly and efficiently. Positive outcomes have been more likely for women acting together in class action suits.

Women have won some dramatic victories through administrative channels and in the courts. For example, the Office for Federal Contract Compliance greatly increased the numbers of women in banking, insurance, and mining following pressure and litigation (Ilchman, 1986). And in 1980, a federal court awarded women working for Western Electric Company in New Jersey close to $9 million in back wages after finding the company guilty of sex discrimination. According to David Rosenbaum (1980), this case

> is one of hundreds in recent years in which companies and government agencies have been forced to pay back wages to women, raise their salaries and make special allowances in the future to overcome the effects of past discrimination. . . . Job discrimination suits [have been brought] on behalf of women in all walks of life . . . [and the] money involved in the settlements runs into hundreds of millions of dollars. (p. E-3)

Among the employers who have been compelled through lawsuits (most of which were settled out of court) to compensate women for sex discrimination are American Airlines; American Telephone & Telegraph; Brown University; General Electric; Lockheed California; Merrill Lynch, Pierce, Fenner & Smith; the New York Times; Northwest Airlines; Uniroyal; United Airlines; the U.S. Government Printing Office; the U.S. Navy; and the University of Minnesota. In 1980 the Department of Labor ordered the University of Rhode Island to equalize the wages of women classified as cleaners with those of men doing the same work but classified as janitors, resulting in an award of $150,000 in retroactive pay. And in 1985, a federal district judge ruled that the University of Rhode Island had systematically discriminated against women faculty members by hiring them at lower ranks and paying them less than men with similar qualifications.

As a consequence of a class action suit brought against the *New York Times,* 23 percent of its reporters and 25 percent of its photographers are now women, and so are some of its editors and managers (Robertson, 1991). Among the most recent successful sex discrimination suits is that against the State Farm Insurance Companies, which brought a record settlement of $157 million in lost wages to be paid to hundreds of women (Bryant, 1992). An indication of the kind of resistance put up by employers in cases of this kind is the 18-year fight by the U.S. Navy. The federal judge who finally ruled against the Navy said that "the Federal Government wasted time and money and were sometimes just plain mean" in prolonging the litigation "by every means possible, both foul and fair" (cf. Douglas, 1991, p. E-7).

An example of a successful suit brought by an individual and finally resolved by the Supreme Court, is that of *Ann Hopkins v. Price Waterhouse.* Despite the fact that Ms. Hopkins "had secured more major contracts than any other candidate for partnership in the year she applied," she was turned down because her demeanor was not considered sufficiently "feminine." She had been advised to "wear make-up, have her hair styled, and wear jewelry." The Supreme Court supported her claim that her gender played a part in her employer's refusal to promote her (cf. Franke & Toll, 1989).

Although some impressive lawsuits have been won by women, litigation requires years to reach completion and takes up enormous amounts of money, energy, and commitment; there is no guarantee of winning. The court victories for women "hardly make a ripple in the ocean of discrimination" (Rosenbaum, 1980). A 1985 judicial decision in favor of the Sears Roebuck Company was a serious setback for women using the law and the courts to fight job discrimination. The EEOC first filed a lawsuit against Sears in 1979. Whereas other big firms charged with sex bias had settled out of court, Sears refused to do so. According to Jon Wiener (1985),

> the complaint covered the years 1973 through 1980. During that period, 60 percent of the applicants for all sales jobs at Sears and 40 percent of those qualified for commission sales posts [selling big-ticket goods, which is better paying] were women. Only 27 percent of those hired for commission jobs were women, however. Although 72 percent of Sears noncommission salespeople

were women, they received only 40 percent of the promotions. (p. 174)

A federal court rejected the statistical evidence and was persuaded by Sears that "women did not want the higher paying commission sales jobs because they had different values from men" ("Sears' Acquittal," 1986, p. A-2), were "afraid of competition with other salespeople and rejection by customers . . . [were] unfamiliar with most product lines sold on commission [which include fencing and auto parts, but also washing machines and draperies], and they didn't want additional responsibilities" (Wiener, 1985, p. 176). With respect to discrimination against women on college and university faculties, Mary Gray (1985) has noted that "in the twelve years since nondiscrimination statutes became applicable to faculty employment, . . . women have had little success in winning legal redress for employment discrimination in hiring, salary, promotion, and tenure. . . . The burdens in time and money faced by those seeking remedies make litigation accessible to only a few" (p. 33).

More positive outcomes may be forthcoming as a result of the Civil Rights Act of 1991, which "provides for increased damages and jury trials [if requested] in cases of intentional sex, religious, and disability bias" (Gamble, 1991, p. S-1). Prior to this act, compensatory and punitive damages were allowed only to racial and ethnic minorities. The 1991 legislation amended Title VII of the Civil Rights Act of 1964 and established a Glass Ceiling Commission to study barriers faced by women and minorities to advancement in the work force.

Union Solidarity

Labor unions in the United States have made less effort to organize workers in industries where most women work than in those where men predominate, even though the struggles of women clothing and textile workers in the early part of this century contributed dramatically to the birth of the labor movement in this country. Nevertheless, women are the fastest-growing segment of new unionists. In 1975, 34.1 percent of women blue-collar workers, 11.5 percent of women clerical workers, 11.1 percent of women service and private household workers, and 6.2 percent of women sales workers belonged to unions (Noble, 1989). Today, while union membership is down (only 12 percent of all workers compared with 35 percent in the late 1950s, and 22 percent in 1980), women comprise 36 percent of all union members (Bender, 1992; Colatosti, 1992).

Until the mid 1970s, as A. H. Raskin (1977) pointed out, "the 'Men Only' sign [was] . . . firmly in place on the staircase leading to unionism's top floor"; but change has come, and women's potential for labor movement leadership—and the importance of organizing women—has been recognized. According to William Serrin (1985),

women have moved into organizing, political lobbying, research and other important staff positions in such unions as the United Automobile Workers, the United Electrical Workers, the American Federation of State, County and Municipal Employees, the United Mine Workers of America and the Service Employees International Union. (p. A-14)

Although thus far only one woman, an African-American, has served as president of a major union (Mary Futrell, of the National Education Association), two women were on the 35-member executive council of the American Federation of Labor and Congress of Industrial Organizations in 1985. The first woman ever to be elected to this council, in 1980, was Joyce Miller, vice president of the Amalgamated Clothing and Textile Workers Union.

In 1973, a small number of clerical workers in Boston, under the leadership of Karen Nussbaum and Ellen Cassedy, organized for "better pay, better training opportunities and greater stature in the workplace" ("Women in Clerical Jobs," 1985). From this local group grew a national organization known as *9to5: The National Association of Working Women,* which now has chapters all across the country. In 1981 it joined forces with the much larger Service Employees International Union to create District 925, dedicated to organizing the "nearly 20 million female secretaries, stenographers, typists, clerks, keypunch operators and other office workers in the United States" ("Working Women Join Forces," 1981). This movement among clerical workers has been successful in changing the image of the secretary, enhancing women workers' self-esteem and confidence, and improving the conditions of work.

Comparable Worth

In an effort to reduce the differential between salaries earned by most women (in "women's jobs") and salaries earned by most men, some have proposed that jobs that involve comparable effort, training, skill, and responsibility should pay comparable wages or salaries. Carolyn Bell (1984) has pointed out that by extending the principle of equal pay for equal work to situations in which jobs are not identical but comparable, a social policy requiring equal

pay for comparable jobs "would remove the impact of existing discriminatory practices" (p. 17). Paying workers in accordance with the value of their work to their employer would significantly enhance job equity.

Proponents of comparable worth have presented illustrations of salary inequities such as the following: in 1979 a clerk (typically a woman) employed by the State of New York earned $7,195 a year, compared to a parking attendant (typically a man) employed by the state who earned $8,825; in Montgomery County, Maryland, a schoolteacher received an average of $12,323, compared to a liquor store clerk earning $12,479; and in Denver, Colorado, a city-employed registered nurse made $12,768, while a building painter employed by the city made $14,292 (Greenhouse, 1981). A study in San Jose, California found that city jobs generally held by women (such as librarian, nurse, recreation supervisor, stenographer) paid significantly less than comparable jobs held by men (such as electrician, plumber, carpenter, mechanic); for example, the biweekly salary of a nurse was $772, while that of a mechanic was $1,152 ("Strikers Demand," 1981). In Nassau County, New York, communication technicians who send out fire trucks (mostly men) had starting salaries of $14,805 a year, while police communication and teletype operators (mostly women) started at $13,188 (Roberts & Slade, 1984). A study of occupational title ratings (cf. Feldberg, 1984) found that child-care workers were rated lower than parking-lot attendants, that nursery schoolteachers were rated far below marine mammal handlers, and nurse-midwives below hotel clerks.

On the basis of such data, the principle of comparable worth has won some dramatic support. In the first of a group of court cases, a suit brought by four Oregon prison matrons because they were paid only 70 percent as much as male prison guards was upheld by the Supreme Court in 1981. The Court thus acknowledged the legal validity of a comparable worth argument. Later that year, in San Jose, California, city workers won $1.5 million in equity raises in "the first successful strike over equal pay for comparable work" (Cassedy & Nussbaum, 1983, p. 45). In 1983, a federal judge put into practice the comparable worth doctrine that had been supported two years earlier by the Supreme Court, by finding the State of Washington guilty of sex discrimination because it did not provide equal pay for jobs of comparable skill, effort, and responsibility. This decision was subsequently struck down by a U.S. court of appeals, but a promise by the union representing the state employees to take the case to the Supreme Court if necessary led to a settlement of $482 million. As noted in the press, this was the largest settlement yet and "a major victory for the comparable work movement" ("Wash. Court," 1986, p. A-3).

Those opposed to the concept of comparable worth argue that it would radically interfere with the natural market process of supply and demand. But proponents point out that the comparable worth principle was first proposed by a federal agency (the War Labor Board, in the 1940s) when the government was eager to attract women workers to industry; and that market factors are not responsible for women's low wages as much as "a tradition that has treated women as temporary and supplementary workers, devalued women's work, and rationalized low wages as all that women qua women need" (Feldberg, 1984, p. 318). A case in point is that of nurses, who although in high demand have traditionally received lower pay than men in comparable jobs. According to economist Marianne Ferber (1982), wages are determined more by employers (and unions) than by market factors; within a single industry "the wide range of wages paid to workers with very similar qualifications cannot be assumed to be the result of impersonal market forces" (p. 292). Widely used methods already exist for calculating the worth of jobs and for determining wages and salaries. Comparable worth advocates are suggesting that these methods be improved in the interest of gender equity. Former congresswoman Claudine Schneider (1985), for example, has pointed out that federal government workers are already classified by GS level, and that two thirds of all U.S. workers are employed by firms where some form of job evaluation already exists.

Family Leave and Child Care

To end sexism in the workplace requires an end to job segregation by gender and an end to discrimination in hiring, salary, and promotion. It also requires a recognition of the comparable worth of different jobs and an enlightened employment policy that guarantees a leave of absence to pregnant women and to parents of both genders to care for biological or adopted children. As noted earlier, the United States has finally, in 1993, adopted a national policy that gives some employed parents a specific time-off period for childbirth and child care with job protection. This program does not provide for paid leave and is less inclusive than programs in most other countries. And only the United States has no federal subsidy for day care. Even some developing countries are ahead of the United States in this respect.

Some states, acting on their own before federal legislation, mandated that family leaves be granted if requested. A study by 9to5 that compared seven states with some form of required parental leave with seven states that did not have such a law found no evidence that parental leave policies hurt the growth of small businesses or had any negative effects on international competitiveness ("9to5 Proves," 1988). The courts also entered into the discussion of family leave. A nearly 20-year-old class-action lawsuit against AT&T was finally settled in 1991, and $66 million was paid to the claimants, who had been forced to take unpaid maternity leave at the end of their sixth or seventh month of pregnancy without assurance that they would get their jobs back (Miller & Stone, 1991).

The urgent need for federal child-care assistance is indicated by the facts: in 1988, 51.5 percent of children under 6 had mothers employed outside the home; and, in 1986, while families earning $45,000 a year spent an average of 4 percent of their income on child care, 22 percent of family income went to child care among poverty level families (Holmes, 1990). An option adopted by some 1,200 companies is to run their own on-site child care facilities (Sherlock, 1990). And an intriguing suggestion to assist young women scientists, made by Carl Djerassi (1988), but not likely to be acted upon in the near future, is to "make available—on a competitive basis related to professional promise or performance—5-year grants . . . for domestic childcare support . . . [Such a program] would signal to American professional women that child bearing is not considered a biological burden but rather a societal benefit deserving societal support" (p. 10).

WOMEN NEED BOTH LOVE AND WORK

Employed women face special stresses and dilemmas not shared by working men. Although men may also be frustrated in their search for meaningful, well-paid work that provides opportunities for advancement, their pursuit of occupational achievement is applauded and unambiguously approved by society. Such is less often the case for women. In addition, women are generally more educated than men in the same occupational category and are therefore more likely to experience the frustration of being underused. In jobs that are equal to women's abilities, the earnings are typically less than those of male colleagues.

The old Yiddish expression "With friends like these, who needs enemies?" may describe how some women feel after having experienced the obstacles to job satisfaction described in this chapter; some may well say, "With problems like these, who needs a job?" Thus, millions of married women continue to labor only in their own homes and to serve their families for no wages and little social recognition, their behavior maintained by the pleasures derived from family life, the hoped-for affection of husband and children, and avoidance of the frustrations awaiting them outside.

Most women in our society, however, do work for money outside of our homes, and expect to do so, contradicting the myth that women will be cared for by men, and that home-baked pies and a pretty face are the routes to a happy life. Among respondents to a nationwide Associated Press poll ("Poll: Women," 1986), 58 percent agreed that women should have an equal chance to do any job that men do; and an equal percentage of men and women said it was good that more women were now working outside the home. Younger respondents were more positive about this trend than older ones, with 60 percent of 18- to 34-year-olds agreeing that the increasing number of working women was a good thing.

But, unless our society and its important institutions actively and explicitly promote the ideal that women should work on an equal basis with men, women will not have the opportunity to acquire skills, attitudes, and objectives that maximize their potential to fully function in the public sphere of work. We must work toward encouraging women to make full use of their skills and aptitudes and toward decreasing the formidable obstacles now faced in the workplace. We must accept the idea that working for pay is part of a woman's identity and eliminate the dilemma of having to choose between love and work, between personal relationships and achievement, between family satisfactions and those attainable through a job or career. Women, like men, should be encouraged to strive for both.

◆ Discussion Questions

1. What can we learn from "Rosie the Riveter"?

2. How do the experiences of girls and women prepare them (or not) for the world of paid employment?

3. Project yourself 7 to 10 years into the future; what do you see yourself doing with respect to work and relationships or family?

4. Distinguish between women as behavers (doers and actors) and women as stimuli or objects—that is, as perceived or reacted to in the work place.

5. What are the barriers to women's achievement in the work force or in careers? Discuss this with some working women you know, of different ages, of different social classes, and in different occupations.

6. What are the positive and negative consequences to women from participating in the paid work force?

ADULT PERSONALITY AND WELL-BEING: FULFILLING AND NOT FULFILLING CULTURAL EXPECTATIONS

A man of about thirty strikes us as a youthful, somewhat unformed individual, whom we expect to make powerful use of the possibilities for development opened to him by analysis. A woman of the same age, however, often frightens us by her physical rigidity and unchangeability. . . . There are no paths open to further development . . . as though, indeed, the difficult development of femininity had exhausted the possibilities of the person concerned.

SIGMUND FREUD (1933/1964, P. 1340)

Why is it only women who go to therapists? If Jack's in a bad mood and you ask him what's wrong he'll say he wanted to play racquetball and the weather's rotten or he's worried [about politics]. . . . If you ask Jessica or me, we'll say our heads are messed up, we don't know why. Men are always looking on the outside to solve problems and women are always looking into . . . our own heads.

JUDITH ROSSNER (1983, P. 282)

[Wellness is] not . . . something one has or doesn't have, but rather . . . an ideal that, in fact, exists along a continuum. . . . It is not a once-and-forever thing. . . . Just as wellness can erode under conditions of adversity, it can be enhanced by favorable conditions or processes, both natural and engineered. This view is at once a source of challenge and hope. The challenge is to identify factors or conditions that advance or restrict wellness, and the hope is that such information, once unearthed, can be used to shape informed effort to promote it.

EMORY L. COWAN (1991, PP. 404, 405)

THE THREE QUOTES THAT OPEN THIS CHAPTER speak to the themes that will be addressed here: the myths and assumptions in our culture about women's "nature" and adult personality; the way women are encouraged to interpret life problems in internal terms without relating them to external contexts; and an approach to well-being that focuses on factors contributing to functional, effective behavior.

In our society, certain motives, attitudes, and behaviors are said to distinguish "feminine" from "masculine" pursuits and persons. The extent to which girls grow into women who fulfill the expectations of our culture depends on the success with which institutionalized sanctions and differential experiences provide girls with information and role models, and the extent to which their learning experiences and situations continue to be arranged in the culturally defined direction. In this chapter we will consider some of the consequences of the social expectations for women's behavior that begin in childhood and continue in adult life.

Psychologists use the term *trait* to refer to behavior that a person tends to exhibit consistently and frequently across diverse situations (reflecting internalized attributes, or personality) and the term *role* to refer to behavior that is specific to situations and to persons of a particular status. How much of what a woman is observed to do reflects one or the other of these categories of behavior is a question currently being addressed by empirical studies and theoretical arguments and will be raised repeatedly in this chapter as we examine the behavior of adult women in various situations. Another important and relevant term is *habit*. While a trait defines a behavioral tendency that, once acquired, remains stable, internal, and cross-situational, the concept of habit ties the performance of a learned response not only to its strength based on prior practice and reinforcement, but also to situational cues and consequences present at the time. The distinction between a trait and a habit is of great significance, since a habit is behavior that is not assumed to be consistent across situations but fundamentally related to context and conditions. As we will see in this chapter, systematically collected data and personal experiences support the conclusions (Lott & Maluso, 1993) (1) that human behavior is typically not well described by traits; and (2) that individuals learn responses in, and to, situations continuously throughout our lives. As conditions and opportunities for practice change, so does our behavior. Emphasized throughout this book is the proposition that socialization is a lifelong process reflecting changing

circumstances and experiences. This view is strengthened by the variations we see in women's lives associated with social class, ethnicity, historical circumstances, and individual differences.

Research suggests that a female body has few predictable consequences for behavior unless paired by culture with a complex set of demands, anticipations, and circumstances. Women and men can (and do) acquire the same habits, attitudes, aspirations, and motives under the same learning conditions, but they acquire different behavioral propensities if their experiences and the way their responses are reinforced systematically differ. In other words, variations in experiences result in variations in the behaviors we learn, a theme present throughout this book. Thus, personality and role consequences for women are not inevitable but are related to cultural and family emphases, training, and opportunities.

FEMININITY

Our culture defines womanhood differently from manhood, equating the former with femininity. As argued by Susan Brownmiller (1984), however, "biological femaleness is not enough. Femininity always demands more. It must constantly reassure its audience by a willing demonstration of difference" (p. 15). Brownmiller reminds us of how often women are admonished not to "lose" their femininity and complimented if they have managed to "retain" their femininity. "To fail at the feminine difference is to appear not to care about men, and to risk the loss of their attention and approval" (p. 15), as well as that of other women, friends, colleagues, and employers. Whatever else one does, women are told, as we see in the advertisement shown on p. 270, we must not compromise our femininity. Even job success depends on it.

Definitions

Dictionary definitions of the word *feminine* are surprisingly vague, typically making reference to the term *womanly* and sometimes giving one or two adjectives describing feminine traits, such as *weak, gentle, modest*. Yet, this word is used frequently in ordinary conversation and in the mass media. Janet Spence (1985) has suggested that people find it difficult to specify particular attributes but use the terms *feminine* and *masculine* to define a "fundamental property

You've never compromised your femininity for your success.

Maybe that's why you're so successful.

Woman should not compromise their "feminity," according to a lingerie company.

ance," and of masculinity as "self-centeredness, formality, hardheadedness, and coolness" (p. 438). This typical earlier view assumed that femininity and masculinity were at opposite ends of a single continuum or dimension, and that the more one is feminine the less one can be masculine, and vice versa. This unidimensional position has been challenged, as we will see later on, but is still part of much everyday thinking.

Stereotypes

Women (and men) tend to describe themselves *but more especially* others in ways that conform to stereotypes about gender. Diverse samples of adults in this country, varying in age, religion, marital status, and education, have been found to generally agree on traits that differentiate the genders when asked to respond to particular items. As summarized by Kristen Yount (1986),

> The evidence across different instruments reveals a common core of stereotypic female characteristics portraying women as warm and expressive (e.g., kind, gentle, sympathetic) and male characteristics depicting men as assertive and goal-oriented (e.g., dominant, competitive, competent). . . . Sex differences in self-ratings frequently emerge on the same items or scales that differentiate the male and female stereotypes, although sex differences with respect to fewer characteristics emerge on self-ratings and the mean self-ratings of each sex are significantly less sex-stereotyped than the mean ratings of the typical male and female." (p. 64)

or aspect of the individual's self-concept" that identifies one as a woman or a man.

Are any personal qualities or characteristics, or specific behaviors, situations, tasks, or jobs, associated with being feminine as distinguished from masculine? Some psychologists have constructed tests that provide respondents with scores indicating their degree of femininity (or masculinity) based on whether their answers to questions about particular activities, interests, or characteristics are in line with stereotyped assumptions. Thus, for example, in an early measure constructed by Harrison Gough (1952), to be scored as "feminine" required agreeing that you become irritated when you see someone spit on the sidewalk, that you find the thought of being in an automobile accident very frightening, that you prefer romantic stories to adventure stories, and that you would not like to be a building contractor! In constructing his test, Gough was guided by a definition of femininity that included "acceptingness, softness, mildness, and toler-

A classic group of studies by one set of investigators (Broverman, Vogel, Broverman, Clarkson, & Rosenkrantz, 1972), in which respondents were asked to rate themselves and the average adult man and the average adult woman on 122 bipolar adjectives (for example, not at all aggressive versus very aggressive), found that women and men agreed in their descriptions of each gender and that characteristics associated with men were perceived as more socially desirable than those associated with women. Women were assigned such traits as the following: does not use harsh language; is talkative, tactful, gentle, aware of the feelings of others, religious, interested in own appearance, neat in habits, and quiet; has strong need for security; appreciates art and literature; and expresses tender feelings. Men, on the other hand, were said to be aggressive, independent, unemotional, objective, active, competitive, logical, worldly, and direct. The positively valued traits attributed to men were found to cluster in a factor identified as competence-assertion-rationality, while the positively valued traits ascribed to women constituted a warmth-expressiveness factor.

More recent studies using a variety of different methods have found little substantial change in the content of gender stereotypes. Thus, for example, one investigation (Werner & LaRussa, 1985), in which the results from a 1978 study were compared with results from 1958, found that 62 percent of adjectives ascribed in 1958 to men, and 77 percent of those ascribed to women, remained part of the stereotypes in 1978. There was some tendency for women in the later study to view women more favorably than they had previously, and more favorably than men viewed women. Among women respondents, 67 percent of the adjectives applied to women were favorable, compared to 57 percent of the adjectives applied to women by men. Although some older adjective descriptions were replaced by new ones, "in no case did an adjective change sexes over the two decades" (p. 1095), and the researchers concluded that "sex-role stereotypes have changed little in recent decades" (p. 1098). The same conclusion was reached by other investigators (e.g., Smith & Midlarsky, 1985) who had equal numbers of African-American and European-American women and men rate adjectives for degree of femaleness and maleness and social desirability. They found that "current conceptions of femaleness and maleness . . . [had] marked similarities to earlier conceptions" (p. 325) with men viewed as aggressive, work-minded, and capable of leadership and women as sensitive, affectionate, and conscious of appearance. Compared with men's views of women, women saw themselves more positively and in terms of activities rather than traits, but in general all conformed to the same gender stereotypes. Other investigators have also reported that change in gender stereotypes is more likely to occur in women's beliefs than in men's beliefs. One study of a college student sample (DeLisi & Soundranayagam, 1990) reported that although the prototypical view of women clustered around niceness and nurturance, and that of men around potency and strength, women's responses to 217 adjectives in terms of how representative they were of adult women and men revealed a "broader conceptualization of women" that was not shared by the male respondents.

Hope Landrine (1985) asked a sample of college students to respond to a series of adjectives by indicating how closely they matched our society's stereotypes of women who were identified as African-American or European-American, and middle-class or lower-class. She found differences related to class and to ethnicity, but she also found that all the profiles were basically similar to the traditional stereotype of women described by earlier researchers. The European-American middle-class woman fit the stereotype for women most closely. While European-American lower-class women were rated as more confused, impulsive, and irresponsible than middle-class women, and African-American women as more hostile and superstitious than European-American women, respondents agreed that, regardless of class or ethnicity, a woman had stereotypically feminine characteristics. Their own judgments tended to be similar to those they viewed as society's, suggesting to Landrine that "general endorsement of social stereotypes persists" (p. 73).

A 1988 replication of a study conducted in 1972 (Bergen & Williams, 1991) found that when college students were asked to indicate the cultural association of each adjective on a list of 300 with women, men, or neither, the correlation between scores in the two studies was close to perfect (.90). The investigators concluded, as have others cited above, that there is "no evidence that the male and female stereotypes in the United States have become generally less differentiated across the time period studied" (p. 422). The "Sylvia" cartoon on p. 272 illustrates the continued robustness of our gender stereotypes and how easy it is to laugh at them (if only they weren't so serious!).

Our definitions of femininity and masculinity, and ascriptions of different traits, activities, and interests to women and men, are related to our learned expectations and to our observations in particular situations in which women and men are found. These definitions and ascriptions thus reflect differential opportunities to take part in activities. This is illustrated by the results of a study by Rachelle Canter and Beth Meyerowitz (1984). They asked a sample of college students to report on their ability, enjoyment, performance, and opportunity to perform 23 "feminine" sex-typed and 22 "masculine" activities and found a positive relationship between the opportunity to engage in an activity or behavior and the frequency of its performance.

When self-reported and observed characteristics are carefully examined, sizable individual differences within genders are found as well as a wide overlap between women and men on all attributes. This suggests that masculinity and femininity do not represent mutually exclusive poles on a single dimension. Another view that has proved to be very popular, and a strong stimulus to research, is that femininity and masculinity are each represented by a set of distinctive traits that are indepen-

sylvia, by Nicole Hollander. Cartoonists & Writers Syndicate.

dent of one another, so that persons may vary in the extent to which they manifest each mode, and both modes, regardless of their gender. In this approach, first proposed by Carl Jung in the early part of this century (see *The Basic Writings,* 1959), persons who describe themselves as displaying some characteristics typically associated with their own gender and some characteristics associated with the other gender are labeled androgynous. Measures have been constructed that assess sex-typed and androgynous orientations by giving persons independent scores on both femininity and masculinity (Bem, 1974, 1978; Spence, Helmreich, & Stapp, 1974). Developers of these measures recognized that many women and men often behave similarly to one another and manifest the same characteristics. Nevertheless, they continued to label some attributes as feminine and others as masculine, thus implying the existence of separate constellations of traits associated with each gender.

In my view, such a separation of characteristics by gender is inaccurate and reinforces the linguistic and cognitive association of certain behaviors with one gender or the other, despite their actual performance by both. We know that any behavior can be learned by any person capable of performing it, given appropriate conditions for its acquisition, and that the behavior will be maintained if it continues to be situationally appropriate and is approved and not punished. No evidence exists that one group of people (distinguished by sex, color, socioeconomic level, or language) is more naturally suited for some responses than are others. To label some behaviors as feminine because our culture attempts to teach them primarily to

girls and women obscures the essential humanness of the behaviors and dulls our appreciation of their fundamental teachability and modifiability.

Some critics (e.g., Lott, 1981; Wallston, 1981) have urged discontinuing the use of masculine and feminine labels because they reinforce false dichotomies. We will return to this issue later in this chapter. And some of the major contributors to the assessment of femininity, masculinity, and androgyny have now concluded that their tests do not, in fact, actually measure such personality constellations. For example, Janet Spence and Robert Helmreich (1980) have clearly stated that their own test, the *Personal Attributes Questionnaire* (PAQ), does not measure masculinity or femininity but rather gender-neutral, "socially desirable instrumental and expressive characteristics" (p. 157). Elsewhere, Janet Spence (1983) has noted that the labels *instrumental* and *expressive,* or *self-assertive* and *interpersonally oriented,* are more descriptive of the content of the PAQ scales than gender labels are, and she has urged researchers to use the terms *instrumental* and *expressive traits* when referring to scores on the masculinity and femininity scales, respectively, of the PAQ (Spence, 1984). What so-called masculinity scales actually measure are self-reported instrumental, assertive, agentic, and task-oriented behaviors, while so-called femininity scales measure self-reported expressive, communal, and interpersonally sensitive behaviors. Some researchers who have factor-analyzed items on femininity and masculinity scales have reported that they measure still other attributes. For example, an analysis of the frequently used Bem Sex Role Inventory (BSRI) found that what it actually measured could best be described as "other-directedness" and "self-directedness" (Ballard-Reisch & Elton, 1992).

We know from observation and self-reports that women and men manifest varied behaviors at different times under appropriate conditions and that there are sizable individual differences within both groups. Some men may be generally more nurturant or other-directed than some women, and some women may be generally more instrumental or self-directed than some men. While women and men in our society may differ on average in their responses to some items on self-report scales, this does not mean that the scales assess womanliness or manliness.

A provocative hypothesis regarding gender stereotypes was proposed and tested by Curt Hoffman and Nancy Hurst (1990). Their view is that these "stereotypes are largely an attempt to rationalize, justify, or explain the sexual division of labor" (p. 199). Given this division, especially with regard to child care, people assume "that there are inherent differences between males and females that make each sex better suited for its role." To test this proposition, Hoffman and Hurst had college students rate persons called city workers and others called child raisers, living on another planet, on a number of dimensions. Although each group was described to the respondents quite similarly, the child raisers were given higher ratings on communal and nurturant traits, whereas the city workers were given higher ratings on agentic and instrumental traits.

Kristen Yount (1986) proposed and tested a very similar hypothesis, that sex role stereotypes reflect the existing gender segregation in the workplace, or in other words that "personality attributes emerging from traditionally female or male occupations are abstracted and generalized to all women and men and are conceived as masculinity and femininity" (p. 65). To test this proposition, 427 women and 266 men were surveyed in rural households in Colorado, and comparisons were made in the self-reports of physical workers, business workers, workers who tend others, and full-time homemakers. It was found that most gender differences "disappear when occupation is controlled" (p. 80). For example, both homemakers and those in tending occupations more often described themselves as sympathetic, whereas physical workers more often described themselves as aggressive, dominant, and forceful, attributes associated with power. Another study of gender stereotypes has provided additional information of interest. Alice Eagly and Mary Kite (1987) found, within a college student sample, that there was a greater similarity between the stereotypes of

nationalities and the stereotypes of the men than of the women in those nationalities, with this more true of those nationalities rated low on gender equality. In other words, the higher the status of men, the more they are taken to be representative of their societies.

Pressures

Nowhere do we see our society's efforts to maintain the false dichotomies of gender expended so tirelessly than in the perpetuation of standards for women's attractiveness and style by the fashion industry and the mass media. The pressure on women to change our looks to conform to feminine ideals and models directs us to use cosmetics, wear the latest fashion in clothes, deodorize, shave body hair, diet, and even undergo surgery to take off or enhance parts of ourselves in order to achieve the feminine image. While the specific content and tactics of the persuasive messages may change from one decade to the next, the intended consequences remain much the same. As of this writing, the fashionable look for women has once again changed dramatically. "The mature, big-haired and big-breasted look is out, and the short, waiflike and waferlike look is in" (Angier, 1993, p. E-2). The newest models, "skinny and childlike," have led some to ask whether this move by the fashion industry represents a backlash against women's achievements in the workplace and gradual increase in status and power.

Perhaps those who prepare the ads and products for women agree with Sigmund Freud (1933) that narcissism is one of the "psychical peculiarities of mature femininity" (p. 132), which he attributed to our envy of the penis. Physical vanity and the high value women place on their charms, he said, are a compensation for their "original sexual inferiority" and contribute to their stronger need to be loved than to love. If this were indeed the case, however, it would hardly be necessary to continue encouraging us from childhood on to show off our physical attributes, to relish flattery, and to attempt to attract attention by our good looks, clothes, and sexy figure. During my stay at Stanford University in 1993, Playboy photographers came to campus and advertised for female students to come forward and be photo-interviewed for a "fall pictorial, Girls of the Pac 10 Conference." Other campuses on which women were being recruited were Arizona, Arizona State, UC Berkeley, Oregon, Oregon State, UCLA, USC, Washington, and Washington State. In the projected Playboy issue, the "girls," according to a Stanford reporter (Stein, 1993), "will be nude, semi-nude or clothed, depending on the simple, easy-to-read application which also asked the size of their bust, cup, waist, hips and shoes. . . . The applicants will be paid on a sliding scale . . . : $500 for complete nudity, $300 for knickers and significantly less for sweaters, jeans and a frilly hat" (p. 1).

African-American women have written with bitterness about the pain, bewilderment, and frustration they have experienced in having to measure their beauty against the standard set by European-American models. A woman in a story by Paule Marshall (1975), for example, comments, "like nearly every little black girl, I had my share of dreams of waking up to find myself with long, blond curls, blue eyes, and skin like buttermilk" (p. 122). European-American girls, too, dream of having hair that is curlier (or straighter), breasts that are larger (or smaller), and faces and figures that are closer to their idea of perfection. But for African-American women, "the idea of beauty as defined by white America has been an assault on . . . personhood" (Washington, 1975, p. xvii). Gloria Joseph (1981c) compared a sample of magazines most popular with African-American women with those read most often by European-American women and found that the poses, clothing, styles, and makeup featured in each were similar.

While many women find these pressures hard to resist, others turn their backs on them. For example, Susan Faludi (1991) has reported on the sharp drop in the sales of women's apparel in the United States in 1987, a time of economic stress but also a year that saw the sales of men's clothing rise by 2.1 percent. That was the year the fashion industry turned out "little-girl" and "baby-doll" looks that women were supposed to embrace as suitable for their feminine image. But they failed to do so. As Faludi noted:

> Perhaps the designers should have expected it. They were pushing "little-girl" dresses and "slender silhouettes" at a time when the average American woman was thirty-two years old, weighed 143 pounds and wore a size 10 or 12 dress. Fewer than one-fourth of American women were taller than five foot four or wore a size smaller than 14—but 95 percent of the fashions were designed to fit these specifications. (p. 171)

One of the largest studies of women's shopping behavior had found "only three groups of women who were loyal followers of fashion: the very young, the very social, and the very anxious" (p. 174).

Yet, each year, the designers continue to push their newest definition of femininity, seemingly oblivious to the needs and desires of real women. As noted by Patricia McLaughlin (1992), the designers behave as though they are "caught in a time warp," presenting clothes for women that will help them "attract a suitable husband" or "to look as much as possible like ladies of leisure when- . . . out in public." McLaughlin argued that although high fashion "has never quite broken out of this double paradigm of opulence and seduction, . . . women have" (p. D-2). Nevertheless, the cajoling and tempting of women to uphold the feminine image both on the outside and on the inside continues. In the 1990s, we read in trend-setting magazines that "girdles are back," with such new names as body slimmers and body shapers (Darnton, 1991, p. 63). A measure of effectiveness of the pressures on women to conform to the new trends is the volume of lingerie sales—$8 million in 1990. Lingerie is the fastest growing division of women's apparel, as illustrated by the booming popularity of the company Victoria's Secret. Interestingly, men are big customers; they are 30 to 40 percent of Victoria's Secret shoppers and account for nearly half the sales in dollars (Faludi, 1991).

Naomi Wolf (1991) has called attention to what she calls the "third shift" for contemporary women—one at home, one at work, and one trying to get that gorgeous figure through cosmetics, exercise, dieting, the right clothes, and even surgery. The exploitation of women as they are pressured to pursue femininity is "fed by a $20 billion-a-year cosmetics industry, a $33 billion diet industry, [and] a $300 million cosmetic surgery industry" (Dowd, 1991, p. E-3). Cosmetic surgery (to alter breasts, noses, hips, chins, thighs, or whatever), the fastest growing specialty in U.S. medicine, is geared primarily toward women, who make up 85 percent of the patients (Faludi, 1991); these patients have included fashion models who, prior to the rise of the gamine image, while otherwise thin "felt such pressure to be voluptuous that they had breast implant surgery" (Angier, 1993, p. E-2). Wolf's argument, that a woman's definition in terms of youth and beauty has been extended into the work world, is supported by examination of advertisements for beauty products in the 1980s. According to Susan Faludi (1991, p. 202), "in ad after ad, the beauty industry hammered home . . . [the message that] women's professional progress had downgraded their looks; equality had created worry lines and cellulite."

The success of our society's pressure on women to achieve femininity by aspiring to the thin body that is the current ideal is indicated by study after study finding women dissatisfied with their weight and working hard for a slim figure. One group of investigators (Silberstein, Striegel-Moore, Timko, & Rodin, 1988), for example, reported that among a sample of college students, while "approximately equal numbers of men wanted to be heavier as thinner . . . virtually no woman wanted to be heavier" (p. 228) and more women than men reported exercising for weight control. Because body dissatisfaction is so normative for women—in other words, it is the unusual woman who is not dissatisfied with her body—these investigators found that body discrepancy scores for women were not related to a measure of self-esteem. The normativeness of women's concern with body weight is well illustrated by findings from another study (Pliner, Chaiken, & Flett, 1990) in which 639 persons between the ages of 10 and 79 responded to questions about their physical appearance. At all ages, women (and girls) differed from men (and boys) in being significantly more concerned with eating, weight, and appearance.

Not only do body image concerns affect women's behavior and self-evaluations but it affects how others, particularly men, respond to women. Thus, Jayne Stake and Monica Lauer (1987) found among a sample of college women and men, matched on body size, that being overweight affected the quantity and quality of women's heterosexual relationships, while this was not the case for men. There seems little question that such gender differences are related to the pressure of media images. One study (Silverstein, Perdue, Peterson, & Kelly, 1986) found that "the standard of bodily attractiveness presented on television and in popular magazines is slimmer and more oriented to dieting and staying in shape for women than it is for men . . . [and] that the standard of bodily attractiveness for women . . . is more noncurvaceous now that it has been in the past" (p. 531).

Promotion of the "hairless ideal" for women, particularly since the 1940s, and directed primarily toward European-American women, has been analyzed and studied by Susan Basow (1991). She questioned 235 professional women, many of whom were feminists, and found that 80 percent shave their leg and underarm hair, mainly "because it is socially normative and . . . is tied to feeling attractive and feminine" (p. 93). Among the African-American respondents 50 percent said they did not remove leg hair, compared to 21 percent of the European-American respondents. In Basow's view, the hairless norm for women serves two functions: to exaggerate the differences between women and men, and to identify women's attractiveness with youth.

With respect to cosmetics, the pressures and their consequences appear to interact with stereotypes for social class. The results of a study by Cathryn Cox and William Glick (1986) are instructive. Samples of college students looked at photographs of the same women wearing no makeup, moderate makeup, or heavy makeup and then rated the women on a variety of attributes and on their expected performance in an accountant's job or secretary's job. While makeup use was found to be positively correlated in general with high ratings on attractiveness, femininity, and sexiness, women with heavy makeup who were said to have applied for the secretarial job were evaluated very negatively on their expected job performance. For traditional jobs, then, "cosmetics use may enhance physical appearance, but . . . detract from perceived competence" (p. 57). It is as though the reaction to working-class women is, "You are wearing all that makeup to look sexy and attract a man, so we know you will not be paying sufficient attention to your work!" Yet, the heaviest users of cosmetics are adolescents and working-class women (Faludi, 1991).

GENDER-SPECIFIC TRAITS OR SITUATIONS?

While one group of feminist psychologists is presenting evidence against links between behavior and gender, another group is arguing that women's life experiences and imposed separateness from men have created a special women's culture. Women's responsibilities and roles are said to reinforce certain ways of behaving, attitudes, and objectives (for example, care and connection), and even certain ways of gaining knowledge about the world (Belenky, Clinchy, Goldberger, & Tarule, 1986), which should be respected and appreciated. This approach, sometimes called "essentialist," recognizes a "female domain" and urges that it be positively valued.

Jean Baker Miller (1986) and Carol Gilligan (1982) represent this position and have proposed that women are more expressive and sensitive than men and more concerned with relationships, the needs of others, interpersonal responsibility, and interpersonal harmony and cooperation. Such concerns, they suggest, can be sources of strength, not weakness, giving women a special outlook or perspective that reflects the valuing of intimacy and attachment rather than separation and autonomy, traits valued by men. These differences, according to Nancy Chodorow (1978), emerge early in life from the infant's relationship with its mother. Chodorow argues that because mothers differ in gender from their sons, mothers provide the conditions that promote separation from sons, encouraging autonomy and differentiation; for daughters, on the other hand, mothers promote identification and attachment. This approach ("object relations theory") accepts femininity and masculinity as separate orientations and attempts to account for them by different patterns of mother-infant bonding, which promote "ego-boundary rigidity" in boys and "boundary diffuseness" in girls so that boys come to value separation and girls, connectedness.

To Sigmund Freud (1933/1964) femininity was a "riddle" he tried to solve in a different way from the theorists mentioned above. He proposed that girls turn away from their mothers because they hold their mothers "responsible for their lack of a penis" (p. 124). Femininity, according to Freud, is characterized by envy, jealousy, narrowness, a weak superego, little sense of justice, and narcissism. His disciple Helene Deutsch (1944) later emphasized a triad of feminine traits—passivity, narcissism, and masochism. This negative and gloomy portrait is very different from the picture of the cooperative, caring, person-oriented adult woman drawn by the newer proponents of a feminine-masculine dichotomy, but both visions share a focus on traits, stable personality components that are presumed to predispose to particular ways of behaving across situations. In addition, both the older psychoanalytic and the newer "female domain" positions give infancy an all-important role in shaping personality, and both tie a particular set of characteristics to each gender. We will see that these views fare badly when tested against observations and investigations of the actual behavior of adult women in diverse situations.

Dependency and Submissiveness versus Leadership and Dominance

Some women grow up expecting and assuming that they will be taken care of; others seek independence and acquire the requisite skills for its successful achievement. A woman may fear independence because she has had little experience in practicing it or because she has learned that women should be protected, defended, and guided by men. Such an assumption, challenged by most contemporary women, is still part of the dominant gender ideology of our culture.

The association that we tend too readily to make between women and dependence ignores men's needs for affection, attention, compassion, and physical and psychological nurturance, which women are expected to provide for them. When men turn to women for satisfaction of these needs, this behavior is not labeled dependence. Why not? What distinguishes a man's need for someone to take good care of him from a woman's

need? We seem to accept the former uncritically, but to view the latter as a weakness and to label it pejoratively. The reality is that interdependence in relationships is sought by both women and men, despite our reluctance to admit it.

That some strong television women (for instance, Claire Huxtable of "The Cosby Show" and Jessica Fletcher of "Murder, She Wrote") have proven popular suggests that for women to behave in a dominant manner, even in the presence of men, is no longer unusual. Nevertheless, such behavior is not yet the norm. Many women do not behave assertively in the company of men and tend to follow men's leadership in group situations. According to Edwin Hollander (1985), who reviewed the relevant literature, "leadership traditionally has been a male domain. . . . The evidence indicates that women and men are more inclined to expect a man rather than a woman to occupy a leader role" (p. 519). Illustrating and reinforcing these conclusions are findings from a study in which pairs of same-gender and mixed-gender college students, who had been pre-tested on dominance, were asked to interact and choose a leader (Hegstrom & Griffith, 1992). In mixed-gender pairs, men assumed the leader position with much greater frequency than women, regardless of either partner's scores on the dominance measure. These data are congruent with those from a study reported 25 years ago (Megargee, 1969).

Yet, women and men who occupy real leadership positions tend to behave similarly. A statistical analysis of studies comparing women and men on leadership style (Eagly & Johnson, 1990) found that, for both interpersonal and task styles of leadership, stereotypic differences were less likely in studies of ongoing organizations than in laboratory studies or ratings. The former take place in real settings in which people are functioning in accord with the demands of their jobs, unlike laboratory studies where participants are strangers who interact for a brief period of time. Only the slight tendency for women to utilize a more democratic style than men was general across settings. In a study in a natural setting (Wheelan & Verdi, in press), of ongoing conference groups that met together for 4½ to 6 hours, no significant gender differences were found in any of seven categories beyond the first 30 to 60 minutes of interaction.

Some earlier studies found that women's speech tended to be more exaggerated, polite, hedged, expressive, supportive, and indirect than men's speech (e.g., Haas, 1979; Lakoff, 1975; McMillan, Clifton, McGrath, & Gale, 1977) and that men's speech was perceived as more dynamic (Mulac, Incontro, & James, 1985). Men have reported using profanity in daily speech more often than women and that they believe such language demonstrates the social power or dominance of the user (Selnow, 1985). More recent research, however, has cast considerable doubt on the existence of a "woman's language" that differs in important ways from men's use of language. In one example (Simkins-Bullock & Wildman, 1991), an audiotape analysis was made of 15-minute conversations between pairs of women, pairs of men, and mixed-gender pairs. The researchers concluded that their results "lent support to the growing literature suggesting that there are no systematic differences in the use of various language features by men and women" (p. 157). Linguistic styles may reflect individual differences, power, culture, and situations, but not gender (e.g., Tannen, 1990). Popular misconceptions in this area continue, however.

It has also been proposed that nonverbal cues such as posture and gestures reveal women's lesser status and deference to men (e.g., Goffman, 1979; Henley, 1977). For example, an analysis of 1296 posed photographs of high school and college students and faculty (Ragan, 1982) revealed that women lowered their heads (canted) significantly more often than men. On the other hand, the findings from more recent investigations have led us to question the assumption that women's nonverbal behavior reflects lesser dominance. In three separate studies (Halberstadt & Saitta, 1987) involving analyses of photographs, advertisements, and unobtrusive observations of behavior, it was found that women do not lower either their heads or bodies toward others more than men do. Only with respect to smiling was a significant gender difference found. The investigators suggested that observers may tend to "read dominance into the situation on the basis of gender" (p. 270), rather than reading dominance from the different nonverbal behaviors of women and men.

Deferential behavior has been found to be related to situations and status, regardless of gender. For example, one study (Deutsch, 1990) of same- and mixed-gender pairs of college students assigned one member of the pair to the role of interviewer and the other to the role of applicant for a part-time job as a news reporter. Unobtrusive observations of pair interactions revealed that in all pairs, and regardless of gender, "applicants, who presumably occupied the low-power role, smiled more than interviewers" (p. 537) and that gender differences in smiling were absent among applicants. Another approach to the investigation of smiling (Wilson & Lloyd, 1990) was used in a study of college

students in Great Britain. A sample of students of both genders from arts schools and science schools (said to differ in prestige) were photographed. The photographs were analyzed for evidence of submissive cues (smiling, head cant, and orientation away from the camera); it was found that arts school undergraduates displayed more submissive nonverbal behavior than science students across all three variables, with little evidence of self-presentation differences between women and men. The school of study, not gender, distinguished smilers from nonsmilers. Still another investigation of smiling (Brennan-Parks, Goddard, Wilson, & Kinnear, 1991) obtained evidence in support of the proposition that "gender differences . . . may not be located so much in gender roles conceived in personality terms but rather in . . . expectations that vary with the situation" (p. 382). When a group of college students were photographed individually, presumably for a facial perception study, those instructed to smile did so significantly more often than those given no instructions, and there were no differences between women and men.

Susceptibility to Social Influence

The common wisdom that women are more likely to be influenced than men, like many other assumptions regarding gender differences, is not supported across situations. Using quantitative methods of analysis, Alice Eagly and Linda Carli (1981) examined a large body of persuasion/conformity research and found that women were more influenced than men only in situations in which their responses were under surveillance by the influencing agent. Although this gender difference was a significant one across studies, it was nevertheless very small and of little practical value in predicting behavior. In an empirical study (Eagly & Chrvala, 1986), in which college students discussed an issue in five-person groups and expressed their opinions under various conditions, younger women were not more conforming than younger men regardless of whether or not they were under surveillance by fellow group members; the stereotypic gender difference was found only among older participants who expected to read their opinions aloud.

Most of the research on gender differences in social influence has used European-American, middle-class participants. One exception is a study by Kathrynn Adams (1980), who paired a European-American or African-American college student with a confederate of the same or different gender and of the same or different ethnicity. The confederates challenged picture preferences expressed by their partners, and Adams assessed the degree to which the naive partners resisted changing their responses in the direction of the confederates. The European-American women were found to be more easily influenced than the European-American men, but the African-American women were less easily influenced than the African-American men or the European-American men or women. These data illustrate that cultural expectations may not be the same for all women in our society and that not all women behave as dominant stereotypes predict.

Other research has shown that the nature of the issue, topic, or task on which influence is attempted may also affect the extent to which the influence will be successful. Persons conform more readily on matters in which they have little interest or expertise. For example, Judy Morelock (1980) found that when individuals were shown the unanimous opinions of a group with whom they anticipated having a discussion, and these opinions were contrary to their own, women conformed more than men on items they knew little about (such as football and the military), while men conformed to the group opinion more than women on items they knew little about (such as day-care centers and social work). The investigator concluded that "as long as social issues are perceived as sex-typed, . . . each sex will continue to have its limited domain of expertise" (p. 547) and be susceptible to social influence on the issues in which they lack knowledge.

Confidence and Self-Esteem

Some research on self-reported personal worth or self-confidence has suggested that women tend to manifest lower general self-esteem than men (e.g., Instone, Major, & Bunker, 1983; Lenney, 1977; Lippa & Beauvais, 1983), and it has been proposed that this is a predictable consequence of women's socialization in a sexist society. Girls in our society certainly learn early and continue to learn as they grow older that they are less important, less powerful, and less effective than men; and adult women find that they have less control over their own lives. A poem by my daughter Sara (Lott, 1985) expresses these consequences for women metaphorically:

> When I got to the station
> I thought there'd be some time
> to call and make the connection
> but my plans were out of line.
>
> Now I'm standing
> by the railroad tracks,
> waiting for a train.

> I don't care where I'm going
> 'cause each place looks the same.
>
> I doubt it's very different
> where I'm going
> from where I've been.
> It's this ache I carry around with me
> that tells me 'bout the
> shape I'm in.

Particular variables that influence women's self-judgments have been identified. Ellen Lenney and Joel Gold (1982), for example, found that on a task involving academic knowledge in which no social comparison was expected, men and women college students performed equally well and did not differ in self-evaluations of their performance. Only when they expected a comparison did the women evaluate themselves more poorly than the men. Jayne Stake (1983a) reported finding no gender differences in how well persons expected to do on a subsequent task in a study of college students who worked on a gender-neutral task under the conditions of clear and unambiguous feedback about initial task success.

The importance of feedback and reduced ambiguity to women's self-judgments is further illustrated by the findings of a field study (Kimball & Gray, 1982). Students at two universities, studying the same subject, were asked to predict their test scores before each of three examinations. In both groups, women predicted significantly lower scores than did men on the first exam. But on the next two exams, following feedback on the first one, no gender differences in expectancy were found among students in the university in which the course was taught entirely by one instructor. In the second university, where the course was taught sequentially by three different instructors, the women students manifested less self-confidence than the men on all three exams and predicted significantly lower scores, despite the fact that the women's scores were actually higher than the men's. The researchers concluded that "the results from both courses support the hypothesis that in the absence of feedback, women have lower performance expectancies than men" (p. 1004). In the university in which there was "a new instructor and a new body of material for each examination . . . [each test became] a new situation in which the feedback from the last examination was not considered relevant" (p. 1005). A clear demonstration of the role played by performance feedback is provided by another study (Hall, 1990). Students were randomly assigned to compete in video games against a female or male opponent and indicated before each trial how well they expected to do. Clear performance feedback was provided in this situation, and the expectancy scores were found not to differ by gender—the self-confidence of the women was equal to that of the men.

Another variable that has been identified as influencing the self-presentation of performance expectations is whether such expectations are presented publicly or privately. One investigation in which college students of varied ethnicity and economic status were asked to estimate their first-semester grade point averages (Daubman, Heatherington, & Ahn, 1992) found that it was only in the public verbal report condition that women underestimated their actual grades while men overestimated them. No gender difference appeared when students gave their estimates anonymously in writing, and there was no gender difference in the public condition when the participants had been led to believe that they were being questioned by a person of high ability.

In another study (Heilman & Kram, 1984), with management employees from an insurance company, a gender difference was found in perception of one's coworkers' judgments of one's performance, but not in self-ratings. Each participant worked on a task and was led to believe that a partner was working on the same task in another room. Women anticipated less credit for success and more blame for failure from their partners than men did, but self-ratings of effectiveness showed no significant gender differences. These data suggest that when women self-report a low performance expectancy, this may reflect what they believe others expect of them, not necessarily what they themselves believe.

One group of studies has assessed self-esteem or self-confidence by examining the reasons given to explain one's own success or failure. A frequently reported conclusion is that women tend to attribute their successes to external, nonstable factors, such as luck, but to attribute their failures to lack of ability, whereas men attribute success to ability and failure to task difficulty or low effort. But a careful review and analysis of the relevant literature (Frieze, Whitley, Hanusa, & McHugh, 1982) found that this generalization has been overstated and that gender differences in causal attributions for success and failure are not strongly supported across situations. A similar conclusion was reached by David Sohn (1982), who analyzed the results of 20 studies of self-attributions for achievement. He noted that "the empirical evidence does not support the proposition that the sexes differ consequentially in their use of any of the four main types of achievement self-attribution (luck, ability, effort, or diffi-

culty of task)" (p. 354). The reader may recall from the last chapter that this conclusion is supported by the study of managers and other decision makers in natural situations. Similarly, a study of the reactions of real athletes to their performances in an intrasquad basketball scrimmage found that "successful females and males did not differ significantly in their self- and team attributions . . . [and] were generally just as inclined to take responsibility for their victory" (Croxton & Klonsky, 1982, p. 406). Cheryl Travis (1982) found the same high correlation for both women and men between objective success on a series of anagrams and expected future success and that both genders tended to attribute their own success to high ability and their failure to task difficulty. She concluded that "sex differences provide very little information about the perception of causality" (p. 379).

Cooperation, Care, and Connection

As noted earlier, Jean Baker Miller (1986) has suggested that many of the behaviors acquired by women as we are socialized to be good daughters, sisters, wives, and mothers provide us with strengths in the interpersonal domain, where we tend to be prosocial and cooperative, to promote interpersonal harmony and discourage discord. Women are expected to be agreeable and to reduce conflict by smiling, acquiescing, compromising, and not arguing too much. To steadfastly and logically defend one's position in an argument or to pay insufficient attention to what others are saying is to risk being perceived as behaving in a "masculine" manner. The traditional woman has been taught to compromise and to consider the needs and feelings of others. Rae Carlson (1972) referred to this outcome for women as a communal, qualititative, and person-oriented mode of living.

Although many observations of women's behavior may support the conclusion that women pursue harmony and concern for others and are more cooperative, helpful, and altruistic than men, we tend to make such observations in limited situations, ones in which cultural expectations for appropriate gender behavior are strong. When we observe people under conditions in which non-gender-related demands are more salient, we find that women can and do behave competitively and egotistically, and men cooperatively and sensitively. Such behavior depends not on gender but on prior experience, cultural expectations, sanctions, opportunities for practice, and situational demands.

The social sanctions for girls and women make some behavior more likely than others. Thus, for example, women tend to score higher than men on self-report measures of facilitating interaction and showing concern for interpersonal relationships. This was found, for example, in a study of high school and college students in several settings, in different time periods (Gill, Stockard, Johnson, & Williams, 1987). No gender differences were found in the self-report of behaviors defining instrumentality (goal attainment) or autonomy.

Behavior does not always confirm the stereotypes, and careful reviews of the empirical literature typically fail to support generally accepted conclusions of stable gender differences across situations. An example is research on the amount of money (or other rewards) women and men allocate to themselves relative to others in simulated work situations. For example, Martha Thompson (1981) found that among college students asked to play the role of a boss who took an inequitable portion of the winnings of a group, women and men behaved no differently. When role-playing a subordinate group member, however, women were more supportive of one another than men, while the latter were more concerned with avoiding conflict with the boss. A number of studies have found women to be more likely to distribute rewards between themselves and a coworker equally and men to be more likely to employ the principle of equity—that is, to distribute rewards in accord with effort or results. This is not the case under all conditions, however; in a laboratory situation where participants were given information on how much others paid themselves, no gender differences were found; individuals of "both sexes appeared to use the average amount taken by others as their comparison standard" (Major, McFarlin, & Gagnon, 1984, p. 1404). As noted by Michelle Wittig (1985), "such studies which illuminate the circumstances in which previously well-established gender differences are not found, support interpretations of gender differences based on situation-sensitive norms and values, rather than situation-insensitive traits and motives" (p. 10). Another example of important situational influences on reward distribution behavior, or what Brenda Major has called "personal entitlement," comes from a study (Bylsma & Major, 1992) in which college students were told that others had been either highly paid or not highly paid for doing a task, and some were told they had performed well on the task while others were told that they had performed poorly. Both women and men who were told that others had been well paid said they were entitled to more money than those who were told otherwise; and both women and men who

were told their performance was good said they were entitled to more money than those who were told they had not performed well. Gender differences, in other words, were eliminated when both women and men were given the same comparison and performance feedback.

Some situational factors have been found to minimize gender differences in third-party allocation strategies (allocations to others, not oneself). For example, Jayne Stake (1983b), in a study in which participants were instructed to behave like work managers concerned with maintaining harmonious relationships among their employees, found that women and men used similar allocation strategies. In a subsequent investigation (Stake, 1985), she again found no gender differences when college students pretending to be managers were instructed to be fair; under this condition more rewards were given to the faster workers by both women and men. When instructed to improve relationships between the workers, both women and men moved to an equality principle, but when instructed to increase productivity, both used an equity principle. On the other hand, in a study of 229 working administrators where the women and men had comparable management experience, the women were found to use equity in assigning pay raises to employees in a more discriminating way than the men ("Reward For," 1986). In making salary decisions, the women managers were more objective than the men and more responsive to subtle differences in worker performance. The investigator, Vandra Huber, concluded that women "fine-tuned the appraisal-pay system." Finally, a study of fifth graders and college students, in which they evaluated how hypothetical persons allocated rewards after doing tasks (Boldizar, Perry, & Perry, 1988), found no gender differences overall and one reversal of popular wisdom. In both age groups, female respondents judged an equitable distribution by the person who had contributed less to the task to be fairer than the male respondents did. These data, the investigators concluded, contribute to "putting to rest the pervasive myth that males prefer equity and females prefer equality in reward distributions" (p. 588). The research in this area clearly indicates the relevance of situational factors for behavior, and demonstrates that women and men generally appear to behave similarly and effectively when required to allocate rewards on the basis of performance.

Another body of research has been accumulating on moral judgments, stimulated by Carol Gilligan's (1977, 1979, 1982) proposition that moral development in women and men takes different paths and results in different perspectives. She asserts that men's morality is oriented toward justice and is defined abstractly by the balancing of rules and individual rights, whereas women's moral judgments rest on consideration of others' needs (care) and are influenced by interpersonal connections, responsibility for others, and the personal-social context. This dichotomizing of gender in terms of different moral perspectives—care for women and justice for men—has been criticized for a number of different reasons, including Gilligan's reliance primarily on her assessment of European-American, middle-class women. Thus, Carol Stack (1986), for example, has reported finding more similarities than differences in moral motives and concerns of African-American women and men who were migrants to the rural South. According to Stack, these women and men conceptualize their moral dilemmas in the same terms, and they "describe with force and conviction the strength of their kinship ties . . . and the nature of these ties that bind" (p. 323). Other critics have faulted Gilligan for generalizing about a "woman's voice" without attending to the voices of lesbians (Brown, 1990).

In a direct test of Gilligan's hypothesis, one group of investigators (Friedman, Robinson, & Friedman, 1987) asked a sample of college students to respond to four moral dilemmas by rating the importance of 12 different statements reflecting care and justice considerations. No reliable gender differences were found. In another direct test (Ford & Lowery, 1986), college students were asked to describe three important moral conflicts in their own lives and how they thought about them. Women and men did not differ in their use of language indicating concern with care and justice. For both genders, their more important and more difficult decisions were considered more from a care than a justice perspective, and both generally "considered questions of relationships, care, and responsibility, as well as questions of fairness, justice, and rights, and they considered them fairly equally" (p. 782). Still another empirical study (Pratt, Pancer, Hunsberger, & Manchester, 1990), of a sample of adults, found no gender differences in level of moral reasoning attained or in reasoning about justice. One of my students (Roccio, 1991) found that a sample of women and men similarly tended to use care considerations in dealing with a hypothetical dilemma involving their teenage child and drug use and to use justice considerations in a hypothetical dilemma about abortion.

In evaluating Gilligan's thesis, Mary Brabeck (1983, 1989) has noted that the evidence does not support the equating of women with care or connection, nor the conclusion that women are more concerned with primary relationships than with universal principles.

Though she places a different value on the qualities, Gilligan is arguing as Freud, Erikson, Piaget, and Kohlberg have done before her: Women are the more compassionate sex. . . . There is an intuitive appeal to these claims which speaks to an essential truth in the assertions, a truth which persists even when the evidence contradicts it. (Brabeck, 1983, p. 286)

Much of the evidence contradicting Gilligan's thesis comes from analog or paper-and-pencil self-report studies, but not all of it. Jane Aronson (1992) interviewed a sample of retired and still-working women teachers, ranging in age from 35 to 80, who provided a great deal of physical and emotional care for their mothers. What the interviews revealed was the complexity behind behavior that appears to be caring. Much of what the women did was motivated by the fact that if they didn't provide the needed support for their mothers, no one else would—including brothers, other family members, and public services. For the most part, the

women themselves saw their sense of obligation as a necessity rather than a choice when they posed the question "Who else is going to do it?" . . . [They] were torn between adherence to prevailing cultural values about femininity, care, and family ties and the wish to enhance their own autonomy and interests. (p. 25)

Findings relevant to the present discussion have been reported from a study of how humor is evaluated (Crawford & Gressley, 1991). Both women and men were found to consider caring and real-life anchoring to be important factors in humor. They did not differ in their use of the caring dimension in describing a person they knew who had an outstanding sense of humor. Another study (Mills, Pedersen, & Grusec, 1989), in which adults were asked to make "self" or "other" choices with respect to hypothetical conflicts, also found few gender differences.

Faced with a choice between their own wishes or needs and those of another person, women and men were alike in reporting that they would generally make the same kind of decision, namely, to put the other person first. Women offered more empathy-oriented reasons than men . . . while concern for others' needs was mentioned more frequently by men than by women. (p. 617)

Empathy and Interpersonal Sensitivity

Girls and women are encouraged to look to other persons for evidence of their effectiveness, to be sensitive to the needs of others, to interpret subtle cues, and to behave sympathetically. Interpersonal relationships thus become important contributors to our feelings of self-esteem, and many women devote considerable time and energy to taking part in person-oriented activities. In addition, as noted by Catherine Greeno and Eleanor Maccoby (1986), "it is clear that women have a greater reputation for altruism and empathy than do men, and that women accept its validity. Whether the reputation is deserved is a more complicated question" (p. 313). The research literature does not support such a generalization across situations. Instead, as Greeno and Maccoby point out, while "a man is more likely to offer to change a tire, a woman [is more likely] to soothe a child" (p. 314), in line with differences in their experience.

Some of the antecedent conditions relevant to empathy have been identified in a study of college students (Barnett, Howard, King, & Dino, 1980). High-empathy persons of both genders reported that their parents had spent more time with them, had been more affectionate with them, and had more often discussed feelings than was the case for low-empathy persons. With respect to these variables, women reported more than men that their mothers had discussed feelings with them and that their parents had displayed affection toward them; not surprisingly, then, the women scored reliably higher than the men on an empathy scale. These findings support the conclusion that the same experiences enhance empathy in both genders but are found more often in the socialization of girls.

Despite gender differences in experiences promoting empathy, the literature does not fully or unambiguously support the conclusion that women are more empathic than men across situations and conditions. As is true for other behaviors culturally assigned by gender, women and men have been found to differ in empathy most consistently in studies using self-report measures. This conclusion is supported by a series of analyses of relevant literature by Nancy Eisenberg and Randy Lennon (1983). According to these researchers, few gender differences are found when empathy is assessed by physiological measures or nonobvious behavioral measures. They concluded that "females' reputations for and self-report of empathic responding are much stronger than are their tendencies to respond (physiologically or nonverbally) in an empathic manner" (p. 126).

Women are also expected to be more sensitive than men and more adept at interpreting subtle interpersonal cues. Judith Hall (1978) concluded from an analysis of 75 studies of accuracy in interpreting emotion from nonverbal cues that women are better decoders than men, but that women's advantage or greater sensitivity is small. The results of a study by Sara Snodgrass (1985) provide support for the proposition that it is not a woman's gender but her subordinate position that accounts for her greater interpersonal sensitivity. Among a sample of college students who interacted in leader-subordinate pairs for an hour, subordinates were found to be significantly more sensitive to the leaders' feelings and to the impressions they were making than the reverse. Gender made no difference, except that the role effect of being subordinate was strongest for women when their partners were men. In a follow-up study (Snodgrass, 1992), 96 pairs of college students (half same-gender and half mixed-gender) interacted for approximately 1 hour on three tasks. In each pair, one person had been designated the boss, and the other the employee. No significant differences in sensitivity were found to be associated with gender; the only important variable was status. Employees were more sensitive to how their bosses felt about them, whereas the bosses were more sensitive to how their employees felt about themselves. A naturalistic study (Ickes, Stinson, Bissonette, & Garcia, 1990), in which mixed-gender pairs of college students were videotaped in a 6-minute interaction, also found from a coding of observed behaviors that gender was unrelated to empathic accuracy.

Intimacy and Friendship

The differences between women's and men's friendships or attachments to others have been the subject of considerable research interest in recent years. Jean Baker Miller (1986) and Carol Gilligan (1979, 1982) have proposed that interpersonal bonding is a central element or theme in women's lives and feminine personality, and Nancy Chodorow (1978) has suggested that a woman's capacity for close ties to others has its origin in her earliest relationship with her mother. According to Chodorow, because a girl is similar to and identifies with her mother, she experiences connectedness rather than separation and defines herself in terms of attachment and relationships. A boy, on the other hand, who must repress his relationship to his mother, fears connection, and this fear becomes a key element in masculine personality.

As with other generalizations about gender that posit "essential" differences between women and men, however, the empirical literature provides little support for major distinctions between the friendships of women and men and the values assigned to them. For example, in one study (Wheeler & Neziek, 1977), men's and women's social interactions in their first year of college were compared by having a sample of students living in coed dorms keep daily records of social interactions that lasted 10 minutes or more, for 2 weeks early in the fall semester and then again early in the spring semester. The women were found to have socialized more intensely than the men at the beginning of the year (fall term), but in the second semester differences between the men and women were minimal. Once having established relationships, the women decreased the amount of time they spent in each interaction.

Some studies suggest that women's friendships may be more intimate than men's and include the sharing of more personal information. Questionnaire responses by a sample of parents of college students revealed no gender difference in frequency of contact with friends, but the women more frequently than the men said they talked about personal problems, intimate relationships, and daily activities (Aries & Johnson, 1983). Dorie Williams (1985) found that among a sample of college students, women reported more than men that they confided in close friends, openly expressed vulnerability and affection, emphasized mutual understanding, and discussed personal issues. On the other hand, Mayta Caldwell and Letitia Peplau (1982) found no significant gender differences among college students in total number of friends, number of intimate friends, or in hours spent with friends during an average week; more women than men, however, reported talking about "personal topics such as feelings and problems" and talking about other people.

Most of the empirically collected information on friendship comes from college-age women and men. How representative they may be of older persons we do not really know. It is instructive, therefore, to note differences that were reported in one study (Ryff & Migdal, 1984) between a group of young women (18 to 30 years old) and a group of middle-aged women (40 to 55 years old). Intimacy was found to be more important to the younger women and was recalled by the older women as having been more important to them when they were younger. Paul Wright (1982) reviewed a number of studies of friendship and concluded that, in general, women's friendships tend to be more person-oriented, supportive, self-disclosing, and holistic than men's, but

> these differences are not great and, in many cases, they are so obscure that they are hard to demonstrate. In any case, the differences between women's and men's friendships diminish markedly as the strength and duration of the friendships increase. (p. 19)

Gender differences in intimacy of social interaction are less likely to be reported when information is derived from observing behavior instead of from self-reports. Thus, an investigation using both methods of assessment (Reis, Senchak, & Solomon, 1985) found that women reported more intimate interactions than men, but when observed having "an intimate conversation with their best friend, the sexes did not differ, either in their self-ratings or in the opinion of external judges" (p. 1214). The researchers concluded that "when the situation makes it desirable to do so," both genders manifest similar levels of intimacy.

In a self-report study (Wright & Scanlon, 1991) of a large sample of adults with various occupations, it was found that while women and men differed little in their friendships with men, a difference was apparent in friendships with women. These friendships were found to be "especially strong and especially rewarding" for women and to serve both expressive and instrumental functions. Similarly, another study (Snell, Miller, & Belk, 1988) found that women and men "were remarkably similar in their willingness to discuss their emotions with their male friends" (p. 67) and equally willing to share positive emotions with female friends. In the discussion of negative emotions with women, however, women and men differed significantly; women were more willing to do so than men. Data from these two studies are consonant with the depiction in the 1992 film *Fried Green Tomatoes,* of friendship between women who not only care for one another but "who take chances for each other" (Brown, 1992, p. H-22). It may well be that the strong bonds that some adult women form with one another do not require intra-psychic explanations but can be explained more easily and simply as a consequence of patriarchy, which makes it more difficult for a woman to be valued and cared for by a man than by a woman, a person of similar social status. We will return to this issue later in this chapter.

Expressiveness

Our gender ideology tells us that women express emotions more readily than men do. This generalization is so well accepted that little systematic investigation of its accuracy has been undertaken. That women smile significantly more than men has been reported most often (e.g., LaFrance & Carmen, 1980; Lott, 1987; Ragan, 1982). Our previous discussion of submissiveness and dependency, however, noted that even this finding is not a universal one under all conditions.

With respect to other emotional expressions, one study (Lombardo, Cretser, Lombardo, & Mathis, 1983) found that women self-reported crying more often, with greater intensity, and over a greater range of situations than men.

Nevertheless, women and men were very similar in their perception of what might evoke tears. They "saw the same types of interpersonal relationships as making crying most likely; saw the same types of stimulus situations as most conducive to crying; and chose the same adjectives as most descriptive of their post-crying affect" (p. 994). These data suggest that women and men do not differ in feelings or emotional reactions as much as in their overt expression, or in the degree to which they believe emotional expression is appropriate for their gender. Boys and men are repeatedly told that crying is for sissies.

Thus, Richard Fabes and Carol Martin (1991) found, among a large sample of college students, that females "were perceived to express (but not experience) . . . emotions significantly more often than males . . . regardless of the primacy or complexity of the emotions" (p. 538), with the exception of anger. These beliefs were the same for infants, preschoolers, elementary school children, adolescents, and adults, among whom no differences were assumed to exist in feelings, but only in their overt expression. Our culture's strong belief that women are more expressive than men, as illustrated by these findings, may lead observers to be "more likely to look for and explicitly note the presence or absence of emotional qualities in women's behavior than in men's behavior" (Shields, 1987, p. 247). Stephanie Shields tested this hypothesis by examining references to emotion made by television news commentators immediately following the debate between the 1984 vice-presidential candidates Geraldine Ferraro and George Bush. In the transcripts provided by the three commercial networks and PBS, she found "nearly twice as many references to Ferraro's emotion [both its presence and absence] as to Bush's" (p. 244).

Yet studies that have directly investigated overt expression of emotion do not generally find support for a gender difference. For example, in episodes of everyday interaction, women and men were found to experience anger with equal frequency and intensity and for similar reasons and to differ little in expressing it (Averill, cf. Fabes & Martin, 1991). Contradicting the conclusion that women and men probably do not differ in their experience of emotion (even if they may sometimes differ in expressing it), however, are data reported from another study (Fujita, Diener, & Sandvik, 1991). Using multiple sources of information, the investigators concluded that "women in the United States experience emotion more strongly than do men— . . . both positive and negative emotions" (p. 430). Such a generalization, however, must await verification by other researchers using samples other than college students.

As is true of the other behaviors discussed in this chapter, individual differences within each gender can be found. Thus, Paul Cherulnik and Robert Evans (1984) found within-gender differences and between-gender similarities in facial expressiveness in a study in which participants were videotaped while being interviewed and judges then rated an edited tape for pleasantness, excitement, and spontaneity of facial expression. Men who scored high on a scale measuring the extent to which they monitored their own behavior were judged to be more expressive (smiling, excited, and spontaneous) than men who scored low, whereas the reverse was true for women. Among the women, high self-monitors smiled less than low self-monitors and showed less expression and stronger control over the outward display of their feelings. Persons of both genders who self-reported greater instrumental, autonomous, and agentic behaviors were found in another study (Kopper & Epperson, 1991) to also self-report being more prone to anger and more likely to express it outwardly than other persons. No gender differences were found.

Influence Strategies

Because we are told that by being physically attractive a woman can "get what she wants"—can manipulate men and situations and obtain power, beauty becomes enormously important to women, as noted earlier in our discussion of femininity. Because of women's relative lack of access to resources that directly increase status, women's "modes of influence"—that is, the means of controlling our lives or exerting power—are expected, and sometimes observed, to be different from men's.

Paula Johnson (1976) has proposed that women are expected to influence others by means that are indirect and personal. Indirect influence (or "manipulation") is exerted without direct confrontation, without the other person being aware that he or she is being influenced or persuaded to act in a particular way; it involves wheedling, flattery, and cajoling. It is devious. Johnson points out that "if a woman does use direct power, she may risk becoming known as pushy, overbearing, unfeminine, and/or castrating" (p. 101). The personal mode of influence is exerted by threatening to withdraw love, concern, service, or attention unless something wanted is provided. It may involve trading personal resources (affection or sex) for desired outcomes. In a questionnaire study, she found that respondents associated the use of personal rewards and sexuality as means of gaining influence reliably more often with women than with men.

As with many of the other behaviors discussed thus far, self-reports of influence or power strategies tend to confirm the assumption of gender differences while observation of behavior under varying conditions is less apt to do so. Thus, for example, when college students were asked to assume the role of employee or supervisor and to answer questions about their likely behavior (Offermann & Schrier, 1985), women reported more often than men that they would use personal/dependent or negotiation strategies, and less often than men that they would use reward/coercion strategies. In a departure from the stereotype, the men were more likely to consider using manipulation and other indirect influence techniques. But when college students were actually observed in simulated work groups, influence techniques used by leaders under the same set of instructions were found to be unrelated to gender (Stitt, Schmidt, Price, & Kipnis, 1983).

In two other studies (White, 1988; White & Ronfall, 1989) using different methods, support was found for the conclusion that influence tactics vary with the situation or context, not with gender. Among participants who indicated the frequency with which they used 43 strategies to get their way, both genders were found to use rational strategies most often and manipulative, high-pressure, and reward strategies less often. In line with these data, another study (Bisanz & Rule, 1989) found that women and men did not differ in their degree of approval for a number of different tactics. Similarly, Lynda Sagrestano (1992a), who asked a sample of college students how they would try to influence a nonintimate friend, found that women and men chose similar strategies—primarily persuasion, reasoning, discussing, asking, and persistence. What influenced strategy choice was not gender but whether the person doing the influencing was considered an "expert." Under this condition, direct strategies were most often chosen. Elsewhere, after reviewing studies on the use of power strategies by women and men, Sagrestano (1992b) concluded that indirect strategies are more likely to be used by "people in positions of weakness . . . in attempting to influence a more powerful person" (p. 446). It is a mistake to associate these strategies with women, as we have seen from some of the studies mentioned above, except insofar as the balance of power in a particular situation places a woman in a weak position so that she must rely on weaker strategies.

Aggression

A review of the literature on adult aggressive behavior (Frodi, Macauley, & Thorne, 1977) found that 61 percent of the laboratory studies did not show less aggressiveness by women than by men across all conditions. Once again, only in self-report studies did the authors find "the kind of differences that sex role stereotypes would seem to predict" (p. 654). When the aggressive behavior could be justified, or when persons were acting anonymously, gender differences were less likely to be found. One of my students, Robin Hasenfeld (1982), concluded from a quantitative analysis of aggression studies that there are no reliable gender differences in aggression under experimental conditions in which the aggressive behavior is believed to be justified.

Differences in aggressive behavior, both among women and between women and men, have been related to individual and personal variables as well as to situational factors. In one study, for example, college women who were sex-role traditionalists were found to respond more aggressively to an opponent (by use of electric shock in a laboratory situation) than more liberal women (Richardson, Vinsel, & Taylor, 1980). In another study (Richardson, Bernstein, & Taylor, 1979), women who were alone or women who were with a supportive observer responded "in an increasingly more aggressive manner" in shocking an opponent than did women who were in the presence of a silent observer. The researchers concluded that the aggressiveness of the women in their study "was largely determined by the contingencies present" (p. 204).

Shelagh Towson and Mark Zanna (1982) found that women self-reported responding as aggressively as men to a hypothetical situation involving a frustrating incident concerned with dance exercising, but less aggressively to a frustrating incident concerned with bodybuilding. The first situation was rated by the women as more important to them than the second. Alice Eagly and Valerie Steffen (1986) did a statistical analysis of the literature on gender and aggressive behavior by adults in short-term encounters between strangers in laboratory or field settings. They found a very small difference overall between women and men, that gender differences were more likely to be found in laboratory than field settings, and were "contingent on the particular social norms" that were salient.

Women, like men, have committed all varieties of crimes and have murdered for passion or profit (Weisheit, 1984). As Karen Rosenberg (1984) has pointed out in a review of books on women's role in warfare, women have contributed to intergroup and international violence as supporters and proponents of war efforts, and as active participants in battle. Historical and contemporary data, according to Rosenberg, do not support our culture's "cherished beliefs about female innocence"; she maintains that "conceptions of woman as nurturer, peacemaker, . . . or powerless victim . . . obscure the history of women's complicity in violence" (p. 457). Helen Lewis (1988), in reviewing a collection of articles (by Higonnet, et al.) on women's role in the two world wars, concluded that the articles challenge "the common assumption that only men fight" in wars. Women have engaged in combat and joined guerilla or resistance movements. Women have also participated in acts of terrorism, and their substantial contributions to Nazi ideology and to practices of extermination and genocide have been documented (Bridenthal, Grossman, & Kaplan, 1984; Koonz, 1987).

Thus real world behaviors often contradict the stereotyped expectations for women. Kathleen Blee (1991) documented the role women played in spreading hate in Indiana where in the 1920s almost one third of native-born Protestant, European-American women were members of the Women of the Ku Klux Klan. This group had chapters in 36 states. Calling themselves "a poison squad of whispering women," they spread vicious lies about African-Americans, Catholics, and Jews.

Arnold Buss and Mark Perry (1992) have developed a new scale or assessment instrument that they call *The Aggression Questionnaire*. This scale measures self-reported physical aggression, verbal aggression, hostility, and anger. It is of considerable interest that on anger, which the authors consider the "emotional component" or bridge to aggression, they found no significant difference between women and men. So strong are our conceptions about women's peaceful nature, however, that author Joyce Carol Oates (1981) has noted that wherever she goes, she is asked to explain why her writing is so violent. She finds this question "always insulting . . . always ignorant . . . [and] always sexist" (p. 35), as she also finds the suggestion given to her directly or indirectly that she should focus her writing more on "domestic" and "subjective" material. Whereas the serious male writer is allowed (and expected) to illustrate anger and rage, the woman writer is not. Once, in answer to the question "Why is your writing so violent?" she responded:

"Would you ask that question of a male writer?" . . . After some hesitation, the answer came: "No."
"Why not?" I asked.

Herewith a long pause ensued. My interrogator knew the answer to the question but declined to answer it. Or perhaps he was thinking. I hope he still is. (p. 35)

MASCULINE, FEMININE, ANDROGYNOUS, OR HUMAN?

The fact that women's behavior only sometimes fulfills cultural expectations of femininity illustrates variations among women, and within the same woman, and points up the role of experience and situation in influencing what people do. Behavior depends not on gender but on prior experience, acquired attitudes, cultural expectations, contingencies or consequences, opportunities for practice, and situational demands.

We must also keep in mind, however, that gender is not only a person variable but also a stimulus to which other persons react and that others' expectations and responses can effectively influence behavior in direct or subtle ways. Gender signifies expected normative behavior and, in this way, functions as a complex cue for others' perceptions, expectations, and overt reactions. Kay Deaux and Brenda Major (1987) regard gender as a salient and powerful social category and suggest that three key elements are present in any social interaction in which gender-linked behaviors will be displayed: the beliefs of the perceivers; the gender beliefs of the actors; and the nature of the situation, particularly the extent to which it contains salient gender-relevant cues.

The significance of gender as a stimulus is also central to the social-role analysis of gender proposed by Alice Eagly (1983, 1987), who emphasizes that relative status is a primary characteristic that we learn to associate with, or attribute to, gender. Gender functions as a generalized status cue because it is observed to be correlated with power and prestige across a variety of settings and experiences; in other words, men's positions in most groups and organizations in our society tend to be higher in authority and to offer greater access to resources than women's positions do. Because gender covaries with power and status, we respond to women and men differently, influencing their responses to us and illustrating a phenomenon social psychologists call "fulfilling the prophecies." Other social categories also function as generalized status cues, particularly ethnicity, which also provides cues to social standing (Landrine, 1985). Especially important are the "combined or interactive effects" of gender and ethnicity (Reid & Comas-Diaz, 1990).

We tend to behave as others expect us to in particular situations because we are rewarded for doing what is appropriate and because we have acquired complementary attitudes and responses through relatively consistent experiences. That others' expectations and responses can effectively influence behavior in very subtle ways was explicitly demonstrated in a study (Snyder, Tanke, & Berscheid, 1977) in which undergraduate men were asked to talk on the telephone with a young woman who they believed to be either physically attractive or unattractive, but who was unaware of how she had been described. The researchers later analyzed each conversation and found that the women who were thought to be attractive "came to behave in a friendly, likeable, and sociable manner," in comparison with the women who were believed to be unattractive. In an earlier study that demonstrated the same phenomenon (Zanna & Pack, 1975), undergraduate women who had an opportunity to work on a task with a "desirable" 21-year-old male Princeton senior (with a car and without a girlfriend) portrayed themselves as being either more or less conventional in sex role depending on whether their partner's views were traditional or nontraditional. Furthermore, women who thought their "desirable" male partner was nontraditional outperformed those who thought otherwise in unscrambling anagrams correctly. Women who worked with "undesirable" male partners were not influenced by their partner's sex role beliefs. In another study (Skrypnek & Snyder, 1982), women and men were paired for a task, but some men were led to believe their partner was a man while others were told their partner was a woman. In the latter case, the men selected more stereotypically masculine activities for themselves and feminine activities for their partners. Later, the women whose partners believed they were female were more likely to choose feminine tasks for themselves than the women whose partners thought they were men, although the women did not know what their partners had been told.

Variations from the Normative Model

Gender differences reflect the expectations and responses of many of those with whom we interact. At the same time, most contemporary women behave, at different times and places, in ways quite different from the traditional model. The complexity of modern society—the existence of subcultures and disparate values, pressures, and demands—contributes to varying degrees of deviance from the traditions of the majority culture. We see women everywhere who are active, independent, competitive,

risk-taking, task-oriented, and concerned with achievement (excellence) both inside and outside the home. That many women see these behaviors as appropriate and ideal for women is reported by students in my classes year after year. Further, the majority culture has never expected African-American women, for example, to fit the stereotype of European-American femininity. African-American women have been portrayed as strong, independent, striving, or assertive. And, of course, the conditions of life for a large percentage of African-American women have not been the same as those for most European-American women, and the conditions of life for the poor are different from those for the affluent. As Linda Myers (1978) has noted, everything in the African-American woman's "situation and experience [beginning with slavery] has been contrived to prohibit her fulfilling this [European-American] model of womanhood, even if it were worthy" (p. 3). Bonnie Dill (1979) has pointed out that African-American women were brought as slaves to this country "to work and to produce workers," a role that contrasts sharply with the European-American ideal of domesticity and dependency.

African-American women tend to self-report a relatively equal number of both instrumental and expressive traits, a phenomenon that is not surprising since African-American women have long been accustomed to being wives and mothers who also work outside the home. Joyce Ladner (1971) found that a sample of African-American adolescent girls expected women to take a strong family role as well as to be economically independent, educated, resourceful, self-reliant, and upwardly mobile. Albert Lott and I (1963) studied high school seniors in a Southern community and found that African-American girls and boys were more alike in their values and goals than European-American girls and boys, primarily because of differences between the two groups of girls. African-American women seniors, for example, scored higher than their European-American counterparts on measures of theoretical and political values and lower on aesthetic and religious values as well as on the need for love and affection. In a recent study (Binion, 1990) of a sample of mainly low-income adult African-American women, 36.6 percent scored as both instrumental and expressive on a self-report measure and 23.6 percent scored as primarily instrumental, results consistent with the agentic roles African-American women play in their families and communities. At the same time, the women also expressed traditional beliefs about women's family roles and more traditional sex-role beliefs than a comparable group of European-American women.

Alice Brown-Collins and Deborah Sussewell (1985) have argued that the behavior of African-American women can only be understood in the context of their history and in terms of the interaction between their culture and sex-role socialization. African-American women have functioned as community educators, building schools and maintaining kindergartens, and as community organizers, demonstrating both agentic/instrumental and communal/affiliative attributes and concerns. As noted by Brown-Collins and Sussewell, "the irony of slave women's history is that womanhood was redefined to allow for the exploitation of their labor resulting in the development of independent, self-reliant characteristics" (p. 7). In an important study comparing groups of African-American, Asian-American, European-American, and Latina women students on the meanings they attributed to personality adjectives used on the Bem scale (Landrine, Klonoff, & Brown-Collins, 1992), the authors obtained interesting and challenging results. Despite the fact that the European-American students and the women of color scored similarly on the test—that is, they described themselves in much the same way—they differed substantially in the definitions they selected for some of the terms. Thus, for example, whereas the European-American students preferred to define "passive" as laid-back and easygoing, the women of color tended to define it as not saying what one really thinks.

In addition to differences between European-American and African-American women (or Asian-American, Latina, and Native American women), there are also areas of commonality. As we have seen in earlier chapters, gender expectations sometimes supersede those associated with color, socioeconomic status, or ethnicity. For example, Pamela Reid (1978) noted that African-American girls, too, are trained for motherhood and given the same toys as European-American girls to learn from and practice on; traditional behavior patterns are conveyed in the same ways and by the same agents. The pages of *Ebony* magazine, for example, provide considerable evidence that today's idealized middle-class African-American woman is in many ways indistinguishable from the idealized European-American one. A review of relevant literature (Murray & Mednick, 1977) found that African-American college and middle-class women share the traditional views of women's role held by their European-American counterparts. And, according to Michele Wallace (1979), growing up in Harlem meant listening "no less intently than the little white girls who grew up on Park Avenue, in Scarsdale, or on Long Island" (p. 90) to the messages that

came to both groups from the same magazines, movies, and television.

While common experiences produce common themes associated with gender, variations in behavior among women, and on the part of the same woman, are also found on every behavioral dimension. We know from all available evidence that behavior has no gender. Instrumental, expressive, affiliative, autonomous, self-oriented, or communal-oriented responses are teachable and, under the appropriate conditions, can be learned, maintained, and manifested by girls or boys, women or men. Thus, Jerome Adams (1984) found among cadets in the first three coeducational classes of West Point that no gender differences appeared in educational aspirations, professional career goals, or instrumental, assertive, and agentic personal attributes. And in an altogether different realm, that of personal wishes, one study (Ehrlichman & Eichenstein, 1992) found little evidence of gender differences among ethnically diverse samples of college students and adults. Both women and men wished for "health, wealth, well-being of loved ones, achievement, and power" (p. 418), and in a very similar order. What, then, can we conclude about the adult personality of women?

Careful reviews of the empirical literature typically conclude, as this chapter has documented, that gender differences are less pervasive than has been thought and that gender has relatively weak associations with behavior. Rhoda Unger (1981) has referred to gender differences as having a "now you see them, now you don't" quality—probably because the appearance of gender differences in behavior depends upon the social context or particular conditions of the situation. As Kay Deaux (1984) has suggested, the tasks most likely to disclose gender differences are the same ones that are the sources of difference.

Not Androgynous, but Human

Recognition that individual behavior often fails to confirm gender stereotypes led some psychologists to develop the concept of androgyny, as noted earlier in this chapter. As defined and measured, however, this concept rests on the assumption that masculinity and femininity describe different sets of traits (or different aspects of personality), each one distinctive from and independent of the other. Giving each of these sets of traits a different gender label perpetuates the linguistic and conceptual association between personality and gender. Thus, masculinity and femininity continue to be regarded as dual natures or distinctive ways of behaving, although combinable in various ways. Such a dualistic view of human personality is rooted in sex-role stereotypes and is not supported by careful reviews of the evidence. This evidence led Sandra Bem (1985), a major contributor to the earlier androgyny literature, to a dramatic revision of her approach and to the view that "human behaviors and personality attributes should no longer be linked with gender, and [that] society should stop projecting gender into situations irrelevant to genitalia" (p. 222).

We know that no teachable human behavior belongs exclusively to any one group of persons and that both women and men manifest wide individual differences along all behavioral dimensions. Any behavior can be learned by any person capable of performing it, given appropriate conditions for its acquisition, and the behavior will be maintained if it continues to be situationally appropriate and is approved and not punished. There is no evidence that one group of persons (distinguished by sex, skin color, socioeconomic level, or other social categories) is more naturally suited for some responses than another. To label some behaviors as feminine because our culture attempts to teach them primarily to girls and women obscures the essential humanness of these behaviors.

The ease with which some psychologists slipped into a trap of their own making is evident when a woman who describes herself as self-reliant, ambitious, assertive, and analytical is given points on a test for masculinity, implying that men have a special monopoly on these characteristics. We know full well that these are *human* characteristics, manifested to varying degrees in differing circumstances by both women and men. Women's traditional role in the family, for which girls are typically socialized and which most women eventually practice, is said to be related to the development of nurturance, caring, sensitivity, expressiveness, and connectedness. Not attended to, however, are other probable and significant behaviors learned in this role, namely effective problem solving, management skills, decision making, task-persistence, initiative, and so on. Which of these components of women's work do we highlight as women's strengths and identify as key features of women's personality?

While women and men can both acquire any human behavior, our differing life circumstances in contemporary society must be acknowledged and attended to. A major variable distinguishing the adult lives of most women and men is differential power—that is, access to resources. Socialization and differences in power between groups are interrelated. Socialization describes how we learn to behave as our culture expects us to. Power differences

make differential socialization necessary and are then perpetuated and reinforced by the results of differential learning. This circle can be broken. One requisite for change is recognizing the power differences between groups and knowing how these are related to economic, political, and other conditions. Another requisite is understanding how we learn to behave as we do—that is, the antecedents of particular behaviors.

Recognizing that behavioral polarities are rare enlarges our understanding that responses to complex events tend to be multidimensional. Thus, for example, Mary Brabeck (1983) has suggested that the ideal moral decision can be understood as combining a principle of justice (as claimed for men) and an ethic of care and responsibility (as claimed for women). Moral choices, in other words, can

> reflect reasoned and deliberate judgments that ensure justice be accorded each person while maintaining a passionate concern for the well-being and care of each individual. Justice and care are then joined; . . . and the need for autonomy and for interconnection are united in an enlarged and more adequate conception of morality. (p. 289)

Such an enlarged conception of morality is not one that combines so-called masculine and feminine elements, but one that dispenses with such artificial dualities. Similarly, an enlarged conception of human personality does not first divide human functioning into two pieces and then put them back together again. We know that gender differences may reliably be found for some behaviors, at some ages, in some situations, at some times and places. But such differences are better understood if related to their learning antecedents and situational determinants than if simply related to sex. Historical and current variations among women in life-styles, aspirations, attitudes, and interests, between affluent women and those who are poor, and among women from different ethnic groups provide impressive evidence that we must include all within-gender variations in our understanding of what it means to be a woman, just as we must recognize variations in the behavior of the same woman.

Despite the ubiquity of gender associations and stereotypes, the cultural emphasis on separate spheres and societal arrangements to maintain them, reliable gender differences turn out to be very small and unstable, and their magnitude is not consistent across situations. This suggests that persons learn whenever they have opportunities to practice behavior and supports the conclusion that no human behavior is exclusively the province of one group of persons rather than another. At the same time, we must not forget that gender continues to function as a cue for position in our society and that women and men differ widely in access to resources and to opportunities for personal growth. Gender continues to function as a central organizing principle in social institutions—a salient stimulus signifying relative prestige and power, probable occupation, and connoting expected personal attributes.

DYSFUNCTIONAL BEHAVIOR

Among the most damaging responses that our culture teaches us to make to women are the contradictory expectations we have of women's capacity to tolerate and cope with stress. On the one hand, we learn that women are frail, need protection, are easily upset or frightened, cannot cope with emergencies, worry a lot, visit doctors frequently, and are prone to nervous breakdowns. On the other hand, we also expect that women will know how to "take care" of the problems of their children, partners, or elderly parents; to tend the sick or the troubled; to nurture and soothe; and to handle the stresses of everyday life without falling apart—in other words, that women are more hardy than men in dealing with personal crises. Sometimes our literature and art reflect one image of women, and sometimes the other. And similar contradictions appear in the research and writings of social scientists. In behavior-focused studies, however, as opposed to self-reports of attributes, nonclinical samples of women and men tend not to be distinguishable in terms of how they cope with stress. Sandra Hamilton and Beverly Fagot (1988), for example, studied a group of first-year college students for 8 weeks by means of a telephone interview three times a week and found no important gender differences in actual behavior. The women and men did not engage in stereotypical behavior, did not use different amounts of expressive or instrumental coping strategies, and did not differ in frequency of stressful events or proportion of problem-solving efforts.

The issues we will consider next are traditionally discussed in a context in which mental health and mental illness refer to two ends of a continuum describing general functioning or day-to-day coping with life's stresses and strains. Psychologists typically measure mental health by obtaining answers to questions that assess adjustment, well-being, self-esteem, or life satisfaction. Sometimes overall functioning is assessed by self-reports of symptoms such as headaches, fatigue, and so on. Mental health is also taken to mean the absence of mental illness as diagnosed

on the basis of specific symptoms that occur in conjunction with impairment of function and the experience of distress. Impaired mental health is sometimes inferred from the fact of inpatient or outpatient treatment. My preference is to view behavior not on a continuum of health or illness but on one of effectiveness or optimum functioning. In this view, effective (functional or adaptive) behavior, characteristic of "mental health," is behavior that achieves a person's goals, succeeds in solving problems, reduces conflict, maximizes the attainment of positive consequences in the short run without sacrificing long-term gains, does not lead to an increase in pain or frustration, and does not create new problems or unsolvable conflicts. Dysfunctional behavior is behavior that fails to meet these criteria.

Special Problem Areas for Women

At the end of this chapter we will consider how individual effectiveness can be increased or enhanced and examine some of the requirements for women's well-being, but first we will focus on dysfunctional behavior and address the issue of gender differences in self-reported frequency of symptoms of distress and in psychiatric diagnoses. Overall, data from a variety of sources—community surveys, outpatient clinics, private treatment facilities, general hospitals, mental hospitals, and college or university counseling centers—indicate that women tend to be the most frequent consumers of mental health services in the United States, although not in all types of facilities. Among children, the situation is different; girls are less likely than boys to receive treatment. A comprehensive and important review of relevant data (Russo, 1985) concluded as follows:

[1] Men have higher rates of admission to mental health facilities than do women for all marital status categories, with one exception—married men have lower admission rates than do married women. This reversal is especially dramatic for minority women.

[2] A higher percentage of women than men receive services from various types of facilities. . . . The situation is reversed in state and county mental hospitals and in public mental hospitals.

[3] Women report more worries and say more often than do men that . . . bad things happen to them. . . .

[4] In 1980 for the noninstitutionalized populations . . . women showed substantially higher rates of depressive disorders and phobias by a factor of at least two to

one. In contrast, men showed higher rates of antisocial personality and alcohol abuse/dependence; women were more likely to be diagnosed as having dysthymic disorders, somatization disorders, panic disorders, obsessive/compulsive disorders, and schizophrenia. . . . Compared to men, women have higher prevalence rates of affective disorders at every age. (pp. 5–7)

The findings noted in item 4 came from a major national survey directed by the National Institute of Mental Health that involved door-to-door interviews of approximately 10,000 adults (Fox, 1984). These researchers concluded that although women and men differ in the frequency with which they receive various particular diagnoses, as just indicated, the rate of mental disorders is roughly equal for both genders, as it is for African-Americans and European-Americans.

Depression and Suicide. Among the patterns of dysfunctional behavior manifested by women, depression is the most common. The symptoms—passivity, feelings of hopelessness and helplessness, lowered self-esteem, crying, suicidal feelings, self-accusation, slowed movement, and disturbed sleep—are congruent with women's socialization. Women are taught to look inside ourselves for the cause of unresolved problems, to ask what we have done wrong, and to feel guilt. Women—who lack power, or access to resources, relative to men—may be more likely, when we do not meet objectives, experience success, or overcome barriers, to turn the anger of the frustration experienced against ourselves rather than against others. We may tend to view ourselves as failures and at fault if others have not been loving, attentive, approving, or rewarding to us. Thus, it makes sense to find that the most vulnerable of all to depression are married minority women and low-income female heads of single-parent households; the latter have the highest depression rate of any demographic group (Russo, 1985).

Among nonclinical samples of college students (i.e., students not undergoing treatment), who are typically single, childless, and middle-class, significant gender differences in paper-and-pencil measures of depression are not usually found (e.g., Padesky & Hammen, 1981; Elpern & Karp, 1984; Wise & Joy, 1982). The same lack of gender difference in incidence of depression has been reported among nonclinical samples of adults in the general population, challenging the oft-repeated assumption of greater prevalence among women. In a study of 3,132 European-American adults who were interviewed about symptoms, "distributions of depression scores were generally similar in women and men, with the exception of a small number of extreme scores among women" (Golding, 1988, p. 71); the extreme scoring women were typically disadvantaged in income and social status.

The single most discriminating behavior between women and men has been reported to be the greater tendency on the part of women to cry (Padesky & Hammen, 1981; Kleinke, Staneski, & Mason, 1982). In the latter study, women were also found to be more likely than men to eat, smoke, become short-tempered, and confront their feelings when depressed, while men were more likely to become aggressive or engage in sexual behavior. Among students who scored high in depression, men were more likely to use drugs and spend time alone, whereas women were more likely to blame themselves and seek help. College women have self-reported a greater tendency than college men to eat more when depressed and to seek personal support (Chino & Funabiki, 1984).

Women attempt suicide at a rate approximately 2.3 times greater than men, whereas men complete suicides more than women by the same ratio (Kushner, 1985). The rate of successful suicides is highest for European-American men, followed by African-American men, European-American women, and African-American women. Men are more likely to use guns; women are more likely to use pharmaceuticals (Heshusius, 1980). Howard Kushner (1985) believes that the gender difference in suicidal behavior has been exaggerated and that "if we combine completions and attempts, there is not now, nor has there ever been so far as anyone can demonstrate, any gender-specific difference in suicidal behavior" (p. 546). Kushner argues that combining the numbers of completed and attempted suicides is justified because neither reveals anything about intention. He further argues that the greater use of firearms in suicide by men in this country simply reflects men's greater access to them. "No student of history . . . should be surprised to learn that women have had less access to lethal technology than men" (p. 551).

Alcohol and Drug Abuse. The prevalence of alcohol and drug abuse among women is difficult to assess because many women are in situations in which their chemical dependency can remain hidden. Sherri Matteo's (1988) review of the literature in this area led her to conclude that "the reaction of disgust and repulsion with which an alcoholic woman must contend may well reinforce her reluctance to admit to a drinking problem. She is much more likely to drink alone, at home, early in the mornings or on weekends, [and] to go to great lengths to hide her problem from herself and others" (p. 743).

The data sources that are available—arrest statistics, hospital admissions, physicians' reports, membership in groups like Alcoholics Anonymous, and community surveys—indicate that men outnumber women with respect to dysfunctional behavior involving chemical substance abuse but also that the number of women experiencing alcohol and drug problems has been steadily increasing. Some data have shown that the gender difference in rates of substance abuse is smaller at younger ages, suggesting that future generations may approach equal prevalence (Russo, 1985). Whereas the general male-female ratio for alcohol problems among European-Americans is currently 4 to 1, among African-Americans it is 3 to 2; and although African-American women are more likely to be alcohol abstainers by a 2 to 1 margin, those who drink are more likely to be heavy drinkers.

> More women aged 35 to 64 are drinkers and the percentage of women aged 35 to 49 who are heavy drinkers rose from 5% in 1971 to 9% in 1981. . . . Women . . . [with] higher risks of having drinking problems develop . . . [are] those . . . who were never married, divorced or separated women, unemployed women who were looking for work, and those who lived with partners to whom they were not married. (Matteo, 1988, p. 742).

Women's alcohol problems are less likely to be detected and, therefore, less likely to be treated than men's. Men, whose drinking is typically more visible, have more often been the focus of attention and research. Women who drink heavily may be treated for anxiety and other symptoms of poor functioning and are at risk for being given prescriptions for sedatives or tranquilizers, resulting in multiple addictions.

We know that cocaine usage and addiction problems have increased among women (Brozan, 1985), as indicated by the number of admissions to state-financed programs and the number of telephone calls for help made to cocaine hot lines. Cocaine abuse appears to be more common among younger women than younger men, and women tend to use it in greater quantities. In one psychiatric facility, 53 percent of the women referred for treatment for cocaine abuse were younger than 30, compared with 25 percent of the men (Brozan, 1985).

Although women's rate of alcohol and drug problem behavior is approaching that of men, some evidence shows gender differences in the ways substance abuse is manifested, in its associations with frustrations or life stresses, and in the reactions it elicits from other people. Edith Gomberg (1979) reviewed the relevant literature and noted that women begin heavy drinking somewhat later than men; drink more frequently at home, alone or with their spouse; do less binge drinking; do more solitary drinking; and are at greater risk for drug and alcohol interaction effects. While a study of more than 300 patients treated for alcoholism (Cronkite & Moos, 1984) found no significant gender differences in drinking pattern, impairment, or consumption, it found evidence that the consequences of alcohol dependence for married women are likely to be significantly more negative than those for married men. When the patients were questioned 6 to 8 months after discharge from residential treatment facilities, the researchers found that whereas marriage increased the likelihood of post-treatment abstinence for men, it lowered the likelihood of abstinence for women. Other data indicate that women with alcohol problems frequently marry alcoholic men, that women are more likely than men to be blamed for the alcohol problems of their spouse, and that "husbands of alcoholic women are less tolerant of their spouses' drinking than are wives of alcoholic men [and] . . . are more likely to leave alcoholic spouses and fight for custody of children" (Russo, 1985, p. 23).

Our society has less tolerance and less sympathy for women with alcohol or drug problems than for men. A review of the literature by Jonica Homiller (1977) found that whereas 9 out of 10 women stay with an alcoholic husband, only 1 man out of 10 stays with an alcoholic wife; and women alcoholics are generally believed to be "sicker" than their male counterparts. These findings are supported by a study in which college students read about cases of wife abuse and made judgments about responsibility (Richardson & Campbell, 1980). When the abusive husband was described as drunk, the respondents ascribed significantly more responsibility for the abuse to the situation than when he was sober. On the other hand, "when the wife was drunk, she received more blame for the incident than when she was sober . . . [and] the amount of blame to the husband decreased" (p. 55).

A popular hypothesis in the substance abuse literature is that chemically dependent women have difficulties living up to their standards of traditional femininity, but supporting data are sparse. Sandra Anderson (1980), for example, compared a sample of women in treatment centers for alcoholism with their nonalcoholic sisters, and found no significant differences between them on measures of conscious feminine identification, sex-role style, or unconscious masculine identification. Alcoholic women were also found not to differ from their nonalcoholic sisters in descriptions of their parents (Anderson, 1984), but were more likely to be divorced and living alone, to recall more parental disapproval and childhood unhappiness, and to perceive themselves as less similar to their mothers in attitudes and interests.

Eating Disorders. Among the dysfunctional behaviors in our society that are most associated with women are eating disorders. As we have already seen, all relevant data support the conclusion that "women in general, more than men, spend a great deal of time and energy worrying about appearance and feeling too fat" (Rodin, Silberstein, & Striegel-Moore, 1985, p. 294). Thus, as noted by Rodin and her colleagues, a large-scale survey in 1978 found that 56 percent of all women respondents were on a diet; samples of college women consistently score higher than men on questions assessing body dissatisfaction and desire for thinness; the second most important concern expressed by a sample of elderly women, following memory loss, was increased weight; and among college undergraduates, weight and body shape have been found to be the central determinants of women's (but not men's) perception of their physical attractiveness. A survey by *Glamour* magazine (Wooley & Wooley, 1984) found that 63 percent of the young women among 33,000 respondents reported that weight affected how they felt about themselves, and 42 percent said that losing weight would make them happier than success at work, a date with an admired man, or hearing from an old friend. Such data are echoed by the feelings expressed by a woman in a Marge Piercy (1989) novel:

> At least she hadn't gained weight with all this trauma. At least that. Great. She lost her husband, she felt crazy and on the verge of total disintegration, she couldn't face anyone she knew, she was so angry with Tom she could have killed him herself while she could not even yell at him or demand an explanation or say how hurt she was, but at least she wasn't fat. They could put that on her grave. Her life was miserable, she was a total failure as a woman and an artist, but she kept her weight down. (p. 46)

Concern with weight is prevalent among adolescent girls and children. A national poll in 1989 found that one third of high school girls thought they were overweight compared with only 15 percent of boys, and a study of 200 suburban Boston sixth-graders found that 17 percent of the girls said they dieted frequently while the remaining 83 percent dieted occasionally and 58 percent reported that they think too much about food (cf. "Preteen Girls," 1991). Other researchers have found that European-American girls, especially, report beginning to be worried about their body image as early as the second grade.

While the concern on the part of girls is with being too fat, boys think they're too thin and try to gain weight or build up their muscles (cf. DeAngelis, 1990).

It is to be expected, then, that more women than men will manifest exaggerated patterns of eating. Rodin and her colleagues, as well as others (e.g., Brownmiller, 1984), have argued that women's preoccupation with appearance is normative in our society—that it results from social pressures, from the greater punishments experienced by obese women than men, and from the strong relationship between women's judged attractiveness and thinness. As discussed earlier, attractiveness "has been considered a feminine attribute, and its pursuit a feminine responsibility"; it continues to give "a woman power in terms of having more access to resources (for example, being able to attract and marry a high-status man) and of being more favorably treated in social contexts" (Rodin et al., 1985, pp. 275f.). But women pursuing nontraditional roles and independent careers seem no less vulnerable than others to the exaggerated contribution of weight and appearance to feelings of self-worth. According to some researchers (Wooley & Wooley, 1986), career women, too, appear to use thinness as an indication of ability to control events and as a sign of worthiness.

Many women regard weight as a crucial index of acceptability and attractiveness. Failure to take account of the biological factors that predispose females to accumulate more body fat than males (a greater production of cholesterol-related estrogen and metabolic rate changes during puberty) and our society's pressure on women to be thin take their toll in a high incidence of eating disorders which can be viewed on a continuum with anorexia and bulimia at the extreme end of one pole and normal eating on the other. Anorexia is diagnosed if an individual has lost at least 25 percent of body weight and feels fat even though clearly and seriously underweight. Restrictor anorexics maintain their emaciation by drastically restricting their intake; bulimic anorexics binge and then attempt to compensate by vomiting; using laxatives, diuretics, or amphetamines; exercising excessively; or some combination of these. Susan Squire (1983) has suggested that anorexia is followed on the continuum by normal-weight bulimia, occasional purging, occasional dieting, and finally normal eating and satisfaction with one's body regardless of weight. The last pattern appears to characterize only a small minority of women. Robin Gibbs (1986) found among a sample of high school students that 22 percent of the girls could be classified as having an eating disorder on the basis of their scores on a measure of eating behavior. The current estimate is that

Women are pressured to be "chic" by being thin. (Photograph © Diana Mara Henry, Carmel, CA)

1 out of 200 American girls between 12 and 18 years of age will develop some degree of anorexia and that 10 to 15 percent of these girls will die (cf. "Women's Health," 1985).

Bingeing and purging behavior is common among women on college campuses across the country, and evidence exists that women directly teach this behavior to one another. Self-induced vomiting has been found among all weight groups from the obese to the anorexic. The prevalence of bulimia has been difficult to estimate because the binge eating and vomiting are typically done in secret, and because the shape and weight of bulimics are usually within normal limits and their eating habits in social situations are appropriate (Schlesier-Stropp, 1984). Estimates of prevalence have ranged from 13 to 67 percent among normal nonclinical samples (Polivy & Herman, 1985). A survey of more than 1000 high school women found that 21 percent reported binge-eating episodes at least once a week (cf. Rodin et al., 1985); at one state university, 13 percent of the respondents to a survey reported experiencing all the major symptoms of bulimia (cf. Schlesier-Stropp, 1984). Although some consider overeating and obesity to be problems as serious as anorexia and bulimia, the latter have received far more

attention because they are primarily found among young women and can be life-threatening. The most recent estimates (cf. DeAngelis, 1990) are that bulimic behavior in the United States is declining but that "bulimia affects from 1 to 2 percent of adolescent and young adult women . . . that about 95 percent of bulimics are female, and 86 percent are between 15 and 30 years old" (p. 8). One study found a greater incidence of bulimia among college women than working women of the same ages (between 18 and 30), 5 percent versus 1 percent (Ollendick & Hart, 1985). Others have noted that the behavioral symptoms of disordered eating often occur among college women in the absence of associated psychological characteristics indicative of pathology (Hesse-Biber, 1989).

Efforts to explain disordered eating patterns by women in terms of individual personality dynamics have included the common assumption that women eat to relieve stress (as in the "Sylvia" cartoon on p. 295). More complex interpretations posit that anorexia and bulimia are "a predominantly female defense against the dangers most women experience of devaluation and sexualization" (Friedrichs, 1988, p. 70) or are "related to feelings among young women that in the area of intellectual/professional

SYLVIA, by Nicole Hollander. Cartoonists & Writers Syndicate.

achievement being a female is a disadvantage" (Silverstein, Perdue, Wolf, & Pizzolo, 1988, p. 730). Mothers, as we might expect, have come in for a share of the blame, with one study reporting that mothers of daughters with eating disorders urged them to lose significantly more weight than other mothers and rated their daughters as less attractive than the daughters rated themselves (cf. "Study: Zealous Moms," 1991).

While the American Psychiatric Association is considering the inclusion of binge-eating as a new disorder to be listed in the new edition of the DSM (anorexia is already included) (Youngstrom, 1991), a rather different approach interprets such eating as a consequence of social contagion. Binge-eating, in other words, is viewed as a behavior that is acquired just as other behaviors are and is under social control. In support of this hypothesis, Christian Crandall (1988) found that in one college sorority popularity was positively related to bingeing; the greater the reported frequency, the more popular was the young woman. In another sorority, popularity was associated with bingeing just the right amount, not too often and not too seldom. Furthermore, "by the end of the academic year, a sorority member's binge-eating could be predicted from the binge-eating level of her friends" (p. 588). These data clearly implicate the role played by social factors, as do those obtained by one of my students (Gibbs, 1986). She found, within a high school sample, that eating problem scores were positively related to talking to one's friends about weight.

According to Maria Root (1990), problems associated with disordered eating are not restricted to European-American women. She argues that women of color in today's society are just as vulnerable, and that eating disorders are increasingly common among ethnic minorities, especially African-American women. In our society,

> dieting appears to be a rite of passage into adulthood for females . . . [and] also appears to be a strategy women rather than men use to increase self-esteem, obtain privileges, increase credibility in the workforce, and contend with conflicting gender-role proscriptions. . . . Mythology, fairy tales, television, movies, and advertising lead women to believe that thinness is beauty, success, power, and acceptance, and therefore, dieting is a viable strategy. (p. 526) Women of color . . . [are also] vulnerable to adopting the concrete strategy of making physical appearance conform to the standard displayed in all the fashion magazines. Physical appearance becomes a ticket for acceptance and even promotion. (p. 529)

Other Dysfunctions. Women outnumber men among persons diagnosed as suffering from histrionic personality, the term now used in the official diagnostic manual of the American Psychiatric Association (1987) to replace hysteria (a term that literally means "wandering womb"!). According to Pauline Bart and Diana Scully (1979), a man given the diagnosis of hysteria was almost certain to be homosexual, poor, or an ethnic minority; and the behaviors regarded as symptomatic of hysteria represent a "stark caricature of femininity," with exaggerated dependence, exhibitionism, and manipulativeness. Others have also pointed out the correspondence between the group of symptoms labeled as hysteria and the behaviors our culture teaches to women (e.g., Celani, 1976). Hysteria, according to Howard Wolowitz (1972), described the stereotyped woman whose needs for approval, dependency, and affiliation became overwhelming demands to be satisfied by the use of charm, sex, goodness, and perhaps finally illness and martyrdom. Hope Landrine (1989, 1991), using different methodologies, found that psychotherapists and college students match the diagnosis of histrionic personality with middle- or upper-class single women, and vice versa. These results support Landrine's thesis that personality disorder diagnoses, based on symptom descriptions, represent particular social role stereotypes in our society, organized by gender, social class, and marital status, and that the social role category that matches the symptoms is the one that receives the diagnosis most often. We will return to issues of diagnosis later in this chapter.

Another dysfunction associated primarily with women is agoraphobia, a fear of open spaces. Persons with agoraphobia experience anxiety or panic when they attempt to work, shop, visit, or do anything requiring their presence outside of their own homes; they tend to "fear any situation in which escape to safe territory or to a trusted companion might be hindered" (Chambless & Goldstein, 1980, p. 119). Some have suggested that women are vulnerable to agoraphobia because such behavior is acceptable, and the symptoms may be reinforced by family members who see them as not too inappropriate for a woman. In an Australian study (Hafner & Minge, 1989), a group of women who met the criteria for agoraphobia were found to rate themselves significantly lower on a scale of autonomy than a control group of women.

Richard Lewine (1981) reviewed the literature on schizophrenia and concluded that gender differences exist in age of onset (or diagnosis) and in symptoms. Men appear to receive schizophrenia diagnoses and to be hospitalized at younger ages than women. Whether this reflects a true gender difference in age of onset is not known, since family members may attend sooner to men who manifest the deviant behavior that characterizes schizophrenia (bizarre affective and cognitive responses). Early in this century Leta Hollingworth argued that this was the case with respect to mental retardation; men were institutionalized at earlier ages than women because young retarded women could remain at home, serving useful functions and performing limited tasks. According to Stephanie Shields (1975b), Hollingworth

reasoned that since men were expected to take their place in society as competitive and economically-independent individuals, their deficiencies would be noted earlier.

Women, on the other hand, " . . . are not so readily recognized as defective since they do not have to compete mentally to maintain themselves in the social milieu." (p. 854)

Contributing Factors

Powerlessness. It has long been suspected that high on the list of factors contributing to dysfunctional behavior is powerlessness—a condition of having little or no access to the resources that enable one to influence the behavior of others or the outcomes accruing to oneself. Jeanne Marecek (1977), arguing that "powerlessness engenders a high risk of psychological disorder" (p. 2), has noted that dysfunctional behavior is prevalent in our society among persons who are chronically poor and undereducated; who are powerless because of continued social inequities; and who are experiencing temporary powerlessness as a consequence of "abrupt economic reversals, the death of a spouse or love, or serious illness," life stresses that magnify the lack of control persons have over their environments. As a status group, women have less power than men; and on an individual level, a woman's ability to control her own life decreases with the extent to which she conforms to traditional role expectations, and the extent to which she is discriminated against by economic, political, legal, and educational institutions.

A study of a graduate student sample (Elpern & Karp, 1984), for example, found that for both women and men, greater depression was associated with lower self-reported assertiveness and other instrumental/agentic attributes and that, among women, those who self-reported primarily communal and nurturant attributes were more depressed than others. Similarly, a group of middle-aged European-American women diagnosed as depressive were found to differ from a comparable nonclinical group (Tinsley, Sullivan-Guest, & McGuire, 1984) in being more likely to describe themselves in nurturant, expressive, and communal terms, supporting the researchers' hypothesis that "depression in the middle-aged female is related to her degree of acceptance of the traditional feminine sex role" (p. 30). Found to be associated with physical symptoms and depression in a sample of married professional women with small children (Reifman, Biernat, & Lang, 1991) were lack of authority and influence on the job, sex discrimination, and a heavy work load, all factors that can be said to contribute to relative powerlessness.

Similarly, data on suicide attempts suggest that women may resort to this behavior more than men because they have fewer options for solving problems or changing conditions. Lous Heshusius (1980) summarized this proposition as follows:

> a "woman's place" does not [ordinarily] offer her the resources needed to deal effectively and adaptively with the environment. Where males most often have political power, financial power, power derived from their career status and possibilities, and sheer physical power to bring about changes in their environment, females typically lack such resources. (p. 852)

Contributing to powerlessness are demographic disadvantages, which are more likely to characterize women than men. Thus, the women's health agenda developed by an interdisciplinary group for the National Institute of Mental Health (Russo, 1990) specifically identified poverty as one of five priority research areas. In a large random community sample of adults in Los Angeles (Golding, 1988), high depression scores were found to be prevalent among "the young, less educated, low income, low socioeconomic status, unmarried, and unemployed" (p. 71). Because more women were found among these groups, they were more likely to have extreme depression scores, but these demographic indicators put both women and men at a similar disadvantage. The general assumption of the greater prevalence of depression among women was challenged by Golding's analysis of several studies of large random samples of adults and by her own data. It is women's greater likelihood of being demographically disadvantaged, and not their gender, that puts them at greater risk for depression.

A colleague and I have presented a similar argument (Lott & Maluso, 1993) in discussing a much publicized survey of research on depression (McGrath, Keita, Strickland, & Russo, 1990). To conclude that depression is not gender-neutral because women are twice as likely as men to receive such a diagnosis neglects to take into account women's lesser status and power both in the workplace and in heterosexual relationships, as well as women's greater exposure to uncontrollable negative life events such as sexual and physical victimization and poverty. Gender differences in power are accompanied by differences in exposure to stressors and in access to moderating resources. It is these risk factors for depression that are not gender-neutral, not their outcomes. In other words, it is the accumulation of uncontrollable negative life experiences without access to mediating resources, and not the fact that one is a woman, that is causally implicated in depression.

Powerlessness has been found to be an especially significant factor among women who have newly immigrated to the United States. For example, at least 60 percent of all Asian-American women in the United States have entered the country since 1970. The majority are both married and in the work force but employed in low-wage, low-status occupations, such as domestics, clerks, saleswomen, and seamstresses. "Because of the persistent stereotype of Asian American women as hardworking, uncomplaining handmaidens, they are often exploited at work, denied promotion, and relegated to backroom office work" (True, 1990, p. 479). A low level of access to resources combines with cultural conflicts to put this group of women at risk for dysfunction. Similarly at risk are immigrants from Mexico and Central America; among this group, women have been found to have higher levels of stress than men, associated with breaking ties with families, friends, and communities and with the need to adapt to a new language and culture (DeSnyder, Salgado, Cervantes, & Padilla, 1990).

Restricted Social Role. Another factor, related to powerlessness, that has been proposed as contributing to the distress particularly of married women who are full-time homemakers is their more restricted social role. The role of full-time homemaker is said to provide lesser variety and fewer satisfactions, and to be more ambiguous, than the role of employed husband (Gove & Tudor, 1973). A woman who stays at home for many years with children and housework is expected to derive satisfaction from interaction with family members, the gleam of a polished floor, a report of "no cavities" from her children's dentist, or the whiteness of her husband's laundered shirt. Unless she is also involved in activities outside the home, her sources of satisfaction will be more limited than those of her husband; this gender-restricted social role, it is argued, increases the likelihood of more negative than positive experiences. Whereas raising children and keeping house full-time are low-prestige, frustrating, relatively unstructured, and largely invisible jobs, an employed husband has two major sources of gratification, his family and his work. A study of an adult sample of 178 women provides some insight into the consequences of restricted social roles. The women were asked about their greatest regrets in life thus far; among those who were categorized as least satisfied with their lives, almost half regretted lost educational opportunities, and more than 25 percent regretted not having taken more risks (Metha, Kinnier, & McWhirter, 1989).

Less Sympathy. Related to women's generally lower status relative to men, and the stereotyped expectation of greater female expressiveness, is the probability that women get considerably less sympathy than men when attempting to enlist family members in helping with problems. Since a woman's traditional role may be considered easier than a man's and less stressful, the complaints of a homemaker may be taken less seriously and considered less valid than those of her husband. In addition, women are expected to be nurturers and to know how to tend and heal and protect. We somehow expect that women will know how to take care of the problems of their children or spouses, how to tend the sick or the troubled, how to nurture and soothe, and how to handle financial, emotional, and physical stress without falling apart.

A man with problems is likely to find that his wife will want to help him, be willing to listen, and try to be supportive; this is what wives are supposed to do. Husbands, however, are far less likely to do the same. When a woman turns to her husband for sympathy or reassurance, she may be disappointed because such responses are difficult for him to make. Men have had less practice in nurturance and may experience discomfort and anxiety when asked to give emotional support. Or a man may be "too busy" with more salient concerns and responsibilities centering around his job and the financial needs of his family.

A study by R. B. Warren found that women relied on emotional support and help with personal problems from a spouse less than did men; this discrepancy was particularly characteristic of blue-collar couples (cf. Barnett & Baruch, 1978). Thus, whereas marriage is associated with a drastic reduction in psychological dysfunction among men, this is not the case for women. Using an index based on proportional differences between the married and the never-married, researchers have found that "marriage is associated with a 71 percent reduction in illness rates for minority men, 63 percent for white men, 28 percent for white women, and 8 percent for minority women" (Russo, 1985, p. 8). Men may be uncertain about their effectiveness in the area of emotional support since they have had so little practice. A fine film, *Woman Under the Influence,* about a working-class woman who "goes mad," explores her husband's struggle to be caring and sympathetic. These responses are not easily elicited from men, who have seldom been called upon to make them and who have typically not been rewarded for their sensitivity.

Abuse. Another major problem for women, as we have already seen, is that women are often the targets of abuse by men. To know that you are an object toward which

someone's rage may be directed—not because of what you did or did not do but because as a woman you are weaker, have less status, and are thus a safe scapegoat—is an additional reason to "go mad" or become depressed. If you have personally experienced physical, sexual, or psychological abuse, then it is likely that your ability to function freely, easily, and confidently will be impaired. If you are also a member of a low-status minority group and poor, and have been exploited and terrorized, behavioral dysfunction is even more understandable. One study found that among persons hospitalized for mental illness, 53 percent of the women and 23 percent of the men had histories of abuse; of those who had been sexually abused, 89 percent were women (cf. Russo, 1985). Similarly, another of my students (Bianco, 1984) found that family crises or abuse are an important antecedent or correlate of chemical substance abuse by adolescent girls. She investigated the backgrounds and treatment outcomes of teenage residents of a center for alcohol and drug abuse and found that 84 percent had an alcoholic or absent father and had experienced sexual or physical abuse, or had a mother who had been abused.

Thus, one of the five major variables identified as high-priority research areas in the study of women's health is that of violence (Russo, 1990). A contributor to this area, Mary Koss, found in a study utilizing interviews and medical records that women who were victims of crimes were more likely to suffer, later on, from a variety of health problems (cf. McCarthy, 1990). The severity of the violence against them was the single most important contributor to later health-care visits, with the biggest increase in physician visits occurring not immediately but in subsequent years. Related to these findings is a hypothesis proposed by Susan Cutler and Susan Nolen-Hoeksema (1991). They contend that child sexual abuse, which is more than twice as prevalent among girls than boys, can help explain the greater incidence of depression among women, since depression is a common long-term consequence of such abuse. A similar argument was presented by Bonnie Strickland (1991), a former president of the American Psychological Association, who noted that "survey research in nonclinical populations has found rates of childhood sexual assault ranging from 21.7 percent to 37 percent among women, and that battering by an intimate partner may occur in the lives of as many as 25 percent of women" (p. 3). On the basis of such data, the American Psychological Association's Task Force on Women and Depression concluded that sexual and physical abuse may well contribute dramatically to psychological dysfunction.

Deviating from the Traditional Role. Phyllis Chesler (1972) has argued that women who behave in nontraditional ways run the risk of censure and may be perceived by others as behaving oddly. Our society, even in the 1990s, tolerates but does not actually encourage behaving in ways that deviate too widely from the traditional role. Thus, the same behavior by women and men may have different meanings to observers and be judged differently depending upon how closely they conform to, or deviate from, expectations. For example, a sample of college students who read descriptions of individuals and then rated them on adjustment relative to work, family, sexuality, and so on (Tilby & Kalin, 1980) judged persons whose behavior deviated from traditional sex-role patterns as "significantly more maladjusted" than traditional persons on all measures, describing the former group as more likely to require psychiatric help in the future.

A diagnosis of mental illness may be an effective punishment for deviance, and treatment may be geared toward reestablishing conformity to a socially approved role. Jane Prather and Linda Fidell (1975) examined a sample of drug advertisements that appeared in four U.S. medical journals and found that women were portrayed more often than men as irritating others by their mental illness and reassuming their traditional roles after they recovered. Similarly, David Stockburger and James Davis (1978), who analyzed a 10-year sample of advertisements for psychoactive drugs, noted that a treatment objective for women, strongly suggested by the content of the ads, could be illustrated by one "which indicated that remission of a patient's symptoms would let her get the laundry done" (p. 133).

Conforming to the Traditional Role. While deviating from the traditional role brings with it obvious costs, it has been proposed that, for women, conforming to the traditional role may also increase vulnerability to dysfunction. When a woman behaves in the culturally prescribed stereotypic feminine manner, with dependence, expressiveness, and nonassertiveness, she may be judged as behaving normally for a woman but not in the way one expects a mature and healthy adult to behave. In a now classic study (Broverman, Broverman, Clarkson, Rosenkrantz, & Vogel, 1970), 79 psychologists, psychiatrists, and social workers were asked to respond to 122 bipolar adjectives by choosing the pole that best described a "mature, healthy, socially competent" adult man, adult woman, or adult person. The researchers found that both women and men perceived healthy persons and healthy

men in the same way, but as different from women, and they concluded that women are caught in a double bind. Women who behave in ways considered desirable for mature adults "risk censure" for failing to be appropriately feminine; behaving in feminine ways, however, means being "deficient with respect to the general standards for adult behavior" (Broverman, Vogel, Broverman, Clarkson, & Rosenkrantz, 1972, p. 75).

Since the publication of these findings, many critiques have been published, some critical of the methods and statistical analyses. Other researchers have repeated the study with different samples and varying instructions. The results have been mixed, with some evidence that the bias against women is alive and well and some evidence failing to substantiate it. By and large, it has become increasingly difficult, in the 1980s and 1990s, to find mental health workers who are not familiar with the Broverman work and who would naively respond differently to mental health questions about women and men. One pair of critics of the Broverman work (Widiger & Settle, 1987) has argued that respondents were provided with more adjectives describing socially desirable or valued behavior for men than for women, thus increasing the probability that mental health would be described in terms associated with men. On the other hand, it seems to be the case that "the male stereotype [actually] comprises a larger number of elements—and a larger number of favorable attributes—than does that for the female" (DelBoca, Ashmore, & McManus, 1986, p. 125), a conclusion reached from a review of relevant literature.

The question of how traditionally behaving women are perceived has been approached in other ways. Since we judge or interpret the behavior of an individual in the context of our expectations and assumptions about his or her life patterns, goals, and general nature, it is sometimes found that the same behaviors exhibited by a woman and a man are evaluated quite differently. For example, in one study (Borys & Perlman, 1985), college students who read a brief description of a lonely first year student rated this student significantly more positively on a number of dimensions if a woman than a man, suggesting that loneliness is a more acceptable attribute for the former since the general stereotype for women includes shyness, reserve, and modesty. Another group of researchers (Israel, Raskin, Libow, & Pravder, 1978) found that a sample of college undergraduates judged female clients described as suffering from mild and common types of disturbance as being less responsible people than comparable male clients, and judged depressed female clients as more disturbed than comparable men. Another research strategy has been to obtain judgments of behavior without indicating whether this behavior is performed by a woman or man. Using this procedure, it has been found that stereotypical feminine behavior is more often associated with maladjustment, regardless of who exhibits it. Thus, for example, Linda Teri (1982) found that a large sample of clinical psychologists of both genders rated hypothetical clients who were described as feeling worthless and depressed ("stereotypically feminine behavior") as more maladjusted and as functioning less adequately both socially and on the job than clients described as hostile and aggressive ("stereotypically masculine").

There is evidence that members of subordinate social groups who conform very closely to the stereotypes about them adhered to by the majority culture are likely to be labeled "mad" or mentally ill, as illustrated in our earlier discussions of hysteria and depression. To test this hypothesis—that a judgment of mental illness is likely to be made when individuals of low status groups are described as totally conforming to their stereotyped roles—Hope Landrine (1991) asked a sample of practicing psychotherapists to make psychiatric evaluations of individuals described in varying ways. Among her findings was that a person described as "primarily concerned with cultivating an alluring attractive physical appearance . . . [with] a romantic view of life, and of relationships . . . [and whose] sense of self is not clearly defined" (the stereotype of a young middle-class woman) was diagnosed as having a histrionic personality disorder by 80 percent of the respondents. A person described like the stereotype of an older middle-class woman was judged to be a dependent personality 78 percent of the time and depressive 44 percent of the time. Landrine's research illustrates and supports her thesis that the diagnostic categories used to label mental illness reflect the ways in which the dominant social group describes and attempts to socialize persons differing in gender, age, social class, and ethnicity from the European-American male middle-class cultural standard.

A somewhat similar hypothesis has been proposed by Richard Cloward and Frances Piven (1979). They argue that a society's norms govern dysfunctional as well as functional behavior and that each gender responds to stress in culturally approved ways. For women, this means privately and stoically enduring pain, or becoming disabled by events viewed as reflecting personal failure. "Stresses are refracted through an ideology which encourages women to search within their psyches and their bodies for the sources of their problems" (p. 668). Women are encouraged to view our problems as originating from within due to incompetence, inferiority, or weakness and to respond with inner strength or endurance, or to self-destructively blame ourselves for our inability to cope. Both modes of response are tied closely to the definition of women's traditional role.

Being Discarded. Also related to the traditional role, and another factor that contributes to women's dysfunction, is the ease with which we are discarded when no longer considered useful. Women who have learned too well the behaviors descriptive of the feminine mode, who have been most accepting of the cultural definition of women as nurturing, self-sacrificing, family-oriented adjuncts of their men, may feel seriously dislocated and confused when no longer needed by those they previously served. When conditions no longer facilitate the attainment of gratification for doing the womanly, wifely, or motherly things women are expected to do, one's value is questioned by others and oneself. Such changed conditions may result from age or illness; loss of a partner through death, divorce, or disinterest; departure of one's children; poverty; excessive fatigue from being overburdened; or unreachable standards of feminine accomplishment. When the perception of being no longer useful is added to that of a woman's generally low status, she may blame herself for being unloved. The consequences may be tragic for a woman for whom traditional motives and behaviors have not been augmented by a wider range of competencies.

Pauline Bart (1971) studied depression among a group of middle-aged women and found that those most likely to experience distress were the most traditional, most sacrificing wives and mothers who had always "done the right thing." With their children gone and forgetful about letters and phone calls, traditional mothers felt "letdown," abandoned, and useless. Especially if their husbands were no longer alive, there were few familiar guidelines for their behavior, and no one left to serve (except themselves). Bart found that depressed reactions were more likely to occur among full-time homemakers than among employed wives, and more likely among middle-class than among less affluent working-class women.

Material from various sources lends support to the proposition that a woman's value is related to how well she fulfills her family responsibilities. In The Women's Room, Marilyn French (1977) introduced us to Lily, whose husband found her increasingly unsatisfactory. As she became uncertain, confused, and frightened, her husband became more and more resentful, and finally sent her to a mental hospital for "treatment." When Lily's friend Mira visited her, she saw her in the company of other young women with heavy makeup and freshly dyed hair. "'They're like me.' Lily laughed. 'What this place really is is a country club for women whose husbands don't want them anymore'" (p. 236). Later, after returning home from the hospital, Lily told Mira, "Carl says I can't do anything . . . I try. I clean and clean and clean. If I don't, they'll send me back" (p. 261).

Diagnostic Labels. An additional issue relevant to any discussion of the factors contributing to dysfunctional behavior is the meaning of diagnostic labels. The reader may have assumed that a diagnosis always reflects some specific set of symptoms—some clear dysfunction, mal-adjustment, or maladaptive behavior—but there is good reason to question this assumption. We must remember when discussing a diagnosis of psychopathology that this label, which has been applied to an individual presumably to facilitate treatment, may also serve other purposes. Psychiatric diagnoses are well known to be unreliable (to vary among those making them) and to reflect biases associated with therapists' training and clients' social class and ethnicity. As mentioned earlier, Hope Landrine (1991), one of my students, found support for her hypothesis that psychotherapists tend to describe certain diagnostic categories with the same terms they use to independently describe members of certain status groups. For example, single European-American middle-class women are likely to be described as having the same attributes as persons with histrionic personality disorders, whereas African-American lower-class men are likely to be described as having the same attributes as persons with character disorders.

The current edition of the *Diagnostic and Statistical Manual of Mental Disorders* (DSM-III-R) (American Psychiatric Association, 1987), used by all psychotherapists in North America, suggests that the following disorders are more prevalent among women than among men: agoraphobia, anxiety states, borderline personality, dependent personality, depression, histrionic personality, multiple personality, psychogenic pain disorder, sexual dysfunction, simple phobias, and somatization disorders. Men, on the other hand, are more diagnosed as suffering from alcoholism, antisocial personality, compulsive personality, drug abuse, intermittent explosive disorder, paraphilia, pathological gambling, and pyromania. Carol Landau (1986) has pointed out the remarkable fit between the

categories of mental disorder said to be more prevalent among women (or among men) and our culture's gender stereotypes and gender socialization. This fit has been empirically demonstrated, as for example in the more likely diagnosis of histrionic personality for women than for men exhibiting identical behavior (Hamilton, Rothbart, & Dawes, 1986).

In 1987, the American Psychiatric Association revised the DSM-III. Among the changes was the addition of a number of new diagnoses, some of which raised strong objections from a group of feminist psychotherapists on the grounds that little empirical evidence supported them and that they would serve to pathologize the behavior of women reacting in a traditional way to the stressful circumstances of their lives. The public controversy surrounding these diagnoses succeeded in getting them placed in the Appendix of DSM-III-R, presumably for further study, but as of this writing some fear that they will continue to be listed in the forthcoming DSM-IV (DeAngelis, 1991).

One example of such a new diagnosis, "premenstrual dysphoric disorder" (PMDD) was discussed in a previous chapter. Another example of a new diagnostic category is "self defeating personality disorder" (SDPD), a thinly veiled substitute for the now discarded diagnostic category of "masochistic personality." The proposed symptoms—guilt, self-punishment, and serving others before taking care of oneself—have long been associated with stereotyped femininity, and there is little doubt that this diagnosis would be used far more often for women than for men. Critics (e.g., Caplan & Gans, 1991) have argued that very little empirical evidence supports such a diagnosis and that its criteria are designed for women. Who else is likely to be viewed as having been "drawn to situations or relationships in which he or she will suffer, and prevent others from helping," as specified in the DSM-III-R (American Psychiatric Association, 1987)? As pointed out by Deborah Franklin (1987), the new diagnosis is potentially damaging to women not only in a therapeutic setting, in which they will be labeled "sick" for doing what they have learned to do, but also legally. She cites a federal assistant attorney general who notes that such a diagnostic label

> might be enough to strip [a woman] . . . of the custody of her children . . . [The DSM] has . . . evolved into an extremely powerful basis for decisions in court cases. Insurance companies, too, now require that anyone seeking reimbursement for psychiatric treatment submit the name and number of their mental disorder, as listed in the DSM-III. (p. 56)

Jeanne Marecek and Rachel Hare-Mustin (1991) have put the issue surrounding diagnosis into clear focus.

> Beyond the battles won and lost regarding specific diagnostic categories, the deeper issue is the political meaning of diagnosis. Far from resting solely on scientific evidence, decisions about what behaviors are acceptable or unacceptable, and what behaviors demand intervention or restraint, have moral and political dimensions. Diagnostic categories provide the language that therapists speak, and thus the very framework for their judgments and actions. Moreover, the conventional diagnostic system identifies the individual as the locus of pathology. The influence of the social context . . . is effectively removed from view . . . We ask not only what ends are served, but more pointedly, *whose* ends are served. To what extent are diagnoses a means of social control, ensuring conformity to the interests of those in power, and denying the connection between social inequities and psychological distress? (p. 525)

One example of the "moral and political" dimensions of diagnoses is the removal of homosexuality from the list of "mental disorders," following protests and criticism, by a vote of the American Psychiatric Association in 1974.

One final factor contributing to women's dysfunction is negative treatment from the medical profession. This contributes to women's poor health and detracts from our well-being. We will discuss this issue more fully in the section that follows.

TREATMENT ISSUES

As we have already noted, our culture tends to view psychological disturbance as an expected feminine reaction to life problems. Some have suggested that illness for women is encouraged, as preferable to more collective (and effective) forms of reaction to stress or frustration (Cloward & Piven, 1979). Phyllis Chesler (1972) noted that portraits of madness highlighted by both psychiatrists and novelists in this century have been primarily of women. This seems to be a continuing phenomenon in films and television. It is ironic that while women are encouraged to interpret personal problems in ways that underestimate their cultural meaning and overemphasize their internal components, women's complaints tend to be trivialized and interpreted as transitory, or exaggerated as signs of instability. Compounding such perceptions of women's "emotional" problems is the

underattention to serious medical problems, underfunding of research, and exclusion of women from large-scale medical investigations.

Mood-Altering Drugs

Seeing women's problems as internal and temporary, trivial, or as a sign of excessive emotionality, has led to a tendency by doctors to overprescribe mood-altering drugs. It is not unusual for a doctor to advise a troubled woman to go back home, smile at her husband or lover more often, and when things get tough, "take a pill." Barbara Gordon's (1979) story of her addiction to prescribed Valium and its tragic consequences, told in *I'm Dancing as Fast as I Can,* and a 1970s song by Mick Jagger and Keith Richard about "mother's little helper," the little yellow pill, reflect a continuing reality of contemporary life (cf. Matteo, 1988; Travis, 1988). A study by the National Institute of Drug Abuse (cf. Scanlan, 1978) found that 80 percent of the mood-altering drugs taken by women were prescribed for them by internists, general practitioners, and obstetricians-gynecologists. The tendency of doctors to help women by prescribing tranquilizers or sedatives has been found nationwide.

Studies indicate that although women account for only 58 percent of all visits to doctors' offices, they receive 73 percent of all prescriptions written for mood-altering, psychotropic drugs (Russo, 1985). One study (Svarstad et al., cf. Matteo, 1988) found from an examination of pharmacy records during a 2-year period that women received more prescribed drugs than men, particularly during their childbearing years. A content analysis (Prather & Fidell, 1975) of drug advertisements that appeared over a 5-year period in four leading medical journals found that the ads tended to associate psychoactive drugs with women patients and nonpsychoactive drugs with men, implying that women's illnesses reflect mental problems more than men's. There was also a significant difference in the symptoms men and women users of psychoactive drugs were said to manifest, men being more likely to be presented in association with specific and work-related symptoms and women with diffuse anxiety, tension, or depression.

Sexist Discrimination in Medicine

Women have suffered from neglect in medical research as well as from unnecessary surgical interventions and inadequate access to high quality treatment. Examples, unfortunately, abound. Sexism in medicine adversely affects women's physical health and, directly and indirectly, women's general well-being.

While heart disease, for example, "kills women and men in almost equal numbers" (Ames, Hager, Wilson, & Buckley, 1990, p. 60), women were routinely excluded for many years from research (clinical trials) on this and other serious diseases and were not given equal access to the newest forms of diagnosis and treatment. Even though heart disease is the leading cause of death in women, accounting for 28 percent of all deaths, more deaths than all forms of cancer (Litt, 1993; Stefanick, 1992), "a man is three times more likely than a woman to be referred for cardiac catheterization and four times more likely to be treated with bypass surgery" (Rosenthal, 1989, p. 60).

Research on diseases specific to women, like endometriosis, cervical cancer, breast cancer, and chlamydia, or diseases more common in women, like osteoporosis, is poorly funded. As pointed out by Iris Litt (1993), despite the fact that "women contribute equally with men through their tax dollars to the budget of the NIH [National Institutes of Health], which directs most medical research in the United States . . . only 13 percent of the medical research in this country is on women's health" (p. 153). Yet, 1 in 8 women in the United States will develop breast cancer (a rate that increased in the 1980s from 1 in 12) and, of these, 1 in 4 will die from it at a rate of one every 12 minutes. This disease has been seriously neglected in terms of research funds, medical attention, and insurance company payment for experimental treatments (Beck, Yoffe, Carroll, Hager, Rosenberg, & Beachy, 1990).

Surgery appears to be the quickest and easiest response to too many of women's medical problems. For many years reports have established that hysterectomies (surgical removal of the uterus) are often performed unnecessarily. Once again in 1992 (cf. "Hysterectomies Found," 1992) a study reiterated this conclusion, finding that large numbers of women in this country with noncancerous fibroid tumors without other symptoms were still being advised to have surgery even though such invasive treatment was not required. Elsewhere we noted the overuse of cesarean sections during childbirth, as well as the tragic consequences of implanting silicone in women's breasts, to which the FDA finally ordered a halt in 1992 (except for reconstructive purposes following breast surgery for cancer).

With respect to AIDS, the newest killer of women, the seriousness of women's neglect is underscored by the World Health Organization's prediction that 80 percent of all AIDS cases in the future will be transmitted heterosexually and that a woman is over 14 times more likely to contract the HIV virus heterosexually than a man is. In 1990, 51 percent of women with AIDS "were infected through injected drug use and 29 percent through heterosexual contact" (O'Leary, Jemmott, Suarez-Al-Adam, Al Roy, & Fernandez, 1993). Women, who now represent 15 percent of all AIDS cases in the United States, are typically diagnosed so late that their survival averages from 15 weeks to 6 months from the time of diagnosis, whereas men's survival averages 2 to 3 years (O'Leary et al., 1993; "Women with AIDS," 1991). AIDS is now one of the five leading causes of death for women between the ages of 15 and 44 (Byron, 1991). In New York City, AIDS is the leading cause of death among women between 25 and 29 years of age (Crimp, 1988). African-American and Latina women were reported in 1991 to constitute 73 percent of the 15,493 women diagnosed with AIDS in the United States, while only 17 percent of the female population ("Minority Women," 1991); yet they have been virtually omitted from clinical trials in the testing of new drugs, not admitted to many hospital facilities, and diagnosed too late for effective treatment. More than 50 percent of HIV-infected minority women contract the virus from intravenous drug use (Cochran & Mays, 1989).

Bias against women in medical research and treatment is also illustrated by a study of the recipients of kidney transplants among patients suffering from End-Stage Renal Disease (Kutner & Brogan, 1990). Data from the Medicare program across the United States and from South Carolina and Georgia were analyzed. The authors found that European-American men had the highest probability of receiving a kidney transplant, considered the "best-outcome treatment," while this treatment was least probable for older African-American women. "Being a man, being white rather than black, and being younger increase a patient's chances of being treated by kidney transplantation rather than by kidney dialysis" (p. 283f). The authors also found that the gender discrepancy in kidney transplant rates had increased between 1978 and 1985! A similarly shocking report has come from U.S. courts; they were found to be more likely to reject the request to turn off life support when made by a dying woman than by a man. Appellate courts followed the wishes of 6 out of 8 men in such cases, but of only 2 out of 14 women (cf. "Death Bias?" 1990).

We have already noted that low-income and ethnic minority women are especially unlikely to have access to prompt diagnosis and treatment. One indicator of access to medical treatment is medical insurance coverage. In the United States, approximately 31 million have no coverage of any kind, and millions more have coverage that is not adequate. Within this group women are the majority. One study of national survey data (Seccombe & Beeghley, 1992) found that among adults aged 25 or over who were employed for at least 20 hours each week, women were less likely to have private employer medical coverage than were men. Least likely to have insurance were single, divorced, and low-earning women. Compared with European-Americans, among whom 12 percent have no health insurance, the figures for African-Americans, Mexican-Americans, and Asian-Americans are 22 percent, 35 percent, and 16 percent, respectively ("AMA Changes," 1991). Hopefully, a new health insurance plan to be proposed to Congress by the Clinton administration will tackle these inequities.

Good news for women, as of this writing, is the federal government's announcement that "it plans to conduct the most sweeping study of women's health problems ever attempted . . . in a research effort expected to cost $500 million over 10 years. . . . The study intends to examine the major causes of illness and death among women" ("'Most Far-Reaching,'" 1991). It is instructive that this massive project (The Women's Health Initiative) that will study several hundred thousand women between the ages of 50 and 79 ("APA Testifies," 1991), was spearheaded by a woman, Bernardine Healy, when she was director of the National Institutes of Health.

Traditional Values in Psychotherapy

Helplessness and despair, the most common correlates of dysfunctional behavior, can be overcome by learning how to control the events in our lives, by developing skills that will give us access to resources, and by acquiring responses that will permit effective problem solution and the attainment of desired results. But when we look at the kind of treatment women are likely to receive from mental health professionals, such objectives are not always apparent.

Phyllis Chesler (1972), in *Women and Madness,* was among the first to examine how women are treated by a mental health profession dominated by men and by patriarchal attitudes. She pointed out that psychotherapy as traditionally practiced with women emphasizes individual solutions to problems that have societal components, and reinforces dependence on an authority figure. Demonstrating differences in the treatment of women and men has been difficult, however, and investigations of

therapists' attitudes toward women, their adherence to gender stereotypes, and the relationship between evaluation and treatment and the gender of client or therapist have produced ambiguous findings.

As Christine Abramowitz and Paul Dokecki (1977) noted, there has been an "outpouring of feminist concerns in the professional literature"; and while this outpouring has perhaps fallen short of its "goal of eliminating sex bias from clinical practice," it may have made therapists more sensitive about what they say they believe and more alert to the significance of their attitudes. A review of the literature by Abramowitz and Dokecki did not support the conclusion that client gender is a consistent influence on therapists' judgments in simulated situations. And other reviewers (Brodsky, 1980; Davidson & Abramowitz, 1980; Lopez, 1989; Mogul, 1982) have concluded that the therapist-client gender interaction has not been established as a clear factor in therapy. Client gender no longer appears to influence general judgments of mental health in simulated situations. For example, when 104 psychological service providers were asked to rate the behaviors of an average "mature, healthy, socially competent" woman or man in a home environment or a work environment, gender was found to make no difference (Poole & Tapley, 1988). This study, like others of its kind, relies on self-reports to questionnaires, which may or may not accurately reflect how therapists respond to their real clients. The current conclusion, as expressed by Carol Mowbray and Elissa Benedek (1988, p. 10) is that "research studies about the relevance of therapist's gender to assessment, duration of treatment, and satisfaction of treatment or its outcome provide no clear replicable results salient to decision-making." We do know, however, that under certain circumstances client gender makes a difference and that specific diagnoses continue to be made differentially for women and men, as previously discussed.

A likely conclusion is that therapists who hold traditional beliefs about the differential nature and roles of women and men, regardless of their own gender, are apt to reflect these beliefs in their work with clients. It is now generally acknowledged that psychotherapy is not a value-free process and that it reflects our society's dominant views and expectations. Bernard Whitley (1979) concluded, from his survey of the literature, that clinicians appear to share the sex role stereotypes of non-clinicians; and Mary Lee Smith's (1980) analysis of relevant studies also led her to conclude that "clinicians hold negative stereotypes about women" (p. 405). How different these beliefs are now in the 1990s is something we are not sure of, and how these views affect client treatment and outcomes has thus far not been clearly or reliably demonstrated.

What actually occurs during interaction between client and therapist over the course of many meetings, both directly and subtly, is difficult to study. While the goal of psychotherapy (to increase an individual's effective social behaviors, the probability of satisfying relationships, and successful outcomes) may be the same for women and men, how these goals are interpreted may differ. A consumer handbook, prepared by the Association for Women in Psychology and the American Psychological Association (*Women and Psychotherapy*, 1981) notes that "therapists are products of our society and as such may be influenced by societal values . . . [which] may reinforce a standard of 'normalcy' that encourages women and/or minorities to adjust to traditional, sometimes sexist/racist roles" (pp. 3f.). The handbook provides advice on selecting and evaluating a psychotherapist, on alternatives to psychotherapy, and on "how to tell whether sexism is interfering with therapy."

Feminist Therapies

A radical approach to psychotherapy, developed in the 1970s, is practiced by therapists who share common feminist values and strategies. As noted by Jeanne Marecek and Rachel Hare-Mustin (1991), diverse philosophies and approaches can be considered examples of feminist therapy, including a revised psychoanalytic approach that has attempted "to rewrite the account of women's development in an affirmative, woman-centered way" (p. 529). Although there are multiple approaches, or "different versions of feminist therapy practice" (Brown, 1991), feminist therapies can generally be said to differ in theory and objectives from traditional therapy in the following ways:

1. Feminist therapists have an obligation to make their values explicit to their clients (Rawlings & Carter, 1977).

2. The central element of feminist therapy is a focus on society and social institutions and an emphasis on the link between personal change and sociopolitical change (Marecek & Kravetz, 1977). Such a sociological perspective discourages the use of individual psychopathology labels (Rador, Masnick, & Hauser, 1977), and focuses instead on the sources of stress within the culture. This position is vital to feminist therapy and puts into practice the core belief of feminism that "the personal is political." As Hannah Lerman (1976) has pointed out, "separating the internal and the external [or seeing their interrelation-

ship] . . . serves to help a woman learn that she is not crazy" (p. 380).

3. Feminist therapists recognize women's inferior social status as an important component of psychological distress and attribute it not to biology but to the lack of political and economic power (Rawlings & Carter, 1977).

4. In feminist therapy, therapist-client differences in status are deemphasized and "equal sharing of resources, power and responsibility" are promoted (Marecek & Kravetz, 1977). The therapy process is "democratized." The therapist does not function as an expert; rather, the client is assumed to be competent and knowledgeable about her own feelings and needs and decides what behaviors she wants to change. "Feminist values and techniques promote equalitarian rather than hierarchical relationships [and] respect for the client's expertise about herself" (Lerman, 1985, pp. 6f.).

This aspect of the feminist approach has proved problematic and, according to Laura Brown (1991), has sometimes led to "boundary problems" and the "overlap of personal and professional roles, identities, and relationships" (p. 325). The possibility of such overlap is increased when both client and therapist live and work in the same relatively small community. The *Feminist Therapy Ethical Code*, written by the Feminist Therapy Institute (cf. Brown, 1991), discusses this issue and mandates that the therapist must always behave in the best interests of the client, noting that the risk of boundary problems is reduced if attention is clearly paid to power dynamics and a respect for diversity. As Brown points out, "the feminist model requires the therapist to imagine the impact of her actions on the client, on that person in relationship to herself (the therapist) and on the interpersonal matrix in which they both participate" (p. 334).

5. Feminist therapists see themselves as participants in the women's movement, as supporters of equality between women and men, and as questioners of traditional roles. They often take social action and are advocates on behalf of their clients (Rawlings & Carter, 1977).

6. Feminist therapists assume that all social roles (and behaviors) are open to women; they encourage clients to evaluate and define their choices and to differentiate between what they have learned is gender appropriate and what is appropriate to them as individuals. "Feminist therapists strive to restore a balance in the emphasis on work and relationships" (Rador, Masnick, & Hauser, 1977, p. 509).

7. Women are encouraged to deal with anger, to assume responsibility for their actions and feelings, and to learn how to assert power openly. They urge the client to

take responsibility for doing what is needed to get what she wants for herself and to communicate her needs to others in a straightforward manner.

8. An important goal of feminist therapy is achievement of respect and trust for other women. Feminist therapists understand that while a relationship with a man can be enriching, it is not necessary or central to a woman's mental health (Rawlings & Carter, 1977) and encourage women to view other women not as competitors for men but as sources of emotional support.

9. Feminist therapists do not view men as the enemy (Rawlings & Carter, 1977), and a relationship with a man in or outside of marriage is considered to be a "partnership of equals."

10. In feminist therapy, issues and experiences unique to women, such as menstruation, childbirth, and assault, are raised and discussed.

The major therapeutic goal is the discovery and pursuit of personal strengths and the achievement of independence. There is an emphasis on power, and the client is helped to "reclaim power in the workplace and the bedroom" (Fishel, 1979, p. 79). Ellyn Kaschak (1990) has described the mission of The Feminist Therapy Institute as "the development of complex feminist theory and therapy, . . . to discern the patterns and commonalities of women's lives, while never losing sight of their diversity and specificity" (p. 1).

FACTORS CONTRIBUTING TO WELL-BEING

The emphasis of feminist therapy on women's power points to the central importance of control and access to resources to mental health and well-being. A considerable amount of research in recent years has been concerned with identifying the ingredients of positive feelings about oneself and one's life, and the conclusion seems to be that these ingredients are the same for women as for men. For example, data from large national interview studies of representative samples of adults indicate that the dominant factors contributing to reductions in the subjective well-being of married parents of both genders are: strain from ill health and worries and feelings of personal inadequacy (Bryant & Veroff, 1982). Women and men were both affected by future-oriented, work-related, and family-life issues.

The personal traits that have been shown to relate positively to measures of self-esteem or subjective well-being are the same for women as for men; these traits include assertiveness, independence, self-responsibility, and efficacy. A high "good functioning" score is earned by a respondent who self-reports behaving in an assertive, autonomous, and effective manner. These characteristics that are typically associated with men and are the characteristics our society values, but they are also the attributes that mediate the successful attainment of personal goals.

Marylee Taylor and Judith Hall (1982) statistically analyzed and reviewed studies of nonclinical adult samples that compared indices of mental health with self-reported behavior. For both women and men, the major contributor to well-being scores was found to be high scores on instrumentality, which, as the researchers concluded, "pays off for individuals of both sexes . . . [and] yields positive outcomes for individuals in American society" (p. 362). Bernard Whitley (1983, 1985) has reached similar conclusions. In statistical reviews of research, he found that self-esteem and psychological well-being are related to self-reported assertive, independent, agentic, and instrumental attributes among both women and men. As an example of such a study, Vonda Long (1986) had four diverse groups of women rate themselves on various traits and found that instrumental attributes were a better predictor of self-esteem than occupation or educational level.

Mental health or life satisfaction is considerably diminished by circumstances in which individuals lack power or control, as noted earlier. Thus, studies find that the important link to well-being is not the sheer number of life changes (or stressors) but certain factors that mediate between the life events and their consequences, such as the degree to which the events were controllable, access to community or other resources, and the existence of emotional or social supports. Thus, for example, a study of college students (Ganellen & Blaney, 1984) found that those with social supports were more "hardy"—that is, more resistant to the ill effects of life stress.

For parents, children at home are a significant source of stress and uncontrollable life changes. Not surprisingly, therefore, recent studies have found that among married persons of both genders, the "empty nest" is associated with heightened well-being and satisfaction. Thus, for example, Lenore Radloff (1980) found among a large representative sample of married European-American adults that those with no children living at home were significantly less depressed than those with children at home or those who had never had them. This was true for full-time homemakers as well as for employed women, and for women and men regardless of income or age. Similarly, Rosalind Barnett and Grace Baruch (1985) found, among a sample of European-American women between the ages of 35 and 55, that the role of parent rather than that of paid worker was their major source of stress. "Regardless of employment status, mothers experienced higher levels of role overload and anxiety than did childless women" (p. 144).

Data from a national survey of more than 2,000 adults were analyzed by Carolyn Morgan (1980) to determine which of several variables best correlated with an index of "satisfaction" derived from respondents' descriptions of their lives as interesting or boring, friendly or lonely, full or empty, and so on. The three best predictors of satisfaction with life were found to be gender (men were more satisfied than women), work satisfaction, and personal competence. In general, women reported themselves to be significantly lower than men in personal competence, work satisfaction, and marital adjustment. Morgan concluded that "there is little difference between the sexes in what contributes to their satisfaction with life . . . [but that] females experience more obstacles in attaining life-satisfying goals" (p. 379). Also found to be important in its relationship with life satisfaction in this study was ethnicity. In the low satisfaction category were 40 percent of all the women of color, compared with 26 percent of the European-American women; in the high satisfaction category were 10.6 percent of the women of color and 13 percent of the European-American women.

The picture beginning to emerge from a variety of studies is that, in general, for women (as for men), being involved in activities that use "one's skills and education, that offer social contacts and intimacy, and that provide income" help to maintain or foster good psychological and physical health. This conclusion was reached by Lois Verbrugge and Jennifer Madans from the results of a national health interview study (cf. "Busy Women," 1985). Employment was found to have the strongest and most consistent positive association with women's good health, followed by marriage, with parenthood "a weak third." Working women reported less illness and that they felt better than women not engaged in paid employment. Another study, by Lerita Coleman and Toni Antonucci (cf. "Women's Well-Being," 1982), reached similar conclusions by comparing a group of working married women between 40 and 59 years of age with a group of full-time homemakers. Of all the variables tested in this study, employment was "the only significant predictor of levels of self-esteem in midlife women . . . [and] one of the most important predictors of physical health and lack of

psychological anxiety" (p. 5). Grace Baruch and Rosalind Barnett (1985b) reached the same conclusion. They found only one social role to be related to an index of well-being within their sample of 35- to 55-year-old women; self-esteem was positively related to being a paid worker.

In general, the data indicate that the satisfactions women derive from employment contribute significantly to general well-being and happiness. This relationship has been documented among women in a variety of different subgroups or populations (e.g., Baruch, Barnett, & Rivers, 1983; Erdwins & Mellinger, 1984; Horwitz, 1982; Rosen, Ickovics, & Moghadam, 1990). European-American and African-American women have been found to share the same predictors of well-being; income, occupational status, and job satisfaction (Crohan, Antonucci, & Adelmann, 1989). Paid employment appears to provide direct benefits to women by offering sources of potential pleasure or satisfaction (beyond family life and friends), just as it does for men; it may also help ameliorate the stresses associated with launching children into adulthood, marital problems, divorce, or widowhood. Physical well-being, too, is positively impacted by paid employment. Among a sample of 242 affluent, middle-aged European-American women, those who worked were found, in a long-term study (12 to 15 years) to be less prone to heart attacks and to have "lower blood pressure, cholesterol, blood sugar, and other predictors of heart disease" ("Women Who Work," 1992).

For many women paid employment appears to provide access to resources, a sense of control over one's life, and a source of satisfaction. Not all jobs, however, contribute equally to enhanced self-satisfaction. Allan Horwitz (1982) found that, in general, employed married adults reported significantly fewer symptoms of psychological distress than married women and men who were unemployed; he concluded that "the resources gained through employment lead to psychological benefits for both sexes" (p. 614). But the more dominant or powerful one's position, the fewer symptoms of distress were reported, suggesting a strong positive relationship between well-being and control or dominance. "Every group in the sample with significantly fewer symptoms than average—married men and women who are chief breadwinners, married employed men, and married employed women—occupy roles high in resources and low in subordination" (Horwitz, 1982, p. 619). The link between depression and low status is clearly supported by the literature. As summarized by Susan Faludi (1991), "whether they are professional or blue-collar workers, working women experience less depression than housewives; and the more challenging the career, the better their mental and physical health" (p. 38).

Contrary to popular assumptions, multiple roles have been found to have benefits for women and to be accompanied by good health and positive spirits, provided that the positions occupied are ones that increase the likelihood of success and effectiveness. The same is true for men. Estelle Ramey, who has studied the effects of stress, noted in an interview that "top-level, high-paid, successful women and men live longer than anyone else. . . . People at the top are in control of their lives, and people in control live longer" ("Success, Health Linked," 1984). Thus, among a sample of women between 35 and 55 years of age (Baruch, Barnett, & Rivers, 1983), it was found that the women with the highest degree of life satisfaction had both families and high-prestige jobs. Similarly, among a sample of well-educated, affluent women studied by Abigail Stewart and Patricia Salt (1981), those who were married with children and careers reported the least illness of any group.

It is likely that the more varied one's behavioral repertoire is, the more sources of satisfaction one will experience. Joann Rodgers (1985) has cited a number of studies to support her thesis that what may be best for a woman's health is "juggling roles, making change, [and] taking charge" (p. 57). Among the studies cited by Rodgers is one by Suzanne Kobasa that found that men and women who stayed healthy under stress were "committed (to self, work, family, religion, or other values); in control (over one's life); and challenged (by life's ups and downs and by change)" (p. 58).

Emory Cowan (1991) has proposed that wellness (a feeling of purpose and belongingness, and satisfaction with one's life) is an outcome of four general factors: competence (doing well what one should be doing); resilience (coping with major life stressors); social system modification; and empowerment. With respect to the latter two factors, one must recognize that social institutions play a part in enhancing wellness or in posing obstacles to its attainment—that is, wellness does not depend exclusively or primarily on individual qualities. As Cowan has noted, "for many people the roots of maladaptation or problems in living reside less in failings in individuals . . . and far more in de facto aspects of a macrosystem that deprives them of power, justice, and opportunity" (p. 407). In like vein, Albert Bandura has suggested that persons experience two forms of "futility," one deriving from self-doubt about one's competence or capacities, and the other deriving from doubt about

Prescription for women's mental health. (From Nicole Hollander, *I'm in Training to Be Tall and Blonde.* Copyright © 1979 by Nicole Hollander. Reprinted by permission of St. Martin's Press, Inc.)

outcomes, the fear that one's efforts will not produce the desired results because of "the unresponsiveness, negative bias, or punitiveness of the environment" (p. 140). To decrease doubts about one's competence requires expansion of an individual's behavioral repertoire, with opportunities for practice, reinforcement, and correction; while a decrease in outcome-based futility requires a social environment that provides equitable rewards based on performance and that does not discriminate against persons on the basis of status (gender, ethnicity, social class, and so on).

Involvement and activity contribute to health. Jobs or life situations that provide the opportunity for responsibility, control, variety, and supportive relationships enhance or help maintain psychological and physical health. Love and work, as Sigmund Freud suggested, are the twin poles around which human adult lives rotate; it is through our active engagement with their challenges, and our experience with the satisfactions that they mediate, that we derive respect for ourselves and maintain well-being. Nicole Hollander's cartoon speaks not to an impossible dream but to the raw material of personal satisfaction and health.

◆ Discussion Questions

1. What would observers from Mars conclude is true of adult women in our society? Place these observers in different places, observing women in different situations, in the media, and so on.

2. What characteristics would you like your daughter to exhibit? Discuss the concepts of femininity, masculinity, and androgyny.

3. Provide examples of variation in behavior in yourself, your mother, women in different social classes and occupations, etc.

4. Distinguish among traits, habits, and roles. Define personality.

5. Define mental health.

6. What factors contribute to the well-being of women?

7. How is mental health related to gender? In what ways does your gender affect your experiences?

8. How has gender influenced your life?

9. How are you influenced by the assumptions and practices of the mental health profession and by the DSM?

CHAPTER 13

THE MIDDLE AND LATER YEARS: CHANGES AND SATISFACTIONS

Women today make choices and go through life stages in a radically different way from their mothers and grandmothers. . . . The midlife woman of current social science literature is . . . a far cry from the traditional psychoanalyst's woman mourning the loss of her reproductive powers. One hears less today about women's "mid-life crisis" and more about "post-menopausal zest."

BETH HESS (1985, p. 7)

Many women worry about losing attractiveness and/or physical appeal. Wrinkles, loss of breast and abdominal elasticity, . . . skin changes, graying . . . , weight gain, . . . are poignant reminders of aging. In a society and culture that values youth and beauty over wisdom and maturity, growing older can be difficult. . . . On the other hand, many women approach middle age with optimism and enthusiasm, and experience it as a time of enhanced personal liberation, power, and opportunity.

SANDRA LEIBLUM (1990, p. 497)

CONTEMPORARY OLDER WOMEN DISCONFIRM and defy the stereotypes of them as worn-out, unattractive, sickly, sexless, boring, or foolish crones. Many are experiencing the rewards of confidence and economic and emotional independence that accompany paid employment; many have returned to school and completed training for a previous or new career; many are vigorously involved in social interaction and a variety of community interests. For these women, life continues to be vital and engaging after 50, 60, 70, and beyond; for some, it only begins to be so in the years following full-time child rearing or devotion to family. At the same time, women confront a number of special and potentially problematic issues or challenges as we grow older that require our special attention.

What the dividing lines are between young adulthood, middle age, and old age has become increasingly unclear, since people live longer and behave quite differently from their parents or grandparents in these life periods. As pointed out by Bernice Neugarten and Dail Neugarten (1987):

> More men and women marry, divorce, remarry and divorce again up through their 70s. . . . People are becoming grandparents for the first time at ages ranging from 35 to 75. . . . More women . . . exit and reenter school, enter and reenter the work force and undertake second and third careers up through their 70s. It therefore becomes difficult to distinguish the young, the middle-aged and the young-old—either in terms of major life events or the ages at which those events occur. (p. 30)

In this chapter we will be considering issues relevant to the middle and later years without clear definition of these terms but focusing, in general, on women who are "growing older."

Older women constitute the fastest-growing portion of the U.S. population. One out of every 10 or 11 persons in the United States is over 65 years old (Rodin & Ickovics, 1990), compared to only 4 percent in 1900. Within this group, women predominate, with 84 percent of women and 70 percent of men alive at age 65. The preponderance of women at older ages is true throughout the industrialized world, where women outlive men by a margin of 4 to 10 years (cf. Holden, 1987). Women over 50 constitute 38 percent of all adult women in the United States, and within the next 20 to 25 years it is estimated that almost 20 percent of the U.S. population will be made up of women over 50 (Steenland, 1988).

Two hundred years ago the life expectancy for women in the United States was 35 (and 33 for men); by 1900 it had climbed to 48 for women and 46 for men. In this century, the longevity for both genders has steadily increased and in 1987 the average woman could expect to live to age 78.3 and the average man to 71.5 ("Men Catching Up," 1990). Impressive as these figures are, in 1988 women in the United States "had a shorter average life expectancy than women in 15 other countries" (Dutton, 1993, p. 98). Among those who live to be 100 there are five women for every man; and, at every age, more men than women die at an average ratio of 1.15 to 1 across the life span (Rodin & Ickovics, 1990). At age 65, women currently outnumber men by 100 to 83, and by 100 to 39 by age 85 (Carstensen & Pasupathi, 1993). These ratios include all persons, but longevity for African-Americans and other disadvantaged minorities has continued to lag dramatically behind that of European-Americans. Thus, the average life expectancy for African-American women is 73 years, and that for African-American men is 64 (Carstensen & Pasupathi, 1993).

Among women over 50 in this country, 89 percent are European-American, 9 percent are African-American, and 2 percent are Latina and Asian-American (Steenland, 1988). Living alone are 55 percent of nonminority elderly women, 50 percent of Latinas, between 40 and 50 percent of African-Americans and Native Americans, and only a small percentage of Asian-Americans (Leavitt & Welch, 1989). Among all elderly women and men, 95 percent live in the community by themselves, with spouses, other relatives or friends. Thus, only about 5 percent are in nursing homes, where women, because of their greater longevity, make up three fourths of the residents. It seems also to be the case, however, that families are more apt to institutionalize older women than men. "In people 85 and over, one in four women lives in a nursing home, whereas only one in seven men lives in a nursing home" (Carstensen & Pasupathi, 1993, p. 73).

CULTURAL RESPONSES TO OLDER WOMEN

Public images do not generally present older women as physically attractive, sensual, vibrant, or interesting. As Ethel Kahn (1984) has noted:

> Today's older woman is [typically] seen by society as a "wrinkled, greying old bag," no longer . . . sexually attractive. She finds herself in sharp contrast to the "distinguished, grey-haired, eligible bachelor" whose loss of spouse increases his attractiveness and whose work

history still conveys status. She is undervalued by employers, frequently rejected in social situations, and psychologically misdiagnosed and treated. (p. 2)

Our society reacts differently to aging in women and men, and both folk culture and developmental theories in psychology suggest, as Mary Gergen has put it, that "a woman's life is basically downhill, or regressive, from 40 on" (1990, p. 477). Gergen points out that there has been a lack of serious attention to understanding the development of midlife and maturing women, a state of affairs in which stereotypes can flourish. One consequence is that many older women try "to cover up aging as an obscenity," and react to it with fear and disgust. For example, in Margaret Drabble's (1977) novel *The Ice Age*, the heroine, a beautiful, intelligent, and very modern upper-middle-class woman, says of herself, "I am a vain, a wicked woman . . . I cannot face old age, I cannot face ugliness and decay."

That such feelings are alive and well in the liberated 1990s is illustrated by a popular film with Goldie Hawn and Meryl Streep *(Death Becomes Her)* in which two women in their 50s go to bizarre and macabre lengths to stay forever young. Interestingly, Meryl Streep and Michael Douglas are used as contrasts in posters that appeared in the spring of 1993 along Sunset Boulevard in Hollywood to protest the unfair treatment of women in films. Above a photograph of Douglas are the words "In His Prime?" while "Past Her Peak?" appears above a photograph of Streep. "Below the photos run these words: 'Only 9 percent of roles in films in 1992 went to women over 40' " (Smith, 1993, p. C-3).

Youth is clearly highly valued by both genders in our current society, and men as well as women work to retain youthful figures and zest by watching their diets, exercising, keeping up with the fashions in dress and recreation, and resisting being categorized as old. Women, however, are cajoled more than men to focus on our external personas, and the culture's message that it is crucial for us to be slim and attractive to find love and personal happiness continues as we age. As Alice Rossi (1980) has pointed out, for women

> indicators of age are important to the social self presented to others: gray hair, wrinkles, dentures, drowsiness, age spots, thickening of the waistline, sagging of abdomen and breasts, and bifocal glasses may touch aspects of aging that matter in social and, particularly, intimate interactions. (p. 21)

It has been argued that whereas the youth-preserving products used by women are typically marketed as linked to beauty and health, those for men are "linked to power dynamics" and that women begin trying to avoid looking old long before they are. "Wrinkle creams, calcium supplements, and reconstructive surgeries are utilized by women both young and old" (Rodeheaver & Stohs, 1991, p. 151). Barbara Macdonald (1989) has suggested that our culture's largely negative response to older women is intimately related to the "motherhood myth." The older woman, who is no longer performing her "primary" role, is perceived as though

> she has no personhood, no desires or values of her own. She must not fight for her own issues — if she fights at all, it must be for "future generations." Her greatest joy is seen as giving all to her grandchildren. And to the extent that she no longer directly serves a man — can no longer produce his children, is no longer sexually desirable to men — she is erased more completely as grandmother than she was as mother. (p. 10)

Gender stereotypes can be particularly crippling for older women. Doris Lessing's (1984) book, *The Diaries of Jane Somers,* tells the stories of old women whose proud determination to live independent and meaningful lives despite their age is not respected, is misunderstood, and frustrated by circumstances and social institutions. The tragic disparity between how an old woman may feel about herself and how she appears to others is also described in a story by Pat Barker (1983). Alice Bell is 76 years old.

> She had hid herself from the mirror. For years she had avoided looking into it: the hag it showed bore no relation to the person she was. Inside herself, she was still sixteen. She had all the passion, all the silliness . . . Now the dislocation between what the mirror showed and what she knew herself to be was absolute. She would have to break the glass. (p. 255)

The media often present images of older women who are unpleasant or unimportant. In the American theater, for example, older women are treated as "not sexy, not interesting, not exciting, not worth writing a play about" (Robertson, 1985). And positive images of powerful older women are also rare in contemporary novels. As noted by Nancy Porter (1989), "in fictional plots, old women are relegated to subordinate and subservient roles. Few are self-defining, independent characters" (p. 99). But not all the current popular images of older women are negative, although the more positive stereotypes also ignore individual differences and fail to recognize the wholeness or reality of life for older women. Barbara Macdonald (1989) has explored this subject and argued that

> you who are younger see us as either submissive and childlike or as possessing some unidentified vague wisdom. As having more "soul" than you or as being overemotional and slightly crazy. As weak and helpless or as a pillar of strength. As "cute" and funny or as boring. As sickly sweet or dominating and difficult. You pity us, or you ignore us . . . [or] you want to honor us. . . . None of these images has anything to do with who we are. (p. 10)

Research has uncovered multiple stereotypes of older people in general and older women in particular (Gatz & Pearson, 1988): positive ones, like wise person or perfect grandparent; and negative ones, like senile, nosy, or depressed old woman, or bag lady.

The television industry appears to have taken a dramatic turn away from its earlier dreary and sad portrayal of older women to its current portrayal of them as well-to-do and still looking for Mr. Right. In the 1970s, the predominant images were of older women staving off obsolescence with Geritol or aspirin, baking cookies for their grandchildren, or retreating into the world of soap operas and reminiscences about unfulfilled expectations and lost dreams. One study that monitored the image of old people on television found what they saw to be "something to dread and feel threatened by. . . . We are shown as stubborn, rigid, unflexible, forgetful and confused . . . as dependent, powerless, wrinkled babies, unable to contribute to society" (cf. Roberts, 1977, p. E-4). But a study of prime-time entertainment television in 1986 (over a 6-week period) by the National Commission on Working Women (Steenland, 1988) found an altogether different state of affairs.

In this later study, women over 50 were found to constitute 20 percent of all women characters on TV, twice the number they were in the mid-1970s; of these older women on TV, 23 percent were over 65. The study revealed that among the over-50 women on prime-time entertainment TV (excluding ads), 68 percent were presented as widows and 16 percent as divorced, numbers that are in sharp contrast with the reality of 32 percent widowed and 6 percent divorced. With respect to economic status, the TV screen also presented a grossly inaccurate picture. None of the fictional over-50 TV women were poor: 26 percent were millionaires, 68 percent were middle-class, and 5 percent were working-class. In reality, only 0.2 percent of women over 50 have annual incomes over $75,000, 11 percent have incomes over $20,000, and 40 percent have incomes under $5,000. Among the TV women over 50, 11 percent were

African-American but none were Latina or Asian-American. The over-50 women characters on the 1986 TV screen were shown as leading affluent lives, healthy, attractive, and ready for romance; they "wear negligees, kiss passionately, and have love affairs" (Steenland, 1988, p. 12). No social barriers were shown as hindering the older woman in the work force. In the world of TV entertainment there appears to be no age discrimination, unemployment, or low pay. Thus newer images, like the ones that preceded them, still seem to have little to do with the real lives and concerns of older women.

PHYSIOLOGICAL CHANGES AND SPECIAL CONCERNS

A number of feminist writers have been critical of the usual approach to discussion of women's middle and later years, pointing out the overemphasis on biological changes, the use of language that medicalizes and pathologizes normal processes, and the relative lack of attention to variations among women and the significance of social and personal factors. Thus, for example, Mary Gergen (1990) has rightly noted that "where women's midlife development does receive attention, the concern is almost exclusively biological. . . . Women seem to be identified first of all by their sexual reproductive relations" (p. 476). Similarly, Ellen Cole and Esther Rothblum (1990) have decried the usual reference to menopausal *symptoms* rather than *signs,* the description of women's reproductive organs as "atrophying," and the heterosexist bias in this literature that ignores lesbians. "It is untrue," they argue, "that a woman's skin decays as she ages, or that her vagina wastes away. We must stop . . . equating age with 'rotting' " (p. 510). I agree with these critics and present the discussion on physiological issues that follows in the context of nonpathological, natural, and normal experiences.

Menopause

The climacteric is a gradual aging process in both sexes that includes changes affecting the entire body in hormonal output, in metabolism, and in the efficiency of physiological and structural functioning. Only females, however, experience menopause, which refers very specifically to the cessation of ovulation and menstruation. The gradual reduction in levels of progesterone and estrogen is a result of the slowdown in their production by the ovaries.

Contemporary women can expect to reach menopause, defined specifically by no menstruation for the previous 12 months, sometime in their late 40s or early 50s. The average age is 51.4 (cf. Morokoff, 1988), somewhat later than it was in the early years of this century (Weideger, 1976). The primary physiological changes begin when the ovarian follicles stop maturing. The reader will recall from the discussion in Chapter 5 that during the menstrual cycle an ovum is released monthly from one of the follicles when stimulated by hormones from the pituitary. At menopause, this process ceases and the ova no longer function in this way, a phenomenon for which there is no clear explanation. The anterior pituitary continues to release the hormones that have played their part in the menstrual cycle, but the ovaries lose their responsiveness, and so the production of estrogen is gradually diminished. Although some estrogen continues to be produced by the follicles and by the adrenal glands, it is not enough to trigger the next phase of the menstrual cycle and the manufacture of progesterone. Menopause thus marks the end of menstruation.

Women who require surgical removal of both ovaries (for treatment of cancer or other serious problems) experience early and sudden menopause. But for most others the reduction of estrogen and progesterone is gradual, as is the reduction of testosterone and other gonadal hormones, all of which continue to be produced but at diminished levels. Part of the misinformation and myths about menopause is the belief that it results in the complete absence of estrogen and progesterone. This is not the case. There are three types of estrogen—estrone, estradiol, and estriol. Of these, only estradiol (synthesized in the ovaries) is dramatically decreased. As noted by Anne Fausto-Sterling (1985):

> The other estrogenic hormones, as well as progesterone and testosterone, drop off to some extent but continue to be synthesized at a level comparable to that observed during the early phases of the menstrual cycle. Instead of concentrating on the notion of estrogen deficiency . . . it is more important to point out that: (1) postmenopausally the body makes different kinds of estrogen; (2) the ovaries synthesize less and the adrenals more of these hormones; and (3) the monthly ups and downs of these hormones even out following menopause. (p. 115)

Estrone synthesis declines somewhat but not as sharply as estradiol, and estrone

> becomes the principal estrogen in the postmenopausal woman and has a production rate four times that of estradiol. . . . Almost all production of estrone in late

menopause results from a conversion of the precursor androstenedione [an androgen], mostly of adrenal origin, while the primary source of estradiol is the peripheral conversion of estrone. (Morokoff, 1988, p. 491).

Estrogen is also produced in fat cells (adipose tissue) and by cholesterol (cf. Gannon, 1988), probably accounting for the positive correlation between the weight of postmenopausal women and both estrone and estradiol levels.

At the same time that the total level of estrogen is decreasing, FSH (follicle-stimulating hormone) and LH (luteinizing hormone) levels increase so that the post-menopausal woman eventually has "one-and-one-half times more LH and seven times more FSH circulating in her blood than when she menstruated regularly" (Fausto-Sterling, 1985, p. 115). The consequences of the increase in the level of these hormones are not yet understood, but one view is that they are somehow implicated in the production of hot flashes (or flushes). The hot flash, "a sudden expansion of the blood flow into the skin" (Fausto-Sterling, 1985, p. 117), is the sign most often linked to menopause and, for many women, serves as its symbol. It is reportedly experienced to some extent by about 75 percent of menopausal women but remains a medical mystery. While treatment with estrogen can suppress hot flashes, the normal thermal mechanism in the hypothalamus is believed to be triggered at the same time as the pituitary releases bursts of LH (Brozan, 1983), the hormone that spurs the ovaries into action. While ova are no longer released after menopause, parts of the cycle may continue on a random basis with action by the pituitary. The hypothalamic neurons controlling the release of LH by the pituitary are very near the temperature-regulating center, suggesting that the LH surge and hot flashes may result from alterations in hypothalamic functions (Marx, 1979b).

Hot flashes vary widely in frequency and duration, in the number of months or years during which they occur, and in women's reactions to them. Some women come to recognize precipitating factors such as hot drinks, alcohol, emotional upset, hot weather, or a warm bed. And in all women the flashes eventually disappear as the body naturally adjusts to the changed relative levels of LH, estrogen, and other hormones.

While the scientific literature on menopause was, until recently, both "sparse and inconclusive" (Posner, 1979, p. 189), the popular view that menopause is a difficult, troublesome, confusing, and depressing period continues. According to Sadja Greenwood (1985), "the popular image of the middle-aged woman as an emotional wreck, drenched in sweat and unable to cope, has been played up by pharmaceutical companies to persuade doctors and their patients to use drugs for this condition" (p. 79). But recent studies by psychologists and sociologists have found little evidence to support these beliefs. Nonetheless, frightening and inaccurate information continues to be presented by popular authors (e.g., Sheehy, 1991) and by some medical practitioners. Thus, according to Ann Voda and Mona Eliasson (1985), current medical literature describes menopausal women as "hypogonadal, castrates, or as estrogen deficient" (p. 138) and treats menopause as a disease, while advertisements in clinical journals "project an image of the typical menopausal woman as worried, with wrinkled forehead, looking sad, and despairing."

The data accumulating on women's experience during and after menopause are in sharp contrast to the traditional medical view. Menopause is rarely perceived as a crisis to women, and many women feel relief to have their menstrual years behind them. One study (Black & Hill, 1984), for example, of more than 200 women between the ages of 46 and 61 in intact marriages found that among the 71 percent who reported any signs of menopause, only 24 percent experienced them as negative. With respect to general happiness and marital and work satisfaction, 90 percent of this sample of well-educated and fairly affluent women rated themselves as positive. Similar data have been reported by Karen Frey (1981) from a study of 40- to 60-year-old women of varied background, ethnicity, and socioeconomic level, among whom 88 percent were employed. Within this sample, those going through menopause had no greater frequency of physical complaints than pre- or postmenopausal women, and the women generally did not indicate an illness orientation toward menopause or view it as a "central distressing event" (p. 31).

An important prospective study of 2500 randomly sampled women in Massachusetts between the ages of 45 and 55 (the Massachusetts Women's Health Study) followed them from pre- to postmenopause and found that both their health status and use of health services were predicted primarily by premenopausal health factors and that natural (i.e., nonsurgical) menopause was not a significant predictor of either psychological or physical well-being (cf. Morokoff, 1988). An analysis of two large-scale national community surveys of married women between 40 and 54 (Lennon, 1987) similarly found that menopause was not related to the report of depression when other variables were controlled. Only lower levels of

education predicted higher depression scores, not menopausal status.

The psychological and emotional correlates of menopause reported by some women, while not directly attributable to physiological or structural changes, may be a function of how bodily changes are interpreted, the evaluation of their significance, and the further changes anticipated in one's life. Most women, according to findings from the Massachusetts Health Study (cf. Adler, 1991a), "report feeling neutral or relieved when they stop menstruating and increasingly positive as their menopause proceeds," but some women believe menopause will lead to depression. This study obtained evidence linking prior expectations to later reports of negative menopausal signs. For example,

> among [premenopausal] women who agreed with the statement: "Menopause does not change most women in any important way," only 19 percent [later] got night sweats. But 37 percent of women who disagreed with the statement did. Among women who agreed that many women worry about losing their mind during menopause, 33 percent got night sweats. Only 17 percent of those who disagreed got night sweats.

Another researcher, Karen Matthews (cf. Adler, 1991a) also found a correlation between the negative expectations women had prior to menopause and increases in postmenopausal feelings of anger and depression. Thus, as we have seen before, what we anticipate influences interpretations and feelings about bodily and other events.

Hormone Replacement Therapy (HRT)

Robert Wilson, whose 1966 book *Feminine Forever* "influenced thousands of physicians to prescribe estrogen to millions of women" (Fausto-Sterling, 1985, p. 112), considered menopause to be an estrogen-deficiency disease and proclaimed estrogen replacement therapy to be the only "cure." Other popular medical writers, like David Reuben (1969), also presented horrifying images of postmenopausal women as sexless and shriveled: "Not really a man but no longer a functional woman, these individuals live in the world of intersex" (p. 292). Such views, as might be imagined, have helped pharmaceutical companies sell huge quantities of estrogen products to cure the "disease of menopause" despite lack of supporting data or careful investigations of the physiological and social correlates of aging. Although estrogen replacement therapy has been available since the 1940s, it is still the case that "little is known about its long-term health benefits or consequences" (National Women's Health Report, 1992, p. 1).

First presented by the pharmaceutical industry as a way to stay "forever feminine" and to prevent the "living decay" of menopause, estrogen replacement was subsequently promoted in connection with the prevention of osteoporosis. According to Anne Fausto-Sterling (1985), "by 1975 some six million women had started long-term treatment with Premarin (Ayerst Labs' brand name for estrogen), making it the fourth or fifth most popular drug in the United States" (p. 112). Ayerst Labs were reported to have hired a public relations firm to run a campaign about osteoporosis, which succeeded in getting congressional and media attention, and financed a tour of medical experts to large cities to publicize the possible link between this condition and estrogen decline (Dejanikus, 1985).

Osteoporosis, or progressive bone loss, accompanies the aging process in both sexes. As a result of a drop in the blood calcium level, bones become thin and porous, with a consequent reduction in bone mass. Sufficient calcium is required to maintain an equilibrium between the rate of normal bone breakdown and the rate of new bone formation. The blood calcium level is sensitive to, or influenced by, multiple factors, such as "chronic illness, immobilization, alcohol abuse, heavy smoking, stress, certain drugs, sedentary lifestyle, and poor nutrition" (MacPherson, 1984, p. 8). Because osteoporosis is most common among postmenopausal women, estrogen has been implicated, but the precise relationship between estrogen and the use of calcium for new bone formation is not known. What is known is that bone loss is very rapid for about 10 years after menopause, and then slows down to about the rate it was at about age 35 (Eagan, 1989).

According to Joan Beck (1983), about 25 to 40 percent of women develop osteoporosis. It appears to be more prevalent in fair-skinned, thin, and small-boned European-American women and Asian-American women (Voda & Eliasson, 1985; Cook, 1986). African-American women, who produce more of the hormone calcitonin, are relatively immune (Greenwood, 1985). The so-called "dowager's hump" results from collapse of fractured spinal vertebra, with subsequent loss of height and a humped upper back, and is said to occur in 5 to 10 percent of women in the 25 years following menopause. By age 80, a woman has a 1 in 6 chance of breaking a hip and by 90 a 1 in 3 chance (Eagan, 1989). Figure 13.1 shows the typical percent of bone loss with age for women and men.

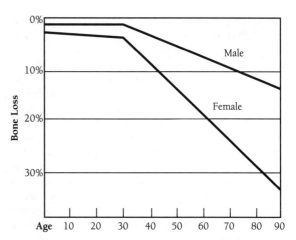

FIGURE 13.1 *Bone loss with age. Bone mass declines dramatically after about age 30. The loss is greater for women than for men and affects mostly the trabecular layer, causing bones to become brittle. By age 70, women have lost more than 20 percent of the bone they had at age 30, and men have lost about 10 percent.* (SOURCE: American Medical Association. From *The Good Health Magazine, New York Times*, April 28, 1991, p. 20.)

Natural and safe ways to prevent osteoporosis involve making sure that one's body is getting enough calcium and using it most efficiently. This can be done by eating high-calcium foods like dairy products, yogurt, cocoa, tofu, green leafy vegetables, canned salmon, and sardines; taking calcium supplements; and avoiding cigarettes, alcohol, salt, protein, and caffeine, which interfere with calcium use. Vitamin D is also necessary for new bone formation and is obtainable from the sun or from foods rich in this vitamin. Since phosphorous contributes to bone loss, avoiding excessive use of red meat, cola drinks, and processed food with phosphorous additives is important. We now know that "bones do better if you are not too thin" (Greenwood, 1985, p. 82) since fatty tissue is a source of estrogen. A reliable link has also been found between strong bones and regular exercise, especially weight-bearing exercises and those that involve movement, pull, and stress on the long bones such as walking, jogging, bicycling, and jumping rope (MacPherson, 1984; Greenwood, 1985).

In the view of some (e.g., Eagan, 1989), prevention of osteoporosis by diet, exercise, and a few extra pounds "is probably much more effective than any treatment" (p. 43). Weight lifting, in particular, is considered important in this regard because it helps to build a reserve of bone mass. It thickens bone by increasing blood flow which carries more nutrients to bone-building cells, and by putting stress on bones, thus creating an electrical charge which also stimulates bone-building cells (Kaufman, 1991). Some scientists have questioned the recommendation for calcium supplements, urging instead the intake of high-calcium foods and pointing out that too much calcium can lead to kidney stones and interfere with the body's use of vitamin D, necessary for the activation of bone cells (cf. Kolata, 1986).

Increasing a woman's supply of estrogen does appear to arrest bone loss, but it never replaces lost bone and has not been conclusively related to a decreased incidence of osteoporotic bone fractures (Seidler, 1984; Voda & Eliasson, 1985). On the other hand, a sizable number of studies have shown a causal connection between estrogen intake and both endometrial and breast cancer (Seidler, 1984). As a result of publication of the research linking estrogen treatment to uterine and breast cancer, "many women stopped taking estrogen and many physicians became more cautious about prescribing it, [but] the idea of hormone replacement therapy remains with us" (Fausto-Sterling, 1985, p. 112). In 1989, estrogens were being taken by over 3.5 million women ("Focus on Estrogen," 1992), or 20 percent of menopausal and postmenopausal women (National Women's Health Report, 1992).

It has been suggested that the danger of estrogen replacement therapy can be offset by combining estrogen with progesterone (or progestin), but according to Sadja Greenwood (1985), progestin "raises the blood level of a type of fat that may predispose to heart disease" and the long-term consequences of exogenous estrogen and progestins "are still questioned by responsible investigators" (p. 82). Critics of pharmaceutical interventions emphasize the uncertain effects of HRT and the fact that increased calcium intake and regular exercise are cheaper and safer ways to prevent osteoporosis. Although estrogen does alleviate hot flashes, these return when the estrogen is stopped, so that it appears as though HRT "merely postpones passage through the transitional period" (Voda & Eliasson, 1985, p. 148). This transitional period is one in which internally produced estrogen, progestin, FHS, and LH reach new levels of balance. As noted earlier in our description of normal menopausal changes, menopause does not result in the absence of any hormone, but in the relative decline of some and an increase in others.

Andrea Eagan (1989) has argued that medicine appears to have had a continuing "love affair with estrogen," recommending it in one form or another over the past 50 years to prevent miscarriage, as a morning-after pill, to suppress lactation, in birth-control pills, to keep a woman sexually active and forever feminine, and most recently to prevent osteoporosis and heart disease. Eagan describes a roller-coaster phenomenon—high positive publicity followed by negative research findings. Research findings remain mixed, with some evidence indicating that estrogen therapy has benefits for slowing osteoporosis and preventing heart disease, and other evidence that it may speed up gall bladder and liver disease, cause blood clots, and pose serious risks for breast and endometrial cancer (National Women's Health Report, 1992; Rodin & Ickovics, 1990). For example, a joint U.S.-Swedish study (cf. Marx, 1989) on a large group of women found that, overall, women who took estrogen developed about 10 percent more than the expected number of breast cancers and that the risk increased sharply and significantly with increased estrogen use after 9 years. The hope that progestin would protect against breast cancer did not turn out to be the case; in fact, the combination of estrogen and progestin increased the breast cancer risk more than estrogen alone. While progestin counteracts the negative effect of estrogen on uterine cells, it appears to act with estrogen to stimulate the growth of breast cells. Despite the increased risk of breast cancer, projected to be the case for 1 of every 20 estrogen users, the FDA in 1990 gave limited support to the contentions of the Wyeth-Ayerst pharmaceutical company that its product Premarin prevents heart disease, a projected benefit for 1 in every 10 estrogen users (Pearson, 1990).

The current state of affairs, and the lack of clear answers, has been summarized by Marcia Stefanick (1992).

> Estrogen has been shown to prevent bone loss and reduce the incidence of osteoporosis. . . . Unfortunately, estrogen increases the risk of endometrial (uterine) cancer three to five times . . . unless estrogen is combined with progestin therapy, which protects the uterus. . . . Unfortunately, progestins have been shown to lower HDL [the "good" cholesterol] and raise LDL [the "bad" cholesterol]; therefore, to protect the uterus from estrogenic effects that increase cancer risk might negate the beneficial effects of estrogen on heart disease. (p. 2)

Complicating the picture even further, according to Stefanick, the recent studies reporting less risk of coronary heart disease among postmenopausal estrogen users were confounded by the fact that users tended to be more educated than nonusers. Hope for the unraveling of this complex picture rests on a new project currently begun by the National Institutes of Health. This project, the Women's Health Initiative, will directly investigate the effects on older women not only of hormone therapy but also of a lowfat diet and calcium supplements.

Other Medical Interventions

Hysterectomy, the surgical removal of the uterus (and sometimes also the ovaries and fallopian tubes) is a common surgical procedure for older women in the United States. A National Institutes of Health conference reported in 1979 that "by the time American women reach 60, upwards of one-half have had a hysterectomy" (Voda & Eliasson, 1985, p. 138). Others have estimated that 62 percent of U.S. women can expect to have a hysterectomy by the time they are 70 (cf. Bjornson, 1984), and that 31 percent of women between 45 and 49 have had hysterectomies, more than a quarter of them for nonmalignant fibroids (Nakhnikian, 1992). Hysterectomies and oopherectomies (surgical removal of the ovaries) are often performed as elective surgery—for example, to prevent cancer—and not as a procedure essential for the patient's immediate health and well-being. As noted by Joanne West (1984):

> Many women as they near or pass menopause are told that they no longer need a uterus because its only function is to carry a baby, that the ovaries are not needed because they "shrivel up and die" after menopause, that the hormones that ovaries produced can be replaced with drugs . . . and that this surgery will leave their sexual lives unchanged or improved. The inference that "at this age" the uterus, cervix, and ovaries might become cancerous and that it is safer and healthier to take it all out leads many women into the operating room. (p. 4)

Some doctors promote the removal of healthy ovaries at the time of hysterectomy in all women over 40 or 45 as a "prophylactic" against possible future cancer, even though studies show that chances are only 1 in 1000 that such a cancer would occur (Bjornson, 1984).

The frequency with which U.S. surgeons perform these operations relative to doctors in other countries has been widely criticized and has aroused suspicions that greed may be an underlying motive. Critics have argued that such surgery should be performed only when the organs are diseased and constitute a danger to continued health. Hysterectomies and oopherectomies are not reversible procedures; they have potential life-altering consequences, and the missing organs may disrupt the body's

biochemical balance and decrease sexual motivation and responsiveness (Morgan, 1982). An alternative to hysterectomy for women with fibroid tumors is now available. The vaginal myomectomy permits a surgeon to remove the fibroids through the vagina by cutting them out of the uterus with a small instrument. This new procedure has two major advantages over the hysterectomy: the uterus remains intact, and there is no surgical recovery time. Yet, according to Elise Nakhnikian (1992), "five out of six women who have surgery for fibroids [are] still getting hysterectomies" (p. 37).

Another problem area that affects older women (as well as older men) is the current tendency to exaggerate and overestimate the prevalence of Alzheimer's disease.

> Gerontologists now are concerned about mistaken assumptions of the prevalence of Alzheimer's disease . . . which is still non-normative in all age groups. The disorder has assumed the wastebasket status once held by the term *senility* and reflects the same misinformation, misunderstanding, and stereotyping about the aging process. (Rodeheaver & Datan, 1988)

Moderate to severe dementias are found in only 4 to 6 percent of persons 65 and older and just about half of these are of the Alzheimer's type (Gatz & Pearson, 1988). The overdiagnosis of Alzheimer's is a special problem for women because there are more women than men in older age groups.

With respect to other medical issues, it has been reported that older women are less likely than younger women to be tested for cervical cancer with a Pap smear. Yet, this is an especially important test for women who have had multiple sexual partners; these women are at greater risk for cervical cancer ("Pap Smears," 1990). Older women are also found in great numbers among the disabled. According to the National Institute on Aging (cf. Howard, 1991), women constitute three fourths of disabled adults aged 65 or older (4 million women). A 7-year federally financed study has been launched to study disabilities in women, their causes, moderating factors, and treatment.

Another problem that has remained largely hidden until recently, and estimated to be twice as common among older women than men, is urinary incontinence (Zones, 1990). Although urinary incontinence increases in prevalence with age, it is not considered a normal consequence of aging, and most cases can be cured or improved by behavioral techniques including a regular schedule for going to the toilet, eliminating foods that irritate the bladder, or changing medications, or by a regular program of exercises (Kegel exercises) that strengthen the vaginal muscles.

SOCIAL AND PERSONAL ISSUES

Beyond the physiological changes that accompany aging, older women's lives may be influenced by a number of significant social and personal changes.

Widowhood

Widows comprise almost 5 percent of the U.S. population, and outnumber widowers by a ratio of 2.45 to 1.0, reflecting both the greater longevity of women and the custom of women marrying men older than themselves (Luria & Meade, 1984). The mean age at widowhood is 66 for women and 69 for men. Among persons aged 65 or older, 51 percent of women and 13 percent of men are widowed, and the mean duration of widowed life is 14 years for women and 7 for men (Hansson & Remondet, 1988). Of the 5.9 million women over age 65 living alone in a separate residence, 80 percent are widows (O'Bryant, 1988).

Widowhood may bring loneliness, and some earlier researchers viewed it as "the most consistent problem widows endure" (Barrett, 1981, p. 476). But newer data dispute this conclusion. For example, Karen Rook (1984), who interviewed over 100 widows between the ages of 60 and 89, found that loneliness was significantly related to having few social supports, not just to widowhood. Similarly, a study of the psychological well-being of 226 European-American widows aged 60 to 89 who remained alone in their own homes following their husbands' death found that only health was significantly related to measures of both positive and negative well-being. The researchers concluded that "a great proportion of the variance in widows' well-being remains unexplained" (McGloshen & O'Bryant, 1988, p. 113).

For some women, widowhood brings enforced independence and the necessity to solve problems alone. While the loss of a spouse is problematic for both women and men, some women may be more vulnerable to temporary despair and panic because of their relative lack of worldliness and knowledge about mortgages, insurance, loans, and so on. Lynn Caine (1974), whose husband died when she was still a young mother of small children, wrote movingly of how widowhood forced her to regain a lost identity. Caine, who was educated, European-American, middle-class, and employed, was forced by widowhood and the necessity of caring for herself and her children to develop new skills, to acquire new behaviors, and to rediscover old strengths. For older widows who are poorly educated this transition may be more difficult, but widows invariably talk about experiencing the change from dependence to autonomy and often marvel at their unanticipated competence at handling aspects of living previously attended to by their husbands.

In a novel by Elizabeth Hailey (1979) the heroine writes to a friend after her husband's death, "I am just beginning to learn how to live alone as an adult" (p. 123). And in a poem entitled "The Widow Steps Out," Eve Merriam (1991, p. 27) lets us feel the joy of a woman who has just begun to appreciate her personal power. She describes her experience at a folk dance class for seniors.

> . . . to her surprise
> the widow steps forth,
> takes the male side,
> swings the granny with the wiggy curls,
> switches to the withered grape and
> . . .
> feeling strong and powerful,
> she could knock down the caller,
> punch the puny husbands,
> [and] raise a tower of shrunken old women to the sun.

Despite the loneliness experienced by some widows and the necessity of dealing with aspects of the world previously handled by their husbands, current research is finding that women tend to cope with the death of a spouse more successfully than do men. A review of the relevant literature (Stroebe & Stroebe, 1983) found that, regardless of the index used to assess well-being, whether depression, psychiatric disorders, physical illness, mortality, or suicide, men suffered more negative consequences after a spouse's death than women did. As noted by Nancy Datan (1989), "if a man is widowed, his mortality rises by 67 percent in the first year after the death of his spouse, while if a woman is widowed, her mortality rises by only about 3 percent . . . because women are more effective in maintaining the social networks that sustain life" (p. 16).

Comparisons of widowers to married men, and comparisons of widows to married women, indicate that differences between the men are invariably greater than between the women, suggesting a greater psychological and physical effect of bereavement on men. A 12-year survey of more than 4,000 widowed people (Helsing, Szklo, & Comstock, 1981) found that the negative effects of widowhood for men disappeared if they remarried.

Among widowed men who remarried the mortality rate was as low as, or lower than, among nonwidowed men, whereas those who did not remarry had a 60 percent higher chance of dying sooner than nonwidowed men in the same age group. Too few widows had remarried for a reliable assessment to be made of the effect of remarriage on their mortality, but there was a suggestion of the same phenomenon. A more recent study (cf. "Study: Wife," 1990) of 7,651 U.S. adults reported similar findings for people aged 45 to 64. Men living without a wife were twice as likely as married men to die within 10 years; women without a husband were less at risk, and the risk was associated more with a lower income than with loss of a partner.

Even without remarriage, which is unlikely for widows, women do better than men in adjusting to their spouse's death and in caring for their social, emotional, health, and practical needs. This adjustment is all the more remarkable in view of the significant negative impact widowhood has on the average woman's economic resources. Compared to a widowed man, a widowed woman is far more likely to be poor. "Estimates suggest a widow's income decreases to approximately 66% of former income, yet the living costs for a single person are projected to be approximately 80% of that of a married person" (O'Bryant, 1988, p. 93). The Massachusetts Women's Health Survey (cf. Dietz, 1988), which involved 5 years of interviews with 2,500 midlife women, found that while recently widowed women were no more likely to get sick than other women, the physical health problems of some were related, not to depression, "but to economic factors: reduced income, loss of health insurance, [and] loss of access to health care" (p. 33).

Widowed women differ from widowed men primarily with respect to income, with women being more likely to experience poverty after a spouse's death (Markson & Hess, 1980; Rodeheaver & Datan, 1988). Otherwise, few gender differences are reported on measures of social and psychological well-being, life satisfaction, or distress following widowhood. A decline in psychological health is not considered normative for older persons of either gender, or for widowed persons in particular. Helen Lopata (1988) concluded that "there is a great heterogeneity of lifestyles and support systems among modern American widows" (p. 127). And, consistent with other research, data from a large national sample (McCrae & Costa, 1988), supported the conclusion that,

in the long run, although it affects lifestyle, widowhood does not appear to have any enduring effect on psycho-

social functioning. . . . Older widowed men and women have as many friends and confidants, believe themselves to be as healthy, and are as able to perform daily activities as are older married individuals. . . . [They] learn to accept their loss, and . . . widowhood ultimately ceases to have much effect on day-to-day mood and functioning. (pp. 137, 138)

Divorce

In Chapter 7 we examined divorce in general, in terms of statistics and issues. Here we want to consider it again with special reference to older women. An estimated 100,000 people over the age of 55 get divorced in this country each year (Cain, 1982). These marriage dissolutions are said to be "overwhelmingly initiated by men" and to produce greater psychological upheaval for older women than for younger women. For a woman over 60, a divorce typically comes after 30 to 40 years of marriage. Self-blame is common, and the divorce exacerbates the stress of aging. In addition, few states recognize the role of homemaker, wife, and mother in their divorce laws, and most judges are not directed by law to take into account the contributions made by a woman in these roles when redistributing a divorcing couple's assets. One exception is New York State, which in 1980 passed an "equitable distribution" law to protect the financial security of women after divorce.

One woman interviewed by Barbara Cain (1982) noted that "divorce after 60 is a double whammy" (p. 90).

Unlike the elderly widow, the elderly divorcee must live with the realization that her loss was deliberate, volitional, intended. . . . Moreover, the divorcee, unlike the widow, must disengage from a partner who continues to walk the face of the earth often in the same town, even the same neighborhood. (p. 92)

Similar feelings are expressed by a middle-aged woman psychotherapist in a novel by Judith Rossner (1983). At a party she notes the presence of newly divorced male colleagues and their much younger second wives or companions.

These men were leaving women who were often, by the men's own admission, more than satisfactory wives. For women, this epidemic lent to the aging process a sense of doom beyond its normal difficulties and humiliations. Women looked at a gray-haired man and saw father; men looked at a gray-haired woman and ran from death. (p. 36)

Martha Kirkpatrick (1989) has pointed out that the breakup of an established relationship is generally much more difficult for a heterosexual than a homosexual woman. While divorce for the former generally means a

> lowering of her standard of living, . . . loss of the family home, loss of credit, . . . loss of a sexual partner, . . . [and] also the loss of the supportive network of married women friends . . . the lesbian community responds very differently . . . [and] tends to rush to the aid of the separated members and provide comfort and participation in the search for new relationships. (p. 93)

Poverty

We have already noted that poverty is a serious problem for widows and divorced women of any age. Poverty affects the lives of far more women over 65 than men. In 1985, for example, one out of every six elderly women had an annual income of less than $5,600, the official poverty level for single-person households (Jaycox, 1985). According to more recent census data (cf. Steenland, 1988), the median annual income for women in their 50s is less than $8,500 and for women over 65 it is $6,000. Statistics on the poverty of older women come from many sources, utilize various indices, and paint a consistently depressing picture. On every measure, African-American, Latina, and Native American older women are worse off than European-American women, among whom 25 percent are considered to be poor (Carstensen & Pasupathi, 1993).

The Gray Panthers, a national advocacy organization for older people, maintains that health care for the elderly costs four times as much as it does for others and that the elderly pay an average of 34 percent of their income for housing that is often well below standards for decency, maintenance, safety, and hygiene. Women, who have fewer financial resources than men, are more affected by these high costs. Robert Butler, a geriatrics specialist, estimated that "women today have a 60 percent chance of being destitute in old age because of low earnings, inequalities in pensions and the tendency of couples to exhaust their assets during the last illness of the mate who dies first, usually the husband" (cf. Johnson, 1984). Among all ethnic groups, approximately 50 percent of elderly women live alone. Those who are homeowners typically live in poorly maintained single-family houses in need of serious repair (Leavitt & Welch, 1989).

According to the Older Women's League (OWL), one half of all older widows and two thirds of all older divorced women have no private health insurance, 4 out of 5 women over 65 have no access to pensions, and 6 out of 10 women over 65 who live alone depend upon social security as their only source of income (Glasse, 1988). To receive full social security benefits, however, one must have been employed for 35 years, and the payment one receives is based on the average earned during that time (Suh, 1991). The current Social Security system short-changes women, especially those who worked outside the home but earned less than their husbands. "A wife who worked often does not get any more in her Social Security check than she would have gotten if she had not worked even though she paid Social Security taxes" (Peterson, 1983) because a nonemployed spouse is entitled to 50 percent of the employed spouse's benefits. In 1985, the average monthly social security benefits received by women over 65 was $420 (Jaycox, 1985). Proposals to reform the Social Security system by permitting each spouse to qualify independently for a benefit based on half the couple's total earnings have still not been adopted.

Being a Grandmother

There is a paucity of research on grandparenting, despite its significance and the pleasures almost universally reported in association with this role. Anecdotal evidence abounds to support the assertion that a woman's relationship with her daughter generally becomes more positive after the latter experiences motherhood and that relationships with grandchildren are generally more relaxed and mutually appreciative than with one's children. My own experience supports these generalizations; the reader can get a hint of the fun my granddaughter Samone and I have with one another from the photograph on p. 322.

One interesting study (Eisenberg, 1988) obtained information from young adult children about their relationships with grandparents. From these reports, grandmothers were found to have more contact with their grandchildren, and to engage in more positive activities with them, than grandfathers did. Grandmothers were also rated higher on scales of closeness and liking. Maternal grandmothers were liked the most, got the highest ratings on closeness, saw their grandchildren most often, and were said to make themselves particularly accessible to their grandchildren. "Maternal grandmothers engage in a wider variety of activities with grandchildren than any other grandparents . . . [and] score particularly high on . . . being someone to talk to or share secrets with, giving advice, and providing a sense of family continuity" (p. 215).

This positive portrait of grandmothers, from the perspective of their grandchildren, reflecting the experiences of many, exists side by side with the more negative

Being a grandmother: Three-year-old Samone and me. (Photograph by Judith Lott.)

My mother, Annie, sparkling and smiling in the sun shortly before her death. (Photograph by Shoshana Rothaizer.)

stereotypes discussed earlier in this chapter. The reader may recall the words of Barbara Macdonald (1989): "The old woman['s] . . . greatest joy is seen as giving all to her grandchildren. . . . She is erased more completely as grandmother than she was as mother" (p. 10). This stereotype, like many others, seems to be at variance with reality. Although grandchildren are a source of great pleasure for older women, so too, as we will see in the next section, are friends, job, travel, and social and community activities.

WELL-BEING AND EFFECTIVENESS

Despite the institutional discrimination and personal slights often experienced by older women, there are numerous indications that the middle and later years can be even more satisfying, rewarding, exciting, and produc-

tive than the years of early adulthood. Some women discover strengths and skills they had never previously tested and redefine their personal identities. Other women pick up interests and objectives where they had left them for marriage and a family. The photograph of my mother was taken when she was 77, a year before she died. Although she was physically ill toward the end of her life, she maintained her sense of personal integrity, dignity, charm, and involvement.

Older women have many new role models. The writer May Sarton, for example, lived alone most of her life and was ignored by the critics, but in her later years she is still beautiful, energetic, and at the height of her fame and popularity. Her most recent book, *Endgame* (Sarton, 1992), is subtitled "A journey of the seventy-ninth year." In it she continues to chronicle, as noted by Sue Halpern (1992), her struggles "to make a life, a fertile life, without the conventional soil of marriage and children" (p. 18). Maggie Kuhn and some friends founded the Gray Panthers in 1970 after she was forced to retire from her job at the age of 65. Other older women are "coming out" and publically proclaiming that they are vital and interesting, with special strengths and attributes. As poetically phrased by Natasha Josefowitz (1984):

> Your skins are taut
> Your faces smooth
>   like fresh plums
> My skin is wrinkled
> My brow furrowed
>   like a prune
> Prunes are sweeter. (p. 12)

Among contemporary older women, Mary Gergen (1990) has noted, are many who organize their lives in new, nontraditional ways. "Traditional forms cannot do justice to babies born to mothers of 40, grandmothers enrolled in graduate school, and women with multiple careers and relational histories" (p. 486).

Sexuality

Recent studies have shown that both women and men who are in generally good health and who are motivated can continue to respond sexually and obtain gratification in their 60s, 70s, 80s, and probably indefinitely throughout their lives. A study conducted at Duke University (cf. Lobsenz, 1974) found that one in three women reported sexual interest in their 60s, but only one in five were having heterosexual relationships. The difference between interest and heterosexual activity was attributed to such factors as the lack of available men, anxiety over physical appearance, and a willingness to believe that sex should end after menopause. A subsequent study of women and men between the ages of 60 and 82 (cf. "Studying Love," 1985) reported that all but a few of the persons interviewed were sexually active and experimented more with sex than they did when they were younger. The respondents described creative activities on dates: going camping, walking, going to the theater, taking weekend trips, and so on. The researchers concluded that with respect to intimacy, dating behavior, and sexuality, "old people are just younger people who have gotten older."

Zella Luria and Robert Meade (1984) have noted that the extent of sexual functioning in middle age is related to early experience and enjoyment of sex and that in both the middle and later years sexuality also depends upon good health and the availability of partners. An expanded sense of sexuality for older women may include masturbation and lesbian relationships. A number of researchers have reported a greater enjoyment of sex among older women than in earlier years. Lillian Rubin (1981), for example,

conducted long interviews with 160 heterosexual women between 35 and 54 years of age and found that most told her that their sexual pleasure had increased with age; sex for them had "gotten better and better" (p. 74). A national survey (cited in Luria & Meade, 1984) of almost 200 middle- and upper-class women over age 50 found that 91 percent expressed interest in sex and 84 percent reported themselves to be coitally active. These results are in sharp contrast with one study (Alston & Rose, 1981) of a sample of African-American women between the ages of 40 and 65 who said they found sex less enjoyable than they used to and implicated menopause as a causal factor.

Some writers have focused on the presumed difficulty of heterosexual pleasure associated with vaginal dryness (dyspareunia) due to decreased estrogen after menopause, which in turn is associated with less vascular engorgement in the labia and clitoris and less vaginal lubrication. Such a condition, however, can be safely treated with non-estrogen creams and jellies, cocoa butter, or unsaturated oils; as Anne Fausto-Sterling (1985) noted, "continued sexual activity also helps—yet another example of the interaction between behavior and physiology" (p. 118). Heterosexual intercourse is likely to be painful for the sexually abstinent older woman, not for the sexually active one (Leiblum, 1990). The capacity for sexual arousal and orgasm remains intact after menopause with no decrease in the likelihood of pleasure from physical relationships. Patricia Morokoff (1988) has concluded from her studies of sexuality in postmenopausal women that the role of estrogen in sexual functioning is not well known or clearly established and that "women continue to engage in and enjoy sexual activity during and after menopause" (p. 506).

Ellen Cole and Esther Rothblum (1990) have pointed out that older lesbian women do not need to be concerned about dyspareunia or the erectile difficulties of older male partners. Among a sample of older lesbians, they found that 76 percent said they did not have sexual problems, and most discussed their sexuality in the context of an intimate relationship and said that sex was as good as or better than ever. These data are congruent with those reported by others. Martha Kirkpatrick (1989) reviewed the relevant literature and found that older lesbians look forward to having sexual partners in their later years and continue to seek physical intimacy with or without genital contact. One segment of the older lesbian community is made up of previously heterosexual women who, after conventional marriage and childbearing, adopt a new life-style that includes sexual intimacy with women and a lesbian partnership.

It is important to put the information obtained from older heterosexual women in a historical perspective. These are women born before World War II; before television; before the "sexual revolution" of liberated attitudes, sexual knowledge, and practice; and before the easy availability of reliable contraception. As Zella Luria and Robert Meade (1984) have pointed out, such women differ from young women "not only in biology but also in the different scripts they learned for sexual experience and initiation" (p. 385). Young women of the current generation generally have far greater sexual experience than their grandmothers did. It is likely, then, that as newer generations of women age, their sexuality will continue to be robust and an even more important part of their lives than is true for the present cohort of older women.

Social Relationships and Satisfying Work

Researchers have concluded that older women often experience a heightened sense of self-esteem, a phenomenon believed to be related to the current social climate and the enhanced expectations and choices for women of all ages (Baruch, Barnett, & Rivers, 1983). The "empty nest" has not been found to be a source of depression for women; on the contrary, "the end of the active mothering function is greeted with relief" (Rubin, 1981, pp. 28f.). Among the 160 women between 35 and 54 years of age interviewed at length by Lillian Rubin, "not one . . . yearned for another chance [at motherhood]. For good or ill, they were glad the job was done, ready to move on to the next stage of life" (p. 38). Middle-aged and older women consistently report that they look forward to pleasures attainable from work, study, travel, and sociability, provided that they are in good health and not living in poverty.

The Massachusetts Women's Health Study, referred to earlier, found that

> the typical woman at midlife [between 45 and 55] is an extremely busy person . . . , two-thirds still had children living at home and 6 percent had an elderly parent living with them. Twenty-five percent were providing regular care for an older relative. About 75 percent held fulltime or parttime jobs. (Dietz, 1988, p. 33)

Studies of women aged 45 to 60 (e.g., Harris, Ellicott, & Holmes, 1986) report that those who are educated, not poor, and healthy often experience increases in life satisfaction and "positive personality changes such as increased mellowing, patience, assertiveness, and expressivity" (p. 415). Similarly, Ravenna Helson and Geraldine

Moane (1987) found, in a longitudinal study of a sample of college women, general normative changes with age that included increased self-discipline, commitment to responsibilities, independence, coping skills, and confidence. These women in their 50s were described as being vitally engaged in their present lives, as showing a relative absence of negative affect, and pursuing "a lifestyle that prioritizes an intimate relationship along with a sense of autonomy—being oneself and taking charge of one's life" (Mitchell & Helson, 1990, p. 467).

An investigation of 7,000 persons in California, carefully monitored since 1965, found that the factors associated with increased chance of death were not the same for women as for men. The most significant risk factors for men were smoking, heavy alcohol usage, and not having a spouse, while the risk factors for women were physical inactivity, few social contacts, dissatisfaction with life, and self-perceived poor health (cf. Fisher, 1984). Other sources of data reinforce the significance of social interaction and activity for the well-being of older women. A national survey of adults between the ages of 50 and 95 (Antonucci & Akiyama, 1987) found that whereas men tend to rely almost exclusively on their wives for social support, women rely on children and friends in addition to husbands. Although one may intuitively expect relationships with children to be a source of support and comfort to older women, the data indicate that this is not generally the case. For example, Linda Beckman (1981), who interviewed more than 700 European-American women between the ages of 60 and 75 living in their own households, found that, contrary to what one might expect, the amount of contact with children had an insignificant effect on the women's well-being, while contact with other persons was positively and reliably related to feeling good. More important than quantity of contact was its quality. Similarly, Karen Rook (1987) found in an interview study of 115 widows, mostly European-American, between the ages of 60 and 89, that reciprocal social exchange and satisfaction was greater in the women's interactions with their friends than with their adult children. Satisfaction with children was positively related to the amount of practical, instrumental help they provided for their mothers, and negatively related to the amount of instrumental support the elderly mothers were providing for their children. The researcher concluded that "kin and peer relations . . . may be most satisfying in old age if they provide complementary resources" (p. 152).

The Massachusetts Women's Health Study found that the major source of worry and stress among midlife women was their families, parents or parents-in-law, and especially their children (a cause of stress for 39 percent of the sample). In contrast, work was a positive factor in the lives of most of the women and served to reduce the stress caused by family members (cf. Dietz, 1988). This finding supports Mary Gergen's (1990) argument that "women's attachment to their work may be as significant as men's" (p. 476) and that we need to pay more attention to the effect of retirement on older women's well-being. It is instructive in this regard, and disappointing, to note that a research agenda on older women prepared for the National Institute of Mental Health (Cohen, 1987) makes no mention of work or retirement issues.

Researchers have shown an increased interest in older persons in the past decade and have obtained findings that belie stereotypes of senility and decay. For example, Claire Brody (1990) led small groups of women in nursing homes in reminiscing sessions over the course of 3 years and found evidence of "a capacity for emotional survival and vitality" (p. 579). These institutionalized elderly women, she concluded, had untapped strengths; they discovered that they could still give something meaningful to others and experience a sense of hope. Another study of nursing home residents, women aged 68 to 97, found that, as is true of younger women, self-esteem and hopeful expectations for the future were positively related to self-reported instrumentality and agency (Krames, England, & Flett, 1988).

Older lesbian women, like older heterosexual women, face issues of aging that involve physical, physiological, and social changes and are also typically called upon to care for parents who are ill or needy. But researchers (cf. Benjamin, 1989; Johnson, 1989) have been finding that the social supports of older lesbian women tend to be strong and well-developed and that their social identity is tied to work and career. Older "always single" women have been found to be generally vigorous, satisfied, resourceful, resilient, and independent and to have close friendships with peers of equal status. "Women who have always been single" are reported to be "better off financially and less likely to be depressed or lonely" than older women who have been married (Carstensen & Pasupathi, 1993, p. 67).

There is evidence that contemporary older women in general tend to conform less to gender stereotypes than younger women, and some researchers have suggested that as both genders in our culture get older, they converge more and more in self-described personal attributes. One study (Fischer & Narus, 1981) found that persons who gave non-sex-typed self-descriptions were significantly older than those giving sex-typed self-descriptions. Older women saw themselves as more autonomous and competent than younger women, and older men saw themselves as more communal and expressive than younger men. Similarly, Jan Sinnott (1984) interviewed a large sample of people over 60 years of age who were in good health and living in their communities and found that the women and men described themselves in very similar ways, including attributes both stereotypically masculine and feminine. These older persons of both genders tended to see themselves as "balanced," or not sex-typed, and they indicated that they believed others expected them to be that way.

Personal and Political Objectives

As women born in the 1950s, 60s, and 70s mature and grow older, their expectations and assumptions will likely differ from those of women born in earlier decades. The daughters of today's women are also likely to be better educated than their mothers, to have explored several personal options, to have experienced and observed radical social changes, and to have had longer years of employment experience. But today's older women are living in a vastly different social world from the one they were part of when younger. As Pamela Perun (1981) noted, for many older women, investment in family did not bring the security and support that was promised. Thus, many older women are changing their lives and circumstances, and many are entering or reentering the work force or colleges and universities.

Women over 25 who are entering or reentering college after a significant period of time following high school graduation, whose educations were likely interrupted by marriage, child rearing, employment, or a geographic move because of their husband's job, now constitute a sizable proportion of the undergraduate population. This phenomenon, which began in the 1960s, appears to be continuing unabated.

Older women in college, known as reentry women, face a variety of special problems, ranging from the acceptance of transfer credits for courses taken many years earlier to feeling uneasy in classrooms with 20-year-olds whose lives and interests are vastly different from their own. Many reentry women have reported feeling stupid, confused, and anxious about their ability to cope with requirements and assignments. One woman interviewed by Lillian Rubin (1981) described herself as "an absolute infant" in school. "I feel dumb, dumb, dumb—like an intellectual basket case. I don't know how to do a term paper; I didn't even know what a term paper was" (p. 155). Rubin herself returned to school after age 40, going all the way to a doctorate in sociology. Such stories are no longer uncommon. Despite the problems of initial adjustment and minority status, reentry women invariably do extraordinarily well in college. They are active participants in their education, hard workers, and responsible students. One study (Badenhoop & Johansen, 1980) found that a sample of reentry undergraduate women had significantly higher grade point averages than a comparable group of younger women students; other studies have obtained similar results.

Although remarkable for their motivation, persistence, and achievements, reentry women do not seem to differ in other important ways from other women of their generation. For example, when a sample of 30- to 50-year-old women enrolled in a B.A. program were compared with a sample of same-aged homemakers without college educations who were not in school (Amstey & Whitbourne, 1981), the two groups were found to be similar in measures of identity, sex-role orientation, and political views. Similarly, in another study (Ballmer & Cozby, 1981), the marital adjustment of reentry women and a comparable group of homemakers was reported not to differ although, among the reentry women, both spouses perceived their families as characterized by more conflict, more independence, and a greater intellectual or cultural and active recreational orientation than was the case among the homemaker group. Judith Gerson (1985) compared a sample of 30- to 50-year-old married or divorced women college students with a sample of full-time homemakers and found that although the students reported more role strain, they also reported more personal benefits and general gratification than the homemakers did.

Besides pursuing higher education, older women in the 1990s can be found leading vigorous lives and participating fully in the workplace, in politics, and in organized efforts for social change. In the forefront of efforts to improve housing, neighborhoods, schools, and community life in rural and urban areas around the country one finds creative and committed women who see social change as intimately related to private well-being. The goals of the Gray Panthers, an articulate and militant organization in which women hold important positions of leadership, include the abolition of poverty, reform of pension plans, better health care and housing for the elderly, better monitoring of nursing care facilities, and better police protection. This group has been effective in raising public consciousness about older people's skills and needs and in influencing Con-

Activist women of all ages. (Photograph © Diana Mara Henry, Carmel , CA)

gress to investigate and legislate. Working with people of all ages on programs to expand human rights and to improve the human environment has maintained and enhanced the effectiveness and dignity of older women like the anti-war demonstrators shown above.

A case-study investigation of three politically committed midlife women (Stewart & Gold-Steinberg, 1990) found that they came from families with a strong and explicit sense of "social engagement," shared the desire to contribute to society, and saw midlife as providing them with new resources and opportunities. Another study (Todd, Friedman, & Kariuki, 1990) that compared European-American, African-American, and Kenyan women on their responses to a projective test of power motivation found that older women who are advantaged in social or economic status show a positive shift in power with age. These older women told more stories about strong women than younger women in response to ambiguous picture cards.

Barbara Macdonald (1989) has noted that older women today organize "from a lobby watch of 132 women in a Detroit housing project to protect themselves from male violence, to the Older Women's League of 12,000 women throughout the United States who work to make legislative changes that affect the economic oppression of old women" (p. 6). It is clear that many of today's women, when gray hair and wrinkles appear, effectively resist being pushed aside.

◆ Discussion Questions

1. How does gender interact with age in our society to produce special problems and issues for women? Discuss these issues.

2. Complete the following sentence: "I will consider myself old when I . . . "

3. Interview four women of different ages (50s, 60s, 70s, 80s). With each, explore the following subjects: past and present priorities; regrets; past and present challenges; accomplishments; failures; the role of family, work, friends, politics, and so on—past and present; sense of well-being and what is relevant to it.

4. Observe a sample of grandmothers and grandchildren in some natural settings.

CHAPTER 14

WHAT WOMEN WANT:
NEW DIRECTIONS
AND STRATEGIES

*I myself have never been able to find out precisely what fem-
inism is: I only know that people call me a feminist whenever I express sentiments that differentiate me from a
doormat.*

REBECCA WEST (1913)

*Gloria Steinem, six months shy of her fiftieth . . . told
me . . . that women may be the one group that grows more
radical with age. "As students," she said, "women are probably treated with more equality than we ever will be
again . . . " But later . . . come the important "radicalizing"
stages in a woman's life. The first is when she enters the
labor force and discovers that men, by and large, still control the workplace. The second is when she marries and
learns that marriage is not yet a completely equal partnership. The third is when she has children and finds out who
is the principal child-rearer. And the fourth is when she
ages, which still involves greater penalties for women than
for men.*

ELISABETH BUMILLER (1990, p. 287)

EVERYWHERE WE SEE CLEAR INDICATIONS THAT women's lives will not return to the status quo of earlier generations. Today's older woman is wiser, more articulate, and more skilled; and today's younger woman expects that her options will not be restricted because of her gender. American women have come a long way since the 19th century when Harriet Tubman put her life on the line in the underground railroad helping slaves to escape, when Harriet Beecher Stowe's book prodded abolitionists into greater action, and when Lucretia Mott and Elizabeth Cady Stanton organized the first women's rights convention in 1848 at Seneca Falls, New York. The National Organization of Women (NOW), begun in 1966 with 300 members, currently claims 250,000, and for every woman affiliated with NOW or some other feminist group, hundreds more are sympathetic to feminist goals and act on them in diverse ways.

The answer to Freud's famous question (still asked by many men with annoyance) "What does a woman want?" is that we want a fair share of everything in an equitable humane world in which access to resources does not depend on gender, ethnic background, or social position. As Michelle Murray (1973) wrote, women want "to cast a shadow . . . [that is] long and . . . rich" (p. 14), and we want others to have an opportunity to do the same.

My niece and my sister: Daughter and mother in sisterhood. (Photograph by Bernice Lott.)

SISTERHOOD ACROSS THE BARRIERS OF SOCIAL CATEGORY

Among the most far-reaching and significant objectives of the second wave of the women's movement in the United States that began in the late 1960s was its insistence on respect for, and empathy with, all women—regardless of marital status, color, sexual orientation, occupation, or age. This has not been easy to achieve but as women began talking to one another openly, we discovered common fears, problems, and aspirations. We found each other likable, interesting, and capable of strong and loving friendship. As the smiles shown above suggest, daughters rediscovered their mothers and mothers, their daughters. In the words of Mary Daly (1978b):

A feminist thinks of her close friends as sisters, but she knows that she has many sisters . . . whom she has never met. Sometimes she meets such women and some conversation unmasks the similarities between them. . . . The proximity that she feels is not merely geographic/

spatial. . . . She senses gynesthetically that there is a convergence of personal histories, of wavelengths. (p. 29)

Sisterhood is thus a means both to group understanding and to self understanding, a dual objective articulated by many chroniclers and theorists of the women's movement.

Raising Consciousness

Consciousness of common experience has been directed toward personal change and goal achievement and also toward militant change and political organization. Modern life in a patriarchal society tends to keep women isolated, in the nuclear family home or alone in a city apartment, and to convince women they are in competition with one another for men. The women's movement has given women a way to break out of isolation and encouraged us to see through the myths and to recognize personal strengths and common objectives. In Mary Daly's (1978b) words, "whenever two or three Self-affirming women are gathered together in our own names we are lighting our Fire" (p. 33).

Women gathering for enlightenment and support is not an altogether new phenomenon. One of the charges the churchmen of the early Massachusetts Bay Colony made against Anne Hutchinson was that women gathered regularly in her home to discuss the scriptures and other matters of mutual interest and to comment on the weekly sermons without benefit of male leadership or guidance. For this, Hutchinson, a midwife, herbal healer, and mother of 15 children, was banished from Massachusetts in 1638, excommunicated from the Church, and forced to flee with her family to Rhode Island. Anne Hutchinson threatened the male clergy because "she dared to assert the right of

329

women to instruct others" (Lerner, 1977, p. 465). In Nathaniel Hawthorne's (1850/1948) classic story of Puritan life, *The Scarlet Letter,* we read that Hester Prinn, who was publicly shamed for participating in adultery, was sought after toward the end of her life by women who came to her isolated cottage to share their problems, disappointments, and pain.

Women . . . came to Hester's cottage, demanding why they were so wretched, and what the remedy! Hester comforted and counselled them, as best she might. She assured them, too, of her firm belief that, at some brighter period, when the world should have grown ripe for it . . . a new truth would be revealed, in order to establish the whole relation between man and woman on a surer ground of mutual happiness. (pp. 271f.)

Raising Consciousness

Among contemporary women, what started two decades ago simply as informal and spontaneous "rap sessions"—the discussion of mutual concerns in more-or-less regularly scheduled leaderless group meetings—became a powerful tool for social change. The New York group Redstockings is credited with having introduced consciousness raising (CR) in the late 1960s as an American feminist version of the Chinese revolutionary practice of "speaking bitterness." It has brought women together and encouraged analyses of the interdependent relationship between self and society, the personal and the political. As noted by Catharine MacKinnon (1982):

Through consciousness raising, women grasp the collective reality of women's condition from within the perspective of that experience, not from outside it. . . . [And] women learn they have learned that men are everything, women their negation, but that the sexes are equal. (pp. 536, 542)

Almost from the very beginning, the women's movement had a dual purpose—social change on a mass scale and changes in individual lives; and the "organizational bridge between the two foci," as Naomi Rosenthal (1984) has pointed out, was consciousness raising. Among the personal consequences of CR groups is that one's perception of oneself and the social environment is never the same again. Collective action directed toward change has often followed.

An analysis of data on the outcome of CR groups (Kravetz, Marecek, & Finn, 1983) found that the most important reason for joining a group was the desire to explore women's experiences. Rose Weitz (1982) ques-

tioned a large group of women 3 months after they joined CR groups and found "a number of beneficial changes—decreased feelings of depression, isolation, helplessness, worthlessness, and self-reproach—as well as . . . increased positive attitudes towards women and feminism" (p. 237). Although largely a European-American, middle-class phenomenon at the outset, consciousness raising has also been used by working-class groups that focus more often on community problems, the need for jobs, and the desire for more education. Regardless of what brings them together, once women explore common issues and their position in society, how they relate to one another invariably changes; they share ideas with increased ease and confidence and give one another respectful attention. For example, in Carolyn Slaughter's (1985) novel *A Perfect Woman,* a man who has come unexpectedly to visit a woman and finds her among a group of friends, describes his surprise at their behavior.

They had all welcomed him. . . . They moved back to include him, but they went on talking, in a way he wasn't familiar with. They probed and pried at one another, protected, teased, laughed. But no one was in charge. No loud male voice guided the proceedings. Everyone had a turn to talk, no one dominated. (p. 102)

Most participants in CR groups would probably agree that they "fostered a sense of collective power and responsibility, political solidarity [and awareness], and sisterhood among members" (Marecek & Hare-Mustin, 1991, p. 528). Consciousness raising has been criticized by some for emphasizing personal lives, thus diverting attention and energy away from actively working for institutional changes that would benefit all women. But changes in personal attitudes and behavior are correlates of changes in culture, and pressures for social changes come from women (and men) who insist on leading fuller lives than those prescribed by the dominant gender ideology. An inventory of significant changes in the lives of members of my CR group (still intact after more than 20 years) would include decisions to work for higher degrees; the launching of a nationally known and respected women's cooperative art gallery; improved paid employment—jobs with greater responsibility and status; and participation within the larger community in political action and service to women. We have all taken greater risks and moved more assertively into the world outside of our homes. We are more confident and more responsible for our own behavior, and we perceive more options. We have experienced disappointments and frustrations, job losses, divorces, problems with children, and deaths, but also marriages, births, career changes, life-style changes, and more satisfying personal relationships and work responsibilities.

Learning from the Experience of Lesbians

Charlotte Bunch, an important feminist theorist, is reputed to have said, "no woman is truly free to be anything unless she is also free to be a lesbian." Because lesbians are women who do not orient their lives around men, they present an affront and a challenge to men and a serious threat to patriarchal institutions. Lesbianism is thus said by some to represent the essence of women's struggle against sexism. Many active feminists report having been accused by someone at some time of being a lesbian and have had that label hurled at them angrily or seen the suspicion in bitter eyes. "Cagney and Lacey," a widely acclaimed and popular television show in the 1980s about two women detectives, was altered after its first season to "soften" the main characters who, according to CBS, were too tough, hard, unfeminine, and aggressive. A spokesman for CBS was quoted as saying that the characters "were too harshly women's lib . . . more intent on fighting the system than doing police work. We perceived them as dykes" (cf. Swertlow, 1982, p. A-1).

In 1977, the representatives to the National Women's Conference in Houston voted overwhelmingly in favor of a sexual preference resolution, an event described by Anne Fleming (1977) as follows:

> The proposition passed easily and the aisles were suddenly full of women kissing each other, on the cheek, on the mouth. . . . One had to remind oneself that at least 75 percent of the women celebrating were heterosexual. They were celebrating because for that one moment, with that one vote, they knew they were better than men. (p. 33)

Approval of the lesbian rights resolution at the Houston conference was more than an affirmation of civil rights; it represented recognition by heterosexual feminists of the special place occupied by lesbians in the women's liberation movement, of the important lessons to be learned from lesbian lives and struggles, and of the absolute necessity for unity and understanding among women.

In learning from the lesbian experience, feminists have turned the spotlight on heterosexuality, questioning both the reasons for its dominance and its centrality to a patriarchal, sexist society in which men wield power over women. Charlotte Bunch, among others, called the attention of heterosexual women to the privileges they tend not to examine but to take for granted. She pointed out that heterosexual women "gain much of their social status . . . through their relationship with men . . . [which provides] legitimacy, economic security, social acceptance, legal and physical protection" (cf. Sapiro, 1990, p. 289). And Adrienne Rich (1980) argued that women experience heterosexuality as compulsory and, therefore, that it "needs to be recognized and studied as a *political institution*" (p. 637). She suggested that lesbianism be viewed as a continuum or range of woman-identified behaviors and attitudes that enhance power and include sharing, supporting, and bonding among women and resistance to marriage.

While agreeing that lesbianism represents resistance to patriarchy, some urge that its sexual core not be understated, and that explicit attention also be given to the "deeply felt eroticism of female love and friendship that has persisted for centuries" (Zita, 1981, p. 186). Still others stress the life-style aspect of lesbian identity. In an attempt to provide mutual support and empowerment, lesbian communities or networks have formed, in which women maintain a high level of political consciousness, shared values, and intimacy. From the energy generated in such communities has come a great deal of contemporary "women's culture"—music, art, and literature (Zimmerman, 1984). According to Susan Krieger (1982), lesbian communities enhance

> sense of self . . . [and] provide a haven or home in a hostile or distrusting outside world. They lend support for what is frequently a stigmatized life-style choice. They command recognition of a distinctively lesbian sensibility—a sensibility that is unusual because of the value it places on intimacy between women. (p. 91)

Lesbian communities are not immune from externally or internally generated problems, however, and Krieger has noted some of these: intolerance of individual differences, exclusion, exploitation, and demands for commitment and intimacy, all of which "*may threaten as well as support the development of individual identity*" (p. 105). As with other communities, there are variations among lesbian communities as well as among the individuals who comprise them.

The earlier medical view of lesbians as sick and perverted has finally been discredited. The search for antecedents or determinants has not uncovered a link between homosexuality and pathological parent-child relationships or evidence of any one "critical period." In fact, Evelyn Hooker (1972), who chaired the National Institute of Mental Health's Task Force on Homosexuality, concluded that "adult homosexual roles may be formed by a continuous process of social-sexual learning, from early childhood to adolescent and early adult life" (p. 13). The contemporary view based on psychological, sociological, and medical evidence, as Susan Krieger (1982) noted, is that lesbianism is

> neither a sexual nor a social disease but, rather, a life-style choice closely linked with a sense of personal identity . . . [and] a product of multiple influencers rather than . . . traceable to a single cause. Indeed, . . . [social scientists] look less at causes than at behaviors and perceptions of experience. . . . They consider lesbianism to be a matter of total personality identity . . . changeable in definition rather than as something that is a given. (pp. 93, 95)

As was mentioned in an earlier chapter, the American Psychiatric Association officially removed homosexuality from its classifications of mental illness on December 15, 1973, ending a long and bitter dispute. Five years later the U.S. surgeon general declared that homosexuality was no longer considered a mental disease or defect, and the Immigration and Naturalization Service ordered its agents to stop preventing foreign homosexuals from coming into the country ("Ban on Homosexuals," 1979). In 1975, the American Psychological Association issued an official policy statement that homosexuality does not imply "impairment in judgment, stability, reliability, or general social or vocational capabilities" (cf. Morin & Rothblum, 1991, p. 947); similar resolutions were passed by the American Sociological Association, the National Association for Mental Health, and the National Association of Social Workers. The search for genetic, hormonal, or brain differences between heterosexuals and homosexuals, however, keeps periodically resurfacing. In the 1990s, this topic is once again the subject of media attention (e.g., Emery, 1991), despite conclusions from experts in the field like John Money, whose survey of the literature led him to conclude that "you are barking up the wrong tree if you're looking for differences in hormones" (cf. Adler, 1990b).

Homosexuals typically grow up in straight, not gay, families and social environments. Lesbians and heterosexual women are socialized in a common culture and have acquired similar gender-related beliefs and ways of behaving that are reinforced and maintained by social institutions. Not surprisingly, then, research has shown few reliable differences between heterosexual women and lesbians outside the area of sexual preference. Research supports the conclusions that (a) comparisons between heterosexual and homosexual women of comparable background and social status generally indicate more similarities than differences; and (b) lesbians vary widely in background and experiences.

One study that compared lesbian and heterosexual women on perception of their parents (Johnson, Stockard, Rothbart, & Friedman, 1981) found the women to be "remarkably similar." Most of the women, regardless of sexual preference, reported that their mother was the more supportive parent—more protective, affectionate, and tolerant of expressions of anger. Lesbians did differ from heterosexual women, however, in reporting less affection, respect, and encouragement from their fathers. Andrea Oberstone and Harriet Sukoneck (1976) found no differences between a group of lesbians (recruited through referral by friends) and a comparable group of single heterosexual women on a standard measure of "total psychological adjustment" and in their responses to interview questions dealing with such items as living situation, relationships, friendship patterns, and use of drugs and alcohol. Differences were found only on items directly related to sexual orientation. All the women were European-American, single, between 20 and 45 years old, and equivalent in education and occupation. Expert judges were not able to find any distinctively lesbian characteristics that would differentiate the personality profiles of homosexual women from others, but the lesbians reported greater satisfaction in their relationships and vocations than the heterosexual women. Both groups had had very similar heterosexual experiences, but at some point the lesbians appeared to have made a choice that was not related to seduction or any other distinctive single event. Another group of investigators (Cardell, Finn, & Marecek, 1981) found that lesbians describe themselves in a less sex-typed and stereotyped way with regard to personality attributes than gay men or heterosexuals of either gender.

If lesbians are generally similar to heterosexual women of similar background, they are also, like heterosexual women, a very diverse group. For example, Brenda Vance and Vicki Green (1984) interviewed 43 predominantly European-American, well-educated, self-defined lesbians and concluded that the participants were "a very heterogeneous group, with divergent backgrounds, divergent sexual and social experiences, and divergent avenues of identifying and defining themselves as 'lesbian'" (p. 306). Sophie Loewenstein's (1978) clinical observations and research led her to a similar conclusion. Lesbians, like heterosexual women, she wrote,

> are extremely diverse in personality, family constellation and developmental experiences and categorizing them as a group becomes as meaningless as categorizing all hetero-

sexual women would be. Stereotypes of lesbians as man-haters, as obsessed with sex, as immature, as masculine or aggressive apply to some lesbians (as well as to some heterosexual women) while they are false for others. (pp. 8f.)

According to Judy Klemesrud (1971), the membership of the New York City chapter of the Daughters of Bilitis, a lesbian organization, included "college professors, scientists, unemployed women on welfare, editors, singers, actresses, secretaries, students, doctors, nurses, certified public accountants, housewives, and city employees."

While there is as much diversity and individual variability among lesbians as among heterosexual women, in couple relationships lesbians have been found to behave with more flexibility, cooperation, and equal sharing of responsibility and power; these studies were discussed in the chapter on relationships. As is true among heterosexual couples, however, among lesbian couples where equal power is the ideal, for those who do not achieve it inequality has been found to be associated with less satisfaction in the relationship (Caldwell & Peplau, 1984). Others (Schullo & Alperson, 1984) have found "no evidence that the underlying dynamics of heterosexual and homosexual relationships are different" (p. 1000).

It is estimated that there are anywhere from 6 to 13 million lesbians in the United States, living in rural and urban communities all across the country (Henry, 1990), among whom about 1.5 million are mothers. Yet lesbians who are "out" (and gay men) continue to be discriminated against in employment and housing, and to experience serious negative personal and social consequences. More than 85 cities and 6 states (Connecticut, Hawaii, Massachusetts, New Jersey, Vermont, and Wisconsin) provide formal legal guarantees of equal protection and nondiscrimination (Noble, 1992), but Congress has thus far failed to pass federal civil rights legislation for lesbians and gay men. An amendment to the Civil Rights Act of 1964 that would extend its prohibitions and protect lesbians and gay men from discrimination in housing and employment was first introduced in 1976, but has not yet gained sufficient support to be passed (Morin & Rothblum, 1991). Thus, cities like Dallas, Texas, can continue legally banning homosexuals from working in their police departments ("Deep in the Heart," 1992), and the Georgia attorney general can fire a highly competent lesbian attorney in his office after learning that she planned to marry her lover in a private religious ceremony (Harlow, 1991–1992).

The expectation that lesbians must lose custody of their children following divorce is being challenged, as are the assumptions that lesbians are uninterested in their children or poor mothers or that their children will suffer ill effects. Still, in custody cases in which one parent's sexual preference is raised as an issue, the homosexual parent is likely to lose. Sometimes the loss of custody is accompanied by reduction of visiting rights or the stipulation that a third party of the other gender must always be present during visits. In one case, a Pennsylvania appeals court ruled against a lesbian mother and upheld the principle that homosexuality can be used against a parent in determining the custody of children ("Homosexuality Held a Bar," 1985). To help lesbian mothers assert their legal rights in custody cases, a group called CALM (Custody Action for Lesbian Mothers) currently offers legal counseling and psychological support. Another nonprofit legal group, Lambda, assists lesbians and gay men in asserting their civil rights in all areas and the right of couples to be recognized as a family and to enjoy the benefits of health insurance coverage, child custody, and adoption rights (Lambda, n.d.).

Children in the 1990s are learning that some have one mother, or one father, or one of each, or two dads or two moms, like the young boy in the photograph on p. 334. At the same time, as Lindsy Van Gelder (1992) noted, the concept of a lesbian mother is still far from acceptable. One example she presented is that of a school board in New York City that "banned all references to gay parents from the curriculum on the grounds that such things are 'not appropriate' for children" (p. 94). Yet research indicates that children raised by homosexual parents do not differ from children raised in more conventional family settings with respect to sexual identity, behavior, or preferences (Green, 1978). One 1989 study found that the only way lesbian parents differ from straight parents is in using less physical punishment and more reasoning in disciplining their children (cf. Van Gelder, 1992).

It is clearly homophobia or heterosexism, and not homosexuality, that is dangerous to society and hurtful to individuals. Lesbians are discriminated against in the legal system, the workplace, and the community. Martin Levine and Robin Leonard (1984) reported from a review of the literature that the vast majority of lesbians hide their sexual preference from employers and that 10 to 12 percent have been asked to resign or have been fired after disclosure. From their own research in New York City, Levine and Leonard concluded that "employment discrimination is a serious problem" (p. 705). One fourth of the lesbians studied reported discrimination in salary or promotions, verbal harassment, or some combination of these; 29 percent had not been hired or had been fired because they

Proud lesbian moms and their son. (Photograph by Cynthia Johnson/Time Magazine.)

were known to be lesbians; 77 percent were "closeted" on the job; and 27 percent were closeted to everyone. According to Randy Shilts (1993), although all women in the military experience discrimination and harassment, lesbians suffer the most cruel treatment. They have been subjected to coercive tactics to "confess" their homosexuality and expelled from the armed services at far higher rates than gay men.

To counter heterosexist attitudes and behaviors, lesbians and gay men have joined forces for active community organizing, Gay Pride marches and other demonstrations, and lobbying to demand equal rights in housing, employment, and all areas of social, political, and economic life. In addition, some national organizations have begun to educate their members. For example, the Boston chapter of NOW published a handbook designed to combat prejudice against lesbians and to help members understand the significance of "heterosexual privilege" (*Lesbians: A Consciousness Raising Kit,* 1980). A new division (Division 44) devoted to the psychological study of lesbian and gay issues is now part of the American Psychological Association. And, at the 1980 national

meetings of the American Association for the Advancement of Science, the National Organization of Lesbian and Gay Scientists was formed to communicate "with . . . heterosexual colleagues, and with society-at-large, about the effects of homophobia on their well-being" (Escoffier, Malyon, Morin, & Raphael, 1980, p. 340).

Learning from Prostitutes and Women in Prison

One consequence of consciousness raising is the discovery by middle-class women of their commonalities with other women who differ from them in income, background, and experience. For example, there is similarity in the motivations of prostitutes and other women, and we can empathize with women for whom sex provides employment. As pointed out by Christine Overall (1992),

> Prostitution is a commercial enterprise, and evidence strongly suggests that the women who engage in it do so primarily, and often exclusively, for economic gain. . . . Yet female cooks, secretaries, and university professors also sell their labor power, and for many of them economic

gain may be their chief or only motive. . . . Why then should prostitution be considered morally any worse than cooking, secretarial service, or professorial work? (p. 709)

Others have argued that, in addition to the shared economic motive of all working women, being treated as a sexual object by men, and exchanging sex for favors of various kinds, is not unique to one class of women. Nineteenth-century Victorian feminists, too, apparently understood that the bond linking prostitutes with all other women was men's attitudes and their view of women "as sexual objects to be bought and sold" (Walkowitz, 1980, p. 125). And contemporary women can both laugh and cry at a joke told by stand-up comic Elayne Boosler that goes like this: "Hookers! How do they do it? How could any woman sleep with a man without having a dinner and a movie first?" (cf. Berger, 1984, p. 38).

For an ordinary woman to be treated in ways similar to a prostitute is not unusual. Ellen Strong (1970), an ex-hooker, has argued persuasively that most adolescent girls learn "the basic principle of hustling"—that one can exchange what men want (sex) for what women want (attention, gifts, security). Many women experience some pressure at some time to take part in such an exchange. Sex, we are told, is something we can "give" to lovers or husbands in order to make them happy and satisfied; in return we will be rewarded by harmony, good treatment, or other special expressions of gratitude. In a work by Kate Millett (1971), "J" tells the following story:

> [Miles] Davis was playing in a club, and someone outside wanted to take me . . . asked me if I wanted to go in. And I knew that if I went in with him I'd have to sleep with him. But I figured it was worth it; I wanted to see Miles Davis. I had no feeling for this guy; I just wanted the ticket to get in there. I realized I'd whored—there was no way of denying the truth to myself. So when the time came a few years later and I was absolutely broke, I was ready. (p. 24)

Such an exchange, offered by many men, although not universally accepted, is not an unusual experience for women across diverse social categories. Priscilla Alexander (cf. Anthony, 1992) has told about being a student at a small and very elite college in Vermont where women wait to be picked up randomly by fraternity men from nearby colleges. Similar stories by college women are not uncommon.

The geisha of Japan, like the hetairai of ancient Athens, were women who were set apart from others in order to provide special attention and entertainment for men of wealth and high position. These women, versed in the arts

of love and conversation, who were also talented and specially educated musicians, poets, or dancers, were regarded not with disrespect but with some awe. Geisha lived in separate communities and typically taught their daughters the elegant and artful behaviors they had learned. There are stories of geisha who were brilliant confidantes of, and advisors to, powerful and influential men of state and industry. Some contemporary women begin a life of prostitution with the illusion that, like the courtesans of old, such a life brings glamour and independence from a husband. But invariably and inevitably, the realities of prostitution override the illusion and promise of good times and easy money. Most women who have talked about their experiences tell much the same story of alienation, self-hatred, and increased hostility toward men. Prostitutes are abused and exploited by pimps, roughed up and victimized by their clients and the police, and taken advantage of by hotel operators, lawyers, pornographers, and organized crime. It is the rare prostitute who can live like the romanticized courtesans of old, who can survive and flourish and sometimes even work herself out of the business.

Gail Sheehy (1974) spent 2 years exploring the world of prostitution in New York and concluded that a streetwalker rarely sees more than 5 percent of her earnings; the rest goes primarily to a pimp, for police or gangster protection, and to pay court fines. A study of street prostitutes in San Francisco cited by Kathleen Barry (1979) found that they had begun the life at an average age of 17, and that 63 percent had been runaways. Prior to prostitution, 80 percent had been victims of physical or sexual abuse; 37 percent had been victims of incest. The vast majority were working for pimps and had no savings. Another study cited by Barry found that 67 percent of a group of interviewed prostitutes had been seriously injured by customers. She concluded that "life in the brothel is not plush, erotic excitement" (p. 116). A study of 100 San Francisco prostitutes (cf. "Not Victimless," 1980) reported that nearly half were under 16 years old; most were from middle-class backgrounds; more than half had been victims of incest or sexual abuse; and 70 percent had been raped in an incident unrelated to their work.

Jane Anthony (1992), an ex-prostitute, considers prostitution a "cornerstone of patriarchy" and has argued movingly against the notion that it is simply a job freely chosen by a woman. She disagrees strongly with those who defend commercial sex and with those who believe that "women exploited and abused by not one but many men for the sake of economic survival are making a 'real choice'" (p. 86). Most prostitutes, she points out, make this "choice" after having suffered previous sexual abuse, and as a way out of poverty. Although Anthony, too, felt "empowered" when she turned her first trick, she soon lost this illusion and reports still finding herself in vulnerable moments "living with the ghost of prostitution—the sense of being nonhuman" (p. 87).

When feminists express empathy for, or solidarity with, prostitutes, the intent is not to romanticize this so-called "oldest profession" but to emphasize women's common experiences. Both the paid whore and the average woman are sexually exploited in a society that promotes the image of women as servicers of men. The prostitute magnifies one facet of our culture's picture of women and symbolizes women's exploitation and role in society. Christine Overall (1992), has answered the question "What's wrong with prostitution?" as follows:

> Prostitution epitomizes male dominance: it is a practice that is constructed by and reinforces male supremacy, which both creates and legitimizes the "needs" that prostitution appears to satisfy . . . . (p. 724)

The prostitute is often the target of hostility. It is she—rarely her customer—who is derided, arrested, and liable to a fine, a jail sentence, and a police record. The infamous Jack the Ripper murdered prostitutes in London's streets a century ago, and the preying on prostitutes by serial killers is too often repeated in today's cities and towns. Male police officers, also, have long considered prostitutes fair game for mauling and sexual abuse. Society's harassment of prostitutes and benign neglect of their customers and pimps is the focus of a report by Arlene Carmen and Howard Moody (1985), who spent 8 years talking to street prostitutes in Manhattan.

The American Psychological Association's Division on the Psychology of Women approved a resolution calling for the decriminalization and destigmatization of prostitution ("Resolution For," 1984). The resolution argues that women and people of color are discriminated against in enforcement of antiprostitution laws, and that stigmatization of prostitution jeopardizes the prostitute's physical and mental well-being. By decriminalizing and destigmatizing prostitution, the intent is to reduce the victimization of women who are currently doubly oppressed and humiliated, by their customers *and* by the justice system.

Discrimination against women by the justice system is also illustrated by its treatment of juvenile offenders, among whom far more girls than boys get in trouble with the law for sex offenses. These sex offenses are usually the basis of a formal charge of being a "runaway" or

"intractable." Rosemary Sarri (cf. "Girls Are Different," 1977) found that girls are frequently (but boys are never) charged with promiscuity. Furthermore, once arrested, girls receive tougher penalties. According to Kenneth Wooden (1976), a study of 722 juvenile institutions found that two thirds of the girls, compared with one third of the boys, were imprisoned for "status offenses"—offenses that are not considered crimes when committed by adults, such as promiscuity and running away. Many of the girls became runaways because they were escaping from the sexual advances of male relatives. Wooden concluded that while boys often received harsh and brutal treatment, the girls suffered greater psychological abuse, received less food, poorer education, and were subjected to vaginal examinations for venereal disease "with outrageous frequency."

As of the end of the 1980s, there were 90,000 women in state and federal prisons, three times more than at the beginning of the decade (Applebome, 1992). Thus, women's share of the prison population has been rising, from about 3 percent in 1981 to the present 6 percent (Harris, 1993). A study of Michigan prisons (cf. "Society's Losers," 1981) found that the women inmates typically came from poor families, were unskilled with little education, and often had a history of mental problems or drug addiction. More than half were minority women; and the major offenses for which the women were sent to jail were larceny, forgery, drug offenses, or prostitution. Most state prisons would yield a similar picture. The large increase in women's incarceration in the 1980s is attributed by the experts to drugs. "About 60% of all women in federal prisons have been convicted of drug-related offenses . . . [and] many other crimes—theft, prostitution, armed robbery—are also drug related" (Church, 1990, p. 20).

As in the world outside of jail, incarceration is not an equivalent experience for women and for men. Rosemary Sarri concluded that "women who commit serious crimes usually are given the same penalties as men . . . [but those] convicted of less severe crimes, such as shoplifting, drug use . . . and fraud, sometimes are given stiffer sentences" (cf. Barclay, 1984, p. A-6). Inside prison, women and men are treated differently, to the disadvantage of women. Suzanne Sobel (1982) noted that while women's prisons are generally more physically attractive, in rural areas, and without concrete walls and gun towers, they are also more punitive. In many state prisons, more petty restrictions are imposed on women, and they can earn fewer privileges than men. In addition to being punishment-oriented, women's prisons provide inadequate medical and psychological or counseling services, and in general "lack the opportunities for vocational, educational, social, and personal development that are present in many prisons for male offenders" (Sobel, 1982, p. 108). One study cited by Sobel reported that the average women's prison offers 2.7 vocational programs compared to 10 offered for men. The programs for women are typically limited to cosmetology, clerical training, food services, or nurse's aide, whereas male inmates are often able to obtain training in "more lucrative trades, such as plumbing, auto repair and electrical work" (Barclay, 1984, p. A-6). There was little change in this situation during the 1980s.

> While male lockups may train inmates for such high-paying trades as welding and mechanics, courses in women's facilities still concentrate on homemaking or low-paid skills like beautician and launderer. . . . Too often a woman leaves prison even less equipped to earn an honest living than her male counterpart. [And] health care, or the lack of it, is a crisis in some women's prisons. . . . Pregnant inmates typically get little or no prenatal care, though many are drug abusers with a high risk of medical complications. (Church, 1990, p. 21)

Women inmates are more likely than men to be parents and have custody of their children. About 75 percent of women in state and federal prisons are parents (Applebome, 1992), and separation from their children, they say, is their harshest punishment. According to Jean Harris (1993), about 9 percent of incarcerated women give birth in prison. The children must be left with relatives, placed in foster care, or put up for adoption, and they rarely visit. "Women's prisons, like those for men, are often all but inaccessible by public transportation. When children do manage to get there, the sessions can be heartrending" (Church, 1990, p. 21). Only some institutions have pleasant visiting rooms for children; a small number allow babies born to prisoners to stay with their mothers for a year; and some have parenting and children's outreach programs, many run by private organizations. Only New York State permits infants to stay with their mothers in a prison nursery until they reach their first birthday or, if parole is expected within that time, until the infant is 18 months (Harris, 1993).

Because of the gender inequities in our prison system, some groups of incarcerated women have filed sex discrimination suits in federal courts. As a result of one decision, Kentucky's state prison for women instituted a unique program to provide eligible women an opportunity to learn to be truck drivers (Kash, 1984a). The success of this program in training and job placement illustrates the many possibilities for improving the lives of imprisoned women and increasing the probability of a dignified and responsible return to their communities. This new approach to the treatment of imprisoned women is a direct consequence of social action encouraged by the women's movement and its insistence that women identify with one another and appreciate the special problems of particular groups.

Learning from Minority Women and Working-Class Women

For women differing in special circumstances, skin color, sexual orientation, social class, or ethnic background to understand one another and to see the similarity in our relationships to men has not been easy. Articulate minority women like Shirley Chisholm (the first African-American woman to serve in Congress, elected in 1968) have been in the forefront of the women's liberation movement, but some critics have noted important differences between the immediate concerns of the average African-American woman and those of European-American, middle-class women. According to Julianne Malveaux (1985), for example, "since black women head 42% of black households, the distribution of income, not the distribution of housework, is a more critical issue for black women" (p. 27). African-American women face discrimination in jobs, access to public services, health care, and housing, and have "virtually no power" in mainstream public institutions (Taylor & Smitherman-Donaldson, 1989). According to Wilhelmina Leigh (1989), housing discrimination, although outlawed two decades ago, remains in its subtle forms "the major form of discrimination that confronts black women today" (p. 82). And, regardless of color or ethnicity, some concerns of working-class women differ sharply from those of more affluent women. For example, working-class urban women see urban planning as an issue that directly affects them and their families. They have "become increasingly more active in community issues and self-help movements to improve living conditions related to housing, child care, food cooperatives, and neighborhood planning . . . in tenant organizing and rent strikes" (Wekerle, 1980, p. S211). As noted by Marilyn Gittell and Nancy Naples (1982), and others, the women's movement is seen by many working-class women as having failed to understand the significance of "the barriers to education and employment faced by minority and low-income women" (p. 25).

Distrust of middle-class European-American women may be found especially among poor women of color who have cooked the meals and cleaned the toilets in European-American homes. "It is a source of amusement . . . to black women to listen to [white] feminists talk of liberation while somebody's nice black grandmother shoulders daily responsibility of child rearing and floor mopping" (Morrison, 1971, p. 64). Just as heterosexuality is associated with greater privilege in our society, so too is white skin and middle-class status. As pointed out by Aida Hurtado (1989), "the avenues of advancement through marriage that are open to white women who conform to prescribed standards of middle-class femininity are not even a theoretical possibility for most women of color" (pp. 842f.). European-American women's privileges give many of them access to better incomes and social positions through marriage than they would have on their own; it is only when such previously privileged women lose their spouses through divorce or death that they can appreciate the position of the women who do not have access to an income other than their own (Palmer, 1983).

In a novel by Gail Godwin (1982), Azalea, an African-American housekeeper, leaves her own home to come to live with her longtime European-American employer, Theodora, since they are both alone and aging. Theodora remarks:

> "The old order changes, Azalea. Why look at us. Who would ever have thought you and I'd be coughing each other to sleep on the opposite sides of our wall?" Azalea gave Theodora a level look . . . "You know and I know there's still that wall." (p. 580)

Thus, some feminists have challenged the meaning of the word *women,* arguing, like Chela Sandoval (1984)

> that it is impossible to utter the word . . . as if it holds some common, unified meaning. Every woman is subject to . . . desires, values, and meanings that have been shaped—not only by her experiences of sexuality and gender—but by her particular experience of the intersections of race, culture, and class. (p. 728)

Nevertheless, unity among women is considered essential if sexism, experienced across ethnicities and social class, is to be effectively challenged. Unity is regarded as attainable, even among those who are most passionate in raising the issues of class and ethnic diversity, if it is based on respect for differences, recognition of common objectives, and appreciation of within-group heterogeneity. Most women of color, for example, do not

believe that it is necessary to stand several steps behind their men in order to advance the movement for civil rights and the elimination of discrimination. Barbara Smith (1985) has eloquently articulated the position of contemporary African-American feminists as follows:

> Denying that sexual oppression exists or requiring that we wait to bring it up until racism, or in some cases capitalism, is toppled, is a bankrupt position. A Black feminist perspective has no use for ranking oppressions. . . . The feminist movement and the anti-racist movement have in common trying to insure decent human life. . . . Until Black feminism, very few people besides Black women actually cared about or took seriously the demoralization of being female and colored and poor and hated. (pp. 6, 9)

At the same time, African-American women, as is true of other women, are not all the same in life-style and circumstances, in social class, religion, values, or interests. According to Julianne Malveaux (1985), this heterogeneity tends not to be appreciated, but is instead presented by the media as an apparent contradiction.

> We black women are considered "twofers." . . . On one hand, we are superwomen who manage both child and career. On the other hand, we represent a good number of the pregnant teens who "cause" long-term social problems. On one hand, we are castrating "bitches" who emasculate our men, oppress them with our strength. On the other hand, we are lonely ladies, facing ten-to-one odds in finding a man. (p. 27)

Pamela Reid (1984) has argued that African-American women in general, who have long functioned competently both within their families and in the work force, are good role models for young women of all ethnic backgrounds. What young woman can fail to be inspired, for example, by this poem by Gloria Gayles (1979, pp. 363f.)?

> *black sturdy shoulders*
> *we are monuments that refuse to crumble*
> *deep-rooted oaks from which the generations*
> *like thick-leaved branches grow and thrive*
> *we are the strong ones*
> *having balanced the weight of the tribe*
> *having made our planting as deep as anyman's*
>
> *and yet*
> *as women*
> *we have known only meager harvests*
> *we sing strong songs*
> *and the world hums a sweet lullaby*
> *we write rich poems*
> *and the world offers muted applause*

for a jingling rhyme
sometimes
as women only
do we weep
we are brought to whisper
when we wish to scream
assent
when we wish to defy
dance pretty
    (on tiptoe)
when we would raise circles of dust
before the charge

It is instructive that national polls indicate that African-American women tend to support feminist goals and that most descriptions of their own lives stress the role that work has played in promoting independence and autonomy (despite the underuse of their skills in low-status, low-paying jobs). As noted by Deborah King (1988),

> African-American women have been prime movers in both community life and liberation politics—from Sojourner Truth and Harriet Tubman during slavery to Ida Wells Barnett, who led the fight against lynching, to Fannie Lou Hamer and Rosa Parks of the civil rights movement. We founded schools, operated social welfare services, sustained churches, organized collective work groups and unions, and . . . established banks and commercial enterprises. . . . We were the back bone of racial uplift, and we also played critical roles in the struggles for racial justice. (p. 54)

While recognizing the need for cross-ethnic alliances, women of color are demanding their fair share of power within the women's liberation movement, and are resisting having their priorities set by others. "Feminist women of color have spent their energies counteracting racism and sexism and reaffirming their multiple identities. . . . Thus, women of color's feminism may take a different shade" (Comas-Diaz, 1991, p. 600). This "different shade" has been termed "womanist" by Alice Walker (1983) and others in order to underscore the "peculiar burden" of a woman of color who "is deprived of her rights by sexist attitudes" in her own community, "the domestic domain, and by Euro-American patriarchy in the public sphere," and who must be "concerned with the ethics of surviving rather than the aesthetics of living" (Ogunyemi, 1985, p. 79). Many have written about the lives and consciousness of women of color in terms of a triple jeopardy—racism, sexism, and classism. Deborah King (1988), for example, argues that the conditions of African-American women's lives and their history of resisting oppression have made them "feminists since the early 1800s" (p. 70). She notes

Activist Angela Davis. (Photograph by AP/Wide World Photos.)

that the hallmark of "black feminist thought" is the "necessity of addressing all oppressions. . . . The dual and systematic discrimination of racism and sexism [which] remain pervasive, and, for many, class inequality [that] compounds these oppressions" (p. 43).

Pictured above, Angela Davis (1982), in a speech before the National Women's Studies Association, emphasized that "women's issues . . . must revolve, first of all, around the majority of women and those women who have the most to gain: working-class women and women of color" (p. 7). Such words have been taken seriously, and issues of special concern to working-class women and to women of color appear more and more to be priorities in the U.S. women's movement. As Lillian Comas-Diaz (1991) noted,

> presently, women of color are participating in crafting the feminist agenda. Some of the most prominent include

Mary Berry and Patsy Mink in education and civil rights, Shirley Chisholm and Barbara Jordan in employment and civil rights, and Faye Wattleton in reproductive rights, among others. (p. 600)

She argues that feminist women of color are *"the other's other."* Just as women have been typically defined in reference to men (as pointed out by Simone de Beauvoir in 1961), women of color have been defined in reference to European-American women. An advantage of being an outsider, however, is that it "affords a different perspective and a clearer vision" (p. 606) and encourages the questioning of definitions, universal, and general conclusions.

Along with African-American women, Latina, Asian-American, and Native American women have been demanding recognition, respect, appreciation, and special attention to their particular problems. Maxine Zinn (1982) has pointed out that Mexican-American women have been misrepresented as long-suffering, simple women, dependent upon insecure macho men. But careful study suggests that, like other women, "Chicanas can be active, adaptive human beings despite their subordination" (p. 260) and that their oppression is a function not only of cultural tradition but of contemporary institutional discrimination that excludes them from public life. Similarly, Rayna Green (1980) has argued that our picture of the lives of Native American women is unrealistic and unclear. Indian women must be seen within the context of Native American life, in which they are largely responsible for maintaining "the resilient intratribal and pan-Indian networks . . . on and off reservation, networks which keep migratory and urban Indians working, educated and in touch with their Indian identities" (p. 266). Native American women have been writing eloquently about their lives, as in Louise Erdrich's (1984, 1987) novels, *Love Medicine* and *The Beet Queen*, and the poetry and fiction of others (cf. Green, 1984). Correcting misrepresentations about Asian-American women has also been a feminist objective (e.g., Cheng, 1984; Kingston, 1977; Kumagai, 1978; Tan, 1991a), and we are learning that traditions of women warriors exist side by side with expectations of docility and deference to men.

Jewish feminists (e.g., Pogrebin, 1982b; Scheinmann, 1981) have been calling attention to the existence of deeply rooted anti-Jewish attitudes and stereotyped beliefs among other women. Special issues and problems salient for Jewish feminists are discussed in the magazine *Lilith,* named for Eve's legendary predecessor who insisted on equality with Adam. According to Susan Schneider (1984), the women's movement has been powerfully served by the energy of Jewish women who tend to identify strongly with feminist goals.

Thus, the message emanating from all the separately identifiable groups within the women's movement is largely the same. Each seems to be saying, "Respect where we have come from; recognize our special needs; guard against the negative stereotypes you have learned; and welcome our contributions and leadership." Diversity presents challenges that enhance strength as women move toward solving shared and specific problems.

MOVING FORWARD

Women can answer Freud's question—we know what we want. We may apply different labels to our positions and come from different backgrounds, but our agenda for the 1990s and beyond is one on which most women will agree.

Equality under the Law and Access to the Public Arena

Women want equal opportunities and treatment in employment, education, and all aspects of social and political life; we support the need for affirmative action to help redress the negative consequences of past discrimination. Women's efforts in the United States to clarify our status and extend our legal rights are not new. Proposals for equal rights

> extend historically from 1776 and Abigail Adams' famous letter to her husband at the Second Continental Congress admonishing lawmakers to "Remember the Ladies" to present-day efforts to add an Equal Rights Amendment to the Constitution. In the nineteenth century, an attempt was made to include equality for women in the Fourteenth Amendment, which had been designed to guarantee rights and privileges to newly liberated black males. . . . In 1878, an amendment was proposed specifically affirming the right of women to vote, which became the "Suffrage" or Nineteenth Amendment upon ratification in 1920. (Gladstone, 1991, p. 2)

The first vote of the first woman in Congress (prior to passage of the 19th Amendment) was cast on April 6, 1917, by a Montana legislator, Jeannette Rankin, who voted against U.S. involvement in World War I, saying,

"We cannot settle disputes by eliminating human beings" (cf. McCarthy, 1991, p. C-21).

In more recent times, women's efforts to achieve equality in the public sphere are exemplified by our work on behalf of the Equal Rights Amendment (ERA). This amendment, proposed as the 27th to the U.S. Constitution, was written by Alice Paul for the National Women's Party and was first introduced in the Congress in 1923. When it was reintroduced after World War II, it was twice passed by the Senate, but the House Judiciary Committee refused to hold hearings on it. In 1967, "a stubborn Paul, then 82, persuaded the National Organization for Women to endorse the amendment" (Toufexis, 1982, p. 32), and the modern campaign began. The ERA was finally passed by both houses of Congress in 1972, and a 7-year deadline was set for ratification. Section 1 of the ERA states clearly and simply that "equality of rights under the law shall not be denied or abridged by the United States or by any state on account of sex." Section 2 gives Congress the power to enforce the provisions, and Section 3 specifies that they will take effect 2 years after ratification. "In 1978, when it had been approved by 35 states, three less than the necessary three-quarters (38), Congress voted to extend the deadline. No additional states voted for ratification . . . , however, and the measure died on June 30, 1982" (Gladstone, 1991, p. 2).

That the effort to ratify the ERA failed is a shocking lesson in U.S. politics, since national polls consistently favored its adoption (Katzenstein, 1984) and it had been endorsed by all presidents, from Eisenhower through Carter, and by 450 national, religious, labor, civic, and educational groups "from the AFL-CIO to the Y.M.C.A." (Toufexis, 1982, p. 32). Ronald Reagan was the first of the recent presidents to oppose ratification. The failure in the United States to gain a constitutional endorsement of women's rights contrasts sharply with success in Canada where, in 1981, a new constitution was approved that includes an explicit guarantee of gender equality under the law.

Failure to win approval of the ERA has been a disappointment to the U.S. women's movement and has stimulated reanalysis and reassessment of strategies. Some believe that one lesson to be learned is the importance of direct dialogue with legislators and the necessity of more active participation in the electoral process. Others point to a more fundamental problem, the ever-present tension in our society between women's roles as mothers and as citizens.

Although the results of national surveys indicated that the majority of Americans of both genders favored the objectives of ERA, one significant problem was that many people did not understand just what the ERA was. Some people who said they disapproved of the ERA indicated by their responses to other questions that they actually supported its aims. For example, Marsha Jacobson (1983) found that college students presented with the actual text of the amendment indicated significantly greater approval of it and fewer negative misconceptions about its meaning and probable consequences than students presented just with the title. Another striking example is provided by a study (Bers & Mezey, 1981) of more than 200 women leaders of community organizations in a suburban area outside of Chicago. The researchers found that "although 98 percent agree that 'the U.S. and individual states should not deny any person his or her rights on account of the person's sex,' only 50.9 percent agree that the ERA should be ratified" (p. 740). Thus, some people who endorsed the words of the amendment did not realize that this was the way the ERA was written.

In 1984, Geraldine Ferraro was the first woman nominated for a high office by a major political party and the first woman who stood a real chance of winning. Among Ferraro's predecessors were Belva Lockwood, who ran for president in 1884 and 1888, and Victoria Woodhull, who ran in 1892, both on the Equal Rights Party ticket; Angela Davis, who ran for vice president on the Communist Party ticket in 1984; and Sonia Johnson, who ran for President on the Citizen's Party ticket in 1984. Margaret Chase Smith was among the Republican Party's nominees for president at the GOP convention in 1964, and Shirley Chisholm was a candidate in 1978 for the Democratic Party's presidential nomination.

For generations, women have run duplicating machines, stuffed envelopes, made telephone calls, written speeches, planned strategy, and brewed coffee for male colleagues who ran for political office. Women in the 1990s are emerging more and more from behind the scenes and putting energy and knowledge to use for our own political advantage. In an earlier chapter we talked about the large number of women who ran for office in the 1992 national elections and the resulting significant gain in women's representation.

A lack of funds has historically hampered women in their pursuit of political office. A research group at Rutgers University reported that in 1984 there were 20 political action committees whose primary goal was the election of women to U.S. political office. But such committees were too few to effectively counter the typical denial of funds to women by established sources. As simply put by the political director of the Democratic National

Committee, "the three biggest obstacles for women candidates . . . [are] money, money and money" (cf. "PACs Give Women," 1984, p. A-14). To counteract the limited financial backing typically given to women candidates, women have organized their own networks. Emily's List is a national fundraising group that supports Democratic women candidates. "'Emily' stands for 'Early Money Is Like Yeast.' The idea is that 'it makes the dough rise'—that early money makes for a stronger start and, in the long run, a better organized, better financed campaign" (McKay, 1992, p. A-3). Part of women's success in the 1992 elections is attributed to the financial support provided by Emily's List.

Affirmative action programs in business, industry, government, and education have made women more visible and enabled us to demonstrate our competence. Our creativity and effectiveness has been shown in all areas—from accounting and the arts to zoology and zoning, in religion, science, management, the professions, skilled hard-hat labor, and sports. Women's competent presence in the mass media, the worlds of commerce, national affairs, entertainment, law enforcement, production, and service is due to women's own efforts; as this presence is observed and reflected upon, it has the further consequence of changing attitudes, beliefs, and expectations. For example, a longitudinal study of 1,200 European-American women interviewed four times between 1962 and 1977 indicated that there had been "a dramatic increase in . . . liberal attitudes about appropriate roles for men and women in the home and at work" ("Fifteen-Year Study," 1980, p. 3). In 1977, two thirds of the respondents disagreed that most of the important family decisions should be made by the "man of the house," compared with just under one third in 1962. While egalitarian attitudes were most likely to be expressed by younger, more educated women and those in the work force, the researchers concluded that all women had been affected by the social changes of the 1960s and 70s. Other studies support this conclusion.

A special issue of *Time* in 1990, devoted to women, highlighted the accomplishments of 10 women in very diverse fields: an AIDS activist, baseball club owner, bishop, choreographer, fashion tycoon, Indian chief, police chief, rap artist, rock climber, and saxophonist (the photographs of 3 of these women are on p. 343). It is the accomplishments of such women and others that constitutes the good news for women in the 1990s. Jackie Joyner-Kersee, shown on p. 344, was the first woman to win a second consecutive gold medal in the seven event heptathlon competition. Women still have a long way to go, however, in our quest for equality and a more humane society. As Barbara Ehrenreich (1990) argued,

> To a certain extent, women have "won." In medicine, law and management, they have increased their participation by 300% to 400% since the early '70s. . . . for all the pioneering that brave and ambitious women have done, the female majority remains outside, earning 70¢ to man's $1 in stereotypically female jobs. That female majority must still find a way to survive the uncaring institutions, the exploitative employers and the deep social inequities the successful few have not yet got around to challenging. (p. 15)

According to the U.S. Labor Department, in 1990 the top 10 jobs for women were precisely the same as in 1940, except that the occupation of maid has dropped off the list ("Little Progress," 1992). In 1990, the most common jobs held by women were in waitressing, retail sales, teaching, and nursing. Women earn 74 cents for every dollar earned by men, get about half of what men do when they rehire and, according to a report by Ralph Nader's Center for Responsive Law, "are consistently charged more than men for cars, haircuts, clothes, etc." (Roe, 1993, p. A-15).

Other bad news for women in the workplace includes the continued prevalence of sexual harassment. In the 1990s, however, such mistreatment of women is recognized and deplored by many—at least in public forums. For example, the Armed Services Committee of the House of Representatives held a hearing on "gender discrimination" in July 1992, to which it invited personal testimony from the chiefs of the four military branches. Each "was called on to recite the steps he was taking to end discrimination against and harassment of women in the services" (Gordon, 1992). The step none of them was yet prepared to take was to permit women to be eligible for combat roles, seen by many as necessary to counter women's "second-class status that invites harassment" (Schmitt, 1992, p. E-3). Less than a year later, however, "Defense Secretary Les Aspin ordered all the services to remove restrictions on women flying combat aircraft and said he would ask Congress to lift the ban on women serving aboard warships at sea" (Nelan, 1993, p. 38).

Women's desires for legal, political, and social equity; for respectful admission to all the ways of making a living; and for access to resources necessary for a good life may seem eminently fair and reasonable to some of us, but they appear to be a source of distress for others. For example, critics have commented on the many television and movie dramas in the early 1990s that presented a strange portrait

Indian Chief Wilma Mankiller.
(Photograph by Gwendolen Cates.)

Bishop Barbara Harris. (Photograph by UPI/Bettman.)

Saxophonist Jane Ira Bloom. (Photograph by Amy Etra.)

Olympic gold medalist Jackie Joyner-Kersee. (Photograph by Reuters/Bettmann.)

of women: as menacing, psychopathic, deadly she-devils, or as cringing, pitiable, helpless victims. "Could it be," asked John Martin (1991, p. C-5), "that the men who make television are having their revenge against competent women who are rising through the power circuits of our society?" Or, have TV and movie producers concluded, as Harry Waters (1991b, p. 74) suggested, that "what today's woman wants . . . is to watch other women suffer." I do not believe this desire would emerge high on a list of women's current priorities.

An End to Our Exploitation as Sex Objects

The idea that women exist "for the use and appreciation of men" (Greer, 1970) has had a strong hold on the consciousness of both genders. Very likely, visitors from another planet would still reach the same conclusion in

the early 1990s from examining our advertisements, watching our television, and listening to our popular music. That women in our society are everywhere on display is a subject we have explored throughout this book in many different contexts.

To dramatize feminist opposition to the expectation that women's bodies must be enhanced to lure men, women were invited to gather in Atlantic City 25 years ago, on September 7, 1968, for a "day-long boardwalk-theatre event" to protest the image of Miss America ("No More Miss America," 1970). The conveners urged those who came to bring with them, for disposal into "a huge Freedom Trash Can," such items as "bras, girdles, curlers, false eyelashes, wigs" and other "such woman-garbage you have around the house" (p. 521). Despite the media headlines, no bras were burned, just thrown away as symbols of women's enslavement to standards of sexual attractiveness influenced by men.

Feminists continue to work for changes in media representations of women and have raised public awareness about advertisements and pornography. Some have used dramatic means to emphasize their message. For example, a group of women and men in Santa Cruz, California, that has grown in number from 4 in 1980 to about 1,000 in 1984, has been staging a counter-pageant to that of Miss California. Contestants have appeared as "'Miss Used,' 'Miss Informed,' and 'Miss Directed.' One protester, 'Miss Steak,' modeled a 35-pound gown of scalloped bologna and olive loaf with a hot-dog neckline garnished with parsley. 'Judge Meat, Not Women,' demonstrators chanted" (Howard, 1984, p. 24). In 1986, the Miss California pageant was moved from Santa Cruz to San Diego to avoid the counter-pageant, but the latter followed. To protest the "girlie show" in 1987, Ann Simonton, a leader of the Myth California demonstrations since they began and "a former model who once graced the cover of a *Sports Illustrated* swimsuit issue, shaved off her long blonde hair and draped turkey slices across her torso," dramatizing the argument that "beauty pageants 'treat people like meat'" ("Miss Calif.," 1987). Simonton travels across the United States with a 200-slide presentation entitled "Sex, Power and the Media."

One of her slides is of an ad that claims a bra gives a career woman much-needed freedom; another shows a ditzy gal who takes control of her life by using the right hair conditioner. This is followed by clothing ads that Simonton believes make light of inhuman treatment of women—a model tied up with belts, a teenager with a hot iron on her stomach . . . [and] photos of raped and dismembered women. (Liebman, 1989, p. 133)

Women's consciousness with regard to the issue of objectification has been raised considerably in recent years, a development apparent in many areas and especially in women's humor. The "Cathy" cartoon above is one example: even Cathy, who is always being pushed and pulled by the conflicting expectations for today's woman, refuses to obey fashion's call to return to the miniskirt. Resistance can be seen on other fronts as well. A flight attendants' union has filed a complaint with the Equal Employment Opportunities Commission against United Airlines, arguing that the airline's policy of a maximum weight for flight attendants "perpetuates a sex-based stereotype that female flight attendants must be slim bodied, attractive women, rather than competent employees" (cf. Quindlen, 1993b, p. E-17). United suspended one attendant without pay for being 12 pounds over her maximum of 133 after the birth of her second baby.

Affirmation of Joy and Adventure

Contemporary women are asking for fun, ripping off our ladylike white gloves (if we ever wore them), and kicking up our heels. WITCH (1970), one of the earliest feminist groups in the "second wave," called on women to be "groovy, courageous, aggressive, intelligent, nonconformist, explorative, curious, independent, sexually liberated, revolutionary, . . . untamed, angry, [and] joyous" (pp. 539f.). The contemporary women's movement has "poets, songsters, clowns, dancers, writers and image makers" (Smith, 1991, p. 156). It also has activists who

are "staging extremely unorthodox, highly effective, and very visible events that dramatize women's issues with wit and wildness" (Antrobus, 1993, p. 17). Groups like the Guerrilla Girls in New York City, Ladies of the Lake in Buffalo, and the Riot Girls Network (high school girls) are blasting stereotypes and presenting hilarious images in public appearances and posters designed to publicize women's agendas.

This may surprise readers who have accepted the media's depiction of feminists as women with "braided hair and short nails . . . [as] humorless, dour, and . . . unblinkingly earnest women" (Barreca, 1991). But women comics, for example, who "tell it like it is," now make up 20 percent of the nightclub circuit (Bland, 1990). In the late 1980s and in the 1990s, Lily Tomlin and Whoopi Goldberg were joined by many other funny women who, as described by Stefan Kanfer (1990) "have power smiles, well-toned bodies, and social commentary that ticks before it detonates" (p. 62).

The superwoman image is an especially popular target for feminist humor—for example, the cartoon on p. 346. Another example is a joke told by Carol Leifer: "Hi! I just had a baby an hour ago, and I'm back at work already. And while I was delivering, I took a seminar on tax-shelter options" (cf. Kanfer, 1990, p. 63). Women can laugh at these jokes at ourselves for two reasons: first, because the image of juggling family, career, friends, housekeeping, and recreation all at once is so funny; and, second, because so many women are really doing it and finding that "having it all" is possible if we understand that the pleasures and satisfactions will be well mixed

DORIS K. ELSTON

BRAIN SURGEON·PROFESSIONAL
MODEL·ARTIST·LAWYER·
plus
MOTHER OF FOUR

R·Chast

Drawing by R Chast, © 1987 The New Yorker Magazine Inc.

with fatigue and stress. We also know that with help from our partners, children, employers, and community resources, "having it all" could be made a lot more fun!

It is no longer unusual to read about women like Janet Guthrie who drive race cars, long-distance swimmers like Diana Nyad, runners like Joan Benoit and Florence Griffith Joyner and tennis players like Martina Navratilova. Following Sally Ride, the first U.S. woman in space, in 1983 (20 years after Valentina Tereshkova, the Russian woman cosmonaut), other women have worked in teams in outer space, and women now constitute more than 10 percent of the U.S. astronaut corps. In all areas, women's insistence on being recognized as persons who are challenged by nature, by adventure, and by both intellectual and physical goals continues to increase.

New Ideals for Behavior and the Humane Use of Skills and Power

Stereotyped depictions of women are still omnipresent in the media but, as we have seen, they are being challenged

by women's skilled performance in the labor force and by assertions of equality in personal relationships. As we observe women (and men) functioning in ways that belie the stereotypes, beliefs have begun to change.

One place where such a change is apparent is in self-reported views of "ideal persons." College student samples in the 1980s and 1990s have described ideal women and men as more similar to one another than average or typical women and men. I consistently get this result from an exercise with my undergraduate students; sometimes I ask them to check off attributes they would like to see in their own children and the students are surprised to see how much their (anticipated) daughters and sons would resemble one another. It has also been reported (Major, Carnevale, & Deaux, 1981) that adults described as being both instrumental and expressive, independent as well as concerned about others, tend to be liked best and to be rated as most well-adjusted.

In a world in which oppression and suffering are realities for a majority of people, many of today's women want humane use of skills and power to be valued and cultivated by men as well as by women. A major obstacle to this goal has been the perception that women have a monopoly on humane behavior. Robin Morgan has noted (1982b) that women have been assigned "the positive values of 'humanism,' pacifism, nurturance, ecoconsciousness, and reverence for life. While these values have been (1) regarded by Man as amusingly irrelevant, and (2) understood by women not to be inherently 'womanly,' they are objectively positive values" (p. 101). These objectively positive values are ones we must teach to our sons as well as to our daughters; they are gender-neutral and available to any human being. Both women and men can reflect in their work, whatever its nature, humane values and a respect and concern for the welfare of others. As Belva Lockwood, the first woman attorney to plead before the United States Supreme Court and a candidate for U.S. president, expressed it a century ago, "I do not believe in sex discrimination in literature, law, politics, or trade; or that modesty and virtue are more becoming to women than to men; but wish we had more of it everywhere" (cf. Lerner, 1977, p. 419).

If the conditions of women's and men's lives did not differ systematically as a function of gender, there would be little reason to expect that a woman sailor, physician, plumber, bureaucrat, or corporation executive would be distinguishable from a man doing the same job. But women's life experiences differ considerably from men's, and some women reflect, in their work and in their approach to human problems, particular values and attitudes different from those of some men.

It has been proposed (e.g., Gilligan, 1982; Miller, 1986) that women are especially concerned with the welfare of others, connectedness, and other interpersonal issues and more likely to be guided by an assessment of consequences and responsibilities to people than by abstract principles. Others have suggested that a woman's position as "outsider," or as adapter to low status, promotes a special way of looking at issues, so that in positions of authority or power or in the use of skills, women will show a greater sensitivity to people and a greater concern with equity and process. The evidence, however, suggests that it is less the fact of a woman's gender and more her analysis of her experiences as a woman that makes the quality of work some women do in areas previously dominated by men special and different from the quality of men's work in those fields.

Two women private detectives in San Francisco, for example, called their agency The People's Eye and were reported to specialize in working for "underdog" clients—poor people, lesbians, and radicals ("Two Women Survive," 1978). Similarly, Eleanor Helin, who discovered a new asteroid that circles the sun once every 9 months, named it Ra-Shalom, combining the name of the ancient Egyptian sun god Ra, symbol of enlightenment, with the Hebrew greeting of peace, Shalom ("New Asteroid," 1978). In one study (Merritt, 1982), 51 women municipal legislators from suburban areas and a matched group of comparable men were interviewed. Although no relationship was found between political ambition and gender, the women gave some indications of focusing more on the public interest and less on private advancement than the men, and could be characterized more by a "public serving instrumentality" (p. 1035). A more recent study by Dorothy Cantor and Toni Bernay of women in high elected office concluded that these women manifested "a competent self," "creative (constructive) aggression," and "woman power" (cf. DeAngelis, 1992b). The women interviewed said that they had entered politics to "make society a better place" environmentally, educationally, or economically, and the researchers concluded that the women saw politics as public service.

But many studies of the political views of women and men find small differences. For example, polls conducted between 1984 and 1988 found that 9 percent more women than men opposed the use of force, but only 1.1 percent more women than men opposed a strong defense, while 3.6 percent more women than men supported federal spending for social programs (cf. McLaughlin, Shryer, Goode, & McAuliffe, 1988). Such a "gender gap" is not striking. A larger gap was reported in a study of attitudes toward a nuclear power plant in a North Carolina community (Solomon, Tomascovic-Devey, & Risman, 1989); women were more opposed to such a plant than men and more concerned about its safety. On the other hand, a study of concern about acid rain among Kentucky adults found no gender difference (Arcury, Scollay, & Johnson, 1987). It is also of interest that *New York Times*/CBS telephone polls between November 1979 and January 1993 have consistently found that women nationwide are more pessimistic than men about "the present state of things" and the future ("Men and Women," 1993).

Whether being a woman makes one a "better" legislator, doctor, or what have you, remains an intriguing subject. According to the *Feminist Majority* ("Women Crack," 1992)

> The newly elected congresswomen [to the 103rd Congress] are primarily feminist. They are all pro-choice and pro–women's rights. Of all the women in Congress, 93% of them—51 out of 55—support abortion rights. (p. 8)

These attitudes tell us something about the women in Congress but also, of course, something about the voters who elected them. In an area far removed from politics, it has been claimed that, because women are patient and careful observers, the study of primate behavior has amassed remarkable new information from the field reports of scientists like Dian Fossey, Jane Goodall, and Birute Galdikas (cf. Starowica, 1992). In medicine, we can point to a surgeon like Susan Love, who "typically holds the hand of her patient as anesthesia is administered"; but we must also heed the words of another surgeon, Marilyn Richardson, who "doubts that being a female has affected her mode of doctoring" (Klass, 1988, p. 35). Pediatrician Perri Klass (1988) argues that because women doctors have "trouble assuming the mantle of all-knowing, paternal medical authority . . . [they] have found themselves searching for new ways to interact with patients, with nurses and with fellow doctors" (p. 96). This conclusion is reinforced by studies that find that women doctors spend significantly more time with each patient, interrupt their patients less often, and are more willing to treat poor patients and work in poor neighborhoods than men doctors. At the same time, women doctors are no more homeopathic than men—that is, they are no more inclined to use natural methods and no less inclined to be interventionist in their treatment—and women doctors do not differ from men in number of surgical procedures performed or drugs prescribed (Angier, 1992).

Another aspect of women's presumed "specialness" is the report by some professional women that more is expected of them than of male colleagues with respect to staff and client relationships. Thus, for example, a group of women managers from 50 organizations were compared with men in similar positions (Josefowitz, 1980) and found to be more tolerant and encouraging of interruptions by their staff members. Each of the managers studied was observed carefully on the job, and the women were found to be more likely to have their doors open (literally and figuratively) and to walk out of their offices to talk to their subordinates. This greater availability of women executives, however, was perceived by them not only as a positive strength, but also as a source of strain about which they complained. Women lawyers, too, have reported feeling that more is expected of them in terms of time and energy than is expected of their male colleagues (Epstein, 1981). Feminist lawyers who wish to provide maximum support and assistance for clients have expressed feelings of frustration about clients' sometimes unreasonable expectations.

Experience certainly supports the conclusion that not all women bring a so-called "woman's perspective" to their work. Throughout this book we have stressed the commonalities in women's experiences across social categories, but also the variations among women and the enormous role played by situations, practice, and the demands of status or position. Thus, although there is little question that art, literature, science, medicine, law, business, and politics inevitably reflect the experiences and values of their practitioners, it does not follow that all or most women bring to their work (inside or outside the home) a unique perspective reflecting similar concerns.

Values, attitudes, and behavior are acquired through a unique pattern of interaction with other people and with social institutions in circumstances and conditions that vary over time. As the contingencies influencing behavior vary, so too do our perspectives, points of view, and subsequent actions and reactions. The evidence supporting wide differences among women must temper our enthusiasm for gender comparisons and an exaggerated emphasis on differences between the genders, which distort what we know and observe in daily life. As I noted elsewhere (Lott, 1985),

> to know, for example, that Phyllis Schlafly, Margaret Thatcher, Shirley Chisholm, and Kate Millett are all women will permit reliable prediction of only some behavior. . . . Can we predict that each of these women is similar in her concern for relationships, caring, harmony, and responsibility? My guess is that we could more easily match Thatcher and Chisholm, for example, to two different men than to each other on values, interests, beliefs, and moral position. (pp. 161f.)

Linda Kerber (1986) noted an important lesson we should have learned from the suffragist argument, that once women were given the vote

> the streets would be clean, child labor would be eliminated, war would be at an end. . . . [While] suffragists were right in expecting that support for peace movements and progressive legislation would come from newly enfranchised women, . . . they were wrong to predict that most women would support a political agenda drawn up from the concerns central to women's sphere. Newly enfranchised women voted as the interests of their race and class dictated. (pp. 308f.)

Thus, Sandra Day O'Connor, the first woman Justice of the U.S. Supreme Court, shared the conclusions of conservative Justice William Rehnquist in 123 of the 137 cases she participated in during her first year on the bench. "Of the 29 cases that sharply divided the Court—those 5-4 opinions that are taken by the press as ideological barometers with Rehnquist as a benchmark conservative and William Brennan as a benchmark liberal—she voted with Rehnquist in 26, with Brennan in three" (Kerr, 1982, p. 52).

Feminist Objectives

If we want a more humane world, we must provide the appropriate conditions for both genders to learn positive pro-social behaviors; as argued throughout this book, these are gender-neutral and available to any human being. Women have already begun to make a difference; now we must include men in our agenda. Feminists, Naomi Wolf (1992) reminds us, are not defined by our sexual identities, experiences, background, social status, or chromosomes, but by our values and objectives. "In the fight against sexism, it's those who are for us versus those who are against us—of either gender" (p. 31).

Women have been pursuing personal and social change at a rapid pace during the past two decades. Some may view these changes as feminist while others will be uncomfortable with this word, but there can be little debate about what has been accomplished. As Barbara Ehrenreich (1990) has pointed out, women have spearheaded "reforms in the treatment of female victims of rape and of battering," have sensitized "corporations to the need for flexible hours, child care and parental leave," and have succeeded in getting "women's concerns out of the 'style section' and onto the front page" (p. 15). Women in community leadership positions were found in one study (Bers & Mezey, 1981) to favor specific efforts to strengthen women's status through programs for rape victims, battered wives, and displaced homemakers; equal educational opportunities for girls and boys; and sexual equality in employment. While most of the women did not label themselves as feminists and did not necessarily want to change their own lives, they supported feminist goals.

A survey of a sample of working-class (mainly European-American) women by Myra Ferree (1983) also found largely positive attitudes toward the goals of the women's liberation movement, and a large-scale national study of women and men (Doherty & Baldwin, 1985) found that women have become increasingly more aware of structural inequalities in society that influenced their lives. Women whose consciousness has been raised with respect to the connection between their personal lives and social institutions and who act on their beliefs may not necessarily identify themselves as feminists. Although such an identification is important, what is more meaningful is what women do on their own behalf. As pointed out by bell hooks (1992), "we can act in feminist resistance without ever using the word 'feminism'" (p. 80).

> Community organization [working-class] women may or may not see themselves as feminists, [but] they all see themselves as strong women who have fought for what they believe. Many acknowledge that the women's movement was influential in promoting their ability to develop as competent community leaders. (Gittell & Naples, 1982, p. 27)

Some women are moving into high places and are realizing their potential for public effectiveness and power. Whether defined in terms of one's ability to get others to do what you want, or one's influence over others, or one's access to resources, *power* is now a word used by more and more women with less and less self-consciousness and apology. Power is clearly something more women want more of! At the same time, feminists insist that men, too, will gain from greater gender equality in opportunities and from greater gender flexibility. Although men as a group (especially middle-class, European-American men) have profited from their position of power, individual men are not "the enemy." All of us are denied aspects of our common humanity by sex-typing. As the suffrage leader Crystal Eastman told an audience in 1920 (cf. Kerber, 1977, p. 48): "We must bring up feminist sons." Brothers must come to share their sisters' commitment to equality if that objective is to be realized and to agree that it is "womanly as well as manly to earn your own living, to

stand on your own feet. And it must be manly to know how to cook and sew and clean."

Major feminist objectives are to teach women and men to share power equally; to change institutions so that this sharing is possible and probable; and to sever the connection between power and gender (or other arbitrary categories like race or ethnicity). The goal has never been to punish men or to assert women's superiority. Ellen Willis (1981) articulated the primary feminist objective elegantly and simply: extending "to women—and to the entire realm of familial and social life—the democratic principles of self-determination, equality and the right to the pursuit of happiness" (p. 494). To this end, she argued, we must reject assumptions about "opposing masculine and feminine natures" and assumptions that men and women have monopolies on different behaviors or human capacities.

A significant aspect of feminism, often noted, is that theory emerges from everyday life experiences, but then goes further to examine how these experiences are related to the social order and to institutions. "Personal testimony," bell hooks (1992) has pointed out, provides "fertile ground for the production of liberatory feminist theory." But although feminist thinking allows individual women "to transform their lives . . . any feminist transformational process is easily co-opted if not rooted in a political commitment to a mass-based feminist movement" (p. 82).

In other words, it is not enough to make assertions and to state objectives. It is also not enough for individual women to acquire personal power within the existing system if that system continues to oppress most other women. The New Woman is presented to us by the media as well-groomed, in a business suit, cool, efficient, with perfect makeup, and ready for the day's challenges. We must ask, however, how she will change the life of the mother who washes the dishes at home before beginning a day in the typing pool or the restaurant, who carries her lunch in a paper sack, not papers in an attache case. Enhanced personal lives for some women must be accompanied by changes in the social, economic, and political institutions that affect all of us.

Many women who are now realizing their personal dreams and ambitions, doing responsible and worthwhile work and involved in satisfying personal relationships do not connect their present possibilities and satisfactions with the earlier struggles of women before them or with the continued oppression of other women. The media myth "that feminism means being . . . anti-men and ultimately alone" (Gilman, 1991) has been too easily accepted and has encouraged some women to distance themselves from such an identification. Thus, a *Time/CNN* poll found in February 1992 that 63 percent of U.S. women did not consider themselves feminists (cf. Gibbs, 1992). This means, however, that 37 percent were willing to self-identify as feminists. The same poll also found that 57 percent of the women respondents answered "yes" to the question "Is there still a need for a strong women's movement?" and 82 percent answered "yes" to the question "Do women today have more freedom than their mothers did?"

As Laura Shapiro (1991) noted,

> During the '80s a long, slow chill settled over the word feminism as the press, the advertising industry, the New Right, the religious right, television and movies all decided that the women's movement was dead and nobody was mourning it. In fact a smiling new "post feminist" American woman was supposed to have risen from its ashes. Under scrutiny, post feminism turned out to look a lot like prefeminism, give or take a briefcase. (p. 4)

Much of this movement to deny, discredit, and destroy the gains made by feminism in the United States has been carefully chronicled by Susan Faludi (1991) in her book *Backlash,* which I have frequently cited. Although the media have been all too eager to proclaim that feminism is dead, it really isn't. As put so well by Anna Quindlen (1992), "like any distance runner with a long way to go, . . . [feminism] was just getting a second wind" (p. E-14). And, as Gloria Steinem reminds us, "the future depends on what each of us does every day! After all, a movement is only people moving" (cf. Gibbs & McDowell, 1992, p. 57).

In a speech at Stanford University on April 28, 1993, Susan Faludi

> offered tips on how to spot the backlash [against women and feminism] in the media, popular culture and political rhetoric. [She proposed] nine rules . . . that might have been compiled by backlash propagators. . . .
>
> "If anything can go wrong for women, it will be the fault of feminism and female independence." . . .
>
> "When you attack feminism, always refer to scientific evidence and studies by supposed experts." . . .
>
> "When studies and statistics don't work, get personal or get malicious." . . .
>
> "Never let facts get in the way of a good backlash story." . . .
>
> "Denounce feminist organizations for things they never did or said." . . .
>
> "Divide and conquer. Get women to do the dirty work by setting them against each other." . . .
>
> "Pretend you're on women's side." . . .

> "When feminists catch you in the act of backlashing, claim you are just joking." . . .
>
> "When all else fails, just pretend feminism is dead and maybe it will go away." (Seawell, 1993, p. 6)

Women's interest in issues of comparable worth, economic justice, violence and harassment, family leave, child care, health care, and reproductive rights remains strong, according to polls. In addition, there continues to be much evidence in rural and urban areas, among women of diverse ethnicities, of women's activism (Ireland, 1992; Manegold, 1992a, 1992b; Shapiro, 1991), that some interpret as a new "surge of feminism" both on the streets and in less visible areas. One example is the success of *Ms.* magazine, which after having ceased publication because of financial difficulties returned to circulation in 1990 with a new policy of not accepting advertising. That the magazine is now making a profit and had a circulation of approximately 150,000 as of August 1991 "defies not only publishing wisdom but also the frequent pronouncements that the women's movement is over" (Denworth, 1991, p. 60). Another sign of the movement's vitality is the continued vigor of NOW. Although a *New York Times* story on NOW's ninth president Patricia Ireland began with the boldly headlined caution that "The new head of the women's rights organization faces a country where she and her cause have become a hard sell, even to some feminists," (Gross, 1992), the details in the lengthy article do not really reinforce this pronouncement.

Others have pointed to a small but significant feminist influence on television and movies in terms of themes that appear in dramas and talk shows. Elayne Rapping (1993) has argued that "we're doing very well indeed in the hearts and minds department, . . . where gender issues and cultural values are concerned" (p. 20). Films like *Thelma and Louise, The Accused, Fried Green Tomatoes, Rambling Rose,* and *Dogfight* are cited as having been influenced by the women's movement even though the word "feminist" is not a popular one in Hollywood. On the other hand, the "F word" can be heard—not in whispers but out loud—at professional conferences in the social sciences and the humanities, and in international conferences like the Congress on Women I attended in February 1993 in San Jose, Costa Rica. A sure sign of life is the word's appearance in *Cosmopolitan,* where Regina Barreca (1991) asserted that

> Feminists are not a lonely tribe of women fenced off from the rest of society. . . . Feminists don't wish they were men; they celebrate their womanhood. I think I've always been one. I'm glad I've finally come out of the closet.

While enjoying lives that promise personal rewards, young middle-class women must also participate with other women in a movement to abolish gender inequities. These are not easy times for women. Many aspire to meet impossible goals without societal supports: to be perfect mothers, wives, and responsible, successful workers, while also keeping slim, attractive, exercised, healthy, and calm. Crescent Dragonwagon (1985) satirized these expectations in describing "Today's Woman":

> A nurturing mother who works by day, goes to law school by night, lifts weights, works hard at your marriage, and makes tortellini with fresh basil. You're equally at home in pinstripes, decolletage, and sweats, and you weigh less than you did at 12. (p. 158)

This image is a tragicomic distortion of a postfeminist future. Only a robot can blithely and confidently vacuum the rugs, go hiking with her children or friends, visit museums, pick wildflowers, work for political candidates, listen to music, repair automobiles, do the food shopping, and hold down a full-time job without assistance.

I prefer a different image of a feminist utopia, one outlined by Jane Flax (1981) that is characterized by (a) equal sharing and valuing by women and men of all socially useful work ("caring for people and interpersonal relationships, beautifying personal environments, raising children and maintaining daily life" [p. 131]); (b) redistribution of socially necessary work (such as science, engineering, medicine, and trade) among all groups; (c) dissolution of the division between private and public work; and (d) equitable rewards for all those who participate in doing work of benefit to society.

Feminist objectives are reachable and worth working for. In a society such as feminists envision, both women and men can realize the full promise of our humanity. Thus, this book ends with the same promise with which it began. Sojourner Truth knew that having plowed and planted, having worked in the fields and borne the lash, made her no less a woman than one whose hands bore rings, whose face was powdered, or who sewed, cooked, and tended only her own children. This book has traced the general life experiences of contemporary women in the United States as we continue to learn how to behave in accordance with our culture's definition of our character and role. We have seen that the traditional definition does an injustice to our possibilities. Let us move toward a new definition and assert that to be a woman is to be a biological complement to man, and to share with him equally a repertoire of behavior and motives bounded only by time, circumstance, and physical limitation, but not by imagination, self-esteem, or power.

◆ Discussion Questions

1. What do women want? How can women achieve their objectives, individually and collectively?

2. What is gained and lost by the achievement of feminist objectives?

3. Can there be sisterhood between women of different ethnicities, social class, background, and sexual preference—sisterhood that includes drug abusers, pro-choice and anti-choice women, mothers and daughters, and so on?

4. Do an informal survey among friends and relatives regarding the meaning of the word *feminism*.

5. What new insights can you credit to this book and to this course?

6. What in this book and course did you find most upsetting?

REFERENCES

The AAUW Report. (1992). *How schools shortchange girls.* Washington, DC: American Association of University Women Educational Foundation.

Abbey, Antonia. (1982). Sex differences in attributions for friendly behavior: Do males misperceive females' friendliness? *Journal of Personality and Social Psychology, 42,* 830–838.

Abbey, Antonia, & Melby, Christian. (1986). The effects of nonverbal cues on gender differences in perceptions of sexual intent. *Sex Roles, 15,* 283–298.

Abcarian, Robin. (1990, February 7). Something fishy about 'Little Mermaid'? *Providence Journal Bulletin.*

Abplanalp, Judith M. (1983). Premenstrual syndrome: A selective review. In S. Golub (Ed.), *Lifting the curse of menstruation* (pp. 107–123). New York: Haworth.

Abrahamson, Alan. (1992, January 29). Study: Working women are healthier than homemakers. *Providence Journal Bulletin,* pp. C-1, C-2.

Abramowitz, Christine V., & Dokecki, Paul R. (1977). The politics of clinical judgment. *Psychological Bulletin, 84,* 460–476.

Abu-Laban, Sharon M. (1981). Women and aging: A futurist perspective. *Psychology of Women Quarterly, 6,* 85–98.

Acker, Ally. (1992, March/April). Arts: Women behind the camera. *Ms.,* pp. 64–67.

Acock, Alan C., & Ireland, Nancy K. (1983). Attribution of blame in rape cases: The impact of norm violation, gender, and sex-role attitude. *Sex Roles, 9,* 179–193.

Adams, Jerome. (1984). Women at West Point: A three-year perspective. *Sex Roles, 11,* 525–541.

Adams, Kathrynn A. (1980). Who has the final word? Sex, race, and dominance behavior. *Journal of Personality and Social Psychology, 38,* 1–8.

Adler, Nancy E. (1979). Abortion: A social-psychological perspective. *Journal of Social Issues, 35*(1), 100–119.

Adler, Nancy E. (1989, March 16). *Testimony before the United States House of Representatives on the Medical and Psychological Impact of Abortion on Women.* American Psychological Association, 1200 17th St., NW, Washington, DC 20036.

Adler, Nancy E. (1992). Unwanted pregnancy and abortion: Definitional and research issues. *Journal of Social Issues, 48*(3), 19–35.

Adler, Nancy E., David, Henry P., Major, Brenda N., Roth, Susan H., Russo, Nancy F., & Wyatt, Gail E. (1990). Psychological responses after abortion. *Science, 248,* 41–44.

Adler, Nancy E., & Tschann, Jeanne M. (1993). The abortion debate: Psychological issues for adult women and adolescents. In S. Matteo (Ed.), American women in the nineties: Today's critical issues (pp. 193–212), Boston: Northeastern University Press.

Adler, Tina. (1989, March). Sex-based differences declining, study shows. *APA Monitor,* p. 6.

Adler, Tina. (1990a, January). Causes, cure of PMS still elude researchers. *APA Monitor,* p. 10.

Adler, Tina. (1990b, January). Differences explored in gays and straights. *APA Monitor,* p. 27.

Adler, Tina. (1990c, January). PMS diagnosis draws fire from researchers. *APA Monitor,* p. 12.

Adler, Tina. (1991a, July). Women's expectations are menopause villains. *APA Monitor.*

Adler, Tina. (1991b, September). Parents' jobs linked to childrearing style. *APA Monitor.*

Adler, Tina. (1991c, December). Abuse within families emerging from closet. *APA Monitor,* p. 16.

Agonito, Rosemary. (1977). *History of ideas on women.* New York: Capricorn.

Allport, Gordon W. (1955). *Becoming.* New Haven: Yale University Press.

Alston, Doris N., & Rose, Natalie. (1981). Perceptions of middle-aged black women. *Journal of General Psychology, 104,* 167–171.

Alta. (1973). Penus envy, they call it. In F. Howe & E. Bass (Eds.), *No more masks! An anthology of poems by women* (p. 295). New York: Anchor.

Alther, Lisa. (1976). *Kinflicks.* New York: Knopf.

Alther, Lisa. (1990). *Bedrock.* New York: Ballentine.

Altman, Sydney L., & Grossman, Frances K. (1977). Women's career plans and maternal employment. *Psychology of Women Quarterly, 1,* 365–376.

AMA changes course, asks U.S. to provide health coverage for all. (1991, May 14). *Providence Journal Bulletin*, p. A-7.

Amaro, Hortensia. (1986, April 14). *A profile of Hispanic women in the United States: Health and mental health needs*. Paper read at University of Rhode Island, Kingston.

American Health and Psychology Today Service. (1990, January 17). Study: Sexual motivation changes with age. *Providence Journal Bulletin*, p. E-3.

The American woman 1988–89: A status report. (1988). New York: Norton.

American Psychiatric Association. (1987). *Diagnostic and statistical manual of mental disorders* (3rd ed., Revised). Washington, DC: Author.

Ames, Katrine, Hager, Mary, Wilson, Larry, & Buckley, Linda. (1990, December 17). Our bodies, their selves. *Newsweek*, p. 60.

Amstey, Frederica H., & Whitbourne, Susan K. (1981). Continuing education, identity, sex role, and psychosocial development in adult women. *Sex Roles, 7*, 49–58.

Anderson, Claire J., & Fisher, Caroline. (1991). Male-female relationships in the work place: Perceived motivations in office romance. *Sex Roles, 25*, 163–180.

Anderson, Sandra C. (1980). Patterns of sex-role identification in alcoholic women. *Sex Roles, 6*, 231–243.

Anderson, Sandra C. (1984). Alcoholic women: Sex-role identification and perceptions of parental personality characteristics. *Sex Roles, 11*, 277–287.

Andrisani, Paul J. (1978). Job satisfaction among working women. *Signs, 3*, 588–607.

Angelou, Maya. (1971). *I know why the caged bird sings*. New York: Bantam.

Angier, Natalie. (1992, June 21). Bedside manners improve as more women enter medicine. *New York Times*, p. E-18.

Angier, Natalie. (1993, April 11). Fashion's waif look makes strong women weep. *New York Times*, p. E-2.

The annual report on the economic status of the profession 1983–84. (1984, July/August). *Academe*, pp. 1–64.

Ansen, David. (1991, May 13). Madonna lets it all hang out. *Newsweek*, pp. 66–67.

Anstett, Patricia. (1991, July 2). Armed with birth control. *Providence Journal Bulletin*, pp. B-1, B-3.

Anthony, Jane. (1992, January/February). Prostitution as "choice." *Ms.*, pp. 86–87.

Antill, John K. (1983). Sex role complementarity versus similarity in married couples. *Journal of Personality and Social Psychology, 45*, 145–155.

Antonucci, Toni C. & Akiyama, Hiroko. (1987). An examination of sex differences in social support among older men and women. *Sex Roles, 17*, 737–749.

Antrobus, Helen. (1993, March/April). Revolution girl-style now! *Utne Reader*, pp. 17–18.

Anyan, Walter J. Jr., & Quillan, Warren W. II. (1971). The naming of primary colors by children. *Child Development, 42*, 1629–1632.

APA testifies before NIH scientists on Women's Health Initiative. (1991, November/December). *Psychological Science Agenda*, American Psychological Association.

Applebome, Peter. (1992, December 27). Holding fragile families together when mothers are inmates. *New York Times*, p. E-2.

Archer, Cynthia J. (1984). Children's attitudes toward sex-role division in adult occupational roles. *Sex Roles, 10*, 1–10.

Archer, Dane, Iritani, Bonita, Kimes, Debra D., & Barrios, Michael. (1983). Face-ism: Five studies of sex differences in facial prominence. *Journal of Personality and Social Psychology, 45*, 725–735.

Arcury, Thomas A., Scollay, Susan J., & Johnson, Timothy P. (1987). Sex differences in environmental concern and knowledge: The case of acid rain. *Sex Roles, 16*, 463–472.

Ardener, Shirley. (1977). Perceiving women. New York: Halsted.

Arendell, Terry J. (1988). Women and the economics of divorce in the contemporary United States. *Signs, 13*, 121–135.

Aries, Elizabeth J., & Johnson, Fern L. (1983). Close friendship in adulthood: Conversational content between same-sex friends. *Sex Roles, 9*, 1183–1196.

Arleu, Sharyn R. (1992). Surrogacy: For love but not for money? *Gender & Society, 6*, 30–48.

Armstrong, Louise. (1978). *Kiss daddy goodnight: A speak-out on incest*. New York: Hawthorn.

Arnow, Harriette. (1954). *The dollmaker*. New York: Avon.

Aronoff, Joel, & Crano, William D. (1975). A re-examination of the cross-cultural principles of task segregation and sex role differentiation in the family. *American Sociological Review, 40*, 12–20.

Aronson, Jane. (1992). Women's sense of responsibility for the care of old people: "But who else is going to do it?" (1992). *Gender & Society, 6*, 8–29.

Arvey, Richard D. (1979). Unfair discrimination in the employment interview: Legal and psychological aspects. *Psychological Bulletin, 86*, 736–765.

Ashton, Eleanor. (1983). Measures of play behavior: The influence of sex-role stereotyped children's books. *Sex Roles, 9*, 43–47.

Astin, Alexander W. (1977). *Four critical years*. San Francisco: Jossey-Bass.

Astin, Helen S. (1978, March). *Women and achievement: Occupational entry and persistence*. Paper presented at the meeting of the Eastern Psychological Association, Washington, DC.

Atkin, David J., Moorman, Jay, & Lin, Carolyn A. (1991). Ready for prime time: Network series devoted to working women in the 1980s. *Sex Roles, 25*, 677–685.

Atkinson, Jean M. (1982). Anthropology. *Signs, 8*, 236–258.

Atkinson, Jean, & Huston, Ted L. (1984). Sex role orientation and division of labor early in marriage. *Journal of Personality and Social Psychology, 46*, 330–345.

Attanucci, Jane S. (1982, March). *"How would you describe yourself to yourself?" Mothers of infants reply*. Unpublished paper, Harvard Graduate School of Education, Cambridge, MA.

Attanucci, Jane. (1989). Review of David Guttmann's *Reclaiming Powers*. *Sex Roles, 20*, 598–601.

Attie, Ilana, & Brooks-Gunn, Jeanne. (1989). Development of eating problems in adolescent girls: A longitudinal study. *Developmental Psychology, 25*, 70–79.

Atwood, Margaret. (1984). *Bluebeard's Egg*. Toronto: Seal.

Atwood, Margaret. (1988). *Cat's eye*. Garden City, NJ: Doubleday.

Aube, Jennifer, & Koestner, Richard. (1992). Gender characteristics and adjustment: A longitudinal study. *Journal of Personality and Social Psychology, 63*, 485–493.

Augustoni, MaryLynn, Barnett, Rosalind C., & Baruch, Grace K. (1988, March). *Never married women: Factors contributing to their well-being/distress*. Presented at meeting of Association for Women in Psychology, Bethesda, MD.

Australian court: Wife is not obligated to have sex with husband. (1991, December 5). *The Good 5¢ Cigar*, p. 2.

Average Salary for Men and Women Faculty . . . , 1991–92. (1992, March–April). *Academe*, p. 20.

AWP Brochure (no date). Association for Women in Psychology.

A baby learns mother's scent. (1980, January 8). *Providence Evening Bulletin*.

Bachman, Jerald G. (1987, July). Adolescence: An eye on the future. *Psychology Today*, pp. 6–8.

Bachtold, Louise M. (1976). Personality characteristics of women of distinction. *Psychology of Women Quarterly, 1*, 70–78.

Badenhoop, M. Suzanne, & Johansen, M. Kelly. (1980). Do reentry women have special needs? *Psychology of Women Quarterly, 4*, 591–595.

Bailey, William C., Hendrick, Clyde, & Hendrick, Susan S. (1987). Relation of sex and gender role to love, sexual attitudes, and self-esteem. *Sex Roles, 16*, 637–648.

Bajt, Theresa R., & Pope, Kenneth S. (1989). Therapist-patient sexual intimacy involving children and adolescents. *American Psychologist, 44*, 455.

Baker, Susan W. (1980). Biological influences on human sex and gender. *Signs, 6*, 80–96.

Bakst, M. Charles. (1984, June 7). Walsh pledges to ease restrictions on abortion. *Providence Evening Bulletin*.

Ballard-Reisch, Deborah, & Elton, Mary. (1992). Gender orientation and the Bem Sex Role Inventory: A psychological construct revisited. *Sex Roles, 27*, 291–330.

Ballmer, Helene, & Cozby, Paul C. (1981). Family environments of women who return to college. *Sex Roles, 7*, 1019–1026.

Balswick, Jack, & Ingoldsby, Bron. (1982). Heroes and heroines among American adolescents. *Sex Roles, 8*, 243–249.

Bambara, Toni C. (1974). Commentary: Sexuality of black women. In L. Gross (Ed.), *Sexual behavior: Current issues* (pp. 39–42). Flushing, NY: Spectrum.

Ban on homosexuals eased. (1979, August 19). *New York Times*.

Ban, Peggy L., & Lewis, Michael. (1974). Mothers and fathers, girls and boys; attachment behavior in the one-year-old. *Merrill-Palmer Quarterly, 20*, 195–204.

Bandura, Albert. (1982). Self-efficacy mechanism in human agency. *American Psychologist, 37*,122–147.

Bandura, Albert, & Schunk, Dale H. (1981). Cultivating competence, self-efficacy, and intrinsic interest through proximal self-motivation. *Journal of Personality and Social Psychology, 41*, 586–598.

Bane, Mary Jo, & Ellwood, David T. (1989). One fifth of the nation's children: Why are they poor? *Science, 245*, 1047–1053.

Banikiotes, F. G., Montgomery, A. A., & Banikiotes, P. G. (1972). Male and female auditory reinforcement of infant vocalizations. *Developmental Psychology, 6*, 476–481.

Banks, Adelle M. (1988, May 1). Is rape sometimes OK? *Providence Sunday Journal*, pp. A-1, A-29.

Barb. (1984, May 28). Victim blames libbers [Letter to Good Neighbors column]. *Providence Evening Bulletin*, p. A-16.

Barber, Bonnie L., & Eccles, Jacqueline S. (1992). Long-term influence of divorce and single parenting on adolescent family- and work-related values, behaviors, and aspirations. *Psychological Bulletin, 111*, 108–126.

Barclay, Dolores. (1984, April 2). Women in prison—the numbers are increasing. *Providence Evening Bulletin*, pp. A-1, A-6.

Bardwell, Jill R., Cochran, Samuel W., & Walker, Sharon. (1986). Relationship of parental education, race, and gender to sex role stereotyping in five-year-old kindergartners. *Sex Roles, 15*, 275–281.

Barker, Pat. (1983). *Union street*. New York: Putnam.

Barnes, Michael L., & Buss, David M. (1985). Sex differences in the interpersonal behavior of married couples. *Journal of Personality and Social Psychology, 48*, 654–661.

Barnes, Steve. (1989, October 15). The crusade of Dr. Elders. *New York Times Magazine*, pp. 39–41, 74–75, 90–91.

Barnett, Mark A. (1978, September). *Situational influences and sex differences in children's reward allocation behavior*. Paper presented at the meeting of the American Psychological Association, Toronto.

Barnett, Mark A., Howard, Jeffrey A., King, Laura M., & Dino, Geri A. (1980). Antecedents of empathy: Retrospective accounts of early socialization. *Personality and Social Psychology Bulletin, 6*, 361–365.

Barnett, Rosalind C. (1981). Parental sex-role attitudes and child-rearing values. *Sex Roles, 7*, 837–846.

Barnett, Rosalind C., & Baruch, Grace K. (1978). Women in the middle years: A critique of research and theory. *Psychology of Women Quarterly, 3*, 187–197.

Barnett, Rosalind C., & Baruch, Grace K. (1983, August). *Determinants of fathers' participation in family work*. Paper presented at the meeting of the American Psychological Association, Anaheim, CA.

Barnett, Rosalind C., & Baruch, Grace K. (1985). Women's involvement in multiple roles and psychological distress. *Journal of Personality and Social Psychology, 49*, 135–145.

Baron, Pierre, & Joly, Elisabeth. (1988). Sex differences in the expression of depression in adolescents. *Sex Roles, 18*, 1–7.

Barreca, Regina. (1991, April). Who says being a feminist isn't fun? *Cosmopolitan*.

Barreca, Gina. (1991, September 1). In celebration of the bad girl. *New York Times*, p. H-21.

Barrett, Carol J. (1981). Intimacy in widowhood. *Psychology of Women Quarterly, 5*, 473–487.

Barrett, David E. (1979). A naturalistic study of sex differences in children's aggression. *Merrill-Palmer Quarterly, 25*, 193–204.

Barrett, Karen. (1982, September). Date rape: A campus epidemic? *Ms.*, pp. 48–51, 130.

Barrett, Martha B. (1990). *Invisible lives*. New York: Harper & Row.

Barringer, Felicity. (1991, June 9). The fissioning of the nuclear family. *New York Times*, p. E-7.

Barry, Kathleen. (1979). *Female sexual slavery*. Englewood Cliffs, NJ: Prentice Hall.

Bart, Pauline B. (1971). Depression in middle-aged women. In V. Gornick & B. K. Moran (Eds.), *Woman in sexist society* (pp. 99–117). New York: Basic Books.

Bart, Pauline B., & O'Brien, Patricia H. (1985). *Stopping rape*. New York: Pergamon.

Bart, Pauline B., & Scully, Diana H. (1979). The politics of hysteria: The case of the wandering womb. In E. S. Gomberg & V. Franks (Eds.), *Gender and disordered behavior* (pp. 354–380). New York: Brunner/Mazel.

Bar-Tal, Daniel, & Saxe, Leonard. (1976). Physical attractiveness and its relationship to sex-role stereotyping. *Sex Roles, 2*, 123–133.

Barth, Ramona. (1976). *Why we burn: A feminist exercise in exorcism*. Pittsburgh, PA: KNOW, Inc.

Bartlett, Kay. (1981, April 4). Out of the eye of the beholder and into the courtroom. *Providence Journal*, p. E-3.

Baruch, Grace K. (1976). Girls who perceive themselves as competent: Some antecedents and correlates. *Psychology of Women Quarterly, 1*, 38–49.

Baruch, Grace K., & Barnett, Rosalind C. (1985b). *Role quality, multiple role involvement and psychological well-being in midlife women*. Unpublished paper, Wellesley College, Center for Research on Women, Wellesley, MA.

Baruch, Grace K., & Barnett, Rosalind C. (1986). Consequences of fathers' participation in family work: Parents' role strain and well-being. *Journal of Personality and Social Psychology, 51*, 983–992.

Baruch, Grace K., Barnett, Rosalind C., & Rivers, Caryl. (1983). *Life prints: New patterns of love and work for today's women*. New York: McGraw-Hill.

Basler, Barbara. (1986, December 7). Putting a career on hold. *New York Times Magazine*, pp. 152–153, 158–159.

Basow, Susan A. (1991). The hairless ideal: Women and their body hair. *Psychology of Women Quarterly, 15*, 83–96.

Baum, Charlotte, Hyman, Paula, & Michel, Sonya. (1975). *The Jewish woman in America*. New York: New American Library.

Baumrind, Diana. (1971). Current patterns of parental authority. *Developmental Psychology Monograph, 4*(2).

Baumrind, Diana. (1980). New directions in socialization research. *American Psychologist, 35*, 639–652.

Beach, Frank. (1969, July). It's all in your mind. *Psychology Today*, pp. 33–35, 60.

Beck, Evelyn T. (1983). The motherhood that dare not speak its name. *Women's Studies Quarterly, 11*(4), 8–11.

Beck, Joan. (1983, October 8). When greater risk is no risk at all. *Providence Evening Bulletin*.

Beck, Joan. (1990, September 25). Lesbians, gays and partners: Their quest for marital benefits. *Providence Journal Bulletin*, p. A-9.

Beck, Melinda, Yoffe, Emily, Carroll, Ginny, Hager, Mary, Rosenberg, Debra, & Beachy, Lucille. (1990, December 10). The politics of breast cancer. *Newsweek*, pp. 62–65.

Becker, Judith V., & Abel, Gene G. (1978). Men and the victimization of women. In J. R. Chapman & M. Gates (Eds.), *The victimization of women* (pp. 29–52). Beverly Hills, CA: Sage.

Beckman, Linda J. (1978). The relative rewards and costs of parenthood and employment for employed women. *Psychology of Women Quarterly, 2*, 215–234.

Beckman, Linda J. (1981). Effects of social interaction and children's relative inputs on older women's psychological well-being. *Journal of Personality and Social Psychology, 41*, 1075–1086.

Belenky, Mary F., Clinchy, D., Goldberger, N., & Tarule, J. (1986). *Women's ways of knowing*. New York: Basic Books.

Bell, Carolyn S. (1984, September). After equal pay, equal worth. *The Women's Review of Books*, pp. 17–18.

Bellinger, David C., & Gleason, Jean B. (1982). Sex differences in parental directives to young children. *Sex Roles, 8*, 1123–1139.

Bem, Sandra L. (1974). The measurement of psychological androgyny. *Journal of Consulting and Clinical Psychology, 42*, 155–162.

Bem, Sandra L. (1978). *The short Bem Sex Role Inventory*. Palo Alto, CA: Consulting Psychologists Press.

Bem, Sandra L. (1981). Gender schema theory: A cognitive account of sex typing. *Psychological Review, 88*, 354–364.

Bem, Sandra L. (1983). Gender schema theory and its implications for child development: Raising gender-aschematic children in a gender-schematic society. *Signs, 8*, 598–616.

Bem, Sandra L. (1985). Androgyny and gender schema theory: A conceptual and empirical integration. In T. B. Sonderegger (Ed.), *Nebraska symposium on motivation 1984: Psychology and gender*, vol. 32 (pp. 179–226). Lincoln: University of Nebraska Press.

Benbow, Camilla P., & Stanley, Julian. (1980). Sex differences in mathematical ability: Fact or artifact? *Science, 210*, 1261–1264.

Bender, Penny. (1992, June 25). Labor unions look for ways to survive in a changing world. *Providence Journal Bulletin*, p. D-9.

Benderly, Beryl L. (1989, November). Don't believe everything you read. *Psychology Today*, pp. 67–69.

Benedict, Helen. (1991, July/August). When to blame the victim—The media's rules on rape. *Ms.*, pp. 102–103.

Beneke, Timothy. (1982, July). Men talk about rape. *Mother Jones*, pp. 13–16, 20–23.

Benjamin, Ruby. (1989). Smoother transitions for "Always Single" women. *Hot Flash, 8*(2).

Benoit-Samuelson, woman marathoner, wins Sullivan award. (1986, February 25). *Providence Journal-Bulletin*.

Berch, Daniel B., & Bender, Bruce G. (1987, December). Margins of sexuality. *Psychology Today*, pp. 54–57.

Berg-Cross, Linda, Berg-Cross, Gary, & McGeehan, Deborah. (1979). Experience and personality differences among breast- and bottle-feeding mothers. *Psychology of Women Quarterly, 3*, 344–356.

Bergen, David J., & Williams, John E. (1991). Sex stereotypes in the United States revisited: 1972–1988. *Sex Roles, 24*, 413–424.

Berger, Phil. (1984, July 19). The new comediennes. *New York Times Magazine*, pp. 26–29, 32, 38, 51.

Berman, Phyllis W., & Smith, Vicki L. (1984). Gender and situational differences in children's smiles, touch, and proxemics. *Sex Roles, 10*, 347–355.

Bernard, Jessie. (1981). The good-provider role: Its rise and fall. *American Psychologist, 36*, 1–12.

Bernard, Jessie (with Dorothy Lee, Claude, & David). (1978). *Self-portrait of a family*. Boston: Beacon.

Berryman-Fink, Cynthia, & Verderber, Kathleen S. (1985). Attributions of the term feminist: A factor analytic development of a measuring instrument. *Psychology of Women Quarterly, 9*, 51–64.

Bers, Trudy H., & Mezey, Susan G. (1981). Support for feminist goals among leaders of women's community groups. *Signs, 6*, 737–748.

Berscheid, Ellen, & Walster, Elaine H. (1978). *Interpersonal attraction*. Reading, MA: Addison-Wesley.

Bersoff, David, & Crosby, Faye. (1984). Job satisfaction and family status. *Personality and Social Psychology Bulletin, 10*, 79–83.

Biaggio, Mary Kay, Mohan, Philip J., & Baldwin, Cynthia. (1985). Relationships among attitudes toward children, women's liberation, and personality characteristics. *Sex Roles, 12*, 47–62.

Bianco, Dorothy. (1984). Adolescent female drug abusers and their families: Some variables associated with successful treatment outcome. Dissertation Abstracts International, 45B, 1005. (University Microfilms No. 03).

Biernat, Monica, & Wortman, Camille B. (1991). Sharing of home responsibilities between professionally employed women and their husbands. *Journal of Personality and Social Psychology, 60*, 844–860.

Binion, Victoria J. (1990). Psychological androgyny: A Black female perspective. *Sex Roles, 22*, 487–507.

Birnbaum, Dana W., & Croll, William L. (1984). The etiology of children's stereotypes about sex differences in emotionality. *Sex Roles, 10*, 677–691.

Birns, Beverly. (1976). The emergence and socialization of sex differences in the earliest years. *Merrill-Palmer Quarterly, 22*, 229–254.

Bisanz, Gay L., & Rule, Brendan G. (1989). Gender and the persuasion schema: A search for cognitive invariants. *Personality and Social Psychology Bulletin, 15*, 4–18.

Bishop, Katherine. (1992, April 3). Sweet victory for feminist pioneer at law school. *New York Times*, p. A-19.

Bjornson, Edith. (1984, March/April). Sex after hysterectomy-oopherectomy: An old wives' tale revisited. *Network News*, pp. 5, 15.

Black, Sionag M., & Hill, Clara E. (1984). The psychological well-being of women in their middle years. *Psychology of Women Quarterly, 8*, 282–292.

Black women complain of pressure on abuse. (1992, February 21). *Providence Journal Bulletin*, p. A-16.

Blakely, Mary Kay. (1991, July/August). Living on the land. *Ms.*, pp. 22–26.

Blakemore, Judith E.O. (1990). Children's nurturant interactions with their infant siblings: An exploration of gender differences and maternal socialization. *Sex Roles, 22*, 43–57.

Blee, Kathleen M. (1991). *Women of the Klan: Racism and gender in the 1920s*. Berkeley: University of California Press.

Bleier, Ruth. (1984). *Science and gender: A critique of biology and its theories on women*. New York: Pergamon.

Bloch, Marianne N. (1987). The development of sex differences in young children's activities at home: The effect of the social context. *Sex Roles, 16*, 279–301.

Block, Jeanne H. (1976). Debatable conclusions about sex differences. *Contemporary Psychology, 21*, 517–522.

Blumenfeld, Laura. (1991, August 11). Lesbo-A-Go-Go: Where women treat women as sex objects. *San Francisco Chronicle*, Sunday Punch Section, p. 2.

Blumstein, Philip, & Schwartz, Pepper. (1977). Bisexuality: Some psychological issues. *Journal of Social Issues, 33*(2), 30–45.

Blumstein, Philip, & Schwartz, Pepper. (1983). *American couples: Money, work, sex*. New York: Morrow.

Blyth, Dale A., & Foster-Clark, Frederick S. (1987). Gender differences in perceived intimacy with different members of adolescents' social networks. *Sex Roles, 17*, 689–718.

Boldizar, Janet P., Perry, David G., & Perry, Louise C. (1988). Gender and reward distributions: A test of two hypotheses. *Sex Roles, 19*, 569–579.

Bolotin, Susan. (1982, October 17). Voices from the post-feminist generation. *New York Times Magazine*, pp. 28–31, 103–107, 114–117.

Borys, Shelley, & Perlman, Daniel. (1985). Gender differences in loneliness. *Personality and Social Psychology Bulletin, 11*, 63–74.

Bose, Christine E. (1987). Dual spheres. In B. B. Hess & M. M. Ferree (Eds.), *Analyzing gender: A handbook of social science research*. Sage: Newbury Park, CA.

Bouchard, Thomas J. Jr., & McGee, Mark G. (1977). Sex differences in human spatial ability: Not an X-linked recessive gene effect. *Social Biology, 24*, 332–335.

Bower, Bruce. (1991, March 23). Teenage turning point. *Science News, 139*.

Brabant, Sarah. (1976). Sex role stereotyping in the Sunday comics. *Sex Roles, 2*, 331–337.

Brabant, Sarah, & Mooney, Linda. (1986). Sex role stereotyping in the Sunday comics: Ten years later. *Sex Roles, 14*, 141–148.

Brabeck, Mary. (1983). Moral judgment: Theory and research on differences between males and females. *Developmental Review, 3*, 274–291.

Brabeck, Mary M. (1989). Comment on Scarr. *American Psychologist, 44*, 846.

Brackbill, Yvonne, & Schroder, Kerri. (1980). Circumcision, gender differences, and neonatal behavior: An update. *Developmental Psychology, 13*, 607–614.

Bradbard, Marilyn R., & Endsley, Richard C. (1983). The effects of sex-typed labeling on preschool children's information-seeking and retention. *Sex Roles, 9*, 247–260.

Bradley, Harriet. (1989). *Men's work, women's work*. Minneapolis: University of Minnesota Press.

Brady, Katherine. (1979). *Father's days*. New York: Dell.

Bram, Susan. (1984). Voluntarily childless women: Traditional or nontraditional? *Sex Roles, 10*, 195–206.

Brasher, Philip. (1983, January 21). Jane Roe: Battle was still worth it. *Providence Evening Bulletin*.

Bray, Rosemary L. (1991, November 17). Taking sides against ourselves. *New York Times Magazine*, pp. 56, 94–95, 101.

Breast implants: Deadly news. (1990, November/December). *Ms.*, p. 25.

Brehm, Sharon S., & Weinraub, Marsha. (1977). Physical barriers and psychological reactance: Two-year-olds' responses to threats to freedom. *Journal of Personality and Social Psychology, 35*, 830–836.

Brennan-Parks, Kimberley, Goddard, Murray, Wilson, Alexander E., & Kinnear, Lori. (1991). Sex differences in smiling as measured in a picture taking task. *Sex Roles, 24*, 375–382.

Breslin, Jimmy. (1986). *Table money*. NY: Ticknor & Fields.

Bretl, Daniel J., & Cantor, Joanne. (1988). The portrayal of men and women in U.S. television commercials. *Sex Roles, 18*, 595–609.

Brewer, Rose N. (1988). Black women in poverty: Some comments on female-headed families. *Signs, 13*, 331–339.

Brickman, Edith, & Beckwith, Jonathan. (1982, March 14). Letters. *New York Times*.

Bridenthal, Renata, Grossman, A., & Kaplan, M. (1984). *When biology became destiny: Women in Weimar and Nazi Germany*. New York: Monthly Review Press.

Bridges, Judith S. (1987). College females' perceptions of adult roles and occupational fields for women. *Sex Roles, 16*, 591–604.

Bridgwater, Carol A. (1983, November). Sex and the prestigious job. *Psychology Today*, p. 74.

Briere, John, & Malamuth, Neil M. (1983). Self-reported likelihood of sexually aggressive behavior: Attitudinal versus sexual explanations. *Journal of Research in Personality, 17*, 315–323.

Briscoe, Anne M. (1978). Hormones and gender. In E. Tobach & B. Rosoff (Eds.), *Genes and gender I* (pp. 31–50). New York: Gordian Press.

Briscoe, Jerry B. (1989). Perceptions that discourage women attorneys from seeking public office. *Sex Roles, 21*, 557–567.

Brison, Susan. (1993, March 21). Survival course. *New York Times Magazine*, pp. 20, 22.

Brodsky, Annette M. (1980). A decade of feminist influence on psychotherapy. *Psychology of Women Quarterly, 4*, 331–344.

Brody, Claire R. (1990). Women in a nursing home: Living with hope and meaning. *Psychology of Women Quarterly, 14*, 579–592.

Brody, Jane E. (1981, January 21). Personal health. *New York Times*.

Brody, Jane E. (1983a, May 11). Personal health. *New York Times*, p. C-6.

Brody, Jane E. (1983b, October 17). Research on easy-to-use male contraceptive lags. *Providence Evening Bulletin*.

Brody, Jane E. (1986, April 16). Treatment techniques vary for premenstrual syndrome. *New York Times*.

Brody, Leslie R. (1984). Sex and age variations in the quality and intensity of children's emotional attributions to hypothetical situations. *Sex Roles, 11*, 51–59.

Bronstein, Phyllis, & Pfennig, Joyce. (1988). Misperceptions of women and affirmative action principles in faculty hiring: Response to Elliot's comment on Bronstein et al. *American Psychologist, 43*, 668–669.

Brooks-Gunn, Jeanne. (1986). The relationship of maternal beliefs about sex typing to maternal and young children's behavior. *Sex Roles, 14*, 21–35.

Brooks-Gunn, Jeanne, & Ruble, Diane N. (1983). Dysmenorrhea in adolescence. In S. Golub (Ed.), *Menarche* (pp. 251–261). Boston: Lexington Books.

Broverman, Inge K., Broverman, Donald M., Clarkson, Frank E., Rosenkrantz, Paul S., & Vogel, Susan R. (1970). Sex-role stereotypes and clinical judgments of mental health. *Journal of Consulting Psychology, 34*, 1–7.

Broverman, Inge K., Vogel, Susan R., Broverman, Donald M., Clarkson, Frank E., & Rosenkrantz, Paul S. (1972). Sex-role stereotypes: A current appraisal. *Journal of Social Issues, 28*(2), 59–78.

Brown, Diane R., & Gary, Lawrence E. (1985). Social support network differentials among married and nonmarried black females. *Psychology of Women Quarterly, 9*, 229–241.

Brown, Laura S. (1990, Summer). Mapping the moral domain: A review and a critique. *The Interchange*, pp. 5–6, 4527 1st Ave NE, Seattle, WA 98105.

Brown, Laura S. (1991). Ethical issues in feminist therapy. *Psychology of Women Quarterly, 15*, 323–336.

Brown, Linda K. (1979). Women and business management. *Signs, 5*, 266–268.

Brown Project. (1980, April). *Men and women learning together: A study of college students in the late 70's*. Providence, RI: Office of the Provost, Brown University.

Brown, Rita Mae. (1973). *Rubyfruit jungle*. New York: Bantam.

Brown, Rosellen. (1976). *The autobiography of my mother*. Garden City, NJ: Doubleday.

Brown, Rosellen. (1984). *Civil wars*. New York: Knopf.

Brown, Rosellen. (1992, April 19). Why audiences hunger for 'Fried Green Tomatoes.' *New York Times*, p. H-22.

Brown-Collins, Alice R., & Sussewell, Deborah R. (1985). *Afro-American woman's emerging selves: A historical and theoretical model of self-concept*. Unpublished paper, Brown University, Providence, RI.

Browne, Angela, & Finkelhor, David. (1986). Impact of child sexual abuse: A review of the research. *Psychological Bulletin, 99*, 66–77.

Brownmiller, Susan. (1975). *Against our will: Men, women and rape*. New York: Simon & Schuster.

Brownmiller, Susan. (1984). *Femininity*. New York: Linden Press.

Brozan, Nadine. (1983, January 12). Hot flashes are topic for research and group therapy. *New York Times*, pp. C-1–C-14.

Brozan, Nadine. (1985, February 18). Women and cocaine: A growing problem. *New York Times*, p. C-18.

Bruer, John T. (1983). Women in science: Lack of full participation. *Science, 221*, 1339.

Bryan, Janice W., & Luria, Zella. (1978). Sex-role learning: A test of the selective attention hypothesis. *Child Development, 49*, 13–23.

Bryant, Adam. (1992, April 30). The woman who sued State Farm and won. *New York Times*.

Bryant, Fred B., & Veroff, Joseph. (1982). The structure of psychological well-being: A sociohistorical analysis. *Journal of Personality and Social Psychology, 43*, 653–673.

Bryden, M. P. (1979). Evidence for sex-related differences in cerebral organization. In M. A. Wittig & A. C. Petersen (Eds.), *Sex-related differences in cognitive functioning* (pp. 121–143). New York: Academic Press.

Bryson, Rebecca B., Bryson, Jeff B., Licht, Mark H., & Licht, Barbara G. (1976). The professional pair: Husband and wife psychologists. *American Psychologist, 31*, 10–16.

Budoff, Penny W. (1982). Zomepirac sodium in the treatment of primary dysmenorrhea syndrome. *New England Journal of Medicine, 307*, 714–719.

Buehler, Cheryl. (1988). The social and emotional well-being of divorced residential parents. *Sex Roles, 18*, 247–257.

Bullough, Bonnie. (1974). Some questions about the past and the future. In V. Bullough, *The subordinate sex: A history of attitudes toward women* (pp. 335–354). New York: Penguin.

Bullough, Vern L. (1974). *The subordinate sex: A history of attitudes toward women*. New York: Penguin.

Bullough, Vern L. (1983). Menarche and teenage pregnancy: A misuse of historical data. In S. Golub (Ed.), *Menarche* (pp. 187–193). Boston: Lexington Books.

Bumiller, Elisabeth. (1990). *May you be the mother of a hundred sons*. New York: Fawcett Columbine.

Burgess, Ann W., & Holmstrom, Lynda L. (1976). Rape: Its effect on task performance at varying stages in the life cycle. In M. J. Walker & S. L. Brodsky (Eds.), *Sexual assault* (pp. 23–33). Lexington, MA: Heath.

Burlew, Ann K. (1982). The experiences of black females in traditional and nontraditional professions. *Psychology of Women Quarterly, 6*, 312–326.

Burt, Martha R. (1980). Cultural myths and supports for rape. *Journal of Personality and Social Psychology, 38*, 217–230.

Burt, Martha R., & Estep, Rhoda E. (1981). Apprehension and fear: Learning a sense of sexual vulnerability. *Sex Roles, 7*, 511–522.

Bush, Sherida. (1976, May). Day care is as good as home care. *Psychology Today*, pp. 36–37.

Buss, Arnold H., & Perry, Mark. (1992). The aggression questionnaire. *Journal of Personality and Social Psychology, 63*, 452–459.

Buss, David M. (1988). The evolution of human intrasexual competition: Tactics of mate attraction. *Journal of Personality and Social Psychology, 54*, 616–628.

Buss, David M., & Barnes, Michael. (1986). Preferences in human mate selection. *Journal of Personality and Social Psychology, 50*, 559–570.

Busse, Curt, & Hamilton, William J. III. (1981). Infant carrying by male chacma baboons. *Science, 212*, 1281–1282.

Bussey, Kay, & Bandura, Albert. (1984). Influence of gender constancy and social power on sex-linked modeling. *Journal of Personality and Social Psychology, 47*, 1292–1302.

Bussey, Kay, & Perry, David G. (1982). Same-sex imitation: The avoidance of cross-sex models or the acceptance of same-sex models? *Sex Roles, 8*, 773–784.

Busy women are healthier. (1985, February 20). *Providence Evening Bulletin*, pp. A-1f.

Buttenwieser, Susan. (1991a, May/June). Reprotech and the law. *Ms.*, p. 46.

Buttenwieser, Susan. (1991b, May/June). Reprospeak defined. *Ms.*, p. 33.

Bylsma, Wayne H., & Major, Brenda. (1992). Two routes to eliminating gender differences in personal entitlement. *Psychology of Women Quarterly, 16*, 193–200.

Byron, Peg. (1991, January/February). HIV: The national scandal. *Ms.*, pp. 24–29.

Cahill, Spencer E. (1983). Reexamining the acquisition of sex roles: A social interactionist approach. *Sex Roles, 9*, 1–15.

Cain, Barbara S. (1982, December 19). Plight of the gray divorcee. *New York Times Magazine*, pp. 89–95.

Caine, Lynn. (1974). *Widow*. New York: Morrow.

Caine, Lynn. (1985). *What did I do wrong? Mothers, children, guilt*. New York: Arbor House.

Caldwell, Donna. (1988). *Factors differentiating teenage mothers from successful contraceptors*. Master's thesis, University of Rhode Island.

Caldwell, Mayta A., & Peplau, Letitia A. (1982). Sex differences in same-sex friendship. *Sex Roles, 8*, 721–732.

Caldwell, Mayta A., & Peplau, Letitia A. (1984). The balance of power in lesbian relationships. *Sex Roles, 10*, 587–599.

Calvin, William H. (1991). *The ascent of mind*. New York: Bantam.

Calvin, William H. (1991). *The throwing madonna: Essays on the brain*. New York: McGraw Hill.

Calway-Fagen, Norma, Wallston, Barbara S., & Gabel, Harris. (1979). The relationship between attitudinal and behavioral measures of sex preferences. *Psychology of Women Quarterly, 4*, 274–280.

Campbell, Anne. (1984). *Girls in the gang*. New York: Basil Blackwell.

Canby, Vincent. (1986, June 1). Inside 'Cobra' may dwell a pussycat. *New York Times*, p. H-21.

Cancian, Francesca M. (1986). The feminization of love. *Signs, 11*, 692–709.

Canter, Rachelle J., & Ageton, Suzanne S. (1984). The epidemiology of adolescent sex-role attitudes. *Sex Roles, 11,* 657–676.

Canter, Rachelle J., & Meyerowitz, Beth E. (1984). Sex-role stereotypes: Self-reports of behavior. *Sex Roles, 10,* 293–306.

Cantor, Aviva. (1976, Fall). The Lilith question. *Lilith,* pp. 5–10, 38.

Caplan, Paula J. (1977). Sex, age, behavior, and school subject as determinants of report of learning problems. *Journal of Learning Disabilities, 10,* 60–62.

Caplan, Paula J. (1979). Beyond the box score: A boundary condition for sex differences in aggression and achievement striving. In B. A. Maher (Ed.), *Progress in experimental personality research,* vol. 9 (pp. 42–87). New York: Academic Press.

Caplan, Paula J. (1986, October). Take the blame off mother. *Psychology Today,* pp. 70–71.

Caplan, Paula J. (1993, March 25). Personal communication (letter).

Caplan, Paula J., & Gans, Maureen. (1991). Is there empirical justification for the category of "Self-Defeating Personality Disorder"? *Feminism & Psychology, 1,* 263–278.

Caplan, Paula J., MacPherson, G. M., & Tobin, P. (1985). Do sex-related differences in spatial abilities exist? A multilevel critique with new data. *American Psychologist, 40,* 786–799.

CAPline. (1991, June). Poverty guidelines. 1991. South County Community Action, Peacedale, RI 02883.

Caputi, Jane, & Russell, Diana E. H. (1990, September/October). "Femicide": Speaking the unspeakable. *Ms.,* pp. 34–37.

Cardell, Mona, Finn, Stephen, & Marecek, Jeanne. (1981). Sex-role identity, sex-role behavior, and satisfaction in heterosexual, lesbian, and gay male couples. *Psychology of Women Quarterly, 5,* 488–494.

Cardoza, Desdemona. (1991). College attendance and persistence among Hispanic women: An examination of some contributing factors. *Sex Roles, 24,* 133–147.

Careers and paychecks. (1984, May 29). *USA Today,* p. D-4.

Carli, Linda L. (1991). Gender, status, and influence. *Advances in Group Processes, 8,* 89–113.

Carlson, Rae. (1972). Understanding women: Implications for personality theory and research. *Journal of Social Issues, 28,* 17–32.

Carmen, Arlene, & Moody, Howard. (1985). *Working women: The subterranean world of street prostitution.* New York: Harper & Row.

Carnage of violence challenges diseases as top health threat. (1984, November 27). *Providence Evening Bulletin.*

Carpenter, C. Jan, & Huston-Stein, Aletha. (1980). Activity structure and sex-typed behavior in preschool children. *Child Development, 51,* 862–872.

Carpenter, C. Jan, Huston, Aletha C., & Holt, Wilma. (1986). Modification of preschool sex-typed behaviors by participation in adult-structured activities. *Sex Roles, 14,* 603–615.

Carr, Peggy G., & Mednick, Martha T. (1988). Sex role socialization and the development of achievement motivation in Black preschool children. *Sex Roles, 18,* 169–180.

Carrie, Cherylynn M. (1981). Reproductive symptoms: Interrelations and determinants. *Psychology of Women Quarterly, 6,* 174–186.

Carstensen, Laura L. & Pasupathi, Monish. (1993). Women of a certain age. In S. Matteo (Ed.), *American women in the nineties: Today's critical issues* (pp. 67–78). Boston: Northeastern University Press.

Cassedy, Ellen, & Nussbaum, Karen. (1983). *9 to 5: The working woman's guide to office survival.* New York: Penguin.

Celani, David. (1976). Interpersonal approach to hysteria. *American Journal of Psychiatry, 113,* 1414–1418.

Census says college women have chance of marrying. (1987, February 24). *The Good 5¢ Cigar,* University of Rhode Island, Kingston, RI.

Census: Women waiting. (1989, June 28). *Providence Journal Bulletin,* p. E-3.

Chambless, Dianne L., & Goldstein, Alan J. (1980). In A. M. Brodsky & R. T. Hare-Mustin (Eds.), *Women and psychotherapy* (pp. 113–134). New York: Guilford Press.

Chan, W. Y. (1983). Prostaglandins in primary dysmenorrhea: Basis for the new therapy. In S. Golub (Ed.), *Menarche* (pp. 243–249). Boston: Lexington Books.

Change over a decade. (1985, March 10). *New York Times,* p. E-24.

Changing the rules on abortion. (1993, January 23). *San Francisco Chronicle,* p. A-19.

Charnes, Ruth, Hoffman, Kay E., Hoffman, Lyla, & Meyers, Ruth S. (1980). The Sesame Street library—bad books bring big bucks. *Young Children, 35*(2), 10–12.

Chavez, Deborah. (1985). Perpetuation of gender inequality: A content analysis of comic strips. *Sex Roles, 13,* 93–102.

Chavez, Lydia. (1987, July 17). Women's movement, its ideals accepted, face subtler issues. *New York Times,* p. A-10.

Check, James V. P., & Malamuth, Neil M. (1983). Sex role stereotyping and reactions to depictions of stranger versus acquaintance rape. *Journal of Personality and Social Psychology, 45,* 344–356.

Check, James V. P., & Malamuth, Neil M. (1985). An empirical assessment of some feminist hypotheses about rape. *International Journal of Women's Studies, 8*(4), 414–423.

Cheney, Dorothy, Seyfarth, Robert, & Smuts, Barbara. (1986). Social relationships and social cognition in nonhuman primates. *Science, 234,* 1361–1366.

Cheng, Lucie. (1984, February). Asian American women and feminism. *Sojourner, 10*(2), 11–12.

Cherry, Louise. (1975). The pre-school teacher-child dyad: Sex differences in verbal interaction. *Child Development, 46,* 532–535.

Cherulnik, Paul D., & Evans, Robert M. (1984). Facial expressive behaviors of high self-monitors are less sex-typed. *Sex Roles, 11,* 435–449.

Chesler, Phyllis. (1972). *Women and madness.* New York: Doubleday.

Chesler, Phyllis. (1985). *Mothers on trial: The battle for children and custody.* New York: McGraw-Hill.

Children's lives deteriorated in the 1980s, study finds. (1991, February 2). *Providence Journal Bulletin,* p. B-9.

The children of the shadows: Shaping young lives. (1993, April 4). *New York Times,* p. Y-17.

Chino, Allan F., & Funabiki, Dean. (1984). A cross-validation of sex differences in the expression of depression. *Sex Roles, 11,* 175–187.

Chodorow, Nancy. (1978). *The reproduction of mothering: Psychoanalysis and sociology of gender.* Berkeley: University of California Press.

Choosing baby's sex is closer to reality. (1979, February 15). *Providence Evening Bulletin.*

Chrisler, Joan C. (1990, Fall). Menstrual humor: Funny or not? *AWP Newsletter,* p. 9.

Church, George J. (1990, Fall). The view from behind bars. *Time* (Special Issue), pp. 20–22.

Chusmir, Leonard H., Koberg, Christine S., & Stecher, Mary D. (1992). Self-confidence of managers in work and social situations: A look at gender differences. *Sex Roles, 26,* 497–512.

Chute, Carolyn. (1985). *The Beans of Egypt, Maine.* New York: Ticknor & Fields.

Clarke-Stewart, K. Alison. (1989). Infant day care: Maligned or malignant? *American Psychologist, 44,* 266–273.

Clayton, Obie Jr., Baird, Anne C., & Levinson, Richard M. (1984). Subjective decision making in medical school admissions: Potentials for discrimination. *Sex Roles, 10,* 527–532.

Clements, Marcelle. (1992, September). Childless and second class. *Glamour,* p. 208.

Cleveland clinic to aid infertile with donor eggs. (1987, July 15). *Providence Journal-Bulletin,* p. A-7.

Cloward, Richard A., & Piven, Frances F. (1979). Hidden protest: The channeling of female innovation and resistance. *Signs, 4,* 651–669.

Cobb, Nancy J., Stevens-Long, Judith, & Goldstein, Steven. (1982). The influence of televised models on toy preference in children. *Sex Roles, 8,* 1075–1080.

Cochran, Susan D., & Mays, Vickie M. (1989). Women and AIDS-related concerns. *American Psychologist, 44,* 529–535.

Cohen, Donna. (1987, October 24). *Mental health and older women: A research agenda.* National Institute of Mental Health, Washington, DC.

Colangelo, Nicholas, Rosenthal, David M., & Dettman, David F. (1984). Maternal employment and job satisfaction and their relationship to children's perceptions and behaviors. *Sex Roles, 10,* 693–702.

Colatosti, Camille. (1992). Making 65¢ on the dollar. *Labor Notes,* 7435 Michigan Ave., Detroit, MI 48210.

Cole, Ellen, & Rothblum, Esther. (1990). Commentary on "Sexuality and the midlife woman." *Psychology of Women Quarterly, 14,* 509–512.

Coleman, Marilyn, & Ganong, Lawrence H. (1985). Love and sex role stereotypes: Do macho men and feminine women make better lovers? *Journal of Personality and Social Psychology, 49,* 170–176.

Coles, Frances S. (1986). Forced to quit: Sexual harassment complaints and agency response. *Sex Roles, 14,* 81–95.

Coles, Robert, & Coles, Jane H. (1978). *Women of crisis: I.* New York: Delacorte.

Collins, Glenn. (1986, March 28). New generation of working women learn what it is to retire. *Providence Journal Bulletin,* p. B-11.

Collins, Jean E. (1978, April 30). Publishers depict women in new ways. *New York Times,* sec. 12, p. 19.

Collins, Patricia H. (1991). *Black feminist thought, knowledge, consciousness, and the politics of empowerment.* Perspectives on gender, vol. 2. New York: Routledge.

Coltrane, Scott. (1992). The micropolitics of gender in nonindustrial societies. *Gender & Society, 6,* 86–107.

Comas-Diaz, Lillian. (1991). Feminism and diversity in psychology. The case of women of color. *Psychology of Women Quarterly, 15,* 597–609.

Computer revolution: Why it's a man's world. (1989, February 13). *Providence Journal Bulletin,* p. A-1.

Condry, John C. (1984). Gender identity and social competence. *Sex Roles, 11,* 485–511.

Connelly, Sherryl. (1981, March 5). What's not good for the unborn. *Providence Evening Bulletin.*

Connor, Jane M., Schackman, Maxine, & Serbin, Lisa A. (1978). Sex-related differences in response to practice on a visual-spatial test and generalization to a related test. *Child Development, 49,* 24–29.

Connor, Jane M., Serbin, Lisa A., & Ender, Regina A. (1978). Responses of boys and girls to aggressive, assertive, and passive behaviors of male and female characters. *Journal of Genetic Psychology, 133,* 59–69.

Constantinople, Anne. (1979). Sex-role acquisition: In search of the elephant. *Sex Roles, 5,* 121–133.

Contraceptives: The Pill acquitted. (1989, February). *University of California, Berkeley Wellness Letter,* p. 1.

Contratto, Susan. (1992). Review of "Women, girls, and psychotherapy," edited by Carol Gilligan, Annie G. Rogers, and Deborah L. Tolman. *Psychology of Women Quarterly, 16,* 543–545.

Cook, Alice S., Fritz, Janet J., McCornack, Barbara L., & Visperas, Cris. (1985). Early gender differences in the functional usage of language. *Sex Roles, 12,* 909–915.

Cook, Jennifer. (1986, December). Bone strength. *Self,* pp. 114–119.

Cooper, Harris M., Burger, Jerry M., & Good, Thomas L. (1981). Gender differences in the academic locus of control beliefs of young children. *Journal of Personality and Social Psychology, 40,* 562–572.

Copenhaver, Stacey, & Grauerholz, Elizabeth. (1991). Sexual victimization among sorority women: Exploring the link between sexual violence and institutional practices. *Sex Roles, 24,* 31–41.

Corballis, Michael C. (1980). Laterality and myth. *American Psychologist, 35,* 284–295.

Corcoran, Mary, Duncan, Greg J., & Hill, Martha S. (1984). The economic fortunes of women and children: Lessons from the panel study of income dynamics. *Signs, 10,* 232–248.

Cordes, Colleen. (1986b, June). Test tilt: Boys outscore girls on both parts of SAT. *APA Monitor,* pp. 30–31.

Corea, Gena. (1980, July). The caesarean epidemic. *Mother Jones,* pp. 28–42.

Corrigan, Patricia. (1992, March 25). Do little girls need a pregnancy doll? *Providence Journal Bulletin,* pp. C-1, C-3.

Cottle, Charles E., Searles, Patricia, Berger, Ronald J., & Pierce, BethAnn. (1989). Conflicting ideologies and the politics of pornography. *Gender & Society, 3,* 303–333.

Council of Representatives Resolutions on Reproductive Choice and Abortion. (1989). American Psychological Association, 1200 17th St. NW, Washington, DC 20036.

Cowan, Gloria. (1984). The double standard in age-discrepant relationships. *Sex Roles, 11,* 17–23.

Cowan, Gloria, & Hoffman, Charles D. (1986). Gender stereotyping in young children: Evidence to support a concept-learning approach. *Sex Roles, 14,* 211–224.

Cowan, Gloria, Lee, Carole, Levy, Daniella, & Snyder, Debra. (1988). Dominance and inequality in X-rated videocassettes. *Psychology of Women Quarterly, 12,* 299–311.

Cowen, Emory L. (1991). In pursuit of wellness. *American Psychologist, 46,* 404–408.

Cowley, Geoffrey. (1990, December 24). A birth-control breakthrough. *Newsweek,* p. 68.

Cowley, Geoffrey, & Hager, Mary. (1991, December 9). Sleeping with the enemy. *Newsweek,* pp. 58–59.

Cox, Cathryn L., & Glick, William H. (1986). Resume evaluations and cosmetics use: When more is not better. *Sex Roles, 14,* 51–58.

Cramer, Phebe, & Skidd, Jody E. (1992). Correlates of self-worth in preschoolers: The role of gender-stereotyped styles of behavior. *Sex Roles, 26,* 369–390.

Crandall, Christian S. (1988). Social contagion of binge eating. *Journal of Personality and Social Psychology, 55,* 588–598.

Crawford, Mary, & Gressley, Diane. (1991). Creativity, caring, and context: Women's and men's accounts of humor preferences and practices. *Psychology of Women Quarterly, 15,* 217–232.

Crichton, Sarah. (1983, October). Sex and self-discovery. *Ms.,* pp. 68–69.

Crimp, Douglas. (1988). *AIDS: Cultural analysis, cultural activism.* Cambridge, MA: MIT Press.

Crocker, Phyllis L. (1982). Annotated bibliography on sexual harassment in education. *Women's Rights Law Reporter, 7,* 91–106.

Crohan, Susan E., Antonucci, Toni D., & Adelmann, Pamela K. (1989). Job characteristics and well-being at midlife: Ethnic and gender comparisons. *Psychology of Women Quarterly, 13,* 223–235.

Cronkite, Ruth C., & Moos, Rudolf H. (1984). Sex and marital status in relation to the treatment and outcome of alcoholic patients. *Sex Roles, 11,* 93–112.

Crook, Joan. (1986). Family functioning in families of origin of survivors of father-daughter incest. Unpublished master's thesis, University of Rhode Island, Kingston.

Crouter, Ann C. (1987). *Developmental Psychology, 23,* 431–440.

Croxton, Jack S., & Klonsky, Bruce G. (1982). Sex differences in causal attributions for success and failure in real and hypothetical sport settings. *Sex Roles, 8,* 399–409.

Cummings, Scott, & Taebel, Delbert. (1980). Sexual inequality and the reproduction of consciousness: An analysis of sex-role stereotyping among children. *Sex Roles, 6,* 631–644.

Cunningham, Susan. (1984, January). Suit leads to study of sexual harassment on job. *APA Monitor,* p. 29.

Cutler, Susan E., & Nolen-Hoeksema, Susan. (1991). Accounting for sex differences in depression through female victimization: Childhood sexual abuse. *Sex Roles, 24,* 425–438.

Daly, Mary. (1978a). *Gyn/Ecology.* Boston: Beacon.

Daly, Mary. (1978b). Sparking: The fire of female friendship. *Chrysalis, 6,* 27–35.

Danziger, Nira. (1983). Sex-related differences in the aspirations of high school students. *Sex Roles, 9,* 683–695.

Darnton, Nina. (1990, June 4). Mommy vs. mommy. *Newsweek,* pp. 64–67.

Darnton, Nina. (1991, May 13). The ultimate squeeze play. *Newsweek,* p. 63.

Dash, Joan. (1973). *A life of one's own.* New York: Harper & Row.

Data Points. (1992). *Science, 255,* 1376.

Datan, Nancy. (1989). Aging women: The silent majority. *Women's Studies Quarterly, 17* (1 & 2), 12–19.

Daubman, Kimberly A., Heatherington, Laurie, & Ahn, Alicia. (1992). Gender and the self-presentation of academic achievement. *Sex Roles, 27,* 187–204.

Davidson, Christine V., & Abramowitz, Stephen I. (1980). Sex bias in clinical judgment: Later empirical returns. *Psychology of Women Quarterly, 4,* 377–395.

Davidson, Sara. (1978). *Loose change.* New York: Pocket Books.

Davis, Albert J. (1984). Sex-differentiated behaviors in nonsexist picture books. *Sex Roles, 11,* 1–16.

Davis, Angela. (1982). Women, race and class: An activist perspective. *Women's Studies Quarterly, 10*(4), 5–9.

Davis, Angela Y. (1983). *Women, race, and class.* New York: Vintage.

Davis, Donald M. (1990). Portrayals of women in prime-time network television: Some demographic characteristics. *Sex Roles, 23,* 325–332.

Davis, Glen E., Leitenberg, Harold. (1987). Adolescent sex offenders. *Psychological Bulletin, 101,* 417–427.

D.C. rates highest in infant mortality. (1993, January 8). *Providence Journal Bulletin,* p. A-5.

Dean, Nancy, & Stark, Myra (Eds.). (1977). Introduction. In *the looking glass* (pp. xiii–xxii). New York: Putnam.

DeAngelis, Tori. (1990, December). Who is susceptible to bulimia, and why? *APA Monitor,* p. 8.

DeAngelis, Tori. (1991, June). DSM being revised, but problems remain. *APA Monitor,* pp. 12–13.

DeAngelis, Tori. (1992a, April). APA's amicus brief attempts 'to educate' high court on abortion. *APA Monitor,* pp. 6–7.

DeAngelis, Tori. (1992b, August). Book on women in power strikes chord with media. *APA Monitor,* p. 11.

DeAngelis, Tori. (1992c, September). APA brief has an effect on decision in *Casey. APA Monitor,* p. 1.

Death bias? (1990, July 2). *Newsweek,* p. 6.

Deaux, Kay. (1984). From individual differences to social categories: Analysis of a decade's research on gender. *American Psychologist, 39,* 105–116.

Deaux, Kay, & Hanna, Randel. (1984). Courtship in the personals column: The influence of gender and sexual orientation. *Sex Roles, 11,* 363–375.

Deaux, Kay, & Major, Brenda. (1987). Putting gender into context: An interactive model of gender-related behavior. *Psychological Review, 94,* 369–389.

de Beauvoir, Simone. (1961). *The second sex.* New York: Bantam. (Original work published in 1949.)

DeBold, Joseph F., & Luria, Zella. (1983). Gender identity, interactionism, and politics: A reply to Rogers and Walsh. *Sex Roles, 9,* 1101–1108.

Decade of the woman. (1992, December 31). *Providence Journal Bulletin,* p. A-8.

DeCasper, Anthony J., & Fifer, William P. (1980). Of human bonding: Newborns prefer their mothers' voices. *Science, 208,* 1174–1176.

Deep in the heart. (1992, January 26). *New York Times,* p. E-9.

Deitz, Sheila R., Littman, Madeleine, & Bentley, Brenda J. (1984). Attribution of responsibility for rape: The influence of observer empathy, victim resistance, and victim attractiveness. *Sex Roles, 10,* 261–280.

Dejanikus, Tacie. (1985, May/June). Major drug manufacturer funds osteoporosis public education campaign. *Network News,* p. 1.

DeLacoste-Utamsing, Christine, & Holloway, Ralph L. (1982). Sexual dimorphism in the human corpus callosum. *Science, 216,* 1431–1432.

Delaney, Janice, Lupton, Mary J., & Toth, Emily. (1976). *The curse.* New York: New American Library.

DeLisi, Richard, & Soundranayagam, Luxshmi. (1990). The conceptual structure of sex role stereotypes in college students. *Sex Roles, 23,* 593–611.

Del Boca, Frances K., Ashmore, Richard D., & McManus, Margaret A. (1986). Gender-related attitudes. In R. D. Ashmore & F. K. Del Boca (Eds.), *The social psychology of female-male relations: A critical analysis of central concepts* (pp. 121–163). Orlando, FL: Academic Press.

DeLoache, Judy S., Cassidy, Deborah J., & Carpenter, C. Jan. (1987). The three bears are all boys: Mothers' gender labeling of neutral picture book characters. *Sex Roles, 17,* 163–178.

Deluty, Robert H. (1985). Consistency of assertive, aggressive, and submissive behavior for children. *Journal of Personality and Social Psychology, 49,* 1054–1065.

DeMarchi, W. G. (1976). Psychophysiological aspects of the menstrual cycle. *Journal of Psychosomatic Research, 20,* 279–287.

Denmark, Florence L., Shaw, Jeffrey S., & Ciali, Samuel D. (1985). The relationship among sex roles, living arrangements, and the division of household responsibilities. *Sex Roles, 12,* 617–625.

Denworth, Lydia. (1991, August 26). Sisterhood is profitable. *Newsweek,* p. 60.

DePalma, Anthony. (1993, January 24). Rare in Ivy League: Women who work as full professors. *New York Times,* pp. Y-1, 11.

Dermody, Colleen. (1992, Winter). Gag rule to be enforced by executive branch. *Feminist Majority Report,* p. 5.

DeSnyder, V. Nelly S., Cervantes, Richard C., & Padilla, Amado M. (1990). Gender and ethnic differences in psychosocial stress and generalized distress among Hispanics. *Sex Roles, 22,* 441–453.

Deutsch, Claudia H. (1990, January 28). Saying no to the 'Mommy Track.' *New York Times,* p. F-29.

Deutsch, F. M. (1990). Status, sex, and smiling: The effect of role on smiling men and women. *Personality and Social Psychology Bulletin, 16,* 531–540.

Deutsch, Helene. (1944). *The psychology of women: A psychoanalytic interpretation,* vol. 1. New York: Grune & Stratton.

Developing a national agenda to address women's mental health needs. (1985). Washington, DC. American Psychological Association.

Development of the law of sexual harassment. (1992, November 4). *Labor Relations Week.* The Bureau of National Affairs, Rockville, MD 20850.

de Wolf, Virginia A. (1981). High school mathematics preparation and sex differences in quantitative abilities. *Psychology of Women Quarterly, 5,* 555–567.

Diamond, Pam. (1985, May). Medical news. *Ms*, p. 64.

DiBlasio, Frederick A., & Benda, Brent B. (1992). Gender differences in theories of adolescent sexual activity. *Sex Roles, 27,* 221–239.

Dick-Read, Grantly. (1959). *Childbirth without fear* (2nd ed.). New York: Harper & Row.

Dietz, Jean. (1985, November 14). Family job stress found in Hub study. *Boston Globe*, pp. 1, 17.

Dietz, Jean. (1988, May 30). What *really* bothers women in midlife. *Boston Globe*, pp. 33–34.

DiFilippo, Dana, & Wexler, Laura E. (1991, March). Feminist movement may suffer as today's students shun label. *U. The National College Newspaper*, p. 1).

Dill, Bonnie T. (1979). The dialectics of black womanhood. *Signs, 4,* 543–555.

Dinnerstein, Dorothy. (1977). *The mermaid and the minotaur*. New York: Harper & Row.

Dino, Geri A., Barnett, Mark A., & Howard, Jeffrey A. (1984). Children's expectations of sex differences in parents' responses to sons and daughters encountering interpersonal problems. *Sex Roles, 11,* 709–717.

DiPerna, Paula. (1984, January). Balancing high school and motherhood. *Ms*, pp. 57–62.

Disclosure of sexual abuse: A process. (1990). *Grand Rounds: Brookside Hospital Review, 4*(3), 1–2.

Division 35 Brochure. (n.d.). Psychology of Women. Washington, DC: American Psychological Association.

Divorce rate is only 1 in 8, says Harris poll. (1987, June 29). *Providence Journal Bulletin*, pp. A-1, A-2.

Dix, Theodore. (1991). The affective organization of parenting: Adaptive and maladaptive processes. *Psychological Bulletin, 110,* 3–25.

Djerassi, Carl. (1981). *The politics of contraception*. San Francisco: Freeman.

Djerassi, Carl. (1988). "My mom, the professor." *Science, 239,* 10.

Djerassi, Carl. (1989). The bitter pill. *Science, 245,* 356–361.

Dobzhansky, Theodosius. (1967). Of flies and men. *American Psychologist, 22,* 41–48.

Dobzhansky, Theodosius. (1972). Genetics and the diversity of behavior. *American Psychologist, 27,* 523–530.

Docket Report. (1983–1984). New York: Center for Constitutional Rights.

Doctors: 1st caesarean should be mother's last. (1988, October 27). *Providence Journal Bulletin*, p. A-9.

Doherty, William J., & Baldwin, Cynthia. (1985). Shifts and stability in locus of control during the 1970s: Divergence of the sexes. *Journal of Personality and Social Psychology, 48,* 1048–1053.

Dohrenwend, Barbara S. (1973). Social status and stressful life events. *Journal of Personality and Social Psychology, 28,* 225–235.

Donenberg, Geri R., & Hoffman, Lois W. (1988). Gender differences in moral development. *Sex Roles, 18,* 701–717.

Donnerstein, Edward I. (1980). Pornography and violence against women: Experimental studies. *Annals of the New York Academy of Sciences, 347,* 277–288.

Donnerstein, Edward I. (1983). Aggressive pornography: Can it influence aggression toward women? In G. W. Albee, S. Gordon, & H. Leitenberg (Eds.), *Promoting sexual responsibility and preventing sexual problems* (pp. 220–237). Hanover, NH: University Press of New England.

Donnerstein, Edward I., & Linz, Daniel G. (1986, December). The question of pornography. *Psychology Today*, pp. 56–59.

Douglas, Carlyle C. (1991, December 1). Firing big guns, the Navy loses. *New York Times*, p. E-7.

Dowd, Maureen. (1991, May 26). The politics of beauty at work: Yes, but can she make them swoon? *New York Times*, p. E-3.

Dowie, Mark. (1990, March 20). RU 486 creator has an easy delivery. *Providence Journal Bulletin*, pp. B-1, B-3.

Downs, A. Chris. (1983). Letters to Santa Claus: Elementary school-age children's sex-typed toy preferences in a natural setting. *Sex Roles, 9,* 159–163.

Downs, A. Chris, & Gowan, Darryl C. (1980). Sex differences and punishment on prime-time television. *Sex Roles, 6,* 683–694.

Doyle, Miranda. (1993, April 12). MBA inequity: Recent study shows men out-earn women. *The Stanford Daily*, p. 1.

Drabble, Margaret. (1977). *The ice age*. New York: Knopf.

Drabman, Ronald S., Robertson, Stephen J., Patterson, Jana N., Jarvie, Gregory J., Hammer, David, & Cordua, Glenn. (1981). Children's perception of media-portrayed sex roles. *Sex Roles, 7,* 379–389.

Dragonwagon, Crescent. (1985, May). The last word on sleepless, foodless . . . and endless good health. *Ms*, p. 158.

Dreher, George F., Dougherty, Thomas W., & Whitely, William. (1989). Influence tactics and salary attainment: A gender-specific analysis. *Sex Roles, 20,* 535–550.

Dreifus, Claudia. (1975, December). Sterilizing the poor. *Progressive*, pp. 13–19.

Dropping out harder on girls than boys. (1987, March 16). *Providence Journal-Bulletin*, p. A-5.

Ducker, Dalia G. (1980). The effect of two sources of role strain on women physicians. *Sex Roles, 6,* 549–559.

Duckworth, Ed. (1985, April 9). Woman jockey succeeds—her way. *Providence Evening Bulletin*.

Duffy, Karen G. (n.d.). *Facilitating discussions of human sexuality among undergraduate students*. (mimeo., SUNY, Geneseo, NY)

Dutton, Diana B. (1993). Poorer and sicker: Legacies of the 1980s, lessons for the 1990s. In S. Matteo (Ed.), *American women in the nineties: Today's critical issues* (pp. 98–138). Boston: Northeastern University Press.

Dweck, Carol S., Davidson, William, Nelson, Sharon, & Enna, Bradley. (1978). Sex differences in learned helplessness: II. The contingencies of evaluative feedback in the classroom, and III. An experimental analysis. *Developmental Psychology, 14,* 268–276.

Dweck, Carol S., Goetz, Therese E., & Strauss, Nan L. (1980). Sex differences in learned helplessness: IV. An experimental and naturalistic study of failure generalization and its mediators. *Journal of Personality and Social Psychology, 38,* 441–452.

Dworkin, Andrea. (1978, July). The bruise that doesn't heal. *Mother Jones*, pp. 31–36.

Dye, Nancy S. (1980). History of childbirth in America. *Signs, 6,* 97–108.

Dzeich, Billie W., & Weiner, Linda. (1984). *The lecherous professor: Sexual harassment on campus*. Boston: Beacon.

Eagan, Andrea B. (1983, October). The selling of premenstrual syndrome. *Ms.*, pp. 26–31.

Eagan, Andrea B. (1989, April). The estrogen fix. *Ms.*, pp. 38–43.

Eagly, Alice H. (1983). Gender and social influence: A social psychological analysis. *American Psychologist, 38,* 971–981.

Eagly, Alice H. (1987). *Sex differences in social behavior: A social-role interpretation*. Hillsdale, NJ: Erlbaum.

Eagly, Alice H., & Carli, Linda L. (1981). Sex of researchers and sex-typed communications as determinants of sex differences in influencibility: A meta-analysis of social influence studies. *Psychological Bulletin, 90,* 1–20.

Eagly, Alice H., & Chrvala, Carole. (1986). Sex differences in conformity:

Status and gender role interpretations. *Psychology of Women Quarterly,* *10,* 203–220.

Eagly, Alice H., & Johnson, Blair T. (1990). Gender and leadership style: A meta-analysis. *Psychological Bulletin, 108,* 233–256.

Eagly, Alice H., & Karau, Steven J. (1991). Gender and the emergence of leaders: A meta-analysis. *Journal of Personality and Social Psychology, 60,* 685–710.

Eagly, Alice H., & Kite, Mary E. (1987). Are stereotypes of nationalities applied to both women and men? *Journal of Personality and Social Psychology, 53,* 451–462.

Eagly, Alice H., & Steffen, Valerie J. (1986). Gender and aggressive behavior: A meta-analytic review of the social psychological literature. *Psychological Bulletin, 100,* 309–330.

Ebeling, Kay. (1990, November 19). The failure of feminism. *Newsweek,* p. 9.

Eckholm, Erik. (1984, September 18). New view of female primates assails stereotypes. *New York Times,* pp. C-1, C-3.

Effective, not overpowering. (1986, September). Tranxene advertisement. *American Journal of Psychiatry, 143,* back cover.

Ehrlichman, Howard, & Eichenstein, Rosalind. (1992). Private wishes: Gender similarities and differences. *Sex Roles, 26,* 399–422.

Ehrenreich, Barbara. (1983). *The hearts of men.* Garden City, NY: Anchor/Doubleday.

Ehrenreich, Barbara. (1990, Fall). Sorry, sisters, this is not the revolution. *Time* (Special Issue), p. 15.

Ehrenreich, Barbara, Hess, Elizabeth, & Jacobs, Gloria. (1986). *Re-making love: The feminization of sex.* New York: Anchor.

Ehrhardt, Anke A., & Meyer-Bahlburg, Heino F. L. (1981). Effects of prenatal sex hormones on gender-related behavior. *Science, 211,* 1312–1318.

Eisenberg, Ann R. (1988). Grandchildren's perspectives on relationships with grandparents: The influence of gender across generations. *Sex Roles, 19,* 205–217.

Eisenberg, Nancy, & Lennon, Randy. (1983). Sex differences in empathy and related capacities. *Psychological Bulletin, 94,* 100–131.

Eldridge, Natalie S., & Gilbert, Lucia A. (1990). Correlates of relationship satisfaction in lesbian couples. *Psychology of Women Quarterly, 14,* 43–62.

Ellis, Lee, & Ames, M. Ashley. (1987). Neurohormonal functioning and sexual orientation: A theory of homosexuality-heterosexuality. *Psychological Bulletin, 101,* 233–258.

Elpern, Sarah, & Karp, Stephen A. (1984). Sex-role orientation and depressive symptomatology. *Sex Roles, 10,* 987–992.

Eme, Robert F. (1979). Sex differences in childhood psychopathology: A review. *Psychological Bulletin, 86,* 574–595.

Emery, C. Eugene Jr. (1983, April 14). Balance of hormones critical to "pill" safety. *Providence Journal-Bulletin.*

Emery, C. Eugene Jr. (1984, March 22). Dissent is strange to Soviets. *Providence Evening Bulletin.*

Emery, C. Eugene Jr. (1985, April 11). 2 studies find IUDs raise infertility risk in childless women. *Providence Journal-Bulletin.*

Emery, C. Eugene Jr. (1986, September 4). Fetal monitors not really needed during long-risk births, study says. *Providence Journal-Bulletin,* p. B-8.

Emery, C. Eugene Jr. (1991, February 14). Disparity in AIDS care cited. *Providence Journal-Bulletin,* pp. A-1, A-10.

Emery, C. Eugene Jr. (1991, December 18). New study: Homosexuality genetic. *Providence Journal-Bulletin,* p. D-9.

Emmerich, Walter, & Shepard, Karla. (1984). Cognitive factors in the development of sex-typed preferences. *Sex Roles, 11,* 997–1007.

Engel, Marian. (1979). *The glassy sea.* New York: St. Martin's Press.

Englander-Golden, Paula, & Barton, Glenn. (1983). Sex differences in absence from work: A reinterpretation. *Psychology of Women Quarterly, 8,* 185–188.

English, Deirdre. (1981, February/March). The war against choice. *Mother Jones,* pp. 16–21, 26, 28, 31–32.

Epstein, Cynthia F. (1982). *Women in law.*

Erdrich, Louise. (1984). *Love medicine.* New York: Holt, Rinehart & Winston.

Erdrich, Louise. (1987). *The beet queen.* New York: Bantam.

Erdwins, Carol J., & Mellinger, Jeanne C. (1984). Mid-life women: Relation of age and role to personality. *Journal of Personality and Social Psychology, 47,* 390–395.

Erikson, Erik H. (1968). *Identity: Youth and crisis.* New York: Norton.

Ernster, Virginia L. (1975). American menstrual expressions. *Sex Roles, 1,* 3–13.

Eron, Leonard D. (1980). Prescription for reduction of aggression. *American Psychologist, 35,* 244–252.

Escoffier, Jeffrey, Malyon, Alan, Morin, Stephen, & Raphael, Sharon. (1980). Homophobia: Effects on scientists. *Science, 209,* 340.

Estellachild, Vivian. (1971, Winter). Hippie communes. *Women: A Journal of Liberation, 2,* 40–43.

Estrich, Susan. (1991, April 19). Victims who go on trial. *Providence Journal Bulletin,* p. A-14.

Etaugh, Claire. (1980). Effects of nonmaternal care on children: Research evidence and popular views. *American Psychologist, 35,* 309–319.

Etaugh, Claire, & Harlow, Heidi. (1975). Behaviors of male and female teachers as related to behaviors and attitudes of elementary school children. *Journal of Genetic Psychology, 127,* 163–170.

Etaugh, Claire, & Liss, Marsha B. (1992). Home, school, and playroom: Training grounds for adult gender roles. *Sex Roles, 26,* 129–147.

Etaugh, Claire, & Nekolny, Karen. (1990). Effects of employment status and marital status on perceptions of mothers. *Sex Roles, 23,* 273–280.

Etaugh, Claire, & Poertner, Patricia. (1991). Effects of occupational prestige, employment status, and marital status on perceptions of mothers. *Sex Roles, 24,* 345–354.

Etaugh, Claire, & Whittler, Tommy E. (1982). Social memory of preschool girls and boys. *Psychology of Women Quarterly, 7,* 170–174.

Evans, Beverly K. (1990). Mothering as a lesbian issue. *Journal of Feminist Family Therapy, 2,* 43–52.

Executive summary: National study of the incidence and severity of child abuse and neglect. (1982). Washington, DC: Children's Bureau.

'F' is for infants favor fathers' favors. (1982, October 26). *Providence Evening Bulletin.*

Fabes, Richard A., & Laner, Mary R. (1986). How the sexes perceive each other: Advantages and disadvantages. *Sex Roles, 15,* 129–143.

Fabes, Richard A., & Martin, Carol L. (1991). Gender and age stereotypes of emotionality. *Personality and Social Psychology Bulletin, 17,* 532–540.

Fagot, Beverly I. (1974). Sex differences in toddlers' behavior and parental reaction. *Developmental Psychology, 10,* 554–558.

Fagot, Beverly I. (1981a). Male and female teachers: Do they treat boys and girls differently? *Sex Roles, 7,* 263–271.

Fagot, Beverly I. (1981b). Stereotypes versus behavioral judgments of sex differences in young children. *Sex Roles, 7,* 1093–1096.

Fagot, Beverly I. (1984a). The child's expectations of differences in adult male and female interactions. *Sex Roles, 11,* 593–600.

Fagot, Beverly I. (1984b). Teacher and peer reactions to boys' and girls' play styles. *Sex Roles, 11,* 691–702.

Fagot, Beverly I. (1984c). The consequences of problem behavior in toddler children. *Journal of Abnormal Child Psychology, 12,* 385–396.

Fagot, Beverly I., & Hagan, Richard. (1985). Aggression in toddlers:

Responses to the assertive acts of boys and girls. *Sex Roles, 12*, 341–351.

Fagot, Beverly I., Leinbach, Mary D., & Hagan, Richard. (1986). Gender labeling and the adoption of sex-typed behaviors. *Developmental Psychology, 22*, 440–443.

Falk, Ruth, Gispert, Maria, & Baucom, Donald H. (1981). Personality factors related to black teenage pregnancies and abortions. *Psychology of Women Quarterly, 5*, 737–746.

Faludi, Susan. (1991). *Backlash: The undeclared war against American women*. NY: Crown.

Family Life Information Service. (1988, November). *STDS*. PO Box 10716, Rockville, MD, 20850.

Family size drops. (1993, January 4). *Providence Journal Bulletin*, p. D-1.

Fanzo, Michelle. (1987–1988, Fall/Winter). Sex and the teenage girl. *Hampshire Reports*, pp. 4, 5, 14. Hampshire College, Amherst, MA.

Farb, Peter. (1978). *Humankind*. Boston: Houghton Mifflin.

Farley, Jennie. (1985). Book reviews. *Signs, 10*, 585–588.

Farley, Lin. (1978). *Sexual shakedown*. New York: McGraw-Hill.

Fascinating facts. (1989, June). *University of California, Berkeley Wellness Letter, 5*(9).

Fathers are more fun. (1986, May 20). *Providence Evening Bulletin*, p. A-1.

Fausto-Sterling, Anne. (1985). *Myths of gender: Biological theories about women and men*. New York: Basic Books.

The favored infants. (1976, June). *Human Behavior*, pp. 49–50.

FDA calls for halt to breast implants. (1992, January 7). *Providence Journal-Bulletin*, pp. A-1, A-6.

FDS advertisement. (1984, April). *Seventeen*.

Federation CECOS, Schwartz, D., & Mayaux, M. J. (1982). Female fecundity as a function of age. *New England Journal of Medicine, 306*, 404–406.

Feild, Hubert S. (1978). Attitudes toward rape: A comparative analysis of police, rapists, crisis counselors, and citizens. *Journal of Personality and Social Psychology, 36*, 156–179.

Feild, Hubert S. (1979). Rape trials and jurors' decisions. *Law and Human Behavior, 3*, 261–284.

Feinauer, Leslie L. (1988). Relationship of longterm effects of childhood sexual abuse to identity of the offender: Family, friend, or stranger. *Women & Therapy, 7*(4), 89–107.

Feinblatt, John A., & Gold, Alice R. (1976). Sex roles and the psychiatric referral process. *Sex Roles, 2*, 109–122.

Feingold, Alan. (1988). Cognitive gender differences are disappearing. *American Psychologist, 43*, 95–103.

Feinman, Saul. (1981). Why is cross-sex-role behavior more approved for girls than for boys? A status characteristic approach. *Sex Roles, 7*, 289–300.

Feiring, Candice, & Lewis, Michael. (1980). Temperament: Sex differences and stability in vigor, activity and persistence in the first three years of life. *Journal of Genetic Psychology, 136*, 65–75.

Feldberg, Roslyn. (1984). Comparable worth: Toward theory and practice in the United States. *Signs, 10*, 311–328.

Feldman, S. Shirley, & Nash, Sharon C. (1984). The transition from expectancy to parenthood: Impact of the firstborn child on men and women. *Sex Roles, 11*, 61–78.

Feldstein, Jerome H. (1976). Sex differences in social memory among preschool children. *Sex Roles, 2*, 75–79.

Ferber, Marianne A. (1982). Women and work: Issues of the 1980s. *Signs, 8*, 273–295.

Ferguson, Trudi, & Dunphy, Joan S. (1991). *Answers to the mommy track*. New York: New Horizon Press.

Ferree, Myra M. (1983). The women's movement in the working class. *Sex Roles, 9*, 493–505.

Fetler, Mark. (1985). Sex differences on the California statewide assessment of computer literacy. *Sex Roles, 13*, 181–191.

Few women getting top jobs at newspapers, study shows. (1993, April 19). *San Jose Mercury News*, p. A-12.

Few women lawyers make the top. (1988, August 8). *Providence Journal Bulletin*, p. B-2.

Fewer teenagers having abortions. (1991, September 14). *Providence Journal-Bulletin*, p. A-11.

Field, Tiffany M., Woodson, Robert, Greenberg, Reena, & Cohen, Debra. (1982). Discrimination and imitation of facial expressions by neonates. *Science, 218*, 179–181.

Fifteen-year study documents tremendous change in women's sex-role attitudes. (1980, Winter). *ISR Newsletter*, p. 3. (Institute for Social Research, University of Michigan, Ann Arbor).

Finkelhor, David. (1979). *Sexually victimized children*. New York: Free Press.

Finlay, Barbara, Starnes, Charles E., & Alvarez, Fausto B. (1985). Recent changes in sex-role ideology among divorced men and women: Some possible causes and implications. *Sex Roles, 12*, 637–653.

Finn, Jerry. (1986). The relationship between sex role attitudes and attitudes supporting marital violence. *Sex Roles, 14*, 235–244.

Fiorentine, Robert. (1988). Increasing similarity in the values and life plans of male and female college students? Evidence and implications. *Sex Roles, 18*, 143–158.

Firestone, Shulamith. (1971). *The dialectic of sex*. New York: Bantam.

Fischer, Gloria J. (1987). Hispanic and majority student attitudes toward forcible date rape as a function of differences in attitudes toward women. *Sex Roles, 17*, 93–101.

Fischer, Judith L., & Narus, Leonard R. (1981). Sex-role development in late adolescence and adulthood. *Sex Roles, 7*, 97–106.

Fischman, Joshua. (1986, June). The wounds of war. *Psychology Today*, pp. 8–9.

Fishel, Anne. (1979, June). What is a feminist therapist? and How to find one. *Ms.*, pp. 79–81.

Fisher, Elizabeth. (1979). *Women's creation: Sexual evolution and the shaping of society*. New York: McGraw-Hill.

Fisher, Kathleen. (1984, August). Role choice linked to health. *APA Monitor*, p. 39.

Fisher, Kathleen. (1985, November). Parental support vital in coping with abuse. *APA Monitor*, p. 12.

Fisher, William A., & Byrne, Donn. (1978). Sex differences in response to erotica? Love versus lust. *Journal of Personality and Social Psychology, 36*, 117–125.

Fisher-Thompson, Donna. (1990). Adult sex-typing of children's toys. *Sex Roles, 23*, 291–303.

5 acquitted of 1980 Mass. rape-beating. (1983, June 18). *Providence Journal*, p. A-2.

Fitzgerald, Louise F. (1992). *The cultural mythology of sexual victimization*. (Unpublished manuscript, Department of Psychology, University of Illinois, Champagne, IL)

Fivush, Robyn. (1989). Exploring sex differences in the emotional content of mother-child conversations about the past. *Sex Roles, 20*, 675–691.

Flax, Jane. (1981). A materialist theory of women's status. *Psychology of Women Quarterly, 6*, 123–136.

Fleming, Anne T. (1977, December 25). That week in Houston. *New York Times Magazine*, pp. 10–13, 33.

Fleming, Anne T. (1986, October 26). The American wife. *New York Times Magazine*, pp. 29–39.

Fleming, Arline A. (1992, March 24). How kids distinguish moms from dads. *Providence Journal Bulletin,* p. B-2.

Flerx, Vicki C., Fidler, Dorothy S., & Rogers, Ronald W. (1976). Sex role stereotypes: Developmental aspects and early intervention. *Child Development, 47,* 998–1007.

Flexner, Eleanor. (1975). *Century of struggle* (Revised edition). Cambridge, MA: Belknap.

Foa, Uriel G., Anderson, Barbara, Converse, John Jr., Urbansky, William, A., Cawley, Michael J. III, Muhlhausen, Solveig M., & Tornblom, Kjell Y. (1987). Gender-related sexual attitudes: Some crosscultural similarities and differences. *Sex Roles, 16,* 511–519.

Focus on estrogen replacement therapy. (1992, Winter). *Rhode Island Women's Health Collective Newsletter,* p. 1.

Folb, Edith A. (1980, November/December). Runnin' down some lines. *Society,* pp. 63–71.

Ford, Maureen R., & Lowery, Carol R. (1986). Gender differences in moral reasoning: A comparison of the use of justice and care orientations. *Journal of Personality and Social Psychology, 50,* 777–783.

Fowers, Blaine J. (1991). His and her marriage: A multivariate study of gender and marital satisfaction. *Sex Roles, 24,* 209–221.

Fowler, Elizabeth M. (1982, November 10). Women as senior executives. *New York Times.*

Fox, Bonnie J. (1990). Selling the mechanized household: 70 years of ads in *Ladies Home Journal. Gender & Society, 4,* 25–40.

Fox, Jeffrey L. (1984). NIMH study finds one in five have disorders. *Science, 226,* 324.

Frame, Janet. (1982). *To the is-land.* New York: Braziller.

Francke, Linda B. (1982). *The ambivalence of abortion.* New York: Laurel/Dell.

Frank, Ellen J. (1988). Business students' perceptions of women in management. *Sex Roles, 19,* 107–118.

Franke, Ann H., & Toll, Martha A. (1989, July–August). Court decisions hinder women's, minorities' rights. *Academe,* p. 47.

Franken, Mary W. (1983). Sex role expectations in children's vocational aspirations and perceptions of occupations. *Psychology of Women Quarterly, 8,* 59–68.

Franklin, Deborah. (1987, January). The politics of masochism. *Psychology Today,* pp. 53–57.

Frazier, Patricia A. (1990). Victim attributions and post-rape trauma. *Journal of Personality and Social Psychology, 59,* 298–304.

Freedman, Victoria H. (1983). Update on genetics. In M. Fooden, S. Gordon, & B. Hughley (Eds.), *Genes and gender IV: The second X and women's health* (pp. 29–37). New York: Gordian Press.

Freeman, Harvey R., Schockett, Melanie R., & Freeman, Evelyn B. (1975). Effects of gender and race on sex role preferences of fifth-grade children. *Journal of Social Psychology, 95,* 105–108.

Freeman, Patricia. (1983, August). Triathlete—a new breed of superwoman. *Ms.,* pp. 62–65, 101.

Freeman-Longo, Robert E., & Wall, Ronald V. (1986, March). Changing a lifetime of sexual crime. *Psychology Today,* pp. 58–64.

Freiberg, Peter. (1990a, November). APA testifies: Rape estimates far too low. *APA Monitor,* p. 25.

Freiberg, Peter. (1990b, November). Outreach helps women at risk for AIDS. *APA Monitor,* pp. 28–29.

Freiberg, Peter. (1990c, December). Lesbian moms can give kids empowering models. *APA Monitor,* p. 33.

French, Marilyn. (1977). *The women's room.* New York: Summit.

French, Marilyn. (1987). *Her mother's daughter.* New York: Ballantine.

Freud, Sigmund. (1938). Three contributions to the theory of sex. In A. A. Brill (Ed.), *The basic writings of Sigmund Freud* (pp. 553–629). New York: Modern Library. (Original work published in 1905.)

Freud, Sigmund. (1964). Femininity. In *New introductory lectures on psychoanalysis* (pp. 112–135). New York: Norton. (Original work published in 1933.)

Frey, Karen A. (1981). Middle-aged women's experience and perceptions of menopause. *Women and Health, 6,* 25–36.

Friday, Nancy. (1973). *My secret garden.* New York: Pocket Books.

Friday, Nancy. (1991). *Women on top: How real life has changed women's fantasies.* New York: Simon & Schuster.

Friedan, Betty. (1963). *The feminine mystique.* New York: Norton.

Friedan, Betty. (1985, November 3). How to get the women's movement moving again. *New York Times Magazine,* pp. 26–28, 66–67, 84–85, 89, 98, 106–108.

Friederich, Mary A. (1983). Dysmenorrhea. In S. Golub (Ed.), *Lifting the curse of menstruation* (pp. 91–106). New York: Haworth.

Friedman, William J., Robinson, Amy B., & Friedman, Britt L. (1987). Sex differences in moral judgments? A test of Gilligan's theory. *Psychology of Women Quarterly, 11,* 37–46.

Friedrich, Otto. (1983, August 15). What do babies know? *Time,* pp. 52–59.

Friedrichs, Mary. (1988). The dependent solution: Anorexia and bulimia as defenses against danger. *Women & Therapy, 7(4),* 53–73.

Friendly, David T. (1985, March 18). This isn't Shakespeare. *Newsweek,* p. 62.

Frieze, Irene H. (1979, April). Power and influence in violent and nonviolent marriages. Paper read at the meeting of the Eastern Psychological Association, Philadelphia, PA.

Frieze, Irene H. (1983). Investigating the causes and consequences of marital rape. *Signs, 8,* 532–553.

Frieze, Irene H., Whitley, Bernard E. Jr., Hanusa, Barbara H., & McHugh, Maureen C. (1982). Assessing the theoretical models for sex differences in causal attributions for success and failure. *Sex Roles, 8,* 333–343.

Frodi, Ann, Macauley, Jacqueline, & Thorne, Pauline R. (1977). Are women always less aggressive than men? A review of the experimental literature. *Psychological Bulletin, 84,* 634–660.

Fuchs, Victor R. (1986). Sex differences in economic well-being. *Science, 232,* 459–464.

Fuentes, Annette. (1991, October 28). Women warriors? Equality, yes—militarism, no. *The Nation,* pp. 516–519.

Fujita, Frank, Diener, Ed, & Sandvik, Ed. (1991). Gender differences in negative affect and well-being: The case for emotional intensity. *Journal of Personality and Social Psychology, 61,* 427–434.

Full-time work, part-time pay. (1991, July/August). *Ms.,* p. 103.

Funiciello, Theresa. (1990, November/December). The poverty industry. *Ms.,* pp. 33–39.

Furby, Lita, Weinrott, Mark P., & Blackshaw, Lyn. (1989). Sex offender recidivism: A review. *Psychological Bulletin, 105,* 3–30.

The future of the family. (1981, Winter). *ISR Newsletter.* (Institute for Social Research, University of Michigan, Ann Arbor)

Gaelick, Lisa, Bodenhausen, Galen V., & Wyer, Robert S. Jr. (1985). Emotional communication in close relationships. *Journal of Personality and Social Psychology, 49,* 1246–1265.

Galloway, Paul. (1991, August 27). Blondie Bumstead gets a career. *Providence Journal-Bulletin,* pp. E-1, E-4.

Gamarekian, Barbara. (1985, May 27). Women's caucus: Eight years of progress. *New York Times.*

Gamble, Barbara. (1991, November 13). Civil Rights Act of 1991. *Labor Relations Week,* pp. S1-S4.

Ganellen, Ronald J., & Blaney, Paul H. (1984). Hardiness and social supports as moderators of the effects of life stress. *Journal of Personality and Social Psychology, 47,* 156–163.

Gannon, Linda. (1988). The potential role of exercise in the alleviation of menstrual disorders and menopausal symptoms: A theoretical synthesis of recent research. *Women & Health, 14*(2), 105–127.

Garcia, Luis T. (1982). Sex-role orientation and stereotypes about male-female sexuality. *Sex Roles, 8,* 863–876.

Garcia, Luis T., & Derfel, Barbara. (1983). Perception of sexual experience: The impact of nonverbal behavior. *Sex Roles, 9,* 871–878.

Garcia, Stella, Stinson, Linda, Ickes, William, Bissonnette, Victor, & Briggs, Stephen R. (1991). Shyness and physical attractiveness in mixed-sex dyads. *Journal of Personality and Social Psychology, 61,* 35–49.

Garties, George. (1989, February 13). All dolled up for her 30th. *Providence Journal-Bulletin,* pp. B-1, B-4.

Gartrell, Nanette, & Mosbacher, Diane. (1984). Sex differences in the naming of children's genitalia. *Sex Roles, 10,* 867–876.

Gatz, M., & Pearson, C. G. (1988). Ageism-revised and the provision of psychological services. *American Psychologist, 43,* 184–188.

Gavey, Nicola, Florence, Joy, Pezaro, Sue, & Tan, Jan. (1990). Mother-blaming, the perfect alibi: Family therapy and the mothers of incest survivors. *Journal of Feminist Family Therapy, 2*(1), 1–25.

Gayles, Gloria. (1979). Sometimes as women only. In R. P. Bell, B. J. Parker, & B. Guy-Sheftall (Eds.), *Sturdy black bridges* (pp. 363–364). Garden City, NY: Anchor.

Gazzaniga, Marin. (1991, March 31). Until working father joins superwoman. *New York Times,* p. E-12.

Gee, Pauline W. (1983). Ensuring police protection for battered women: The Scott v. Hart suit. *Signs, 8,* 554–567.

Gehlen, Frieda L. (1977). Legislative role performance of female legislators. *Sex Roles, 3,* 1–18.

Geis, F. L., Brown, Virginia, Jennings (Walstedt), Joyce, & Porter, Natalie. (1984). TV commercials as achievement scripts for women. *Sex Roles, 10,* 513–525.

Geist, William E. (1985, October 2). About New York: Equality of the sexes, Playboy style. *New York Times,* p. B-3.

Gelles, Richard J. (1974). *The violent home.* Beverly Hills, CA: Sage.

Gelles, Richard J. (1979, October). The myth of battered husbands. *Ms.,* pp. 65–66, 71–73.

Gelles, Richard J., & Straus, Murray A. (1979). Violence in the American family. *Social Issues, 35*(2), 15–39.

Gelman, David. (1990a, July 2). Fixing the 'between'. *Newsweek,* pp. 42–43.

Gelman, David. (1990b, December 24). A is for apple, P is for shrink. *Newsweek,* pp. 64–66.

Gerber, Gwendolyn L. (1991). Gender stereotypes and power: Perceptions of the roles in violent marriage. *Sex Roles, 24,* 439–458.

Gerdes, Eugenia P., & Garber, Douglas M. (1983). Sex bias in hiring: Effects of job demands and applicant competence. *Sex Roles, 9,* 307–315.

Gergen, Mary M. (1990). Finished at 40: Women's development within the patriarchy. *Psychology of Women Quarterly, 14,* 471–493.

Gerrard, Meg. (1987). Sex, sex guilt, and contraceptive use revisited: The 1980s. *Journal of Personality and Social Psychology, 52,* 975–980.

Gerson, Judith. (1985). Women returning to school: The consequences of multiple roles. *Sex Roles, 13,* 77–92.

Gerson, Kathleen. (1986, November). Briefcase, baby or both? *Psychology Today,* pp. 30–36.

Gerson, Mary-Joan. (1980). The lure of motherhood. *Psychology of Women Quarterly, 5,* 207–218.

Gerson, Mary-Joan. (1984). Feminism and the wish for a child. *Sex Roles, 11,* 389–398.

Gerson, Mary-Joan. (1986). The prospect of parenthood for women and men. *Psychology of Women Quarterly, 10,* 49–62.

Gerson, Mary-Joan, Alpert, Judith L., & Richardson, Mary Sue. (1984). Mothering: The view from psychological research. *Signs, 9,* 434–453.

Getting ideas. (1991, March 3). *New York Times,* p. E-7.

Gettys, Linda D., & Cann, Arnie. (1981). Children's perceptions of occupational sex stereotypes. *Sex Roles, 7,* 301–308.

Geyer, Georgie Anne. (1989, December 8). Is feminism dead? *Providence Journal Bulletin,* p. A-24.

Giacopassi, David J. & Dull, R. Thomas. (1986). Gender and racial differences in the acceptance of rape myths within a college population. *Sex Roles, 15,* 63–75.

Giarrusso, Roseann, Johnson, Paula, Goodchilds, Jacqueline, & Zellman, Gail. (1979, April). Adolescents' cues and signals: Sex and assault. Paper read at the meeting of the Western Psychological Association, San Diego, CA.

Gibbs, Nancy. (1992, March 9). The war against feminism. *Time,* pp. 50–55.

Gibbs, Nancy. (1993, January 18). 'Til death do us part. *Time,* pp. 38–45.

Gibbs, Nancy, & McDowell, Jeanne. (1992, March 9). How to revive a revolution. *Time,* pp. 56–57.

Gibbs, Robin. (1986). Social factors in exaggerated eating behavior among high school students. *International Journal of Eating Disorders, 5,* 1103–1107.

Giele, Janet. (1984).

Gigy, Lynn L. (1980). Self-concept of single women. *Psychology of Women Quarterly, 5,* 321–340.

Gilbert, Lucia A. (1985). *Men in dual-career families: Current realities and future prospects.* Hillsdale, NJ: Erlbaum.

Gilbert, Lucia A., Gallessich, June M., & Evans, Sherri L. (1983). Sex of faculty role model and student's self-perceptions of competency. *Sex Roles, 9,* 597–607.

Gilbert, Sandra M. (1984, December 30). Feisty femme, 40, seeks nurturant paragon. *New York Times Book Review,* p. 11.

Gilbert, Susan. (1993, April 25). Waiting game. *New York Times Magazine,* pp. 70–72, 92.

Gill, Sandra, Stockard, Jean, Johnson, Miriam, & Williams, Suzanne. (1987). Measuring gender differences: The expressive dimension and critique of androgyny scales. *Sex Roles, 17,* 375–400.

Gilligan, Carol. (1977). In a different voice: Women's conception of the self and of morality. *Harvard Educational Review, 47,* 481–517.

Gilligan, Carol. (1979). Woman's place in man's life cycle. *Harvard Educational Review, 49,* 431–446.

Gilligan, Carol. (1982). *In a different voice: Psychological theory and women's development.* Cambridge, MA: Harvard University Press.

Gilligan, Carol, Lyons, Nona P., & Hammer, Trudy J. (1990). *Making connections: The relational worlds of adolescent girls at Emma Willard School.* Cambridge, MA: Harvard University Press.

Gillis, John S., & Avis, Walter E. (1980). The male-taller norm in mate selection. *Personality and Social Psychology Bulletin, 6,* 396–401.

Gilman, Susan J. (1991, September 1). Why the fear of feminism? *New York Times,* p. E-11.

Girls are different, look at the law. (1977, September 12). *Providence Evening Bulletin.*

Girls lose their lead. (1981, November). *Science 81,* pp. 6f.

Gitelson, Idy B., Petersen, Anne C., & Tobin-Richards, Maryse H. (1982). Adolescents' expectations of success, self-evaluations, and attributions about performance on spatial and verbal tasks. *Sex Roles, 8,* 411–419.

Gittell, Marilyn, & Naples, Nancy. (1982, Summer). Activist women: Conflicting ideologies. *Social Policy,* 25–27.

Gladstone, Leslie W. (1991, October 30). Equal rights for women. *CRS Issue Brief.* The Library of Congress, Washington, DC.

Glaser, Robert L., & Thorpe, Joseph S. (1986). Unethical intimacy: A survey of sexual contact and advances between psychology educators and female graduate students. *American Psychologist, 41,* 43–51.

Glass, Shirley P., & Wright, Thomas L. (1985). Sex differences in type of extramarital involvement and marital dissatisfaction. *Sex Roles, 12,* 1101–1120.

Glasse, Lou. (1988, Fall). Letter. Older Women's League, 730 11th St. NW, Washington, DC 20001.

Glazer, Nona Y. (1990). The home as workshop: Women as amateur nurses and medical care providers. *Gender & Society, 4,* 479–499.

Glenn, Evelyn N. (1987). Racial ethnic women's labor: The intersection of race, gender, and class oppression. In C. Bose, R. Feldberg, and N. Sokoloff (Eds.), *Hidden aspects of women's work* (pp. 14–45). New York: Praeger.

Glenwick, David S., Johansson, Sandra L., & Bondy, Jeffrey. (1978). A comparison of the self-images of female and male assistant professors. *Sex Roles, 4,* 513–524.

Glick, Peter, Zion, Cari, & Nelson, Cynthia. (1988). What mediates sex discrimination in hiring decisions? *Journal of Personality and Social Psychology, 55,* 178–186.

Glossary. (1990). *Connexions, 32,* 2.

Godwin, Gail. (1978). *Violet Clay.* New York: Knopf.

Godwin, Gail. (1983). *A mother and two daughters.* New York: Avon.

Godwin, Gail. (1991). *Father Melancholy's daughter.* New York: Avon.

Goffman, Erving. (1979). *Gender advertisements.* New York: Harper & Row.

Gold, Dolores, & Berger, Charlene. (1978). Problem-solving performance of young boys and girls as a function of task appropriateness and sex identity. *Sex Roles, 4,* 183–193.

Goldberg, Andrea S., & Shiflett, Samuel. (1981). Goals of male and female college students: Do traditional sex differences still exist? *Sex Roles, 7,* 1213–1222.

Golding, Jacqueline M. (1988). Gender differences in depressive symptoms. *Psychology of Women Quarterly, 12,* 61–74.

Golding, Jacqueline M. (1990). Division of household labor, strain, and depressive symptoms among Mexican American and non-Hispanic whites. *Psychology of Women Quarterly, 14,* 103–117.

Goldman, Juliette D. G., & Goldman, Ronald J. (1983). Children's perceptions of parents and their roles: A cross-national study in Australia, England, North America, and Sweden. *Sex Roles, 9,* 791–812.

Goleman, Daniel. (1987, August 2). Girls and math: Is biology really destiny? *New York Times,* Sec. 12, pp. 42–43.

Golub, Sharon. (1983). Menarche: The beginning of menstrual life. In S. Golub (Ed.), *Lifting the curse of menstruation* (pp. 17–36). New York: Haworth.

Golub, Sharon, & Harrington, Denise M. (1981). Premenstrual and menstrual mood changes in adolescent women. *Journal of Personality and Social Psychology, 41,* 961–965.

Gomberg, Edith S. (1979). Problems with alcohol and other drugs. In E. S. Gomberg & V. Franks (Eds.), *Gender and disordered behavior* (pp. 204–240). New York: Brunner/Mazel.

Good, Paul R., & Smith, Barry D. (1980). Menstrual distress and sex-role attributes. *Psychology of Women Quarterly, 4,* 482–491.

Goodman, Madeline J., Griffin, P. Bion, Estioko-Griffin, Agnes A., & Grove, John S. (1985). The compatibility of hunting and mothering among the Agta hunter-gatherers of the Philippines. *Sex Roles, 12,* 1199–1209.

Goodnow, Jacqueline J. (1988). Children's household work: Its nature and functions. *Psychological Bulletin, 103,* 5–26.

Goolkasian, Paula. (1985). Phase and sex effects in pain perception: A critical review. *Psychology of Women Quarterly, 9,* 15–28.

Gordon, Barbara. (1979). *I'm dancing as fast as I can.* New York: Harper & Row.

Gordon, Michael R. (1993, April 25). Another blow to cohesiveness. *New York Times,* p. E-2.

Gordon, Michael R. (1992, July 31). Military chiefs contrite about sexual harassment. *Providence Journal Bulletin,* p. A-1.

Gormly, Anne V., Gormly, John B., & Weiss, Helen. (1987). Motivations for parenthood among young adult college students. *Sex Roles, 16,* 31–39.

Gornick, Vivian. (1982, April). Watch out: Your brain may be used against you. *Ms.,* pp. 14–20.

Gornick, Vivian. (1987). *Fierce attachments.* New York: Farrar Straus Giroux.

Gornick, Vivian. (1990, April 15). Who says we haven't made a revolution? *New York Times Magazine,* pp. 24–27, 52–53.

Gough, Harrison G. (1952). Identifying psychological femininity. *Educational and Psychological Measurements, 12,* 427–439.

Gould, Lisa L. (1979, August/September). Adverse effects of obstetrical drugs. *Newsletter, Association for Women in Psychology.*

Gould, Stephen J. (1978, November 2). Women's brains. *New Scientist,* pp. 364–366.

Gove, Walter. (1979). Sex, marital status, and psychiatric treatment: A research note. *Social Forces, 58,* 89–93.

Gove, Walter R., & Tudor, Jeannette F. (1973). Adult sex roles and mental illness. *American Journal of Sociology, 78,* 812–835.

Grant, Eleanor. (1988, January). The housework gap. *Psychology Today,* p. 10.

Grauerholz, Elizabeth, & Serpe, Richard T. (1985). Initiation and response: The dynamics of sexual interaction. *Sex Roles, 12,* 1041–1059.

Gray, Ellen. (1993). *Unequal justice: The prosecution of child sexual abuse.* NY: The Free Press.

Gray, Janet D. (1983). The married professional woman: An examination of her role conflicts and coping strategies. *Psychology of Women Quarterly, 7,* 235–243.

Gray, Janice D., & Silver, Roxane C. (1990). Opposite sides of the same coin: Former spouses' divergent perspectives in coping with their divorce. *Journal of Personality and Social Psychology, 59,* 1180–1191.

Gray, Mary W. (1985, September/October). The halls of ivy and the halls of justice: Resisting sex discrimination against faculty women. *Academe,* pp. 33–41.

Gray-Little, Bernadette, & Burks, Nancy. (1983). Power and satisfaction in marriage: A review and critique. *Psychological Bulletin, 93,* 513–538.

Green, Rayna. (1977). Magnolias grow in dirt. *Southern Exposure, 4*(4), 29–33.

Green, Rayna. (1980). Native American women. *Signs, 6,* 248–267.

Green, Rayna (Ed.). (1984). *That's what she said.* Bloomington: Indiana University Press.

Green, Richard. (1978). Sexual identity of 37 children raised by homosexual or trans-sexual parents. *American Journal of Psychiatry, 135,* 692–697.

Greenfield, Patricia M. (1981). Child care in cross-cultural perspectives: Implications for the future organization of child care in the United States. *Psychology of Women Quarterly, 6,* 41–54.

Greenhaus, Philip S. (1983, January 23). Letter to the editor. *New York Times Magazine,* p. 74.

Greenhouse, Linda. (1981, March 22). Equal pay debate now shifts to a far wider concept. *New York Times.*

Greenhouse, Steven. (1984, October 31). Former steel workers' income falls by half. *New York Times,* p. A-17.

Greenhouse, Steven. (1991, June 2). French Supreme Court rules surrogate-mother agreements illegal. *New York Times.*

Greeno, Catherine G., & Maccoby, Eleanor E. (1986). How different is the "Different Voice"? *Signs, 11,* 310–316.

Greenwood, Sadja. (1985, May). Hot flashes: How to cope when the heat is on. *Ms.,* pp. 79, 82, 151–152.

Greer, Germaine. (1970). *The female eunuch.* New York: McGraw-Hill.

Greer, William R. (1986, February 22). The changing women's marriage market. *New York Times.*

Gregory, Chester. (1974). *Women in defense work during World War II.* Hicksville, NY: Exposition Press.

Gregory, Mary K. (1977). Sex bias in school referrals. *Journal of School Psychology, 15,* 5–8.

Griffin, Susan. (1981). *Pornography and silence.* New York: Harper & Row.

Griffitt, William, & Kaiser, Donn L. (1978). Affect, sex guilt, gender, and the rewarding-punishing effects of erotic stimuli. *Journal of Personality and Social Psychology, 36,* 850–858.

Gross, Jane. (1984, August 12). Women athletes topple sports myths. *New York Times,* p. E-22.

Gross, Jane. (1986, February 16). In federal war on drug trafficking, women are playing a greater role. *New York Times,* p. 52.

Gross, Jane. (1991, July 14). Female surgeon's quitting touches nerve at medical schools. *New York Times.*

Gross, Jane. (1992, March 1). Patricia Ireland, president of NOW: Does she speak for today's women? *New York Times Magazine,* pp. 17–18, 38, 54.

Groth, A. Nicholas. (1979). *Men who rape: The psychology of the offender.* New York: Plenum.

Guffy, Ossie, & Ledner, Caryl. (1971). *Ossie: The autobiography of a black woman.* New York: Norton.

Gupta, Nina, Jenkins, G. Douglas Jr., & Beehr, Terry A. (1983). Employee gender, gender similarity, and supervisor-subordinate cross-evaluations. *Psychology of Women Quarterly, 8,* 174–184.

Gutek, Barbara. (1985). *Sex and the workplace.* San Francisco: Jossey-Bass.

Gutek, Barbara A. (1992, February). *Responses to sexual harassment.* Paper read at Claremont Graduate School Symposium on Applied Social Psychology, chaired by S. Oskamp & M. Costanzo.

Gutek, Barbara A., & Koss, Mary P. (1993). Changed women and changed organizations: Consequences of and coping with sexual harassment. *Journal of Vocational Behavior,* 1–21.

Gutierres, Sara E., Patton, Deanna S., Raymond, Jonathan S., & Rhoads, Deborah L. (1984). Women and drugs: The heroin abuser and the prescription drug abuser. *Psychology of Women Quarterly, 8,* 354–369.

Gutis, Philip S. (1989, May 28). Family redefines itself; and now the law follows. *New York Times,* p. E-6.

Guttman, Leslie. (1991, September 19). Magazine covers undress for success. *Providence Journal Bulletin,* p. E-8.

Haas, Adelaide. (1979). Male and female spoken language differences: Stereotypes and evidence. *Psychological Bulletin, 86,* 616–626.

Hafner, R. Julian, & Minge, Priscilla J. (1989). Sex role stereotyping in women with agoraphobia and their husbands. *Sex Roles, 20,* 705–711.

Halberstadt, Amy G., & Saitta, Martha B. (1987). Gender, nonverbal behavior, and perceived dominance: A test of the theory. *Journal of Personality and Social Psychology, 53,* 257–272.

Half of caesarean-section births in U.S. unnecessary, report says. (1989, January 27). *Providence Journal Bulletin,* p. A-6.

Hahn, Jon. (1977, November 2). Sex is fun; so is more, report says. *Providence Evening Bulletin,* p. D-4.

Hahn, William K. (1987). Cerebral lateralization of function: From infancy through childhood. *Psychological Bulletin, 101,* 376–392.

Hailey, Elizabeth F. (1979). *A woman of independent means.* New York: Avon.

Hall, Eleanor R., Howard, Judith, A., & Boezio, Sherrie L. (1986). Tolerance of rape: A sexist or antisocial attitude? *Psychology of Women Quarterly, 10,* 101–118.

Hall, Evelyn G. (1990). The effect of performer gender, performer skill level, and opponent gender on self-confidence in a competitive situation. *Sex Roles, 23,* 33–41.

Hall, Evelyn G., & Lee, Amelia M. (1984). Sex differences in motor performance of young children: Fact or fiction? *Sex Roles, 10,* 217–230.

Hall, Judith A. (1978). Gender effects in decoding nonverbal cues. *Psychological Bulletin, 85,* 845–857.

Hall, Roberta M., & Sandler, Bernice R. (1982). The classroom climate: A chilly one for women? *Project on the Status and Education of Women.* (Association of American Colleges, Washington, DC)

Hall, Roberta M., & Sandler, Bernice R. (1984). Out of the classroom: A chilly campus climate for women? *Project on the Status and Education of Women.* (Association of American Colleges, Washington, DC)

Hall Carpenter Archives Lesbian Oral History Group. (1989). *Inventing ourselves.* New York: Routledge.

Halpern, Diane F. (1986). A different answer to the question, "Do sex-related differences in spatial abilities exist?" *American Psychologist, 41,* 1014–1015.

Halpern, Sue. (1992, June 21). From a cocoon of pain. *New York Times Book Review,* p. 18.

Hamilton, Mykol C. (1991). Masculine bias in the attribution of personhood: People = male, male = people. *Psychology of Women Quarterly, 15,* 393–402.

Hamilton, Sandra, & Fagot, Beverly I. (1988). Chronic stress and coping styles: A comparison of male and female undergraduates. *Journal of Personality and Social Psychology, 55,* 819–823.

Hamilton, Sandra, Rothbart, Myron, & Dawes, Robyn M. (1986). Sex bias, diagnosis, and DSM-III. *Sex Roles, 15,* 269–274.

Hammer, Signe. (1976). *Daughters and mothers: Mothers and daughters.* New York: New American Library.

Hammond, Judith A., & Mahoney, Constance W. (1983). Reward-cost balancing among coal miners. *Sex Roles, 9,* 17–29.

Hansson, Robert O., & Remondet, Jacqueline H. (1988). Old age and widowhood: Issues of personal control and independence. *Journal of Social Issues, 44(3),* 159–174.

Harding, M. Esther. (1972). *Woman's mysteries: Ancient and modern.* New York: Putnam.

Harjo, Joy. (1991, July/August). Three generations of Native American women's birth experience. *Ms.,* pp. 28–30.

Harlow, Ruth. (1991–1992, Winter). A young lawyer's wedding plans become the basis for job bias. *Civil Liberties, 375.*

Harper, Lawrence V., & Sanders, Karen M. (1975). Preschool children's use of space: Sex differences in outdoor play. *Developmental Psychology, 11,* 119.

Harris, Janet. (1976). *The prime of Ms. America.* New York: New American Library.

Harris, Jean. (1993, March 28). The babies of Bedford. *New York Times Magazine,* p. 26.

Harris, Marvin. (1977, November 13). Why do men dominate women. *New York Times Magazine.*

Harris, Rochelle L., Ellicott, Abbie M. & Holmes, David S. (1986). The timing of psychosocial transitions and changes in women's lives: An examination of women aged 45 to 60. *Journal of Personality and Social Psychology, 51,* 409–416.

Harris, Victor A., & Katkin, Edward S. (1975). Primary and secondary emotional behavior: Analysis of the role of autonomic feedback on affect, arousal, and attribution. *Psychological Bulletin, 82,* 904–916.

Harris, William H., & Levey, Judith S. (Eds.). (1975). *The new Columbia encyclopedia.* New York: Lippincott.

Harrison, Albert A. (1977). Let's make a deal: An analysis of revelations and stipulations in lonely hearts advertisements. *Journal of Personality and Social Psychology, 35,* 257–264.

Hartmann, Heidi I. (1981). The family as the locus of gender, class, and political struggle: The example of housework. *Signs, 6,* 366–394.

Hartmann, Sandra J., Griffeth, Rodger W., Crino, Michael D., & Harris, O. Jeff. (1991). Gender-based influences: The promotion recommendation. *Sex Roles, 25,* 285–300.

Hasenfeld, Robin. (1982). Empathy and justification: Two contextual cues related to gender differences in aggressive behavior. Unpublished paper, Department of Psychology, University of Rhode Island, Kingston.

Haskell, Molly. (1974). *From reverence to rape: The treatment of women in the movies.* New York: Penguin.

Hatcher, Maxine A. (1991). The corporate woman of the 1990s. *Psychology of Women Quarterly, 15,* 251–260.

Hatfield, Elaine, & Sprecher, Susan. (1987). *Journal of Adolescence, 9,* 383–410.

Haugh, Susan S., Hoffman, Charles D., & Cowan, Gloria. (1980). The eye of the very young beholder: Sextyping of infants by young children. *Child Development, 51,* 598–600.

Hawkins, Beth. (1991, August 9). U.S. study acknowledges corporate 'glass ceiling.' *San Francisco Chronicle,* p. A-1.

Hawthorne, Nathaniel. (1948). *The scarlet letter.* New York: Dodd, Mead. (Original work published in 1850.)

Hawthorne, Nathaniel. (1973). The birthmark. In M. Murray (Ed.), *A house of good proportion: Images of women in literature* (pp. 351–366). New York: Simon & Schuster. (Original work published in 1843.)

Hayden, Dolores. (1984, January). Making housing work for people. *Ms.,* pp. 69–71.

Hayfield, Nancy. (1980). *Cleaning house.* New York: Farrar, Straus & Giroux.

Hays, Hoffman R. (1964). *The dangerous sex: The myth of feminine evil.* New York: G. P. Putnam's.

Hays, Terence E. (1987). Menstrual expressions and menstrual attitudes. *Sex Roles, 16,* 605–614.

Healy, Bernardine. (1992). Women in science: From panes to ceilings. *Science, 255,* 1333.

Hegstrom, Jane L., & Griffith, W. I. (1992). Dominance, sex, and leader emergence. *Sex Roles, 27,* 209–220.

Heilbrun, Carolyn G. (1973). *Toward a recognition of androgyny.* New York: Harper & Row.

Heilman, Joan R. (1980, September 7). Breaking the caesarean cycle. *New York Times Magazine,* pp. 84, 86, 88, 90–93.

Heilman, Madeline E., & Kram, Kathy E. (1984). Male and female assumptions about colleagues' views of their competence. *Psychology of Women Quarterly, 7,* 329–337.

Heiman, Julia R. (1975, April). Women's sexual arousal: The physiology of erotica. *Psychology Today,* pp. 91–94.

Heimovics, Richard D., & Herman, Robert D. (1988). Gender and the attributions of chief executive responsibility for successful or unsuccessful organizational outcomes. *Sex Roles, 18,* 623–635.

Helsing, Knud J., Szklo, Moyses, & Comstock, George W. (1981). Factors associated with mortality after widowhood. *American Journal of Public Health, 71,* 802–809.

Helson, Ravenna. (1986, March). *Advancing the social clock.* Paper presented at the meeting of the Association for Women in Psychology, Oakland, CA.

Helson, Ravenna, Mitchell, Valory, & Moane, Geraldine. (1984). Personality and patterns of adherence and nonadherence to the social clock. *Journal of Personality and Social Psychology, 46,* 1079–1096.

Helson, Ravenna, & Moane, Geraldine. (1987). Personality change in women from college to midlife. *Journal of Personality and Social Psychology, 53,* 176–186.

Hemmer, Joan D., & Kleiber, Douglas A. (1981). Tomboys and sissies: Androgynous children? *Sex Roles, 7,* 1205–1211.

Henahan, Donal. (1983, January 23). Women are breaking the symphonic barriers. *New York Times,* pp. 1, 19.

Hendrick, Susan, Hendrick, Clyde, Slapion-Foote, Michelle J., & Foote, Franklin H. (1985). Gender differences in sexual attitudes. *Journal of Personality and Social Psychology, 48,* 1630–1642.

Hendrick, Clyde, & Hendrick, Susan. (1986). A theory and method of love. *Journal of Personality and Social Psychology, 50,* 392–402.

Hendricks, Paula. (1987, September). Condoms: A straight girl's best friend. *Ms.,* pp. 98–102.

Hendrix, Lewellyn, & Hossain, Zakir. (1988). Women's status and mode of production: A cross-cultural test. *Signs, 13,* 437–453.

Hendrix, Lewellyn, & Johnson, G. David. (1985). Instrumental and expressive socialization: A false dichotomy. *Sex Roles, 13,* 581–595.

Henley, Nancy M. (1977). *Body politics: Power, sex and nonverbal communication.* Englewood Cliffs, NJ: Prentice Hall.

Henley, Nancy M., & Freeman, Jo. (1976). The sexual politics of interpersonal behavior. In S. Cox (Ed.), *Female psychology: The emerging self* (pp. 171–179). Chicago: Science Research Associates.

Henry, William A., III. (1990, Fall). The lesbians next door. *Time,* pp. 78–79.

Herman, Jeanne B., & Gyllstrom, Karen K. (1977). Working men and women: Inter- and intra-role conflict. *Psychology of Women Quarterly, 1,* 319–333.

Herman, Judith L. (1992). *Trauma and recovery.* New York: Basic Books.

Herman, Judith, & Hirschman, Lisa. (1977). Father-daughter incest. *Signs, 2,* 735–756.

Herman, Judith, & Hirschman, Lisa. (1981). Families at risk for father-daughter incest. *American Journal of Psychiatry, 138,* 967–970.

Heshusius, Lous. (1980). Female self-injury and suicide attempts: Culturally reinforced techniques in human relations. *Sex Roles, 6,* 843–857.

Hess, Beth B. (1985, June). Prime time. *Women's Review of Books,* pp. 6–7.

Hess, Beth B., & Ferree, Myra M. (Eds.) (1987). *Analyzing gender: A handbook of social science research.* Newbury Park, CA: Sage.

Hess, Robert D., & Miura, Irene T. (1985). Gender differences in enrollment in computer camps and classes. *Sex Roles, 13,* 193–203.

Hesse-Biber, Sharlene. (1989). Eating patterns and disorder in a college population: Are college women's eating problems a new phenomenon? *Sex Roles, 20,* 71–89.

Hicks, Jonathan P. (1991, November 3). Women in waiting. *New York Times,* sec. 4A, p. 19.

Hier, Daniel B. (1979). Genetic explanation for no sex difference in spatial ability among Eskimos. *Perceptual and Motor Skills, 48,* 593–594.

High court rejects definition of porn as violation of civil rights. (1986, February 25). *Providence Evening Bulletin,* p. A-4.

Hilts, Philip J. (1990, December 16). Birth-control backlash. *New York Times Magazine,* pp. 41, 55, 70–74.

Hines, Melissa. (1982). Prenatal gonadal hormones and sex differences in human behavior. *Psychological Bulletin, 92,* 56–80.

Hirsch, Kathleen. (1990, September/October). Fraternities of fear: Gang rape, male bonding, and the silencing of women. *Ms.,* pp. 52–56.

Hispanic children poor at higher rate. (1991, August 27). *Providence Journal Bulletin,* p. A-5.

Hite, Shere. (1976). *The Hite report.* New York: Dell.

Hite, Shere. (1987). *Women and love: A cultural revolution in progress.* New York: Knopf.

Hochschild, Arlie, & Machung, Anne. (1989). *The second shift.* New York: Viking.

Hoffman, Curt, & Hurst, Nancy. (1990). Gender stereotypes: Perception or rationalization? *Journal of Personality and Social Psychology, 58,* 197–208.

Hoffman, Jan. (1993, January 10). The morning-after pill: A well-kept secret. *New York Times Magazine,* pp. 12–15, 30–32.

Hoffman, Joan C. (1982). Biorhythms in human reproduction: The not-so-steady states. *Signs, 7,* 829–844.

Hoffman, Lois W. (1977). Changes in family roles, socialization, and sex differences. *American Psychologist, 32,* 644–657.

Hoffman, Lois W. (1989). Effects of maternal employment in the two parent family. *American Psychologist, 44,* 283–292.

Hoff-Wilson, Joan. (1988). The unfinished revolution: Changing legal status of U.S. women. *Signs, 13,* 7–36.

Hogrebe, Mark C. (1987). Gender differences in mathematics. *American Psychologist, 42,* 265–266.

Holden, Constance. (1984). Will home computers transform schools? *Science, 225,* 296.

Holden, Constance. (1987). Why do women live longer than men? *Science, 238,* 158–160.

Hollander, Edwin P. (1985). Leadership and power. In G. Lindzey & E. Aronson (Eds.), *Handbook of social psychology,* vol. 2 (3rd ed.) (pp. 485–537). New York: Random House.

Hollender, John, & Shafer, Leslie. (1981). Male acceptance of female career roles. *Sex Roles, 7,* 1199–1203.

Holmes, Steven A. (1990, April 8). Day care bill marks a turn toward help for the poor. *New York Times,* p. E-4.

Holmstrom, Lynda L., & Burgess, Ann W. (1978). *The victim of rape.* New York: Wiley.

Holroyd, Jean C., & Brodsky, Annette M. (1977). Psychologists' attitudes and practices regarding erotic and non-erotic physical contact with patients. *American Psychologist, 32,* 843–849.

Holten, Jamie D. (1990). When do we stop mother-blaming? *Journal of Feminist Therapy, 2,* 53–60.

Holy or wholly wedlock: Maimonides 1174 A.D. (1972, November). *Intellectual Digest,* p. 53.

Holy Bible (Revised Standard Version). (1952). New York: Nelson & Sons.

Homiller, Jonica D. (1977). *Women and alcohol: A guide for state and local decision makers.* Washington, DC: The Council of State Authorities, Alcohol and Drug Problems Association of North America.

Homosexuality held a bar to the custody of children. (1985, June 20). *Providence Journal Bulletin.*

Honey, Maureen. (1983). The working-class woman and recruitment propaganda during World War II: Class differences in the portrayal of war work. *Signs, 8,* 672–687.

Hooker, Evelyn. (1972). Homosexuality. In *National Institute of Mental Health Task Force on Homosexuality: Final report and background papers* (pp. 11–21). Rockville, MD: National Institute of Mental Health.

hooks, bell. (1992, July/August). Out of the academy and into the streets. *Ms.,* pp. 80–82.

Hopkins, Ellen. (1992, March 15). Tales from the baby factory. *New York Times Magazine,* pp. 40–41, 78–84, 90.

Hopkins, J. Roy. (1977). Sexual behavior in adolescence. *Journal of Social Issues, 33*(2), 67–85.

Hopkins, Joyce, Marcus, Marsha, & Campbell, Susan B. (1984). Postpartum depression: A critical review. *Psychological Bulletin, 95,* 498–515.

Hopson, Janet L. (1987, August). Boys will be boys, girls will be . . . *Psychology Today,* pp. 60–66.

Horgan, Dianne. (1983). The pregnant woman's place and where to find it. *Sex Roles, 9,* 333–339.

Horn, Patrice. (1974, August). Newsline: Parents still prefer boys. *Psychology Today,* pp. 29–30.

Horney, Julie. (1979). Menstrual cycles and criminal responsibility. *Law and Human Behavior, 2,* 25–36.

Horney, Karen. (1967). Premenstrual tension. In H. Kelman (Ed.), *Feminine psychology* (pp. 99–106). New York: Norton. (Original work published in 1931.)

Hort, Barbara E., Leinbach, Mary D., & Fagot, Beverly I. (1991). Is there coherence among the cognitive components of gender acquisition? *Sex Roles, 24,* 195–207.

Horwitz, Allan V. (1982). Sex-role expectations, power, and psychological distress. *Sex Roles, 8,* 607–623.

Hot news from the Hotline. (1991, March–April). *9to5 Newsline,* p. 2.

Houppert, Karen. (1991, September/October). Wildflowers among the ivy. *Ms.,* pp. 52–58.

How firms use sex to win government contracts. (1980, June 26). *Providence Evening Bulletin.*

Howard, Ann. (1987, May). The pendulum swings. *APA Monitor,* p. 40.

Howard, Elizabeth M. (1984, November). Miss Steak—and other beauties. *Ms.,* p. 24.

Howard, Judith A., Blumstein, Philip, & Schwartz, Pepper. (1987). Social or evolutionary theories? Some observations on preferences in human mate selection. *Journal of Personality and Social Psychology, 53,* 194–200.

Howard, Maureen. (1983, March). Forbidden fruits. *Vogue,* pp. 385–386, 428.

Howard, Wanda. (1991, October 10). Disabilities that afflict older women to be studied. *Providence Journal Bulletin,* p. 1.

Hrdy, Sarah B. (1980). *The woman that never evolved.* Cambridge, MA: Harvard University Press.

Hughes, J. O., & Sandler, Bernice R. (1988). *Peer harassment: Hassles for women on campus.* Washington, DC: Project on the Status and Education of Women, Association of American Colleges.

Hughes, Linda A. (1988). "But that's not *really* mean": Competing in a cooperative mode. *Sex Roles, 19,* 669–687.

The Hunger Project. (1985). *Ending hunger: An idea whose time has come.* NY: Praeger.

Hurst, Marsha, & Zambrana, Ruth E. (1980). The health careers of urban women: A study in East Harlem. *Signs, 5* (Suppl.), 112–126.

Hurtado, Aida. (1989). Relating to privilege: Seduction and rejection in the subordination of white women and women of color. *Signs, 14,* 833–855.

Hurwitz, Robin E., & White, Mary A. (1977). Effect of sex-linked vocational information on reported occupational choices of high school juniors. *Psychology of Women Quarterly, 2,* 149–156.

Huston, Ted L., & Vangelisti, Anita L. (1991). Socioemotional behavior and satisfaction in marital relationships: A longitudinal study. *Journal of Personality and Social Psychology, 61,* 721–733.

Hyde, Janet S. (1981). How large are cognitive gender differences? *American Psychologist, 36,* 892–901.

Hyde, Janet S. (1984). How large are gender differences in aggression? A developmental meta-analysis. *Developmental Psychology, 20,* 722–736.

Hyde, Janet S., Fennema, Elizabeth, & Lamon, Susan J. (1990). Gender differences in mathematics performance: A Meta-analysis. *Psychological Bulletin, 107,* 139–155.

Hyde, Janet S., Fennema, Elizabeth, Ryan, Marilyn, Frost, Laurie A., & Hopp, Carolyn. (1990). Gender comparisons of mathematics attitudes and affect: A meta-analysis. *Psychology of Women Quarterly, 14,* 299–324.

Hyde, Janet A., & Linn, Marcia C. (1988). Gender differences in verbal ability: A meta-analysis. *Psychological Bulletin, 104,* 53–69.

Hyde, Janet S., Rosenberg, B. G., & Behrman, JoAnn. (1977). Tomboyism. *Psychology of Women Quarterly, 2,* 73–75.

Hysterectomies found often unnecessary, doctors report. (1992, April 2). *Providence Journal Bulletin,* p. D-14.

"I survived," says former Miss America. (1991, May 10). *Providence Journal Bulletin,* pp. D-1–D-2.

IBM advertisement. (1985, January). *Psychology Today,* pp. 14–15.

Ickes, William, & Barnes, Richard D. (1977). The role of sex and self-monitoring in unstructured dyadic interactions. *Journal of Personality and Social Psychology, 35,* 315–330.

Ickes, William, Stinson, Linda, Bissonnette, Victor, & Garcia, Stella. (1990). Naturalistic social cognition: Empathic accuracy in mixed-sex dyads. *Journal of Personality and Social Psychology, 59,* 730–742.

If I were a woman. (1991, April). *Self,* pp. 160–161.

Ihinger-Tallman, Marilyn. (1982). Family interaction, gender, and status attainment value. *Sex Roles, 8,* 543–556.

Ilchman, Alice. (1986, January 7). Sex bias in the work place. *Providence Evening Bulletin,* p. A-11.

Imbrie, Katherine. (1986, November 23). Saying "no" might not protect her from date rape. *Providence Journal,* pp. E-1, 4.

Imperato-McGinley, Julianne, Guerrero, Luis, Gautier, Teofilo, & Peterson, Ralph E. (1974). Steroid 5.101-reductase deficiency in man: An inherited form of male pseudohermaphroditism. *Science, 186,* 1212–1215.

Improving longevity may have side effects. (1985, February 17). *New York Times.*

Incest injury & discovery. (1989, May). *The facts.* NOW, 99 Hudson St., New York, NY 10013.

Increase seen in number of lesbians having children. (1989, January 30). *Providence Journal Bulletin,* p. B-3.

Inequality persists on Women's Equality Day. (1990, August–September). *9to5 Newsline,* p. 1.

Instone, Debra, Major, Brenda, & Bunker, Barbara B. (1983). Gender, self-confidence, and social influence strategies: An organizational simulation. *Journal of Personality and Social Psychology, 44,* 322–333.

Ireland, Patricia. (1992, July/August). The state of NOW. *Ms.,* pp. 24–27.

Ireson, Carol J. (1984). Adolescent pregnancy and sex-role. *Sex Roles, 11,* 189–201.

Isaacs, Susan. (1990, January 14). Sisterhood isn't so powerful in the movies. *New York Times,* pp. H-1, H-37.

Israel, Allen C., Raskin, Pamela A., Libow, Judith A., & Pravder, Marsha D. (1978). Gender and sex-role appropriateness: Bias in the judgment of disturbed behavior. *Sex Roles, 4,* 399–413.

It's taking longer for couples to tie the knot, survey confirms. (1991, June 7). *Providence Journal Bulletin,* p. A-4.

Jacklin, Carol N. (1989). Female and male: Issues of gender. *American Psychologist, 44,* 127–133.

Jacobs, Jerry A., & Powell, Brian. (1985). Occupational prestige: A sex-neutral concept? *Sex Roles, 12,* 1061–1071.

Jacobson, Marsha B. (1981). Effects of victim's and defendant's physical attractiveness on subjects' judgments in a rape case. *Sex Roles, 7,* 247–255.

Jacobson, Marsha B. (1983). Attitudes toward the Equal Rights Amendment as a function of knowing what it says. *Sex Roles, 9,* 891–896.

Jacobson, Marsha B., & Popovich, Paula M. (1983). Victim attractiveness and perceptions of responsibility in an ambiguous rape case. *Psychology of Women Quarterly, 8,* 100–104.

Jaffee, Annette W. (1988). *Recent history.* New York: Putnam's.

Jaycox, Vicki. (1985). Letter to friends of Older Women's League. (1325 G Street, NW, Washington, DC 20005)

Jeffords, Charles R. (1984). The impact of sex-role and religious attitudes upon forced marital intercourse norms. *Sex Roles, 11,* 543–552.

Jehl, Douglas, & Gerstenzang, James. (1988, November 21). Can Quayle quell ridicule? *Providence Journal Bulletin,* pp. A-2, A-3.

Jennings, Kay D. (1977). People versus object orientation in preschool children: Do sex differences really occur? *Journal of Genetic Psychology, 131,* 65–73.

Jhally, Sut. (1991). *Dreamworlds* (videotape). The Foundation for Media Education, PO Box 2008, Amherst, MA 01004.

Johnson, Allan G. (1980). On the prevalence of rape in the United States. *Signs, 6,* 136–146.

Johnson, Catherine B., Stockdale, Margaret S., & Saal, Frank E. (1991). Persistence of men's misperceptions of friendly cues across a variety of interpersonal encounters. *Psychology of Women Quarterly, 15,* 463–475.

Johnson, Dirk. (1986, June 15). Abused women get leverage in Connecticut. *New York Times,* p. E-9.

Johnson, James D., & Jackson, Lee A. Jr. (1988). Assessing the effects of factors that might underlie the differential perception of acquaintance and stranger rape. *Sex Roles, 19,* 37–45.

Johnson, Jean. (1989). Transitions experienced by midlife and older lesbians. *Hot Flash, 8,*(2).

Johnson, Maria M. (1985, November 8). Girls' aggression earns them recess separation. *Providence Journal-Bulletin.*

Johnson, Miriam M., Stockard, Jean, Rothbart, Mary K., & Friedman, Lisa. (1981). Sexual preference, feminism, and women's perceptions of their parents. *Sex Roles, 7,* 1–18.

Johnson, Paula. (1976). Women and power: Toward a theory of effectiveness. *Journal of Social Issues, 32,* 99–110.

Johnson, Sandy, Flinn, Jane M., & Tyer, Zita E. (1979). Effect of practice and training in spatial skills on embedded figures scores of male and females. *Perceptual and Motor Skills, 48* (part 1), 975–984.

Johnson, Sharon. (1984, May 22). Difference in life expectancy widens between the sexes. *New York Times,* p. C-10.

Johnson, William R. & Skinner, Jonathan. (1986). *American Economic Review, 73* (3).

Jones, Ann. (1980). *Women who kill.* New York: Fawcett Columbine.

Jones, Ernest. (1955). *The life and work of Sigmund Freud* (Vol. 2). New York: Basic Books.

Jones, Rebecca. (1991, June 10). One more pregnant professional. *Providence Journal Bulletin,* p. D-5.

Jong, Erica. (1973). *Fear of flying.* New York: Signet.

Jong, Erica. (1984). *Parachutes and kisses.* New York: Signet.

Jong, Erica. (1990). *Any woman's blues.* New York: Harper & Row.

Josefowitz, Natasha. (1980). Management men and women: Closed vs. open doors. *Harvard Business Review, 58*(5), 56–58, 62.

Josefowitz, Natasha. (1984, May). Plums and prunes. *The Owl Observer,* p. 12.

Joseph, Gloria I. (1981a). Black mothers and daughters: Their roles and functions in American society. In G. I. Joseph & J. Lewis, *Common differences: Conflicts in black and white feminist perspectives* (pp. 75–126). Garden City, NY: Anchor.

Joseph, Gloria I. (1981b). Styling, profiling, and pretending: The games before the fall. In G. I. Joseph & J. Lewis, *Common differences: Conflicts in black and white feminist perspectives* (pp. 178–230). Garden City, NY: Anchor.

Joseph, Gloria I. (1981c). The media and blacks—selling it like it isn't. In G. I. Joseph & J. Lewis, *Common differences: Conflicts in black and white feminist perspectives* (pp. 151–165). Garden City, NY: Anchor.

Joseph, Gloria I., & Lewis, Jill. (1981). *Common differences: Conflicts in black and white feminist perspectives.* Garden City, NY: Anchor.

Joyce, Laurel. (1993, January 27). Commitment needed to tackle gender inequity, panel says. *Campus Report* (Stanford University), pp. 9–10.

Judge defends comments on abuse of children. (1982, March 6). *Providence Evening Bulletin.*

Judge's recall sought. (1982, January 12). *Providence Evening Bulletin.*

Jung, Carl G. (1959). In V. deLaszlo (Ed.), *The basic writings of C. G. Jung.* New York: Random House.

Kagan, Jerome, & Moss, Howard. (1962). *Birth to maturity.* New York: Wiley.

Kahn, Ethel. (1984, March/April). The time has come for mid-life and older women. *Network News,* p. 2.

Kahn, Madeline. (1993). The politics of pornography. In S. Matteo (Ed.), *American women in the nineties: Today's critical issues* (pp. 235–252). Boston: Northeastern University Press.

Kanarian, Mary A. (1980). Attributions about rape. Unpublished master's thesis, University of Rhode Island, Kingston.

Kanarian, Mary A., & Quina, Kathryn. (1984, April). Sex-related differences in mathematics: Aptitude or attitude? Paper read at the meeting of the Eastern Psychological Association, Baltimore, MD.

Kanowitz, Leo. (1969). *Women and the law.* Albuquerque: University of New Mexico Press.

Kanter, Rosabeth M. (1977). *Men and women of the corporation.* New York: Basic Books.

Kantrowitz, Barbara et al. (1991a, April 29). Naming. *Newsweek,* pp. 26–32.

Kantrowitz, Barbara, Quade, Vicki, Fisher, Binnie, Hill, James, & Beachy, Lucille. (1991b, April 29). The pregnancy police. *Newsweek,* pp. 52–53.

Kantrowitz, Barbara et al. (1991c, October 21). Striking a nerve. *Newsweek,* pp. 34–40.

Kaplan, David A., McDaniel, Ann, Glick, Daniel, & Picker, Lauren (1991, June 3). Just say no advice. *Newsweek.* p. 18.

Kaschak, Ellyn. (1990, Summer). Future visions: A chairside view of FTI's first decade. *The Interchange,* 4527 1st Ave. NE, Seattle, WA 98105.

Kash, Sara D. (1984a, January). Birth-control survey. *Ms.,* p. 17.

Kash, Sara D. (1984b, January). On the road to a second chance. *Ms.,* p. 19.

Kasindorf, Jeanie. (1989, December 29). New moms at 40 something. *San Francisco Chronicle,* p. B-5.

Kassner, Marcia W. (1981). Will both spouses have careers?: Predictors of preferred traditional or egalitarian marriages among university students. *Journal of Vocational Behavior, 18,* 340–355.

Katzenstein, Mary F. (1984). Feminism and the meaning of the vote. *Signs, 10,* 4–26.

Kaufmann, Elizabeth. (1991, April 28). The new case for woman power. *New York Times Magazine,* Part 2, pp. 18–22.

Keil, Sally V. W. (1982, April 18). Letter to the Editor. *New York Times Magazine,* p. 130.

Keller, Evelyn F. (1983, September/October). Feminism as an analytic tool for the study of science. *Academe,* pp. 15–21.

Keller, James F., Elliott, Stephen S., & Gunberg, Edwin. (1982). Premarital sexual intercourse among single college students: A discriminant analysis. *Sex Roles, 8,* 21–32.

Kellerman, Jonathan, & Katz, Ernest R. (1978). Attitudes toward the division of child-rearing responsibility. *Sex Roles, 4,* 505–512.

Kelly, Rita Mae. (1983). Sex and becoming eminent as a political/organizational leader. *Sex Roles, 9,* 1073–1090.

Kenrick, Douglas T. (1987). Gender, genes, and the social environment: A biosocial interactionist perspective. In P. Shaver & C. Hendrick (Eds.), *Sex and gender* (pp. 14–43). Newbury Park, CA: Sage.

Kenrick, Douglas T., Stringfield, David O., Wagenhals, Walter L., Dahl, Rebecca H., & Ransdell, Hilary J. (1980). Sex differences, androgyny, and approach responses to erotica: A new variation on the old volunteer problem. *Journal of Personality and Social Psychology, 38,* 517–524.

Kerber, Linda K. (1977, September 6). Point of View: "It must be womanly as well as manly to earn your own living." *Chronicle of Higher Education,* p. 48.

Kerber, Linda K. (1986). Some cautionary words for historians. *Signs, 11,* 304–310.

Kerr, Virginia. (1982, December). Supreme Court Justice O'Connor: The woman whose word is law. *Ms.,* pp. 52, 80–84.

Kessler, Seymour, & Moos, Rudolf H. (1969). XYY chromosome: Premature conclusions. *Science, 165,* 442.

Kimball, Meredith M. (1989). A new perspective on women's math achievement. *Psychological Bulletin, 105,* 198–214.

Kimball, Meredith M., & Gray, Vicky A. (1982). Feedback and performance expectancies in an academic setting. *Sex Roles, 8,* 999–1007.

Kimmel, Douglas C. (1988). Ageism, psychology, and public policy. *American Psychologist, 43,* 175–178.

Kimura, Doreen. (1985, November). Male brain, female brain: The hidden difference. *Psychology Today,* pp. 50–58.

Kimura, Doreen. (1989, November). Monthly fluctuations in sex hormones affect women's cognitive skills. *Psychology Today,* pp. 63–66.

King, Deborah K. (1988). Multiple jeopardy, multiple consciousness: The context of a black feminist ideology. *Signs, 14,* 42–72.

King, H. Elizabeth, & Webb, Carol. (1981). Rape crisis centers: Progress and problems. *Journal of Social Issues, 37*(4), 93–104.

Kingston, Maxine H. (1977). *The woman warrior: Memoirs of a girlhood among ghosts.* New York: Vintage.

Kinsbourne, Marcel. (1982). Hemispheric specialization and the growth of human understanding. *American Psychologist, 37,* 411–420.

Kinsey, Alfred C., Pomeroy, Wardell B., Martin, Clyde E., & Gebhard, Paul H. (1953). *Sexual behavior in the human female.* Philadelphia: Saunders.

Kinsman, Cheryl A., & Berk, Laura E. (1979). Joining the block and housekeeping areas. Changes in play and social behavior. *Young Children, 35,* 66–75.

Kirby, Darrell F., & Julian, Nancy B. (1981). Treatment of women in high school history textbooks. *Social Studies, 72,* 203–207.

Kirkpatrick, Martha. (1989). Middle age and the lesbian experience. *Women Studies Quarterly, 17* (1&2), 87–96.

Kirshenbaum, Gayle. (1990, September/October). Abortion: Is there a doctor in the clinic? *Ms.,* pp. 86–87.

Kitzinger, Sheila. (1979). *Women as mothers.* New York: Vintage.

Klass, Perri. (1988, April 10). Are women better doctors? *New York Times Magazine,* pp. 32–35, 46–48, 96–97.

Klass, Perri. (1989, January 29). The perfect baby? *New York Times Magazine,* pp. 45–46.

Klebanov, Pamela K., & Jemmott, John B., III. (1992). Effects of expectations and bodily sensations on self-reports of premenstrual symptoms. *Psychology of Women Quarterly, 16,* 289–310.

Klein, Julia M. (1977, March). Is there a child in their future? *Radcliffe Quarterly.*

Kleinke, Chris L., Staneski, Richard A., & Mason, Jeanne K. (1982). Sex differences in coping with depression. *Sex Roles, 8,* 877–889.

Kleiman, Carol. (1983, July 26). Gender gap grows in educational executive posts. *Providence Evening Bulletin.*

Kleiman, Carol. (1988, August 29). More women managers being fired than men. *Providence Journal Bulletin,* p. E-1.

Kleiman, Carol. (1989a, June 12). Despite gains, few women are found in blue-collar jobs. *Providence Journal Bulletin,* p. B-5.

Kleiman, Carol. (1989b, August 28). How to get ahead in career? Women, men give similar replies. *Providence Journal Bulletin,* p. A-12.

Kleiman, Carol. (1991, January 21). Women stopped by 'glass ceiling.' *Providence Journal Bulletin,* p. A-12.

Kleiman, Carol. (1992, January 13). Women workers speak out on harassment. *Providence Journal Bulletin,* p. A-8.

Klemesrud, Judy. (1971, March 28). The disciples of Sappho, updated. *New York Times Magazine.*

Klemmack, Susan H., & Klemmack, David L. (1976). The social definition of rape. In M. J. Walker & S. L. Brodsky (Eds.), *Sexual assault* (pp. 135–148). Lexington, MA: Heath.

Knaub, Patricia K., Eversoll, Deanna R., & Voss, Jacqueline H. (1983). Is parenthood a desirable adult role? An assessment of attitudes held by contemporary women. *Sex Roles, 9,* 355–362.

Koblinsky, Sally A., & Sugawara, Alan I. (1984). Nonsexist curricula, sex of teacher, and children's sex-role learning. *Sex Roles, 10,* 357–367.

Koedt, Anne. (1973). The myth of the vaginal orgasm. In A. Koedt, E. Levine, & A. Rapone (Eds.), *Radical Feminism* (pp. 19–20). New York: Quadrangle.

Koeske, Randi K. (1983). Lifting the curse of menstruation: Toward a feminist perspective on the menstrual cycle. In S. Golub (Ed.), *Lifting the curse of menstruation* (pp. 1–16). New York: Haworth.

Koeske, Randi K., & Koeske, Gary F. (1975). An attributional approach to moods and the menstrual cycle. *Journal of Personality and Social Psychology, 31,* 473–478.

Koestner, Richard, Zuckerman, Miron, & Koestner, Julia. (1989). Attributional focus of praise and children's intrinsic motivation: The moderating role of gender. *Personality and Social Psychological Bulletin, 15,* 61–72.

Kohl, Linda. (1988, October 10). FloJo streaks past Barbie image. *Providence Journal-Bulletin,* p. B-1.

Kohlberg, Lawrence A. (1966). A cognitive-developmental analysis of children's sex-role concepts and attitudes. In E. E. Maccoby (Ed.), *The development of sex differences* (pp. 82–173). Stanford, CA: Stanford University Press.

Kohn, Alfie. (1987a, February). Shattered innocence. *Psychology Today,* pp. 54, 56–58.

Kohn, Alfie. (1987b, December). Making the most of marriage. *Psychology Today,* pp. 6–8.

Kohn, Alfie. (1988, July/August). Parenthood pablum. *Psychology Today,* pp. 64–65.

Kolata, Gina B. (1980a). Math and sex: Are girls born with less ability? *Science, 210,* 1234–1235.

Kolata, Gina B. (1980b). NIH panel urges fewer cesarian births. *Science, 210,* 176–177.

Kolata, Gina B. (1983). First trimester prenatal diagnosis. *Science, 221,* 1031–1032.

Kolata, Gina B. (1984a). Puberty mystery solved. *Science, 223,* 272.

Kolata, Gina B. (1984b). Studying learning in the womb. *Science, 225,* 302–303.

Kolata, Gina B. (1986). How important is dietary calcium in preventing osteoporosis? *Science, 233,* 519–520.

Kolata, Gina B. (1987). What babies know, and noises parents make. *Science, 237,* 726.

Kolata, Gina. (1991, August 5). When grandmother is the mother, until birth. *New York Times,* pp. A-1, A-11.

Komarovsky, Mirra. (1982). Female freshmen view their future: Career salience and its correlates. *Sex Roles, 8,* 299–314.

Koonz, Claudia. (1987). *Mothers in the fatherland: Women, family-life, and Nazi ideology., 1900–1945.* New York: St. Martin's Press.

Kopper, Beverly A., & Epperson, Douglas L. (1991). Women and anger. *Psychology of Women Quarterly, 15,* 7–14.

Korpivaara, Ari. (1982, February). Play groups for dads. *Ms.,* pp. 52–54.

Koslow, Robert E. (1987). Sex-related differences and visual-spatial mental imagery as factors affecting symbolic motor skill acquisition. *Sex Roles, 17,* 521–527.

Koss, Mary P. (1981, September). *Hidden rape on a university campus.* Unpublished final report to the National Institutes of Mental Health, Rockville, MD.

Koss, Mary P. (1985). The hidden rape victim: Personality, attitudinal, and situational characteristics. *Psychology of Women Quarterly, 9,* 193–212.

Koss, Mary P. (1992). The underdetection of rape: Methodological choices influence incidence estimates. *Journal of Social Issues, 48 (1),* 61–75.

Koss, Mary P., & Burkhart, Barry R. (1989). A conceptual analysis of rape victimization: Long-term effects and implications for treatment. *Psychology of Women Quarterly, 13,* 27–40.

Koss, Mary P., Dinero, Thomas E., Seibel, Cynthia A., & Cox, Susan L. (1988). Stranger and acquaintance rape: Are there differences in the victim's experience? *Psychology of Women Quarterly, 12,* 1–24.

Koss, Mary P., Gidycz, Christine A., & Wisniewski, Nadine. (1987). The scope of rape: Incidence and prevalence of sexual aggression and victimization in a national sample of higher education students. *Journal of Consulting and Clinical Psychology, 55,* 162–170.

Koss, Mary P., Leonard, Kenneth E., Beezley, Dana A., & Oros, Cheryl J. (1985). Non-stranger sexual aggression: A discriminant analysis of the psychological characteristics of undetected offenders. *Sex Roles, 12,* 981–992.

Koss, Mary P., & Oros, Cheryl J. (1982). The Sexual Experiences Survey: A research instrument investigating sexual aggression and victimization. *Journal of Consulting and Clinical Psychology, 50,* 455–457.

Kotkin, Mark. (1983). Sex roles among married and unmarried couples. *Sex Roles, 9,* 975–985.

Kourilsky, Marilyn, & Campbell, Michael. (1984). Sex differences in a simulated classroom economy: Children's beliefs about entrepreneurship. *Sex Roles, 10,* 53–66.

Kozinn, Allan. (1985, March 24). An American woman conductor on the way up. *New York Times,* p. H-23.

Krames, Lester, England, Rebecca, & Flett, Gordon L. (1988). The role of masculinity and femininity in depression and social satisfaction in elderly females. *Sex Roles, 19,* 713–721.

Kravetz, Diane, Marecek, Jeanne, & Finn, Stephen E. (1983). Factors influencing women's participation in consciousness-raising groups. *Psychology of Women Quarterly, 7,* 257–271.

Krieger, Susan. (1982). Lesbian identity and community: Recent social science literature. *Signs, 8,* 91–108.

Kropp, Jerri J., & Halverson, Charles F. (1983). Preschool children's preferences and recall for stereotyped versus nonstereotyped stories. *Sex Roles, 9,* 261–272.

Krulewitz, Judith E. (1978, August). Sex differences in the perception of victims of sexual and nonsexual assault. Paper presented at the meeting of the American Psychological Association, Toronto.

Kuhn, Deanna, Nash, Sharon C., & Brucken, Laura. (1978). Sex role concepts of two- and three-year-olds. *Child Development, 49,* 445–451.

Kumagai, Gloria L. (1978). The Asian woman in America. *Explorations in Ethnic Studies, 1,* 27–39.

Kurdek, Lawrence A. (1991). Correlates of relationship satisfaction in cohabiting gay and lesbian couples. *Journal of Personality and Social Psychology, 61,* 910–922.

Kurdek, Lawrence A., & Schmitt, J. Patrick. (1986a). Interaction of sex role self concept with relationship quality and relationship beliefs in married, heterosexual cohabiting, gay, and lesbian couples. *Journal of Personality and Social Psychology, 51,* 365–370.

Kurdek, Lawrence A., & Schmitt, J. Patrick. (1986b). Relationship quality of partners in heterosexual married, heterosexual cohabiting, and gay and lesbian relationships. *Journal of Personality and Social Psychology, 51,* 711–720.

Kushner, Howard I. (1985). Women and suicide in historical perspective. *Signs, 10,* 537–552.

Kutner, Nancy G., & Brogan, Donna. (1990). Sex stereotypes and health care: The case of treatment for kidney failure. *Sex Roles, 24,* 279–290.

Kutner, Nancy G., & Levinson, Richard M. (1978). The toy salesperson: A voice for change in sex-role stereotypes? *Sex Roles, 4,* 1–8.

Kweskin, Sally L., & Cook, Alicia S. (1982). Heterosexual and homosexual mothers' self-described sex-role behavior and ideal sex-role behavior in children. *Sex Roles, 8,* 967–975.

Labor Department reports increase of working women is slowing after 2 decades. (1990, November 24). *Providence Journal Bulletin,* p. A-2.

Lacayo, Richard. (1993, March 22). One doctor down, how many more? *Time,* pp. 46–47.

Lacayo, Richard. (1992, May 4). Abortion: The future is already here. *Time,* pp. 26–32.

Ladner, Joyce A. (1971). *Tomorrow's tomorrow: The black woman.* Garden City, NY: Doubleday.

LaFrance, Marianne, & Carmen, Barbara. (1980). The nonverbal display of psychological androgyny. *Journal of Personality and Social Psychology, 38,* 36–49.

Lake, Randall A. (1986). The metaethical framework of anti-abortion rhetoric. *Signs, 11,* 478–499.

Lakoff, Robin. (1975). *Language and woman's place.* New York: Harper & Row.

Lamb, Patricia F. (1985, April). Heroine addicts. *Women's Review of Books,* pp. 16–17.

Lambda. (n.d.). *Put bigots on trial.* Lambda Legal Defense and Education Fund, 666 Broadway, New York, NY 10012.

Lambert, Helen H. (1978). Biology and equality: A perspective on sex differences. *Signs, 4,* 97–117.

Lamphere, Louise. (1977). Anthropology. *Signs, 2,* 612–627.

Landau, Carol. (1986, May). Critique of DSMIII-R. Paper read at the meeting of the Rhode Island Association for Women in Psychology, Cranston, RI.

Landers, Susan. (1987, February). Panel urges teen contraception. *APA Monitor,* p. 6.

Landers, Susan. (1989, April). NY: Scholarship awards are ruled discriminatory. *APA Monitor,* p. 14.

Landis, Bruce. (1983, September 20). Rapes increase in RI; Young girls at risk. *Providence Evening Bulletin.*

Landrine, Hope. (1985). Race x class stereotypes of women. *Sex Roles, 13,* 65–75.

Landrine, Hope. (1988). Depression and stereotypes of women: Preliminary empirical analyses of the gender-role hypothesis. *Sex Roles, 19,* 527–541.

Landrine, Hope. (1989). The politics of personality disorder. *Psychology of Women Quarterly, 13,* 325–339.

Landrine, Hope. (1991). *The politics of madness.* New York: Peter Lang.

Landrine, Hope, Klonoff, Elizabeth A., & Brown-Collins, Alice. (1992). Cultural diversity and methodology in feminist psychology: Critique, proposal, empirical example. *Psychology of Women Quarterly, 16,* 145–163.

Lang, Perry. (1991, October 16). Black prof.: Pick marriage over career. *Providence Journal Bulletin,* p. D-3.

Langlois, Judith H., & Downs, A. Chris. (1980). Mothers, fathers, and peers as socialization agents of sex-typed play behaviors in young children. *Child Development, 51,* 1237–1247.

Lanier, Hope B., & Byrne, Joan. (1981). How high school students view women: The relationship between perceived attractiveness, occupation, and education. *Sex Roles, 7,* 145–148.

L'Armand, K., & Pepitone, Albert. (1982). Judgments of rape: A study of victim-rapist relationships and victim sexual history. *Personality and Social Psychology Bulletin, 8,* 134–139.

Lasker award stirs controversy. (1979). *Science, 203,* 341.

Latham, Caroline. (1985, February). How to live with a man. *Cosmopolitan,* pp. 98, 106–107, 112.

LaTorre, Ronald A., Yu, Lauren, Fortin, Louise, & Marrache, Myriam. (1983). Gender-role adoption and sex as academic and psychological risk factors. *Sex Roles, 9,* 1127–1136.

Lawrence, Frances C., Draughn, Peggy S., Tasker, Grace E., & Wozniak, Patricia H. (1987). Sex differences in household labor time: A comparison of rural and urban couples. *Sex Roles, 17,* 489–502.

Laws, Judith L., & Schwartz, Pepper. (1977). *Sexual scripts: The social constructions of female sexuality.* New York: Dryden.

Laws, Sophie. (1983). The sexual politics of pre-menstrual tension. *Women's Studies International Forum, 6,* 19–31.

Lawson, Carol. (1986, August 25). Women, success and romantic advice. *New York Times.*

Lawyer-client sex: Unethical, illegal, helpful. (1992, Winter). *Nolo News,* p. 3.

Lazarre, Jane. (1985, March 10). Writers as mothers. *New York Times Book Review,* p. 30.

Leader, Jody. (1991, November 16). For comedienne Diane Ford, unequal pay isn't funny. *Providence Journal Bulletin,* p. A-10.

Lear, Martha W. (1972, January 30). Q. If you rape a woman and steal her TV, what can they get you for in New York? A. Stealing her TV. *New York Times Magazine.*

Leavitt, Jacqueline, & Welch, MaryBeth. (1989). Older women and the suburbs: A literature review. *Women Studies Quarterly, 17* (1 & 2), 35–47.

Leavitt, Judith W. (1980). Birthing and anesthesia: The debate over twilight sleep. *Signs, 6,* 147–164.

Lederer, Laura. (1980). Introduction. In L. Lederer (Ed.), *Take back the night* (pp. 15–20). New York: Morrow.

Lee, Harper. (1960). *To kill a mockingbird.* Philadelphia: J. B. Lippincott.

Lee, Patrick C., & Gropper, Nancy B. (1974). Sex-role culture and educational practice. *Harvard Educational Review, 44,* 369–407.

Leiblum, Sandra R. (1990). Sexuality and the midlife woman. *Psychology of Women Quarterly, 14,* 495–508.

Leibowitz, Lila. (1970, February). Desmond Morris is wrong about breasts, buttocks and body hair. *Psychology Today,* pp. 16, 18, 22.

Leibowitz, Lila. (1978). "Universals" and male dominance among primates: A critical examination. In E. Tobach, & B. Rosoff (Eds.), *Pitfalls in research on sex and gender, No. 2.* Staten Island, NY: Gordian Press.

Leifer, Myra. (1980). Pregnancy. *Signs, 5,* 754–765.

Leigh, Wilhelmina A. (1989). Barriers to fair housing for black women. *Sex Roles, 21,* 69–84.

Lemkau, Jeanne P. (1979). Personality and background characteristics of women in male-dominated occupations: A review. *Psychology of Women Quarterly, 4,* 221–240.

Lemkau, Jeanne P. (1983). Women in male-dominated professions: Distinguishing personality and background characteristics. *Psychology of Women Quarterly, 8,* 144–165.

Lemkau, Jeanne P. (1988). Emotional sequelae of abortion. *Psychology of Women Quarterly, 12,* 461–472.

Lemkau, Jeanne P., & Landau, Carol. (1986). The "selfless syndrome": Assessment and treatment considerations. *Psychotherapy: Theory, Research, and Practice, 23,* 227–233.

Lenney, Ellen. (1977). Women's self-confidence in achievement settings. *Psychological Bulletin, 84,* 1–13.

Lenney, Ellen. (1981). What's fine for the gander isn't always good for the goose: Sex differences in self-confidence as a function of ability area and comparison with others. *Sex Roles, 7,* 905–924.

Lenney, Ellen, & Gold, Joel. (1982). Sex differences in self-confidence: The effects of task completion and of comparison to competent others. *Personality and Social Psychology Bulletin, 8,* 74–80.

Lennon, Mary C. (1987). Is menopause depressing? An investigation of three perspectives. *Sex Roles, 17,* 1–16.

Leone, Christopher, & Robertson, Kevin. (1989). Some effects of sex-linked clothing and gender schema on the stereotyping of infants. *Journal of Social Psychology, 129,* 609–619.

Lerman, Hannah. (1976). What happens in feminist therapy? In S. Cox (Ed.), *Female psychology: The emerging self* (pp. 378–384). Chicago: Science Research Associates.

Lerman, Hannah. (1985). Some barriers to the development of a feminist theory of personality. In L. B. Rosewater & L. E. A. Walker (Eds.), *Handbook of feminist therapy: Women's issues in psychotherapy* (pp. 5–12). New York: Springer.

Lerner, Gerda. (1977). *The female experience: An American documentary.* Indianapolis: Bobbs-Merrill.

Lesbians: A consciousness raising kit. (1980). Cambridge, MA: Boston NOW.

Lessing, Doris. (1984). *The diaries of Jane Somers.* New York: Vintage.

Leung, Jupian J. (1990). Aspiring parents' and teachers' academic beliefs about young children. *Sex Roles, 23,* 83–90.

Levenson, Robert W., & Gottman, John M. (1985). Physiological and affective predictors of change in relationship satisfaction. *Journal of Personality and Social Psychology, 49,* 85–94.

Lever, Janet. (1978). Sex differences in the complexity of children's play and games. *American Sociological Review, 43,* 471–482.

Levertov, Denise. (1973). From Stepping westward. In B. Segnitz & C. Rainey (Eds.), *Psyche: The feminine poetic consciousness* (pp. 100–102). New York: Dell.

Levine, Martin P., & Leonard, Robin. (1984). Discrimination against lesbians in the work force. *Signs, 9,* 700–710.

Levitin, Teresa E., & Chananie, J. D. (1972). Responses of female primary school teachers to sex-typed behaviors in male and female children. *Child Development, 43,* 1309–1316.

Lewin, Miriam. (1985). Unwanted intercourse: The difficulty of saying no. *Psychology of Women Quarterly, 9,* 184–192.

Lewin, Tamar. (1986, November 9). A grueling struggle for equality. *New York Times,* pp. F-12–F-13.

Lewin, Tamar. (1991, January 20). In crime, too, some gender-related inequities. *New York Times,* p. E-9.

Lewin, Tamar. (1992a, February 28). Canada court says pornography harms women. *New York Times,* p. B-7.

Lewin, Tamar. (1992b, March 15). Hurdles increase for many women seeking abortions. *New York Times,* p. 1.

Lewine, Richard R. J. (1981). Sex differences in schizophrenia: Timing or subtypes? *Psychological Bulletin, 90,* 432–444.

Lewis, Anthony. (1991, April 3). Transplant for the ghettos. *Providence Journal-Bulletin,* p. A-12.

Lewis, Helen. (1988, January). A battlefield of one's own. *Women's Review of Books.*

Lewis, Jill. (1981a). The subject of struggle: Feminism and sexuality. In G. I. Joseph & J. Lewis, *Common differences: Conflicts in black and white feminist perspectives* (pp. 231–273). Garden City, NY: Anchor.

Lewis, Jill. (1981b). Sexual division of power. In G. I. Joseph & J. Lewis, *Common differences: Conflicts in black and white feminist perspectives* (pp. 43–71). Garden City, NY: Anchor.

Lewis, Michael. (1975). Early sex differences in the human: Studies of socio-emotional development. *Archives of Sexual Behavior, 4,* 329–335.

Lewis, Peter H. (1984, August 26). What's on babies' minds when they come into the world. *New York Times,* p. E-8.

Lewontin, R. C., Rose, Steven, & Kamin, Leon J. (1984). *Not in our genes: Biology, ideology, and human nature.* New York: Pantheon.

Libby, Marion N., & Aries, Elizabeth. (1989). Gender differences in preschool children's narrative fantasy. *Psychology of Women Quarterly, 13,* 293–306.

Lieber, Jill. (1989, February). The woman warrior. *Sports Illustrated,* pp. 132–134.

Liebert, Robert M., McCall, Robert B., & Hanratty, Margaret A. (1971). Effects of sex-typed information on children's toy preferences. *Journal of Genetic Psychology, 119,* 133–136.

Liebmann-Smith, Joan. (1987, April). Sex. *Ms.,* pp. 78, 89.

Life of fishing appeals to women. (1980, May 28). *Providence Evening Bulletin.*

Lindsey, Robert. (1976, September 12). Women entering job market at an "extraordinary" pace. *New York Times.*

Lindsey, Robert. (1984, April 4). Sexual abuse of children draws experts' increasing concern nationwide. *New York Times,* p. A-21.

Linn, Marcia C. (1985). Fostering equitable consequences from computer learning environments. *Sex Roles, 13,* 229–240.

Linz, Daniel G., Donnerstein, Edward, & Penrod, Steven. (1988). Effects of long-term exposure to violent and sexually degrading depictions of women. *Journal of Personality and Social Psychology, 55,* 758–768.

Linz, Daniel, Wilson, Barbara J., & Donnerstein, Edward. (1992). Sexual violence in the mass media: Legal solutions, warnings, and mitigation through education. *Journal of Social Issues, 48* (1), 145–171.

Lippa, Richard, & Beauvais, Cheryl. (1983). Gender jeopardy: The effects of gender, assessed femininity and masculinity, and false success/failure feedback on performance in an experimental quiz game. *Journal of Personality and Social Psychology, 44,* 344–353.

Lipsitt, Lewis P. (1977). The study of sensory and learning processes of the newborn. *Clinics in Perinatology, 4,* 163–186.

Lisak, David, & Roth, Susan. (1988). Motivational factors in nonincarcerated sexually aggressive men. *Journal of Personality and Social Psychology,*

Litt, Iris. (1992, Spring). Gender differences in adolescents' alcohol use. *Institute for Research on Women and Gender Newsletter,* Stanford University.

Litt, Iris F. (1993). Health issues for women in the 1990s. In S. Matteo (Ed.), *American women in the nineties: Today's critical issues* (pp. 139–157). Boston: Northeastern University Press.

Little progress for women in job market. (1992, August 12). *Providence Journal Bulletin,* p. D-9.

Littlefield, Christine H., & Rushton, J. Philippe. (1986). When a child dies: The sociobiology of bereavement. *Journal of Personality and Social Psychology, 51,* 797–802.

Living alone. (1984, August). *ISR Newsletter.* (Institute for Social Research, University of Michigan, Ann Arbor.)

Lobsenz, Norman M. (1974, January 20). Sex and the senior citizen. *New York Times Magazine.*

Lockheed, Marlaine E. (1985). Women, girls, and computers: A first look at the evidence. *Sex Roles, 13,* 115–122.

Lockheed, Marlaine E. (1986). Reshaping the social order: The case of gender segregation. *Sex Roles, 14,* 617–628.

Loden, Marilyn. (1986, February 9). Disillusion at the corporate top: A machismo that drives women out. *New York Times,* p. F-2.

Loewenstein, Sophie F. (1977, November). Passion in women's lives. Paper presented at Butler Hospital, Providence, RI.

Loewenstein, Sophie F. (1978). *Understanding lesbian women.* Unpublished paper, Simmons College, School of Social Work, Boston.

Loewenstein, Sophie F., Bloch, Natalie E., Campion, Jennifer, Epstein, Jane S., Gale, Peggy, & Salvatore, Maggie. (1981). A study of satisfactions and stresses of single women in midlife. *Sex Roles, 7,* 1127–1141.

Lombardo, William K., Cretser, Gary A., Lombardo, Barbara, & Mathis, Sharon L. (1983). For cryin' out loud—there is a sex difference. *Sex Roles, 9,* 987–995.

Long, Vonda O. (1986). Relationship of masculinity to self-esteem and self-acceptance in female professionals, college students, clients, and victims of domestic violence. *Journal of Consulting and Clinical Psychology, 54,* 323–327.

Lont, Cynthia. (1990). The roles assigned to females and males in non-music radio programming. *Sex Roles, 22,* 661–668.

"A look at abortion laws around the world." (1981, May 20). *Providence Evening Bulletin.*

Looft, William R. (1971). Sex differences in the expression of vocational aspirations by elementary school children. *Developmental Psychology, 5,* 366.

Lopata, Helena Z. (1987). In Hess, Beth B., & Ferree, Myra M. (Eds.). (1987). *Analyzing gender: A handbook of social science research.* Newbury Park, CA: Sage.

Lopata, Helena Z. (1988). Support systems of American urban widowhood. *Journal of Social Issues, 44* (3), 113–128.

Lopez, Steven R. (1989). Patient variable biases in clinical judgment. *Psychological Bulletin, 106,* 184–203.

Lorber, Judith. (1981). On The Reproduction of Mothering: A methodological debate. *Signs, 6,* 482–486.

Lorimer, Linda K. (1990, May 13). The pluses of women's colleges. *Richmond Times-Dispatch,* p. F-7.

Lott, Albert J., & Lott, Bernice E. (1963). *Negro and white youth.* New York: Holt, Rinehart & Winston.

Lott, Albert J., & Lott, Bernice E. (1968). A learning theory approach to interpersonal attitudes. In A. G. Greenwald, T. C. Brock, & T. M. Ostrom (Eds.), *Psychological foundations of attitudes* (pp. 67–88). New York: Academic Press.

Lott, Albert J., & Lott, Bernice E. (1972). The power of liking: Consequences of interpersonal attitudes derived from a liberalized view of secondary reinforcement. In L. Berkowitz (Ed.), *Advances in experimental social psychology* (pp. 109–148). New York: Academic Press.

Lott, Albert J., & Lott, Bernice E. (1974). The role of reward in the formation of positive interpersonal attitudes. In T. L. Huston (Ed.), *Foundations of interpersonal attraction* (pp. 171–192). New York: Academic Press.

Lott, Bernice. (1973). Who wants the children? Some relationships among attitudes toward children, parents, and the liberation of women. *American Psychologist, 28,* 573–582.

Lott, Bernice. (1978). Behavioral concordance with sex role ideology related to play areas, creativity, and parental sextyping of children. *Journal of Personality and Social Psychology, 36,* 1087–1100.

Lott, Bernice. (1979). Sex role ideology and children's drawings: Does the jack-o'-lantern smile or scare? *Sex Roles, 5,* 93–98.

Lott, Bernice. (1981). A feminist critique of androgyny: Toward the elimination of gender attributions for learned behavior. In C. Mayo & N. M. Henley (Eds.), *Gender and nonverbal behavior* (pp. 171–180). New York: Springer-Verlag.

Lott, Bernice. (1985a). The devaluation of women's competence. *Journal of Social Issues, 41*(4), 43–60.

Lott, Bernice. (1985b). The potential enrichment of social/personality psychology through feminist research, and vice versa. *American Psychologist, 40,* 155–164.

Lott, Bernice. (1987). Sexist discrimination as distancing behavior: I. A laboratory demonstration. *Psychology of Women Quarterly.*

Lott, Bernice. (1988). Sexist discrimination as distancing behavior: II. Primetime television. *Psychology of Women Quarterly.*

Lott, Bernice. (1990). Dual natures or learned behavior. In R. T. Hare-Mustin, & J. Marecek (Eds.), *Making a difference: Psychology and the construction of gender* (pp. 65–101). New Haven, CT: Yale University Press.

Lott, Bernice. (1991). Social psychology: Humanist roots and feminist future. *Psychology of Women Quarterly, 15,* 505–519.

Lott, Bernice. (1993). Sexual harassment: Consequences and remedies. *Thought & Action, 8*(2), 89–103.

Lott, Bernice, & Lott, Albert J. (1985). Learning theory in contemporary social psychology. In E. Aronson & G. Lindzey (Eds.), *Handbook of social psychology, vol. III* (pp. 109–135). Reading, MA: Addison-Wesley.

Lott, Bernice, & Maluso, Diane. (1993). The social learning of gender. In A. E. Beall & R. J. Sternberg (Eds.), *The psychology of gender.* New York: Guilford.

Lott, Bernice, Reilly, Mary Ellen, & Howard, Dale R. (1982). Sexual assault and harassment: A campus community case study. *Signs, 8,* 296–319.

Lott, Sara. (1978). Mountains. Unpublished poem.

Lott, Sara. (1985). Shape I'm in. Unpublished poem.

Lowe, Geoff. (1987, July). Scaling the heights of passion. *Psychology Today,* p. 10.

Lowe, Marian. (1978). Sociobiology and sex differences. *Signs, 4,* 119–125.

Lowe, Marian. (1983). The dialectic of biology and culture. In M. Lowe & R. Hubbard (Eds.), *Woman's nature: Rationalizations of inequality* (pp. 39–62). New York: Pergamon.

Luebke, Barbara F. (1989). Out of focus: Images of women and men in newspaper photographs. *Sex Roles, 20,* 121–133.

Luginbuhl, James, & Mullin, Courtney. (1981). Rape and responsibility: How and how much is the victim blamed? *Sex Roles, 7,* 547–559.

Luker, Kristin. (1984). *Abortion and the politics of motherhood.* Berkeley: University of California Press.

Luker, Kristin. (1986). Losers in a zero-sum game. *New York Times Book Review,* pp. 7, 9.

Luria, Zella, & Meade, Robert G. (1984). Sexuality and the middle-aged woman. In G. Baruch & J. Brooks-Gunn (Eds.), *The middle-aged woman* (pp. 371–397). New York: Plenum.

Lutz, John S. (1991, Spring). Feminism: Cornerstone of political correctness. *Campus,* p. 1.

Lynch, Jean M., & Reilly, Mary E. (1985–1986). Role relationships: Lesbian perspectives. *Journal of Homosexuality, 12*(2), 53–69.

Lynn, Michael, & Shurgot, Barbara A. (1984). Responses to lonely hearts advertisements: Effects of reported physical attractiveness, physique, and coloration. *Personality and Social Psychology Bulletin, 10,* 349–357.

Lyons, Judith A., & Serbin, Lisa A. (1986). Observer bias in scoring boys' and girls' aggression. *Sex Roles, 14,* 301–313.

Lyons, Richard D. (1984, May 30). It's a boy? That's no surprise. *Providence Evening Bulletin.*

Lytton, Hugh, & Romney, David M. (1991). Parents' differential socialization of boys and girls: A meta-analysis. *Psychological Bulletin, 109,* 267–296.

Maccoby, Eleanor E. (1990). Gender and relationships: A developmental account. *American Psychologist, 45,* 513–520.

Maccoby, Eleanor E., & Jacklin, Carol N. (1974). *The psychology of sex differences.* Stanford, CA: Stanford University Press.

Maccoby, Eleanor E., & Jacklin, Carol N. (1980). Sex differences in aggression: A rejoinder and reprise. *Child Development, 51,* 964–980.

Macdonald, Barbara. (1989). Outside the sisterhood: Ageism in women's studies. *Women's Studies Quarterly, 17* (1 & 2), 6–11.

MacKay, Scott. (1992, June 13). Women Democrats raise funds. *Providence Journal Bulletin,* p. A-3.

Mackey, Aurora. (1989, March 26). Breaking ranks. *Providence Journal Bulletin,* pp. J-1, J-4.

MacKinnon, Catharine A. (1979). *Sexual harassment of working women.* New Haven: Yale University Press.

MacKinnon, Catharine A. (1982). Feminism, Marxism, method, and the state: An agenda for theory. *Signs, 7,* 515–544.

MacKinnon, Catharine A. (1989). *Toward a feminist theory of the state.* Harvard University Press: Cambridge, MA.

MacKinnon, Catherine A. (1991, December 15). The Palm Beach hanging. *New York Times,* p. E-15.

MacPherson, Kathleen I. (1984, March/April). Is osteoporosis inevitable? *Network News,* p. 8.

Macris, Gina. (1992, March 16). Helping children of divorce. *Providence Journal Bulletin,* pp. A-1, A-5.

Maio, Kathi. (1990, September/October). Hooked on hate? *Ms.,* pp. 42–44.

Major, Brenda, Carnevale, Peter J. D., & Deaux, Kay. (1981). A different perspective on androgyny: Evaluations of masculine and feminine personality characteristics. *Journal of Personality and Social Psychology, 41,* 988–1001.

Major, Brenda, McFarlin, Dean B., & Gagnon, Diana. (1984). Overworked and underpaid: On the nature of gender differences in personal entitlement. *Journal of Personality and Social Psychology, 47,* 1399–1412.

Major, Jack. (1983, February 27). If it's new it's cool. *The Providence Sunday Journal.*

Malamuth, Neil M. (1981). Rape proclivity among males. *Journal of Social Issues, 37*(4), 138–157.

Malamuth, Neil M. (1983). Factors associated with rape as predictors of laboratory aggression against women. *Journal of Personality and Social Psychology, 45,* 432–442.

Malamuth, Neil M. (1986). Predictors of naturalistic sexual aggression. *Journal of Personality and Social Psychology, 50,* 953–962.

Malamuth, Neil M., Heim, Maggie, & Feshbach, Seymour. (1980). Sexual responsiveness of college students to rape depictions: Inhibitory and disinhibitory effects. *Journal of Personality and Social Psychology, 38,* 399–408.

Malamuth, Neil M., Sockloskie, Robert J., Koss, Mary P., & Tanaka, J. S. (1991). Characteristics of aggressors against women: Testing a model using a national sample of college students. *Journal of Consulting and Clinical Psychology, 59,* 670–681.

Male birth control pill. (1991, July 2). *Providence Journal Bulletin,* p. B-2.

Malveaux, Julianne. (1985). Current economic trends and black feminist consciousness. *Black Scholar, 16*(2), 26–31.

Mamay, Patricia D., & Simpson, Richard L. (1981). Three female roles in television commercials. *Sex Roles, 7,* 1223–1232.

Mandelbaum, Dorothy R. (1978). Women in medicine. *Signs, 4,* 136–145.

Mandler, Jean M. (1990). A new perspective on cognitive development in infancy. *American Scientist, 78,* 236–244.

Manegold, Catherine S. (1992a, July 12). No more nice girls. *New York Times,* pp. 25, 31.

Manegold, Catherine S. (1992b, August 2). The battle over choice obscures other vital concerns of women. *New York Times,* p. E-1, E-3.

Mansfield, Phyllis K., Koch, Patricia B., Henderson, Julie, Vicary, Judith R., Cohn, Margaret, & Young, Elaine W. (1991). The job climate for women in traditionally male blue-collar occupations. *Sex Roles, 25,* 63–80.

A man-sized resistance to housework. (1981, February 5). *Providence Evening Bulletin.*

Mansnerus, Laura. (1989, February 19). The rape laws change faster than perceptions. *New York Times,* p. E-20.

Mansnerus, Laura. (1991). Don't tell. *New York Times Magazine.*

Manstead, A. S. R., Proffitt, C., & Smart, J. L. (1983). Predicting and understanding mothers' infant-feeding intentions and behaviors. *Journal of Personality and Social Psychology, 44,* 657–671.

Marecek, Jeanne. (1977). Power and women's psychological disorders: Preliminary observations. Unpublished paper, Swarthmore College, Swarthmore, PA.

Marecek, Jeanne, & Hare-Mustin, Rachel T. (1991). A short history of the future: Feminism and clinical psychology. *Psychology of Women Quarterly, 15,* 521–536.

Marecek, Jeanne, & Kravetz, Diane. (1977). Women and mental health: A review of feminist change efforts. *Psychiatry, 40,* 323–329.

Margolick, David. (1990, March 25). A name, a face and a rape: Iowa victim tells her story. *New York Times,* pp. 1, 28.

Margolin, Gayla, & Patterson, Gerald R. (1975). Differential consequences provided by mothers and fathers for their sons and daughters. *Developmental Psychology, 11,* 537–538.

Marini, Margaret M. (1978). Sex differences in the determination of adolescent aspirations: A review of research. *Sex Roles, 4,* 723–753.

Markson, Elizabeth W., & Hess, Beth B. (1980). Older women in the city. *Signs, 5* (Suppl.), 127–141.

Markstrom-Adams, Carol. (1989). Androgyny and its relation to adolescent psychosocial well-being: A review of the literature. *Sex Roles, 21,* 325–340.

Marriages down in 1985; divorce up after a slide. (1986, March 27). *Providence Evening Bulletin,* p. A-5.

Marshall, Megan. (1986, December). The Boston marriage. *New England Monthly*, pp. 71–73.

Marshall, Paule. Reena. In M. H. Washington (Ed.), Black-Eyed Susans (pp. 114–138). Garden City, NY: Anchor.

Martin, Del. (1976). *Battered wives*. San Francisco, CA: Glide.

Martin, John. (1991, November 6). Not-so-subtle messages about women. *Providence Journal Bulletin*, p. C-5.

Martin, Patricia Y., & Hummer, Robert A. (1989). Fraternities and rape on campus. *Gender & Society, 3,* 457–473.

Martocchio, Joseph J., & O'Leary, Anne M. (1989). Sex differences in occupational stress: A meta-analytical review. *Journal of Applied Psychology, 74,* 495–501.

Martz, Larry, & Reiss, Spencer. (1991, April 22). Legal sleaze in Palm Beach. *Newsweek*, p. 34.

Marx, Jean L. (1979a). Dysmenorrhea: Basic research leads to a rational therapy. *Science, 205,* 175–176.

Marx, Jean L. (1979b). Hormones and their effects in the aging body. *Science, 206,* 805–806.

Marx, Jean L. (1989). Estrogen use linked to breast cancer. *Science, 245,* 593.

Maslin, Janet. (1990, June 17). Bimbos embody retro rage. *New York Times*, p. H-13.

Maslin, Janet. (1991, June 16). Lay off 'Thelma and Louise.' *New York Times*, pp. H-11, H-16.

Mason, Avonne, & Blankenship, Virginia. (1987). Power and affiliation motivation, stress, and abuse in intimate relationships. *Journal of Personality and Social Psychology, 52,* 203–210.

Mass. scientists identify human gene determining sex. (1987, December 23). *Providence Journal-Bulletin*, p. A-5.

Massachusetts Coalition of Battered Women Service Groups. (1981). *For shelter and beyond*. Boston: Author.

Masson, Jeffrey M. (1983). *The assault on truth*. New York: Farrar, Straus & Giroux.

Masters, John C., & Wilkinson, Alexander. (1976). Consensual and discriminative stereotypes of sex-type judgments by parents and children. *Child Development, 47,* 208–217.

Masters, William, & Johnson, Virginia. (1966). *Human sexual response*. Boston: Little, Brown.

Matacin, M. L., & Burger, J. M. (1987). A content analysis of sexual themes in *Playboy* cartoons. *Sex Roles, 17,* 179–186.

Mathieu, John E., & Zajac, Dennis M. (1990). A review and meta-analysis of the antecedents, correlates, and consequences of organizational commitment. *Psychological Bulletin, 108,* 171–194.

Matteo, Sherri. (1987). The effect of job stress and job interdependency on menstrual cycle length, regularity, and synchrony. *Psychoneuroendocrinology 12,* 467–476.

Matteo, Sherri. (1988). The risk of multiple addictions: Guidelines for assessing a woman's alcohol and drug use. *Western Journal of Medicine, 149,* 741–745.

Matteo, Sherri, & Rissman, Emilie F. (1984). Increased sexual activity during the midcycle portion of the human menstrual cycle. *Hormones and Behavior, 18,* 249–255.

Matthews, Karen A., & Carra, Joseph. (1982). Suppression of menstrual distress symptoms: A study of Type A behavior. *Personality and Social Psychology Bulletin, 8,* 146–151.

Matthews, Wendy S. (1981). Sex-role perception, portrayal, and preference in the fantasy play of young children. *Sex Roles, 7,* 979–987.

Maybelline advertisement. (1984, April). *Teen*.

Maynard, Joyce. (1993, January 31). Housebroken. *New York Times Magazine*, p. 18.

McBride, Angela B., & Black, Kathryn N. (1984). Differences that suggest female investment in, and male distance from, children. *Sex Roles, 10,* 231–246.

McCarroll, Thomas. (1993, March 15). Taking the bad rap. *Time*, p. 63.

McCarthy, Colman. (1991, December 10). Remembering an act of courage in '41. *Washington Post*, p. C-21.

McCarthy, Kathleen. (1990, November). Victims of crimes incur rise in health problems. *APA Monitor*, p. 43.

McClanahan, Sara S. (1989). Sex differences in poverty, 1950–1980. *Signs, 15,* 102–122.

McClintock, Martha. (1979). Considering "A biosocial perspective on parenting." *Signs, 4,* 703–710.

McClure, Gail T., & Piel, Ellen. (1978). College-bound girls and science careers: Perceptions of barriers and facilitating factors. *Journal of Vocational Behavior, 12,* 172–183.

McConahay, Shirley, & McConahay, John B. (1977). Sexual permissiveness, sex-role rigidity, and violence across cultures. *Journal of Social Issues, 33,* 134–143.

McCormack, Arlene. (1985). The sexual harassment of students by teachers: The case of students in science. *Sex Roles, 13,* 21–32.

McCormick, Naomi B. (1979). Come-ons and put-offs: Unmarried students' strategies for having and avoiding sexual intercourse. *Psychology of Women Quarterly, 4,* 194–211.

McCormick, Naomi B., Brannigan, Gary G., & LaPlante, Marcia N. (1984). Social desirability in the bedroom: Role of approval motivation in sexual relationships. *Sex Roles, 11,* 303–314.

McCoy, Elin. (1980, June 19). More mothers joining support groups. *New York Times*.

McCrae, Robert R., & Costa, Paul T. Jr. (1988). Psychological resilience among widowed men and women: A 10-year follow-up of a national sample. *Journal of Social Issues, 44* (3), 129–142.

McDermott, Alice. (1987). *That night*. New York: Perennial.

McFarland, Cathy, Ross, Michael, & DeCourville, Nancy. (1989). Women's theories of menstruation and biases in recall of menstrual symptoms. *Journal of Personality and Social Psychology, 57,* 522–531.

McFarlane, Jessica, Martin, Carol L., & Williams, Tannis M. (1988). Mood fluctuations: Women versus men and menstrual versus other cycles. *Psychology of Women Quarterly, 12,* 201–223.

McGee, Mark G. (1979). Human spatial abilities: Psychometric studies and environmental, genetic, hormonal, and neurological influences. *Psychological Bulletin, 86,* 889–918.

McGhee, Paul E., & Frueh, Terry. (1980). Television viewing and the learning of sex-role stereotypes. *Sex Roles, 6,* 179–188.

McGloshen, Thomas H., & O'Bryant, Shirley L. (1988). The psychological well-being of older, recent widows. *Psychology of Women Quarterly, 12,* 99–116.

McGrath, Ellen, Keita, Gwendolyn P., Strickland, Bonnie R., & Russo, Nancy F. (1990). *Women and depression: Risk factors and treatment issues*. Washington, DC: American Psychological Association.

McGuire, Linda S., Ryan, Kimberly O., & Omenn, Gilbert S. (1975). Congenital adrenal hyperplasia. II. Cognitive and behavioral studies. *Behavior Genetics, 5,* 175–188.

McKay, Scott. (1992, June 13). Women Democrats raise funds; Aurora club admits females. *Providence Journal Bulletin*, p. A-3.

McLaughlin, Mary M. (1974). Survivors and surrogates: Children and parents from the ninth to the thirteenth centuries. In L. deMause (Ed.), *The history of childhood* (pp. 101–181). New York: Harper & Row.

McLaughlin, Merrill, Shryer, Tracy L., Goode, Erica E., & McAuliffe,

Kathleen. (1988, August 8). Attitude. In politics and management, the "gender gap" is real. *U.S. News & World Report*, p. 56.

McLaughlin, Patricia. (1992, June 25). High fashion's 'lady of leisure' time warp. *Providence Journal Bulletin*, pp. D-1, D-2.

McMillan, Julie R., Clifton, A. Kay, McGrath, Diane, & Gale, Wanda S. (1977). Women's language: Uncertainty or interpersonal sensitivity and emotionality? *Sex Roles, 3*, 545–559.

McMullin, Lorraine, & Offen, Liz. (n.d.). Letter.

McNulty, Faith. (1981). *The burning bed*. New York: Bantam.

Mead, Margaret. (1950). *Sex and temperament in three primitive societies*. New York: Mentor. (Original work published in 1935.)

Mead, Margaret. (1968). *Male and female*. New York: Dell. (Original work published in 1949.)

Meece, Judith L., Parsons, Jacquelynne E., Kaczala, Caroline M., Goff, Susan B., & Futterman, Robert. (1982). Sex differences in math achievement: Toward a model of academic choice. *Psychological Bulletin, 91*, 324–348.

Melson, Gail F. (1977). Sex differences in use of indoor space by preschool children. *Perceptual and Motor Skills, 44*, 207–213.

Melson, Gail F., & Fogel, Alan. (1988, January). Learning to care. *Psychology Today*, pp. 39–45.

Melton, Gary B. (1987). Legal regulation of adolescent abortion. *American Psychologist, 42*, 79–83.

Men and women. (1993, January 31). *New York Times*, p. E-3.

Men catching up in population as women move up in work force. (1990, April 11). *Providence Journal-Bulletin*, p. A-1.

Menke, Edna M. (1983). Menstrual beliefs and experiences of mother-daughter dyads. In S. Golub (Ed.), *Menarche* (pp. 133–137). Boston: Lexington Books.

Men's life expectancy raised to 71.1 years. (1985, June 6). *Providence Evening Bulletin*.

Meredith, Dennis. (1985, June). Mom, dad, and the kids. *Psychology Today*, pp. 62–65.

Merriam, Eve. (1991, July/August). The widow steps out. *Ms.*, p. 27.

Merritt, Shayne. (1982). Sex roles and political ambition. *Sex Roles, 8*, 1025–1036.

Merritt, Susan M. (1986, July 27). For women, a central role in computers. *New York Times*, p. E-22.

Metha, Arlene T., Kinnier, Richard T., & McWhirter, Ellen H. (1989). A pilot study on the regrets and priorities of women. *Psychology of Women Quarterly, 13*, 167–174.

Meyer, C. Buf, & Taylor, Shelley E. (1986). Adjustment to rape. *Journal of Personality and Social Psychology, 50*, 1226–1234.

Meyer, Shannon-Lee, Murphy, Christopher M., Cascardi, Michele, & Birns, Beverly. (1991). Gender and relationships: Beyond the peer group. *American Psychologist, 46*, 537.

Michell, Gillian. (1988). The reproduction of narcissism. *Women & Therapy, 7*(4), 35–52.

Millenson, Michael L. (1992, January 14). Condom for women available soon. *Providence Journal Bulletin*, pp. B-1, B-3.

Miller, Annetta, & Stone, Joanna. (1991, July 29). With child, without a job. *Newsweek*, p. 39.

Miller, Annetta, & Tsiantar, Dody. (1991, November 25). Mommy tracks. *Newsweek*, pp. 48–49.

Miller, Cynthia L. (1987). Qualitative differences among gender-stereotyped toys: Implications for cognitive and social development in girls and boys. *Sex Roles, 16*, 473–487.

Miller, Jean B. (1986). *Toward a new psychology of women*, 2nd ed. Boston: Beacon.

Miller, Patricia Y., & Fowlkes, Martha R. (1980). Social and behavioral constructions of female sexuality. *Signs, 5*, 783–800.

Millett, Kate. (1971). Prostitution: A quartet for female voices. In V. Gornick & B. K. Moran (Eds.), *Women in sexist society* (pp. 21–69). New York: Basic Books.

Millett, Kate. (1978, November). Reply to "What do you think is erotic?" *Ms.*, p. 80.

Mills, Rosemary S. L., Pedersen, Jan, & Grusec, Joan E. (1989). Sex differences in reasoning and emotion about altruism. *Sex Roles, 20*, 603–621.

Milow, Vera J. (1983). Menstrual education: Past, present, and future. In S. Golub (Ed.), *Menarche* (pp. 127–132). Boston: Lexington Books.

Miner, Robert. (1980, June 15). Do fathers make good mothers? *Family Weekly*, pp. 4–6.

Minority women at bottom of law faculty. (1992, April 3). *New York Times*, p. A-19.

Minority women at risk. (1991, March 29). *Providence Journal Bulletin*, p. A-2.

Misconceptions about women Ph.D.s challenged. (1982, Spring). *Project on the Status and Education of Women, 34*, pp. 6–7. (Association of American Colleges, Washington, DC)

Miss. Calif. pageant protestor shaves locks, wears deli meat. (1987, June 18). *Providence Journal Bulletin*.

Mitchell, Valory, & Helson, Ravenna. (1990). Women's prime of life. Is it the 50s? *Psychology of Women Quarterly, 14*, 451–470.

Mitgang, Lee. (1989, May 10). National merit bias alleged. *Providence Journal-Bulletin*, p. C-1.

Mithers, Carol L. (1990, October 21). Incest and the law. *New York Times Magazine*, pp. 44, 53, 58, 62–63.

Mogul, K. M. (1982). Overview: The sex of the therapist. *American Journal of Psychiatry, 139*, 1–11.

Molestation story puts Fla. senator in spotlight. (1984, May 3). *Providence Evening Bulletin*.

Mom, please cheer up. (1990, November 19). *Newsweek*, p. 6.

Money, John. (1972, December). Nativism versus culturalism in gender-identity differentiation. Paper presented at the meeting of the American Association for the Advancement of Science, Washington, DC.

Monroe, Alice. (1991, December). Elizabeth Morgan update. *National NOW Times*, p. 14.

Montemayor, Raymond. (1974). Children's performance in a game and their attraction to it as a function of sex-typed labels. *Child Development, 45*, 152–156.

Montepare, Joann M., & Vega, Cynthia. (1988). Women's vocal reactions to intimate and casual male friends. *Personality and Social Psychology Bulletin, 14*, 103–113.

Mooney, Linda, & Brabant, Sarah. (1987). Two martinis and a rested woman: "Liberation" in the Sunday comics. *Sex Roles, 17*, 409–420.

Moore, Helen A. (1985). Job satisfaction and women's spheres of work. *Sex Roles, 13*, 663–678.

More one-parent families, Census Bureau says. (1986, November 5). *Providence Journal Bulletin*, p. A-17.

More people are living alone. (1985, November 20). *Providence Evening Bulletin*.

More women postponing marriage. (1986, December 10). *New York Times*, p. A-22.

Morelock, Judy C. (1980). Sex differences in susceptibility to social influence. *Sex Roles, 6*, 537–548.

Morgan, Carolyn S. (1980). Female and male attitudes toward life: Implications for theories of mental health. *Sex Roles, 6*, 367–380.

Morgan, Michael. (1982). Television and adolescents' sex role stereotypes: A longitudinal study. *Journal of Personality and Social Psychology, 43*, 947–955.

Morgan, Robin. (1970). *Sisterhood is powerful.* New York: Random House.

Morgan, Robin. (1982a). *The anatomy of freedom.* Garden City, NY: Anchor/Doubleday.

Morgan, Robin. (1982b, December). A quantum leap in feminist theory. *Ms.,* pp. 101–106.

Morgan, Susanne. (1982, March). Sex after hysterectomy—what your doctor never told you. *Ms,* pp. 82–85.

Morin, Stephen F., & Rothblum, Esther D. (1991). Removing the stigma: Fifteen years of progress. *American Psychologist, 46,* 947–949.

Morokoff, Patricia J. (1985). Effects of sex guilt, repression, sexual "arousability," and sexual experience on female sexual arousal during erotica and fantasy. *Journal of Personality and Social Psychology, 49,* 177–187.

Morokoff, Patricia J. (1988). Sexuality in perimenopausal and postmenopausal women. *Psychology of Women Quarterly, 12,* 489–511.

Morrison, Ann M., & Van Glinow, MaryAnn. (1990). Women and minorities in management. *American Psychologist, 45,* 200–208.

Morrison, Toni. (1971, August 22). What the black woman thinks about women's lib. *New York Times Magazine,* pp. 14–15, 63–64, 66.

Morrison, Toni. (1987). *Beloved.* New York: Knopf.

Moses, Susan. (1990, November). Teen girls can have 'crisis of connection.' *APA Monitor,* p. 26.

Moses, Susan. (1991, July). Ties that bind can limit minority valedictorians. *APA Monitor,* p. 47.

Moss, Cynthia. (1978, January). Law of the jungle (revised). *Ms.,* pp. 65–67, 89–90.

Moss, Howard A. (1967). Sex, age, and state as determinants of mother-infant interaction. *Merrill-Palmer Quarterly, 13,* 19–36.

Moss, Ruth J. (1987, February). Good grades for day-care. *Psychology Today,* p. 20.

Most depend on social security. (1986, March 20). *New York Times,* p. C-8.

Most far-reaching study to examine women's health. (1991, April 20). *Providence Journal Bulletin,* p. A-1.

Motherhood. (1992, February 2). *Providence Journal Bulletin,* p. E-7.

Mowbray, Carol T., & Benedek, Elissa P. (1988). *Women's mental health research agenda.* Washington, DC: National Institute of Mental Health.

Muehlenhard, Charlene L., & Falcon, Polly L. (1990). Men's heterosexual skill and attitudes toward women as predictors of verbal sexual coercion and forceful rape. *Sex Roles, 23,* 241–259.

Muehlenhard, Charlene L., & Hollabaugh, Lisa C. (1988). Do women sometimes say no when they mean yes? The prevalence and correlates of women's token resistance to sex. *Journal of Personality and Social Psychology, 54,* 872–879.

Muehlenhard, Charlene L., & Linton, Marigold A. (1987). Date rape and sexual aggression in dating situations: Incidence and risk factors. *Journal of Counseling Psychology, 34,* 186–196.

Mulac, Anthony, Incontro, Carol R., & James, Margaret R. (1985). Comparison of the gender-linked language effect and sex role stereotypes. *Journal of Personality and Social Psychology, 49,* 1098–1109.

Munro, Alice. (1977). Red dress—1946. In N. Dean and M. Stark (Eds.), *In the looking glass* (pp. 199–211). New York: G. P. Putnam's.

Murphy, Mary. (1986, March 29). Sexual harassment in Hollywood. *TV Guide,* pp. 2–6, 10–11.

Murray, Ann D. (1979). Infant crying as an elicitor of parental behavior: An examination of two models. *Psychological Bulletin, 86,* 191–215.

Murray, Michele (Ed.). (1973). *A house of good proportion: Images of women in literature* (2nd ed.). New York: Simon & Schuster.

Murray, Saundra R., & Mednick, Martha T. S. (1977). Black women's achievement orientation: Motivational and cognitive factors. *Psychology of Women Quarterly, 1,* 247–259.

Mydans, Seth (1993, May 30). California denies clemency pleas of 14 women who killed spouses. *New York Times,* p. Y-14.

Myers, Linda J. (1978). Black women in double jeopardy. Unpublished paper, Ohio State University, Columbus.

Myers, Harriet H., & Siegel, Paul S. (1985). The motivation to breast feed: A fit to the opponent-process theory? *Journal of Personality and Social Psychology, 49,* 189–193.

Nakhnikian, Elise. (1992, May/June). Heading off hysterectomy. *Health,* pp. 36–38.

Nash, Sharon C. (1975). The relationship among sex-role stereotyping, sex-role preference and the sex difference in spatial visualization. *Sex Roles, 1,* 15–32.

Nation ignoring problem of teenage pregnancies, says House subcommittee. (1986, February 10). *Providence Evening Bulletin.*

National Advisory Council on Economic Opportunity. (1981, September). *The American promise: Equal justice and economic opportunity.* Final Report. Washington, DC, U.S. Government Printing Office.

National Commission on Working Women. (1983). *Women's work: Undervalued, underpaid.* Washington, DC: Center for Women and Work.

National NOW Times. (1991, December). Martina questions women and AIDS double standard. p. 4.

National women's Health Report. Risks vs. Benefits: How does hormonal replacement therapy measure up? (1992, July/August) Vol. 3, no. 4.

Nation's birthrate up in '84. (1985, March 30). *Providence Evening Bulletin.*

Naylor, Gloria. (1985). *Linden Hills.* New York: Ticknor & Fields.

Naylor, Gloria. (1988). *Mama Day.* New York: Ticknor & Fields.

Need for mother's touch is brain-based. (1988). *Science, 239,* 142.

Neiswender-Reedy, M., Birren, James E., & Schaie, K. Warner. (1981). Age and sex differences in satisfying love relationships across the adult life span. *Human Development, 24,* 52–66.

Nelan, Bruce W. (1993, May 10). Annie get your gun. *Time,* pp. 38, 43.

Nelson, Gayle. (1975). The double standard in adolescent novels. *English Journal, 64,* 53–56.

Nettles, Elizabeth J., & Loevinger, Jane. (1983). Sex role expectations and ego level in relation to problem marriages. *Journal of Personality and Social Psychology, 45,* 676–687.

Neugarten, Bernice L., & Neugarten, Dail A. (1987, May). The changing meanings of age. *Psychology Today,* pp. 29–33.

Nevid, Jeffrey S. (1984). Sex differences in factors of romantic attraction. *Sex Roles, 11,* 401–411.

New asteroid is found within our solar orbit. (1978, September 10). *Providence Evening Bulletin.*

New Miss America was beaten. (1991, September 18). *Providence Journal Bulletin,* p. D-1.

New police policy to stem domestic violence triples arrests. (1984, July 19). *Providence Evening Bulletin,* p. A-4.

New TV roles for women applauded. (1984, December 5). *Providence Evening Bulletin.*

New Woman. (1987, October). A new woman is an attitude, not an age. p. 18.

New York Times. (1988, January 17). Sec. 4, p. 1.

Newcomb, Michael D. (1986). Nuclear attitudes and reactions: Associations with depression, drug use, and equality of life. *Journal of Personality and Social Psychology, 50,* 906–920.

Newcomb, Michael D., & Bentler, P. M. (1983). Dimensions of subjective female orgasmic responsiveness. *Journal of Personality and Social Psychology, 44,* 862–873.

Newcombe, Nora, Bandura, Mary M., & Taylor, Dawn G. (1983). Sex differences in spatial ability and spatial activities. *Sex Roles, 9,* 377–386.

Newman, Louise M. (1985). *Men's ideas/women's realities.* New York: Pergamon.

Newman, Lucile F. (1972). Birth control: An anthropological view. *Addison-Wesley Modular Publications, Module 27.* Reading, MA: Addison-Wesley.

News from the United Nations. (1991, November). *SPSSI Newsletter,* p. 11.

Newton, Niles. (1970, November). Childbirth and culture. *Psychology Today,* pp. 74–75.

Newton, Niles, & Modahl, Charlotte. (1978, March). Pregnancy: The closest human relationship. *Human Nature,* pp. 40–49.

Nicola-McLaughlin, Andree. (1985). White power, black despair: Vanessa Williams in Babylon. *Black Scholar, 16*(2), 32–39.

Nigro, Georgia N., Hill, Denia E., Gelbein, Martha E., & Clark, Catherine L. (1988). Changes in the facial prominence of women and men over the last decade. *Psychology of Women Quarterly, 12,* 225–235.

The 1989 *9to5* profile of working women. (1989, May/June). *9to5 Newsletter,* p. 1.

9to5 proves parental leave does not hurt business. (1988, September/October). *9to5 Newsletter,* p. 1.

99 ways to attract the right man. (1985, May 7). *TV Guide.*

Njeri, Itabari. (1990). *Every good-bye ain't gone: Family portraits and personal escapades.* New York: Random House.

No more Miss America! (1970). In R. Morgan (Ed.), *Sisterhood is powerful* (pp. 521–524). New York: Vintage.

Noble, Barbara P. (1992, June 21). Legal victories for gay workers. *New York Times,* p. F-23.

Noble, Barbara. (1993a, February 7). The family leave bargain. *New York Times,* p. F-25.

Noble, Barbara P. (1993b, April 18). Worthy child-care pay scales. *New York Times,* p. F-25.

Noble, Kenneth B. (1985, December 12). Low-paying jobs foreseen for most working women. *New York Times,* p. A-20.

Noble, Kenneth B. (1989, January 8). The Black ascent in union politics. *New York Times,* p. E-4.

Nochlin, Linda. (1979, October 28). Women painters and Germaine Greer. (Review of *The Obstacle Race* by G. Greer.) *New York Times Book Review,* pp. 3, 46.

Norman, Ralph D. (1974). Sex differences in preferences for sex of children: A replication after 20 years. *Journal of Psychology, 88,* 229–239.

Norsigian, Judy. (1989, November/December). Testimony before the . . . Food and Drug Administration. *The Network News,* pp. 4–5.

Northeast has lowest levels of rape, "legitimate violence," researchers say. (1985, June 20). *Providence Evening Bulletin,* p. A-2.

Not victimless; The prostitutes are the victims. (1980, June 26). *Providence Evening Bulletin.*

Number of poor children rose 2.2 million in '80s—study. (1991, June 3). *Providence Journal-Bulletin,* p. A-2).

Nyquist, Linda, Slivken, Karla, Spence, Janet T., & Helmreich, Robert L. (1985). Household responsibilities in middle-class couples: The contribution of demographic and personality variables. *Sex Roles, 12,* 15–34.

Oates, Joyce C. (1981, March 29). Why is your writing so violent? *New York Times Book Review,* pp. 15, 35.

Oates, Joyce C. (1985). *Solstice.* New York: Dutton.

Oates, Joyce C. (1986). *Marya: A life.* New York: Dutton.

Oates, Joyce C. (1987). *You must remember this.* New York: Harper & Row.

Oates, Mary J., & Williamson, Susan. (1978). Women's colleges and women achievers. *Signs, 3,* 795–806.

Oberstone, Andrea K., & Sukoneck, Harriet. (1976). Psychological adjustment and life style of single lesbians and single heterosexual women. *Psychology of Women Quarterly, 1,* 172–188.

O'Brien, Eileen M. (1989, December 7). Date rape. *Black Issues in Higher Education,* pp. 6–10.

O'Bryant, Shirley L. (1988). Self-differentiated assistance in older widows' support systems. *Sex Roles, 19,* 91–106.

Odent, Michel. (1984). *Birth reborn.* New York: Pantheon.

Offerman, Lynn R., & Bell, Cheryl. (1992). Achievement styles of women leaders and their peers. *Psychology of Women Quarterly, 16,* 37–56.

Offermann, Lynn R., & Schrier, Pamela E. (1985). Social influence strategies: The impact of sex, role, and attitudes toward power. *Personality and Social Psychology Bulletin, 11,* 286–300.

Ogunyemi, Chikwenye O. (1985). Womanism: The dynamics of the contemporary black female novel in English. *Signs, 11,* 63–80.

O'Keefe, Eileen S. C., & Hyde, Janet S. (1983). The development of occupational sex-role stereotypes: The effects of gender stability and age. *Sex Roles, 9,* 481–492.

Olds, Sharon. (1980). From the language of the brag. In *Satan says* (pp. 44–45). Pittsburgh, PA: Pittsburgh University Press.

O'Leary, Ann, Jemmott, Loretta S., Suarez-Al-Adam, Mariana, AlRoy, Carolyn, & Fernandez, M. Isa. (1993). Women and AIDS. In S. Matteo (Ed.), *American women in the nineties: Today's critical issues* (pp. 173–192). Boston: Northeastern University Press.

Olejnik, Anthony B. (1980). Socialization of achievement: Effects of children's sex and age on achievement evaluations by adults. *Personality and Social Psychology Bulletin, 6,* 68–73.

Ollendick, Thomas, & Hart, Kathleen. (1985). . . . *American Journal of Psychiatry, 142,* . . . .

On the legislative front. (1990, September/October). *Ms.,* p. 45.

1 out of 8 women raped, victims' rights groups report. (1992, April 24). *Providence Journal Bulletin,* p. A-1.

O'Reilly, Jane. (1982). *The girl I left behind.* New York: Bantam.

Ortner, Sherry B. (1974). Is female to male as nature is to culture? In M. Z. Rosaldo & L. Lamphere (Eds.), *Woman, culture and society* (pp. 67–87). Stanford, CA: Stanford University Press.

Ortner, Sherry B., & Whitehead, Harriet (Eds.). (1981). *Sexual meanings: The cultural construction of gender and sexuality.* Cambridge, MA: Cambridge University Press.

Ostriker, Alicia. (1986, March 9). American poetry, now shaped by women. *New York Times Book Review,* pp. 1, 28, 30.

Overall, Christine. (1992). What's wrong with prostitution? Evaluating sex work. *Signs, 17,* 705–724.

PACs give women crucial assistance during campaigns. (1984, July 13). *Providence Evening Bulletin,* p. A-14.

Padesky, Christine A., & Hammen, Constance L. (1981). Sex differences in depressive symptom expression and help-seeking among college students. *Sex Roles, 7,* 309–320.

Pagelow, Mildred D. (1992). Adult victims of domestic violence. *Journal of Interpersonal Violence, 7* (1), 87–120.

Paige, Karen E. (1973). Women learning to sing the menstrual blues. In *Psychology Today* (Eds.), The female experience (pp. 17–21). Del Mar, CA: Communications/Research/Machines.

Painton, Priscilla. (1993, May 10). The maternal well. *Time,* pp. 44-45.

Palca, Joseph. (1989). The pill of choice? *Science, 245,* 1319–1323.

Pallak, Suzanne R., & Davies, Jacqueline M. (1982). Finding fault versus attributing responsibility: Using facts differently. *Personality and Social Psychology Bulletin, 8,* 454–459.

Palmer, Phyllis. (1983). "The racial feminization of poverty": Women of color as portents of the future for all women. *Women's Studies Quarterly, 11*(3), 4–6.

Pap smears for the elderly can save lives and money. (1990, Spring). *National Women's Health Report,* p. 5.

Papalia, Diane E., & Tennent, Susan S. (1975). Vocational aspirations in preschoolers: A manifestation of early sex role stereotyping. *Sex Roles, 1,* 197–199.

Paper urges therapists to remember wife. (1982, Summer). *Bradley Scope,* p. 7. (Emma Bradley Hospital, East Providence, RI)

Paradise, Louis V., & Wall, Shavaun M. (1986). Children's perceptions of male and female principals and teachers. *Sex Roles, 14,* 1–7.

The paradox of well-being. (1981, Spring). *ISR Newsletter.* (Institute for Social Research, University of Michigan, Ann Arbor)

Parental notification and consent laws and their effect on minors. (1990). *Reproductive choice and abortion: A resource packet.* American Psychological Association, 1200 17th St, NW, Washington, DC 20036.

Parker, Kathleen. (1991, September 4). The working mother's lie: She's in a meeting. *Providence Journal Bulletin,* p. C-3.

Parlee, Mary B. (1973). The premenstrual syndrome. *Psychological Bulletin, 80,* 454–465.

Parlee, Mary B. (1982). Changes in moods and activation levels during the menstrual cycle in experimentally naive subjects. *Psychology of Women Quarterly, 7,* 119–131.

Parlee, Mary B. (1983). Menstrual rhythms in sensory processes: A review of fluctuations in vision, olfaction, audition, taste, and touch. *Psychological Bulletin, 93,* 539–548.

Parsons, Jacquelynne E., Ruble, Diane N., Hodges, Karen L., & Small, Ava W. (1976). Cognitive-developmental factors in emerging sex differences in achievement-related expectancies. *Journal of Social Issues, 32,* 47–61.

Patinkin, Mark. (1983, March 25). Hormone disharmony makes us do what we do. *Providence Evening Bulletin,* p. A-3.

Patinkin, Mark. (1984, April 26). Grazing generation is changing the nation's tastes. *Providence Evening-Bulletin,* p. A-3.

Patinkin, Mark. (1986, December 18). The division of labor in an enlightened, liberated household. *Providence Journal Bulletin.*

Patinkin, Mark. (1987, May 20). Polls have the power to conjure surprising glimpses of ourselves. *Providence Journal-Bulletin,* p. C-1.

Patrick, G. T. W. (1979). The psychology of women. In J. H. Williams (Ed.), *Psychology of women: Selected readings* (pp. 3–11). New York: Norton. (Original work published in 1895.)

Paul, Lois. (1974). The mastery of work and the mystery of sex in a Guatemalan village. In M. Z. Rosaldo & L. Lamphere (Eds.), *Woman, culture and society* (pp. 281–299). Stanford, CA: Stanford University Press.

Payer, Lynn. (1989, March). Hell week: What's new, what's old, and what we still don't know about PMS. *Ms.,* pp. 28–31.

Pearce, Diana M. (1993). Something old, something new: Women's poverty in the 1990s. In S. Matteo (Ed.), *American women in the nineties: Today's critical issues.* Boston: Northeastern University Press.

Pearce, Diana M. (1985). Toil and trouble: Women workers and unemployment compensation. *Signs, 10,* 439–459.

Pearson, Cynthia. (1990, July/August). FDA waffles on premarin decision. *National Women's Health Network,* p. 1.

Pearson, Jessica. (1980). Women who farm: A preliminary portrait. *Sex Roles, 6,* 561–574.

Pedersen, Frank A., & Bell, Richard Q. (1970). Sex differences in preschool children without histories of complications of pregnancy and delivery. *Developmental Psychology, 3,* 10–15.

Peirce, Kate. (1990). A feminist theoretical perspective on the socialization of teenage girls through Seventeen magazine. *Sex Roles, 23,* 491–500.

Peirce, Kate, & Edwards, Emily D. (1988). Children's construction of fantasy stories: Gender differences in conflict resolution. *Sex Roles, 18,* 393–404.

Pelka, Fred. (1991, Winter). "Dreamworlds": How the Media Abuses Women. *On the Issues.*

Peplau, Letitia A. (1979). Power in dating relationships. In J. Freeman (Ed.), *Women: A feminist perspective* (2nd ed.) (pp. 106–121). Palo Alto, CA: Mayfield.

Peplau, Letitia A. (1981, March). What homosexuals want. *Psychology Today,* 28–34, 37–38.

Peplau, Letitia A. (1982). Research on homosexual couples: An overview. *Journal of Homosexuality, 8*(2), 3–8.

Peplau, Letitia A., Rubin, Zick, & Hill, Charles T. (1977). Sexual intimacy in dating relationships. *Journal of Social Issues, 33,* 86–109.

Perman, Lauri, & Stevens, Beth. (1989). Industrial segregation and the gender distribution of fringe benefits. *Gender & Society, 3,* 388–404.

Perry, David G., & Bussey, Kay. (1979). The social learning theory of sex differences: Imitation is alive and well. *Journal of Personality and Social Psychology, 37,* 1699–1712.

Person, Ethel S. (1980). Sexuality as the mainstay of identity: Psychoanalytic perspectives. *Signs, 5,* 605–630.

Personal Products Corp. (1957). *Growing up and liking it* (pamphlet). Milltown, NJ: Author.

Perun, Pamela J. (1981). Comment on Rossi's "Life-span theories and women's lives." *Signs, 7,* 243–248.

Petersen, Anne. (1983). Menarche: Meaning of measures and measuring meaning. In S. Golub (Ed.), *Menarche* (pp. 63–76). Boston: Lexington Books.

Peterson, Jonathan. (1983, February 8). Social security: A bias against working wives? *Providence Evening Bulletin.*

Peterson, Rolf A. (1983). Attitudes toward the childless spouse. *Sex Roles, 9,* 321–331.

Peterson, Sharyl B., & Kroner, Traci. (1992). Gender biases in textbooks for introductory psychology and human development. *Psychology of Women Quarterly, 16,* 17–36.

Pfost, Karen S., & Fiore, Maria. (1990). Pursuit of nontraditional occupations: Fear of success or fear of not being chosen. *Sex Roles, 23,* 15–24.

Phillips, Gerald M. (1983). *Loving and living.* Englewood Cliffs, NJ: Prentice Hall.

Phillips, Sheridan, King, Suzanne, & DuBois, Louise. (1978). Spontaneous activities of female versus male newborns. *Child Development, 49,* 590–597.

Phillis, Diane E., & Stein, Peter J. (1983). Sink or swing? The lifestyles of single adults. In E. R. Allgeier & N. B. McCormick (Eds.), *Changing boundaries: Gender roles and sexual behavior* (pp. 202–225). Palo Alto, CA: Mayfield.

Phipps-Yonas, Susan. (1980). Teenage pregnancy and motherhood: A review of the literature. *American Journal of Orthopsychiatry, 50,* 403–431.

Piercy, Marge. (1975). *Small changes.* New York: Fawcett.

Piercy, Marge. (1976a). *Woman on the edge of time.* New York: Fawcett.

Piercy, Marge. (1976b). Rape poem. In *Living in the open* (pp. 88–89). New York: Knopf.

Piercy, Marge. (1979). *Vida.* New York: Summit.

Piercy, Marge. (1983). *Braided lives.* New York: Fawcett.

Piercy, Marge. (1984a). *Fly away home.* New York: Summit.

Piercy, Marge. (1984b). The inquisition. In *The moon is always female*. New York: Knopf.

Piercy, Marge. (1984c). Under red Aries. In *The moon is always female*. New York: Knopf.

Piercy, Marge. (1984d). Right to life. In *The moon is always female*. New York: Knopf.

Piercy, Marge. (1989). *Summer people*. New York: Ballantine.

The Pill—back in style. (1982, November). *The Harvard Medical School Health Letter*, pp. 2, 5.

Pinzler, Isabelle K. (1989, Fall/Winter). Liberty, equality, and maternity. *Civil Liberties*, pp. 1, 3.

Pitchford, Kenneth. (1978, October). The manly art of child care. *Ms.*, pp. 96–99.

Pizzey, Erin. (1974). *Scream quietly or the neighbours will hear*. Harmondsworth, England: Penguin.

Plath, Sylvia. (1972). *The bell jar*. New York: Bantam.

Pliner, Patricia, Chaiken, Shelly, & Flett, Gordon L. (1990). Gender differences in concern with body weight and physical appearance over the life span. *Personality and Social Psychology Bulletin, 16*, 263–273.

Plumb, Pat, & Cowan, Gloria. (1984). A developmental study of destereotyping and androgynous activity preferences of tomboys, nontomboys, and males. *Sex Roles, 10*, 703–712.

Pogrebin, Letty C. (1972, September). Down with sexist upbringing. *Ms.*, pp. 18, 32.

Pogrebin, Letty C. (1982a, February). Big changes in parenting. *Ms.*, pp. 41–46.

Pogrebin, Letty C. (1982b, June). Anti-Semitism in the women's movement. *Ms.*, pp. 66–67.

Pogrebin, Letty C. (1990, September/October). The teflon father. *Ms.*, pp. 95–96.

Policy vs. polls. (1991, September 15). *New York Times*, p. E-5.

Poliry, Janet, & Herman, C. Peter. (1985). Dieting and binging: A causal analysis. *American Psychologist, 40*, 193–201.

Poll shows teens have sex, many don't use birth control. (1986, December 17). *Providence Evening Bulletin*, p. A-24.

Poll: Women belong in the workplace. (1986, June 17). *Providence Evening Bulletin*, pp. A-1–A-2.

Pollis, Nicholas P., & Doyle, Donald C. (1972). Sex role, status, and perceived competence among first graders. *Perceptual and Motor Skills, 34*, 235–238.

Pollitt, Katha. (1985, December 12). Hers. *New York Times*, p. C-2.

Pollitt, Katha. (1990, May 13). What women want from feminism. *New York Times Magazine*, p. 12.

Pollitt, Katha. (1991, April 7). The Smurfette principle. *New York Times Magazine*, pp. 22–23.

Pomerleau, Andree, Bolduc, Daniel, Malcutt, Gerard, & Cossette, Louise. (1990). Pink or blue: Environmental gender stereotypes in the first two years of life. *Sex Roles, 22*, 359–367.

Poole, Debra A., & Tapley, Anne E. (1988). Sex roles, social roles, and clinical judgments of mental health. *Sex Roles, 19*, 265–272.

Pope, Kenneth S., Levenson, Hanna, & Schoer, Leslie R. (1979). Sexual intimacy in psychological training: Results and implications of a national survey. *American Psychologist, 34*, 682–689.

Porter, Nancy. (1989). The art of aging: A review essay. *Women's Studies Quarterly, 17* (1 & 2), 97–108.

Porter, Sylvia. (1985, August 23). What's a housewife worth? More than numbers show. *Providence Evening Bulletin*.

A positive approach helps. (1979, April 27). *Journal of the American Medical Association, 241*, 1763.

Posner, Judith. (1979). It's all in your head: Feminist and medical models of menopause (strange bedfellows). *Sex Roles, 5*, 179–190.

Poverty scars kids at an early age, particularly blacks, study says. (1993, March 27). *San Jose Mercury News*.

Powers, Marla N. (1980). Menstruation and reproduction: An Oglala case. *Signs, 6*, 54–65.

Prather, Jane, & Fidell, Linda S. (1975, January). Sex differences in the content and style of medical advertisements. *Social Science and Medicine, 9*, 23–26.

Pratt, Michael W., Pancer, Mark, Hunsberger, Bruce, & Manchester, Judy. (1990). Reasoning about the self and relationships in maturity: An integrative complexity analysis of individual differences. *Journal of Personality and Social Psychology, 59*, 575–581.

Presser, Harriet B. (1980). Sally's corner: Coping with unmarried motherhood. *Journal of Social Issues, 36*(1), 107–129.

Preston, Kathleen, & Stanley, Kimberley. (1987). "What's the worst thing . . . ?": Gender-directed insults. *Sex Roles, 17*, 209–219.

Preteen girls say they try to be slim, worry about image. (1991, December 9). *Providence Journal Bulletin*, p. D-14.

Preventing sexual harassment: A fact sheet for employees. (1992, November 4). *Labor Relations Week*, The Bureau of National Affairs, Rockville, MD 20850.

Prisoners. (1992, March 29). *New York Times*, p. E-7.

Probber, Joan, & Ehrman, Lee. (1978). Pertinent genetics for understanding gender. In E. Tobach & B. Rosoff (Eds.), *Genes and gender: I* (pp. 13–30). New York: Gordian Press.

The problem of rape on campus. (1978, Fall). *Project on the Status and Education of Women*. (Association of American Colleges, Washington, DC)

Project on the Status and Education of Women. (1978, June). *Sexual harassment: a hidden issue*. Washington, DC: Association of American Colleges.

Prose, Francine. (1990, January 7). Confident at 11, confused at 16. *New York Times Magazine*, pp. 22–25, 37–40, 45–46.

Pryor, J. B. (1987). Sexual harassment proclivities in men. *Sex Roles, 5/6*, 269–289.

Purcell, Piper, & Stewart, Lara. (1990). Dick and Jane in 1989. *Sex Roles, 22*, 177–185.

Pyke, S. W., & Kahill, S. P. (1983). Sex differences in characteristics presumed relevant to professional productivity. *Psychology of Women Quarterly, 8*, 189–192.

Quadagno, David M., Briscoe, Robert, & Quadagno, Jill S. (1977). Effect of perinatal gonadal hormones on selected nonsexual behavior patterns: A critical assessment of the nonhuman and human literature. *Psychological Bulletin, 84*, 62–80.

Queen, Stuart A., & Adams, John B. (1952). *The family in various cultures*. Philadelphia: Lippincott.

Quina, Kathryn, & Carlson, Nancy. (1989). *Rape, incest and sexual harassment*. New York: Greenwood.

Quina, Kathryn, & Lott, Bernice. (1986, March). Post-abortion personal issues and changes in life direction. Paper presented at the meeting of the Association for Women in Psychology, Oakland, CA.

Quindlen, Anna. (1991a, February 3). Women warriors. *New York Times*.

Quindlen, Anna. (1991b, August 6). Two on trial in the Palm Beach case. *San Francisco Chronicle*, p. A-15.

Quindlen, Anna. (1992, February 23). Getting a second wind. *New York Times*, p. E-14.

Quindlen, Anna. (1993a, April 11). The good guys. *New York Times*, p. E-3.

Quindlen, Anna. (1993b, May 16). In thin air. *New York Times*, p. E-17.

Rachlin, Susan K., & Vogt, Glenda L. (1974). Sex roles as presented to children by coloring books. *Journal of Popular Culture, 8*, 549–556.

Radloff, Lenore S. (1980). Depression and the empty nest. *Sex Roles, 6,* 775–781.

Rador, Carol G., Masnick, Barbara R., & Hauser, Barbara B. (1977, November). Issues in feminist therapy: The work of a women's study group. *Social Work,* 507–509.

Radway, Janice A. (1984). *Reading the romance: Women, patriarchy, and popular literature.* Chapel Hill: University of North Carolina Press.

Rafkin, Louise. (1993, April/May). The parenting plunge. *Out,* p. 20.

Ragan, Janet M. (1982). Gender displays in portrait photographs. *Sex Roles, 8,* 33–44.

Ragins, Belle R., & Sundstrom, Eric. (1989). Gender and power in organizations: A longitudinal perspective. *Psychological Bulletin, 105,* 51–88.

Rakowsky, Judy. (1987, June 10). 'Flagman' becomes a misnomer. *Providence Journal Bulletin,* p. A-13.

Ramey, Estelle R. (1976). Sex hormones and executive ability. In S. Cox (Ed.), *Female psychology: The emerging self* (pp. 20–30). Chicago: Science Research Associates.

Rape attempts decreasing, study finds. (1991, January 14). *Providence Journal Bulletin,* p. A-14.

Rapin, Lynn S., & Cooper, Merri-Ann. (1980). Images of men and women: A comparison of feminists and nonfeminists. *Psychology of Women Quarterly, 5,* 186–194.

Rapping, Elayne. (1992, March/April). TV Highlights: Feminism and the media in an age of reaction. *Democratic Left,* pp. 8–9, 20.

Raskin, A. H. (1977, June 5). Women are still absent from labor's top ranks. *New York Times.*

Raskin, Barbara. (1990). *Current affairs.* New York: Random House.

Rawlings, Edna I., & Carter, Dianne K. (Eds.). (1977). *Psychotherapy for women: Treatment toward equality.* Springfield, IL: Charles C Thomas.

Rayman, Paula. (1990, June). The meaning of work in women's lives. *Radcliffe Quarterly,* pp. 11–14.

Raymond, Janice G. (1986). Man-made reproduction. *Choices, 6,* 4–5, 7, 13, 17.

Raymond, Janice G. (1991, May/June). International traffic in reproduction. *Ms.,* pp. 29–33.

Real incest and real survivors: Readers respond. (1993, February 14). *New York Times Magazine,* pp. 3, 27.

Recovery of women workers from recession lags greatly. (1984, March 23). *Providence Evening Bulletin,* p. A-15.

Refusing to bear the pain. (1990, April 17). *Providence Journal Bulletin,* pp. F-3, F-4.

Reid, Libby. (1988). *Do you hate your hips more than nuclear war?* New York: Penguin.

Reid, Pamela T. (1978, August). Black matriarchy: Young and old. Paper presented at the meeting of the American Psychological Association, Toronto.

Reid, Pamela T. (1984). Feminism versus minority group identity: Not for black women only. *Sex Roles, 10,* 247–255.

Reid, Pamela T., & Comas-Diaz, Lillian. (1990). Gender and ethnicity: Perspectives on dual status. *Sex Roles, 22,* 397–408.

Reifman, Alan, Biernat, Monica, & Lang, Eric L. (1991). Stress, social support, and health in married professional women with small children. *Psychology of Women Quarterly, 15,* 431–446.

Reilly, Mary Ellen. (1976). The family. *Population Profiles.* Unit No. 17. Washington, CT: The Center for Information on America.

Reilly, Mary Ellen, Lott, Bernice, & Gallogly, Sheila M. (1986). Sexual harassment of university students. *Sex Roles, 15,* 333–358.

Reilly, Mary Ellen, Lott, Bernice, Caldwell, Donna, & DeLuca, Luisa. (1992). Tolerance for sexual harassment related to self-reported sexual victimization. *Gender & Society, 6,* 122–138.

Reinhold, Robert. (1985, December 15). Cherokees install first woman as chief of major American Indian tribe. *New York Times.*

Reinisch, June M. (1981). Prenatal exposure to synthetic progestins increases potential for aggression in humans. *Science, 211,* 1171–1173.

Reinisch, June M., & Karow, William G. (1977). Prenatal exposure to synthetic progestins and estrogens: Effect on human development. *Archives of Sexual Behavior, 6,* 257–288.

Reis, Harry T., Senchak, Marilyn, & Solomon, Beth. (1985). Sex differences in the intimacy of social interaction: Further examination of potential explanations. *Journal of Personality and Social Psychology, 48,* 1204–1217.

Reis, Harry T., & Wright, Stephanie. (1982). Knowledge of sex-role stereotypes in children aged 3 to 5. *Sex Roles, 8,* 1049–1056.

Renne, Karen S., & Allen, Paul C. (1976). Gender and the ritual of the door. *Sex Roles, 2,* 167–174.

Repetti, Rena L. (1984). Determinants of children's sex stereotyping: Parental sex-role traits and television viewing. *Personality and Social Psychology Bulletin, 10,* 457–468.

Report details TV's inadequate depiction of women. (1990, November 15). *Providence Journal Bulletin,* p. G-1.

Report says U.S. lags in care of children. (1990, March 19). *Providence Evening Bulletin,* p. A-8.

Reppucci, N. Dickon, & Haugaard, Jeffrey J. (1989). Prevention of child sexual abuse: Myth or reality. *American Psychologist, 44,* 1266–1275.

Research dispels incestuous family myth. (1984, March). *NASW News,* pp. 3–4.

Resolution for the decriminalization and destigmatization of prostitution. (1984, August). Adopted by Division 35, American Psychological Association, at conference in Toronto.

Reuben, David. (1969). *Everything you always wanted to know about sex but were afraid to ask.* New York: McKay.

Reuss, Patricia B. & Goldfarb, Sally F. (1992, Spring). Violence against women is national health problem. *LDEF in Brief, 1*(3), 5.

Reward for top work? Look for woman boss. (1986, June/July). *University of Utah Review.*

Reynolds, Simon. (1992, February 9). Belting out that most unfeminine emotion. *New York Times,* p. H-27.

Rheingold, Harriet L., & Cook, Kaye V. (1975). The contents of boys' and girls' rooms as an index of parents' behavior. *Child Development, 46,* 459–463.

Rhode Island Women's Health Collective. (1991, Holiday). Focus on sexually transmitted disease. *Newsletter,* pp. 1, 4–7. (90 Printery St., Providence, RI 02904).

Ribble, Margaret A. (1944). Infantile experience in relation to personality development. In J. McV. Hunt (Ed.), *Personality and the behavior disorders,* vol. 2 (pp. 621–651). New York: Ronald.

Rice, Berkeley. (1980, December). Enlightened talk, chauvinist action. *Psychology Today,* pp. 24–25.

Rice, Joy K., & Hemmings, Annette. (1988). Women's colleges and women achievers: An update. *Signs, 13,* 546–559.

Rich, Adrienne. (1977). *Of woman born.* New York: Bantam.

Rich, Adrienne. (1980). Compulsory heterosexuality and lesbian existence. *Signs, 5,* 631–660.

Richardson, Deborah C., Bernstein, Sandy, & Taylor, Stuart P. (1979). The effect of situational contingencies on female retaliative behavior. *Journal of Personality and Social Psychology, 37,* 2044–2048.

Richardson, Deborah C., & Campbell, Jennifer L. (1980). Alcohol and wife abuse: The effect of alcohol on attributions of blame for wife abuse. *Personality and Social Psychology Bulletin, 6,* 51–56.

Richardson, Deborah C., & Campbell, Jennifer L. (1982). Alcohol and rape: The effect of alcohol on attributions of blame for rape. *Personality and Social Psychology Bulletin, 8,* 468–476.

Richardson, Deborah C., Vinsel, Anne, & Taylor, Stuart P. (1980). Female aggression as a function of attitudes toward women. *Sex Roles, 6,* 265–271.

Richardson, John T. E. (1990). Questionnaire studies of paramenstrual symptoms. *Psychology of Women Quarterly, 14,* 15–42.

Richardson, John G., & Mahoney, E. R. (1981). The perceived social status of husbands and wives in dual-work families as a function of achieved and derived occupational status. *Sex Roles, 7,* 1189–1198.

Ride claims she educated media. (1985, July 23). *Providence Evening Bulletin.*

Riedle, Joan E. (1991). Exploring the subcategories of stereotypes: Not all mothers are the same. *Sex Roles, 24,* 711–724.

Rierdan, Jill, Koff, Elissa, & Silverstone, Esther. (1978, March). *Human figure drawings of premenarcheal and postmenarcheal girls.* Paper read at the meeting of the Eastern Psychological Association, Washington, DC.

Riger, Stephanie, & Gordon, Margaret T. (1981). The fear of rape: A study in social control. *Journal of Social Issues, 37*(4), 71–92.

Riley, Pamela J. (1981). The influence of gender on occupational aspirations of kindergarten children. *Journal of Vocational Behavior, 19,* 244–250.

The risks that women took. (1989, April 23). *New York Times,* p. E-6.

Risks vs. benefits: How does hormone replacement therapy measure up? (1992, July/August). *National Women's Health Report,* p. 1.

Risman, Barbara J. (1987). Intimate relationships from a microstructural perspective: Men who mother. *Gender & Society, 1987, 1,* 6–32.

Roach, Sharyn L. (1990). Men and women lawyers in in-house legal departments: Recruitment and career patterns. *Gender & Society, 4,* 207–219.

Roberts, Katherine, & Slade, Margot. (1984, April 29). Women's work in Nassau County. *New York Times.*

Roberts, Leslie. (1988). Zeroing in on the sex switch. *Science, 239,* 21–23.

Roberts, Steven V. (1977, October 30). The old-age lobby has a loud voice in Washington. *New York Times,* p. E-4.

Robertson, Nan. (1985, March 18). Theater festival for older women at the Public. *New York Times.*

Robertson, Nan. (1991). *The girls in the balcony.* New York: Random House.

Robinson, Clyde C., & Morris, James T. (1986). The gender-stereotyped nature of Christmas toys received by 36-, 48-, and 60-month-old children: A comparison between nonrequested vs requested toys. *Sex Roles, 15,* 21–32.

Robison, Joan T. (1989, Fall). Noncoital reproduction. *Psychology of Women Newsletter,* pp. 1, 3–5.

Roccio, Lisa. (1991). Moral reasoning related to gender and dilemma content. (1992). Master's thesis, Department of Psychology, University of Rhode Island, Kingston.

Rodeheaver, Dean, & Datan, Nancy. (1988). The challenge of double jeopardy: Toward a mental health agenda for aging women. *American Psychologist, 43,* 648–654.

Rodeheaver, Dean, & Stohs, Joanne. (1991). The adaptive misperception of age in older women: Sociocultural images and psychological mechanisms of control. *Educational Gerontology, 17,* 141–156.

Rodgers, Joann E. (1985, May). The best health kick of all. *Ms.,* pp. 57–60, 140–141.

Rodin, Judith. (1976). Menstruation, reattribution, and competence. *Journal of Personality and Social Psychology, 33,* 345–353.

Rodin, Judith, & Ickovics, Jeannette R. (1990). Women's health: Review and research agenda as we approach the 21st century. *American Psychologist, 45,* 1018–1034.

Rodin, Judith, Silberstein, Lisa, & Striegel-Moore, Ruth H. (1985). Women and weight: A normative discontent. In T. B. Sonderegger (Ed.), *Nebraska symposium on motivation 1984: Psychology and gender,* vol. 32 (pp. 267–307). Lincoln: University of Nebraska Press.

Roe, Myrne (1993, June 7). Women still lack a fair share. *Providence Journal Bulletin,* p. A-15.

Rogers, Deborah. (1988, August 28). AIDS spreads to the soaps, sort of. *New York Times,* p. H-29.

Rogers, Lesley, & Walsh, Joan. (1982). Shortcomings of the psychomedical research of John Money and co-workers into sex differences in behavior: Social and political implications. *Sex Roles, 8,* 269–281.

Rogers, Tony. (1992, June 2). All-girls schools foster interests in math, science. *Providence Journal Bulletin,* p. F-2.

Rohter, Larry. (1991, March 17). Are women directors an endangered species? *New York Times,* pp. H-14, H-20–H-21.

Rollins, Judy, & White, Priscilla N. (1982). The relationship between mothers' and daughters' sex-role attitudes and self-concepts in three types of family environment. *Sex Roles, 8,* 1141–1155.

Romer, Nancy, & Cherry, Debra. (1980). Ethnic and social class differences in children's sex-role concepts. *Sex Roles, 6,* 245–263.

Romero, Mary. (1985). A comparison between strategies used on prisoners of war and battered wives. *Sex Roles, 13,* 537–547.

Rommel, Elizabeth. (1984, January). Grade school blues. *Ms.,* pp. 32–35.

Rook, Karen S. (1984). The negative side of social interaction: Impact on psychological well-being. *Journal of Personality and Social Psychology, 46,* 1097–1108.

Rook, Karen S. (1987). Reciprocity of social exchange and social satisfaction among older women. *Journal of Personality and Social Psychology, 52,* 145–154.

Roopnarine, Jaipaul L. (1986). Mothers' and fathers' behaviors toward the toy play of their infant sons and daughters. *Sex Roles, 14,* 59–68.

Root, Maria P. P. (1990). Disordered eating in women of color. *Sex Roles, 22,* 525–536.

Rosaldo, Michelle Z. (1974). Woman, culture and society: A theoretical overview. In M. Z. Rosaldo & L. Lamphere (Eds.), *Woman, culture and society* (pp. 17–42). Stanford, CA: Stanford University Press.

Rosaldo, Michelle Z. (1980). The use and abuse of anthropology: Reflections on feminism and cross-cultural understanding. *Signs, 5,* 389–417.

Rose, Judy. (1990, August 14). The manly version of PMS. *Providence Journal-Bulletin,* p. B-3.

Rosen, Leora N., Ickovics, Jeannette R., & Moghadam, Linda Z. (1990). Employment and role satisfaction: Implications for the general well-being of military wives. *Psychology of Women Quarterly, 14,* 371–385.

Rosen, Marjorie. (1973). *Popcorn Venus: Women, movies and the American dream.* New York: Avon.

Rosenbaum, David E. (1980, July 27). Working women still seek man-sized wages. *New York Times,* sec. 4, p. E-3.

Rosenberg, Florence R., & Simmons, Roberta G. (1975). Sex differences in the self-concept in adolescence. *Sex Roles, 1,* 147–159.

Rosenberg, Karen. (1984, April 14). Peaceniks and soldier girls. *The Nation,* pp. 453–457.

Rosenblatt, Roger. (1992, January 19). How to end the abortion war. *New York Times Magazine,* pp. 26, 41–42, 50, 56.

Rosenthal, Elisabeth. (1989, September 17). Different but deadly. *New York Times Magazine,* pp. 60, 120–121.

Rosenthal, Herman M., & Rudolph, Ileane. (1991, November 2–8). Newswoman syndrome: Big money, little clout. *TV Guide*, pp. 29–30.

Rosenthal, Naomi B. (1984). Consciousness raising: From revolution to re-evaluation. *Psychology of Women Quarterly, 8,* 309–326.

Ross, Ellen. (1980). "The love crisis": Couples' advice books of the late 1970s. *Signs, 6,* 109–122.

Ross, Joanna, & Kahan, James P. (1983). Children by choice or by chance: The perceived effects of parity. *Sex Roles, 9,* 69–77.

Ross, Laurie, Anderson, Daniel, & Wisocki, Patricia A. (1982). Television viewing and adult sex-role attitudes. *Sex Roles, 8,* 589–592.

Ross, Loretta J. (1981, July/August). Black women ponder: Why feminism? *New Directions for Women*, pp. 5, 16.

Rossi, Alice. (1980). Life-span theories and women's lives. *Signs, 6,* 4–32.

Rossi, Joseph S. (1983). Ratios exaggerate gender differences in mathematical ability. *American Psychologist, 38,* 348.

Rossner, Judith. (1976). *Looking for Mr. Goodbar*. New York: Pocket Books.

Rossner, Judith. (1983). *August*. New York: Houghton Mifflin.

Rothman, Barbara K. (1986). *The tentative pregnancy: Prenatal diagnosis and the future of motherhood*. New York: Viking.

Routh, Donald K., Schroeder, Carolyn S., & O'Tuama, Lorcan A. (1974). Development of activity level in children. *Developmental Psychology, 10,* 163–168.

Rowe, Mary P. (1973, December). *The progress of women in educational institutions: The Saturn's rings phenomenon*. Unpublished paper, Massachusetts Institute of Technology, Cambridge.

Rowland, Robyn. (1987). Technology and motherhood: Reproductive choice reconsidered. *Signs, 12,* 512–528.

Rowland, Robyn. (1991, May/June). Decoding reprospeak. *Ms.*, pp. 38–41.

Rowley, James. (1992, April 20). Violent crime in U.S. jumped 7.9% in 1991. *Providence Journal Bulletin*, p. A-1.

Roy, Maria (Ed.). (1977). *Battered women: A psychosociological study of domestic violence*. New York: Van Nostrand Reinhold.

Royal photo lacks stamp of reality. (1981, June 11). *Providence Evening-Bulletin*.

Rubenstein, Carin. (1980, July). Menstruation: The shame of it all. *Psychology Today*, p. 38.

Rubenstein, Carin. (1989, October 8). The baby bomb. *New York Times Magazine*, Part 2, pp. 34, 36, 38, 40–41.

Rubin, Jeffrey Z., Provenzano, Frank J., & Luria, Zella. (1974). The eye of the beholder: Parents' views on sex of newborns. *American Journal of Orthopsychiatry, 44,* 512–519.

Rubin, Lillian. (1976). *Worlds of pain: Life in the working class family*. New York: Basic Books.

Rubin, Lillian. (1981). *Women of a certain age*. New York: Harper & Row.

Rubin, Lillian. (1986). A feminist response to Lasch. *Tikkun, 1*(2), 89–91.

Rubin, Robert T., Reinisch, June M., & Haskett, Roger F. (1981). Postnatal gonadal steroid effects on human behavior. *Science, 211,* 1318–1324.

Rubin, Sylvia. (1991, February 5). Better birth control. *Providence Journal Bulletin*, pp. F-3, F-5.

Rubin, Zick. (1970). Measurement of romantic love. *Journal of Personality and Social Psychology, 16,* 265–273.

Rubin, Zick, Peplau, Letitia A., & Hill, Charles T. (1981). Loving and leaving: Sex differences in romantic attachments. *Sex Roles, 7,* 821–835.

Ruble, Diane N. (1977). Premenstrual symptoms: A reinterpretation. *Science, 197,* 291–292.

Ruble, Diane N., Balaban, Terry, & Cooper, Joel. (1981). Gender constancy and the effects of sex-typed televised toy commercials. *Child Development, 52,* 667–673.

Ruble, Diane N., Boggiano, Ann K., & Brooks-Gunn, Jeanne. (1982). Men's and women's evaluations of menstrual-related excuses. *Sex Roles, 8,* 625–638.

Ruble, Diane N., Fleming, Alison S., Hackel, Lisa S., & Stangor, Charles. (1988). Changes in the marital relationship during the transition to first time motherhood. *Journal of Personality and Social Psychology, 55,* 78–87.

Ruddick, Sara. (1989). *Maternal thinking: Toward a politics of peace*. Boston: Beacon Press.

Ruggiero, Josephine A., & Weston, Louise C. (1985). Work options for women in women's magazines: The medium and the message. *Sex Roles, 12,* 535–547.

Rushton, J. Philippe. (1976). Socialization and the altruistic behavior of children. *Psychological Bulletin, 83,* 898–913.

Ruskai, Mary Beth. (1991). Guest comment: Are there innate cognitive gender differences: Some comments on the evidence in response to a letter from M. Levin. *American Journal of Physics, 59* (1), 11–14.

Russell, Diana E. H. (1982). *Rape in marriage*. New York: Macmillan.

Russell, Diana E. H., & Howell, Nancy. (1983). The prevalence of rape in the United States revisited. *Signs, 8,* 688–695.

Russell, John. (1983, July 24). It's not "women's art," it's good art. *New York Times*, sec. 2, pp. 1, 25.

Russo, Nancy F. (Ed.) (1985). *A women's mental health agenda*. Washington, DC: American Psychological Association.

Russo, Nancy F. (1990). Overview: Forging research priorities for women's mental health. *American Psychologist, 45,* 368–373.

Russo, Nancy F. (1992, Fall). Abortion and unwanted childbearing: The impact of Casey. *Psychology of Women Newsletter*, pp. 1–4.

Russo, Nancy F., Horn, Jody D., & Schwartz, Robert. (1992). U.S. abortion in context: Selected characteristics and motivations of women seeking abortions. *Journal of Social Issues, 48,* (3), 183–202.

Russo, Nancy F., Kelly, Rita M., & Deacon, Melinda. (1991). Gender and success-related attributions: Beyond individualistic conceptions of achievement. *Sex Roles, 25,* 331–350.

Ryan, Mary P. (1979). *Womanhood in America: From colonial times to the present* (2nd ed.). New York: New Viewpoints.

Ryff, Carol D., & Migdal, Susan. (1984). Intimacy and generativity: Self-perceived transitions. *Signs, 9,* 470–481.

Saal, Frank E., Johnson, Catherine B., & Weber, Nancy. (1989). Friendly or sexy? *Psychology of Women Quarterly, 13,* 263–276.

Sacks, Karen. (1970). Social bases for sexual equality: A comparative review. In R. Morgan (Ed.), *Sisterhood is powerful* (pp. 455–469). New York: Vintage.

Sacks, Karen. (1979). *Sisters and wives*. Westport, CT: Greenwood.

Sadalla, Edward K., Kenrick, Douglas T., & Vershure, Beth. (1987). Dominance and heterosexual attraction. *Journal of Personality and Social Psychology, 52,* 730–738.

Sadker, Myra, & Sadker, David. (1985, March). Sexism in the schoolroom of the '80s. *Psychology Today*, pp. 54–57.

Sagrestano, Lynda M. (1992a). Power strategies in interpersonal relationships. *Psychology of Women Quarterly, 16,* 481–495.

Sagrestano, Lynda M. (1992b). The use of power and influence in a gendered world. *Psychology of Women Quarterly, 16,* 439–447.

St. John-Parsons, Donald. (1978). Continuous dual-career families: A case study. *Psychology of Women Quarterly, 3,* 30–42.

St. Lawrence, Janet S., & Joyner, Doris J. (1991). The effects of sexually violent rock music on males' acceptance of violence against women. *Psychology of Women Quarterly, 15,* 49–63.

St. Peter, Shirley. (1979). Jack went up the hill . . . but where was Jill? *Psychology of Women Quarterly, 4,* 256–260.

Salholz, Eloise, Beachy, Lucille, Miller, Susan, Annin, Peter, Barrett, Todd, & Foote, Donna. (1992, December 28). Did America 'get it'? *Newsweek,* pp. 20–22.

Sanday, Peggy R. (1981a). *Female power and male dominance: On the origins of sexual inequality.* New York: Cambridge University Press.

Sanday, Peggy R. (1981b). The socio-cultural context of rape: A cross-cultural study. *Journal of Social Issues, 37*(4), 5–27.

Sanday, Peggy. (1990). *Fraternity gang rape.* New York: New York University Press.

Sandberg, David E., Ehrhardt, Anke A., Mellins, Claude A., Ince, Susan E., & Meyer-Bahlburg, Heino F. L. (1987). The influence of individual and family characteristics upon career aspirations of girls during childhood and adolescence. *Sex Roles, 16,* 649–668.

Sandidge, Susanne, & Friedland, Seymour J. (1975). Sex-role-taking and aggressive behavior in children. *Journal of Genetic Psychology, 126,* 227–231.

Sandoval, Chela. (1984). Comment on Krieger's "Lesbian identity and community: Recent social science literature." *Signs, 9,* 725–729.

Sanger, Margaret. (1920). *Woman and the new race.* New York: Truth.

Sapiro, Virginia. (1990). *Women in American society* (2nd ed.). Mountain View, CA: Mayfield.

Sarton, May. (1992). *Endgame.* New York: W.W. Norton.

Savin-Williams, Ritch C., & Demo, David H. (1983). Situational and transituational determinants of adolescent self-feelings. *Journal of Personality and Social Psychology, 44,* 824–833.

Sayers, Janet. (1987). Science, sexual difference, and feminism. In B. B. Hess & M. M. Ferree (Eds.), *Analyzing gender: A handbook of social science research* (pp. 68–91). Newbury Park, CA: Sage.

Sayre, Anne. (1975). *Rosalind Franklin and DNA.* New York: Norton.

Scanlan, Christopher. (1978, May 15). "Mother's little helpers" exact heavy wages. *Providence Evening Bulletin.*

Scarr, Sandra, Phillips, Deborah, & McCartney, Kathleen. (1990). Facts, fantasies and the future of child care in the United States. *Psychological Science, 1,* 26–35.

Scarf, Maggie. (1980, July). The promiscuous woman. *Psychology Today,* pp. 78–87.

Schafer, Alice T., & Gray, Mary W. (1981). Sex and mathematics. *Science, 211,* 231.

Schein, Virginia E., Mueller, Ruediger, & Jacobson, Carolyn. (1989). The relationship between sex role stereotypes and requisite management characteristics among college students. *Sex Roles, 20,* 103–110.

Scheinmann, Vivian J. (1981, August). Jewish feminists demand equal treatment. *New Directions for Women,* pp. 5, 16.

Schlesier-Stropp, Barbara. (1984). Bulimia: A review of the literature. *Psychological Bulletin, 95,* 247–257.

Schlesinger, Arthur M. Jr. (1981). Introduction. In J. L. Stratton, *Pioneer women.* New York: Touchstone.

Schmeck, Harold M. Jr. (1980, February 24). Genetic flaws can come from father. *New York Times,* p. E-20.

Schmidt, Peggy. (1985, March 24). For the women, still a long way to go. *New York Times,* sec. 12, pp. 14–15.

Schmitt, Eric. (1992, August 2). The military has a lot to learn about women. *New York Times,* p. E-3.

Schneider, Beth E., & Gould, Meredith. (1987). Female sexuality: Looking back into the future. In B. B. Hess & M. M. Ferree (Eds.), *Analyzing gender: A handbook of social science research* (pp. 120–153), Newbury Park, CA: Sage.

Schneider, Claudine. (1985, November 21). Realities about comparable worth. *Providence Evening Bulletin.*

Schneider, Margaret S. (1986). The relationships of cohabiting lesbian and heterosexual couples: A comparison. *Psychology of Women Quarterly, 10,* 234–239.

Schneider, Susan W. (1984). *Jewish and female.* New York: Simon & Schuster.

Schreiner, Tim. (1984, May 29). A revolution that has just begun. *USA Today,* p. 40.

Schullo, Stephen A., & Alperson, Burton L. (1984). Interpersonal phenomenology as a function of sexual orientation, sex, sentiment, and trait categories in long-term dyadic relationships. *Journal of Personality and Social Psychology, 47,* 983–1007.

Schwadel, Francine. (1985, March 14). Women move up in the military, but many jobs remain off limits. *Wall Street Journal,* p. 33.

Schwartz, Lori A., & Markham, William T. (1985). Sex stereotyping in children's toy advertisements. *Sex Roles, 12,* 157–170.

Schwartz, Lynne. (1989). *Leaving Brooklyn.* Boston: Houghton Mifflin.

Schwartz, Lynne S. (1985). *Disturbances in the field.* New York: Bantam.

Sciolino, Elaine. (1985, September 11). Equality remains an elusive goal for U.N. women. *New York Times,* pp. C-1, C-4.

Scott, Ronald L., & Tetreault, Laurie A. (1987). Attitudes of rapists and other violent offenders toward women. *Journal of Social Psychology, 127,* 375–380.

Scully, Diana. (1988). Convicted rapists' perceptions of self and victim: Role taking and emotions. *Gender and Society, 2,* 200–213.

Scully, Diana, & Marolla, Joseph. (1981, December). *Convicted rapists' attitudes toward women and rape.* Paper presented at the meeting of the First International Interdisciplinary Congress on Women, Haifa, Israel.

Sears' acquittal ends more than just a case. (1986, February 10). *Providence Evening Bulletin,* pp. A-1, A-2.

Sears, Pauline S. & Barbee, A. H. (1977). Career and life satisfaction among Termans gifted women. In J. C. Stanley, W. D. George, & C. H. Solano (Eds.), *The gifted and the creative: A fifty-year perspective.* Baltimore: Johns Hopkins University Press.

Seavey, Carol A., Katz, Phyllis A., & Zalk, Sue R. (1975). Baby X: The effect of gender labels on adult responses to infants. *Sex Roles, 1,* 103–109.

Seawell, Mary Ann. (1993, May 5). Battling the backlash: Faludi offers tips on strategy. *Campus Report* (Stanford University), p. 6.

Sebold, Alice. (1989, February 26). Speaking of the unspeakable. *New York Times Magazine,* pp. 16–18.

SEC enforcer quits after wife-beating story. (1985, February 27). *Providence Evening Bulletin.*

Seccombe, Karen, & Beeghley, Leonard. (1992). Gender and medical insurance: A test of human capital theory. *Gender & Society, 6,* 283–300.

Seegmiller, Bonni R. (1980a). Sex-typed behavior in preschoolers: Sex, age, and social class effects. *Journal of Psychology, 104,* 31–33.

Seegmiller, Bonni R. (1980b). Sex-role differentiation in preschoolers: Effects of maternal employment. *Journal of Psychology, 104,* 185–189.

Seidler, Susan. (1984, March/April). ERT: Drug company sales vs. women's health. *Network News,* p. 7.

Selkin, James. (1975, January). Rape. *Psychology Today,* pp. 71–76.

Selkow, Paula. (1984). Effects of maternal employment on kindergarten and first-grade children's vocational aspirations. *Sex Roles, 11,* 677–690.

Selnow, Gary W. (1985). Sex differences in uses and perceptions of profanity. *Sex Roles, 12,* 303–312.

Selvin, Paul. (1991). Does the Harrison case reveal sexism in math? *Science, 252,* 1781–1783.

Selvin, Paul. (1992). Heroism is still the norm. *Science, 255,* 1382–1383.

Serbin, Lisa A., & Connor, Jane M. (1979). Sex-typing of children's play preferences and patterns of cognitive performance. *Journal of Genetic Psychology, 134,* 315–316.

Serbin, Lisa A., Connor, Jane M., Burchardt, Carol J., & Citron, Cheryl C. (1979). Effects of peer presence on sex-typing of children's play behavior. *Journal of Experimental Child Psychology, 27,* 303–309.

Serbin, Lisa A., Connor, Jane M., & Citron, Cheryl C. (1978). Environmental control of independent and dependent behaviors in preschool girls and boys: A model for early independence training. *Sex Roles, 4,* 867–875.

Serbin, Lisa A., Connor, Jane M., & Citron, Cheryl C. (1981). Sex-differentiated free play behavior: Effects of teacher modeling, location, and gender. *Developmental Psychology, 17,* 640–646.

Serbin, Lisa A., Connor, Jane M., & Iler, Iris. (1979). Sex-stereotyped and non-stereotyped introduction of new toys in the preschool classroom: An observational study of teacher behavior and its effects. *Psychology of Women Quarterly, 4,* 261–265.

Serbin, Lisa A., O'Leary, K., Daniel, Kent, Ronald N., & Tonick, Illene J. (1973). A comparison of teacher response to the preacademic and problem behavior of boys and girls. *Child Development, 44,* 796–804.

Serrin, William. (1984, November 25). Experts say job bias against women persists. *New York Times.*

Serrin, William. (1985, January 31). Women are turning to collective action as a key to power and protection. *New York Times,* p. A-14.

Sex habits of single women detailed in national survey. (1986, June 2). *Providence Evening Bulletin,* p. A-4.

Sexual assault reports in R.I. increased 14.8% in last year. (1986, February 26). *Providence Evening Bulletin,* p. A-2.

Sexual harassment stirs high court's wrath. (1986, June 24). *Providence Evening Bulletin.*

Shakin, Madeline, Shakin, Debra, & Sternglanz, Sarah H. (1985). Infant clothing: Sex labeling for strangers. *Sex Roles, 12,* 955–964.

Shange, Ntozake. (1985). *Betsey Brown.* New York: St. Martin's Press.

Shapiro, Laura. (1991, October 21). Why women are angry. *Newsweek,* pp. 41–44.

Shapiro, Laura, Murr, Andrew, & Springen, Karen. (1991, June 17). Women who kill too much: Is 'Thelma and Louise' feminism, or fascism? *Newsweek,* p. 63.

Sharff, Jagna W. (1983). Sex and temperament revisited. In M. Fooden, S. Gordon, & B. Hughley (Eds.), *Genes and gender IV. The second X and women's health* (pp. 49–62). Staten Island, NY: Gordian Press.

Shaver, Philip, & Hendrick, Clyde. (1987). *Sex and gender.* Newbury Park, CA: Sage.

Sheehy, Gail. (1974). *Hustling.* New York: Dell.

Sheehy, Gail. (1991). *The silent passage.* New York: Random House.

Shenon, Philip. (1986, May 18). A second opinion on pornography's impact. *New York Times.*

Shepard, Winifred. (1980). Mothers and fathers, sons and daughters: Perceptions of young adults. *Sex Roles, 6,* 421–433.

Shepherd-Look, Dee L. (1982). Sex differentiation and the development of sex roles. In B. B. Wolman (Ed.), *Handbook of Developmental Psychology.* Englewood Cliffs, NJ: Prentice Hall.

Shepperd, James A., & Stratham, Alan J. (1989). Attractiveness and height: The role of stature in dating preferences, frequency of dating, and perceptions of attractiveness. *Personality and Social Psychology Bulletin, 15,* 617–627.

Sherfey, Mary Jane. (1970). A theory on female sexuality. In R. Morgan (Ed.), *Sisterhood is powerful* (pp. 220–230). New York: Random House.

Sherman, Julia A. (1971). *On the psychology of women: A survey of empirical studies.* Springfield, IL: Charles C Thomas.

Sherman, Julia A. (1980). Mathematics, spatial visualization, and related factors: Changes in girls and boys, grades 8–11. *Journal of Educational Psychology, 72,* 476–482.

Sherman, Julia A. (1982, January). Premenstrual Syndrome. *Division 35 Newsletter* (American Psychological Association, Washington, DC), pp. 10–11.

Sherman, Julia A. (1983). Factors predicting girls' and boys' enrollments in college preparatory mathematics. *Psychology of Women Quarterly, 7,* 272–281.

Sherman, Julia A., & Fennema, Elizabeth. (1978). Distribution of spatial visualization and mathematical problem solving scores: A test of Stafford's X-linked hypotheses. *Psychology of Women Quarterly, 3,* 157–167.

Sherman, Susan R., & Rosenblatt, Aaron. (1984). Women physicians as teachers, administrators, and researchers in medical and surgical specialties: Kanter versus "Avis" as competing hypotheses. *Sex Roles, 11,* 203–209.

She's single—and prefers it. (1984, July 13). *Providence Evening Bulletin.*

She's the chief. (1985, January 27). *New York Times,* p. E-6.

Shields, Stephanie A. (1975a). Functionalism, Darwinism, and the psychology of women: A study in social myth. *American Psychologist, 30,* 739–754.

Shields, Stephanie A. (1975b). Ms. Pilgrim's progress: The contributions of Leta Stetter Hollingworth to the psychology of women. *American Psychologist, 30,* 852–857.

Shields, Stephanie A. (1987). Women, men, and the dilemma of emotion. In P. Shaver & C. Hendrick (Eds.), *Sex and gender* (pp. 229–250). Newbury Park, CA: Sage.

Shields, Stephanie A., & Cooper, Pamela E. (1983). Stereotypes of traditional and nontraditional childbearing roles. *Sex Roles, 9,* 363–376.

Shilts, Randy (1993). Conduct unbecoming: Lesbians and gays in the military, Vietnam to the Persian Gulf. New York, St. Martin's Press.

Shipp, E. R. (1991, July 28). Bearing witness to the unbearable. *New York Times,* pp. E-1–E-2.

Shotland, R. Lance, & Straw, Margaret K. (1976). Bystander response to an assault: When a man attacks a woman. *Journal of Personality and Social Psychology, 34,* 990–999.

Shows blasted for depicting teen bimbos. (1988, August 25). *Providence Journal-Bulletin,* pp. F-1–F-2.

Shreve, Anita. (1982, November 21). Careers and the lure of motherhood. *New York Times Magazine,* pp. 38–43, 46–52, 56.

Shusterman, Lisa R. (1976). The psychosocial factors of the abortion experience: A critical review. *Psychology of Women Quarterly, 1,* 79–106.

Signorelli, Nancy, & Lears, Margaret. (1992). Children, television, and conceptions about chores: Attitudes and behaviors. *Sex Roles, 27,* 157–170.

Silberstein, Lisa R., Striegel-Moore, Ruth H., Timko, Christine, & Rodin, Judith. (1988). Behavioral and psychological implications of body dissatisfaction: Do men and women differ? *Sex Roles, 19,* 219–232.

Silverstein, Brett, Perdue, Lauren, Peterson, Barbara, & Kelly, Eileen. (1986). The role of the mass media in promoting a thin standard of bodily attractiveness for women. *Sex Roles, 14,* 519–532.

Silverstein, Brett, Perdue, Lauren, Wolf, Cordulla, & Pizzolo, Cecilia. (1988). Bingeing, purging, and estimates of parental attitudes regarding female achievement. *Sex Roles, 19,* 723–733.

Silverstein, Louise B. (1991). Transforming the debate about child care and maternal employment. *American Psychologist, 46,* 1025–1032.

Simon, Kate. (1982). *Bronx Primitive.* New York: Harper & Row.

Simon, Kate. (1986). *A wider world: Portraits in adolescence.* New York: Harper & Row.

Simon, Kate. (1990). *Etchings in an hourglass.* New York: Harper & Row.

Simon, William, & Gagnon, John. (1977). Psychosexual development. In D. Byrne & L. A. Byrne (Eds.), *Exploring human sexuality* (pp. 117–129). New York: Crowell.

Simkins-Bullock, Jennifer A., & Wildman, Beth G. (1991). An investigation into the relationships between gender and language. *Sex Roles, 24,* 149–160.

Simpson, Gwyned. (1984). The daughters of Charlotte Ray: The career development process during the exploratory and establishment stages of black women attorneys. *Sex Roles, 11,* 113–139.

Simpson, Peggy. (1991, January/February). Election 1990: A mixed bag. *Ms.,* pp. 88–89.

Singer, Jerome L., & Singer, Dorothy G. (1980). Television viewing, family style and aggressive behavior in preschool children. In M. R. Green (Ed.), *Violence and the family* (pp. 37–65). Boulder, CO: Westview.

Singer, Judith E., Westphal, Milton, & Niswander, Kenneth R. (1972). Sex differences in the incidence of neonatal abnormalities and abnormal performance in early childhood. In J. Bardwick (Ed.), *Readings on the psychology of women* (pp. 13–17). New York: Harper & Row.

Singles enjoy more active social life. (1985, May 8). *Providence Evening Bulletin.*

Singles in 30s a growing phenomenon. (1987, September 10). *Providence Journal Bulletin,* p. A-9.

Sinnott, Jan D. (1984). Older men, older women: Are their perceived roles similar? *Sex Roles, 10,* 847–856.

Skolnik, Ricki. (1983, March). A safe method lovers can share. *Whole Life Times,* pp. 24–25.

Skrypnek, Berna, & Snyder, Mark. (1982). On the self-perpetuating nature of stereotypes about men and women. *Journal of Experimental Social Psychology, 18,* 277–291.

Skultans, Vieda. (1979). The symbolic significance of menstruation and the menopause. In J. H. Williams (Ed.), *Psychology of women: Selected readings* (pp. 115–128). New York: Norton.

Slaughter, Carolyn. (1985). *A perfect woman.* New York: Ticknor & Fields.

Smedley, Agnes. (1973). *Daughter of earth.* Old Westbury, NY: Feminist Press. (Original work published in 1929.)

Smith, Barbara. (1985). Some home truths on the contemporary black feminist movement. *Black Scholar, 16*(2), 4–13.

Smith, Caroline, & Lloyd, Barbara. (1978). Maternal behavior and perceived sex of infant: Revisited. *Child Development, 49,* 1263–1265.

Smith, Dorothy E. (1991). Writing women's experience into social science. *Feminism and Psychology, 1,* 155–170.

Smith, Elsie J. (1982). The black female adolescent: A review of the educational, career and psychological literature. *Psychology of Women Quarterly, 6,* 261–288.

Smith, Jane E., Waldorf, Ann V., and Trembath, David L. (1990). "Single white male looking for thin, very attractive . . ." *Sex Roles, 23,* 675–685.

Smith, Joan. (1984). The paradox of women's poverty: Wage-earning women and economic transformation. *Signs, 10,* 291–310.

Smith, Liz. (1993, April 3). Grapevine: Women make a point on Sunset Boulevard. *San Jose Mercury News,* p. C-3.

Smith, Mary Lee. (1980). Sex bias in counseling and psychotherapy. *Psychological Bulletin, 87,* 392–407.

Smith, Patricia A., & Midlarsky, Elizabeth. (1985). Empirically derived conceptions of femaleness and maleness: A current view. *Sex Roles, 12,* 313–328.

Smith, Patricia L., Smits, Stanley J., & Hoy, Frank. (1992). Female business owners. *Sex Roles, 26,* 485–496.

Smith, Roberta. (1990, June 17). Waging guerilla warfare against the art world. *New York Times,* pp. H-1, H-31.

Smye, Marti D., & Wine, Jeri D. (1980). A comparison of female and male adolescents' social behaviors and cognitions: A challenge to the assertiveness literature. *Sex Roles, 6,* 213–230.

Snell, William E. Jr., Miller, Rowland S., & Belk, Sharyn S. (1988). Development of the emotional self-disclosure scale. *Sex Roles, 18,* 59–73.

Snitow, Ann B. (1980). The front line: Notes on sex in novels by women. *Signs, 5,* 702–718.

Snitow, Ann. (1991, May/June). Motherhood—reclaiming the demon texts. *Ms.,* pp. 34–37.

Snodgrass, Sara E. (1985). Women's intuition: The effect of subordinate role on interpersonal sensitivity. *Journal of Personality and Social Psychology, 49,* 146–155.

Sara E. Snodgrass. (1992). Further effects of role versus gender or interpersonal sensitivity. *Journal of Personality and Social Psychology, 62,* 154–158.

Snyder, Mark, Tanke, Elizabeth D., & Berscheid, Ellen. (1977). Social perception and interpersonal behavior: On the self-fulfilling nature of social stereotypes. *Journal of Personality and Social Psychology, 35,* 656–666.

Sobel, Suzanne B. (1982). Difficulties experienced by women in prison. *Psychology of Women Quarterly, 7,* 107–118.

Society's losers. (1981, Autumn). *ISR Newsletter,* pp. 4–5. (Institute for Social Research, University of Michigan, Ann Arbor.)

Sohn, David. (1982). Sex differences in achievement self-attributions: An effect-size analysis. *Sex Roles, 8,* 345–357.

Sokoloff, Natalie J. (1987). What's happening to women's employment: Issues for women's labor struggles in the 1980s–1990s. In C. Bose, R. Feldberg, and N. Sokoloff (Eds.), *Hidden aspects of women's work* (pp. 14–45). New York: Praeger.

Solomon, Lawrence S., Tomaskovic-Devey, Donald, & Risman, Barbara J. (1989). The gender gap and nuclear power: Attitudes in a politicized environment. *Sex Roles, 21,* 401–414.

Sommer, Barbara. (1983). How does menstruation affect cognitive competence and psychophysiological response? In S. Golub (Ed.), *Lifting the curse of menstruation* (pp. 53–90). New York: Haworth.

Sontag, Susan. (1979). The double standard of aging. In J. H. Williams (Ed.), *Psychology of women: Selected readings* (pp. 462–478). New York: Norton.

Spacks, Patricia M. (1975). *The female imagination.* New York: Knopf.

Spacks, Patricia M. (1981). *The adolescent idea.* New York: Basic Books.

Spade, Joan Z., & Reese, Carole A. (1991). We've come a long way, maybe: College students' plans for work and family. *Sex Roles, 24,* 309–321.

Spears, Gregory. (1991, October 1). Breast-feeding is on the decline. *Providence Journal Bulletin,* p. F-4.

Specter, Joan. (1986, February 16). Philadelphia leads the way in parental leave. *New York Times,* p. E-16.

Spence, Janet T. (1983). Comment on Lubinski, Tellegen, and Butcher's "Masculinity, femininity, and androgyny viewed and assessed as distinct concepts." *Journal of Personality and Social Psychology, 44,* 440–446.

Spence, Janet T. (1985). Gender identity and its implications for the concepts of masculinity and femininity. In T. B. Sonderegger (Ed.), *Nebraska symposium on motivation 1984: Psychology and gender,* vol. 32 (pp. 59–96). Lincoln, NE: University of Nebraska Press.

Spence, Janet T., & Helmreich, Robert L. (1980). Masculine instrumentality and feminine expressiveness: Their relationships with sex role attitudes and behavior. *Psychology of Women Quarterly, 5,* 147–163.

Spence, Janet T., Helmreich, Robert L., & Stapp, Joy. (1974). The personality attributes questionnaire: A measure of sex role stereotypes and masculinity-femininity. *Journal Supplement Abstract Service Document,* Ms. No. 617.

Sperry, Roger. (1982). Some effects of disconnecting the cerebral hemispheres. *Science, 217,* 1223–1226.

Sprecher, Susan. (1989). The importance to males and females of physical attractiveness, earning potential, and expressiveness in initial attraction. *Sex Roles, 21,* 591–607.

Squire, Susan. (1983, October). Is the binge-purge cycle catching? *Ms.,* pp. 41–46.

Stack, Carol B. (1974). *All our kin: Strategies for survival in a Black community.* New York: Harper & Row.

Stack, Carol B. (1986). The culture of gender: Women and men of color. *Signs, 11,* 321–324.

Stake, Jayne E. (1983a). Ability level, evaluative feedback, and sex differences in performance expectancy. *Psychology of Women Quarterly, 8,* 48–58.

Stake, Jayne E. (1983b). Factors in reward distribution: Allocator motive, gender, and Protestant ethic endorsement. *Journal of Personality and Social Psychology, 44,* 410–418.

Stake, Jayne E. (1985). Exploring the basis of sex differences in third-party allocations. *Journal of Personality and Social Psychology, 48,* 1621–1629.

Stake, Jayne, & Lauer, Monica L. (1987). The consequences of being overweight: A controlled study of gender differences. *Sex Roles, 17,* 31–47.

Staples, Robert. (1977). Male-female sexual variations: Functions of biology or culture? In D. Byrne & L. A. Byrne (Eds.), *Exploring human sexuality* (pp. 185–193). New York: Crowell.

Stapley, Janice C., & Haviland, Jeannette M. (1989). Beyond depression: Gender differences in normal adolescents' emotional experiences. *Sex Roles, 20,* 295–308.

Stark, Elizabeth. (1985, June). Androgyny makes better lovers. *Psychology Today,* p. 19.

Stark, Elizabeth. (1986a, April). Stand up to your man. *Psychology Today,* p. 68.

Stark, Elizabeth. (1986b, October). Young, innocent and pregnant. *Psychology Today,* pp. 28–35.

Starowicz, Mark (1992, August 16). Leakey's last angel. New York Times Magazine, pp. 29ff.

Starr, Barbara S. (1979). Sex differences among personality correlates of mathematical ability in high school seniors. *Psychology of Women Quarterly, 4,* 212–220.

State Dept. admits bias against female officers. (1989, April 20). *Providence Journal Bulletin,* p. A-12.

State of Rhode Island, 1979. Criminal offenses, Title II, Chapter 11–37. *An Act Relating to Rape and Seduction.*

Steel, Lauri, Abeles, Ronald P., & Card, Josefina J. (1982). Sex differences in the patterning of adult roles as a determinant of sex differences in occupational achievement. *Sex Roles, 8,* 1009–1024.

Steenland, Sally. (1988). *Prime time women: An analysis of older women on entertainment television.* National Commission on Working Women, 1325 G St. NW, Washington, DC 20005.

Stefanick, Marcia L. (1992, Winter). Women's issues. *Institute for Research on Women and Gender Newsletter,* Stanford University, pp. 1–3.

Steil, Janice M., & Weltman, Karen. (1991). Marital inequality: The importance of resources, personal attributes, and social norms on career valuing and the allocation of domestic responsibilities. *Sex Roles, 24,* 161–179.

Stein, Aletha H., Pohly, Sheila R., & Mueller, Edward. (1971). The influence of masculine, feminine, and neutral tasks on children's achievement behavior, expectancies of success and attainment values. *Child Development, 42,* 195–207.

Stein, Joel. (1993, May 12). *Playboy* searching for "model students." *Stanford Daily,* p. 1.

Steinem, Gloria. (1978a, February). A flash of power. *Ms.,* pp. 87–88.

Steinem, Gloria. (1978b, October). If men could menstruate. *Ms.,* p. 110.

Steinem, Gloria. (1978c, November). Erotica and pornography: A clear and present difference. *Ms.,* pp. 53–54, 75, 76.

Steinmetz, Suzanne K. (1977–1978). The battered husband syndrome. *Victimology, 2,* 499–509.

Stephen, Beverly. (1984, November). Rites of independence. *Ms.,* p. 55.

Stericker, Anne, & LeVesconte, Shirley. (1982). Effect of brief training on sex-related differences in visual-spatial skill. *Journal of Personality and Social Psychology, 43,* 1018–1029.

Stern, Marilyn, & Karraker, Katherine H. (1989). Sex stereotyping of infants: A review of gender labeling studies. *Sex Roles, 20,* 501–522.

Sternberg, Robert J., & Grajeck, S. (1984). The nature of love. *Journal of Personality and Social Psychology, 47,* 312–329.

Steward, Margaret S., Steward, David S., & Dary, Judith A. (1983). Women who choose a man's career: Women in ministry. *Psychology of Women Quarterly, 8,* 166–173.

Stewart, Abigail J., & Salt, Patricia. (1981). Life stress, life-styles, depression, and illness in adult women. *Journal of Personality and Social Psychology, 40,* 1063–1069.

Stewart, Abigail J., & Gold-Steinberg, Sharon. (1990). Midlife women's political consciousness: Case studies of psychosocial development and political commitment. *Psychology of Women Quarterly, 14,* 543–566.

Stiles, Deborah A., Gibbons, Judith L., Hardardottir, Sara, & Schnellman, Jo. (1987). The ideal man or woman as described by young adolescents in Iceland and the United States. *Sex Roles, 17,* 313–320.

Stipek, Deborah J. (1984). Sex differences in children's attributions for success and failure on math and spelling tests. *Sex Roles, 11,* 969–981.

Stitt, Christopher, Schmidt, Stuart, Price, Karl, & Kipnis, David. (1983). Sex of leader, leader behavior, and subordinate satisfaction. *Sex Roles, 9,* 31–42.

Stockburger, David W., & Davis, James O. (1978). Selling the female image as mental patient. *Sex Roles, 4,* 131–134.

Stokes, Henry S. (1982, October 17). Life and limbs are growing longer in Japan. *New York Times,* sec. 4.

Stone, Merlin. (1979). *Ancient mirrors of womanhood,* vol. 1. New York: New Sibylline Books.

Stoneman, Zolinda, Brody, Gene H., & MacKinnon, Carol E. (1986). Same-sex and cross-sex siblings: Activity choices, roles, behavior, and gender stereotypes. *Sex Roles, 15,* 495–511.

Straus, Murray A. (1978, December). Stress and assault in a national sample of American families. Paper read at Colloquium on Stress and Crime, National Institute of Law Enforcement and Criminal Justice, MITRE Corporation, Washington, DC.

Straus, Murray A., Gelles, Richard J., & Steinmetz, Suzanne K. (1981). *Behind closed doors.* Garden City, NY: Anchor/Doubleday.

Streissguth, Ann P., Landesman,-Dwyer, Sharon, Martin, Joan C., & Smith, David W. (1980). Teratogenic effects of alcohol in humans and laboratory animals. *Science, 209,* 353–361.

Streshinsky, Shirley. (1975, September). The not so weaker sex. *McCall's,* p. 33.

Stress causes premature births—study. (1990, August 15). *Providence Journal Bulletin,* pp. E-1, E-2.

Strickland, Bonnie R. (1991, April 23). *Testimony of the American Psychological Association regarding women's health research priorities.* Washington, DC: American Psychological Association.

Strikers demand equal pay for women. (1981, July 6). *Providence Evening Bulletin,* pp. A-1, A-6.

Stroebe, Margaret S., & Stroebe, Wolfgang. (1983). Who suffers more? Sex differences in health risks of the widowed. *Psychological Bulletin, 93,* 279–301.

Strong, Ellen. (1970). The hooker. In R. Morgan (Ed.), *Sisterhood is powerful* (pp. 289–297). New York: Vintage.

Strube, Michael J. (1981). Meta-analysis and cross-cultural comparison: Sex differences in child competitiveness. *Journal of Cross-Cultural Psychology, 12,* 3–20.

Strube, Michael J. (1988). The decision to leave an abusive relationship: Empirical evidence and theoretical issues. *Psychological Bulletin, 104,* 236–250.

Strum, Shirley C. (1987). *Almost human: A journey into the world of baboons.* New York: Random House.

Study: Men's attitudes slow to change. (1990, November 8). *Providence Journal Bulletin,* p. A-2.

Study: No link between the Pill, breast cancer in middle-aged. (1989, September 6). *Providence Journal Bulletin,* p. A-4.

Study: 1 in 8 U.S. children hungry. (1991, March 27). *Providence Journal Bulletin.*

Study shows inequality in male-female financial aid. (1984, January 24). *Good 5¢ Cigar.* (University of Rhode Island, Kingston)

Study: Wife means life for older men. (1990, October 17). *Providence Journal Bulletin.*

Study: Zealous moms influence eating disorders. (1991, April 30). *Providence Journal Bulletin,* p. A-1.

Studying love: Older set is enjoying new spirit of courtship. (1985, June 7). *Providence Evening Bulletin.*

Success, health linked in study. (1984, May 10). *Providence Evening Bulletin.*

Suh, Mary. (1991, November/December). When I'm 65. *Ms.,* pp. 58–62.

Suisman, Sherry J. (1990, September/October). Restrictive abortion laws and teenage women. *The Network News,* pp. 1, 6.

Suleiman, Susan R. (1988). On maternal splitting. *Signs, 14,* 25–41.

Summers, Timothy P., & DeCotiis, Thomas A. (1988). An investigation of sex differences in job satisfaction. *Sex Roles, 18,* 679–689.

Superstition crumbles underground. (1981, December 14). *Providence Evening Bulletin.*

Survey: Most teens sexually active. (1992, January 4). *Providence Journal-Bulletin,* p. A-2.

Survey: Women lawyers earn less than men. (1990, September 24). *Providence Journal Bulletin,* p. B-3.

Swandby, Janet R. (1979). Daily and retrospective mood and physical symptom self-reports and their relationship to the menstrual cycle. Unpublished master's thesis, University of Wisconsin, Milwaukee.

Swerdlow, Marian. (1989). Men's accommodations to women entering a nontraditional occupation: A case of rapid transit operatives. *Gender & Society, 3,* 373–387.

Swertlow, Frank. (1982, June 12). TV update: Hollywood. *TV Guide,* p. A-1.

Swim, Janet, Borgida, Eugene, Maruyama, Geoffrey, & Myers, David G. (1989). Joan McKay versus John McKay: Do gender stereotypes bias evaluations? *Psychological Bulletin, 105,* 409–429.

Tan, Amy. (1991a). *The joy luck club.* New York: Vintage Books.

Tan, Amy. (1991b). *The kitchen god's wife.* New York: Putnam.

Tangri, Sandra S., Burt, Martha R., & Johnson, Leanor B. (1982). Sexual harassment at work: Three exploratory models. *Journal of Social Issues, 38*(4), 33–54.

Tannen, Deborah. (1990). *You just don't understand: Women and men in conversation.* New York: William Morrow.

Tanner, Nancy, & Zihlman, Adrienne. (1976). Women in evolution. Part I: Innovation and selection in human origins. *Signs, 1,* 585–608.

Tanzer, Deborah. (1973). Natural childbirth: Pain or peak experience? In *Psychology Today* (Eds.), The female experience (pp. 4–32). Del Mar, CA: Communications/Research/Machines.

Tavris, Carol. (1993a, January 3). Beware the incest-survivor machine. *New York Times Magazine.*

Tavris, Carol. (1993b, February 14). Carol Tavris replies. *New York Times Magazine,* p. 27.

Taylor, Dalmas A., & Smitherman-Donaldson, Geneva. (1989). "And, ain't I a woman?": African-American women and affirmative action. *Sex Roles, 21,* 1–12.

Taylor, Marylee C., & Hall, Judith A. (1982). Psychological androgyny: Theories, methods, and conclusions. *Psychological Bulletin, 92,* 347–366.

Taylor, Shelley E., & Langer, Ellen J. (1977). Pregnancy: A social stigma? *Sex Roles, 3,* 27–35.

Taylor, Stuart. (1986, June 15). Abortion is affirmed, but in a lower voice. *New York Times,* p. E-1.

Teenage fathers not poor providers, new study indicates. (1985, October 2). *Providence Journal Bulletin.*

Teenaged boys and girls suffer different—but equally serious—psychological problems. (1977, Summer). *ISR Newsletter.* (Institute for Social Research, University of Michigan, Ann Arbor, MI)

Teltsch, Kathleen. (1985, September 19). Today's engineer is often a woman. *New York Times,* p. C-1.

Terborg, James R. (1985). Working women and stress. In T. A. Beehr & R. S. Bhagat (Eds.), *Human stress and cognition in organizations* (pp. 245–286). New York: Wiley.

Teri, Linda. (1982). Effects of sex and sex-role style on clinical judgment. *Sex Roles, 8,* 639–649.

Tetenbaum, Toby J., & Pearson, Judith. (1989). The voices in children's literature: The impact of gender on the moral decisions of storybook characters. *Sex Roles, 20,* 381–395.

There she goes, Miss America. (1984, August 4–11). *The Nation.*

Theroux, Phyllis. (1987, May 17). TV women have come a long way, baby—sort of. *New York Times,* p. H-35.

A third of high school girls say they're fat. (1991, November 1). *Providence Journal Bulletin,* p. A-5.

Thom, Mary. (1988, May). Dilemmas of the new birth technologies. *Ms.,* pp. 70–76.

Thomas, Constance. (1985). The age of androgyny: The new views of psychotherapists. *Sex Roles, 13,* 381–392.

Thompson, Edward H., Jr. (1991). The maleness of violence in dating relationships: An appraisal of stereotypes. *Sex Roles, 24,* 261–278.

Thompson, Martha E. (1981). Sex differences: Differential access to power or sex-role socialization? *Sex Roles, 7,* 413–424.

Thompson, Spencer K. (1975). Gender labels and early sex role development. *Child Development, 46,* 339–347.

Thompson, Spencer K., & Bentler, P. M. (1973). A developmental study of gender constancy and parent preference. *Archives of Sexual Behavior, 2,* 379–385.

Tidball, M. Elizabeth. (1980). Women's colleges and women achievers revisited. *Signs, 5,* 504–517.

Tieger, Todd. (1980). On the biological basis of sex differences in aggression. *Child Development, 51,* 943–963.

Tiffany, Sharon W. (1982). *Women, work and motherhood.* Englewood Cliffs, NJ: Prentice Hall.

Tilby, Penelope J., & Kalin, Rudolf. (1980). Effects of sex-role deviant lifestyles in otherwise normal persons on the perception of maladjustment. *Sex Roles, 6,* 581–592.

Tinsley, Emiley G., Sullivan-Guest, Sandra, & McGuire, John. (1984). Feminine sex role and depression in middle-aged women. *Sex Roles, 11,* 25–32.

Tittle, Carol K. (1986). Gender research and education. *American Psychologist, 41,* 1161–1168.

Todd, Judith, Friedman, Ariella, & Kariuki, Priscilla W. (1990). Women growing stronger with age: The effect of status in the United States and Kenya. *Psychology of Women Quarterly, 14,* 567–577.

Toner, Robin. (1993, April 4). A shift of focus on abortion law. *New York Times,* p. E-2.

Top, Titia J. (1991). Sex bias in the evaluation of performance in the scientific, artistic, and literary professions: A review. *Sex Roles, 24,* 73–106.

Toth, Emily. (1984, February). Who'll take romance? *The Women's Review of Books,* pp. 12–13.

Toufexis, Anastasia. (1982, July 12). What killed equal rights? *Time,* pp. 32–33.

Towbes, Lynn C., Cohen, Lawrence H., & Glyshaw, Kathy. (1989). Instrumentality as a life-stress moderator for early versus middle adolescents. *Journal of Personality and Social Psychology, 57,* 109–119.

Towson, Shelagh M. J., & Zanna, Mark P. (1982). Toward a situational analysis of gender differences in aggression. *Sex Roles, 8,* 903–914.

The Toy Cellar Christmas catalog. (1990). 7 Main St., Wickford, RI 02852.

Tracy, Dyanne M. (1987). Toys, spatial ability, and science and mathematics achievement: Are they related? *Sex Roles, 17,* 115–138.

Trausch, Susan. (1986, April 20). Terrorism shakes the American psyche. *Boston Globe,* pp. 75–76.

Travis, Cheryl B. (1982). Sex comparisons on causal attributions: Another look at the null hypothesis. *Sex Roles, 8,* 375–380.

Travis, Cheryl B. (1988). *Women and health psychology: Mental health issues.* Hillsdale, NJ: Lawrence Erlbaum.

Treadway, C. Richard, Kane, Francis J. Jr., Jarrahi-Zadeh, Ali, & Lipton, Morris A. (1975). A psychoendocrine study of pregnancy and puerperium. In R. K. Unger & F. L. Denmark (Eds.), *Woman: Dependent or independent variable?* (pp. 591–604). New York: Psychological Dimensions.

Tremaine, Leslie S., Schau, Candace G., & Busch, Judith W. (1982). Children's occupational sex-typing. *Sex Roles, 8,* 691–710.

Trepanier, Mary L., & Romatowski, Jane A. (1985). Attributes and roles assigned to characters in children's writing: Sex differences and sex-role perceptions. *Sex Roles, 13,* 263–272.

Trotter, Robert J. (1987, December). Project day-care. *Psychology Today,* pp. 32–38.

Trotter, Robert. (1982, March). Sex and the psychiatrist. *Science, 82,* pp. 78–79.

True, Reiko H. (1990). Psychotherapeutic issues with Asian American women. *Sex Roles, 22,* 477–486.

Turkington, Carol. (1984, January). Ideology affects approach taken to alleviate PMS. *APA Monitor,* pp. 28–29.

Turner, Charles W., Hesse, Bradford W., & Preston-Lewis, Sonja. (1986). Naturalistic studies of the long-term effects of television violence. *Journal of Social Issues, 42* (1). 51–73.

2 gay adoptions in higher courts. (1993, April 18). *New York Times,* p. Y-19.

Two women survive in a macho world. (1978, September 20). *Providence Evening Bulletin.*

Udry, J. Richard, & Talbert, Luther M. (1988). Sex hormone effects on personality at puberty. *Journal of Personality and Social Psychology, 54,* 291–295.

Ullian, Dora. (1984). "Why girls are good": A constructivist view. *Sex Roles, 11,* 241–256.

Ungar, Sheldon B. (1982). The sex-typing of adult and child behavior in toy sales. *Sex Roles, 8,* 251–260.

Unger, Rhoda K. (1981). Sex as a social reality: Field and laboratory research. *Psychology of Women Quarterly, 5,* 645–653.

U. of Virginia considers wide ban on intimate teacher-student ties. (1993, April 4). *New York Times,* p. Y-13.

U.S. Bureau of the Census. (1976, April). *A statistical portrait of women in the U.S.* Current Population Reports, Series P-23, No. 58. Washington, DC: U.S. Government Printing Office.

U.S. Bureau of the Census. (1985a). *Marital status and living arrangements: March 1984.* Current Population Reports, Series P-20, No. 399. Washington, DC: U.S. Government Printing Office.

U.S. Bureau of the Census. (1985b). *Statistical abstract of the United States.* Washington, DC: U.S. Government Printing Office.

U.S. Department of Labor. (1980, August). *Brief highlights of major federal laws on sex discrimination in employment.* Washington, DC: U.S. Government Printing Office.

U.S. Federal Bureau of Investigation. (1982). *Uniform crime reports.* Washington, DC: U.S. Government Printing Office.

U.S. study finds one in five births out of wedlock. (1985, September 29). *New York Times,* p. 65.

Unwanted births decline. (1985, May 14). *Providence Evening Bulletin.*

Vader, J. E. (1988, June). Riding high. *Ms.,* pp. 28–30.

Vance, Brenda K., & Green, Vicki. (1984). Lesbian identities: An examination of sex behavior and sex role attribution as related to age of initial same-sex sexual encounter. *Psychology of Women Quarterly, 8,* 293–307.

Vance, Carole S. (Ed.). (1984). *Pleasure and danger: Exploring female sexuality.* Boston: Routledge & Kegan Paul.

Vance, Carole S., & Snitow, Ann B. (1984). Toward a conversation about sex in feminism: A modest proposal. *Signs, 10,* 126–135.

Van Gelder, Lindsy. (1990, July/August). The importance of being eleven. *Ms.,* pp. 77–79.

Van Gelder, Lindsy. (1992, July/August). Mothers of convention. *Ms.,* pp. 94–95.

Van Hecke, Madelaine, Tracy, Robert J., Cotler, Sheldon, & Ribordy, Sheila C. (1984). Approval versus achievement motives in seventh-grade girls. *Sex Roles, 11,* 33–41.

Vatican seeks out U.S. nuns. (1986, March 20). *Providence Evening Bulletin,* p. C-22.

Veevers, Jean E. (1982). Voluntary childlessness: A critical assessment of the research. In E. D. Macklin & R. H. Rubin (Eds.), *Contemporary families and alternative lifestyles* (pp. 75–96). Beverly Hills, CA: Sage.

Vetter, Betty M. (1978). New data show uneven progress for women and minorities in science. *Science, 202,* 507–508.

Vetter, Betty M. (1981). Degree completion by women and minorities in sciences increases. *Science, 212,* 35.

Views on sex still liberal—pollster. (1985, April 25). *Providence Evening Bulletin,* p. A-2.

Villemur, Nora K., & Hyde, Janet S. (1983). Effects of sex of defense attorney, sex of jurors, and age and attractiveness of the victim on mock juror decision making in a rape case. *Sex Roles, 9,* 879–889.

Voda, Ann M., & Eliasson, Mona. (1985). Menopause: The closure of menstrual life. In S. Golub (Ed.), *Lifting the curse of menstruation* (pp. 137–156). New York: Haworth.

Vold, Mona. (1987, November). This land is their land. *Ms.,* pp. 76–81.

VonBergen, Jane M. (1990, January 31). 'Learning' to breast-feed. *Providence Journal Bulletin,* p. E-1.

Voydanoff, Patricia. (1980). Perceived job characteristics and job satisfaction among men and women. *Psychology of Women Quarterly, 5,* 177–185.

Vrazo, Fawn. (1984, August 14). Joys and sadnesses of older mothers. *Providence Evening Bulletin.*

Wade, Nicholas. (1975). Discovery of pulsars: A graduate student's story. *Science, 189,* 358–364.

Wage gap closing between women, men. (1989, February 8). *Providence Journal Bulletin,* p. A-5.

Waggett, Gerard J. (1989, May 27). A plea to the soaps: Let's stop turning rapists into heroes. *TV Guide,* pp. 10–11.

Wagner, Irene. (n.d.). Formerly battered women: A follow-up study. (Available from 4761 22nd Ave. NE, Seattle, WA 98105)

Walker, Alice. (1976). *Meridian.* New York: Washington Square Press.

Walker, Alice. (1982). *The color purple.* New York: Washington Square Press.

Walker, Alice. (1983). *In search of our mothers' gardens.* New York: Harcourt Brace Jovanovich.

Walker, Lawrence. (1984). Sex differences in the development of moral reasoning: A critical review. *Child Development, 55,* 667–691.

Walker, Lenore E. (1978). Treatment alternatives for battered women. In J. R. Chapman & M. Gates (Eds.), *The victimization of women* (pp. 143–174). Beverly Hills, CA: Sage.

Walker, Lenore E. (1979). *The battered woman.* New York: Harper & Row.

Walker, Lenore E. (1989a). Psychology and violence against women. *American Psychologist, 44,* 695–702.

Walker, Lenore E. (1989b). *Terrifying love.* New York: Harper Perennial.

Walkowitz, Judith R. (1980). The politics of prostitution. *Signs, 6,* 123–135.

Wallace, Amy. (1985, August 11). Schooldays, workdays. *New York Times.*

Wallace, Michele. (1979). *Black macho and the myth of the superwoman.* New York: Dial.

Wallis, Claudia, & McDowell, Jeanne. (1987, October 12). Back off, buddy. *Time,* pp. 68–73.

Wallston, Barbara S. (1981). What are the questions in psychology of women? A feminist approach to research. *Psychology of Women Quarterly, 5,* 597–617.

Walsh, John. (1984). Total doctorates edge up in science, engineering. *Science, 226,* 815.

Walsh, Mary R. (1985). The psychology of women course: A continuing catalyst for change. *Teaching of Psychology, 12,* 198–203.

Walshok, Mary L. (1981). *Blue-collar women: Pioneers on the male frontier.* New York: Doubleday/Anchor.

Walzer, Stanley, & Gerald, Park S. (1975). Social class and frequency of XYY and XXY. *Science, 190,* 1228–1229.

Ware, Mary Catherine, & Stuck, Mary F. (1985). Sex-role messages vis-a-vis microcomputer use: A look at the pictures. *Sex Roles, 13,* 205–214.

Warr, Peter, & Parry, Glenys. (1982). Paid employment and women's psychological well-being. *Psychological Bulletin, 91,* 498–516.

Warshaw, Robin. (1991, May 5). Ugly truths of date rape elude the screen. *New York Times,* pp. H-17, H-22.

Wash. court approves plan to end sex bias in state worker pay. (1986, April 12). *Providence Evening Bulletin,* p. A-3.

Washington, Mary H. (Ed.). (1975). *Black-eyed Susans.* Garden City, NY: Anchor.

Washington, Mary H. (1982, October). Working at single bliss. *Ms.,* pp. 55–59.

Wasserman, Gail A., & Lewis, Michael. (1985). Infant sex differences: Ecological effects. *Sex Roles, 12,* 91–95.

Waters, Harry F. (1991a, May 13). Sisterhood, frankly speaking. *Newsweek,* p. 65.

Waters, Harry F. (1991b, November 11). Whip me, beat me . . . *Newsweek,* pp. 74–75.

The way we live. (1986, December 14). *New York Times,* p. E-9.

Webb, Thomas E., & Van Devere, Chris A. (1985). Sex differences in the expression of depression: A developmental interaction effect. *Sex Roles, 12,* 91–95.

Weber, Ellen. (1977, April). Sexual abuse begins at home. *Ms.,* pp. 64–67.

Wedding planner. (1990, Spring). *Narragansett Times.*

Weideger, Paula. (1976). *Menstruation and menopause.* New York: Knopf.

Weingarten, Kathy, & Daniels, Pamela. (1981). *Sooner or later: The timing of parenthood in adult lives.* New York: Norton.

Weisheit, Ralph A. (1984). Women and crime: Issues and perspectives. *Sex Roles, 11,* 567–581.

Weisstein, Naomi. (1982, November). Tired of arguing about biological inferiority? *Ms.,* pp. 41–46, 85.

Weitz, Rose. (1982). Feminist consciousness raising, self-concept, and depression. *Sex Roles, 8,* 231–241.

Weitzman, Lenore J. (1985). *The divorce revolution.* New York: Free Press.

Weitzman, Lenore J., Eifler, Deborah, Hokada, Elizabeth, & Ross, Catherine. (1972). Sex-role socialization in picture books for pre-school children. *American Journal of Sociology, 77,* 1125–1150.

Wekerle, Gerda R. (1980). Women in the urban environment. *Signs, 50* (Supp.), S188–S214.

Weld reviews 11 cases of abused women jailed in deaths of mates. (1991, September 30). *Providence Journal Bulletin,* p. A-8.

Wells, Anna J. (1988). Variations in mothers' self-esteem in daily life. *Journal of Personality and Social Psychology, 55,* 661–668.

Wells, Linda. (1988, February 14). The wedding. *New York Times Magazine,* pp. 65, 72, 76.

Wenk, Deeann, & Garrett, Patricia. (1992). Having a baby: Some predictions of maternal employment around childbirth. *Gender & Society, 6,* 49–65.

Wenner, Kate. (1977, May 8). How they keep them down on the farm. *New York Times Magazine,* pp. 74, 80–83.

Wentzel, Kathryn R. (1988). Gender differences in Math and English achievement: A longitudinal study. *Sex Roles, 18,* 691–69.

Werner, Dennis. (1984). Child care and influence among the Mekranoti of Central Brazil. *Sex Roles, 10,* 395–404.

Werner, Paul D., & LaRussa, Georgina W. (1985). Persistence and change in sex-role stereotypes. *Sex Roles, 12,* 1089–1100.

West, Joanne. (1984, March/April). Hysterectomy and the mid-life and older women. *Network News,* p. 4.

West, Rebecca. (1913). Quoted in *Mother Jones* (1991, September/October), p. 29.

Westerlund, Elaine. (1986). Freud on sexual trauma: An historical review of seduction and betrayal. *Psychology of Women Quarterly, 10,* 297–310.

Westoff, Charles F., & Rindfuss, Ronald R. (1974). Sex preselection in the United States: Some implications. *Science, 184,* 633–636.

Wheelan, S. A., & Verdi, A. (in press). Gender differences in groups: A methological artifact? *Sex Roles*.

Wheeler, Ladd, & Nezlek, John. (1977). Sex differences in social participation. *Journal of Personality and Social Psychology, 35*, 742–754.

White, Jacquelyn W. (1988). Influence tactics as a function of gender, insult, and goal. *Sex Roles, 18*, 433–448.

White, Jacquelyn W., & Ronfail, Mary. (1989). Gender and influence strategies of first choice and last resort. *Psychology of Women Quarterly, 13*, 175–189.

Whiting, Beatrice B., & Edwards, Carolyn P. (1988). *Children of different worlds: The formation of social behavior*. Cambridge, MA: Harvard University Press.

Whiting, John W. M. (1941). *Becoming a Kwoma*. New Haven: Yale University Press.

Whitley, Bernard E. Jr. (1979). Sex roles and psychotherapy: A current appraisal. *Psychological Bulletin, 86*, 1309–1321.

Whitley, Bernard E. Jr. (1983). Sex role orientation and self-esteem: A critical meta-analytic review. *Journal of Personality and Social Psychology, 44*, 765–778.

Whitley, Bernard E. Jr. (1985). Sex-role orientation and psychological well-being: Two meta-analyses. *Sex Roles, 12*, 207–225.

Whitley, Bernard E. Jr. (1985). The relation of gender-role orientation to sexual experience among college students. *Sex Roles, 19*, 619–638.

Whitney, Margaret A. (1988, July 3). Playing to win. *New York Times Magazine*, pp. 8, 37.

Widiger, Thomas A., & Settle, Shirley A. (1987). Broverman et al. revisited: An artificial sex bias. *Journal of Personality and Social Psychology, 53*, 463–469.

Wiener, Jon. (1985, September 7). The Sears case: Women's history on trial. *The Nation*, pp. 174–176, 178–180.

Wieser Educational Inc. (1988). *Reality education catalogue*. P.O. Box 1269, El Toro, CA 92630.

Wiest, William M. (1977). Semantic differential profiles of orgasm and other experiences among men and women. *Sex Roles, 3*, 399–403.

Williams, Audrey. (1989). Research on black women college administrators: Descriptive and interview data. *Sex Roles, 21*, 99–112.

Williams, Dorie G. (1985). Gender, masculinity-femininity, and emotional intimacy in same-sex friendship. *Sex Roles, 12*, 587–600.

Williams, Lenore R. (1983). Beliefs and attitudes of young girls regarding menstruation. In S. Golub (Ed.), *Menarche* (pp. 133–137). Boston: Lexington Books.

Williams, Marjorie. (1991, August 11). Barbie and Miss America pull off the gloves. *San Francisco Chronicle*, p. 2.

Williamson, Nancy E. (1976). Sex preferences, sex control, and the status of women. *Signs, 1*, 847–862.

Willis, Ellen. (1981, November 14). Betty Friedan's "Second Stage": A step backward. *The Nation*, pp. 494–496.

Wilmore, Jack H. (1977). The female athlete. *Journal of School Health, 47*, 227–233.

Wilmoth, Gregory H., DeAlteriis, Martin, & Bussell, Danielle. (1992). Prevalence of psychological risks following legal abortion in the U.S.: Limits of the evidence. *Journal of Social Issues, 48* (3), 37–66.

Wilson, Amanda, & Lloyd, Barbara. (1990). Gender vs. power: Self-posed behavior revisited. *Sex Roles, 23*, 91–98.

Wilson, Jean D., George, Frederick W., & Griffin, James E. (1981). The hormonal control of sexual development. *Science, 211*, 1278–1284.

Wilson, Melvin N. (1990). Flexibility and sharing of child care duties in Black families. *Sex Roles, 22*, 409–425.

Wilson, Reginald. (1989). Women of color in academic administration: Trends, progress, and barriers. *Sex Roles, 21*, 85–97.

Wise, George W. (1978). The relationship of sex-role perception and levels of self-actualization in public school teachers. *Sex Roles, 4*, 605–617.

Wise, Paula S., & Joy, Stephany S. (1982). Working mothers, sex differences, and self-esteem in college students' self-descriptions. *Sex Roles, 8*, 785–790.

WITCH. New York Covens. (1970). In R. Morgan (Ed.), *Sisterhood is powerful* (pp. 539–540). New York: Vintage.

Withorn, Ann. (1986, June). New poor, old problems. *Women's Review of Books*, pp. 8–9.

Witkin, Herman A. (1979). Socialization, culture and ecology in the development of group and sex differences in cognitive style. *Human Development, 22*, 358.

Witkin, Herman A., Mednick, Sarnof A., Schulsinger, Fini, Bakkestrom, Eskild, Christiansen, Karol O., Goodenough, Donald R., Hirschhorn, Kurt, Lundsteen, Claes, Owen, David R., Philip, John, Rubin, Donald B., & Stocking, Martha. (1976). Criminality in XYY and XXY men. *Science, 193*, 547–555.

Wittig, Michele A. (1985). Sex-role norms and gender-related attainment values: Their role in attributions of success and failure. *Sex Roles, 12*, 1–13.

Wolf, Naomi. (1991). *The beauty myth: How images of beauty are used against women*. New York: William Morrow.

Wolf, Naomi. (1992, July/August). Radical heterosexuality. *Ms.*, pp. 29–31.

Wolfe, Linda. (1981, December 28–1982, January 4). The good news: The latest expert word on what it means to be single. *New York*, pp. 33–35.

Wolitzer, Meg. (1986). *Hidden pictures*. Boston: Houghton Miffin.

Wolowitz, Howard M. (1972). Hysterical character and feminine identity. In J. M. Bardwick (Ed.), *Readings on the psychology of women* (pp. 307–314). New York: Harper & Row.

Woman to head Columbia Law. (1986, January 5). *New York Times*.

Woman uses PMS defense; drunk driving case dropped. (1991, June 7). *Providence Journal Bulletin*, p. A-14.

Women changing the Army's look. (1978, December 21). *Providence Evening Bulletin*.

Women crack political glass ceiling. (1992, December). *Feminist Majority Report*.

Women face low pay after losing steel jobs. (1984, May 17). *New York Times*.

Women in clerical jobs band together to learn 9-to-5 rights. (1985, February 20). *New York Times*, p. C-9.

Women Marines a gang that can shoot straight. (1986, January 22). *Providence Evening Bulletin*, p. A-15.

Women now hold most professional jobs. (1986, March 20). *Providence Evening Bulletin*, p. A-1.

Women on Words and Images. (1972). *Dick and Jane as victims: Sex stereotyping in children's readers*. Princeton, NJ: Author.

Women on Words and Images. (1975). *Channeling children*. Princeton, NJ: Author.

Women want more equality, more help around the house. (1986, June 10). *Providence Evening Bulletin*, p. A-1.

Women with AIDS decry lack of care. (1991, April 20). *Providence Journal Bulletin*, p. A-7.

Women who work: Healthier hearts. (1992, May/June). *Health*, p. 16.

Women working less, filling dead-end jobs. (1984, July 18). *Providence Evening Bulletin*.

Women's health. Report of the Public Health Service Task Force on Women's Health Issues. (1985). *Public Health Reports, 100*(1), 73–106.

Women's pay still much below men's. (1982, February 6). *Providence Evening Bulletin.*

Women's well-being at midlife. (1982, Winter). *ISR Newsletter.* (Institute for Social Research, University of Michigan, Ann Arbor)

Women's world investigates. (1991, April 9). *Women's World,* pp. 40–41.

Wood, Clive. (1986, October). Hormone dominance. *Psychology Today,* p. 75.

Wood, Elizabeth. (1980). Women in music. *Signs, 6,* 283–297.

Wood, P. S. (1980, May 18). Sex differences in sports. *New York Times Magazine,* pp. 30–33, 38, 96–104.

Woodall, Martha. (1983, October 4). Late pregnancy risks exaggerated. *Providence Evening Bulletin,* p. B-12.

Wooden, Kenneth. (1976). *Weeping in the playtime of others.* New York: McGraw-Hill.

Woods, Nancy F., Dery, Gretchen K., & Most, Ada. (1983). Recollections of menarche, current menstrual attitudes, and perimenstrual symptoms. In S. Golub (Ed.), *Menarche* (pp. 87–97). Boston, MA: Lexington Books.

Wooley, S. C., & Wooley, O. W. (1984, February). Feeling fat in a thin society. *Glamour,* pp. 198–252.

Wooley, Susan, & Wooley, O. Wayne. (1986, October). Ambitious bulimics: Thinness mania. *American Health,* pp. 68–74.

Worell, Judith. (1988). Single mothers: From problems to policies. *Women & Therapy, 7*(4), 3–14.

Working moms, slouching kids. (1992, April 7). *Providence Journal Bulletin,* p. By B-2.

Working Women's Institute. (1980). *Sexual harassment on the job: Questions and answers.* (Available from 593 Park Ave., New York, NY 10021)

Working Women joins forces with national union. (1981, March 20). *Providence Evening Bulletin.*

The World Bank. (1990). *Poverty: World Development Report 1990.* New York: Oxford University Press.

The world's women, 1970–1990: Trends and statistics. (1992). New York: United Nations.

Wright, Paul H. (1982). Men's friendships, women's friendships and the alleged inferiority of the latter. *Sex Roles, 8,* 1–20.

Wright, Paul H., & Scanlon, Mary Beth. (1991). Gender role orientations and friendship: Some attenuation, but gender differences abound. *Sex Roles, 24,* 551–566.

Wyatt, Gail E. (1992). The sociocultural context of African American and White American women's rape. *Journal of Social Issues, 48* (1), 77–91.

Wyatt, Gail E., Notgass, Cindy H., & Newcomb, Michael. (1990). Internal and external mediators of women's rape experiences. *Psychology of Women Quarterly, 14,* 153–176.

Wyche, Karen F., & Graves, Sherryl B. (1992). Minority women in academia: Access and barriers to professional participation. *Psychology of Women Quarterly, 16,* 429–437.

Wyer, Robert S. Jr., Bodenhausen, Galen V., & Gorman, Theresa F. (1985). Cognitive mediators of reactions to rape. *Journal of Personality and Social Psychology, 48,* 324–338.

Yee, Doris K., & Eccles, Jacqueline S. (1988). Parent perceptions and attributions for children's math achievement. *Sex Roles, 19,* 317–333.

Yoder, Janice D. (1983). Another look at women in the United States Army: A comment on Woelfel's article. *Sex Roles, 9,* 285–288.

Yogev, Sara. (1982). Happiness in dual-career couples: Changing research, changing values. *Sex Roles, 8,* 593–605.

Yogev, Sara, & Vierra, Andrea. (1983). The state of motherhood among professional women. *Sex Roles, 9,* 391–396.

Yorburg, Betty, & Arafat, Ibtihaj. (1975). Current sex role conceptions and conflict. *Sex Roles, 1,* 135–146.

Youngstrom, Nina. (1991, July). Scientists probe traits of binge-eating. *APA Monitor,* p. 15.

Youngstrom, Nina. (1992a, February). Laws to aid battered women backfire. *APA Monitor,* p. 45.

Youngstrom, Nina. (1992b, September). Women in military given little aid after sex assaults. *APA Monitor,* pp. 22–24.

Yount, Kristen R. (1986). A theory of productive activity: The relationships among self-concept, gender, sex role stereotypes, and work-emergent traits. *Psychology of Women Quarterly, 10,* 63–88.

Zammichieli, Maria E., Gilroy, Faith D., & Sherman, Martin F. (1988). Relation between sex-role orientation and marital satisfaction. *Personality and Social Psychology Bulletin, 14,* 747–754.

Zanna, Mark P., & Pack, Susan J. (1975). On the self-fulfilling nature of apparent sex differences in behavior. *Journal of Experimental Social Psychology, 11,* 583–591.

Zedeck, Sheldon, & Mosier, Kathleen L. (1990). Work in the family and employing organization. *American Psychologist, 45,* 240–251.

Zellman, Gail L., Goodchilds, Jacqueline D., Johnson, Paula B., & Giarusso, Roseann. (1981, August). *Teenagers' application of the label "rape" to nonconsensual sex between acquaintances.* Paper presented at the meeting of the American Psychological Association, Los Angeles, CA.

Zellman, Gail L., Johnson, Paula B., Giarusso, Roseann, & Goodchilds, Jacqueline D. (1979, September). *Adolescent expectations for dating relationships: Consensus between the sexes.* Paper read at the meeting of the American Psychological Association, New York.

Zeman, Ned. (1991, September 23). Limited access. *Newsweek,* p. 6.

Zimmerman, Bonnie. (1984). The politics of transliteration: Lesbian personal narratives. *Signs, 9,* 663–682.

Zinn, Maxine B. (1982). Mexican-American women in the social sciences. *Signs, 8,* 259–272.

Zita, Jacqueline N. (1981). Historical amnesia and the lesbian continuum. *Signs, 7,* 172–187.

Zones, Jane S. (1990, May/June). Urinary incontinence emerges as a significant health issue. *National Women's Health Network,* pp. 1–2, 4, 7–8.

Zuckerman, Diana M., & Sayre, Donald H. (1982). Cultural sex-role expectations and children's sex-role concepts. *Sex Roles, 8,* 853–862.

TO THE OWNER OF THIS BOOK:

We hope that you have found *Women's Lives: Themes and Variations in Gender Learning, Second Edition*, useful. So that this book can be improved in a future edition, would you take the time to complete this sheet and return it? Thank you.

School and address: _____

Department: _____

Instructor's name: _____

_____

1. What I like most about this book is: _____

_____

2. What I like least about this book is: _____

_____

_____

3. My general reaction to this book is: _____

_____

4. The name of the course in which I used this book is: _____

_____

5. Were all of the chapters of the book assigned for you to read? _____

    If not, which ones weren't? _____

6. In the space below, or on a separate sheet of paper, please write specific suggestions for improving this book and anything else you'd care to share about your experience in using the book.

_____

_____

_____

_____

_____

_____

_____

Optional:

Your name: _____ Date: _____

May Brooks/Cole quote you, either in promotion for *Women's Lives: Themes and Variations in Gender Learning, Second Edition*, or in future publishing ventures?

Yes: _____ No: _____

Sincerely,

Bernice Lott

FOLD HERE

-         - - - - - - -

||||||

BUSINESS REPLY MAIL

FIRST CLASS   PERMIT NO. 358   PACIFIC GROVE, CA

POSTAGE WILL BE PAID BY ADDRESSEE

ATT: _____ *Bernice Lott* _____

Brooks/Cole Publishing Company
511 Forest Lodge Road
Pacific Grove, California 93950-9968

||.|....||.|.|...|.|.||....|.|..|.|..||.|.|..|.||

- -

FOLD HERE